DATE DUE

MAY 15 2013

DEMCO, INC. 38-2931

SHAKESPEAREAN
SCHOLARSHIP

SHAKESPEAREAN SCHOLARSHIP

A Guide for Actors and Students

Leslie O'Dell

Greenwood Press
Westport, Connecticut • London

Library of Congress Cataloging-in-Publication Data

O'Dell, Leslie.
    Shakespearean scholarship : a guide for actors and students / by Leslie O'Dell.
      p. cm.
    Includes bibliographical references and index.
    ISBN 0–313–31146–3 (alk. paper)
      1. Shakespeare, William, 1564–1616–Criticism and
interpretation–History–Handbooks, manuals, etc. 2. Shakespeare, William,
1564–1616–Dramatic production–Handbooks, manuals, etc. 3. Shakespeare, William,
1564–1616–Criticism, Textual–Handbooks, manuals, etc. 4. Shakespeare, William,
1564–1616–Stage history–Handbooks, manuals, etc. 5. Shakespeare, William,
1564–1616–Bibliography–Handbooks, manuals, etc. I. Title.
PR2965.O34 2002
822.3'3–dc21   2001018032

British Library Cataloguing in Publication Data is available.

Library of Congress Catalog Card Number: 2001018032
ISBN: 0–313–31146–3

First published in 2002

Greenwood Press, 88 Post Road West, Westport, CT 06881
An imprint of Greenwood Publishing Group, Inc.
www.greenwood.com

Printed in the United States of America

The paper used in this book complies with the
Permanent Paper Standard issued by the National
Information Standards Organization (Z39.48–1984).

10 9 8 7 6 5 4 3 2 1

Contents

Preface

In writing this book, I have attempted to share with the reader some of the riches I have found in books, which has proven useful in the preparation of the plays of Shakespeare for public performance in the last years of the twentieth century. I encourage readers to use this book in the same manner I suggest for all books: browse, use the index and table of contents, and take from it only what enhances your work as an actor.

BIBLIOGRAPHY

At the end of all but the first and last chapters you will find a long list of books under the heading Recommended Reading, divided into general categories to match the contents of that chapter. In addition, at the end of the book you will find a lengthy list of works from which I have quoted or to which I have referred but not recommended, for one reason or another. I intend no disrespect by thus proverbially separating the sheep from the goats. Rather, I wish to acknowledge that the standards of excellence in academia at times can interfere with the usefulness of certain publications for a more general readership and, in particular, for actors working on a specific role or students seeking to acquire an understanding of how Shakespeare works in the theatre.

In the Recommended Reading section for the second chapter you will find information about various editions of Shakespeare's plays. At the end of the book I have listed only those editions from which I have quoted editorial notes; for that reason, they appear under the name of the editor rather than the author.

CITATIONS

I often quote from one of Shakespeare's plays and note the act, scene, and number of the first line in parentheses immediately following the quotation; I have used the line numbers found in *The Riverside Shakespeare*, edited by G. Blakemore Evans. I include the title of the play if that has not yet been indicated. For convenience, I have used a shortened version of many of the play titles, as follows:

12th Night	*Twelfth Night*
1HIV	*The first part of Henry IV*
2HIV	*The second part of Henry IV*
1HVI	*The first part of Henry VI*
2HVI	*The second part of Henry VI*
3HVI	*The third part of Henry VI*
A&C	*Antony and Cleopatra*
All's Well	*All's Well That Ends Well*
AYLI	*As You Like It*
Dream	*A Midsummer Night's Dream*
Errors	*The Comedy of Errors*
HV	*Henry V*
HVIII	*Henry VIII*
JC	*Julius Caesar*
John	*King John*
Lear	*King Lear*
LLL	*Love's Labour's Lost*
Measure	*Measure for Measure*
Merchant	*The Merchant of Venice*
Much Ado	*Much Ado about Nothing*
R&J	*Romeo and Juliet*
RII	*Richard the Second*
RIII	*Richard the Third*
Shrew	*The Taming of the Shrew*
T&C	*Troilus and Cressida*
Timon	*Timon of Athens*
Titus	*Titus Andronicus*
Two Gents	*The Two Gentlemen of Verona*
Wives	*The Merry Wives of Windsor*
WT	*The Winter's Tale*

I have also used the character names as they appear in *The Riverside Shakespeare* so that, for example, the heroine of *Cymbeline* is Imogen, not Innogen, and the man who eventually becomes King Henry IV is known as Bolingbroke, not Bollingbrook or Bullingbrooke.

I have assumed a familiarity with Shakespeare's plays and so have explained the context of the quotations only if that is significant to what I am discussing. It is very difficult to avoid interpretation in these discussions; I cannot help but envision the scene in performance, the product of innumerable decisions, every one of which can only be right for that one performance (imaginary or remembered), and none of which should be viewed as any more or less correct or valid than the decisions you might make in your productions.

QUOTATIONS

Although I have made use of *The Riverside Shakespeare* for line numbers, I have reproduced the quotations from Shakespeare based upon the 1623 folio edition, with some modifications. I have modernized most spellings for ease of reading aloud. I have also, on occasion, adjusted the punctuation when it might completely mislead the modern reader. When the First Folio is clearly incorrect or when I wish to quote lines only found in a quarto edition, I have made use of whichever alternative text is best regarded by experts in early modern printing practices.

There are a few significant differences, therefore, between the quotations in this book and those found in most editions of Shakespeare's plays. Close comparison between modern practices and those of Shakespeare's contemporaries reveal the following patterns:

- The early texts use far more capitalized words, usually nouns which we consider general and which they make proper, with some adjectives and fewer verbs also so modified.

- The early texts use commas to mark places for the actor to breathe. Modern editors regularly modify these in accordance with rules of grammar.

- The early texts use other punctuation marks quite differently than we do today. Modern editors regularly "normalize" these, privileging grammar and correct usage over an evocation of the flow of ideas in spoken communication.

- The early texts seldom made a clear differentiation between the plural and the possessive, another grammatical "error" corrected by modern editors. Unfortunately, this requires them to choose between one of the two following interpretations of Ophelia's famous line, as in *The Riverside Shakespeare* where it appears as: "The courtier's, soldier's, scholar's, eye, tongue, sword" [*Hamlet* 3.1.151], when the folio reads: "The Courtiers, Soldiers, Scholars: Eye, tongue, sword," leaving it open whether the eye, tongue, and sword in question belong to one or all courtiers, soldiers, and scholars.

- The early texts create compound words or present as two separate words some common compound words, such as "myself" or "tomorrow."

• The early texts sometimes break up the lines of poetry differently than is customary in modern texts. In extreme cases, they present as prose entire passages which are reproduced as poetry by modern editors. In *Romeo and Juliet*, the Nurse's long meander down memory lane, in which a toddling Juliet gets a bump on her forehead, appears as prose in all three early editions. Mercutio's famous evocation of Queen Mab appears as poetry only in the first (1603) quarto; the second (1604) quarto and the First Folio both present this as prose.

Because I have recreated the choices made by the first editors, the quotations in this book might strike the modern reader as unexpected or even incorrect.

CAPITALIZATIONS

The First Folio presents no coherent pattern of making proper nouns of various objects and concepts, tempting modern editors to conclude that the practice was influenced as much by the availability of upper and lower case letters in the typesetter's box as it was by anything in the original manuscript. By including the First Folio capitals in this book, I have made it possible for you to judge for yourself, and glean what information you wish from these markers.

In making a comparison between modern punctuation and that found in the early texts, I have observed that modern editors quite often add an exclamation mark to reflect the strong emotion clearly expressed in the situation, when the first editor loaded on the capital letters and used a humble period. Consider, for example, that most famous of lines, "A horse! a horse! my kingdom for a horse!" [*RIII* 5.4.7] which in the First Folio appears as, "A Horse, a Horse, my Kingdom for a Horse." The four capital letters in that line evoke, for me, the shouting of a desperate man, a tidy equivalent to the three exclamation marks in the modern version.

Another speech from this play reminds us of the effect of linking individual and specific words to universal concepts. Here is the Duchess of York, mother of the title character, describing his childhood:

> No by the holy Rood, thou know'st it well,
> Thou camest on earth, to make the earth my Hell.
> A grievous burthen was thy Birth to me,
> Tetchy and wayward was thy Infancy.
> Thy School-days frightful, desp'rate, wild, and furious,
> Thy prime of Manhood, daring, bold, and venturous:
> Thy Age confirmed, proud, subtle, sly, and bloody,
> More mild, but yet more harmful; Kind in hatred:
> What comfortable hour canst thou name,
> That ever graced me with thy company? [*RIII* 4.4.166]

The capitalization in this speech transforms her memories into another "seven ages of man" speech, marking for us the universality of the stages of Richard's life, from his birth and infancy, through school days, to manhood and finally maturity, marked by the word "Age." When Jacques has a go at the same idea, his version makes use of similar capitalizations, describing "the Infant, / Mewling, and puking in the Nurses arms: / Then, the whining School-boy with his Satchel / And shining morning face, creeping like snail / Unwillingly to school" [*AYLI* 2.7.142].

FIRST FOLIO ERRORS

Using the first texts can open up all sorts of fascinating possibilities for the modern actor that arise from a more direct encounter with the irregularities that modern editors customarily remove from the plays. Here, for example, is a wonderful hiccup that appears at the end of an exchange between the young Duke of York and his uncle Richard:

Richard: What, would you have my Weapon, little Lord?

York: I would that I might thank you, as, as, you call me.

Richard: How?

York: Little. [*RIII* 3.1.122]

Modern editors, in an effort to clean up what they have assumed is an error made by the compositor of this particular page, remove the delicate little stutter, so that York is given no opportunity to telegraph his glee at the approaching punch line. I am more inclined to admire Shakespeare for his intuition about juvenile joke-tellers, and honor the "as, as," in performance.

Not all errors are so attractive. Here is the mess that the compositor has made of Romeo's final speech:

> For fear of that, I still will stay with thee,
> And never from this Palace of dim night
> *Depart again: come lie thou in my arms.*
> *Here's to thy health, where ere thou tumblest in.*
> *O true Apothecary!*
> *Thy drugs are quick. Thus with a kiss I die.*
> Depart again; here, here will I remain,
> With Worms that are thy Chambermaids: O here
> Will I set up my everlasting rest:
> And shake the yoke of inauspicious stars
> From this world-wearied flesh: Eyes look your last:
> Arms take your last embrace: And lips, O you
> The doors of breath, seal with a righteous kiss
> A dateless bargain to engrossing death:

> Come bitter conduct, come unsavory guide,
> Thou desperate Pilot, now at once run on
> The dashing Rocks, thy Sea-sick weary Bark:
> Here's to my Love. O true Apothecary:
> Thy drugs are quicke. Thus with a kisse I die. [5.3.106]

The same mess appears in the 1604 quarto, clearly the copy from which this was being set. The highlighted section is customarily deleted in modern editions. However, I can't help but wonder if the two endings represent two different versions of the speech. Maybe the actors quickly discovered that the shorter version was more effective, and the compositors erred in printing out the shorter as well as the longer version.

Much scholarly effort has been expended on comparing the different early texts, in those cases where we have more than one option, and there is something to be said for the theory that Shakespeare's original version was quite a bit longer than the one actually performed. In this, he would be like most playwrights of my acquaintance, whose manuscripts bear the mark of a helpful editing process instigated by the first performers. It's fascinating to find evidence of the original as well as the amended version, one after the other, thanks to an error in the printing process: almost as good as getting our hands on a copy of the manuscript with Burbage's notes in the margins.

THE SIGNIFICANCE OF THE SELF

We are so accustomed to the modern compound pronouns that we are blind to the very special insights available whenever a character speaks of her individual selfhood. When Polonius advised Laertes, "This above all; to thine own self be true" [*Hamlet* 1.3.78], we hear only the maxim, not the originality of the thought. At a time when the individual was judged to be less worthy of primary loyalty than one's god, and one's liege lord, such loyalty to self was almost heresy.

Returning to *Richard III*, we find an exchange that loses much of its rhetorical power if given a modern spin on selfhood. Lady Anne is spitting out her hatred for the murderer of her husband and father-in-law, a man who is at this moment trying to win her love:

Anne: Vouchsafe (defused infection of man)
          Of these known evils, but to give me leave
          By circumstance, to curse thy cursed *Self*.

Richard: Fairer than tongue can name thee, let me have
          Some patient leisure to excuse my *self*.

Anne: Fouler than heart can think thee,
          Thou canst make no excuse current,
          But to hang thy *self*.

Richard: By such despair, I should accuse my *self*.

Anne: And by despairing shalt thou stand excused,
           For doing worthy Vengeance on thy *self*,
           That didst unworthy slaughter upon others. [1.2.78]

By highlighting the separate word "self," we can see the antithesis between the individual and all of his enemies presented in Anne's last lines. We are also reminded of the immense significance of cursing one's own soul to eternal damnation, the sin of despair, that Anne is wishing upon Richard.

HE OR SHE

In my writing I customarily use the word "actor" to refer to men and women; any reader alert to the nuances of language will note that I scatter male and female pronouns in connection with this noun randomly throughout the text. If I'm discussing Cleopatra or Romeo I will be more likely to have imagined a woman playing the first and a man the second, though historically the reverse has been true: the "squeaking Cleopatra" of Shakespeare's own theatre stands in memory beside Sarah Bernhard and Charlotte Cushman, two among many actresses renown for their portraits of Shakespeare's male protagonists. When appropriate, as in the sentence before this, I will use the term "actress" to make a point about the sex of the performer under discussion.

ACKNOWLEDGMENTS

I could not have completed *Shakespearean Scholarship* without the support and encouragement of my academic and theatre colleagues. In particular, I owe an immense debt of gratitude to the Stratford Shakespearean Festival in Stratford, Ontario, where I have had the privilege of working with those very artists whose enthusiasms, insights, and hard work have inspired this book. Above all, it is the support of my family that has allowed me to undertake this project, and it is to my husband Terry Hynes that I dedicate this book.

❧ 1 ❧
Shakespearean Scholarship without Tears

In Natures infinite book of Secrecy, a little I can read.

The Soothsayer [*A&C* 1.2.10]

I am sitting in the corner of a large rehearsal hall, well-thumbed copy of *As You Like It* in hand, watching and waiting for my cue. The leading lady is bringing to life Rosalind's mocking description of the ideal lover, who is expected to have a lean cheek and a neglected beard, which Orlando does not. When she reaches the words "but I pardon you for that, for simply your having in beard, is a younger brother's revenue" [3.2.376], she abruptly stops, laughs, and announces, "I don't have a clue what I just said." All eyes turn to me, and I clear my throat and prepare to offer what assistance I can.

I am present in the rehearsal hall in my capacity as a Shakespearean text consultant. One of my duties, along with giving classes and providing dramaturgical support, is sitting in rehearsal in order to answer the questions that might arise during the rehearsal process. On many an occasion I have prefaced a contribution by saying, "I don't know if this will be helpful, but . . . ," followed by a snippet of history, a definition from a dictionary, a reproduction of a painting or woodcut, a quotation from a letter, ballad, or commonplace book, or a very quick Elizabethan grammar lesson.

Over the years I have gained a reputation for knowing the answer to just about any question I might be asked. The secret to my apparently encyclopedic knowledge: I have learned how to tap into the wealth of information held in a university library. In truth, I just know where to look for interesting facts and inspiring anecdotes or pictures. I have found books that can be counted on to provide fascinating information for a general background, I have discovered which sorts of books are not worth taking off the shelves, and I have acquired all sorts of tricks for efficient browsing so that I can tell the second sort from the first.

Because Shakespearean scholarship has no place in either my academic training or my research interests, I have had to learn to overcome the painful intimidation any rational nonscholar feels when facing the overwhelming number of publications, to say nothing of the obscure jargon and academic density that characterize the majority of books with "Shakespeare" in the title. It is in the context of this anxiety and intimidation that I have decided to offer some guidance to those of us who are active contributors to the theatrical side of the Shakespeare industry by providing actors an entry into the world of the scholars. The actors who have decided to pursue such explorations stand to benefit from the immense labor of their academic cousins, and there is always a possibility that the iconoclastic and enthusiastic invasion of actors into university libraries will breathe some fresh air into the dry and dusty world of academic Shakespeareana.

PREMISES

This book is based upon a few simple premises:

- That the intellect, like the imagination, is a muscle that needs to be exercised regularly, along with the voice and body, if the actor is to be up to the challenge of playing Shakespearean roles.
- That an understanding of Shakespeare's world will prove invaluable in the rehearsal process of any Shakespearean play.
- That scholars and actors do not share the same value system and therefore misunderstand each other's activities and processes.
- That scholars and actors denigrate each other's work at their own peril.
- That the desire to avoid any research about the role one is playing is as likely to be the product of laziness as of creative autonomy.
- That an excess of intellectual baggage can kill one's creative artistry just as effectively as a bad review or an unsympathetic costume designer, if the actor lets it.
- That the more than three hundred years of Shakespearean scholarship have turned up invaluable information that directly pertains to the challenges facing actors of these roles in the modern theatre.
- That the nuggets of gold that interest actors are buried in mountains of dross turned up by scholarly minds working their way through the "publish-or-perish" maze of academia.
- That the Shakespeare industry can be counted on to generate huge numbers of published works every year, ranging from *Shakespeare for Dummies* to the most esoteric of academic musings.

THE AUTHOR'S BIASES

The quickest survey of table of contents and index will reveal the bias of this book. You will find hardly a thematic study, but hundreds of suggestions of possible sources of information that will help you to imagine the life truly lived of the characters of the plays.

In selecting my recommendations, I have had to make some basic assumptions about just what might interest an actor preparing a role in one of Shakespeare's plays. In this, I am guided, of course, by my own interests when I am acting and directing. Anything that sparks my imagination, that gets my "creative juices" going, anything that transforms the words on the page, be they Shakespeare's or the commentary of the experts, into something alive and compelling, and, above all, anything that helps me to solve one of the problems I encounter "on my feet" during the rehearsal process is likely to find a place in this book.

THE MISMATCH OF FOUR CENTURIES

> They never meet, but there's a skirmish of wit between them.
> Leonato [*Much Ado* 1.1.63]

Only someone quite outside either the theatre or academia would ever assume that scholars who discuss Shakespeare's plays and actors who perform them have anything in common. Outweighing the one thing we have in common, the plays, are the countless things that divide us. Actors and scholars have quite different interests and values, and what is exciting and significant to one often alienates or annoys the other.

An Actor's Inspiration

I have been able to expand my familiarity with the connections actors can make with the product of Shakespearean scholarship through a dozen years of serving as the Shakespearean text consultant at the Stratford (Ontario) Shakespearean Festival. Over the years I have gained a sense of what tends to help and what irritates or, worse yet, suppresses creative energy; I have also learned that what excites one actor is quite likely to leave another unmoved. Generally, though, the helpful comments fall into a few general categories:

- Information: These are factual comments, often mentioned in the scholarly editions, that clarify precisely what's what. A variety of reference texts and historical studies exist; the trick is knowing where to look to get an answer as quickly as possible.

- Meaning: These are explanations of the density of meaning associated with a specific word or the complexities of grammatical construction that are momentarily puzzling.

Dictionaries are just the beginning, because they only give you definitions and do not tell you why these particular words, in that order, function as they do at that moment in the play. For that, you need some general books on language and some working familiarity with how rhetoric and grammar shape meaning.

- Weight: These are more open-ended discussions, less of what something means and more why something is important to the characters in the play. Here the many studies of different aspects of Shakespeare's world provide a rich mosaic upon which to draw for insight.

- Background: These are the most wide-ranging discussions, as they draw upon every possible aspect of the world of the play, what I would call "the life truly lived" that demands to be considered as soon as you imagine your character, a fictional construct, as if she or he were a real person.

A Life Truly Lived

Many actors of my acquaintance share with me a fascination with any detail that evokes the life of a character as it was actually lived by the first actors and their audience. This is in large part because we just cannot resist imagining our characters as if they were real people, getting up in the morning (How did I sleep? Where did I sleep? What did I wear to bed? What is my morning routine?), going through the day (How do I pass the time? What do I do for pleasure? What pressures do I experience? What thoughts do I think? How have I been prepared, by education and by life models, to live the life I lead? In what ways do I conform to the norms around me, and in what ways do I challenge the expectations of others?), and falling asleep at night (What dreams may come? What fantasies, hopes, fears, longings, and images absorbed from the world around me permeate my sleep and the still quiet moments, or the tortured hours, waiting for sleep to come? And oh yes, what about my sex life?). This is the life I cannot help but imagine for my character, leading up to and following from my actions as prescribed by Shakespeare. If I am playing a major character, an answer to many of these questions is suggested by the play. If I am a supporting character or, as has been more often the case for me, a silent onlooker to the main action, many of these questions need to be asked in order for me to comprehend, at the most private and profound level of my understanding, just how I react to the main action of the play.

Actors use the term "backstory" to describe the imagined history of the character, in which they blend elements that are suggested by the words of the play and possibilities suggested by the evocation of the world of the play. No one in the audience will ever know the details of this sort of exploration, and therefore the actor is freed from the concerns with verifiability that govern historical research or scholarly analysis. There is no need to prove that any aspect of the backstory might have happened, but even so, many actors prefer to develop an imaginary past by making use of things that did in fact happen in Shakespeare's England. All of this contributes to the grounding of the performance in that element of realist acting that seeks to evoke a life truly lived.

The Scholars' Perspective

While actors sweat out the hours in rehearsal halls seeking ways to bring Shakespeare's plays alive for modern theatregoers, their scholarly cousins slave in library carrels, seeking ways to survive in their cutthroat world, where "publish or perish" is as stressful a dictum as "if no one comes to see the show, you don't get paid."

Footnote Frenzy

> Small have continual plodders ever won,
> Save base authority from others Books.
>
> Berowne [LLL 1.1.86]

Somewhere in the world there are a very few individuals who read everything that is written about Shakespeare in the English language every year; keeping up with the publications of books and articles in the scholarly press alone is a full-time job. These individuals are, of course, scholars, for the majority of writing about Shakespeare today is by scholars for other scholars about what scholars have said.

One of the things that irritates nonacademics is the apparent necessity of demonstrating that the scholar has read everything ever written about the topic in question through extensive cross-referencing to works by other scholars. It makes Shakespeare studies a daunting field for prospective scholars, just as younger actors and directors carry around the weight of all those famous and marvellous performances to which theirs are going to be compared.

Standing upon the Shoulders

The community of Shakespearean scholars suffers from acute introspection, but also benefits from an interconnected web of academic pursuits. Actors can be thankful for the years of slogging, followed by the months of painstaking gleaning, that result in a presentation of the most interesting bits and pieces to enhance our appreciation of some obscure reference in a lesser-known play. Francis Barker, in writing "Treasures of Culture: *Titus Andronicus* and Death by Hanging," provides us with a few interesting comments on the Elizabethan hangings that illuminate the unhappy end of the Clown in 4.4. To do this, he has gone through more than one intimidating tome, including a source he describes almost reverentially: "From 1975 to 1982 Professor Cockburn published the records of the Home Circuit in ten volumes, one for each of the circuit's constituent counties for each of the reigns of Elizabeth and James" (259).

Ideally, the circle would be completed by the publication of an edition of each of the plays with footnotes that draw upon the most interesting of these tidbits, selected from the most interesting gleanings of the most extensive and comprehensive slogging. Although this might be the goal of many of the editors of Shakespeare's plays, several factors stand in the way of such an achievement. First, there is no way for editors to keep up with the pace of scholarly output. Second, editors select from among the gleanings, using as their criteria the academic respectability of the findings rather than their capacity to inspire an actor's creativity. Space limitations require that editors reduce still further the tidbits that are included in notes, and the amount of information included in any given citation. The result is that even the best editions can only point the way toward a rich lode of scholarly production that benefits from almost four hundred years of analysis, exploration, research, and discussion.

The Great Debates

We quarrel in print, by the book.

Touchstone, *AYLI* [5.4.90]

To the outside, professional Shakespearean scholars are a strange breed indeed. The combative tone adopted in the presentation of their ideas is exacerbated by the intensely competitive nature of their field. There are distinct schools of approach, as well as arriving and disappearing fashions in theory and style, so that there seems to be endless jousting as the old-fashioned are mocked into silence and the newcomers fight to receive a serious hearing. As the industry grows, the pressure to uncover everything written, to cite every scholar, to refute the enemy, and to acknowledge intellectual debts transforms the scholarship into an exercise in footnotes. Anxiety pervades the air, because just when you think that you know what sort of article is sure to be published in the most respected journals, you discover that a radical reevaluation has already taken place and whatever you might have had to say has already been refuted.

Although nonscholars find all of the debates pointless, there is a very good reason why scholars spend so much of their energy discussing the theories of others. This is because, in many aspects of Shakespeare studies, theories are all we have. The actual evidence is so fragmented that it is open to a wide variety of interpretations. Placed into one pattern, the surviving manuscripts and first editions tell one story; if they are placed into an alternative pattern, the story changes along with the assumptions then made about Shakespeare, his fellow actors, his audience, and his plays. Outsiders to academia cannot be blamed for their impressions of the primary agenda of most Shakespearean scholarship as "I'm right, you're wrong, and so is everyone else who has ever written on this topic, except those who agree with me."

Presenting Opinions as Facts

Sometimes a rehearsal-room question is best answered by a precise, unequivocal answer. It might be that scholars have debated the issue, and that there is evidence to support several interpretations. These debates are of great interest to scholars but irrelevant to those entrusted with making the plays live over and over again in the theatre.

There are other issues, in contrast, where alternative possibilities are the bread and butter of an actor's experience. Nonacademics can be deeply offended by the absolute tone of many scholars, not realizing that this is the result of the nature of debate within Shakespeare studies. Professor A writes in absolute terms, presenting his "reading" of the play, criticizing those who have read the play differently, and disallowing any argument that contradicts his. Professor B responds with an alternative reading, equally positive that her "reading" is the only possible one and poking all sorts of holes in professor A's book. Outsiders wonder why either scholar is so antagonistic, and how they can be so sure that theirs is the "correct" interpretation. Theatre people know full well that "correct" and "incorrect" are immaterial: something works or it doesn't, and moreover it might work for this production because actress A is playing the role, but when actress B takes it on, something quite different can be found to work just as well.

Here is an example from *Hamlet*. Some scholars have looked at Claudius and have concluded that he is a good king, citing his effective delegation to the king of Norway and the swift containment of the threat of young Fortinbras. Other scholars, looking at exactly the same "evidence," have concluded that Claudius is entirely duped by the crafty old Norway's response to his ambassadors, and that allowing Fortinbras to pass through Denmark with an army is an act of supreme foolishness. Scholars also debate whether Fortinbras's arrival at the end of the play is a resolution that suggests a future of political stability for Denmark, or quite the opposite.

If you were to read only one side of the scholarly argument, you would be left with the impression that only one view could possibly be justified, given the words of the play and the historical context within which Shakespeare wrote it. Furthermore, you would be led to believe that anyone who does not share this view is something of an idiot. Only if you encounter the writing of an equally adamant scholar who argues the opposite would you realize that either interpretation can be supported by the text, something that has been demonstrated in the variety of successful productions of the play, in some of which Claudius is an effective king, though a villain, and in others of which he is a dunce, a drunk, a fool, a lecher, or all of the above. I have seen the final entrance of Fortinbras costumed and staged to evoke the arrival of Nazi storm troopers; I have also seen the heroic and just Fortinbras mopping up the horror of the play to the satisfaction of all.

Ur-characters

In describing the manner in which communication between an actor and a director can run aground in his book on directing, *Prospero's Staff*, Charles Marowitz suggests, "Whether he verbalizes it or not, almost every actor models his role on some figure, real or imaginary, that in a sense 'directs' him from the inner recesses of his mind" (66). Although Marowitz does not apply his observation directly to the plays of Shakespeare, his choice of the term "ur-character" to describe the damage done to the creative process by unacknowledged assumptions about a role is particularly telling. Marowitz is making use of the term scholars use for the versions of plays, now lost, that predate Shakespeare's telling of the story but upon which he inevitably drew. We know, for example, that an earlier version of *Hamlet*, probably by Thomas Kyd, was performed before 1589. Scholars call this play, for which no manuscript survives, the ur-*Hamlet* and speculate about its impact on the *Hamlet* we know.

One of the most damaging effects of academic interpretations of characters and events is that an actor can be unaware of the existence or source of these rigid assumptions, which have come down to us from generations of scholars. An ur-character sits just out of sight in everyone's consciousness and with deadly pressure steers the actor into preestablished interpretations that are no more or less valid than alternative and individualized "readings" of the characters that might occur in the natural course of rehearsal but that the ur-character drowns out.

Every Shakespearean actor should have a look at the irreverent and thought-provoking diatribes that Marowitz has published over the years. Armed with his armory of jabs and put-downs and always alert for the infamous "ur-character" that he describes so vividly, an actor is armed and ready to face head-on the weight of theatre history that otherwise can suck the lifeblood out of the rehearsal process.

The Mirror

> For any thing so over-done, is from the purpose of Playing, whose end both at the first and now, was and is, to hold as 'twere the Mirror up to Nature; to show Virtue her own Feature, Scorn her own Image, and the very Age and Body of the Time, his form and pressure.
>
> Hamlet [*Hamlet* 3.2.19]

For all that divides those who discuss the plays from those who perform them, scholars and actors share the temptation and the longing to see our own faces in the mirror held up in Shakespeare's plays.

When I use the metaphor of a mirror, please do not think of what you have hanging above the sink in your bathroom. Instead, picture one of the mirrors you might have seen in a museum. It is made of bronze or tin and has been hammered into a flat surface, but even from a distance you can still see the pockmarks and indentations on the irregular surface. The reflection is distorted both in color and in shape, but it is sufficiently accurate that, combined with what you expect to see, you feel that you are seeing yourself. By looking in such a mirror you could adjust your clothing, monitor your aging, and reflect upon your shared humanity. By comparing the face of another with the reflection the two of you see when you stand side by side before the mirror, you would know that the mirror is not to be trusted for detail or accuracy, but rather is to be enjoyed in its capacity to let you see the general shape of those parts of your body you cannot see without assistance. By holding one mirror in your hand and looking into it as it reflects a mirror behind your head, you can even see your back.

That is the mirror that Shakespeare holds up to the audience and, in the fragmentary documents, to the scholars who spend their lives searching for the "real" Shakespeare. I like to think of him as someone very like myself, but I am fully prepared to imagine that he was in fact so different not only from me but from anything that I could imagine that any images I glimpse in the assembled evidence are telling me more about myself than about Shakespeare.

Just how fragmentary is the evidence? Keep these facts in mind:

- Scholars have reason to believe that as many as four out of five plays of the period have been lost to us. This would include, we all assume, plays by Shakespeare not collected in the First Folio and not afterwards added to the complete works by various editors over the years.

- Seven detailed production flow charts from Elizabethan theatre companies have survived, but only one is for a play that has also survived, and that was not written by Shakespeare nor performed by Shakespeare's company.

- We have no accurate and detailed drawings for any of Shakespeare's theatres.

- We have no accurate and detailed company lists, casting records, or account books for Shakespeare's company.

- We do not know for sure when any of Shakespeare's plays were actually composed.

- We have no idea of the relationship between the first editions of any of Shakespeare's plays and either the play he wrote or the play his company performed. We also do not know how much that play might have been revised following the first performance and any subsequent revivals.

- We can only speculate about Shakespeare's personal life, including his sexual orientation and his relationships with his wife and children, with his fellow actors, and with his noble patrons.

- Scholars cannot agree as to how many languages Shakespeare understood, how much he might have travelled around England or beyond its borders, what occupations he might have held before ending up in the theatre in London, what books he read, what types of individuals he might have met in his lifetime, his religious affiliations, his political leanings, or his real attitude to any thematic issue raised in his plays.

- Although we have a number of firsthand reports of Shakespeare's plays in performance, we have no way of understanding how these writers defined the terms they used to describe the performances. Also, many of the reports do not correspond with the playtexts that have survived, and so we must acknowledge the high possibility of inaccuracy in these anecdotes.
- For every well-established tradition about Shakespeare's life and theatre, there is hard concrete evidence that has been used by at least one scholar to disprove that very tradition.
- Scholarly theories are almost always presented as entirely reasonable, rational, and self-evident. All it takes is another scholar disputing the first, and the self-evident is revealed as speculation.
- Much of what we take for granted in the shaping of Shakespeare's texts comes to us from the eighteenth-century editors who sought to regularize his genius, that being the taste of the times.

It is perhaps painfully discouraging for newcomers to the world of Shakespearean scholarship to discover that there is no one version of any of the plays that everyone accepts as being the correct one, that there is no one version of Shakespeare's life that everyone agrees is the most detailed and accurate, and that there is no one description of the theatrical practices of his theatre that satisfies even the majority of scholars poring over the surviving documents and artifacts. In fact, the interpretations are as varied as the number of scholars working in the field. For every publication in which the writer announces that the puzzle is now solved for all time, there are thirty scholars waiting to refute, realign, and re-create an entirely different solution with exactly the same few pieces of evidence.

But the truth of the matter is that the fragmentary evidence allows any one of us to rearrange the pieces of the puzzle into a shape that best reflects what we want to see. For most of us, that is an amalgamation of what we know and what we want to be true. This is the means by which Shakespeare is a mirror to us.

Those Who Discuss and Those Who Do

> I have laboured,
> And with no little study, that my teaching
> And the strong course of my Authority
> Might go one way.
>
> Cranmer [*HVIII* 5.2.68]

Anthony Graham-White concludes the introduction to his 1995 study *Punctuation and Its Dramatic Value in Shakespearean Drama* as follows: "This study will, I hope, interest three kinds of readers: first, those who as editors and scholars are involved in the bibliographical study of Renaissance playscripts; second, those who are concerned with staging them; and third, anyone who needs to refer to an account of punctuation in Elizabethan literature" (25). I can think of no two groups of people with less in common than those involved in bibliographical studies of Renaissance playscripts and those concerned with staging them. Although actors need access to some of the information buried in Graham-White's excellent study, most theatre professionals would find that almost everything about *Punctuation and Its Dramatic Value in Shakespearean Drama* gets in the way of their fulfilling Graham-White's hopes for an interdisciplinary readership.

Many scholars and actors share an interest, only to discover that the conventions of their individual professions get in the way of mutual benefit. Graham-White's introductory chapter identifies just such a potential merging of obsessions: "My own concern is primarily with the spoken delivery of the text, and to that the punctuation of the earliest reliable edition is often a better guide than the syntactical correctness of a modern editor" (17). What the scholar does not seem to realize is that the language he uses, which reflects not only the theoretical framework he assumes that he shares with his reader, but also a mastery of a specifically scholarly vocabulary, limits the transmission of his exciting and practical insights to other scholars; actors, who could put his ideas into practice, won't get past the scholarly trappings. These include the layout of the book, the preponderance of evidence presented to impress other scholars with the validity of the observations, and the language used to present the most helpful bits: "The use of punctuation for specifically dramatic effect is not disjunct from the use of punctuation to mark the meter, for the playwright seizes upon the metrical form to indicate the feelings of a character in a specific situation" (78). Actors might well be offended by the implication that they do not have the intelligence to understand such a sentence, just as scholars might be offended by a similar implication, that they do not have the intelligence to understand how theatre works. I would not be able to defend such a premise, but I would be able to make a strong case for the discomfort an actor would feel if he or she were expected to engage in scholarly debate within academia, and the embarrassment a scholar would feel if he or she were expected to perform on the main stage of a major Shakespearean festival theatre. For all their intelligence, scholars and actors are quite simply not at home with the conventions and discourses of the other world, and if the actor cannot find a way to explain theatrical intuitions or the scholar cannot share discoveries freed from scholarly trappings, then the two sides will continue to gaze across an unbridgeable divide with a mixture of longing and distrust.

Some scholars are more aware of the mismatch in agenda and discourse than others. David Bradley, whose exhaustive study of the seven surviving production flow-charts from Shakespeare's generation of theatre companies has the evocative title *From Text to Performance in the Elizabethan Theatre: Preparing the Play for the Stage*, apologizes to any theatrical readers who have survived the first three pages of his introduction: "I shall also try the patience of readers whose interest is in the theatrical outcomes. To them I can only apologise, for, if the evidence of regular theatrical practice is to be more convincing than the bibliographical arguments that confront it, the arguments for it must be equally stringent, and must be shown to operate for the great majority of texts"(4). We can only wish for Bradley to publish an article in which he would feel free to present the information of interest to those working in the theatre, having fulfilled his scholarly obligations in the full-length book. As it stands, it is impossible to recommend Bradley's book for any but the most determined of actors; there is a great deal of dross for a very few nuggets of gold. The one good thing about Bradley's scholarship is that it is informed by his experimentation in the staging of early modern plays on a stage that reproduced the Swan Theatre (24).

Us and Them

The natural difference in the perspectives of actors and scholars is exacerbated by an anti-intellectual prejudice on the part of some theatre professionals and an antitheatrical prejudice on the part of some scholars. I think that we must discount the theatre people who scoff at scholars, just as we discount the scholars who scoff at actors. In my experience they now represent a minority, and a particularly obtuse one at that. Charles Marowitz entitles one section of his 1991 polemic *Recycling Shakespeare* "Free Shakespeare! Jail Scholars!" and, even after acknowledging the many valuable insights unearthed by scholarship, concludes, "But in the past fifty or sixty years, the Shakespeare industry has turned into an academic Godzilla which rapaciously swallows up the Histories, the Tragedies and the Comedies and regularly disgorges a combination of steam and stool which passes for classical lore but is nothing more than the effluence of some raging academic incontinence" (69). Marowitz reserves his greatest scorn for scholars who study punctuation, which suggests that he would not be likely to reach for Graham-White's book.

Some of the scholars who venture into the territory of staging appear never to have seen a production they liked nor talked to an actor whose insights they were prepared to solicit. Martin Buzacott in *The Death of the Actor: Shakespeare on Page and Stage* argues that actors damage our understanding of Shakespeare's plays. Buzacott uses the language of guerilla warfare and international terrorism, writing about being held hostage by the conspiracies of directorial concepts and actors' incapacities:

Usually a hostage is killed because of what she represents, not because of what she has done. This provides an excellent alibi for the aggressor, because it allows responsibility to be deflected from her onto some ideological cause, with the result that, in the case of acting, the performer is usually blameless and enjoys the advantage of being applauded for her good deeds and being excused for her bad. There is usually some powerful faceless person behind the scenes—a director, a playwright, or the terrorist leader who bears the guilt of the atrocities. (34)

It is difficult to know whether to laugh aloud or shudder at the intensity of Buzacott's disgust when one reads such a sensational metaphor.

We all know of boring scholars and self-indulgent actors, as well as self-indulgent scholars and boring actors, some of whom have contributed books to the overburdened shelves of university libraries. Nothing irritates theatre professionals more than a scholar who insists on writing about Shakespeare with complete disregard of the theatrical aspects of the plays. Nothing irritates a scholar more than the anecdotal musings of a theatre professional, wherein great pronouncements are made based on vague impressions and faulty understanding of anything other than the writer's ego fulfillment. Academia must be criticized for placing quantity before quality, and in particular for demanding that scholars churn out annual ruminations whether or not they have anything to contribute. Likewise, the theatre world is guilty of assuming that every member of the Royal Shakespeare Company is, ipso facto, an expert on Shakespeare.

I would rather salute the many scholars and theatre professionals who have attempted to reach beyond the enclosed enclaves of their respective crafts than suspect all scholars of mustiness and all actors of intellectual vacuity. There is much more to be gained from the naïve admiration expressed by a scholar who acknowledges that the plays were written to be acted and then speculates romantically, if ignorantly, about how an actor approaches a role than from complacent theatre professionals who trivialize the discipline and dedication to intellectual debate that characterize academic scholars. By the same token, there is a great deal more to be learned from a theatre professional who has been persuaded to publish the pearls of wisdom acquired after years in rehearsal halls and classrooms than from the equally complacent scholar who sneers at anecdotal musings, disregarding the flashes of insight that can only arise from firsthand experience.

Dust Off Your Shakespeare

With immense effort, scholars labor and produce nuggets of inestimable value. With similarly immense effort, actors produce productions that demonstrate flashes of brilliant insight. But both scholars and actors must wade through knee-high dross to find the nuggets and flashes, and in all honesty, very few of them are really interested in that particular sort of wading.

Scholars have taken advantage of the many forums available to them in which to decry the failings of various productions of Shakespeare that they have had the (mis)fortune to attend. At the same time, it has long been the suspicion of many lovers of Shakespeare that the academic industry associated with the man has somehow become deeply disconnected with whatever it is that makes the plays appealing to readers, actors, directors, and audience members. Scholars are appalled at the latest strategies in updating Shakespeare with hockey or spaceship uniforms, while nonacademics are nauseated by scholarly "theorrhoea," that trend in literary studies that privileges the reading and discussing of theoretical works over literary works, much to the dismay of anyone who has neither the interest nor the patience to acquire the correct jargon.

Meanwhile, productions and publications abound. There seems to be no end to Shakespeare's popularity as an entirely new generation of patrons discovers his characters and stories transposed to the cinema and television. Publishers rush to produce everything from the most esoteric scholarship, such as Robert S. Knapp's *Shakespeare, the Theater and the Book*, a semiotic analysis of trends in contemporary performance, to Norrie Epstein's *The Friendly Shakespeare*, with no entry longer than a few paragraphs, perfect for glancing at during breaks in rehearsal. *Shakespeare for Dummies* by John Doyle and Ray Lischner, has now joined the popular series, and a vast assortment of books that promise to bring Shakespeare to kids have turned up in public school libraries.

In *Kiss Me Kate* the two protagonists of the comic subplot sing a wonderful song entitled "Brush Up Your Shakespeare," which advises that a few well-chosen quotations from the Bard will impress the girls and smooth the way for the con. The duet seldom fails to win applause and the laughter of recognition, such is the aura that surrounds Shakespeare. I would like to update the Cole Porter lyrics to read, "Dust Off Your Shakespeare," in an effort to shed some of the overwhelming weight that has accumulated from all those productions and all those publications. In "The Immortal Bard," a short story by Isaac Asimov reprinted in Marilyn Schoenbaum's *A Shakespeare Merriment: An Anthology of Shakespearean Humor*, Asimov imagines the transportation of Will to our century, where, in response to being shown a book of criticism, he says, "God ha' mercy! What cannot be racked from words in five centuries? One could wring, methinks, a flood from a damp clout!" (189). The punch line of the short comic tale is the news that, having enrolled in a university English department course on himself, he is flunked by the professor.

AN ACTOR'S GUIDE TO SHAKESPEAREAN SCHOLARSHIP

> Knowing I loved my books, he furnished me
> From mine own Library, with volumes that
> I prize above my Dukedom.
>
> Prospero [*Tempest* 1.2.166]

In preparing this book, I have attempted to collect in one place all of the tricks I have learned, all the resources I have found, and all the uses I have discovered for the wealth of information and insight produced by the labor of scholars. I knew before I began that I simply would not be able to keep up with the outpouring of publications, to say nothing of the daily expansion of Shakespeare's presence on the Internet.

Copia

Because I simply cannot shake off the scholarly habits ingrained after years of earning my living in a university, I struggle with the impulse to include every single article and book I have ever consulted. Nonacademic readers will be happy to know that I resisted this temptation and have included only those books that I actually found helpful.

At the same time, I have included a wide range of books, some old and dated in the eyes of modern scholars, some very recent and overburdened with the latest literary theories, to the dismay of my theatrical readers. Although the vast majority of references are to books that are academic in tone and the product of traditional forms of scholarship, I have also occasionally included distinctly nonscholarly works that might fulfill a particular need for the nonscholarly reader.

Accessible Scholarship

The scholarly books I have recommended have been chosen with a general readership in mind. They contain something that is absent from popular books on Shakespeare: a firm grasp of the facts. While less formal writers (and I am surely in that category) are wont to make statements that lead inevitably to the question "Yes, but how do you know that?" these writers are careful to state the firm footing on which they base their analysis and observation.

Such care inescapably adds to the stodginess of the writing, but who is to say what great insights might not be buried there? The scholarly format does provide an important resource for all readers. All such books contain extensive bibliographies; you can use these listings of books on related topics as a guide for your browsing. Most of the book-length works also contain first-rate indexes. Because there is a standard style in scholarly publishing, you will be sure of finding in the introductory chapter all you need to understand the approach (or thesis, that is, the central argument) of the writer. If this appeals, you can check out the index for a listing of citations from the play on which you are working. Tables of contents can also help you go directly to those sections that are most likely to contain useful bits.

Just the Facts, Ma'am

There are also some wonderful Victorian and Edwardian collections of Elizabethan memorabilia, folk legends, anecdotes, and apocrypha at which con-

temporary social historians sneer but that contain such theatrical gems that I
have included them and risked the wrath of more serious historians. I do this
because I firmly believe that it does not matter if a certain tidbit is "true"
provided it serves to bring the play alive for an actor preparing a role in a
specific production. This puts me at odds with almost every seeker of absolute
truth in academia. But what can we poor thespians do with the great debates
about historical truth? It truly does not matter to us what actually happened
four hundred years ago. All that matters is that we find the enduring human
truth within the fiction of these plays and bring the events of the play and the
words of the characters to life as vividly and honestly as we can. If an apocryphal story about Shakespeare and a drunken sailor helps us to believe in the
ribald songs of Trinculo, then any question of the authenticity of the story is
second to the undeniable justification of the means by the end. It would be
quite different if we were lecturing on Elizabethan England and came out with
outlandish statements of fact that have been proven inaccurate by recent research. But we are creating productions, not taking a stand in an academic
debate, and that freedom encourages us to take the widest possible latitude
and roam far and wide for scholarly nuggets that can fuel our art.

Absent Scholars

There are a considerable number of Shakespearean experts whose work will
not make an appearance in this book. These fall into the general category of
literary analysis, in other words, works in which the author has a theoretical
concept or a perspective and then takes the reader through the play discussing
various events, lines of dialogue, or characters to see how they might be understood, given that premise. The author is almost always perceptive and insightful, and the "reading" of the play that results is coherent, cohesive, and
persuasive.

The real problem with "readings" is that they have a nasty tendency to
linger in the mind, just below the level of conscious thought, affecting explorations undertaken in rehearsal with a sullen negativity. The persuasive "reading" of a character, an event, or even a line of dialogue does not demand to
be played. Rather, it shuts doors to alternative, as-yet-unconsidered possibilities. Somehow, without knowing quite how, but all the time feeling that it is
the most natural and obvious solution to the moment, that anything else would
be twisting the play out of shape in search of novelty, the actors find themselves performing aspects of "readings" that they have long forgotten ever
having read.

This is not to suggest that the scholar is incapable of suggesting approaches
to the events, dialogue, or characters that are theatrical, or, as actors like to
say, "playable." Quite the contrary. Of course, given the fact that they can
pore over the play and make connections between a subtle image in act 1 and
an obscure allusion in act 3, neither of which an audience would catch, much

less connect, at the speed of live performance, scholars have a tendency to base their "readings" on a foundation that actors would find tenuous. The tone in which the "reading" is presented might also annoy the nonscholar, because the culture of academia requires that the author put forth what is clearly just one way of looking at the play as if it were the only way of looking at the play. There is some range in the vehemence with which academics trounce the theories or readings of others who have written on the same play, but even the least aggressive are required, by the unspoken law of competitive scholarship, to take a stand, rejecting all other approaches in favor of their own.

Those of us who have participated in more than one rehearsal process for the same play have seen different casts and directors, or even the same director at different times, prove undeniably that any play contains a multitude of coherent, cohesive, persuasive ways of being performed. The journey of rehearsals is going to be limited, however, if even some of the cast have lodged in their intellect a single approach acquired from one of these scholarly readings.

Perhaps the best cure for oppressive scholarly interpretations is not to avoid learning about any but rather to find out about so many that no one interpretation can possibly dominate. There is something to be said for encountering a variety of scholarly "readings" to see how the different approaches play off against each other. Actors can be assisted in their search for a sampling of contrasting approaches by the editors of scholarly editions that include essays on the play and by editors of the casebook-style collections on a single play.

Another subsection of Shakespearean scholarship is that dedicated to the close examination and discussion of Shakespearean scholarship itself. Some books cover the history of how Shakespeare has been considered and discussed, while others explore the various approaches that have come into or out of favor in recent years. Leading scholars who practice a certain type of scholarship might write about the theories and approaches that characterize their "school" while others, who do not share that particular perspective, might write at length about the flaws in the publications generated by that school. As you can imagine, this keeps scholars busy churning out books and articles and attending conferences, but none of it is of any interest to actors, and so it has no place in this particular survey.

THEATRICAL ADVENTURES IN AN ACADEMIC LIBRARY

> Come and take choice of all my Library,
> And so beguile thy sorrow.
>
> Titus [*Titus* 4.1.34]

Now it is time to make our acquaintance with that imposing repository of all these dry and dusty books: the academic library. When I was in grade six, I earned a bit of extra pocket money by putting books away in the school library. I look back on that experience with fondness, because it taught me a basic lesson in navigation that has served me well in the many years since. Once we acquire this essential road map, we will be able to find our way around the varied and complexly interconnected resources in search of those riches that will enhance our capacity to bring alive Shakespeare's plays.

Those of us who love libraries breathe deeply when we enter the stacks, savoring the dusty air, and promptly begin to trot up and down the aisles, zooming in apparently effortlessly on the exact shelf we need, glancing only rarely at the paper in our hand that records the critical set of letters and numbers, and then at the corresponding markings at the end of each aisle. Once we have reached our destination, we are likely to stand there pulling various books off the shelf, for as long as we can, before lugging an armload to the checkout. Much as I enjoy scanning the collections of far-off libraries through electronic search engines, nothing replaces a good lengthy browse along the shelves. Often a wonderful book is lurking there, its useful contents hidden under an elusive title. The librarians are so skilled in grouping books that if you find one book in the catalogue on your topic and trace it to its home on the library shelf, you can be sure to find many more equally interesting ones awaiting you on adjacent shelves.

A Guided Tour

The art of navigating through the library and nibbling at its feast of knowledge is easily acquired if you are adventuresome and follow a few simple guidelines:

- Do not feel under any obligation to do any more than look at tables of contents, indexes, and illustrations. Dip into an interesting book only as long as every turn of the page rewards you with something worth knowing. If you find lots of things, you might consider signing the book out or sitting down with it for a time, but expect a considerable amount of dross and learn to sift through it quickly in search of actors' gold. Remember always that those things that concern scholars, about which they write and read at length, are often not at all interesting to anyone else. If you find a book that does not have a user-friendly index, put it back on the shelf.

- Learn to use the library catalogue system to locate books that are likely to be of interest in sections other than the obvious: the Shakespeare shelves and those dedicated to English history. Don't be shy. Ask for a briefing session by one of the library staff on duty, and ask specifically for the tricks at which such individuals excel for conducting both specific and general book searches.

- Once you find an interesting title listed in the catalogue and then find your way to that section of the library, take a few moments to look at the other books gathered in that area. You will quickly get an idea of what the various books have in common, and as you move along the shelf to the right and left of the book you have come for, you will see how the topics shift. There is always a fairly transparent logic to the cataloguing of a book collection, and the better you understand this, the more likely you will be to stumble upon interesting books on topics for which you would never have thought to search.

• Don't feel obliged to plow through dense academic prose. Perhaps the index lists entries that interest you, but when you go to those pages and all you find is a lengthy discussion that makes no particular sense, put the book back on the shelf. Remember that the highly evolved academic disciplines have developed a language that is impenetrable to all but the initiated, and there is often a direct correlation between the amount of jargon used and the uselessness of the book to anyone but another scholar. If this particular obtuse writer you have been so unlucky to select has anything of real interest to say, you can be sure that some other scholar will have dug it out of this dusty book and presented it in a much more interesting fashion in another book or article. Since digging and regurgitating are what scholars do best, let them do that work for you.

• Ignore footnotes. The primary function of these irritating interruptions is to demonstrate to other scholars that the academic standards of the discipline within which the author is working have been met. Actors need not concern themselves with the tortured self-justification required of scholars by other scholars.

• The introduction to the book usually clarifies what the author wants to accomplish. It is also a demonstration of the writing style. If you are interested in the former and like the latter, the book is probably worth a good browse.

• Remember that some books are dedicated to a discussion of the work of other scholars rather than presenting new information on a topic. Avoid these books like the plague. If an otherwise useful book contains elements of rebuttal, wherein this particular author pointedly states that another scholar got it wrong, ignore the apparent backstabbing. It is not personal, though you would never know it from the tone of the comments overheard at scholarly conferences.

The Shakespeareana Collection

When you first venture into the library stacks in search of books on Shakespeare, you will probably not want to ask for a list of all the books on the subject: there will be several thousand, even in a small holding. But they are arranged in a fairly straightforward fashion on the shelves, following either the Dewey decimal system or the Library of Congress Classification Schedules. As I am most familiar with the latter, we will begin this guided tour at PR2750. First are shelved the original editions, facsimiles of the folio and quarto texts, followed by modern editions of the plays, beginning with copies of the complete works, then individual plays in alphabetical order by title. Alongside the editions of individual plays you will find scholarly books that have that play for a subject, known generally as "criticism." At the end of this section you will find the poems and then what are called the Shakespearean apocrypha: those plays in which Shakespeare had a hand but which have yet to be included by all scholars in the official complete works, or "canon." If the library has any, you will find translations of the plays, and then imitations and adaptations.

What follows next are periodicals, concordances, dictionaries, indexes, and books of quotations, many of which will be shelved either with the periodicals or in the reference section. Libraries vary greatly in the selection of books to be deemed reference, but generally all of the really useful dictionaries are not with the circulating books.

Then come the books on Shakespeare himself. You will find historical sources and documents as well as biographies here, and also books about Shakespeare's England. There are books on his home and haunts, his town and county, London, the theatres in London, and memorials, testimonials, portraits, and relics. Near the end of this section you will find the many volumes that have been written attempting to prove that Shakespeare's plays were written by someone other than the son of a glover from Stratford, followed by books that document the verifiable manuscripts as well as the forgeries.

Next come books about the sources upon which Shakespeare drew for his inspiration, beginning with general collections and essays and followed by specific categories such as emblem literature or wit and humor. The specific authors who figure largely in this category each make an appearance: you can find books about Shakespeare's debt to Holinshed, Montaigne, Ovid, Plutarch, and Seneca, among others. This section is wrapped up by scholars who compare Shakespeare to his contemporaries such as Christopher Marlowe and Ben Jonson.

Now you are in the heart of Shakespearean criticism as it spans the centuries. First there are the general histories of trends in critical approaches, followed by collections of criticism and analysis of the critical approaches organized by century, then by region or country. Snuggled in at the end of the general-criticism section you will find biographies of some of the great Shakespearean scholars.

More criticism follows, arranged now according to genre: studies of comedies, tragicomedies, romances, histories, tragedies, and the poems are followed by studies within philosophical categories such as idealism or naturalism. For a change of pace, there are next some books about teaching Shakespeare before the criticism section continues with books about characters in groups, such as women, children, fools, kings, or villains, and then individually.

The next topics for criticism have a more theatrical bent, though the actual scholarship is only irregularly theatrical in focus. We have books on Shakespeare's wit and humor, followed by his use of various dramatic techniques, such as asides, openings, soliloquies, and suspense. There are also books that analyze various aspects of the plays, such as their narrative patterns, their scenic structure, and their irregular time schemes.

Now follow books about Shakespeare's treatment and knowledge of specialized subjects. Here the actor will be sure to find books that will help flesh out the roles and worlds of the plays. The drier books cover the world of ideas: philosophy, ethics, or religion, though even these can provide fascinating insights into the beliefs of Shakespeare's contemporaries. The most useful books deal with topics like crime and criminals, botany and zoology, astrology, medicine, and sports. In addition, there are books on specific topics such as birds, death, dogs, fathers, honor, incest, Italy, marriage, military life, pregnancy, Rome, sex, and swearing.

After such excitement come the dusty books on textual criticism, and then a selection of books that analyze the language of the plays. At the end of the Shakespeare bookshelves is a collection of studies of the plays in performance, including film and video versions. Do not be disappointed, as many more books about aspects of production are shelved in a different section of the library, PN2589, Renaissance theatre. Here you will find books on everything from the boy actors to theatre at court. Just along the way, at PN2596, you will find books about the theatre in London, including Shakespeare's Globe.

The collection of books comparing Shakespeare to his contemporaries is not that large, because the many books by scholars who look at Shakespeare within the context of all of the playwrights of his era are housed some shelves away, in the PR646 through 678 section. Here you will find all sorts of thematic studies that explore how different writers address certain issues; there are also studies of the evolution of genres such as they might be described by Polonius, "Tragedy, Comedy, History, Pastoral: Pastoral-Comical-Historical-Pastoral: Tragical-Historical: Tragical-Comical-Historical-Pastoral" [*Hamlet* 2.2.396]. These are of less interest to an actor unless the writer also blends in a discussion of how the theatrical presentation of the issues or events might be compared with what the first actors would have experienced in their daily lives. Look instead for studies about things like adultery, dandies, fools and jesters, homosexuality, illegitimacy, Jews, magic, physicians, revenge, and sex. Some of these contain detailed studies of plays that are seldom performed today, but the most interesting include excellent general introductions that apply equally as well to Shakespeare as to the plays under examination.

In quite another section of the library under the letter D you will find books written by historians. The scholarly discipline of history has undergone as significant changes in approach as can be found in literary studies of Shakespeare's plays. Some historians are interested in the lives of the big names; others are interested in discussing at length the big events. Some historians consider economic developments, others the political changes marked by the ebb and flow of power in and out of the hands of various individuals and groups. Some historians delve exhaustively into the available documents of a community or recognizable group of people in order to speculate upon various aspects of their ordinary lives. Some historians study general or specific aspects of cultural activities, including fairs, ballads and broadsheets, or the theatre itself. Actors have much to be thankful for, given the many dusty archives historians have searched through, looking for facts and patterns that bring another time and place alive for our imaginations.

Some scholarly history books have been created to meet the needs of the general reading public, and almost without exception an actor will be able to find just about everything of interest in such books. You can spot them easily because they make extensive use of pictorial reproductions, and what historical information there might be is presented like a story, with minimal reference to statistics, graphs, or extensive references to obscure archives.

The row upon row of bookshelves in a university library stacks may intimidate at first, but once you learn your way around the system, you will be able to browse with pleasure. Be sure to have a look at books in close proximity to the gem you have discovered to see if others writing in that specific subsection of scholarship are equally interesting.

Book Browsing

If you know the author or the title of a book, large collections can be navigated easily. You simply look up one or the other in the catalogue, today a computer-assisted activity that is as user-friendly as possible, with help on hand from human or electronic sources. However, if you would like to see what might be available on a specific topic, the catalogue can be overwhelming. Here are a few hints:

- Once you have found even a single book that seems to be on your topic, look at how it is listed in the subject index and then use the catalogue to search using only these subject words. This is the only way to access the library's subject index, which uses terms set by the Library of Congress.

- If you are browsing through a book by a scholar who makes use of information about which you would like more detail, check the footnotes and bibliography for the sources that have been used. There you will often find specific titles that you can then look up in the catalogue, pull from the shelves, browse, and use as a source of further titles to locate.

- If you find an author whose approach, agenda, and writing style particularly appeal, then you might want to see what else this author has written. If this book is one of a series, it is likely that other books in the series will have similar approaches. Finally, you can see what else that publisher has released if the catalogue allows you to search their collections by linking keywords, such as "Shakespeare" and "acting," with a publisher name.

Journal Articles

One of the most wonderful events for those of us who live a portion of our lives in university libraries is the development of computer-based catalogues and indexes, many of which are available on the Web. This means that we can find all of the obscure books housed on dust-filled library shelves all around the world.

Actors, having other things to do with their time, can still benefit from the resources available to any librarian. Such is the state of Shakespearean scholarship that you would be hard pressed to have a question about a topic that someone, somewhere, has not written about.

Some products of some of the most useful digging and delving have been published in the form of articles in scholarly journals. The best index to such articles is that prepared by the Modern Language Association (MLA). The computerized databases have excellent search engines, so that by typing in "Shakespeare" and "money" you are given immediately twenty-nine entries. Some of these are dissertations, which are difficult to look at unless you can find a library that has purchased a copy. When I come across a dissertation that sounds, from its title, to be filled with all sorts of juicy bits, I next look in *Dissertation Abstracts*, where I can count on finding a more detailed description of exactly what the author attempted in the study. If the degree is a few years old, I try to find any record of an article or book by this person by entering the name into the search engine, because the majority of academics' first publications emerge directly from their doctoral work.

The MLA database does not give an abstract, or brief description of the content of the article, and sometimes it is quite difficult to tell, simply from the title, if the article will actually be worth searching for. I always appreciate those scholars who give a lengthy title that clarifies the approach they have taken. For example, in the twenty-nine entries under "Shakespeare" and "money," there is one for an article by Anne Paolucci entitled "Marx, Money, and Shakespeare: The Hegelian Core in Marxist Shakespeare-Criticism." It is not likely to be of as much interest as "Love, Marriage, and Money in Shakespeare's Theatre and Shakespeare's England."

Many of the articles that pop up in the MLA database search are published in collections of essays, which makes them easier to find if you have access to a university library that purchases such collections. Also, books are available to be sent out on interlibrary loan, whereas journals are kept in the home library.

On the other hand, tracking down a journal article that interests you will take you to the periodicals section of the library, and there you will find much that rewards your browsing. Once you have located the periodical that contains the article you found through the index, and if in fact the article rewards your search by containing nuggets of gold that you find inspiring and thought-provoking, then browse in other issues of the same journal on the understanding that if the editorial board has approved one article for publication that is useful for an actor, it is likely to have approved others written in the same style and/or from a similar scholarly perspective.

An Actor's Guide to Periodicals

Shakespearean scholars have carved out a significant presence in the publishing world, not only with book-length studies that expand the PR3000 shelving in every library, but also in the periodical reading rooms. Even so, it is not easy for a relatively young Shakespeare scholar to get published, given the number of established academics who continue to turn out everything from curriculum vitae padding to startling and important new work. The intense competitiveness of academic life, and in particular Shakespearean scholarship, results in the publishing of dense, esoteric, or jargon-filled articles of minimal use to actors. Some journals are best avoided for that reason; some are worth checking regularly to see just what might be hidden there of interest even to those who are not academics.

Shakespeare Bulletin; A Journal of Performance Criticism and Scholarship provides thoughtful, detailed commentaries on the productions of Shakespeare in the United States and Canada. These tend to provide a good record of staging choices rather than a print-media-style "review" and therefore are useful for production histories of our favorite plays. The few scholarly articles can be quite obscure.

Shakespeare and the Classroom has as its primary audience teachers of Shakespeare, but includes reviews of productions and films. Often the contributors combine practical, theatrical considerations with scholarly and pedagogical ones, resulting in articles of interest to an actor. *Shakespeare*, published by Georgetown University and Cambridge University Press, takes an even more relaxed tone in its presentation of ideas of teachers of Shakespeare.

At the other end of the spectrum, there are the most scholarly journals dedicated to publishing the most esoteric products from the Shakespeare academic factory. There is even a journal dedicated entirely to articles on one play: *Hamlet Studies*. Scholars from sister disciplines are also busy at work writing for such publications as *Emblematica: An Interdisciplinary Journal for Emblem Studies* and *Early Music*.

Some of the most academic scholars, however, regularly report upon the results of their intensive study of Shakespeare's plays, his life, and his world. This is in part because the subgenre of academic criticism known as performance criticism is now so firmly entrenched as to privilege those academics who have more than a passing understanding of how plays are actually rehearsed in real theatres. This in turn places into perspective some of scholars' more intense infighting, which seems to be moving out of fashion, except, as I hear it, at scholarly conferences, which can become quite nasty. Have a look at such staid and prestigious academic publications as *Cahiers Elisabethains*, as well as the best-known Shakespeare publication, *Shakespeare Quarterly*.

Shakespeare Survey

As the title implies, *Shakespeare Survey*, published once a year, features articles by leading scholars on a variety of issues. Many of the articles are of the driest and dustiest sort, but regularly the survey will contain something that blends scholarly discipline with a theatrical perspective. It is almost impossible to identify such articles without at the least a quick skim through them. As each issue also contains reviews of important productions, it is well worth an hour or two of an actor's time to catch up on the issues published in the last ten years or so.

The editorial style of *Shakespeare Survey* dispenses with lengthy bibliographies and places footnotes at the bottom of each column. This means that you cannot easily use these articles to enter into the Shakespeare scholarship web; as an alternative, each issue offers a lengthy review article about recent Shakespearean scholarship. Reading this can help you spot books that you might actually like to read.

As You Like It *Articles*

Thanks to the computerized indexes found in most university library reference sections, it is possible to search quickly and effectively through the thousands of articles published every year in the vast realm of Shakespearean academia. Most of the available search engines allow you to link keywords in order to zoom in on only those articles that might be of interest to someone going into rehearsal rather than preparing to write an article or book.

Sometimes it takes a bit of practice to find a pair or trio of words that neither eliminate too much nor collect too many titles. Very specific searches can net you absolutely nothing, and sometimes a fair amount of ingenuity is required to find just the right synonym to get at the topic in which you are interested.

When I combined a search for *As You Like It* with the keyword "social," I came up with six quite interesting entries, some of which were in rather obscure journals but three of which I could get my hands on quite easily. I also expended my energy locating articles that I was reasonably sure would contain more than just a thematic analysis and less jargon than information. Sometimes I would have to guess by the title, but often the name of the author, if it was familiar, or the title of the journal itself was a better clue.

You can count on *Shakespeare Quarterly* to publish articles that contain just the sort of historical information of interest to an actor. I was happy to locate something by Louis Adrian Montrose, whose book-length work *The Purpose of Playing* I had enjoyed. His article, which appeared in the spring 1981 issue, contained all sorts of interesting observations informed by an in-depth understanding of social history. It is easy to forget the essential point that Montrose makes: Rosalind is a princess, while Orlando is no more than a gentleman, and a third son at that. By drawing on contemporary Elizabethan publications, Montrose is able to demonstrate that Orlando's conflict with Oliver was a familiar situation and one sure to arouse strong feelings in Shakespeare's first actors and audience. This information is useful not only to the two actors most directly involved, but also to others who are required to form an attitude to that relationship. What, for example, does Charles the Duke's Wrestler think

of these two? And what do Rosalind and Celia think, for Orlando seems to
have told them some stories, as Celia reveals when the elder brother is mentioned:

> O I have heard him speak of that same brother,
> And he did render him the most unnatural
> That lived amongst men. [4.3.121]

We know how Duke Frederick responds to Oliver's avowal "I never loved
my brother in my life," "More villain thou" [3.1.14], this from a man who
usurped his brother's dukedom.

Another writer who provided some exciting social history to illuminate the
development of Corin's situation was Richard Wilson. I had found other chapters in his *Will Power* to be filled with historical details that fascinated and
intrigued, and his chapter on this play was just such a resource. It is entitled
"Like the Old Robin Hood: *As You Like It* and the Enclosure Riots," and it
presents a contemporary event that might well have come into the minds of
many in the audience when Charles describes how the old Duke lives "like
the old Robin Hood of England" [1.1.116]. As for Corin, we know very little
of his situation except for this rather cryptic comment in response to Touchstone informing him that his betters are calling him, "Else are they very
wretched," plus his reference to his master as being of a churlish disposition
[2.4.68,80]. The notes in some of the editions suggest that there is a great story
here. Alan Brissenden, in the Oxford edition, comments about "wretched," "In
1600 a common shepherd over twenty-one years of age could earn in a year
up to £1.13s. And a set of clothes" (137). Furness, quoting an 1886 editor,
includes this comment on H. H. Corin's description of his absent master: "We
have here a glimpse of the grasping English capitalist, who, in the sixteenth
century, was depriving the native shepherds of their independence up and
down the country. Corin's complaint finds very voluminous illustration in
contemporary literature" (97). Wilson's chapter gives a much more complete
portrait of the sorts of situations upon which the first actor might have drawn
when he was creating Corin, and the associations the first audience might have
made when it heard his words.

"The Forest, the Wild and the Sacred," a chapter in Richard Marienstras's
New Perspectives on the Shakespearean World, provided me with a compendium of
literary, cultural, and psychological associations Elizabethans customarily made
with the forest of Arden. I was able to set this literary scholar's musings into
a very specific landscape with the help of scholars working in the very specialized discipline of historical geography. In *The Forest of Medieval Romance* by
Corinne J. Saunders, *A History of English Forestry* by N.D.G. James, and *Trees
and Woodland in the British Landscape* by Oliver Rackham, I found maps and
photographs that inspired me and provided "a local habitation, / And a name"
[*Dream* 5.1.16].

Other articles proved disappointing, despite alluring titles. I sent off for a copy of Peter B. Erickson's article that appeared in the spring 1982 issue of *Massachusetts Review* because the title, "Sexual Politics and the Social Structure in *As You Like It*," sounded promising, and I enjoyed reading his comparison of the Rosaline of *Love's Labour's Lost* with our Rosalind, but his concerns were thematic and literary rather than historical and dramatic.

I wanted to find out more about the women in the court, one of whom is mentioned by name, "Hisperia the Princess Gentlewoman" [2.2.10], knowing that these supporting performers would enjoy some inspiration for their back-stories. I was thrilled to locate Sharon Kettering's article "The Household Service of Early Modern French Noblewomen," which was published in the winter 1997 issue of *French Historical Studies*. As I had expected, there was a significant similarity between French and English models, but the French case study that Kettering used was wonderfully specific for the French setting of the play. Of course, it is not likely that Shakespeare had even secondhand knowledge of the life of French noblewomen, but that is not as much a concern for an actor, who is after all only seeking to make the play come alive in private interior landscape.

Keeping Up with the Joneses

Once a year *Shakespeare Quarterly* publishes an issue in which it lists everything published about Shakespeare in the previous calendar year. The bibliography for 1999 was 831 pages in length and contained 4,237 entries. There were twelve new bibliographies and checklists published in that year alone. There were thirty-two biographical studies. There were fifty publications in the area of stage and theatre history. There were twenty-nine new contributions to the authorship controversy. There were seventy-three new things that someone found to say, at length, about *Othello*, and eighty-one about *A Midsummer Night's Dream*. Five people found that they had something significant to say about *Edward III*, the latest play to join the canon, scholars having decided that a sufficient percentage of the surviving playtext was written by Shakespeare.

Even the most dedicated scholars make use of this service by the editors of *Shakespeare Quarterly* in order to pick and choose which of the many articles and books to put on their "must read" lists. Actors and directors can do the same, thanks to the inclusion of such categories as "Actors, Acting, Directing," with forty-nine entries, and "Stage Productions," with fifteen entries. There is even a category for other theatre professionals, entitled "Theatrical Techniques: Staging, Scenery, Lighting, Etc." (four entries).

You will be assisted in your selection process by the brief descriptions that accompany most entries, from which you can get a fairly good idea what the scholar is setting out to prove and the critical theories that will influence the vocabulary used and the approach taken. From this and from the title you can tell with some accuracy the focus of the entry and judge whether it is worth your while to track it down. If you have found a scholar whose work proves useful to yours, you can look up the name in the authors' index and keep track of her or his annual output. Because entries are not limited to English-language publications, you can sample the international scale of the industry and observe the ebb and flow of fads and fiery debates within the industry.

Scholars also make use of the reviews of books that are regularly published in almost every academic journal. A review is an excellent alternative to browsing in the library itself. You can skim the review and discover immediately which of the latest books are likely to reward a visit to a library and a few hours spent checking the index and page hopping in search of interesting bits.

Research in Special Collections

There is no rational reason that an actor would ever need to visit a special collection. There are many irrational reasons, and these might be difficult to explain to those who give out readers' cards. How can you put into words the significance of holding in your hands one of the few surviving copies of the first published editions of one of Shakespeare's plays? What does it mean to an actor to read a letter written in 1594 and see the handwriting and the paper used by one of Shakespeare's contemporaries? We have all seen the pictures of the originals, but only a few of us are permitted to have access to the holdings in special collections.

The Folger Shakespeare Library in Washington, D.C., houses just such an opportunity to be inspired by direct contact with the past. Here is a transcript of a letter I read during the preparation of this book:

Sir

I have many times purposed to visit you, since I heard of your coming into the country, but have been hitherto hindered by unexpected journeys and businesses which have made me a stranger both at my own house, and to my friends, especially to your self, to whom I am so great a debtor as I can no other wise satisfy than by an ingenious acknowledgement of the same, but if according to the old saying, words be no payment, then is my estate more desperate, nevertheless I shall always endeavor to supply the faults of my means with the true faith and affection of my mind towards you. I am to go the next week into Essex from whence so soon as I shall return I will come unto you to Raynham. My mother and my wife desires to salute you with their best wishes and affections and my self serves you with as much true love as can be expressed by your kinsman that truly loves you John Corbett.
Spronston 25 April

The large sheet of paper was folded in half (such extravagance!) and then addressed "To his much honoured and respected kinsman Sir Roger Town-send Barronett at Raynham give this."

As I sat and read this letter, surrounded by hardworking scholars preparing serious books on Shakespeare, I lost the sensation of trespassing in that rarefied enclave. I felt privileged to be offered an opportunity to allow an artifact from the past to have a profound effect on my experience of the present, and I realized that I had more in common with other readers than I had previously realized. By reading the books of scholars who have closely examined hundreds of such documents, the actor can absorb indirectly during the years when a visit to such a place is not possible.

DIGGERS AND DELVERS, GLEANERS AND GROOMS

> They are the Books, the Arts, the Academes,
> That show, contain, and nourish all the world.
>
> Berowne [*LLL* 4.3.299]

Scholars and actors can take advantage of a few hardy individuals willing to do the digging, either sifting through scholarly treatises that are of interest only to other scholars or sitting through hours of tedious acting in hopes of an unforgettable moment. They then write about what they have discovered in the digging and sitting in a manner that is truly of interest to the scholar or actor. The best of these works also organize their discoveries into a resource book for the rest of us.

Folger Shakespeare Library Publications

Anyone interested in learning more about the world in which Shakespeare lived, rehearsed, and wrote his plays has reason to be thankful for the publishing initiatives undertaken over the years by the Folger Shakespeare Library. In the late 1950s it inaugurated a series, published by Cornell University Press, called the Folger Booklets on Tudor and Stuart Civilization. These booklets are the best place to go for a discussion of the topic in question that is more than a brief overview but far less dense and academic than a scholarly book-length work. The titles of the booklets in the series are self-explanatory, and each booklet consists of about twenty-five pages of writing and an equal number of pages of reproductions of illustrations held in the Folger collection. I have found myself consulting a booklet from this series in order to fill in the gaps in the general notes provided in connection with a play, or to answer a question that I had and that I suspected could not be answered by a simple, three- or four-paragraph explanation in a general guide to Shakespeare's world.

Everything You've Wanted to Know

Shakespeare's plays are pretty well picked over from a scholarly point of view. This makes for tough going for any junior academic looking for some viable territory through which to establish a reputation. Since you cannot pub-

lish anything scholarly about Shakespeare without demonstrating, in your commentary and footnotes, that you have read everything ever written on this
topic, the process of preparing an original piece of scholarship is so daunting
as to give pause to any fainthearted scholars, leaving Shakespeare studies to
the arrogant, the bibliophiles, and those who are more interested in debating
with other scholars than in contributing to our understanding of the plays
themselves. A satire of Shakespearean scholarship can be found in *The Compleat
Works of Wllm Shkspr (Abridged)* by Jess Borgeson, Adam Long, and Daniel
Singer. On one page, the editor, Jim Winfield, has a note for "fishmonger"
that explains the etymological roots of the word and its symbolic implications,
a note on "words, words, word" that informs us that scholars have now concluded this was never intended to be spoken by Hamlet, and a lengthy note
on "Though this be madness, yet there's method in't." The actual notes are
much funnier than my explanation.

Of course, some of the details that are dredged up in scholarly studies are
tedious in the extreme, and actors must always remember that what interests
scholars is not what interests actors. But armed with an efficient search engine,
a decent library willing to summon books by interlibrary loan, and the ability
to skim through theoretical discussions and thematic analysis, the actor can
sift the results of scholarly excavations. What is problematical for academics
has created a scholarly environment of great benefit to actors. As scholars roam
further afield for fresh territory, a significant number of them settle for collecting everything anyone might ever want to know about one very specific
aspect of one play. The result is that an actor would be hard pressed to come
up with a question that a scholar somewhere has not mined as richly as possible.

In the category of "everything you've always wanted to know" I would
place the scholarly series that publish doctoral dissertations, which in themselves more and more often exhibit a certain desperation on the part of the
graduate student to find something original to say about Shakespeare. The
series Elizabethan and Renaissance Studies, published by the Salzburg Studies
in English Literature, has contributed several such titles to many university
libraries, everything from *Dido, Queen of Infinite Literary Variety: The English Renaissance Borrowings and Influences* by Adrianne Roberts-Baytop to *Dramatic Quicklyisms: Malapropic Wordplay Technique in Shakespeare's Henriad* by Barbara Hardy.
My favorite is the forty-seventh volume, entitled *Denmark, Hamlet, and Shakespeare: A Study of Englishmen's Knowledge of Denmark towards the End of the Sixteenth
Century with Special Reference to Hamlet.* Cay Dollerup lays out for her readers
every element of *Hamlet* that could be said to be authentic Danish practice and
suggests just how Shakespeare might have come across the information he
would need to get his facts straight. It matters little to the actor if her conclusions hold any water. Her book is chock-full of those details that provide just
the sort of concrete truthfulness that can anchor a performance in the realm
of lives truly lived. For example, with regard to the fencing match that precip-

itates the final bloodbath, she reveals that while the boy king Christian IV was growing up, his councillors seem to have thought that public fencing matches were educational for their young monarch and so invited travelling groups of professional fencers to give exhibition matches on various festive occasions. Later, Danish noblemen, like Laertes, began to take part in such events. Of course, Dollerup points out, such exhibitions were also popular in England, and in fact just such a match was arranged for Christian IV's visit to his sister Anne's court in 1606. An extensive table of contents is more useful for the browser than the index, which lacks the detail useful to an actor seeking an answer to a specific question.

Here is another *Hamlet*-related example of the startling things you might find in a university library. A search using the keywords "court" and "Denmark," looking for information on daily life in a Danish court, teased out a slender volume entitled *Denmark's Coronation Carpets*, edited by Mogens Bencard. Intrigued because I could not imagine an entire book, even a slender one, dedicated to such a narrow topic, I requested it from a sister library and discovered it to be a publication of the Royal Collections at Rosenborg Palace, Copenhagen, from 1987. The last quarter of the book is given over to beautiful, full-color photographs of the carpets in question. A quick look at one or two was sufficient to satisfy my curiosity. The written text describes these carpets in exhausting detail. What proved much more interesting were the reproductions, sadly in black and white, of coronation scenes throughout the ages in which the carpets could be seen. I was much more interested in the assembled monarchs and courtiers, excellent models for a Claudius and a Gertrude, whether it be the Danish monarch of Shakespeare's time, Christian IV, or Danish kings of later centuries, those being used in modern productions as alternative historical periods within which to relocate the events of the play. I found the stance of the assembled courtiers of particular interest: in the 1670 coronation the courtiers stood with one hand on the hip and the other resting on the hilt of the sword, and their weight was on one leg with the other slightly bent. In the 1905 coronation the courtiers stood firmly on both feet, arms at their sides, and the left hand can be seen wearing and holding a white glove. There are no women visible in the photograph of the 1670 coronation painting, though the reproduction hints at figures who might be more visible in the original; in the 1905 coronation painting the women of the court stand with their hands clasped before them just below the waist. In just such obscure places does one find such lovely suggestions of a life truly lived.

Dead Ends

The journey of a theatre person through the dusty tomes of the scholarly library in search of anyone writing from a theatrical perspective often results in some bizarre dead ends. In 1985 the seventeenth volume of *Shakespeare Studies*, an annual collection of interesting articles on Shakespeare, published

"How Should One Read Shakespeare's Verse?" by Margret Popp. I came across a reference to this article and located a copy, eager to add to my understanding of how an actor might best approach the dramatic poetry of Shakespeare's plays. Without commenting on Popp's qualifications in her very specialized field or on the validity of her ideas, I would have to say that this article is the perfect example of all that is least interesting in the huge industry of Shakespeare studies. Popp's primary agenda seems to be shooting down the ideas of other specialists. She writes more about other scholarly publications than she does about Shakespeare. Her article is filled with jargon that only a specialist like herself can understand. Here is a sample, a list of devices she describes in four quotations: "disyllabic full cadence with internal anacrusis (1), trisyllabic full cadence without anacrusis (2), monosyllabic full cadence with disyllabic anacrusis (3a and b), monosyllabic full cadence with rearrangement of the subsequent bar (4)." Even with the examples in front of me and a dictionary to translate her terminology, I could not understand what she was trying to say.

Even with an exciting topic, some scholars can produce a book that is of minimal interest to those who are preparing to act out the highly charged relationships discussed by the scholar. For example, Maurice Charney recently published *Shakespeare on Love and Lust*, a book that, despite a great title, turns out to be an entirely thematic and literary discussion of love conventions, love poetry, and love relationships. He benefits from the liberal spirit of the times and discusses freely the possibly homosexual relationships and the clearly sexual wit and dirty jokes that other scholars have found in the plays, but his is an interpretive study, and his comments are much less interesting than what actors discover every day on the rehearsal floor.

I wish I could describe a system whereby the actor could be sure of avoiding such enervating and irritating examples of all that gives scholars a bad name in the rehearsal hall. However, since pure gold is hidden away in the most unpromising books and journals, and exciting titles turn out to be another exercise like Popp's, all an actor can do is learn to browse efficiently, reshelve promptly, and follow trails that capture the imagination.

Titles of books can be misleading, resulting in frustration and missed opportunities. Ned Lukacher's *Daemonic Figures* catches the eye during rehearsals of *Macbeth*, leading one to hope for a fresh exploration of witchcraft and the supernatural, but after a quick glance at his introduction the book is replaced on the shelf, its focus explained succinctly by the author: "Shakespeare's place in the history of conscience . . . Shakespeare's relation to, and his effect on, the interpretations of conscience by Heidegger and Freud" (1). An admirable project and, one assumes, an achievement for academic reasons, but not much help to the cast of *Macbeth*.

Guest Experts

An important discovery for those seeking inspiration in the products of scholarship is that the sister disciplines can be consulted for just the sort of background information an actor most enjoys. You will want to feel at home in those areas of the library that house books on the social history of Shakespeare's England as well as British and European history not only for Shakespeare's time but for the era of the history plays, on the history of ideas, on British folklore, and on classical mythology, to say nothing of the history of music and dance, clothing and cutlery.

Because of Shakespeare's mystique, a personal interest or fascination on the part of an expert in quite a different field often translates itself into a fascinating contribution to Shakespeare studies. Such passionate lovers of Shakespeare and experts in something quite far removed can offer up some of the knowledge of their profession that turns out to have specific application to the plays. Best of all, these writers have no particular point to make in connection with Shakespeare studies and so regularly deliver just what an actor might want to know in a form that is accessible and appealing. Even a working playwright of the modern theatre, William Gibson, has written *Shakespeare's Game*, not as a contribution to Shakespeare studies, but as a contribution to the teaching of the craft of play writing.

But in the category of "Why on earth did they purchase this book for our university library?" I would offer Mats Ryden's *Shakespearean Plant Names*, a botanical study of exactly which flowers are meant by the references in Shakespeare's plays, and problems of translation of these into Swedish.

In his preface to *Horses in Shakespeare's England*, Anthony Dent points to the short-sightedness of some scholarly editors:

Nowadays knowledge about such things is confined to a minority, a "special interest group," who are in general so little regarded by the learned that their advice is never asked in cases where it might be helpful. The learned glossator will cheerfully write "fives, a disease of horses" without explaining *which* disease; or gloss "riggish" as wanton without thinking it worthwhile to explain that it qualifies, literally, the behaviour of a rig—he has moved so much further away from the horse-borne world than his counterpart of Shakespeare's day as not even to know what a rig is. (ix)

However, because Dent's book lacks an index, the reader is left to look on every page for a reference to rigs, ultimately without success. A quick consultation of the *Oxford English Dictionary* reveals that the earliest usage of "rig" to indicate a horse-drawn carriage is 1831, which suggests that the knowledgeable guest expert is on occasion in need of assistance from the scholar.

One of my favorite examples of just such a collaboration is an article which reveals the attraction Shakespeare has for a discipline even as far afield as astronomy. I can only imagine the eagerness with which these scientists documented the small contribution they too can make to our understanding of, in this case, the night sky over Elsinore. The November 1998 issue of *Sky and Telescope* published an analysis of "The Stars of *Hamlet*," written by Donald W. Olson, Marilynn S. Olson, and Russell L. Doescher, two physicists and an English professor. What a great collaboration! Perhaps it might interest an actor playing one of the characters on the battlements to know exactly what they are observing when, just before the entrance of the ghost, Bernardo says,

> Last night of all,
> When yond same Star that's Westward from the Pole
> Had made his course t'illume that part of Heaven
> Where now it burns, Marcellus and my self,
> The Bell then beating one. [1.1.35]

"The Stars of *Hamlet*" contains historical information about the astrological as well as astronomical implications of that simple image, which they argue persuasively would have been influenced by the widely discussed appearance in 1572 of a new and bright star in the constellation Cassiopeia.

Not every actor will be interested in this sort of information. Some will find irritating the suggestion that anything more than Shakespeare's stirring words and a lively imagination are necessary for the playing of the moment on stage. Many will be amused at the lengths to which scholars go simply to publish something about this well-picked-over play. If, however, you are one of those who is fascinated, and would like to learn more about the vast realm of Shakespearean scholarship, then I invite you to browse the following chapters, in search of such illumination as only esoteric scholarship can provide.

Strange Questions, Scholarly Answers

In *Titus Andronicus* Aaron the Moor chastises the two quarreling sons of Tamara, saying, "Now, by the Gods that warlike Goths adore, / This petty brabble will undo us all" [2.1.61]. The actor playing the role asked me just who those gods might be. There are several answers to this question, depending upon the historical context within which the actor is functioning. What gods might Shakespeare's first actors and audience have thought these to be? What gods did the Goths worship around 400 A.D.?

Although the first books that I consulted claimed that we have no information on the religious practices of the Goths, a computer-assisted search of the university library system brought me to Malcolm Todd's *Everyday Life of the Barbarians: Goths, Franks, and Vandals*, and I was able to offer the actor a specific and thought-provoking context for his line. In his chapter on "Religious Life," Todd describes not only the war god Tiwaz (or Tiw or Tyr) but also the human sacrifices that so horrified the Romans when they first encountered the Goths. This archeological detail sets an ironic tension for the actors in the first scene of *Titus Andronicus*, where it is the Romans performing the human sacrifice. I do not know if this information affected his performance, but the actor was glad to take a close look at Todd's book.

THE ACTOR'S RESPONSIBILITIES

O thou monster Ignorance, how deformed dost thou look.
Holofernes [*LLL* 4.2.23]

Actors need to set aside their own self-indulgences and prejudices in order to seek every opportunity to enrich their work with the resources available to them. The preparation of a major role in any of Shakespeare's plays requires a daunting commitment from the performer, but we must not use the immensity of the task as an excuse for the sort of superficiality that characterizes weak acting in modern plays.

Although I can identify with an actor's need to receive a simple and playable answer to a question, I often find myself in the position of reminding actors of the dangers of generalizations about a historical period other than our own. It is only natural that we examine the past through the lens of our present values, which in themselves are always changing. I do not think that we can ever look at the forced conversion of Shylock at the end of the trial scene in *The Merchant of Venice* as a happy conclusion to the "pound-of-flesh" subplot, which is how it would have been viewed in xenophobic, Christian England. By converting Shylock, Portia in effect saves his soul from eternal damnation; the thought that she might be robbing him of his birthright as a Jew would never have occurred to the audience.

However, I do not believe that simply acknowledging our contemporary lens, which in truth we cannot and do not want to reject, justifies simplistic and superficial generalizations about how people in Shakespeare's England might have thought or felt about important and complex issues. Scholars have made a very important contribution to our understanding of the tensions that existed in what they have labelled early modern England, and it is not particularly helpful to our understanding of the theatrical power of Shakespeare's plays to pretend that everyone at that time believed, without question, in the divine right of kings, for example.

A superficial encounter with the social history of early modern England can result in a strange bipolar attitude of an actor to the characters in the play. On the one hand, the assumptions about the belief systems lead us to conclude that people back then had simpler concerns, more limited perspectives, and clearer attitudes and were generally less complex than we are today. On the other hand, Shakespeare's characters are so rich and complex and feel so "modern" when they are explored in rehearsal that he was evidently a genius far ahead of his time.

In actuality, the reverse is probably true. The times themselves were so complex, filled with immensely vast and varied concerns, with huge tensions working their way into the very language of the age, that it would take a complete dolt of a playwright not to capture at least some of the richness in crafting characters for the stage. Shakespeare, the great borrower, was very much a part of the theatre of his times and demonstrated minimal originality in thought or theatrical strategy. His genius was in his use of the language of his age, shaping it to reflect the richness of his contemporaries.

⤫ 2 ⤪

Which Shakespeare?

The hand of time,
Shall draw this brief into as huge a volume.

King Philip [*John* 2.1.102]

What edition should I use? Why do they include all those confusing footnotes?
Why are there so many versions to choose from? Aren't they all the same?

Editions of individual plays of Shakespeare fall into two distinct categories.
There are the inexpensive versions designed to facilitate the first encounter
with the plays, and there are more expensive versions designed to facilitate a
scholarly encounter with the play. Of the first, the Signet and Penguin editions
are popular and appropriately priced. Of the latter, the Arden, the Oxford,
and the Cambridge series are the most respected.

Other than price, there is one significant difference between the two types
of editions: the footnotes. We call the editions with more complete footnotes
variorum editions because they follow the model of the Variorum series of
editions of Shakespeare plays published in the nineteenth century, which contain the most complete set of editorial comments about specific aspects of each
text, up to the date of publication.

Footnotes are both irritating and helpful, depending on what assistance you
need and what information they contain. At the very least, they translate selected words, providing a meaning that makes sense to a modern reader. They
might also contain information about social history: Elizabethan customs, beliefs, habits of speech, and so on. They can also tell you everything you did
not want to know about what scholars have debated among themselves for
several hundred years.

An actor must always remember that the editors are concerned with the requirements of readers, not actors. For example, Alan Brissenden's note on "There's no clock in the Forest" [3.2.300] in the Oxford edition of *As You Like It* reads, "The question of how long Duke Senior has been banished should not concern us." That may very well be reasonable advice for a reader, but the actors will have quite a different reaction. The length of time they have been in the woods, even if it is not set in precise calendar terms, needs to be established as "a long, long time and we're getting sick of cold wet smelly caves," or "not long enough for the charm to have worn off," or "long enough to have learned the tricks of survival and so we're doing pretty well for ourselves, thank you very much."

Any given copy of a play is, for the most part, remarkably similar to all the others, because Shakespearean scholarship has forced editors into a series of conventional attitudes with regard to reproducing Shakespeare's plays. The only justification for additional editions is therefore the quality of the footnotes and the editor's introduction.

There are two other open-ended aspects of the plays that allow the editors to earn their paychecks: commas and cruxes. The latter are specific words or phrases that have never been explained to everyone's satisfaction. Editors pick their favorite version and then justify that choice. But they save their most creative editorial energies for punctuating the plays.

It always comes as a great shock to readers of Shakespeare when they discover that one edition has a comma where another has a semicolon, or that one editor uses a period (or even an exclamation mark) when another uses a colon or semicolon. How can they do that? The simple truth of the matter is that we have no idea what Shakespeare wrote, because we do not have a single manuscript in his hand, what experts call his foul papers. We do not even have a single promptbook from a theatrical production. There are innumerable theories about how the first recorded publication of any given play, or the first set of collected plays, came about, but that is all they are: theories. We have manuscripts and printed versions of plays by other playwrights who were Shakespeare's contemporaries, so we can see what a mess the printers made of copying handwriting into typesetting. We also have some evidence of the control another contemporary, Ben Jonson, took in the publishing of his own plays. We are left with a picture of a man of the theatre who did not guard his manuscripts and prepare them for accurate publication, and of a process of publishing that virtually guaranteed errors of both small and great magnitude.

Even the most inexpensive edition of a play by Shakespeare usually includes a brief description of exactly what early editions exist upon which the current accepted version of the play is based. Scholars love lengthy discussion of compositors' errors, the discernible hand of a specific publisher, and the relationship of good quartos, bad quartos, and folios to the author's foul papers. To the uninitiated, it can be quite a shock to discover that there is no "correct" version of any of the plays.

In fact, a great deal can be learned about a specific play by comparing the various versions that date from Shakespeare's century. Most modern editors mix and match from these versions to create a soup or stew that we mistakenly assume to be the play that Shakespeare wrote. Every edition of a Shakespeare play should come with a warning label: scholarly modified material. Do not assume that what you see on the page is what Shakespeare wrote, or that we know what he wrote, or that he wrote only one version of the play, or that his theatre company performed only one version of the play, or that there is a "correct" or "complete" version preserved for us to study and perform. Every edition is a compilation, filled with corrections based upon an editor's best guess as to what Shakespeare intended.

THE SCHOLARLY EDITIONS

When one is confronted with the row upon row of scholarly publications on Shakespeare, it is only natural to despair of ever acquiring sufficient information to play even a single minor role in one of Shakespeare's plays. How could you possibly master all of the social and political history, for example, needed to gain the richest possible understanding of the plot, much less the metaphors?

Here is a concrete strategy. Browse general works to immerse yourself in the period, and rely upon the years of scholarship reflected in the various scholarly editions for the direct applications to the play at hand. Although it is very likely that any given editor has missed some specific detail that could enhance your understanding of your character and the language you have been given to speak and hear, you can trust any academic editor to have read widely and to bring to the footnotes a wealth of detail.

Oxford University Press's World Classics Series, Cambridge University Press's New Cambridge Shakespeare Series, and Methuen's Arden Shakespeare series are the three scholarly editions that contain extensive notes. These editions of the plays share similar characteristics, so a preference of one publisher over another might be due to something as simple as the size of the type and the layout of the footnotes.

Each of these editions features a full-length introductory essay, which may contain little or much of interest to an actor. Those sections of the essay that treat the theme of the play, of such great interest to literary analysis, are best skipped by an actor. Similarly, those sections outlining the tortured path from original editions to the one in hand prove deadly dull to any but the specialist in textual studies, other than to remind the actor that a modern editor has made many changes to what was, if the truth be known, a deeply flawed first publication. Some editors include a section in the introduction that draws upon

the social and political issues and events that reflect upon the play. These will
be of interest to those actors who enjoy imagining the real people who watched
and performed these plays.

The notes that accompany the play itself contain several different kinds of
information that can be of great use to actors. Sadly, these nuggets are buried
within even more commentary that is of interest only to scholars. More often
than not, the editor will choose to fill the bottom third of the page with notes
about how different editors have interpreted a famous crux or otherwise in-
decipherable passage, and leave unexplained words or references that are puzzling to the ordinary reader.

Although the simple definition of words no longer in common usage is an
obvious service provided by an editor, there is a significant range in this as in
other aspects of publishing editions of the plays. In the various editions of any
play there will be some words that every editor defines and some that only
one editor spots as needing explanation. Inevitably, there will be words on the
page that none of the editors have chosen to explain, but that a nonacademic
reader does not recognize.

In the same category of simple definitions is what scholars call a "gloss" or
explanation of how a word is being used or what a short phrase means. Sometimes the note is as simple as the presentation of alternative wording; sometimes an editor will offer additional explanation for this gloss, particularly if
there is some controversy about what the word or phrase might mean. Those
editors who choose to go into the nature of the controversy at length have
one agenda: to clarify the long history of scholarly debate. For an actor, another agenda is at work. You do not care which explanation is the correct one,
and therefore you can open yourself to the possibility that every gloss is available to be explored in rehearsal. So it is worthwhile to plow through the names
of scholars and the dates of their commentary in case one of them has hit
upon a gloss that makes the line come alive for you.

In the second confrontation between Isabella and Angelo in *Measure for Measure*, just seconds before Isabella realizes that the debate about the validity of
trading her sexual favors for her brother's life is not hypothetical, she has
some lines in response to Angelo's "We are all frail." The folio version of her
lines is as follows:

> Else let my brother die,
> If not a fedarie but onely he
> Owe, and succeed thy weaknesse. [2.4.122]

Oh my goodness, what on earth does that mean? Here is the note provided
by the editor of the Arden edition, J. W. Lever:

If not . . . weakness] a much-disputed passage. "Feodary" ("Fedarie" F) combines two
meanings: (i) confederate, accomplice (cf. *Cym.*, III.ii.21, F "Foedarie") from Lat. *foedus*;

(ii) feudatory, i.e. hereditary tenant, from Lat. *feodarius*. The sense is thus: "If my brother has no associates in this weakness you refer to, and no man else will in the way of nature inherit it, then let him die". (61)

The Arden editor further changes "fedarie" to "feodary" and removes the comma after "owe."

The Oxford editor, N. W. Bawcutt, gives "fedarie" a modern spelling and provides the gloss "a form of *feudary*, 'feudal tenant, retainer', but used by Shakespeare to mean 'confederate, accomplice', as in *Cymbeline* 3.2.21." In addition, the second line of the speech is explained more completely, as follows: "**if ... he** if Claudio is the sole offender in this way, and has no accomplices in this crime." The editor then moves on to the third line and defines "owe" as "own" and "succeed" as "inherit." The longest comment is reserved for the end of the line: "**thy weakness** Isabella means 'the weakness you refer to', but Angelo assumes she means 'the exclusively male weakness', or even 'the weakness found in you as well as others' (though as yet she does not know this)" (143).

Both editors, in convoluted ways, are leading the actor by a very indirect route to a playable meaning. George Kittredge is available for his clarity. Thanks to the reissue of his notes in a Complete Works edited by Irving Ribner:

> *Else let ... thy weakness* This speech is obscure, and it is likely, as has been suggested, that some lines have been lost from it. The general sense seems to be "let my brother die if he alone, having no accomplices or confederates, possesses this weakness, and no other man is capable of inheriting it." *federy* (a) confederate accomplice (b) feudatory, hereditary tenant on an estate. *Owe* possess. *succeed* succeed to, inherit. (487)

Such general explanations can also cause problems for the actor, as the editor clarifies the general meaning but might not explain what some of the obscure words mean. The Arden editor did not bother to explain that "owe" means "own" and "succeed" means "inherit."

The Crux

Here is just one example of a crux, the sort of scholarly debate that results in the most confusing sort of note. When Cleopatra receives an envoy from Caesar, she sends an all-important message back to her lover's great enemy, prefaced with the phrase "Say to great Caesar this in deputation" [*A&C* 3.13.74], or at least that is how it appears in the Arden edition. The word in the First Folio is "disputation," and the Arden notes clarify that "deputation" is an alteration first made by Lewis Theobald in 1734, though the editor, M.R. Ridley, comments, "Steevens (pointing as Warburton) believed that F's *disputation* might be retained, suggesting the sense: 'I own he has the better in the controversy.' The probabilities seem to me, however, in favour of *dis* being a result of the attractive proximity of *this* and *kiss*" (135). Steevens edited the play in 1858, Warburton in 1747. A modern actor would be justified in wondering why the disagreements between these scholars should be of any interest at all to a modern reader of the play. David Bevington, the editor of the New Cambridge edition, in contrast, simply lists the variations in a separate section for that purpose, beginning with the First Folio, followed by Theobald's version, marked as a conjecture (189).

An actor would be forgiven for missing the simple fact that both the Arden and the New Cambridge editors prefer an eighteenth-century conjecture over the First Folio, since this information is buried in the least interesting type of note. Far more important than weighing in on either side of the editorial debate would be an actor's awareness that the text you are reading is filled with countless choices, any of which might create a barrier between the actor and an important insight into the scene. What would happen if Cleopatra said to Caesar's envoy, "Say to great Caesar this in disputation: I kiss his conquering hand"? Given that she is playing a dangerous game in the face of Caesar's overwhelming military threat to her person and her kingdom, might the slipping in of "disputation" in place of the expected "deputation" be worth exploring? Actors must learn to take such initiatives within the rehearsal process. By working your way through the choices the editors have made, as described in the dense and alienating scholarly notes on the subject, you might just find an alternative wording to suggest as a valid alternative to the published speech.

Allusions Proverbial, Biblical, and Classical

Some glosses deal with the general category of proverbial sayings. For example, in *The Merchant of Venice* Portia says, "Such a hare is madness the youth, to skip o'er the meshes of good counsel the cripple" [1.2.19], and the New Cambridge editor comments, "Compare the proverbial 'mad as a March hare'" (66). The Oxford editor's note includes, "Compare 'Youth will have its course' (Tilley Y48)" (113), and the Arden editor makes no reference to the proverbial content of the passage.

The citation of Tilley refers to *A Dictionary of the Proverbs in England in the Sixteenth and Seventeenth Centuries: A Collection of the Proverbs Found in English Literature and the Dictionaries of the Period*, published by Morris Palmer Tilley in 1950. If you consult this work, you will find the following under Y48:

YOUTH will have its course (swing)

1578 **LILY** *Euph. Anat. Wit*, p. 261: We haue an olde (Prouerb) youth wil haue his course. **1585** E. SANDYS *Serm.* 8, p. 152: Youth, they say, must haue his swing: let old age wax holy. [**1588**] 1617 GREENE *Alcida*, p. 61: Youth must haue his course. *Ibid.*, p. 97: (his swinge). **1594** LYLY *Mother B.* I i 100: Your sons folly . . . being naturall, it will haue his course. **1605** *Lond. Prod.*, s. B1: Ile serue his youth, for youth must haue his course. **1615** BEAUMONT AND FLETCHER *Cupid's Rev.* I, p. 234: But he is a young man. Let him have [his] swinge. **1616** DR., no. 2526: (it swinge). **1617** MORYSON *Itineray* I 1 i, III 359: Many returning from forraigne parts . . . [having] satisfied their disordinate appetites, by giving youth his swinge (as the Proverbe is) doe at home cast off their vices. **1633** MARMION *Fine Companion* I vi, p. 123: Troth, uncle, youth will have his swing. **1639** CL., p. 183: (swing). See APP., p. 721: SM., p. 610; T. 725, p. 343. Cf. N48: Nature will have her course; Y45: Youth must not have its will. (767)

Clearly, all of the available information cannot be squeezed into a note at the bottom of the page. Tilley, if consulted, points us in the direction of an interesting comparison between the madness of a March hare and the "disordinate appetites" of youth, a natural sort of folly that simply must run its course.

Returning to our March hare allusion, the editors are quick to point out the proverb "As mad as a March hare" but miss the parallel aphorism "hare-brained," and not one of them makes the link to the folk legend of the hare that plucked the beard of the lion, an association that might be on Portia's mind as her thoughts turn next to the dead weight of her father's will. Hares were thought to be melancholy animals, despite their association with spring-time (sexual) madness. This connects us to the beginning of this scene, when Portia's first line announces that her little body is aweary of the great world, her version of Antonio's "In sooth I know not why I am so sad," the first line of the play.

Another thing that the actor learns is that some sayings that are proverbial today were proverbs even when Shakespeare was writing. You may have thought that the madness of a March hare was originated by Lewis Carroll in *Alice in Wonderland*. We know that there are many proverbial sayings that we use today that were invented by Shakespeare, so it is important to be able to tell the difference. That is because the way a character says a fresh, new, brilliant invention, something that will become a proverb, is quite different from the way someone will quote, directly or indirectly, a well-known turn of phrase. In this example from Portia, we learn something very important about Portia's character from this example of her wit in taking the boring cliché about mad hares and old people's courses and creating a fresh new image that makes use of the common country practice of catching hares in nets.

All three editors give us some information so that we can understand Portia's image of the meshes or nets and the skipping hares. In the Arden edition we are given the insight from social history that opens up a complete sensory memory: "In winter hares were hunted on foot with nets." The editor then goes on to quote from a book by Edward Topsell published in 1607, called *History of Four-footed Beasts*, from which we get a second lovely detail: "If the hare 'avoide the net, he [the hunter] must follow her by the foot unto her next lodging place' " (16). The Cambridge editor feels obliged to tell us what the image "means" in a way that is much less helpful to an actor who needs to find her own way into what the image might mean for the character and the moment. The Cambridge gloss on meshes is "i.e. a net to catch hares; used as an image of the attempts made to restrain the natural impulses of others on the part of those who no longer feel them for themselves." This editor also gives us an interesting gloss on March hares, "The leaps performed by hares in spring are a form of sexual behaviour" (66). It is not clear from the note whether the leaping hares were an Elizabethan emblem of springtime horniness, or whether the editor is making use of biological studies of more recent vintage. The Oxford editor's gloss is "In the little allegory that follows, youth is compared to a mad March hare leaping over nets, or snares—the restraints set by good counsel, imagined here as a halting cripple" (113).

How might an actress use this to develop Portia's character? Blended into her backstory might be an education that included the reading of emblem books and writing up little moral lessons on the dangers of youthful exuberance. If Nerissa shared her schoolroom lessons, this proverbial reference fuels their intimacy, particularly if the girls shared a good giggle at the naughtier implications of the emblem behind their teacher's back. There might also be room here to add to Portia's life experiences the hunting of hares with a net, something that would have been a common pastime for the children of Belmont, some out of necessity and others merely for adventure. My favorite trick for making proverbs like this come alive in the mind of the actor is to paint a picture of a stern-voiced adult chastising the young Portia and Nerissa after they have been caught in some youthful madness, saying in the clearly remembered voice, "My goodness, Portia, you are acting as mad as a March hare."

Shakespeare's scene, in which Nerissa goes through the list of Portia's suitors and Portia comments on each, is filled with politically incorrect ethnic jokes that are well explained by the editors of scholarly texts. We learn, for example, that southern Italians were famous for their horsemanship, which explains the joke of Portia's description of him: "Ay that's a colt indeed, for he doth nothing but talk of his horse" [1.2.40]. Even the English are not excused from some good-natured teasing: Portia makes fun of the international wardrobe of the young baron of England: "I think he bought his doublet in Italy, his round hose in France, his bonnet in Germany, and his behaviour every where" [1.2.74]. All three editors let us know that this was a stock joke, to the point where it appears as if Shakespeare was paraphrasing from Robert Greene's *Farewell to Folly*, a play that we date from 1591. But we don't care. It's a great joke.

We might not have needed any scholarly assistance to help us get the point of the comment on the Englishman's clothes or the horse-loving Neapolitan, but we will all be grateful, I suspect, for the information the editors provide in their commentaries on Portia's line "I fear he will prove the weeping Philosopher when he grows old, being so full of unmannerly sadness in his youth" [1.2.48]. This is just the sort of line that is not likely to be cut unless the entire scene is being trimmed, because modern audiences can understand in general terms the point Portia is making. But both actresses on stage need to know much more than generalizations, and the information in the notes gives us real insight not only into the nature of Portia's wit and perceptions of human behavior, but also into her education.

The weeping philosopher is not a generic character type, but a specific individual, Heraclitus of Ephesus. Every schoolchild who was forced to study Juvenal's easy Latin works would have learned by rote the lesson of Heraclitus and his counterpart, Democritus, the laughing philosopher. What was Heraclitus weeping about? That too is wonderfully specific. He wept at how badly people were bringing up their children, allowing them far too many liberties and indulgences. Imagine the strict schoolteacher using this example to justify extra punishment for his naughty charges. It is like imagining being married to Ebenezer Scrooge with no Christmas carol in sight.

The scholarly editors point out biblical as well as classical allusions. These might be direct quotations or paraphrases that would not be missed by anyone in the original audience or more obscure allusions, when the modern editor might take an opportunity to remind us of the permeation of Christian values into the culture of the times. When Portia mocks the Scottish suitor, she says, "He hath a neighbourly charity in him" [1.2.79], and both the Oxford and Cambridge editors point out the echo of Romans 13:10, "Charity worketh no ill to his neighbour." As with the proverbs, however, no editor cites all biblical allusions, and so a quick look at the scholars who specialize in this field will always glean more references for the actor who finds such information useful.

Dangerous Explanations

My greatest complaint about most editorial glosses of phrases is that they explain what the phrase means, but not why those exact words in that order mean exactly that. One of the greatest dangers in acting Shakespeare is the temptation to put your mouth on automatic while the rest of you does something to convey the emotional reality of the moment. We might describe this as acting around and in spite of the language rather than through and with it. General explanations of meaning are surefire recipes for just such disconnections: the actor conveys the meaning as understood from the editor while the mouth recites the words that have been memorized without comprehension.

Immediately following the joke about the mad March hares, Portia says, "But this reasoning is not in the fashion to choose me a husband" [1.2.21], and the editors comment as follows: Arden: "no amount of talking will find her a husband for her' " (16); Cambridge: "Portia means 'no amount of talking will find a husband for her" (66); Oxford: no comment. This may be sufficient information for a reader, but a more detailed gloss is needed before an actor can own these words and begin to explore what might be going on for Portia at this moment in the scene.

What does it mean to be "in the fashion" to do something? Are there alternative meanings for reasoning that would explain just what is being discussed? Surely the word means more than simply "talking." We will need to consult our dictionaries to help us find a complete gloss of this phrase that clearly is intended to signal an important aspect of Portia's mood at this moment and her attitude to what she is doing and thinking and feeling. *The Oxford English Dictionary* provides us with a workable definition for "fashion" in 5.c.: "a method of doing anything." In other words, the phrase means "this reasoning is not the method by which the choosing of a husband will take place"; that is, the real meaning is just about exactly the opposite of that suggested by the editors quoted earlier. Portia is saying that her musing on the lack of control her rational thought has over her vibrant emotions is not the means by which to choose, because she is precluded from making any choice by her father's will.

The moral of the story: take great care when using the explanatory notes provided by even the most scholarly of editors. What is sufficient explanation for a reader might not be what an actor requires to integrate meaning and emotion in the act of speaking the words.

Glorious Illuminations

Sometimes a careful reading of the notes can illuminate the subtleties of the language. For example, in this scene Portia says of the Englishman, "He is a proper mans picture" [1.2.72]. The Arden editor explains, "i.e. he looks fine" (18). That general idea was pretty clear, but surely there is more going on than that, or else why this elaborate image rather than simply saying that he is handsome? The Oxford editor comments, "i.e. image of a handsome man," and adds that the word "proper" should be taken to mean the equivalent of "very" (115). The Cambridge editor is much more help: "i.e. the very epitome of a handsome man—with a hint that he is not quite real" (68). But there is still no explanation of why these words mean that, unless we remember something that the Arden editor includes in his note. There are other plays in which Shakespeare uses the idea of being the picture of something to suggest being the mere appearance, for example, in *Hamlet* when Claudius lists the evils that have befallen the court and describes "poor Ophelia / Divided from her self and her fair Judgement, / Without the which we are Pictures, or mere Beasts" [4.5.84]. From this we can piece together the precise implications of Portia's use of the words "proper" and "picture" to suggest that although he looks quite handsome, there is not much of appeal under the surface.

Cross-References

We are quite rightly fascinated by the fact that Shakespeare comes back to certain images or ideas in play after play. Sometimes the information needed to make sense of one line can be found by having a look at how key words are used elsewhere, and the scholarly editors are very good at pointing out interesting and useful cross-references. Very often these multiple citations to other plays reveal the thinking that informs a proverbial thought. When Nerissa comments on the strange instructions in Portia's father's will that so horribly restrict her marital prospects, she borrows the idea behind the proverb "Dying men speak true" when she says, "Your father was ever virtuous, and holy men at their death have good inspirations" [1.2.27]. With help from the scholarly editors, we are pointed in the direction of the death of John of Gaunt in *Richard II*, when Gaunt speaks at length about the common belief:

> Oh but (they say) the tongues of dying men
> Enforce attention like deep harmony;
> Where words are scarce, they are seldom spent in vain,
> For they breathe truth, that breathe their words in pain.
> He that no more must say, is listened more,
> Than they whom youth and ease have taught to glose,
> More are mens ends marked, than their lives before,
> The setting Sun, and Music at the close
> As the last taste of sweets, is sweetest last,
> Writ in remembrance, more than things long past;
> Though Richard my lifes counsel would not hear,
> My deaths sad tale, may yet undeaf his ear. [2.1.5]

This is a service that scholarly editors are uniquely positioned to provide. Their breadth of reading, which includes not only all of Shakespeare's plays but also the plays of his contemporaries, in addition to the wealth of scholarship available for the play they have edited, allows them to make this sort of important connection. Should the topic spark your interest, such resources will point you in the direction of some very useful additional research.

Not every cross-reference is this useful. Scholars have a tendency to pursue thematic echoes that are of little or no interest to actors, except as a sort of general note along the lines of "Who else says something like this? Oh, yes, So-and-so in such-and-such a play." Scholars focus on the fact that Shakespeare said the same thing in another place, which might suggest something about his attitude to the broader subject; for an actor, all that matters is your character's attitude. In fact, it can be quite irritating to be informed by scholars that the character you are working so hard to bring to life is merely a flawed attempt at a type of character more brilliantly executed in a later play. Rosaline in *Love's Labour's Lost* might grow tired of being compared with Beatrice; Don John in *Much Ado about Nothing* might resent being informed how incomplete his character is compared with Edmund of *King Lear* or Iago in *Othello*.

Scholarly editors often include allusions to specific events around the time of the writing of the play. We learn from the Oxford editor, therefore, that in 1596 there was a fresh outbreak of skirmishes between the English and the

Scots, so that both James and Elizabeth issued proclamations to their people to keep the peace. We also learn details of a more general nature; for example, in explanation of the phrase "round hose" we learn that "it was fashionable to pad out stockings to give one a good 'leg' " (115).

The Variorum Editions of H.H. Furness

The three editions we have been looking at, the Oxford, the Cambridge, and the Arden, are called variorum editions, by which we mean an edition for which the editor has collected commentary from a variety of different sources. The models for all modern variorums of Shakespeare were edited by Horace Howard Furness beginning in 1871. There is no possible description for the Furness variorum editions except the single word "exhaustive." He literally collected everything anyone had ever said about every aspect of the plays and arranged the comments either in sections introducing and concluding the text of the play or directly beneath the line to which the comment refers. Much of what is collected in these old editions is of little use to a modern actor, and it is tempting to assume that the best bits have been picked up by the modern editors who have surveyed all possible citations but have selected those that they feel best serve the modern reader.

Dry and overwhelming as they are, however, the Furness editions reward anyone who dares to page through the thick volumes. Because the Victorian Shakespearean scholars were intensely interested in Shakespeare's world, Furness includes more details about social history than any of the modern variorum editors. Because he did not make any selection from among the many commentators, he included information that a literary scholar would consider extraneous, but an actor enjoys. Because the Furness editions are not readily available in paperback, you will need to visit an academic library to find them.

Hamlet is one of the exceptions, having been reprinted by Dover in a two volume paperback edition, and so will serve us well for examples of the commentary Furness provides, as compared with the three other series. In the final moments of the play, Fortinbras enters, surveys the four dead bodies on the stage, and comments, "This quarry cries on havoc" [5.2.364]. The Riverside editor, G. Blakemore Evans, gives the most direct gloss: "This heap of corpses proclaims a massacre" (1185). The Arden editor, Harold Jenkins, notes that quarry refers to a heap of dead, being literally the total number of deer killed in the hunt. The notes about "cries on havoc" include quotations of the other uses of "havoc" in the canon; it was a battle cry meaning "no quarter" and thus an inciting to slaughter and pillage. "To cry on" is defined as to cry out loud, sometimes in outrage, and two other Shakespearean uses are cited (416). The Oxford editor, G. R. Hibbard, clarifies that quarry is the "pile of game at the end of a hunt" and defines "cries on havoc" as "unequivocally speaks of slaughter on a large scale" (353). The Cambridge editor, Philip Edwards, makes reference also to the heap of dead animals after a hunt and cites another usage of "cries on" after providing the gloss "This heap of bodies proclaims a massacre" (241).

In the Furness variorum we discover that the various commentators have three different glosses for the line: that the pile of dead (*a*) cries out against indiscriminate slaughter, (*b*) proclaims an indiscriminate slaughter, or (*c*) urges to merciless slaughter, where no quarter is given. The entry also includes an interesting quotation from the Statutes of War issued by Henry VIII in 1513: "That no man be so hardy to cry havoc, upon pain of him that is so found beginner, to die therefore; and the remnant to be imprisoned, and their bodies punished at the king's will." Furness also includes various suggestions about the etymology of the word "havoc": perhaps from the Welsh *hafog*, destruction, or the Anglo-Saxon *hafoc*, a hawk, or the French *hai, voux!* a cry to hounds (I 455).

NONSCHOLARLY EDITIONS

In addition to the series published by the Oxford and Cambridge University presses and Methuen under the Arden label, the plays of Shakespeare can be encountered in complete works and in inexpensive paperback editions. The various publications range from the most inexpensive, wherein the maximum amount of text is placed upon the minimum number of pages, to the gift editions, with lovely paper and typesetting and perhaps with illustrations by famous artists. In these volumes the quality of the notes is not a selling point; introductions are also less likely to answer questions an actor might have about the language or Shakespeare's England.

There is also a set of collected works and individual plays published with university students in mind. These volumes often include excellent supplementary material and a reasonable number of notes—just enough to explain most passages to the average reader but not so many as to slow down the reading process. The notes tend toward direct translation and are entirely functional. They are not likely to answer all the questions an actor will have, because an actor needs to take ownership of the language much more completely than does someone reading the play to find out what happens next. But actors need to be reading Shakespeare as often as possible and, like university students, can appreciate a good edition of the collected works.

Signet Classics is the all-purpose publisher of the plays in inexpensive editions. As in the collected works, the notes are functional, and the accompanying introductory essays introduce the basic thematic concerns that are most likely to be addressed in the classroom. Penguin has also published a series, with quite good notes at the back. Some readers prefer this, as they can encounter the play without feeling obliged to check out every note; they can also consult the notes if something stumps them.

The Folger Shakespeare Library has combined forces with Washington Square Press to bring out the plays in a rival paperback series, equally inex-

pensive and with some very attractive features. Each volume includes information on Shakespeare's theatre and Shakespeare's life and a solid introduction
to reading Shakespeare's language. The notes are set on the facing page, and
there are quite a few more glosses than in the Signet editions. Interesting woodcuts are reproduced so that references to social history are reinforced with
visual evidence. Each edition closes with an essay on the play that presents
the important thematic considerations, followed by a selection of important
recent publications on the play and on Shakespeare in general, each accompanied by a few sentences explaining what the book is about and how it might
illuminate the play. This annotated bibliography is a very useful feature, and
one can only hope that more editors follow this model. It is of course impossible to keep these bibliographies up-to-date, and the selected publications lean
toward thematic studies, of greatest interest to someone preparing to write a
literary essay on the play. Even so, it is useful to an actor to have this sort of
guide to what an experienced editor considers the most important recent discussions of the play. The descriptions of the different articles are sufficiently
complete that you will know if a publication will interest you in your work
on the play.

The Everyman Library (J.M. Dent) has also entered the market for inexpensive single-play editions, and their notes are the most extensive of any of
the nonscholarly editions. These are set face-to-face like the Folger editions,
and the introductory essay is supplemented by a commentary by an actor or
director, which brings a fresh perspective to the discussion.

Signet and Penguin, the older series, have brought out editions of all of the
plays; the Everyman and Folger series are incomplete, though each has published the most popular and most frequently studied plays first. Soon, however,
we will be able to acquire an edition of any play in any of the four most
popular inexpensive series.

So many and similar are the various editions of Shakespeare that we now
have a handy guide to them. Ann Thompson asks and answers the question
"Which Shakespeare?" listing each of the plays and comparing the various
editions available for each. She provides a summary of the introductory essay
and a list of the supplementary material included, as well as assessing the
appeal of each of the series. Since her guide was published in 1992, an entirely
new generation of editions has hit the bookstores, but her comments are still
invaluable in considering the relative merits of the different series of plays.

ALTERNATIVE STRATEGIES

The Bedford Shakespeare Series, recently launched by Bedford/St. Martin's
Press, has taken a different strategy, which may prove of great interest to some
actors, as well as to the university students for whom the series has been
prepared. As an alternative to extensive footnotes and essays by contemporary
scholars, the editors in this series have collected reprints of writings published

in Shakespeare's time, including maps, court records, ballads, travel stories, and medical, religious, or political tracts. Many of the scholarly and even the inexpensive editions include excerpts from those publications that scholars consider the sources for Shakespeare's play, but Bedford editors expand their collection of documents to provide evidence of the broader social, political, or philosophical context within which the play would have been written, rehearsed, and performed.

By using a version of the text created by another scholar who specializes in the specific area of Shakespeare studies dedicated to commas and cruxes, commonly known as textual studies, each editor is free to focus on selecting interesting supporting material, all of which is presented with modern spelling and notes on obscure words for ease of access. In William C. Carroll's edition, of 368 pages of writing, only 87 are given to a clean, nicely laid-out copy of *Macbeth* with minimal footnotes; the remaining pages are taken up with short introductions to the play and to each section of reprints, which lay out the broad social context of the first performance, and the reprints. Included are everything from *An Homily against Disobedience and Wilful Rebellion* and *An Act against Conjuration, Witchcraft, and Dealing with Evil and Wicked Spirits* to *Childbirth, or the Happy Delivery of Women*. Most of the inclusions are excerpts of relevant material from longer publications, for which the general reader, including the actor, can be thankful. Here you will find a resource not only for some interesting background information, but also for the language of the times. I strongly urge you to read aloud anything that interests you, so that your firsthand encounter with the language supplements your discoveries. Here, for example, is an excerpt from William Harrison's *The Description of Scotland*, which appeared in Holinshed's *The Chronicles of England, Scotland, and Ireland* in 1587:

It was told me once by Doncan Campbell, a noble knight, that out of Garloll, one of the pools of Argyle, there came a terrible beast, in the year of Grace 1510, which was of the bigness of a greyhound, and footed like a gander, and issuing out of the water early in the morning about midsummer time, did very easily and without any visible force or straining of himself overthrow huge oaks with his tail, and thereunto killed three men outright that hunted him with three strokes of his said tail, the rest of them saving themselves in trees thereabouts, whilest the foresaid monster returned to the water. Those that are given to the observations of rare and uncouth sights, believe that this beast is never seen but against some great trouble and mischief to come upon the realm of Scotland. (280)

This early anecdote about a creature like the Loch Ness monster is just one of many current stories about Scotland upon which *Macbeth*'s terrifying atmosphere is created.

The editors are working their way through the most frequently studied plays, making an important contribution to our bookshelves. The only regret is that these editions are far more expensive than either a scholarly variorum or the other student editions of the plays.

WHAT CAN BE LEARNED FROM QUARTOS AND FOLIOS?

Although it appears to be sheer pretension when a theatre person carries into a rehearsal one of the facsimile versions of the First Folio, this is perhaps not entirely the case. These editions, re-creations of the very first publications that have survived from Shakespeare's age, are most often consulted by scholars but also contain clues that are sufficiently useful to actors to justify learning how to read them. The best book on using the First Folio is Neil Freeman's *Shakespeare's First Texts*. Here you will find many examples and a discussion that is richly theatrical.

The most immediate barrier to using these facsimile editions is availability: they are expensive and are usually kept in reference sections of university libraries. The actual books that they recreate are held in special collections. Second, because they are in fact photographic reproductions of the pages of the brittle, delicate texts, they are very difficult to read. Sections are smudged or torn, lines are wrapped round idiosyncratically, and compositors used the old-fashioned script *s* that looks too much like an *f* for comfort. The Furness variorum editions of the plays use modern print and original punctuation and spelling, which make for easier reading, but these editions are also large and expensive or out of print.

Comparing multiple versions of a single play will eliminate forever any lingering assumptions of the accessibility of a definitive text for plays like *Hamlet* and *King Lear*, and so by extension for the rest of the canon. Editors have preferences, strong ones, but a quick look at alternative words, phrases, lines, sentences, speeches, and entire scenes, to say nothing of the ordering of same, might reveal something quite exciting that sparks a modification of the text for your production.

Even the "bad quartos" that scholars like to bar from inclusion on the grounds of inferiority (a subjective evaluation, of course) often contain vivid, striking, beautiful bits of pure theatricality. Have a look. If you like it, use it. You have as much justification for creating a hodgepodge from a variety of versions as the editors do.

The various versions of a play like *Hamlet* differ greatly in length, and it is possible to witness, through comparing versions, theatrical editing undertaken by Shakespeare's own company. If you have ever felt the need to justify not performing every word of a specific edition of one of Shakespeare's plays, the knowledge that Shakespeare's actors also edited their resident playwright should do the trick. But these gleanings of insight and authorization are secondary to the main inspiration available from facsimile editions, and that is the punctuation and spelling systems used by seventeenth-century editors who created these texts.

Punctuation for Performers

We know that the process of typesetting precluded the sort of accuracy we associate with the publication of a modern poet's work. The best we can get from the facsimile punctuation and spelling is a sense of the patterns that were used to transform spoken theatrical poetry into dramatic poetry for a reader. As best we can tell, the typesetters made extensive use of punctuation and spelling to assist in this transformation.

It is likely that actors were involved in some stage of the publication process. Two members of Shakespeare's company are credited with the First Folio, and scholars have long speculated that actors pirated the "bad quartos" or quickly published "good quartos" to protect the company's copyright on a popular piece. Even if the actors were not directly involved, the publisher presumably had some familiarity with the plays in performance. Just as modern editors use punctuation to capture the rhythms of contemporary theatrical speech habits, Shakespeare's first publishers made use of colons, commas, periods, and semicolons to signal pauses of different lengths and different types of connections between thoughts.

How can an actor make use of this? First, you need to alert yourself to the dangers represented by the punctuation in modern editions. Consider how profound an impact such markings make upon your assumptions about the correct delivery of a line. Then consider the agenda of the modern editor, who inserts a brand-new set of markers to help a modern reader follow the thought patterns of the poetry. But reading thought patterns and hearing ideas and emotions are two quite different ways of receiving human communication; sometimes they are so close as to be equally well served by the same punctuation, but only sometimes.

What is exciting about looking at the punctuation in the First Folio is the doors it opens. Thoughts that are always separated by a full stop in modern editions are suddenly linked with the more open-ended colon. Commas, in particular, serve a radically different function. If, as an exercise, an actor breathes only on commas and uses this approach with first a modern punctuation and then a sixteenth-century version, that actor will discover two strikingly different emotional events. Of course, neither set of punctuation markings is "correct" or even "preferable." All that is important is that the door is opened to variation, and hence to creative inspiration.

Shakespeare's Spelling

When you look at the facsimile versions of Shakespeare's plays, you will at once notice that Shakespeare and his contemporaries used a greater flexibility in spelling than we allow ourselves today. In fact, a huge number of words had two different and equally correct spellings, one older and one newer. Generally, the older version was longer, perhaps with an extra *e* or *y* or unsounded consonant.

Why would a publisher spell sin "sin" on one page and "sinne" on another? After all, you cannot hear the different spellings. Or can you? A careful examination of old and new spellings reveals that when the old spelling is used, the word is almost always of great importance to the meaning and the emotional impact of the sentence. Was this a way to suggest emphasis, the way a modern editor might italicize or put in capitals?

Elizabethan typesetters used both capitalized words and italics. They saved italics for names of characters and used capitalized words for philosophical concepts, such as Time and Honour. But here is another fascinating clue revealed in the old texts. Repeatedly, Shakespearean characters talk metaphorically about plucking Honour by the brow or smoothing Time's frowning forehead. The Elizabethan audience, trained in the medieval play tradition that had actors on stage playing human attributes such as Good Deeds, Mercy, Knowledge, and so on and surrounded by an iconographic tradition that had codified everything from the clothing, sex and hairstyle to the activities of Tyranny, Justice, Opportunity, Lechery, and everything in between, would hear not a concept but a name. Time is as real as Lear, Honour as Hotspur, Gluttony as Falstaff. Modern editors tend to remove all of these Elizabethan "accidentals," which would only confuse a modern reader. But a modern actor can untangle many puzzling ideas and transform philosophy into feeling through careful attention to these clues.

Many scholars have blended an interest in minutiae with historical detective work, and the result is a series of books and articles about the first editions and their relationship to Shakespeare's own draft of the play. The debates still rage: one handwriting expert has just claimed that a manuscript previously rejected from the Shakespeare canon is in the playwright's handwriting. We will have to see if it appears in any new collected works published in this century. But for the actor, almost nothing of this scholarship is of any use at all. The bits and pieces that might be useful can be found in the footnotes and introductions to modern variorum editions, and of course you can go directly to the facsimile editions on your own. If you are ever in Britain and can visit the British Museum, you can see one of the few surviving manuscript versions of some Elizabethan plays. That is a thrill, I can tell you.

Here is another example of what can be gained by having a look at the First Folio and trusting it instead of assuming that its reading must be an error and changing it, as do modern editors. John C. Meagher decries the loss of staging clues to editorial traditions that make the corrections and cut theatre people off from the staging that Shakespeare envisioned. I recommend his book *Shakespeare's Shakespeare* for the many interesting insights it provides. Sometimes Shakespeare's version (if that is what is recorded in the folio or quarto editions) works better than the editor's correction. But sometimes Shakespeare's idea, brilliant as he was, simply does not work for a modern production. Still, it is nice to know how to read the plays for the clues.

Say you received a script from a modern playwright in which you are required to sing several songs (you were cast for your excellent voice), but your director had retyped the manuscript to eliminate the playwright's stage directions, so that this is all you received:

Another character: I'll give you something, a verse I wrote yesterday.

Your character: And I'll sing it for you.

Your character: Here's how it goes. (Then follows the verse of a song.)

Your character: What's that last word mean, anyway?

Another character: It's a Greek word.

Now, if you received that, you would assume that the director had not given you some stage directions that justified you speaking three times in a row. In fact, it would make perfect sense. The other character gives you the paper, you offer to sing, maybe you have to practice a bit, or read it quickly, then you sing it, then you ask the other character about the last word in the song (17).

This is Meagher's best example of the interference of editorial traditions. The play is *As You Like It*, and Jacques keeps asking Amiens to sing for him. After Amiens delivers a verse of the song, Jacques says, "I'll give you a verse to this note, / That I made yesterday in despite of my Invention" [2.5.46]. The next line is, "And I'll sing it," and the next line is, "Thus it goes." Then a verse of the song is written into the text, exactly in the same format as the previous verse. Then follows the line "What's that Ducdame?" followed by Jacques's reply, " 'Tis a Greek invocation."

The folio gives three lines in a row to Amiens. Modern editors cannot abide this and change it so that the dialogue headings alternate. This has Jacques singing the verse, rejecting Amiens's offer to sing the verse, and changing the meaning of "give you" from give you a piece of paper with the verse written to give you a performance of the verse sung aloud. This works, and works well, as countless productions have proven. But wouldn't you have liked to encounter the folio version and to explore how you might make it work, rather than the tidying-up "corrections" of the editors who have assumed that the three headings must be a mistake?

Practical Application: Gleanings from the First Texts

Let's have a close look at one speech in folio, quarto, and modern versions to see how an actor can make use of the information contained in early and modern texts. Here is Benvolio, explaining to Romeo's parents where their son was last seen, as it appears in *The Riverside Shakespeare*:

Madam, an hour before the worshipp'd sun
Peer'd forth the golden window of the east,

A troubled mind drive me to walk abroad,
Where, underneath the grove of sycamore
That westward rooteth from this city side,
So early walking did I see your son.
Towards him I made, but he was ware of me,
And stole into the covert of the wood.
I, measuring his affections by my own,
Which then most sought where most might not be found,
Being one too many by my weary self,
Pursued my humour not pursuing his,
And gladly shunn'd who gladly fled from me. [1.1.118]

In the case of *Romeo and Juliet*, we have access not only to the First Folio, but also to not one but two quarto editions, one published in 1597, and another which was published two years later with the announcement, "Newly corrected, augmented, and amended," which suggests that the early publication was not sanctioned by Shakespeare's company, the owners of the manuscript. It appears as if three other early quarto editions were printed directly from the 1599 quarto. Two of these are dated 1609 and 1637; the third is undated but thought by the experts to have appeared in 1622. The First Folio version of the text is virtually identical to the 1609 quarto. For that reason, scholarly editors attribute to the 1599 what they call "textual authority" and, when in doubt, go with that version. A close comparison of the versions of Benvolio's speech which appear in the three early editions of the play is quite revealing (see Figure 2.1).

The first thing that we notice when we compare several versions of this speech, is that editors make choices that have a huge impact upon what information an actor receives overtly and covertly from the text. In this instance, the choices include something as huge as a complete change in the text. "That most are busied when they're most alone" is the simple, effective, efficient modifying phrase that explains why Benvolio chose not to approach Romeo. This is the major difference between the First and Second Quarto versions of the play; the First Folio matches the Second Quarto. Is the First Quarto a "bad" quarto that inaccurately records the speech? Or does it represent a version of the play as edited by the acting company, Shakespeare included? Those editors who use the First Quarto version clearly lean to the side of the latter explanation and prefer the accessibility of the single line to the complex and difficult language of the two-line version, "Which then most sought where most might not be found, / Being one too many by my weary self."

When we compare modern punctuation with the sixteenth-century punctuation, we can see that modern editors are much more likely to use a period to signal the end of a thought when the first editions used a colon or semicolon to suggest the building of a rhetorical argument. In this twelve- or thirteen-line speech the Riverside edition uses three periods where the First Folio and Sec-

Figure 2.1
Three Editions of *Romeo and Juliet*

First Folio

Madam, an houre before the worshipt Sun
Peer'd forth the golden window of the East,
A troubled mind draue me to walke abroad,
Where vnderneath the groue of Sycamour,
That West-ward rooteth from this City side:
So earely walking did I see your Sonne:
Towards him I made, but he was ware of me,
And stole into the couert of the wood,
I measuring his affections by my owne,
Which then most sought, wher most might not be found:
Being one too many by my weary selfe,
Pursued my Honour, not pursuing his
And gladly shunn'd, who gladly fled from me.

First Quarto

Madame, an houre before the worshipt sunne
Peept through the golden window of the East,
A troubled thought drew me from companie:
Where vnderneath the groue *Sicamoure*,
That Westward rooteth from the Citties side,
So earely walking might I see your sonne.
I drew towards him, but he was ware of me,
And drew into the thicket of the wood:
I noting his affections by mine owne,

That most are busied when th'are most alone,
Pursued my honor, not pursuing his.

Second Quarto

Madam, an houre before the worshipt Sun,
Peerde forth the golden window of the East,
A troubled minde driue me to walke abroad,
Where vnderneath the groue of Sycamour,
That Westward rooteth from this Citie side:
So early walking did I see your sonne,
Towards him I made, but he was ware of me,
And stole into the couert of the wood,
I measuring his affections by my owne,
Which then most sought, where most might not be found:
Being one too many by my wearie selfe,
Pursued my humor, not pursuing his,
And gladly shunned, who gladly fled from me.

ond Quarto have just one, at the end of the speech. The First Quarto, however, has a period after "son."

The addition of a period after "son" and "wood" helps to make the simple units of thought clear. Benvolio explains when and where he saw Romeo. Then he tells what happened next: he went toward Romeo, who saw him and slipped into the woods. Then he explains why he left Romeo alone. Three pieces of information.

In the rhetorical version, without periods, the first unit, telling when and where, is offered simply to set up what happens next, which in turn can only be fully understood in the context of the final piece of information. For an actor, the significant links between when/where and what and why are more strikingly felt if there is no marker signalling end of thought, and hence end of breath and cadencing down.

But even a modern editor who is trying to re-create the more rhetorical style of punctuation wants to change the commas of the first editions into colons and semicolons when the grammar of the sentence requires it. The First Folio has only a comma after "abroad" and "wood." The Second Quarto has a comma in these two spots and also after "son." Here we have an example of the use of punctuation in some system that bears no relationship to grammar. Something much more than a comma is needed after "wood" to make sense of the ending of one thought and the beginning of another at that point. No wonder modern editors help out modern readers by changing the comma to either a period, a colon, or a semicolon.

However, if an actor reads the speech aloud, taking a small breath at every comma, then the spoken rhythm of the speech is brought out by the location of the commas. When we have three reasonable versions of the speech, the First Folio plus two quartos, then we can say the speech with three different rhythms. This reminds us that we cannot view the punctuation of even a first edition as the "correct" punctuation. Rather, it is something that we can use as a guide for a pacing of delivery that is not grammatical, something that suits the theatrical nature of the language.

If you use a word-processing program that has a grammatical check, and if you write fiction or drama, you will have learned that you simply cannot use the grammar program on your creative writing. You are not off the hook for proofreading carefully (spelling errors, for example, make you look really dumb rather than really creative), and whatever punctuation system you use to signal the rhythms of the dialogue must be clear and consistent, but whatever you do, it will not be grammatical. If your stories or plays were ever to be published, the editor would be doing the readers a great disservice by making the writing conform to the rules of grammar.

On the other hand, if you have ever acted in a play that made excessive use of exclamation marks and capitalized words to signal emphasis and intensity, you will know the frustration of being led by the nose into the least interesting of acting choices far too early in the rehearsal process. For that reason, I find editions of Shakespeare's plays that resort to "theatrical" punctuation even more irritating. Here is a parody of this tendency:

> Madam . . . an HOUR before the worshipp'd sun
> Peer'd forth the golden window of the east,
> A TROUBLED mind drave me to walk abroad;
> Where, underneath the grove of sycamore
> That westward rooteth from the city's side,
> So early walking did I see your son!
> Towards him I made, but he was ware of me
> And stole into the covert of the wood!!
> I—measuring his affections by my own,
> That most are busied when they're most alone—
> Pursued my humour NOT pursuing his,
> And gladly shunn'd who gladly fled from me.

At first glance, it might seem helpful to read such a version of the speech. The rhythms suggest a specific "reading" of the emotions of the scene, and by pointing out a few significant words, many aspects of the speech become clearer, at first reading. This is, of course, why editors make these choices. Their responsibility is to readers, who want more than anything else to get what is going on as they are reading the words, so that the play unfolds in front of them as it would in a production.

But this is terrible for actors, who do not want someone so far removed from the rehearsal hall imprinting onto their unconscious minds the message that "hour" and "troubled" and "not" must be emphasized, that there needs to be a bit of a pause after "Madam" to suggest hesitation, and that there is a build toward a single exclamation mark's worth of excitement at "son" and a double exclamation mark's worth at "wood."

It is easy to say, "Take all punctuation with a grain of salt," but it is very, very difficult to do so. These markers get into our minds as we encounter the words on the page, and they remain as invisible gates and fences through which the emotion suggested by the words will flow, long after we have memorized the lines. The only effective antidote, which allays the symptoms but does not offer a cure to the infection, is to read aloud from as many different editions as possible while learning lines and to consider no one text as the primary or "correct" text at any point in your work on the role.

Now let us look at the old spelling signals that might be buried in the early editions. We must remember once again that we are working with versions of the play Shakespeare wrote several times removed, even in the earliest printed versions. We have no idea if the extra "ne" on "son" was how Shakespeare spelled the word, or how the compositor spelled the word, and we have no idea if the old spelling had any great significance other than old habits. As a Canadian I was raised to use British spellings for words like "theatre" and "colour"; today more and more formal publications are switching to American spellings, so that we have "meter" and "neighbor." Will some scholar some day argue that when my fingers slip and I type "valour," it means that the word is to be emphasized, but when I avoid the extra keystroke and type "honor," the word is not as significant?

Although we could be basing an acting theory on the Elizabethan equivalent of typos, I think that it is still worth exploring the potential of long spelling as a clue to hypertext. These extra letters would have represented additional labor for the compositors, and my guess is that they would have eliminated even more of them if there were absolutely no difference between the impact of "son" and "sonne" on the eye of the reader. But there is a difference in impact, and that difference draws the eye to the second version, which I can only think was deemed appropriate by the first editors if the ear was to imagine being drawn to the word by the actor's emphasis.

Here is the list of long-spelling words in Benvolio's speech: hour, walk, son, own, self. When these words appear in the quartos, they are spelled the same way. The only obvious emphasis is in "son" as a pun on "sun" and of course as the primary subject of the entire exchange. The other four words are interesting but scarcely worthy of a heightened intensity in delivery. However, if you read the First Folio version aloud, using commas for small breaths, then the five long-spelling words, if they are given the slightest emphasis, help to shape the flow of the thought. In particular, "owne" and "selfe" help the voice to navigate the complex syntax of the sentence at that point.

We find also, in the Second Quarto, long spelling for "mind" and "weary" and the very interesting spelling of "peerde." In the First Quarto we find the word "sycamour" with both a long spelling and italics. "City" and "company" both have the long spelling. Saying these two versions aloud will result in a different flow, with alternative rhythms and emphasis. By saying all three versions aloud and seeing the validity of any of the three versions of emphasized words, pauses, links between thoughts, and even word choice, you will be best positioned to keep all your options open, a far better approach than memorizing the choices made by any one editor.

Actors who enjoy this approach to studying Shakespeare will want to consult Neil Freeman's book for themselves. Freeman has also done a great service by preparing the Folio Series now published by Applause Books. These are individual editions of the plays based upon the First Folio, with the original spellings, punctuation, and capitalization, but without the f for s or the u/v usage that so confuse a modern reader. Footnotes are provided that clarify changes made in later editions of the First Folio, so that what appear to have been outright errors can be corrected. In order to suggest a striking break with every period, a space is inserted into the body of the long speech. As an extra bonus for actors, the text is printed only on the right page, leaving a blank page facing for notes.

Parallel Texts

This exploration of the many differences between versions of Benvolio's speech reminds us that the versions we read in modern editions are always compilations of one sort or another. It is therefore worth a look at several editions to see what choices other editors have made and to remind ourselves that no one version is "correct."

Scholarly opinion has turned away from the composite editions of those multitext plays for which there exists at least one quarto publication in addition to the First Folio. It used to be that the editor blended the various versions, including the best bits from both. Now it is generally felt that when the quarto and the First Folio are strikingly different, we might be looking at a record of two distinct versions of the play. As a result, some publishers are releasing editions of quarto texts, including the so-called bad quartos, and other editors are producing parallel texts, in which the two (or more) versions are presented across the page from each other. Cambridge University Press has issued variorum editions of the First Quarto versions of *Hamlet, Richard III, The Taming of the Shrew,* and *King Lear.* Oxford University Press has published an edition of the quarto version of *A Midsummer Night's Dream,* and there are parallel editions of *King Lear, Hamlet, Richard III,* and *Henry V.*

Parallel texts allow you to see the contrast between the best of the quarto versions and the First Folio. You can contrast punctuation, to remind yourself that even the First Folio's periods and colons were inserted by a compositor and not necessarily by Shakespeare. You can see immediately the minute and massive cuts that someone, possibly Shakespeare himself, while working through the play in rehearsal or for a revival, made to the longest surviving version of the play. Reproductions of the First Folio and quartos can prove such a strain to the eye that a clean copy with the modern use of *s* and *v* can save headaches. Some editors even go so far as to use modern spellings (René Weis for *King Lear*), which shows the different approaches to the play taken by Shakespeare in editions published in 1608 and 1623, but robs the reader of information encoded (if Freeman is correct) in old and new spellings of "hot" words.

IN SEARCH OF SHAKESPEARE'S TEXT

Working as they often do with scripts in progress and living playwrights, actors probably have less trouble than scholars with the idea that the script that Will Shakespeare first brought into the playhouse might have been edited several times and in several different ways as the company changed and as great ideas emerged in rehearsal. Add to the mix the ever-changing political situation that might require some editing and rewriting, and the absence of copyright or even a clear sense of literary ownership in the profession, and it

is no surprise that Will borrowed freely and reshaped dramatically. This aspect
of Shakespeare's writing used to be anathema to scholars. They far preferred
the fantasy of a single, ideal text that they could intuit from reading the plays,
tracing their way back to something called the author's intention. But in recent
years the alternative versions of the plays that have come down to us have
been persuasively demonstrated, by scholars such as Grace Ioppolo in *Revising
Shakespeare*, to be various modifications that a play undergoes in rehearsal. Eric
Sams in *The Real Shakespeare* goes so far as to bring Shakespeare to London as
early as 1564 and to attribute to him the authorship of earlier versions of
many of the plays that we know of by surviving titles and a few manuscripts
that scholars prefer to label Shakespeare's sources.

Actors can feel equally as oppressed as liberated by the idea that the text
they have been educated to worship cannot be, with any certainty, the play
that Shakespeare wrote. The oppression comes from the sensation that the
firm ground upon which they were attempting to honor the playwright's intentions is a quicksand of speculation and uncertainty. The liberation comes
from the feeling that Shakespeare would have been the first to suggest the sort
of cuts and revisions that are necessary to bring these plays to a modern
audience. It is possible that Shakespeare would have found more to admire in
a complete reworking of one of his plays, as, for example, the transformation
of *Romeo and Juliet* into Baz Luhrmann's *Romeo + Juliet*, than in a reverential,
"straight" production of his masterpiece in Elizabethan costume before a dozing
audience of scholars and middle-aged seekers of high culture.

PLAY-SPECIFIC COMMENTARIES

> We are ready
> To use our utmost Studies, in your service.
>
> Campeius [*HVIII* 3.1.173]

As a service to students of Shakespeare, publishers have issued collections
of articles about a single play, reprinted in full or in part, with or without
explanations by an editor. For the most part, these are collections of literary
studies, but some collections contain more theatrical selections. For example,
G. Harold Metz's collection on *Titus Andronicus, Shakespeare's Earliest Tragedy*,
contains everything you might want to know about the various editions of the
play, Shakespeare's sources, productions, and what the play suggests to us
about how it might have been produced in Shakespeare's time.

Casebooks

Several publishers have created series that are made up of collections of
articles on individual plays, which are shelved right next to the individual

editions of the plays. It is worth an actor's while to browse through the table of contents looking for an article that might contain something other than literary studies and thematic analysis. Generally speaking, the more recent the publication date, the better, because the sorts of scholarship that are most likely to be helpful for actors were distinctly out of fashion for some time but are now very much back in fashion. Another benefit of these collections is that the editors have selected articles that are most likely to appeal to the target readership, undergraduate university students. Scholars who have an agenda of debating with other scholars, or who are heavily reliant upon obscure jargon belonging to a specific theoretical approach, tend not to be republished in such collections.

Let us take, for example, the New Casebook series published by St. Martin's Press. Along with casebooks on *Great Expectations, Wuthering Heights*, and *Wordsworth*, it has tackled, to date, *Hamlet, Macbeth, King Lear, The Merchant of Venice, Twelfth Night, A Midsummer Night's Dream, The Tempest, Antony and Cleopatra*, Shakespeare's tragedies, and Shakespeare's history plays.

The New Casebook volume on *Macbeth*, edited by Alan Sinfield, was published in 1992. The articles appear, by their titles, to be worthy of a look, but all it takes is a quick read of the first two or three paragraphs and a page flip through the rest to tell if a particular article is going to have something useful. The first article is Marilyn French's *"Macbeth* and Masculine Values," which might be filled with details about how men and women did things differently in Shakespeare's world. Instead, it turns out to be a theoretical and thematic discussion of French's ideas of masculinity and femininity and how these play out in the literary elements of the play. There is not much here that is "actable," which is no reflection on the scholarly merit of the article on its own terms.

The next article is more useful for those actors who like knowing something about what was happening at the time the play was written. Peter Stallybrass's title, *"Macbeth* and Witchcraft," is sure to catch the eye, but the opening paragraphs disappoint: he seems to have an agenda of refuting other scholars. However, the next section, labelled "Witchcraft and Monarchy," contains some factual information about accusations of witchcraft that were actually made in Shakespeare's time, which would have been available to the first actors and audience as part of the context within which they created and observed the weird sisters. The rest of the article becomes an analysis of the play that is of much less interest to actors, if for no other reason than that they are likely to be discovering on the rehearsal floor much more exciting things about how the witches really function in their production of the play than the conclusions Stallybrass comes to from having read it.

Sinfield then includes excerpts from Sigmund Freud in which he discusses the characters of Macbeth and Lady Macbeth. I always find such documents fascinating for reasons quite removed from the challenges in the rehearsal hall. Actors tend to intuit, with far more complexity and richness, what Freud might "discover," again from merely reading the plays. But this is Freud, whose name carries considerable cachet, even if his observations are less than earthshaking.

The other articles in the collection can be flipped through in a similar fashion. You might be interested, for example, in what Catherine Belsey has to say in her article "Subjectivity and the Soliloquy," which discusses the convention of soliloquy, not just the monologues in *Macbeth*. I quite enjoyed Steven Mullaney's "Lying like Truth: Riddle, Representation, and Treason in Renaissance England" because it contains lots of juicy details about the treason trials and public executions that were so much a part of Shakespeare's world. I was not at all interested in Jonathan Dollimore's discussion of "Tragedy and Literature" because of its entirely literary focus. Graham Holderness's article on *Macbeth* on film, "Radical Potential," I found interesting only for the list it provided of a variety of film versions of the play: I would rather see them firsthand and form my own conclusions about them than read his analysis of how the directors met the challenge of bringing Shakespeare to film.

These are, of course, my interests; what is great about a casebook is that you can flip through it and browse for what interests you. The articles tend to be short, accessible, and based upon the highest standards of academic scholarship, so if you find something that proves helpful, you can be sure that you are getting the facts and reading the observations of a respected expert. If you find a writer whose approach is especially useful, go to the library catalogue and see if you can find a book or other articles by this individual: it is quite likely that you have found someone working in the specific subsection of the Shakespeare industry that will continue to provide truly useful assistance to your work as an actor.

Another new series, Theory in Practice, has been started by Open University Press, edited by Nigel Wood. The title might seem to indicate the least appealing sort of scholarly criticism. An actor's hesitation would be justified, for the articles have been chosen by Wood because they make interesting use of the jargon and agenda of specific theoretical approaches. However, as some contemporary Shakespearean criticism is dedicated to bringing to light details of Elizabethan social history or to discussing the plays from a theatrical perspective, it turns out that actors are likely to find useful articles lurking in some of the volumes. The introductory material is very helpful in explaining the theoretical elements of the articles, so in that regard the series is geared toward nonscholars. So far the series has produced books on *Antony and Cleopatra, Hamlet, Henry IV, Measure for Measure, The Merchant of Venice,* and *The Tempest,* with more promised.

The Greenwood "Literature in Context" series includes volumes not only on such often-studied novels as *Pride and Prejudice* and *The Scarlet Letter,* but also on those Shakespeare plays most likely to be read by high school students. Even though an editor like Jay L. Halio, in putting together *Understanding The Merchant of Venice: A Student Casebook to Issues, Sources, and Historical Documents,* is clearly preparing a book for use by teachers and students in the public schools, his selection of source materials and illustrations is invaluable for a general introduction to the context of the play. Here you will find excerpts from Thomas Coryat's *Crudities*, first published in 1611, as well as from the state documents from the trial of Dr. Roderigo Lopez in 1594, suggesting some of the attitudes towards Jews reflected in and challenged by Shakespeare's portrait of Shylock. *Understanding Macbeth* and *Understanding Othello*, edited by Faith Nostbakken, *Understanding Romeo and Juliet*, edited by Alan Hater, *Understanding Shakespeare's Julius Caesar*, edited by Thomas Derrick, and *Understanding Hamlet*, edited by Richard Corum, all follow the same model.

With these books, we mark the transition from studies of individual plays to studies that introduce the actor of Shakespeare to the broader considerations of the context within which these plays were written. Scattered through the following chapters you will find many books that take a single play as a starting place for an in-depth study of some aspect of Shakespeare's England; because their usefulness reaches far beyond a single text, I have chosen to include them in later chapters, although they might well be housed in the library alongside individual copies of the plays with which they concern themselves.

Specialty Scholarship on *Hamlet*

Literary commentators on Hamlet have expended a great deal of paper debating the quality and form of his revenge. Actors, however, will want to skip these writers in favor of Charles and Elaine Hallett in *The Revenger's Madness*, who focus specifically on how his madness might have been viewed by the first actors and audience as a medical condition with some level of credibility, that is, as more than simply a dramatic device or part of the old legend. The Halletts' book contains not only a discussion of the dramatic conventions of madness within revenge tragedies and a chapter on Hamlet, but also a chapter, their third, entitled "The Revenger's Madness and Renaissance Psychological Theory," that answers just such questions.

In *The Elizabethan Hamlet*, Arthur McGee takes us through the play as it unfolds, finding enticing parallels between the tenets of faith as expressed in the medieval theatrical heritage as well as contemporary sermons and homilies, and providing the actor with a mixture of thought-provoking commentary and traditional literary analysis. This is a book that rewards skimming as the actor hops over the sort of thematic discussion that is best left to the classroom, stopping to absorb another of McGee's connections. Just one example of the riches to be found: having worked his way through the play, he comes to a chapter entitled "Ophelia and Laertes," the first part of which includes a detailed and fascinating explanation for the mad songs of the fourth act.

In *Hamlet and the Word*, Harold Fisch sets out to assist us in reacting to the spiritual journey of Hamlet and the others in this play as if we were contemporaries of Shakespeare. His book contains such an excellent overview of the complexity of Christian thought of this era that, like Frye's study, it rewards a thorough examination by its direct application to all of the other plays. In keeping with this breadth of scope, Fisch includes comments on some of the other plays; you can find these pages by making use of his index.

King Lear and Demonology

Next to *Hamlet*, *King Lear* has generated the greatest number of books of collected critical articles, always a bad sign for the actor looking for something other than an examination of theme or character. One rewarding topic is the demonology studies that have been conducted as a result not only of Edgar's enacting of Poor Tom, during which a number of devils are named, but also of a pattern of imagery that resonates profoundly when it is set in the context of contemporary events. John L. Murphy in *Darkness and Devils* quotes extensively from a variety of possible influences on Shakespeare's creation and ties in contemporary events as well as dramatic and literary conventions at work in the play. F. W. Brownlow's study of the parallels between Samuel Harsnett's 1604 *Declaration of Egregious Popish Impostures* and Shakespeare's play is most useful for its first chapter, "Devils at Denham," which effectively tells the story of the Denham exorcisms that came to light in 1594, almost ten years after they had been conducted in secret by Catholic priests and lay people, only some of whom appear to have been outright charlatans. Brownlow's chapter on the parallels between *King Lear* and Harsnett's documentation of the exorcisms is worth skimming, more for the obvious links between Edgar's enactment of a Poor Tom's possession, which eerily echoes the story from Denham, than for Brownlow's discussion of the scholarly debate about other less obvious connections. The second part of the book contains a reprint of Harsnett's *Declaration* and should be dipped into and read aloud for its thrilling language, in both the passages describing the demonic possessions and the moralizing commentary that justifies the sensationalism.

Macbeth and Scotland

Scholars have been particularly kind to the actors of *Macbeth*. They have accumulated a great deal of useful information about witchcraft; they have considered how the play reflects recent events in England. They have interesting things to share about Scotland at the time Macbeth was supposed to have been king as well as about the new Scottish king on the throne of England and Shakespeare's new patron, James Stuart.

The most extensive study linking the play with James and recent events in England is Henry Paul's *The Royal Play of Macbeth*. Paul's table of contents sets out the chapters you will want to browse for whatever interests you, be it the porter's reference to equivocation or the king's evil mentioned by Malcolm in the English court scene. The index will also help you to spot useful bits of information, such as the fact that Malcolm, who ascends to the throne at the end of the play with these words, "My Thanes and Kinsmen / Henceforth be Earls, the first that ever Scotland / in such an Honour named" [5.9.28], was the ancestor of both King James and his royal guest and brother-in-law King Christian IV of Denmark.

Those interested in the current events that shaped Shakespeare's retelling of the story of this Scottish king might want to have a look at Garry Wills's *Witches and Jesuits*. Wills's approach is to demonstrate how recent events endowed every moment of *Macbeth* with huge political and spiritual significance. If these connections interest you, his extensive endnotes will point you in the direction of the many books of social and political historians specializing in this period.

Character Studies

Of all of Shakespeare's individual characters, Shylock has generated the most scholarly studies, many of which seek to place Shakespeare's portrait of this particular Venetian Jew into the largest possible context. Both James Shapiro's *Shakespeare and the Jews* and Cecil Roth's *History of the Jews in Venice* can be consulted by anyone interested in this perspective. Shylock research might take an actor to a variety of sources, most of which are caught up in the controversy surrounding this play as performed in the modern theatre. No one likes to think of the racism that permeated Shakespeare's world and is reflected in the attitudes of the characters and the resolution of the plot of this play. An actor friend reports his horror at the nightly cheers that greeted his words, in his role as Antonio, that condemned Shylock to immediate conversion to Christianity. However, an actor would be better served by finding out some of the historical context for this racism than by becoming entangled in the scholarly analysis of the anti-Semitism that modern productions of this play reinforce, despite the best intentions of the company. Shapiro's book is the best of its kind, bringing together a great deal of important factual information and a sensitive and thoughtful analysis of the racism encoded in the play. Roth's book about the Jews in Venice will provide the actor with some information for creating Shylock's world as it might have been for a Jewish merchant living in that Italian city.

Harold Bloom has made an important contribution to the work of actors through his collections of articles on specific characters. His book on Shylock assembles examples of a wide range of approaches, including scholars who weigh in on the difficult moral questions raised by modern productions of anti-Semitic stereotypes. His book also reproduces some invaluable specific studies such as Barbara K. Lewalski's "Biblical Allusion and the Allegory in *The Merchant of Venice*."

Other characters about whom Bloom has produced collections of articles in the Major Literary Characters series include Caliban, Cleopatra, Falstaff, Hamlet, Iago, Julius Caesar, King Lear, Macbeth, Othello, and Rosalind. Any of these is well worth a look by actors entrusted with one of these roles or with playing opposite one of these characters. The wide range of scholarly opinion and analysis will demonstrate the many, many options available to the actor and might well suggest equally viable alternatives that have yet to be explored by scholars.

Other characters have elicited book-length special treatment on the basis of some particular interest on the part of the scholar. The first part of *Shakespeare's Mercutio*, by Joseph A. Porter, is the most interesting for an actor. He explores all sorts of fascinating connections with the Greek god Mercury, some thoughts on Mercutio's brother Valentine, who is mentioned in the list of guests invited to Capulet's party but is never further identified, and an intriguing link with Christopher Marlowe. The second part is a more traditional literary "reading" of the play and, like all such interpretive scholarship, offers solutions to performance that an actor needs to discover on the rehearsal floor, not between the covers of a book.

Othello in Context

Virginia Mason Vaughan's *Othello: A Contextual History* provides a similar healthy dollop of cultural history in connection with Elizabethan attitudes toward Venetians, Turks, and Moors, the military, and relationships between husbands and wives. Vaughan's work is less broadly based than Frye's but is very useful for this specific play. The second half of the book traces how the play has been presented in the years since the premiere, a piece of scholarship of less interest to modern actors. Jack D'Amico has produced *The Moor in English Renaissance Drama*, which will interest actors playing or reacting to Othello, as well as Aaron the Moor in *Titus Andronicus* and the Prince of Aragon in *The Merchant of Venice*.

THE ACTOR AND THE TEXT

> Speak the speech I pray you,
> as I pronounced it to you.
>
> Hamlet [*Hamlet* 3.2.1]

It is perhaps distressing to discover that your much-valued complete works or those handy, inexpensive pocket editions are vulnerable to challenges from specialists who compare the first editions of the plays and demonstrate, over and over, that these are simply not what Shakespeare wrote, what his actors performed, and what the first audience heard. When you venture to the shelves in the library that hold the many editions of the plays, alongside the scholarly works that focus on that play, it is difficult to avoid the sinking sensation of despair. Alternatively, we can admire the rarified expertise of the scholarly editors, who make choices from among the many options, double check each and every edition of the play and read what every scholar has ever said about it. I think it is perfectly acceptable simply to accept the choices made by such authorities, provided we realize that these are, in fact, arbitrary choices.

Because an actor's relationship with the words of the text is so complex, extra care must be taken in selecting which edition of the play to carry on the rehearsal floor. I would not recommend one editor's strategies and approaches over another's, but I would always strongly urge a performer to consult more than one modern edition, at least one of which must be a scholarly variorum, and to take the time to explore the very first editions for the special clues they contain.

RECOMMENDED READING

Modern Editions of the Plays

Barnet, Sylvan, general ed. *The Signet Classic Shakespeare.* New York: New American Library, 1963–present.

Bevington, David, ed. *The Complete Works of Shakespeare.* Glenview: Scott, Foresman, 1980.

Brockbank, Philip, and Brian Gibbons, general eds. *The New Cambridge Shakespeare.* Cambridge: Cambridge University Press, 1984–present.

Ellis-Fermor, Una, Harold F. Brooks, Harold Jenkins, and Brian Morris, general eds. *The Arden Shakespeare,* Second Series. London: Methuen, 1946–1982.

Evans, G. Blakemore, ed. *The Riverside Shakespeare.* Boston: Houghton Mifflin, 1974.

Furness, Horace Howard, ed. *A New Variorum Edition of Shakespeare.* Philadelphia: Lippincott, 1871–1955.

Harbage, Alfred, general ed. *The Pelican Shakespeare.* Baltimore: Penguin Books, 1959–present.

Howard, Jean E., general ed. *The Bedford Shakespeare Series: Texts and Contexts.* Boston: Bedford/St. Martin's, 1996–present.

Mowat, Barbara A., and Paul Werstine, eds. *The New Folger Library Shakespeare.* New York: Washington Square Press, 1992–present.

Proudfoot, Richard, Ann Thompson, and David Scott Kastan, general eds. *The Arden Shakespeare,* Third Series. Walton-on-Thames: Thomas Nelson and Sons, 1983–present.

Ribner, Irving, and George Lyman Kittredge, eds. *The Complete Works of Shakespeare.* New York: John Wiley & Sons, 1971.

Spencer, T.J.B., general ed. *The New Penguin Shakespeare.* London: Penguin Books, 1968–present.

Wells, Stanley, general ed. *The Oxford Shakespeare.* Oxford: Oxford University Press, 1982–present.

Reprints of the First Editions

Allen, Michael J.B., and Kenneth Muir. *Shakespeare's Plays in Quarto: A Facsimile Edition of Copies Primarily from the Henry E. Huntington Library*. Berkeley: University of California Press, 1981.

Freeman, Neil, ed. *The Applause First Folio of Shakespeare*. New York: Applause Books, 2001.

———. *Applause Shakespeare Library: Folio Texts*. New York: Applause Books, 1998–2000.

Hinman, Charlton, ed. *The First Folio of Shakespeare: Based on Folios in the Folger Shakespeare Library Collection*. New York: W. W. Norton, 1996.

———. *The Norton Facsimile: The First Folio of Shakespeare*. New York: W. W. Norton, 1987.

Moston, Doug. *The First Folio of Shakespeare* (1623). New York: Applause Books, 1995.

Smidt, Kristian, ed. *The Tragedy of King Richard the Third: Parallel Texts of the First Quarto and the First Folio with Variants of the Early Quartos*. New York: Humanities Press, 1969.

Warren, Michael. *The Parallel King Lear, 1608–1623*. Berkeley: University of California Press, 1989.

Weis, René, ed. *King Lear: A Parallel Text Edition*. London: Longman, 1993.

Evaluating Editions

Freeman, Neil H.M. *Shakespeare's First Texts*. New York: Applause Theatre Book Publishers, 1999.

Ioppolo, Grace. *Revising Shakespeare*. Cambridge, MA: Harvard University Press, 1991.

Meagher, John C. *Shakespeare's Shakespeare: How the Plays Were Made*. New York: Continuum, 1997.

Sams, Eric. *The Real Shakespeare: Retrieving the Early Years, 1564–1594*. New Haven, CT: Yale University Press, 1995.

Thompson, Ann. *Which Shakespeare? A User's Guide to Editions*. Philadelphia: Open University Press, 1992.

Studies of Individual Plays

Bloom, Harold, ed. *Shylock*. New York: Chelsea House, 1991.

Brownlow, F.W. *Shakespeare, Harsnett, and the Devils of Denham*. Newark: University of Delaware Press, 1993.

Corum, Richard. *Understanding Hamlet: A Student Casebook to Issues, Sources, and Historical Documents*. Westport, CT: Greenwood Press, 1998.

Coyle, Martin, ed. *Hamlet: William Shakespeare*. New Casebooks Series. New York: St. Martin's Press, 1992.

———. *The Merchant of Venice: William Shakespeare*. New Casebooks Series. New York: St. Martin's Press, 1998.

D'Amico, Jack. *The Moor in English Renaissance Drama*. Tampa: University of South Florida Press, 1991.

Derrick, Thomas J. *Understanding Shakespeare's Julius Caesar: A Student Casebook to Issues, Sources, and Historical Documents.* Westport, CT: Greenwood Press, 1998.

Drakakis, John, ed. *Antony and Cleopatra: William Shakespeare.* New Casebooks Series. New York: St. Martin's Press, 1994.

Dutton, Richard, ed. *A Midsummer Night's Dream: William Shakespeare.* New Casebooks Series. New York: St. Martin's Press, 1996.

Fisch, Harold. *Hamlet and the Word: The Covenant Pattern in Shakespeare.* New York: Frederick Ungar, 1971.

Hager, Alan. *Understanding Romeo and Juliet: A Student Casebook to Issues, Sources, and Historical Documents.* Westport, CT: Greenwood Press, 1999.

Halio, Jay L. *Understanding The Merchant of Venice: A Student Casebook to Issues, Sources, and Historical Documents.* Westport, CT: Greenwood Press, 2000.

Hallett, Charles A., and Elaine S. Hallett. *The Revenger's Madness: A Study of Revenge Tragedy Motifs.* Lincoln: University of Nebraska Press, 1980.

Holderness, Graham, ed. *Shakespeare's History Plays: Richard II to Henry V.* New Casebooks Series. New York: St. Martin's Press, 1992.

McGee, Arthur. *The Elizabethan Hamlet.* New Haven, CT: Yale University Press, 1987.

Metz, G. Harold, ed. *Shakespeare's Earliest Tragedy: Studies in Titus Andronicus.* Rutherford, NJ: Fairleigh Dickinson University Press, 1996.

Murphy, John L. *Darkness and Devils: Exorcism and King Lear.* Athens: Ohio University Press, 1984.

Nostbakken, Faith. *Understanding Macbeth: A Student Casebook to Issues, Sources, and Historical Documents.* Westport, CT: Greenwood Press, 1997.

———. *Understanding Othello: A Student Casebook to Issues, Sources, and Historical Documents.* Westport, CT: Greenwood Press, 2000.

Paul, Henry N. *The Royal Play of Macbeth: When, Why, and How It Was Written by Shakespeare.* New York: Macmillan, 1950.

Porter, Joseph A. *Shakespeare's Mercutio: His History and Drama.* Chapel Hill: University of North Carolina Press, 1988.

Roth, Cecil. *History of the Jews in Venice.* New York: Schocken Books, 1975.

Ryan, Kiernan. *King Lear: William Shakespeare.* New Casebooks Series. New York: St. Martin's Press, 1992.

Shapiro, James. *Shakespeare and the Jews.* New York: Columbia University Press, 1996.

Sinfield, Alan, ed. *Macbeth: William Shakespeare.* New Casebooks Series. New York: St. Martin's Press, 1992.

Smith, Peter J., and Nigel Woods, eds. *Hamlet: Theory in Practice.* Philadelphia: Open University Press, 1996.

Vaughan, Virginia Mason. *Othello: A Contextual History.* Cambridge: Cambridge University Press, 1994.

White, R.S., ed. *The Tempest: William Shakespeare.* New Casebooks Series. New York: St. Martin's Press, 1999.

———. *Twelfth Night: William Shakespeare.* New Casebooks Series. New York: St. Martin's Press, 1996.

Wills, Garry. *Witches and Jesuits: Shakespeare's Macbeth.* Oxford: Oxford University Press, 1995.

Wood, Nigel, general ed. *Shakespeare's Plays: Theory in Practice.* Philadelphia: Open University Press, 1995–present.

Zimmerman, Susan, ed. *Shakespeare's Tragedies.* New Casebooks Series. New York: St. Martin's Press, 1998.

༄ 3 ༄
Dictionaries, Reference Books, and Guides

Polonius: What do you read my Lord?
Hamlet: Words, words, words.

[*Hamlet* 2.2.191]

On your tour through an academic library, you will want to visit the reference section, where you will find rows of extremely thick books with imposing titles. There is a section specifically dedicated to Shakespeare, where you will find invaluable resources. There are also useful collections of information, in the form of encyclopedias or dictionaries, in the sections of the reference collection set aside for other disciplines. Libraries have different policies with regard to which resources are so valuable that they are restricted to in-library use, and so a book that is in the reference section of one library might be on the regular shelves in another. Every library, however, will keep as in-library resources a variety of excellent dictionaries, both general and specific.

DICTIONARIES FOR SHAKESPEARE

How can actors use Shakespeare dictionaries? Which ones should they keep closest at hand? How should they use the information contained in dictionaries?

Supplementing the Editors' Notes

One of the problems with many editions of Shakespeare is that the editors simply cannot or do not explain every single word that will puzzle a modern reader. Often editors assume that the reader will know what the word means already, because the meaning is the same then as now. This is easily solved by a quick look in any dictionary. Actors can be asked to play a character with a larger vocabulary than the actor's own even in a modern play.

Much more irritating are those words that were used quite differently by the Elizabethans than they are today, but that occur so frequently that they become common knowledge for anyone who reads a great deal of Shakespeare. Editors, being such people, sometimes forget that a word like "anon" is not in the common vocabulary of the average individual. Because an actor knows that this word is archaic, a trip to a Shakespeare glossary is clearly in order, and special care will be taken in delivering the word so that a modern audience gets the meaning.

Neither of these two types of unglossed trick words are particularly dangerous, because the actor knows that the meaning is not known and can find the meaning in a dictionary. The most dangerous unglossed words are those that mean something quite different today than they did in Shakespeare's time. Some of these we spot because the word is used in an unexpected way, and we realize that it simply cannot mean what we think it does. For such words, the shift of meaning has been complete. But the meanings of some words have shifted in degree or intensity only. These words might be used in the same way we use them today, and so it is easy to miss completely the shift in emphasis required to match the word to its Elizabethan meaning.

Glossaries, Lexicons, and Shakespearean Dictionaries

Many scholars have contributed to our understanding of how language usage has shifted over the years, and also how the most frequently occurring "trick words" have shifted meaning over time. The compilation of a specialized dictionary just for Shakespeare is the result of the work of a large number of scholars in esoteric fields of language study, and the modern actor can find the fruits of their labor in the reference section of any university library.

The publication of glossaries dates back to the frenzy of publication of complete works in the eighteenth century, when it was already apparent that the reader would require explanation of certain words in Shakespeare's plays. A modern library will still have on its reference shelves the greatly enlarged glossaries published at the end of the nineteenth century. The need for updating is the result of ongoing changes in usage; words that were still generally known when C.T. Onions published *A Shakespeare Glossary* had slipped out of use by 1996, when Eugene F. Shewmaker's book *Shakespeare's Language* was published.

Beside these glossaries you will find Alexander Schmidt's two-volume *Shakespeare Lexicon*, which has quite a different format. Words are defined according to how Shakespeare used them, and then examples are given to show many, but not all, of the lines in which he used the word.

The alphabetical listing of words followed by citations of every use of that word in the complete works is called a concordance, and there is sure to be one for Shakespeare right next to the Shakespeare dictionaries. Most academic libraries will have purchased Marvin Spevack's nine-volume *A Complete and Systematic Concordance to the Works of Shakespeare*, but you will find the one-volume edition, *The Harvard Concordance to Shakespeare*, just as useful. A concordance allows you to explore the patterns of Shakespeare's use of a single word or cluster of related words; the resulting echoes and fascinating cross-fertilizations can illuminate the complexity of meaning woven into a word or an image. The Internet now offers several cyberspace search engines that you can use for just this sort of research and which, given their speed and use of hyperlinks which take you directly to the full speech and then the scene and the play in which the speech occurs, have rendered Spevack's life-work obsolete.

In addition to these invaluable Shakespeare reference books, you will be able to find close by the most extensive and complete dictionaries for the English language. Look for the twenty or more volumes of *The Oxford English Dictionary*, if for no other reason than to acknowledge the immensity of the task the editors of that project have set themselves. Here you will find exhaustive documentation of the meanings of words over time, along with citations that illustrate the earliest recorded usage of each word, and the tracing of words to their point of entry into the English language and then back to their roots in Old and Middle English or the original language from which they were borrowed.

Until the practical benefits of dictionaries have been demonstrated, an actor might be forgiven for assuming that the interests of lexicographers and the needs of the rehearsal hall are not likely ever to coincide.

An Editor's Definitions and an Actor's Implications

The most obvious benefit of dictionaries is to translate words that are four hundred years out of date, and this job has been absorbed by most editors of the plays themselves. I can open *The Riverside Shakespeare* just about anywhere and find an example like this one from *Hamlet*: "Like quills upon the fearful porpentine" [1.5.20]. The note tells me that porpentine is, as I suspected, a porcupine. It also tells me that fearful here means not frightening, but frightened, full of fear. As we saw in our discussion of editions of the plays in the previous chapter, the footnotes contain much of particular interest to actors, but we must be careful to supplement the information provided in even the most complete set of scholarly notes on a text. The editors have selected one meaning and have presented it as precisely and clearly as possible to allow the reader to access the plays "at speed." But actors read in a very special way and need to have access to as much (or as little) guidance in finding meaning as best serves their purposes.

Practical Application: In Search of Ownership

Follow me as I imagine that I have been cast in the role of Bernardo. Working my way through the first scene in *Hamlet*, I read,

Last night of all,
When yond same Star that's Westward from the Pole
Had made his course t'illume that part of Heaven
Where now it burns, Marcellus and my self,
The Bell then beating one. [1.1.35]

I look to the bottom of the page and discover the note "pole: pole star." If I had not looked down, I would have assumed that "pole" meant north pole and not thought much more about it. Knowing that it is the pole star, I feel confident that at least I was on the right track, and so my audience will probably not be too far off either. I won't have to work very hard delivering that particular word. At the same time, it helps me, because the pole star holds a position in the sky, and a star can be west of it. Great. Now I can point up into the lights above the audience, pick one to be the pole star, and trace along to another star, moving my hand right. It always feels better knowing that I am on solid ground here. I will be able to do the action with precision. Before, I was just pointing in the general direction of the star, or not pointing at all, just looking out in the direction of the audience, making sure the light was fully on my face. If I wanted to, I could even draw a little map of the battlements and mark north on it.

Continuing on, I realize that there is a problem. Why does Bernardo use two different ways of setting the exact time the ghost appeared the night before? If the clock had just struck one, why does he go on about the stars? Is there something more about that particular star? My first instinct is not to look. Haven't the editors done that for me? Haven't they pulled the precise meaning needed for this line? Perhaps I don't need to know any more about using the stars to tell time, or the superstitions and folk legends associated with the North Star, but if I don't get at least some of that information, how am I going to understand why I say what I do, using so many more words than necessary?

Where can I go for more information? And what about another word I have in this opening scene? (If I had known that it was going to be so much work to play such a little part, I would have turned down this job and done summer stock instead.)

Sit down a-while,
And let us once again assail your ears,
That are so fortified against our Story,
What we have two Nights seen. [1.1.30]

What is "assail"? It sounds like assault, and that seems to fit if I am talking about "fortified," like a castle against assault. We are supposed to be on some battlements, and Denmark thinks that Norway is about to attack. I check my Riverside, and oh, oh, no note. Does this guy think that I know what "assail" means? I can guess, but I hate guessing. What if someone asks, or if I guess wrong and say it in a stupid way? While I am at it, I had better check the pronunciation. Fortunately, "assail" is in our Webster's dictionary at home, so I am on safe ground, but what about those words that aren't in common use any more?

Now that I am on a quest to understand for sure every word I am required to say as Bernardo, I start to think about my opening exchange with Francisco, who has an even smaller part than I do. I say to him,

> If you do meet Horatio and Marcellus,
> The Rivals of my Watch, bid them make haste.[1.1.12]

When I first read that, I recognized every word. But now that I have to prepare to say it in rehearsal, and I have to start the whole play, so I had better get it right, I am wondering what I mean by "rivals" in this situation. I recognize "watch" as being my turn on guard duty. The Riverside has "partners" as the definition of "rivals," and I sort of guessed that, but I had thought that the word meant the competition, as in a love triangle: "They were rivals for her love." Did the word mean both? How? Or did the meaning change over time? How did Shakespeare use the word? Did he use it in any other plays?

I have heard about a concordance, where every word is listed alphabetically, with every occurrence then recorded. I look under "rival" and see what is there. There are several examples listed: "My foolish Rival, that her Father likes" [2.4.174] and "For 'tis thy rival: O thou senseless form" [4.4.198], from *Two Gentlemen of Verona*, both describing Thurio who is listed in some editions of the play as "Thurio, a foolish rival to Valentine"; "With rival hating envy, set on you" [1.3.131], from *Richard II*; "To hold a rival place with one of them" [1.1.174], from *The Merchant of Venice*; "Peace Grumio, it is the rival of my love" [1.2.141], from *Taming of the Shrew*; and "I know you two are Rival enemies" [4.1.142], from *A Midsummer Night's Dream*. All this suggests is that "rival" is limited in meaning to two men competing for one woman, and by extension any other sort of competitive envy, as suggested by the *Richard II* quotation. Because that is the only one that is even a little bit different, I decide that I had better take a closer look at the situation. The line occurs in the speech that Richard makes after stopping the trial by combat, specifically, the third reason he gives for his actions,

> And for we think the Eagle-winged pride
> Of sky-aspiring and ambitious thoughts,
> With rival hating envy, set on you
> To wake our peace, [1.3.129]

confirming what I had suspected from reading the single line.

The word "rivals" appears in much the same context. In addition to the

Hamlet line, I find "You both are Rivals, and love Hermia" [3.2.155], "And now both Rivals to mock Helena" [3.2.156], and "And lead these testy Rivals so astray" [3.2.358], from *A Midsummer Night's Dream*; "and be happy rivals in Bianco's love" [1.1.17] and "Suitors to her, and rivals in my Love" [1.2.144], from *The Taming of the Shrew*, "Great Rivals in our youngest daughters love" [1.1.46], from *King Lear*, and one from *Timon of Athens*, "Translates his rivals." The longer passage reads:

> One do I personate of Lord Timons frame,
> Whom Fortune with her Ivory hand wafts to her,
> Whose present grace, to present slaves and servants
> Translates his Rivals. [1.1.69]

The Poet is describing a lengthy work in praise of his patron, Timon, and the last line is explained by a note in *The Riverside Shakespeare*, "transforms his rivals instantly into slaves and servants" (1446).

About this time, I discover Alexander Schmidt's two volume lexicon. His entries combine the features of a dictionary and a concordance. When I look up "rival," I find the first, primary, definition to be "competitor," as I had expected, with the examples listed by act, scene, and line number rather than with the line written out as in the concordance. The second meaning listed is "associate, companion," and here I find a very interesting and unexpected suggestion from Schmidt. Under this meaning he lists the *Hamlet* example, but also the example from *A Midsummer Night's Dream*, "And now both Rivals to mock Helena." Suddenly, the dramatic impact of the shifting meaning in Helena's speech becomes clear:

> O spite! O hell! I see you all are bent
> To set against me, for your merriment:
> If you were civil, and knew courtesy,
> You would not do me thus much injury.
> Can you not hate me, as I know you do,
> But you must join in souls to mock me too?
> If you were men, as men you are in show,
> You would not use a gentle Lady so;
> To vow, and swear, and superpraise my parts,
> When I am sure you hate me with your hearts.
> You both are Rivals, and love Hermia;
> And now both Rivals to mock Helena.
> A trim exploit, a manly enterprise,
> To conjure tears up in a poor maid's eyes,
> With your derision; none of noble sort,
> Would so offend a Virgin, and extort
> A poor soul's patience, all to make you sport. [3.2.145]

Because two meanings can coexist at the same time, Helena is able to point out how much pleasure Lysander and Demetrius gain from their competition to outdo each other. If their mockery of Helena is a sport in which they are companions as much as competitors, could the same be said of their love for Hermia? I cannot help but think of a couple of love triangles I have observed firsthand and admire the subtle psychology that the double use of "rivals" and the overlapping meaning allow.

Schmidt points me toward a brand-new word, at least for me, "rivality," which he defines as partnership and equality. The example is from *Antony and Cleopatra*, when Eros is explaining to Enobarbus the political situation: "Caesar having made use of him in the wars 'gainst Pompey: presently denied him rivality, would not let him partake in the glory of the action" [3.5.7]. He also alerts me to the fact that the word might be used as a noun, an adjective, or a verb, as when King Lear describes the two who rivalled for his daughter Cordelia, or when Nestor, describing the pleasure boats that do fine when the sea is calm but cannot be compared with the great vessels, says they co-rivalled greatness. In this second example I can see how the verb could combine the meanings of competing and being a companion.

Returning now to my work on my small but increasingly interesting role of Bernardo, what is it that I am saying about Marcellus and Horatio? If they are my rivals during this period of time on guard duty, are we companions who also strive for the excellence that only a touch of competition can bring? Or do Francisco and I belong to one branch of the armed forces, while Marcellus represents a rival corps? Perhaps that is what I am trying to suggest to Francisco, so that he will not suspect that I have allied myself with Marcellus in order to bring Horatio to see the ghost. Maybe none of this will turn out to be any use in playing the scene, which has to be more about the atmosphere on the battlements than on the attitudes and alliances of minor characters like me, but for now I am happy to endow poor Bernardo with any scrap of individuality that I can glean from the text. Maybe I will dream up a complicated backstory in which Marcellus and I were both after the same girl, but she dumped us both for Horatio—or maybe not.

It is easy to see why Schmidt's lexicon is so popular with actors, but these two large volumes tend to get left on a desk somewhere. So when I discover a specialized Shakespeare dictionary, called *A Shakespeare Glossary*, that is so small that I can carry it to rehearsal, I put it to the test right away. Onions gives me the same definitions as Schmidt for "rivals." What about "pole"?

Hurray! Onions gives me a lovely bit of information, that the North Star is a guiding star, which makes me think of the three wise men going to Bethlehem, and, moreover, that the "pole" was a symbol of constant determination. I am thinking that, as a soldier, I would admire that attribute. Then I look up "assail" and find just about the opposite of what I expected: "Address with offers of love, woo, attempt to seduce." I am stumped. Back to Schmidt. Yes, there is the meaning of attacking, which I had suspected, as well as the attempted seduction, and the bridge between them, the "amorous siege." This little bit of cross-checking helps me to understand why Onions's glossary is so small. He only includes the meanings that are not the same as today. If I use his dictionary, I am in the same state as when I use the Riverside and the editor assumes that I know what a word like "assail" means because it is still in his vocabulary, though it has never been in mine and has pretty much disappeared from general usage.

But I realize that I am also getting tired of Schmidt's division of examples so that each of Shakespeare's uses of any given word is linked to only one of the definitions. As I found out with "rivals," sometimes the two meanings coexist quite comfortably, with sufficient overlap or even an enjoyable irony, one step removed from a pun. Maybe I want to be the one to decide which definition applies to my example. In fact, I am beginning to suspect that I am going to want to keep all available meanings "on the go," at least for the early days of exploring the words that I am trying to make my own, and through which I am trying to sense my character's unique existence.

I still don't have an answer to how the meaning of words changes over time. That is going to be important when I am doing a play that is four hundred years old. I will need to know if a modern meaning of a word was already in place for Shakespeare, or if it only came later. It would also be exciting to know if a word my character says is one of the many new words recently invented, maybe even for this play. Maybe my character is the first person to use that word. Now that would be a fun sort of energy to bring to a speech: I am so excited here that I have to make up words to communicate what I am feeling.

I find my answer to these questions and more in the huge *Oxford English Dictionary* (OED). Here are pronunciations (which change over time) and meanings and examples, taken from different time periods, showing how the word was used. Quite often Shakespeare's plays provide the examples. The book is filled with additional information such as common phrases.

I check my short list of words: rivals, assail, pole. I learn that an early meaning for "rival" was "a bank, shore, landing-place." How did the same word come to mean competitor? A rival was also a small stream. I don't think I can use either of these, but it is always interesting to know, if nothing else as a reminder of how words can have multiple meanings.

"Assail" gives me lots of meanings to play with, some expected, some not. There are "to make a violent hostile attack upon by physical means" and "to address with offers of love, to woo." There are also some subtle variations on "attack" that interest me very much in this context. After all, I am proposing that we try once again to convince Horatio, who doesn't believe us, and so definitions like "to attack (institutions, customs, opinions, etc.) with hostile action or influence" and "to attack with hostile, opprobrious, or bitter words; to speak or write directly against," though too violent, have the right feel. They suggest that ideas can be attacked, as well as battlements, and words can be weapons, like swords. The best of the meanings offered is "to attack with reasoning or argument; to address with the object of prevailing upon, persuading, convincing, or controverting." Just below this entry I notice something that quite amazes me. There are dates followed by quotations in which the word is used with the meaning just given, and that are offered as examples of the first usage of the word in exactly that way. The first is dated 1400, and the second, dated 1602, is Bernardo's line. Here is exactly what I was hoping to find: Bernardo, given the intensity of his desire to convince Horatio, is using words in a striking and relatively new manner.

Thrilled as I am to discover the "perfect" definition, I am also interested in some of the meanings that sit over in a slightly different emotional territory. One of these is "to attempt, to venture, to put to the test." I like the idea of exploring a touch of a challenging attitude toward Horatio: "OK, buddy, you're so sure you're right about this ghost, let's just put your philosophy to the test!" Still further afield, but connected in an interesting way, is "to attack with temptations." I am not sure how Bernardo could be tempting Horatio, but I want to keep an open mind. Way back up at the top of the entry is the meaning "to leap upon," which comes from the Latin root of the words "ad salire," which meant to leap or spring at. From there the word travelled to Old French and then to Middle English. Because leaping upon someone was almost always hostile, it came to mean attack. The entry gives me information about where the word comes from and where it is going as the various meanings are placed into a time frame of evolving language usage.

One of the tricks of using *The Oxford English Dictionary* is to check the dates on the examples. If the earliest is the next century, then you are looking at one of those shifts of meaning that get in the way of our understanding. After Horatio has seen the ghost, he says, "Before my God, I might not this believe / Without the sensible and true avouch / Of mine own eyes" [1.1.56]. Our modern ear hears "sensible" and thinks of common sense, an attribute we are ready to ascribe to Horatio and his eyes, and so we don't necessarily think to look further. But the *OED* reveals that the word meant "capable of being perceived by the senses" or "something that is strongly felt." In particular, it was used of the organs of sensing, including the eyes, and therefore by extension of our experience of living in a sensing body. This is how, in *Measure for Measure*, Claudio uses the word when he expresses his fears of death: "To lie in cold obstruction, and to rot, / This sensible warm motion, to become / A kneaded clod" [3.1.118]. Another meaning, "sensitive, easily hurt," dates from 1759 and is the meaning suggested by the title of the Jane Austen novel *Sense and Sensibility*, wherein common sense is contrasted with the capacity of delicate or tender feeling. Our modern meaning was just emerging during Shakespeare's lifetime, and in fact he did use the word our way, but it came to be the dominant and then the only meaning around 1850, when it began to be applied to things like shoes.

Out of curiosity, I look up a couple of words that other people use. I am tempted to ignore these puzzles: I have enough to do to sort out what I have to say, and these words are really someone else's problem. If they do their homework and then say the words right, I will figure out the meaning. But I have discovered that I can get quite a bit from an actor's tone, but not exactly what is meant by an out-of-date word. And surely Marcellus would rightly assume that Bernardo knows what he means when he says, "Liege-men to the Dane" [1.1.15].

So I look up "liegeman." I discover its meaning in feudal law: "A vassal sworn to the service and support of his superior lord, who in return was obliged to afford him protection, etc." I am glad that my *The Riverside Shakespeare* has explained that "the Dane" is the ruling monarch of Denmark. That reminds me of what Hamlet says when he pops up at Ophelia's funeral: "This is I, Hamlet the Dane" [5.1.257]. I wonder how Claudius feels when he says that. Come to think of it, I had better figure out how I feel about it, as I suspect that I am going to be in that scene carrying the bier and parting Laertes and Hamlet when they fight over her grave.

Even though it represents a huge amount of work, I am glad that I took the time to "drop in on" some of these words I have to say and hear as Bernardo. I tend to pick on the words that puzzle me, or that seem important somehow to my character and so are worth spending the time on. The real danger, as I find out, is that I tend to skip words that I just ignore as "Shakespeare-speak," the sort of boring filler that he used all the time and that I know functions a certain way.

I am in rehearsal the day that they are working on the scene immediately following the Mousetrap, and Guildenstern comes on and says, "Good my Lord, vouchsafe me a word with you" [3.2.296]. The director stops him and asks him what "vouchsafe" means. Now that is one of those words that you know what it means because it is used all the time in the plays, fifty-four times to be exact. But you don't know what it means because you have never considered it as anything other than a filler word, signalling extra politeness. It turns out that to vouchsafe someone is to bestow a benefit upon someone, and well before 1400 it was used to mean the act of gracious giving performed by someone high up in status and power to someone lower. Just before *Hamlet* was written, the word began to mean even more specifically "To deign or condescend to give (a word, answer, etc.) in reply or by way of friendly notice." It also meant "To acknowledge (a person) in some favourable relationship or manner." Later in this same scene, Rosencrantz will say, "My Lord, you once did love me" [3.2.335]. This last definition of vouchsafe from the *Oxford English Dictionary* suddenly has direct bearing on Guildenstern's use of it in this situation. Now I begin to understand.

A Dictionary for Every Question

A quick survey of the Shakespeare reference shelf will reveal that dictionaries have been created not only for Shakespeare's language, but also for even more specific aspects of Shakespeare's vocabulary. Actors will find that these resources can contribute immeasurably not only to their understanding of the plays, but also to our understanding of the way language works.

Proverbial Sayings

Near the Shakespeare reference shelves you will find the dictionaries of puns, proverbs, and familiar phrases that are going to be useful for any research you might want to do about what words meant and how they were used by Shakespeare's contemporaries. Shakespearean scholars have gone through these sorts of books and have pulled out what they feel applies directly to the plays, as you have found in editors' notes in the scholarly editions. But why not have a look at the bigger source yourself? You will quickly discover additional associations that were very much "in the air" even if they do not qualify as a direct allusion for scholarly editors.

A good place to begin is with R. W. Dent's *Shakespeare's Proverbial Language.* Here you will find an index by play that lists every proverbial allusion Dent has traced, listed by act, scene, and line number. You can then look up the allusion in the appendix, which is an alphabetical listing of proverbs using Morris Palmer Tilley's numbering system in *A Dictionary of the Proverbs in England in the Sixteenth and Seventeenth Centuries.* The letter is taken from a key word, so that "I will believe it when I see it" is listed as B268 and "We soon believe what we desire" is listed as B269. Dent does not include all of Tilley's proverbs, because he disallows anything that is not clearly a direct allusion. For certain key words, therefore, it is interesting to go to Tilley and discover the full range of proverbs. I recommend doing this for a word like "woman" or "gold," because there are several very interesting proverbs that don't make it into Dent's collection.

Othello's murder of Desdemona makes use of a dense overlay of proverbial allusions. Editors are quick to notice that "Still as the Grave" [5.2.94] is proverbial, and by consulting Dent we learn some of the variations of the common saying in his listing for D133.1, "As dumb (silent, still) as DEATH (the grave)" (86); this same listing quotes from writers before and after Shakespeare as well as his contemporaries and notes that Hamlet also uses this allusion in the form of "as hush as death" [2.2.486]. Neither Dent nor the scholarly editors draw upon other Death allusions that are also at work in the scene. For example, D140 is the number of the proverb "Death has a thousand doors to let out a life." What has prompted Othello to say, "Still as the Grave," is the knocking of Emilia at the locked door of the bedchamber. Also at work are the proverbs "To belie the dead is a sin" (D124.1) and "To lament the dead avails not and revenge vents hatred" (D125) as we await the unravelling of Iago's lies and the punishment he so richly deserves.

Some of Shakespeare's characters demonstrate a great reliance on common sayings, with the same comic effect we enjoy today when a character is given a cliché-ridden speech. Other characters demonstrate wit and acuity by their manipulation of common sayings. The refreshing variation or unusual application can be ironic or insightful, as when a modern satirist suggests that an outgoing politician be greeted by raised glasses and the cry "Two cheers!"

One of the most amusing aspects of the history of language usage is locating the source of what today are common phrases. When did people start using the phrase "cowlick" and why? Robert Hendrickson's *The Facts on File Encyclopedia of Word and Phrase Origins* will tell you that this association with the projecting ridge of hairs that a cow licks into shape on its hide dates back to before 1598. He also records the pleasant fact that cowslips take their name from the droppings of cows because the wild yellow flower grows most abundantly in pastures where cows have been grazing. This word dates back at least as far as the year 1000.

Changing Language, Changing Thought

At first thought, the locating of a wide range of available meanings for Shakespeare's words might seem not only a daunting task, but also a dangerous one. The intellectual comprehension of the workings of verbal communication could very easily get in the way of the mastery of the act of speaking in character, which has more to do with linking the needs of the character, as intuited from the text, with the speech acts shaped by the playwright that form the playtext than with knowing how the words you are saying create meaning in the mind of those who hear you.

Much of what we know about language comes to us from our daily encounter with communication events, and as actors, we apply this intuitive understanding to the communication events that make up the plays of Shakespeare. But our modern patterns of language, though similar in kind, are different in content, and scholars can help us to bridge the gap between Shakespeare's language and ours only if we acknowledge that such a gap exists.

Certain dictionaries explain how the meanings of words have changed. Other dictionaries suggest that the way words are used has changed as well. Perhaps the easiest example with which to begin is the double entendre. We are familiar with the injection of innuendo, thinly disguised second meanings, usually sexual, that coexist with relatively neutral surface meanings. What might take us by surprise is the prevalence of such language usage, and the contrast between our modern "nudge-nudge, wink-wink" joking and Shakespeare's celebration of human sexuality in all its guises.

Erotica

The first serious scholar to document the sexual innuendo at work in Shakespeare's plays was a well-established academic specializing in the history of words (etymology) and the construction of word meanings (lexicology). Eric Partridge has created dictionaries of slang and clichés and has written books on correct usage, and it is with these skills and serious intent that he published *Shakespeare's Bawdy*, first in a limited edition in 1947, and only in 1955 for the general public. Half a century later, his simple observations can still shock someone who has been led to consider Shakespeare as the epitome of good taste. But it is true that there are many "dirty bits" that were edited out of the editions you read in high school.

Frankie Rubinstein's *A Dictionary of Shakespeare's Sexual Puns and Their Significance* will also make for a bit of a shock, even if you have come to terms with the rude and crude jokes that are obvious to the modern reader. Her 1984 dictionary builds upon Partridge's original study, but she seeks the most elusive of erotic allusions and goes much further than Partridge in acknowledging the scatology and sexual awareness that permeated the vocabulary of early modern English. She and others who create this sort of dictionary draw heavily upon the work of such scholars as James Henke, who has studied the slang of the underclasses in *Gutter Life and Language in the Early "Street" Literature of England*, and Roderick McConchie, who has studied medical terminology in *Lexicography and Physicke*. Although these works are not directly and specifically about Shakespeare's plays, they make for fascinating browsing, revealing the richness of the language available to Shakespeare in the creation of his characters.

Gordon Williams's exhaustive study of sexual innuendo, *A Dictionary of Sexual Language and Imagery in Shakespearean and Stuart Literature*, in three volumes is prohibitively expensive, much as one might like to own it for constant study. Fortunately, Athlone Press has brought out a handy paperback one-volume edition, *A Glossary of Shakespeare's Sexual Language* that is much handier for carrying to rehearsal. Unlike Rubinstein's work with the convenient play and character index, you will have to look up all suspect words in Williams's book, and even then you might miss some innuendo. Even so, Williams's book is far more useful for actors than Rubinstein's because he avoids the excessively obscure or forced examples and also does not include the complex lexicon tracing each word back to the often-bizarre source of the pun or innuendo.

Another compact dictionary that can be used to confirm suspicions of double entendres is J. Barry Webb's *Shakespeare's Erotic Word Usage*. Webb does without any sort of introductory essay, and entries provide a few quotations from the writings of Shakespeare or his contemporaries to illustrate the erotic connection. You can also consult studies of double entendres in the works of Shakespeare's contemporaries, such as James T. Henke's *Renaissance Dramatic Bawdy (Exclusive of Shakespeare)*, to set these studies into a larger context.

Any use of these dictionaries will reveal some things about Shakespeare that used to be suppressed in an effort to maintain his reputation as a great dramatic poet. Even today, actors who perform David Mamet's expletive-filled dramas or Bob Fosse's sexy choreography are incredulous to discover that Shakespeare too had the capacity to be rude and raunchy. Our assumptions that such crudity was reserved for the clowns and low-class bumpkins is shattered when we encounter Beatrice's witty bantering with Benedick: "Foul words is but foul wind, and foul wind is but foul breath, and foul breath is noisome, therefore I will depart unkissed" [*Much Ado* 5.2.52]. What seems on the surface to be a joke about bad breath is actually a joke that ends with a reference to a fart, which is "noisome" because it can be both heard and smelled.

It quite shatters our image of Beatrice as a well-educated daughter of the nobility to imagine her making such a silly and sophomoric joke. It also quite shatters our image of a naïve, sheltered young woman to discover that Juliet is describing more than just the night sky in her anticipation of her wedding night:

> Give me my Romeo, and, when I shall die,
> Take him and cut him out in little stars,
> And he will make the Face of heaven so fine,
> That all the world will be in Love with night,
> And pay no worship to the Garish Sun. [3.2.21]

The meaning of "die" is evoked by Benedick near the end of his long merry war with Beatrice, "I will live in thy heart, die in thy lap, and be buried in thy eyes" [*Much Ado* 5.2.102]. "I will knock out two of your eight eyes" is a common threat among fishwives, as every woman is said to have two seeing eyes, two bub-eyes, a bell-eye, two pope's eyes, and a "vagine-eye." "Bub" means a drink, and in the first part of *Henry VI* Shakespeare uses the term so that its meaning is undeniable: "When at their mothers' moist eyes babes shall suck" [1.1.49]. Mistress Overdone, the tired old whore of *Measure for Measure*, is comforted by her tapster/pimp Pompey, "Courage! there will be pity taken on you: you that have worn your eyes almost out in the service" [1.2.109]. This refers to the last eye on the list. Sad to say, they still use the phrase "In the Pope's eye" in Belfast as an insult, the association being with the anus.

Such indirect reference to bodily functions and the intimate parts of the body, to our ear, seems insulting, indecorous, sexist, and just about as far as anyone could get from the poetry of lovers. We will never know for sure if genteel young lovers in Shakespeare's England spoke to each other this way, but in the world of the plays they do, and without a leer or nudge.

Sometimes the extravagant sexuality of the language is in keeping with other attributes of the character. When Mercutio, teasing the lovesick Romeo, refers to Rosaline's "Straight leg, and Quivering thigh, / And the Demesnes, that there Adjacent lie" [*R&J* 2.1.19] or says, "this drivelling Love is like a great Natural, that runs lolling up and down to hide his bauble in a hole" [2.3.91], his direct evocation of female and male genitals is clearly intended and intentionally offensive. He doesn't get a rise out of Romeo, if you will excuse the pun, but Benvolio is quick to respond, "Stop there, stop there" [2.3.94].

What is much more upsetting is to find such language coming out of the mouths of those characters we consider the most educated, sensitive, and noble. Here is Hamlet joking with Rosencrantz and Guildenstern:

Hamlet: My excellent good friends? How dost thou Guildenstern? Ah, Rosencrantz; good Lads: How do ye both?

Rosencrantz: As the indifferent Children of the earth.

Guildenstern: Happy, in that we are not over-happy: on Fortunes Cap, we are not the very Button.

Hamlet: Nor the Soles of her Shoe?

Rosencrantz: Neither my Lord.

Hamlet: Then you live about her waist, or in the middle of her favour?

Guildenstern: Faith, her privates, we.

Hamlet: In the secret parts of Fortune? O, most true: she is a Strumpet. [2.2.224]

We can write this off as a regression to the sort of crude joke young boys might make; these three were schoolfellows together and perhaps are reworking an old nudge-nudge giggle. Similarly, we can attribute Hamlet's crudity with Ophelia to a role he is playing in the eyes of the court:

Hamlet: Lady, shall I lie in your Lap?

Ophelia: No my Lord.

Hamlet: I mean, my Head upon your Lap?

Ophelia: Ay my Lord.

Hamlet: Do you think I meant Country matters?

Ophelia: I think nothing, my Lord.

Hamlet: That's a fair thought to lie between Maids legs.

Ophelia: What is my Lord?

Hamlet: Nothing.

Ophelia: You are merry, my Lord? [3.2.112]

Although the dictionaries of erotica cannot offer much help to the actress in figuring out how to play this scene, they can clarify just how crude Hamlet is being. He begins with the same image that Benedick uses, and when Ophelia responds, whether with anger, embarrassment, or naïveté, he plays on the sound as well as the meaning of "country"; rustics were thought to enjoy great sexual freedom. Two apparently neutral words, "nothing" and "merry," turn out to be more of the same. A thing being a penis, nothing suggests a woman's lack of such an organ. The sexual meaning of "merry" is captured by the comparison made between a visit to a moneylender and a visit to a whore: "When men come to borrow of your Masters, they approach sadly, and go away merry: but they enter my Mistress house merrily, and go away sadly" [*Timon* 2.2.99].

Shakespeare does not seem to share our attitudes to that category of language referred to as "double entendres." He includes sexual desire as an active component of his characters' experiences and imagery. He has his characters refer to all of the bodily functions even when they lack the personalities that we would associate with that particular type of humor. I think that we have to conclude that all of this language was simply more common than it is today, and that it reflected an acceptance of the animal aspects of human nature alongside an acknowledgment of the explosions of laughter and desire that such wordplay evokes and reveals.

Slang

Eric Partridge, who contributed to the emergence of Shakespearean erotica as a subsection of Shakespearean lexicology, has also produced a fascinating volume that defines the terminology of the criminal classes, *A Dictionary of the Underworld, British and American*. Here and in other dictionaries of slang you will find assistance in decoding the rich cacophony of the Boar's Head Tavern and similar low-life haunts. When Shakespeare first takes us to this locale, he presents the character of Gadshill the Ostler, who has a great deal to say about the patrons of the inn, including this: "Tut, there are other Trojans that thou dream'st not of, the which (for sport sake are content to do the Profession some grace; that would (if matters should be looked into) for their own Credit sake, make all whole" [*1HIV* 2.1.69]. Partridge's dictionary, which gives the date for the earliest recording of each slang term, dates "Trojan," meaning professional gamblers or swindlers, to 1800. John Farmer's two-volume *A Dictionary of Slang* defines the same word as a plucky fellow or a thief, and as his work lists quotations, you can see various uses of the term, including some from Shakespeare. Paul Beale's updating of Partridge's *A Dictionary of Slang and Unconventional English* adds still another meaning, the one most likely to apply here: a roisterer, a dissolute. The unnamed individual who is content to do the profession (of thievery) some grace is His Grace the Prince of Wales. Therefore, layered upon the cant use of the word "Trojan" is another set of associations, with princes and the tracing of British civilization through Aeneas to ancient Troy.

Shakespeare's Vocabulary

Marvin Spevack's concordance has been replaced by the speed and efficiency of Web-based search engines for many scholars, but you can still find his and other giant concordances in most reference libraries. If you would like to locate a speech and can remember only one key word, by looking up that word in the concordance you can find all the times Shakespeare used the word and probably find the speech you are looking for.

If you are wondering just how often Shakespeare used a specific word like, for example "shame" and in what context, a concordance will give you all of the references and the lines in which they occur. You will have to have a complete works by your side to have a look at the scene. There are 346 uses of "shame," which suggests that it was a word Shakespeare liked to use. The more you can "drop in on" the word, as shaped by Shakespeare's use, the richer will be your connection with the language of the plays.

Paging through the concordance will reveal some fascinating patterns in Shakespeare's vocabulary. Some words have columns, others only one usage. Some are used over and over to convey the same powerful concept or emotion; shame is such a word. Others slip and slide between various meanings, their very fluidity expanding their usefulness.

Shakespeare uses the word "pain" eighty times, sometimes simply as the sensation of bodily discomfort, sometimes more specifically as torture; sometimes it means generally punishment, other times any heavy suffering, mental or physical. It also means work or effort, specially that undertaken for a certain purpose. As a verb, it can mean to cause pain or to put someone to great effort; painful can mean tormenting the body or requiring great labor. When Helena decides to betray her friend Hermia, she merges the meanings of physical and emotional agony with intense effort for a special purpose when she concludes, "But herein mean I to enrich my pain, / To have his sight thither and back again" [*Dream* 1.1.250].

Perhaps your director has asked you to develop some Elizabethan-style commentary to contribute as you form a crowd responding to the central action of the moment. A concordance is a great place to find some lines or phrases to suit any situation. Here is a compilation that I provided for the ensemble to use when all are shouting insults at once:

O monstrous arrogance!

Thou liest, thou thread, thou thimble, thou yard, three-quarters, half-yard, quarter, nail!

Thou flea, thou nit, thou winter-cricket thou!

Thou stool for a witch!

Thou whoreson, impudent, embossed rascal.

There's no more faith in thee than a stewed prune, nor no more truth in thee than in a drawn fox.

A villainous coward! Are not you a coward? Answer me to that!

I call thee coward! I'll see thee damned ere I call thee coward, but I would give a thousand pound I could run as fast as thou canst.

Thou hast no more brain than I have in mine elbows.

There are lots more where these came from if you look under a few key words, such as "rascal" and "coward," and then go to the complete play, find that scene, and see what insults were flying in the air. That way you will meet some of the great masters of the witty put-down, such as Falstaff and his young friend Hal in *Henry IV* and Thersites in *Troilus and Cressida*.

In addition to his concordance, Marvin Spevack has created *A Shakespearean Thesaurus*, which allows you to look up a word that could not be understood by a modern audience and find a selection of Elizabethan words with similar meaning, any one of which might be substituted if you and your director are engaging in some delicate rewriting. For example, in the first part of *Henry IV*, Falstaff and Hal entertain themselves and their drinking companions with a "play extempore," in which Falstaff plays Hal's father the king and waxes rhetorical with "Shall the blessed Son of Heaven prove a Micher, and eat Blackberries? a question not to be asked" [*1HIV* 2.4.407]. A quick look in the index of Spevack's thesaurus reveals that "micher" is listed under the category of 04.04, rogue. We there find a long list of associated words that might be substituted. We know from the note in our trusty *Riverside* that the word means "truant," which also appears in the list, so we could substitute that word and avoid anachronism. But are there any words that are similar in sound to "micher"? On the list we find "miscreant," which is a syllable longer but very close in sound. From a quick check in the *OED*, we learn that "micher" also meant a petty thief or anyone who sneaks around for naughty purposes, as well as a truant. When we go back to the list, the word "sneak-up" leaps out at us. What a great alternative to "micher" if we would like to capture the other meanings, and a modern audience would understand. So now we have three alternatives to try out in rehearsal until the best is chosen or the decision is made to stick with Shakespeare's original.

The selection of alternative words requires even more care when the substitution is contemplated for a line of poetry. Here we are looking for a similar sound, the same number of syllables, and the same accentuation, or we risk paying too high a price for simple comprehension.

Purists argue against changing a single word or cutting a single line, but there is evidence that Shakespeare himself would be the first to snip away excess, and sometimes a single archaic word stands between the audience and comprehension of an important idea. I do not know who is in the right, those who deliver the text with minimal cuts and no substitutions and convey the meaning of complex sentences and archaic words through vivid acting and a crystal-clear understanding of exactly what is being said shared by everyone on stage, or those who snip out the impossible bits, rearrange the tangled bits, and toss out archaic words in favor of carefully chosen and familiar alternatives. All I know is that when the latter course is followed skillfully, the critics compliment those actors on being the best speakers of Shakespeare's verse in the modern theatre. The irony of the situation does not escape those who know just how much help our William has received in order to have his language come alive four hundred years after the words were recorded.

Even if you don't want to change a word, you can still use Spevack's thesaurus to explore patterns in Shakespeare's word usage and, along with the concordance, put together your own Shakespearean dialogue for those pesky crowd scenes. Just look up "rogue" then look up some of the best words in the list using the concordance, and you will find all sorts of fun things to say.

Names

As a Shakespearean text consultant, I am frequently asked for the correct pronunciation of a name of a character. More often than not, the answer is a selection of pronunciations that have been used at one time or another. There are British traditions and American traditions, scholarly and theatrical, and also fashions and changes over the decades and centuries.

The problems are myriad. There are the vowels. Does Hamlet rhyme with omelette or ham (and eggs)? There are the names with a "th" pronounced like "the" or "thing" or "Tom" or "Don." There are the Italian names that might be anglicized to a greater or lesser degree, names with a "c" that might be "ch" or "k" or "s," and French names that might also be anglicized or perhaps not.

Dale Coye has made a much-appreciated contribution to the working actor with the publication of his text *Pronouncing Shakespeare's Words*. Here you will find, play by play, lists of the troublesome words and how you might pronounce them, along with general pronunciation guidelines. This work supplements the older and often-consulted pronunciation guidelines for Shakespeare's characters, such as Helge Kökeritz's *Shakespeare's Names: A Pronouncing Dictionary* and Theodora Ursula Irvine's *How to Pronounce the Names in Shakespeare*.

There is more to a name, however, than how it is pronounced, and several books have attempted to answer an actor's natural curiosity about the associations a character's name might have to everyone else in the play. Murray Levith's *What's in Shakespeare's Names* is a straightforward listing of the plays and the associations that might be made between the names of the principal characters and the themes of the plays. For example, under *Twelfth Night* he includes the fascinating piece of information that Viola's chosen pseudonym for her male disguise is Cesario, from the Latin *caesaries*, meaning "bushy hair," which Levith suggests is appropriate for a girl disguised as a boy (92).

J. Madison Davis and A. Daniel Frankforter have produced a bigger book following Levith's approach. *The Shakespeare Name Dictionary* contains entries not only on character names, but also on official titles, place names, and even nouns that a modern reader would not capitalize, such as ghost, moonshine, and ruffian. As with other character dictionaries, part of the job of such a resource is simply to list the plays in which the name is used. Some lengthy citations include a wealth of information from histories, mythologies, classical texts, and the Bible. Other citations include allusions to Shakespeare's sources or other popular literary works that might have influenced his choice of the name.

In addition to those indexes and guides that address Shakespeare's names, there are also general reference books about names that can be consulted for additional information. I have found Alfred Kolatch's *The Name Dictionary* of particular interest because of his emphasis on classical and biblical roots that would have affected the reaction of Shakespeare's first audience to a name like Beatrice, from the Latin word meaning "blessing." Other helpful reference books are *The Oxford Dictionary of English Christian Names*, compiled by E.G. Withycombe, *Everyman's Dictionary of First Names*, compiled by Leslie Dunking and William Gosling, and Patrick Hanks and Flavia Hodges's *A Dictionary of First Names*. Each of these dictionaries can be counted on to illuminate some aspect of a name. For example, Gregory is from the Greek *gregoros*, meaning "watchful." It was a common name in Britain in medieval times. Shakespeare uses it for two servants, in *Romeo and Juliet* and in *The Taming of the Shrew*. At the other end of the social scale, the Scottish king killed by Macbeth is named Duncan, which we learn is the anglicized form of the Gaelic name Donnchadh, which blends two meanings, "brown" and "battle." This was also the name of a seventh-century Scottish saint and a tenth-century Irish saint.

Places

Shakespeare's plays are set all over the place, everywhere from Athens and Rome to Venice and Verona, as well as London, York, Windsor, and all over Scotland. It is always interesting to find out about any of the locales that Shakespeare chooses to mention, given that he is also free to set any scene in an unnamed location. A topographical dictionary like E. H. Sugden's is a useful place to start, because the alphabetized listings make for convenience. Sugden includes more than just names of towns, counties, and countries; one entry is for "Half-Moon," in which we discover that this was a very common tavern sign in London. Sugden even gives locations of several. There are maps of the city of London in Shakespeare's time, and every entry includes the allusion in Elizabethan drama.

The problem with Sugden's book, and what will lead most theatrical re-searchers to other sources, is that the dictionary entries often do not contain sufficient information about the subjective attributes of any given locale. Was the Moon's Head Tavern a working-class tavern? Was it associated in the popular culture of the times with thieves and vagabonds or hard-drinking sail-ors? Was it a good place to go to pick up a whore and a bout of venereal disease, or to find a group of students interested in an intellectual debate?

When Sugden includes such information, it is a wonderful boon to actors. Here is his entry on Park Corner: "The N.E. corner of Hyde P., Lond., at the junction of Oxford St. and Edgware Rd. Close by stood the Tyburn gal-lows, and the loneliness of the neighbourhood made it a favourite resort of highwaymen"(392). Buried in various entries are tidbits of social history that make this book an interesting place for a more general delving. Under the listing for Parker's Ordinary, for example, we learn that an "ordinary" was an eating house at which a table d'hôte dinner was served at a fixed price. After dinner patrons usually gambled at the tables provided for that purpose.

REFERENCE BOOKS, COMPANIONS, AND GUIDES

> 'Tis in my memory locked,
> An you your self shall keep the key of it.
>
> Ophelia [*Hamlet* 1.3.85]

For an actor seeking to acclimatize herself to the particular linguistic world of Shakespeare, I would recommend a length of time spent with Charles and

Mary Cowden Clarke's opus *The Shakespeare Key.* As with many scholarly un-
dertakings completed before or shortly after the First World War, this represents an exhaustive collecting and listing of examples rather than brilliant
analysis or important new information. Contemporary scholars would find
little use in such lists, as the categories used by the Clarkes are the most
straightforward, but for an actor this makes the book of greatest use. We are
not interested in a fresh new look at Shakespeare's language. We want to grab
hold of the obvious patterns so that we can make them our own, quickly and
effectively.

There is no handy index of plays, which would make this a supremely useful
resource tool. However, there is a table of contents in alphabetical listing, so
you can find such entries as "Coins" or "Dumb Shows" or "Legal Phrases"
or "Supernatural Music." If we look under the last entry, we discover that
the Clarkes have gathered together quotations and plot summaries from five
different plays in which supernatural music occurs. Their analysis of this
phenomenon is not scholarly: "Several times in the course of his dramas
Shakespeare introduces supernatural music; and always with charming effect,
aiding the dramatic impression he intends to convey" is the extent of their
analysis, but even so it is useful to read the five examples all at once, and I,
for one, appreciate not being told what all of this means. The Clarkes leave
me to make my own conclusions, if any at all.

In 1985 John F. Andrews edited a three-volume set entitled *William Shakespeare: His World, His Work, His Influence.* The first volume, *His World,* provides
an excellent collection of articles filled with just the sort of concrete information
useful to an actor. These are general introductions, and specific references are
more likely to be found in the notes in a scholarly edition of each play, but
these articles will provide the actor with the broad overview, creating a framework within which to set the detailed information that might be applied to any
given line of text. The second volume, *His Work,* contains a variety of articles
that analyze various aspects of Shakespeare's writing, and the third volume,
His Influence, traces the emergence of "Bardolatry," that elevation of Shakespeare the working actor to "the greatest poet of the English stage." These
articles provide an overview of Shakespearean literary scholarship and prove
the least useful to the actor.

Shakespeare Companions

Along with Shakespeare reference books, there are some handy collections
of introductory articles that have been prepared with the general readership
of Shakespeare in mind. The reference section of a university library will include at least one general guide to the plays in dictionary form, in which you
can expect to find paragraph-length entries under the heading of each of the
characters, as well as under the names of famous contemporaries of Shakespeare.

Several publishers have made an effort to fill the need for students to have at their fingertips a variety of supplementary information when they are encountering the plays. *The Bedford Companion to Shakespeare*, edited by Russ McDonald, is an excellent handbook that contains useful general introductions to a variety of topics, some of more interest to the classroom than to the rehearsal hall, but what makes this volume most useful is McDonald's selections from a wide variety of archival material reproduced in modern spelling supplemented by photographs of the original. This is a good place to make your first acquaintance with everything from *A Mirror for Magistrates* and *The Book of Common Prayer* to Philip Henslowe's diary and a letter that Edward Alleyn, an actor, sent to his wife. The chapters on "Life in England," "Men and Women," and "Politics and Religion" are very useful for actors seeking a general introduction to the world of Shakespeare.

Look for some general handbooks or companions that might have been placed in the reference section. For many years, Stanley Wells's collection *The Cambridge Companion to Shakespeare Studies* was the most comprehensive and scholarly. In David Kastan's more recent *A Companion to Shakespeare* you will find general introductions to just about everything an actor should know something about in preparation to perform any of Shakespeare's plays. In the section entitled "Living," you will find excellent introductory articles on Shakespeare's England, Shakespeare's London, religious belief, families, and politics. In the section on "Reading," you will find articles on the greatest influences on Shakespeare's writing, the Bible, the classics, and popular literature such as ballads and prose. The sections on "Writing" and "Playing" are also filled with important information for the actor, including the best possible introduction to iambic pentameter by George T. Wright. If you are interested in how the plays were published, Kastan has included articles by leading scholars in this field as well. Each article concludes with a bibliography, so if the topic captures your imagination, you will have a good idea how to find still further benefit from the work of academics.

Shakespeare and Encyclopedias

Another popular type of publication that you can find in a university library reference section is an encyclopedia for Shakespeare, which includes the briefest possible entries on everything the editors think might be useful. Unfortunately, many editors have students rather than actors in mind. For example, Oxford University Press in 1998 reissued Stanley Wells's *A Dictionary of Shakespeare*, first published in 1988, in a relatively inexpensive paperback edition. What Wells considers interesting, however, is limited to the names of famous actors, some of the individuals who might be mentioned in a biography of Shakespeare, and various theatrical terms. There is an entry for "groundlings," but not for the Gunpowder Plot. At the end of the book Wells lists characters from the plays and the plays in which they appear, and within the dictionary each of the plays has an entry, which consists of a history of significant performances. At the very end he provides some interesting facts and figures, such as a listing of the plays by length, from longest to shortest. Measured by lines, *Hamlet* is first at 4,042 and *The Comedy of Errors* is last at 1,787; measured in words, these two hold their positions, but others shift slightly. For those interested, *Hamlet* has 29,551 words and *The Comedy of Errors* 14,369. The text used for this counting was the Riverside Shakespeare. Wells also gives percentages of verse and prose in the plays (*Hamlet* is 73% verse; *The Comedy of Errors* is 12.9% prose), the longest scenes, and, as fodder for boasting, the longest roles (Hamlet is the longest, with 1,507 lines).

Other dictionaries have been prepared by editors with a different sense of what might be of interest. Simon Trussler's *Shakespearean Concepts* turns out to be quite a useful book, in large part because the editor is not a Shakespearean scholar, though he has written extensively on modern dramatists. His focus of interest in Shakespeare is suggested by another book he has written, a history of the Royal Shakespeare Company from 1978 to 1985. Trussler has chosen to focus on the most influential beliefs, philosophies, or modes of behavior that might have influenced Shakespeare's first actors, and the people, places, and theatrical conventions that reflect these concepts. Because Trussler has created his guide for university students, he includes terminology used by Shakespearean scholars, and so words like "deconstruction" and "semiotics" make an appearance. Browsing through *Shakespearean Concepts* will clarify for the actor all sorts of references that are regularly made in, for example, the introduction and notes that accompany an edition of one of the plays. On the first page you will learn about An Act to Restrain Abuses of Players, listed under "Abuse of Players," the 1606 statute prohibiting the use of the word "God." If you have ever wondered about all those "Jove" references, even in one of the history plays, here is the reason. Because the First Folio was published in 1623, the editors had to change words to avoid being charged with blasphemy. The quartos published before 1606 often reveal what we have taken to be the original and intended language, so most modern editions of such plays revert to the quartos' version of such lines as "God for Harry, England, and Saint George" [*HV* 3.1.34]. Also on the first page you will learn this very useful bit of information: the word "accolade" meant the symbolic gesture used in knighting ceremonies, which might be an embrace or the placing of the hand on the neck, in addition to the one we see all the time in movies: the touch of the royal sword to the shoulder.

Although his entries are short and relatively simplistic, I applaud Trussler for flagging words like "honour" and "nature." The danger is that we think that we understand what these words mean when Shakespeare's usage is loaded with significance far in excess of what we might first expect.

Trussler's book is a handy pocket-sized volume; many readers' guides are, in contrast, heavy and small-print volumes containing answers to every question. *The Reader's Encyclopedia of Shakespeare*, edited by Oscar James Campbell, is actually called an encyclopedia. Here you will find an entry on the Gunpowder Plot and on "Groundlings" (under "Audience"), as well as fairly lengthy entries on each of the plays. You will also find entries on "Imagery" and the "Homilies," but nothing on "Honour."

A more recent publication in the same category is Charles Boyce's *Shakespeare A to Z*. Along with an entry for each play, which starts with a synopsis of the plot, followed by a short commentary, and shorter entries on the sources, the text, and the theatrical history of the play, Boyce includes characters and locations from the plays and people and places from Shakespeare's England. Theatre history is represented by names of famous actors and directors. None of "Imagery," "Groundlings," "Audience," or "Gunpowder Plot" make an appearance, although terms such as "Blank Verse" and "Fair Copy," "Soliloquy" and "Bad Quarto" do. Boyce supplements his descriptions of characters with information about the theatrical traditions to which they adhered or that they challenged, as well as comments on the theatrical function of each. It is interesting to learn, for example, that old Adam of *As You Like It* is not only "a figure of unalloyed goodness, loyalty, and faith" but also the "archetype of the loyal servant" (3). With so much emphasis placed upon the function and the conventions of characters, any character comments appear less prescriptive than descriptive and thus less likely to create the sort of ur-characterization described in the first chapter. The actor can see that the traditions are there to be infused with life; Adam might be an archetypal figure, but when one is playing him, the character still has to be fleshed out into his uniqueness.

At the end of the book you will find lists of entries under different categories that conveniently allow you to scan for certain types of entries. The longest list is for "Characters," which sadly is not divided into the plays in which they appear. There is also a good-sized list of actors and other theatre professionals from different time periods, and one of equal length that lists scholars. The most interesting entries are those for people and places, though the absence of an index for play references makes it difficult to discover why some of these places and people have been included. Only by looking at the entry for Annesley, Brian, for example, will you learn that he is a possible model for King Lear. You probably found this information in the notes in your edition of *King Lear*, and this entry will give you very little more than you already know.

Frank Halliday's *A Shakespearean Companion, 1564–1964* was the first such reference book I purchased, and although many entries are now out of date, I still appreciate this compact, wide-ranging resource book. Halliday includes entries in the category of theatre history, such as Fanny Kemble (1809–93), who played a memorable Portia and Beatrice and wrote *Notes on Some of Shakespeare's Plays*. Important Shakespearean scholars also rate a mention alongside the characters of the plays. In his listing for Lady Capulet, Halliday describes her function in the plot, to support her husband, and notes that she is one of the five mothers of heroines who actually appear in the plays, the others being Mistress Page, Hermione, Thaisa, and Innogen. Because these names are cross-listed, the reader can jump to the last of these and discover that she is the silent wife of Leonato and mother of Hero who is mentioned in an early stage direction in *Much Ado about Nothing*.

Halliday also includes entries for what might best be called aspects of social history. Under instrumental music, we discover that the favorite instruments of the period were the lute, the viol, the recorder, and the hautboy. We also learn that strings and reeds were rarely combined, but usually played in consort, in other words, with instruments of the same family. A "broken" consort, therefore, was a mixture of winds and strings. When we encounter the word "consort" in the plays, we give it the associated meaning of "keeping company," and it is exciting to discover the source of such powerful images as created by Andromache or Mercutio. In *Troilus and Cressida*, when Andromache, wife of the doomed Trojan hero Hector, begs Hector's sister Cassandra to join her in her efforts to persuade Hector not to go to battle, she says,

> Consort with me in loud and dear petition:
> Pursue we him on knees: for I have drempt
> Of bloody turbulence, and this whole night
> Hath nothing been but shapes, and forms of slaughter. [5.3.9]

"Consort" here evokes the musicality of women's voices raised together in strong emotion, as well as the possible sisterhood between the two women. Hector rejects their pleas, however, and creates a broken consort, sounding quite a different note with the line "Ho! Bid my Trumpet sound" [5.3.13]. Mercutio, on the other hand, makes use of the musical allusion to build a comic moment in response to Tybalt's line "Mercutio thou consortest with Romeo," the only excuse he needs to head off on a bit of a rant: "Consort? what dost thou make us Minstrels? an thou make Minstrels of us, look to hear nothing but discords: here's my fiddlestick, here's that shall make you dance: zounds, consort" [*R&J* 3.1.45].

Halliday's *Companion* includes interesting bits of information about Shakespeare's theatre, such as the fact that the musicians were employees of the shareholders of the company, but he does not venture into the more dangerous territory uncovered by more recent scholarship. You will have to consult Frankie Rubinstein's *Dictionary* to learn that the verb "consort" was a euphemism for sexual activity, and that minstrels were epitomized as effeminates.

In his entries for each of the plays, Halliday outlines the plot and also a concise and detailed history of the play's publication and performance. His *Companion* is full of other interesting insights, such as the fact that inverted commas were rarely used in early modern printing, except to indicate an aphorism or a proverb.

Some general guides collect the entries under headings of the individual plays, which greatly facilitates browsing. Arthur Baker's comments in *A Shakespeare Commentary* are not up-to-date, but the entries are an interesting collection. He begins with a brief mention of sources and then gives a detailed plot summary with quotations of the best bits. Then follow, in alphabetical order, entries on people and places. Baker includes interesting classical allusions along with the usual.

Character Dictionaries

Almost every library will have in its collection at least one of the dictionaries of characters, such as A. L. Rowse's *Shakespeare's Characters* or *Who's Who in Shakespeare* by Peter Quennell and Hamish Johnson. Often character descriptions are combined with other types of entries. For example, the *Hutchinson Shakespeare Dictionary*, edited by Sandra Clark, includes characters from the plays, people and places mentioned in the plays, and famous people from Shakespeare's world. The entries for each of the plays give a detailed plot summary and cast list as well as a brief production history and listing of Shakespeare's sources. While it might be useful to read her entry on the Inns of Court, the legal societies in London that trained lawyers, Clark's entries on the characters are, in essence, encapsulations of the "ur-characters" that haunt the efforts of a modern actor to bring Shakespeare's characters alive. She labels Iago as "the malignant villain" and announces, "His chief motive is the hatred of goodness and the desire to destroy happiness whenever he sees it" (175). Fortunately, the majority of Clark's entries on characters simply describe the function each plays in the plot.

A far more useful dictionary, if you can find a copy of it, is W.H. Thomson's *Shakespeare's Characters: A Historical Dictionary*, in which he limits his interest to the history plays and *Macbeth* and documents the real people who appear or are referred to in these plays. I am sure that historians would find much to criticize in the entries, which naturally exclude all of the scholarship that has taken place in the last half-century, but as an introduction, Thomson can be counted on to give the essential facts, including, of course, the play for which the information would be needed. There are a few useful genealogical tables, but what the book really needs is an index that would list all of the entries relevant to each of the plays.

Let's have a look at the entries for a few of the supporting cast in *Richard III*, the history play most often performed. I was happy to find an entry for John Dighton, one of the murderers of the princes in the tower, who was James Tyrrel's groom and was described as a big, broad, square knave. He was made a bailiff, probably as a reward for his crime, but during the reign of Henry VIII he and Tyrrel were arrested and executed for the murder of the boys who would have been Henry's uncles if they had lived. The entry on Tyrrel, who planned the murder, reveals that Tyrrel was a lifelong supporter of the Yorkist side in the Wars of the Roses, and so his loyalty to Richard is not surprising. What is interesting, however, is that Henry VII, who defeated Richard at the Battle of Bosworth, continued to trust Tyrrel and included him in the general pardon of 1486. Then Tyrrel became involved in still another plot, for which he was arrested, and it was only then, when he confessed to the murder of the princes in the tower, that Dighton was arrested and the two were executed. The other murderer, Miles Forrest, died soon after of some sort of rotting disease.

Thomson even has entries for unnamed characters, for which the supporting cast will be indebted to his thoroughness. Under "Recorder," Thomson notes that when Buckingham reports the mayor saying, "The people were not used / To be spoke to, but by the Recorder" [3.7.29], he is referring to Thomas Fitzwilliam, described as a sad and honest man, who had just taken office in 1483. What a wonderful place to begin creating a character! Thomson also decides that the page who introduces Tyrrel into the presence of the king was John Green, an esquire of the body to Richard III, who also seems to have been rewarded for complicity in the murders, being appointed receiver of the Lordship of the Isle of Wight; the story goes that Henry VII had him walled up alive.

A more recent publication that is set up the same way but limits the citations to characters is *Shakespeare's Characters for Students*, edited by Catherine C. Dominic. This publication meets the requirements of first-time readers for a plot summary and a set of character descriptions. Actors will find much evidence of "ur-characterization" here, and if your philosophy is to know the face of the enemy, you will want to acknowledge just how influenced you are by the current assumptions about what central and supporting characters are supposed to be.

Shakespearean Who's Who

Several reference books set out to cover the same territory, each providing in its own style a reference for the people named and alluded to in Shakespeare's plays. One of my favorites, for its organization as much as for the content of the various entries, is Alan and Veronica Palmer's *Who's Who in Shakespeare's England*. Their introduction contains a series of categories, followed by all of the listings that fall under that classification and that are contained in the alphabetical sequence that follows. This means that an actor can look for every entry under the category of "Court and Society Women" and thus discover the three brilliant and well-educated daughters of Sir Anthony Coke, tutor to Edward VI. These remarkable women were renowned for their intelligence and political influence. Each made an important marriage and produced children who rose to prominence in their turn, so that many of the important people in Shakespeare's London were members of this powerful web of cousins.

Other exciting categories for research are suggested by the Palmers. "Rebels and Conspirators," "Seamen," or "Soldiers" might provide exciting models for a variety of characters who appear in Shakespeare's plays, just as any of Coke's daughters might be a model for the countess in *All's Well That Ends Well*. If you are interested in Shakespeare's life, you will find useful the Palmers' categories of actors, patrons, playwrights, and publishers, as well as their list of Shakespeare's London and Stratford connections.

HISTORY REFERENCE BOOKS

> For aught that ever I could read,
> Could ever hear by tale or history.
>
> Lysander [*Dream* 1.1.132]

You will want to venture into other areas of the library's reference section after you have browsed through the Shakespeare books. The history shelves make an ideal second stop, for here you will find general resources not only for Shakespeare's England, but also for the broad sweep of history, which can be a little vague in the minds of many of us, before we are called upon to make concrete and specific choices when we are cast as a character in a past era.

Historical Who's Who

The Who's Who in British History series is an excellent place to start. I found *Who's Who in Late Medieval England*, edited by Michael Hicks, to be most helpful when working on Shakespeare's history plays. C.R.N. Routh edited *Who's Who in Tudor England* and C. P. Hill edited *Who's Who in Stuart Britain*. These, along with Ann Hoffmann's *Lives of the Tudor Age* and Edwin Riddell's *Lives of the Stuart Age* provide easy-to-use collections of "big names" whose characters were available for "life study" by Shakespeare's first company of actors.

Do not neglect the sixty-plus-volume *Dictionary of National Biography*, a massive undertaking of late-nineteenth-century scholarship now available on CD-Rom from Oxford University Press. Here you can find any historical character who makes an appearance in the plays, as well as individuals upon whom the characters might have been based. Look for detailed entries for the "big" names such as Dr. John Dee, a possible model for Prospero, or Robert Devereux, earl of Essex, who is listed under his family name rather than his title.

As a little side trip, you might want to cast your eyes on the library's latest edition of that famous publication, *Debrett's Peerage*. This is actually not of much interest to Shakespearean actors, who would be much better served by a handy little book by Arthur F. Kinney, *Titled Elizabethans*, a precise list of the nobility and officeholders in Shakespeare's court.

Historical Encyclopedias

The reference section of a good library is sure to include a few very broad historical encyclopedias, and a Shakespearean actor will enjoy having a look at such books for both the medieval and Renaissance periods. I am most fond of the illustrated encyclopedias put out by Mayflower Books, Aryeh Grabois's *The Illustrated Encyclopedia of Medieval Civilization* and Ilan Rachum's *The Renaissance: An Illustrated Encyclopedia*, in large part because the illustrations are numerous and beautiful. You can browse these books for an overview of the images, the events, and the issues that dominate a historical approach to the age, and you can also look up some of the specific entries that will assist in understanding the plays.

The reason I recommend a medieval resource is twofold. Shakespeare's history plays are all set in a period deemed medieval by historians and for that reason make reference to events such as the Crusades that are quickly and vividly explained in such an encyclopedia. The other reason is that many of the medieval concepts or developments continued to have significance even as England moved into the Renaissance. We can sense a similar residue if we consider the many changes since the Victorian and Edwardian ages and yet think how fascinated we are with these long-ago ages and how these ideals linger in our imagination.

A single example will do. The young man who courts Juliet is known as the County Paris, that being a customary noble title in Europe and therefore appropriate for the Italian setting of the play. Grabois's entry for "county" explains how that geographical designation and title were developed in the Middle Ages, which clarifies a great deal about the precise social and economic status Paris would have enjoyed vis-à-vis not only the Capulets, who are eager to acquire him as a son-in-law, but also the prince, who mourns his death at the end of the play.

First Thomas G. Bergin and Jennifer Speake, and then Paul F. Grendler, compiled a volume titled *Encyclopedia of the Renaissance*, and each is a useful resource. Medieval and Renaissance encyclopedias will by definition include references to many countries over a long period of time. Because many aspects of medieval life were essentially pan-European, entries on jousting, religious plays, and monasteries will be of use even if England is not the only location described. The development of national cultural activities was very much a part of the Renaissance, and so the English entries will be quite different from the Italian or Spanish descriptions. There is one topic, however, where the breadth of such a reference is invaluable, and that is the hugely significant and immensely complex event known as the Reformation.

Because these resource books are organized through alphabetical entries on specific topics, browsing for information becomes an exercise in following the trails suggested by the editors. Having found one entry, perhaps by chance, you discover cross-listings that take you to other entries, which in turn have still more cross-listings branching out in a variety of directions. You might discover important information under such listings as "Original Sin, Doctrine of," "Justification by Faith," or "Predestination." It might be a name that starts you on a journey of exploration of a long list of cross-referenced names of individuals such as Wycliffe, Calvin, Cartwright, Knox, Tyndale, Coverdale, Rogers, Cranmer, Parker, and Bucer and groups such as Lollards, Puritans, Brownists, Barrowists, Recusants, and Presbyterians. You will be led to entries on "Church of England," "Uniformity," "Articles of Religion," "Six Articles," "Hampton Court Conference," "Advertisements, Book of," "Supremacy, Act of," and "Common Prayer, Book of," all of which will help you to understand the complexity of the situation in England and will take you to the entries for the English monarchs: Henry VIII, Edward VI, Mary, and Elizabeth.

This may seem a strange way to learn about an aspect of Shakespeare's world, but I recommend it for the precision and clarity of each entry and the interconnectedness of people and events evoked by the cross-listings. After following all of the suggested trails, you will have a good idea of just how tangled and dangerous an issue personal faith still was when Shakespeare lived.

NONACADEMIC INTRODUCTIONS AND OVERVIEWS

Sometimes scholars are the least helpful to those seeking introductory explanations. We are fortunate that the wide appeal of Shakespeare has prompted the publication of some very unacademic but useful resources. These are not likely to be kept in the reference section and might not even have been purchased by the more snobbish university librarians.

Creators of glossaries often find it difficult to remember their first encounter with early modern English and therefore do not do a particularly good job of simplifying the important elements of language change and identifying a limited number of lost words to master when one is first trying to read the plays. Randal Robinson, a high-school teacher, provides just this sort of "back to the basics" in *Unlocking Shakespeare's Language*.

The name Isaac Asimov is associated in most people's minds with science-fiction novels or perhaps works of nonfiction on scientific matters. In truth, his is a wide-ranging intellect, and when he turned his attention to the plays of Shakespeare, the result was a two-volume collection of essays, now reprinted in the single volume *Asimov's Guide to Shakespeare*. Here, an actor can find a thoughtful and informative chapter on each of the plays. What is most useful about Asimov's approach is that he simply takes you through the story of the play and provides the sort of background information that will help you to understand what is going on. He explains classical images, fills in historical background, and provides all sorts of information on social customs, superstitions, geography, agriculture, and politics. Although he clearly has an opinion about the meaning of each play, that is not what he writes about. This is an excellent way to encounter the essential elements of a play that you are curious about but don't yet want to read. I strongly recommend his volume on the English plays for an overview of the histories.

Norrie Epstein's *The Friendly Shakespeare* is another accessible and user-friendly sort of publication. The layout of this book makes for pleasant browsing; open it to almost any page, and you will find brief, insightful information and commentaries on just about everything. The table of contents and the index are there for a systematic search in connection with a specific topic or for browsing to see just what might be found in the book. Best of all, Epstein has a firm sense of just what questions are most likely to require answering in the minds of the nonscholarly majority of Shakespeare lovers.

The Dummies books are a familiar sight in bookstores, now available on everything from computers in all their variety to every leisure activity imaginable, the law and taxes, and now, thanks to a British director and an American computer nerd, Shakespeare fan, and amateur actor, Shakespeare. John Doyle and Ray Lischner have produced a very useful handbook, with plot summaries for all the plays, but also quite a few pages on Shakespeare's language, his theatrical conventions, and background information on the man and his world. You will probably not find this entertaining book in a university library, but if you spot it in a bookstore, have a good look. Be sure not to miss the cartoons inside the front cover.

A DEBT OF GRATITUDE

> For this relief much thanks.
>
>   Francisco [*Hamlet* 1.1.8]

We must remain ever thankful for, if sometimes puzzled by, the individuals who have elected to spend their days creating the heavy, dense tomes that stand on the reference shelves. What would we do without all those dictionaries? Yet, as a resource for actors, they are at best clumsy tools for the accessing of the emotional energy contained in words.

That is because the dictionary exists to solidify meanings. Actors know that meaning is not a solid substance. When words are coming at you at the speed of sound, encapsulated in a multilayered communication package that includes tone of voice, facial expression, and gesture, in a context that has emotional significance for the speaker, some of which you know and much of which you sense, and when all of this takes place within the context of an immediate situation, the plot, and larger considerations that arise out of the world of the play, to say nothing of the all-pervasive influence of culture and language, how can we reduce the meaning of a word like "common" to a dictionary definition? Gertrude, in speaking to her son about his father's death, says, "Thou know'st 'tis common; all that lives must die, / Passing through nature to eternity," to which Hamlet replies, "Ay, madam, it is common" [1.2.72]. The two meanings "universal" and "ignoble" are just the beginning of all that this word might mean to these two people, all things considered.

Actors know this from working on modern plays, and therefore in rehearsal the only danger is that they will limit their sensitivity to the potential of words to those meanings that are current today, supplemented by the single definition offered by an editor in whichever version of the play they are using. What riches would be unavailable without assistance from our lexicologist friends.

RECOMMENDED READING

Shakespeare Dictionaries

Coye, Dale F. *Pronouncing Shakespeare's Words: A Guide from A to Zounds.* Westport, CT: Greenwood Press, 1998.

Davis, J. Madison, and A. Daniel Frankforter. *The Shakespeare Name Dictionary.* New York: Garland, 1995.

Dent, R.W. *Shakespeare's Proverbial Language: An Index.* Berkeley: University of California Press, 1981.

Irvine, Theodora Ursula. *How to Pronounce the Names in Shakespeare: The Pronunciation of the Names in the Dramatis Personae of Each of Shakespeare's Plays, Also the Pronunciation and Explanation of Place Names and Names of All Persons, Mythological Characters, Etc., Found in the Text.* Ann Arbor, MI: Gryphon Books, 1971.

Kökeritz, Helge. *Shakespeare's Names: A Pronouncing Dictionary.* New Haven, CT: Yale University Press, 1959.

Levith, Murray J. *What's in Shakespeare's Names.* Hamden, CT: Archon Books, 1978.

Onions, C.T. *A Shakespeare Glossary.* Revised by Robert D. Eagleson. Oxford: Clarendon Press, 1986.

Partridge, Eric. *Shakespeare's Bawdy: A Literary and Psychological Essay and a Comprehensive Glossary.* London: Routledge & Kegan Paul, 1968.

Rubinstein, Frankie. *A Dictionary of Shakespeare's Sexual Puns and Their Significance.* London: Macmillan, 1984.

Schmidt, Alexander. *Shakespeare-Lexicon: A Complete Dictionary of All the English Words, Phrases, and Constructions in the Works of the Poet.* Berlin: G. Reimer, 1886.

Shewmaker, Eugene F. *Shakespeare's Language: A Glossary of Unfamiliar Words in Shakespeare's Plays and Poems.* New York: Facts on File, 1996.

Spevack, Marvin. *The Harvard Concordance to Shakespeare.* Cambridge, MA: Belknap Press of Harvard University Press, 1973.

———. *A Shakespeare Thesaurus.* Hildesheim: Georg Olms, 1993.

Sugden, E.H. *A Topographical Dictionary to the Works of Shakespeare and His Fellow Dramatists.* Hildesheim: Georg Olms, 1969.

Webb, J. Barry. *Shakespeare's Erotic Word Usage.* Hastings, East Sussex: Cornwallis Press, 1989.

Williams, Gordon. *A Dictionary of Sexual Language and Imagery in Shakespearean and Stuart Literature.* 3 vols. London: Athlone Press, 1994.

————. *A Glossary of Shakespeare's Sexual Language.* London: Athlone Press, 1997.

General Dictionaries

Beale, Paul, ed. *A Dictionary of Slang and Unconventional English: Colloquialisms and Catch Phrases, Fossilised Jokes and Puns, General Nicknames, Vulgarisms, and Such Americanisms as Have Been Naturalised.* 8th ed. London: Routledge & Kegan Paul, 1984.

Dunkling, Leslie, and William Gosling. *Everyman's Dictionary of First Names.* London: Dent, 1983.

Farmer, John S. *A Dictionary of Slang: An Alphabetical History of Colloquial, Unorthodox, Underground, and Vulgar English.* 2 vols. Ware, Hertfordshire: Wordsworth Editions, 1987.

Hanks, Patrick, and Flavia Hodges. *A Dictionary of First Names.* Oxford: Oxford University Press, 1990.

Hendrickson, Robert. *The Facts on File Encyclopedia of Word and Phrase Origins.* New York: Facts on File, 1987.

Henke, James T. *Gutter Life and Language in the Early "Street" Literature of England: A Glossary of Terms and Topics, Chiefly of the Sixteenth and Seventeenth Centuries.* West Cornwall, CT: Locust Hill Press, 1988.

————. *Renaissance Dramatic Bawdy (Exclusive of Shakespeare): An Annotated Glossary and Critical Essays.* Salzburg: Institut Für Englische Sprache und Literatur, Universität Salzburg, 1974.

Kolatch, Alfred J. *The Name Dictionary: Modern English and Hebrew Names.* New York: J. David, 1967.

McConchie, Roderick W. *Lexicography and Physicke: The Record of Sixteenth-Century English Medical Terminology.* Oxford: Oxford University Press, 1997.

Partridge, Eric. *A Dictionary of the Underworld, British and American: Being the Vocabularies of Crooks, Criminals, Racketeers, Beggars and Tramps, Convicts, the Commercial Underworld, the Drug Traffic, the White Slave Traffic, Spivs.* London: Routledge & Paul, 1950.

Simpson, J.A., and E.S.C. Weiner, eds. *The Oxford English Dictionary.* 20 vols. Oxford: Clarendon Press, 1989.

Tilley, Morris Palmer. *A Dictionary of the Proverbs in England in the Sixteenth and Seventeenth Centuries: A Collection of the Proverbs Found in English Literature and the Dictionaries of the Period.* Ann Arbor: University of Michigan Press, 1950.

Withycombe, E.G. *The Oxford Dictionary of English Christian Names.* Oxford: Clarendon Press, 1971.

Shakespeare Reference Books, Companions, and Guides.

Andrews, John F., ed. *William Shakespeare, Vol. 1: His World.* New York: Scribner, 1985.

Asimov, Isaac. *Asimov's Guide to Shakespeare.* Garden City, NY: Doubleday, 1970.

Baker, Arthur. *A Shakespeare Commentary.* New York: Frederick Ungar, 1957.

Boyce, Charles. *Shakespeare A to Z: The Essential Reference to His Plays, His Poems, His Life and Times, and More.* New York: Facts on File, 1990.

Campbell, Oscar James, ed. *The Reader's Encyclopedia of Shakespeare*. New York: Thomas Y. Crowell, 1966.

Clark, Sandra, ed. *Hutchinson Shakespeare Dictionary: An A–Z Guide to Shakespeare's Plays, Characters, and Contemporaries*. London: Hutchinson, 1986.

Clarke, Charles, and Mary Cowden Clarke. *The Shakespeare Key: A Comprehensive Guide to All Features of Shakespeare's Style, Dramatic Construction, and Expression*. New York: Frederick Ungar, 1961.

Doyle, John, and Ray Lischner. *Shakespeare for Dummies*. Foster City, CA: IDG Books Worldwide, 1999.

Epstein, Norrie. *The Friendly Shakespeare: A Thoroughly Painless Guide to the Best of the Bard*. New York: Viking, 1993.

Halliday, Frank Ernest. *A Shakespeare Companion, 1564–1964*. Harmondsworth: Penguin Books, 1964.

Kastan, David Scott, ed. *A Companion to Shakespeare*. Oxford: Blackwell Publishers, 1999.

McDonald, Russ. *The Bedford Companion to Shakespeare: An Introduction with Documents*. Boston: Bedford Books of St. Martin's Press, 1996.

Quennell, Peter, and Hamish Johnson. *Who's Who in Shakespeare*. New York: Oxford University Press, 1995.

Robinson, Randal. *Unlocking Shakespeare's Language: Help for the Teacher and Student*. Urbana, IL: National Council of Teachers of English, 1989.

Rowse, A.L. *Shakespeare's Characters: A Complete Guide*. London: Methuen, 1984.

Thomson, W.H. *Shakespeare's Characters: A Historical Dictionary*. Altrincham: John Sherratt and Son, 1951.

Trussler, Simon. *Shakespearean Concepts: A Dictionary of Terms and Conventions, Influences and Institutions, Themes, Ideas, and Genres in the Elizabethan and Jacobean Drama*. London: Methuen Drama, 1989.

Wells, Stanley, ed. *The Cambridge Companion to Shakespeare Studies*. Cambridge: Cambridge University Press, 1986.

History Reference Books

Bergin, Thomas G., and Jennifer Speake. *Encyclopedia of the Renaissance*. New York: Facts on File, 1987.

Debrett's Peerage and Baronetage. London: Debrett's Peerage Ltd. Annual Publication.

The Dictionary of National Biography on CD-ROM. Oxford: Oxford University Press, 1995.

Grabois, Aryeh. *The Illustrated Encyclopedia of Medieval Civilization*. New York: Mayflower Books, 1980.

Grendler, Paul F., ed. *Encyclopedia of the Renaissance*. 6 vols. New York: Scribner's, 1999.

Hicks, M.A. *Who's Who in Late Medieval England, 1272–1485*. Chicago: St. James Press, 1991.

Hill, C.P. *Who's Who in Stuart Britain*. Chicago: St. James Press, 1988.

Hoffmann, Ann. *Lives of the Tudor Age, 1485–1603*. New York: Barnes & Noble Books, 1977.

Kinney, Arthur F. *Titled Elizabethans: A Directory of Elizabethan State and Church Officers and Knights, with Peers of England, Scotland, and Ireland, 1558–1603*. Hamden, CT: Archon Books, 1973.

Palmer, Alan, and Veronica Palmer. *Who's Who in Shakespeare's England.* Brighton, Sussex: Harvester, 1981.

Rachum, Ilan. *The Renaissance: An Illustrated Encyclopedia.* New York: Mayflower Books, 1979.

Riddell, Edwin, ed. *Lives of the Stuart Age, 1603–1714.* New York: Barnes & Noble, 1976.

Routh, C.R.N. *Who's Who in Tudor England.* Chicago: St. James Press, 1990.

‎ 4 ‎
Pictures, Reproductions, and Reprints

A thousand moral Paintings I can show,
That shall demonstrate these quick blows of Fortunes,
More pregnantly than words.
The Painter [Timon 1.1.90]

My imagination has always responded to pictorial artifacts. Among the first purchases I made for my private collection of Shakespeare books was Anthony Burgess's *Shakespeare*, because I could not believe my good fortune in finding such a wealth of full-color illustrations at such an inexpensive price. Since that time I have purchased or pored over as many photographs and reproductions as I could find, collected in books on Shakespeare, his England, or any specific aspect of his world that I can find.

Over the years I have come to value reproductions of the woodcuts that graced the publications of Shakespeare's day. Upon first encounter, these crude renderings struck my eye, trained as it was to admire the visual arts of the Italian Renaissance and all that followed, as boring, childish, and entirely incapable of evoking any aspect of reality. In this case, familiarity bred respect for the achievements of the artist, even within this limited medium, and the power of these images to encompass striking archetypal patterns of behavior as well as the minutiae of the ordinary.

Many of the great Renaissance masters from Europe still inspire me when I am working on a Shakespearean production. I don't care that Shakespeare could never have seen the great artworks that I have feasted upon in museums and picture books. The language of the visual arts includes patterns of imagery that influenced the imagination of the untravelled Englishman, and if a painting by Botticelli happens to be a more compelling example of, for example, the iconography of personification, then I am happy to let it inspire me when I am trying to feel my way through a line like the one spoken by the comic servant describing Helen of Troy as "the mortal Venus, the heart-blood of beauty, loves invisible soul" [*T&C* 3.1.32.].

I am a great fan of museums where I can see these artifacts preserved through time and imagine that the very chair I am looking at was once sat upon by someone who was alive when Shakespeare wrote his plays. In this I am not alone, as witness the thousands of tourists who flow through Shakespeare's birthplace every summer. How happy I am when I find a publication that includes lovely illustrations of such collections, for those of us who cannot afford to travel regularly to such fonts of inspiration.

Along with photographs of places and things, museums and libraries have published reproductions and reprints of some of their manuscripts. In addition, some editors have collected visual and literary material, organized into an accessible form and introduced with just the sort of general information that most appeals to the general reader, including actors.

The most significant benefit of any picture of a real place or artifact is the effect it has on the actor's attitude to the language of the plays. Until you see a photograph of the table book held in the Harvard College Library or, better yet, see the real thing by visiting that collection, you might assume that the standard table book was a good-sized, table-sized volume. After all, Julia calls her confidante Lucetta "the Table wherein all my thoughts / Are visibly Charactered, and engraved" [*Two Gents* 2.7.3]. But the photograph reproduced in the Riverside complete works shows us a tiny little thing, suggesting that Julia does not have very many thoughts to be engraved if they would all fit in that little space. In fact, maybe she just has one thought, and his name is Proteus.

It is one thing to read a scholar's note that crossed arms are associated with a sufferer of love melancholy; it is another entirely to see a woodcut of the fashionable and prescribed image and see that it matches what your character is supposed to say or do, as in *The Two Gentlemen of Verona* and *Love's Labour's Lost*. Without this pictorial evidence, it is all too easy to attribute the crossed arms to a joke that Speed or Moth makes because Valentine or Don Armado just happens to be standing there listening with his arms crossed. That might also be the case, but the joke for Shakespeare's audience was also that the comic verbal portrait matched a familiar image.

Modern aerial photographs of preserved Elizabethan stately homes such as Kirby in Northamptonshire illustrate the sort of estate that young Elizabethan aristocrats were busy carving out of traditional agricultural holdings or common lands. Such a visual inspiration might prove helpful to the cast of *As You Like It* as a picture of just what Oliver has inherited and stands to lose if the duke confiscates his inheritance.

PICTURE-FILLED GENERAL INTRODUCTIONS

The year 1964 marked the four hundredth anniversary of Shakespeare's birth, and several publishers took advantage of the date to publish collections of pictures and commentary. *National Geographic*'s May 1964 issue includes just such an article, entitled "The Britain That Shakespeare Knew," containing photographs of scenes from England that document the many opportunities afforded a modern sightseer to connect tourist attractions to Shakespeare's plays. At the other end of the scholarly scale, the seventeenth volume of *Shakespeare Survey*, published by Cambridge University Press in 1964, dedicated the entire volume to "Shakespeare in His Own Age." Allardyce Nicoll, then editor, solicited a collection of articles, supported by pictorial evidence, that serves as an excellent introduction to the major areas of interest. Also just in time for this anniversary, Louis B. Wright assisted Horizon Magazine in creating a volume entitled *Shakespeare's England*, a lovely book which falls somewhere in the middle of the two extremes of academic and popular publications, and so is of great value to actors.

These anniversary publications simply whetted the appetite of the general public for books that offered a richly visual introduction accompanied by a limited amount of factual information in nonacademic language but supported by the weight of scholarship. The result was a series of books, any one of which might serve as a reliable and inspiring resource for actors. Anthony Burgess, better known for *A Clockwork Orange*, entitled his contribution *Shakespeare*, as did Martin Fido. Maurice Hussey selected a longer title, *The World of Shakespeare and his Contemporaries* while François Laroque called his *The Age of Shakespeare*. Michael Justin Davis used a more evocative title, *The Landscape of William Shakespeare*. R. M. Frye, whose *Renaissance Hamlet* is one of the most valuable resources for an actor interested in social history, has also created just such a fine general introduction and pictorial collection, *Shakespeare's Life and Times*. Each of these is a collection of full-color reprints and short explanations and observations and, if still in print, an excellent bargain.

PICTURES OF HISTORY

In addition to the wonderful collections of images from Shakespeare's life and times, there are excellent sources of visual inspiration in the many books that document England's rich history. If everyone could afford a trip to see the many stately homes and medieval ruins, then such books might not find as many readers; I cannot recommend strongly enough, for those who enjoy such imaginings, collections of photographs and reproductions as an alternative to an expensive tour of the English countryside.

It is impossible, of course, to know how many, if any, of the awe-inspiring sights might have influenced Shakespeare's imagination. Clearly, the beautiful homes erected after his death had no place in his mind's eye. But the medieval castles that still stand today would have been available as models for King Lear or Macbeth or Henry VI's domestic settings. I would also suggest that when a production has been relocated to a later time, photographs and reproductions of more recent palaces can also be useful for helping to inspire an interior landscape.

CASTLES AND SHEEPCOTES

England is blessed with castles and cottages, taverns and tankards, and all manner of places and things that have survived the four hundred years since Shakespeare's time relatively intact. There is, of course, also a great deal of faux Shakespeareana on view, and not just in tourist traps. But the National Trust and the Shakespeare Birthplace Trust, to name two organizations, do a pretty good job of authenticating and presenting the historical landmarks and artifacts to the general public.

The English are rightly proud of their historical buildings and have invested a great deal in the preservation and promotion of such sites for the tourist industry and also for those of us who travel in our imaginations, aided by books of photographs. *The National Trust Book of British Castles* by Paul Johnson offers not only a detailed and historically accurate description of the castles, but also some compelling photographs, drawings, and archival material.

In Colin Platt's wonderful *Guide to Late Medieval and Renaissance Britain*, compiled for the National Trust, you will find an aerial photograph of Bodiam Castle in East Sussex, which is labelled "the most perfect and unspoilt of the Hundred Years War castles" (11) and is, for me, the best illustration of John of Gaunt's lines about England:

> This precious stone, set in the silver sea,
> Which serves it in the office of a wall,
> Or as a Moat defensive to a house,
> Against the envy of less happier Lands. [*RII* 2.1.46]

Or how about the photograph of the gatehouse at Thornton Abbey (42)? This imposing structure provides a possible image for the setting of Flint Castle when Bolingbroke first confronts Richard. The action then moves into the courtyard, for which the aerial photograph of Maxstoke Castle, Warwickshire (39), provides a concrete image of a moated and walled castle court.

Castles provide the location for a significant amount of the action in Shakespeare's plays, and there is no generally agreed-upon understanding of just how accurately Shakespeare or his actors might have envisioned the workings of a real castle, much less Hamlet's Elsinore or Richard II's Pomfret Castle. If you are the sort of actor who likes to imagine real rooms and passageways and accurate patterns of behavior that would be appropriate to the era in which the play is set, then you might want to have a look at John Burke's *Life in the Castle in Medieval England* and Philip Warner's *The Medieval Castle*.

Fortunately for those actors cast in medieval productions, there are many wonderful books available that answer the question "What would life be like in a castle?" I am most fond of those books that blend photographs of castles with medieval artwork and artists' renditions of the author's vision of life in a medieval castle. One such book is Tom McNeill's *English Heritage Book of Castles*. This is a wonderful collection of maps, aerial photographs, drawings, quotations, and detailed information about how castles were built, defended, and lived in.

The most useful picture books contain accompanying essays that provide the sort of rich background material that interests actors. Mark Girouard's *Life in the English Country House* is just such a resource, filled with fascinating details, such as the etiquette of arrival on a royal visit, the rituals with which a meal would be served to a monarch, and the sleeping arrangements for the monarch and his most personal servants. In *Macbeth* Duncan pays a visit to Macbeth's castle and is entertained there; the sleeping arrangements of his grooms become an important part of the murder and cover-up.

Girouard's book covers a vast expanse of time, so some care must be taken by the actor to position the production within the correct social context. At the same time, the layering of historical periods is always at work when one is playing Shakespeare. The original company clearly blended references to old ways of doing things, such as the manner of warfare evoked in *Macbeth*, with more modern attitudes, such as the thinly veiled accolade to their current boss, King James, in the description of the imminent arrival of the English king:

> Ay sir: there are a crew of wretched Souls
> That stay his Cure: their malady convinces
> The great assay of Art. But at his touch,
> Such sanctity hath Heaven given his hand,
> They presently amend. [4.3.141]

Girouard's historical approach, therefore, is particularly useful when one is seeking insight that might be medieval, Elizabethan, or Jacobean in origin.

PORTRAITS AND LANDSCAPES

Many actors are inspired by the portraits of Shakespeare's famous contemporaries, seeing in the faces, clothing, and stance exciting possibilities for characterization. Titian's *Portrait of a Young Englishman* provides us with a potential image for Hamlet; the uncredited portrait of the Moorish ambassador who visited Elizabeth's court in 1600, reproduced in Jock D'Amico's *The Moor in English Renaissance Drama*, a contemporary model for Othello. There are also portraits of historical figures such as Richard III, without any sign of a hump. In 1969 the National Portrait Gallery of Great Britain reprinted some of the Tudor and Jacobean paintings in its collection for those of us who would find it difficult to visit London for a studious and inspiring afternoon in the gallery. Sadly, only a few are in color, and the first volume of this two-volume publication is given over to a description of each painting that contains biographical information and some details about the clothing but otherwise is of more interest to artists than to actors. The indexes list only artists and owners/collections because the portraits themselves are presented in alphabetical order.

As a reminder not to get too worried about "factual truth," consider the portrait of Mary Fitton, impregnated by William Herbert, earl of Pembroke; when her condition was discovered, she was expelled from court. In the nineteenth century she was thought to be the Dark Lady of the Sonnets. But not now. A. L. Rowse is sure that he has found the Dark Lady in Simon Forman's diaries (1974, 99), and various biographers make claims for others. The leading contender these days seems to be Emilia Bassano, the daughter of a court musician and mistress of Lord Hunsdon, patron of Shakespeare's theatre company when it was known as the Chamberlain's Men. We will never know, but it doesn't really matter for an actor, because the search for the means by which one can commit to the human truth at the heart of these great works of fiction varies from actor to actor, from play to play, from production to production, and from century to century. So if the portrait of Mary Fitton inspires you to believe in a Dark Lady, then by all means use it in the private interior landscape of your imagination.

ENGRAVINGS AND WOODBLOCKS

The style of reproduction in engravings and woodblocks lacks the rich color and skillful perspective that we associate with European Renaissance masters, but it is of necessity a primary source of images from Shakespeare's England. All sorts of interesting details are explained by those pictures that have survived in contemporary publications. For example, we find in the Riverside complete works a wonderful collection of engravings, including, in connection with *Hamlet*, a fashionable lady wearing chopines (built-up shoes to increase her stature) and a springe catching a woodcock (a very simple and obvious trap to catch a rather stupid bird).

EUROPEAN RENAISSANCE MASTERS

England's graphic artists remained far behind those of Europe during Shakespeare's lifetime, but that does not mean that students of Shakespeare cannot make use of the inspiration available from the great Renaissance masters. We must remember that European artists formed a community that shared something even more important than specific techniques: the sources of biblical and classical imagery. When we are looking for visual clues for the thoughts of the eunuch Mardian, who answers Cleopatra's teasing about his lack of masculine passion by saying,

> Not in deed Madam, for I can do nothing
> But what in deed is honest to be done:
> Yet have I fierce Affections, and think
> What Venus did with Mars. [A&C 1.5.15]

we might do worse than consult Botticelli's 1483 painting of Mars and Venus. We can find echoes of the juxtaposition of the great god of war satiated by the powerful temptress in biblical themes, for example, Samson and Delilah or David and Bathsheba, as Don Armado notes, great lovers both, seduced by the beauty of a woman.

> Yet was Samson so tempted, and he had an excellent strength; yet was Solomon so seduced, and he had a very good wit. [LLL 1.2.173]

Art historians have written extensively on the topic of the interconnectedness of biblical and classical images and characters, and we can, with their support, trust our intuition that sees Venus and Mars in Samson and Delilah and sees both of these in Antony and Cleopatra.

EMBLEMS

Emblem books remind us that Shakespeare soaked up the verbal and visual images of his day and manipulated them as a type of widely understood shorthand. At a remove of four hundred years it is sometimes difficult for us to receive the complex messages encoded in the reference, other than the most obvious ones that have been recorded in a note by the editor of the edition we are using.

For example, when Hamlet speaks of his mother following his father's body "like Niobe, all tears" [1.2.149], the editors offer the basic information: Niobe was a boastful mother whose fourteen children were slain by the gods. She turned into stone with weeping. If we are browsing through a reprint of Geoffrey Whitney's *A Choice of Emblemes*, however, we will find a woodcut depicting the death of the children and a two-stanza moral. The first stanza gives the basic elements of the story; the second, the lesson to be learned:

> This tragedy, though poets first did frame,
> Yet may it be, to every one applied:
> That mortal men, should think from whence they came,
> And not presume, nor purr them up with pride,
>   Lest that the Lord, who haughty hearts doth hate,
>   Doth throw them down, when sure they think their state. (13)

Whitney also includes the reference to Ovid, and if we look in the sixth book of the *Metamorphoses*, we find the verses on her transformation into stone:

> Widowed, and childless, lamentable state!
> A doleful sight, among the dead she sate;
> Hardened with woes, a statue of despair,
> To every breath of wind unmoved her hair;
> Her cheek still red'ning, but its colour dead,
> Faded her eyes, and set within her head.
> No more her pliant tongue its motion keeps,
> But stands congealed within her frozen lips.
> Stagnate, and dull, within her purple veins,
> Its current stopped, the lifeless blood remains.
> Her feet their usual offices refuse,
> Her arms, and neck their graceful gestures lose:
> Action, and life from ev'ry part are gone,
> And even her entrails turn to solid stone;
> Yet still she weeps, and whirled by stormy winds,
> Born thro' the air, her native country finds;
> There fixed, she stands upon a bleaky hill,
> There yet her marble cheeks eternal tears distil. [6:298]

Just how much does Gertrude have in common with Niobe? Unlike Niobe, Gertrude does not boast of seven strong sons and seven beautiful daughters. She has only Hamlet, to whom she says, "Let not thy Mother lose her Prayers Hamlet: I prithee stay with us, go not to Wittenberg" [1.2.118]. Gertrude, whom Claudius names the imperial jointress to the throne, might well be described as Niobe is by Ovid:

> Her husband's fame, their family's descent,
> Their power, and rich dominion's wide extent,
> Might well have justifyed a decent pride. [6:145]

This points us to Whitney's moral: The proud incur the wrath of the gods, who overthrow them when they most think they are secure. If we rest our understanding of the Niobe reference entirely upon the pathetic image of the eternally weeping stone figure, then we miss the other attribute with which Shakespeare's first actors would have associated the Theban queen: her excessive pride and the fourteen deaths that were required to bring her to that state of perpetual mourning.

Practical Application: Emblem Browsing

I recommend paging through some emblem books during your rehearsal period, not necessarily looking for specific explanations, but just to see what associated images and morals were in the air for the first company. Here are some more of the images in Whitney's emblem book that caught my eye while I was working on *Hamlet*.

Just a few pages past Niobe is a woodcut entitled "Ludus, luctus, luxus," underneath which appears this text:

> Behold the fruits of drunkenness, and play:
> Here courage, brawls with Cutthroat for a cast,
> And oft in fine, if that they lack to pay,
> They swear it out, or blade it at the last:
>> This friendship breaks: this, makes us laughed to scorn,
>> And beggary gives, to those what rich are born. (17)

This reminded me of Hamlet's views on the revelry of the Danish court:

> This heavy headed revel east and west
> Makes us traduced, and taxed of other nations,
> They clepe us drunkards, and with Swinish phrase
> Soil our addition, and indeed it takes
> From our achievements, though performed at height
> The pith and marrow of our attribute. [1.4.17]

When Polonius calls Hamlet's love vows to Ophelia mere "springes to catch Woodcocks," [1.3.115], I recalled Whitney's emblem that features a picture of birds being trapped by a net. The first stanza, describing the taking of "simple fowles," tells of the trick of using a tame duck to trick wild ones. The tame duck comes obediently to light near the net, and the wild ones follow along, not fearing any treachery. The moralizing second stanza comments:

> By this is meant, all such as do betray,
> Their kindred near, that do on them depend,
> And oft do make, the innocent a pray,
> By subtle sleight, to them that seek their end
>> Yea unto those, they should most friendship show,
>> They lie in wait, to work their overthrow. (27)

Does this not describe Polonius's use of Ophelia to trap Hamlet into a confession of the true cause of his madness?

"Thus Conscience does make Cowards of us all" [3.1.82], observes Hamlet, and Whitney's emblem teases out the personification with its first verse:

> The wicked wretch, that mischief late hath wrought,
> By murder, theft, or other heinous crimes,
> With troubled mind, he doubts he shall be caught,
> And leaves the way, and over hedges climbs:

> And stands in fear, of every bush, and brake,
> Yea oftentimes, his shadow makes him quake. (32)

The woodcut gives us a portrait of the armed man raising his sword to strike at his own shadow, while Conscience rides the clouds above and behind, with the full glare of the sun emanating from his being. Look closely, and you will see that Conscience is a miniature version of the man himself.

Another line from that most famous of soliloquies, "who would these Fardels bear / To grunt and sweat under a weary life" [3.1.75], leaps out from a woodcut near the end of the book. This picture shows a man floating on the water, some distance from shore, with a pack on his back. Here are the two stanzas that accompany the emblem:

> Desire to have, doth make us much endure,
> In travail, toil, and labour void of rest:
> The merchant man is carried with this lure,
> Through scorching heat, to regions of the East:
>   O thirst of gold, what not? But thou canst do:
>   And make men's hearts for to consent thereto.

> The traveller poor, when ship doth suffer wrack,
> Who hopes to swim unto the wished land,
> Doth venture life, with fardel on his back,
> That if he scape, the same in steed may stand.
>   Thus, hope of life, and love unto his goods,
>   Holds up his chin, with burden in the floods. (179)

Perhaps it is not just the fear of death, but also the hope of life and love of possessions that turn us away from thoughts of death. Most editions of *Hamlet* helpfully define a "fardel" as a heavy burden; the Oxford editor notes the association with the burden or load of sin. A quick look at the *OED* reveals that the word was used to designate a parcel of unimportant things. Life is filled with burdens, but the unique burden of the longing for material possessions that motivates unceasing labor even in those who have no need to grunt and sweat sharpens the social criticism of this most famous of speeches.

Not surprisingly, there is a skull's-head emblem lurking near the end of the book. Here is the text, which recalls Hamlet's words over the skull of Yorick:

> Where lively once, God's image was expressed,
> Wherein, sometime was sacred reason placed,
> The head, I mean, that is so richly blessed,
> With sight, with smell, with hearing, and with taste,
>   Lo, now a skull, both rotten, bare, and dry,
>   A relike meet in charnell house to lie. (229)

Emblem Collections

There are many emblem books that have been reissued in modern editions. The most useful of these are the ones with an index that allows the actor to indulge in efficient spot checks. For example, George Wither's *A Collection of Emblemes, Ancient and Modern*, reissued by the University of South Carolina Press, reproduces Wither's own table "for the better finding out of the principall things and matters, mentioned in these Foure Bookes," in which the actor will find listings for not only the "Bear," and "Bees," the latter who illustrate the moral "By Paine, on Pleasures we doe seize; / And, we by Suff'rance, purchase Ease (23)," but also "A Bore," the beast rather than the irritating acquaintance, who illustrates the moral "A Life, with good-repute, Ile have, / Or, winne an honorable Grave" (110).

Wither's collection first appeared in 1635, but that late date should not deter you. His emblems are taken directly from engravings by Gabriel Rollenhagen first published in Holland in 1611 in a Latin text entitled *Nucleus emblematum selectissimorum*, and Wither's verse morals build upon a well-established interpretive tradition, one within which Shakespeare and his actors were educated and thus absorbed to be used or challenged at every turn.

For that reason, one of my favorite collections of emblems dates from almost 150 years after Shakespeare's death and has been reprinted in an edition by Edward A. Maser titled *Baroque and Rococo Pictorial Imagery* as part of the Dover Pictorial Archives series. This is the 1758 Hertel edition of Cesare Ripa's *Iconologia*, first published in 1593. Garland has also issued a reprint of George Richardson's 1779 edition. Ripa's *Iconologia* includes emblems for Memory, Virtuous Action, Gratitude, Confusion, Cruelty, and Pride, to name just a few I have enjoyed consulting in connection with a line of dialogue in one of the plays. The engravings have more detail than those found in Elizabethan emblem books, in keeping with the developments of the art form in the intervening years, and the moral explication for each is in modern lettering and so is just that little bit easier to skim for inspiration.

When a character like Menenius cries out, "Confusion's near!" [*Coriolanus* 3.1.189], everyone in the modern theatre immediately understands him to mean, "This is getting confusing." The habit of theatrical personification, coupled with the powerful traditions captured in the emblems, might have aroused a parallel image, that of the dramatic approach of a performer enacting Confusion. In Ripa's *Iconologia* we can see her, a young woman with her hair loose and tangled. The Tower of Babel in the distance sets the biblical context for the disintegration of communication that her name suggests.

When I look at this picture and read about this personification, I cannot help but think of the entrance of Constance with her hair unbound, the victim of political betrayal, consumed by grief for her lost child, and the embodiment of Confusion. King Philip of France heralds her entrance:

> Look who comes here? a grave unto a soul,
> Holding th'eternal spirit against her will,
> In the vile prison of afflicted breath. [*John* 3.4.17]

During her time on stage, the king and his courtiers persuade Constance to put up her hair, but as she leaves, she pulls it all down again, and her confused words mirror her distracted reason:

> Grief fills the room up of my absent child:
> Lies in his bed, walks up and down with me,
> Puts on his pretty looks, repeats his words,
> Remembers me of all his gracious parts,
> Stuffs out his vacant garments with his form;
> Then, have I reason to be fond of grief?
> Fare you well: had you such a loss as I,
> I could give better comfort than you do.
> I will not keep this form upon my head,
> When there is such disorder in my wit:
> O Lord, my boy, my Arthur, my fair son,
> My life, my joy, my food, my all the world:
> My widow-comfort, and my sorrows cure. [3.4.92]

I wonder if Constance reflects any other iconographic images. I read the list provided in the index at the back of Maser's edition of *Iconologia* and discover the word "Despair." Sure enough, this too is a woman, this time falling backwards, near to fainting, with a dagger in her breast to signify the suicide that so often follows, and that King Philip fears for Constance, for his next line after the speech just quoted is "I fear some outrage, and I'll follow her." The connection with betrayal is reinforced by the inclusion of Judas hanging himself following his betrayal of Jesus. Another relevant detail: at the feet of Despair there lies a broken compass, signifying that "in despair one loses all reason and cannot even enjoy good guidance" (106). That is an apt description of what Shakespeare shows us in this encounter between Constance and King Philip.

Another personification I associate with Constance, before she is betrayed and sinks into confusion and despair, is that of Memory, shown by Ripa as a middle-aged woman of serenity, education, wealth, and power. When we first meet Constance, she has dedicated her life to the safeguarding of her husband's memory and her son's right to the English throne. Ripa includes a Janus-like statue, facing in two directions, to suggest "Memory's concern with what is happening in the present, and its ability to remember all that happened in the past" (312).

One more emblem demands consideration, that of Constancy. Here we find another young woman of power and strength. We read that she is armed with righteousness and an unshakeable faith in her beliefs, and as an example of someone with the courage of her convictions, she is shown placing her hand in a flaming brazier. The biblical echo is provided by the inclusion of Shadrach, Meshach, and Abednego standing in the fiery furnace, untouched by the flames. Sadly, the Constance of *King John* does not survive her betrayal similarly unscathed.

The Scholarship of Emblems

If you become excited, as I did, by the wealth of evocative imagery contained in these pictorial artifacts, you may want to venture into the scholarly publishing in the territory of emblems and iconography. I would recommend as a starting place Samuel Chew's monumental work *The Pilgrimage of Life*, an excellent introduction to this scholarly field within the general category of art history. You will find in that section of the library some very interesting collections of artwork from the Renaissance that illustrate how the icons that permeated Shakespeare's world played out in the visual arts. In *Allegory and the Migration of Symbols* Rudolf Wittkower explores how emblems gather layers of meaning. His book is filled with illustrations of great interest to the plays, such as an image from John Bulwer's *Anthropometamorphosis* (69), that might have been described to Desdemona by Othello as "The Anthropophagie, and men whose heads / Do grow beneath their shoulders" [1.3.143]. Wittkower's collection of images that depict Time, Chance, and Fortune remind us of the theatricality of these emblems, and the living tradition of personification that the Elizabethan actors and writers inherited from the medieval morality plays.

An Index on Icons in English Emblem Books, 1500–1700 is a useful resource book prepared by Huston Diehl, who examined the surviving English emblem books published between 1500 and 1700 in order to prepare an index that lists alphabetically all of the personifications, followed by appropriate cross-listings, and then the books in which the icons can be found, the accompanying motto, and the epigram. There are only a limited number of illustrations at the end of the book, included to demonstrate the layout of each book and the style of emblematic drawing used by each compiler.

Diehl's book rewards browsing as well as systematic searches. If it opens to the letter *e* we might find the citation for "eel" and learn that one icon shows a woman shaking hands with a man holding an eel. The accompanying epigram is "A woman's constancy is no surer than the slippery, fleeting eel" (85). We might learn that other associations with an eel involve wickedness that is able to hide for a time but is eventually caught, and that flourishes in times of civil unrest, just as the eel can be found in muddy water. Thanks to Diehl, we can bring all of these associations to the witty exchange between Don Armado and his page Moth:

Moth: I will praise an Eel with the same praise.

Don Armado: What? that an Eel is ingenious.

Moth: That an Eel is quick. [*LLL* 1.2.26]

Alternatively, we can pursue all available associations for a personification that we have encountered in the plays. When Viola describes the imaginary lovesick sister and in so doing describes herself, she says:

> She never told her love,
> But let concealment like a worm i'th'bud
> Feed on her damask cheek: she pined in thought,
> And with a green and yellow melancholy,
> She sat like Patience on a Monument,
> Smiling at grief. Was not this love indeed? [*12th Night* 2.4.110]

In a quick check of Diehl's index, we discover that Patience is listed twelve times. If we follow the trail, we learn an association between Patience and bears shaping their young, a bird singing though it is imprisoned in a cage, and the armor that a good man bears against adversity, linked as it is with Christian faith and the true Christian valor as well as with the fortitude of the Virgin Mary. We also discover images of torture by pressing, associated with the crushing of a proud heart to teach it patience and humility. Is this a clue about the character of Viola? Is there a reason she is so quick to recognize Olivia's pride? Perhaps it is an attribute that she herself enjoyed, before the shipwreck, one would assume. Another association that challenges and enriches the familiar Christian model of suffering and endurance is the icon of a lamb butting a child, which carries the motto "Who, Patience tempts, beyond her strength, / Will make it Fury, at the length" (135). The moral: even the patient lamb, when tempted and provoked, will grow enraged. The patience required to tend the rosebush, with its ugly thorns, contains the promise of much beauty and goodness, and so we can observe Viola's gentle education of the self-indulgent Orsino, trusting that their love, when it emerges, will be glorious. The icon of a man walking through thistles reminds us that Patience can find pleasure in affliction, which matches our perception of Viola's pleasure in the torment of loving Orsino without hope of speaking.

An equally useful index is found in the back of Henry Green's *Shakespeare and the Emblem Writers*. Following his list of emblems, their mottos, and their sources, Green lists each of the plays followed by the direct links he has made between specific lines and an emblem in his book. Under his listing for *Hamlet*, Green directs the reader not only to the picture of a fardel, but also to Hans Holbein's *Dance of Death*, which has been reprinted several times and so is available to modern actors to provide emblematic visions to connect to the many occasions in which death is personified in Shakespeare's plays. I have also enjoyed looking at the woodprints, engravings, and drawings collected in Fritz Eichenberg's compendium, also called *Dance of Death*.

The most useful material in Green's book is in his sixth chapter, in which he classifies the various emblems into categories: historical, illustrating the stories of such as Sinon, the archetypal betrayer; heraldic, presenting such devices as the swan who sings before her death; mythological characters such as Niobe; fables such as the bird in borrowed plumes; illustrations of proverbs such as "a snake in the grass"; and emblems that illustrate aspects of the natural world, poetic ideas, or moral concepts. Browsing this section of the book illustrates the many uses to which emblems could be put and the wide range of images created by the visual artists who contributed to the iconography of the era.

SHAKESPEARE'S HAND

Many editions of the collected works include a reproduction of the one manuscript that scholars tend to agree was written by William Shakespeare. S. Schoenbaum has reproduced every available sample of his writing and samples of the writing of the times in his collection of reprints, *William Shakespeare: Records and Images*. Fortunately for the modern reader, he includes a "translation" of each reprint on opposing pages so that you can follow the handwriting and then glance over to see what the letters are that you are looking at.

REPRODUCTIONS AND REPRINTS

Oh that record could with a back-ward look,
Even of five hundred courses of the Sun,
Show me your image in some antique book,
Since mind at first in character was done.

Sonnet 59

One service that historical scholars have undertaken that greatly rewards the browsing time of an actor is the publication of collections of excerpts from the primary source material they have discovered in their exhaustive research. The editors gather interesting excerpts from court documents, diaries, letters, and publications from the time in question and provide just enough of an introduction and explanation to assist the novice in general understanding. Spelling and punctuation are modernized and obscure words are defined, so that each excerpt is easy to read; indexes and detailed tables of contents make it possible to spot relevant excerpts, but general samplings are just as rewarding.

Collections of Primary Sources

Frequently the scholarly and school editions of the plays include additional readings, some of which are excerpts from writings that Shakespeare and his actors might have read or heard talked about at the time of the first production of the plays. The editors have selected the most interesting and relevant sections that best illustrate how the ideas of the writer appear to have influenced Shakespeare. However, a general introduction to the intellectual background of Shakespeare's England, such as Gerald Pinciss and Roger Lockyer's *Shakespeare's World*, is sometimes even more useful to actors, as it does not force a direct connection between the text of the play and a weighty dollop of prose. Rather, it allows the actor to browse and ingest a variety of images, thoughts, perspectives, and ways of writing that then form the rich and subtle blend of mental processes that can make the words of the character come alive as reflections of the thoughts of the character. For example, as background reading for the cast of *The Merchant of Venice*, George B. Harrison's *England in Shakespeare's Day* includes, among many such samples of contemporary documents, this selection from *Coryat's Crudities*, first published in 1611. Here Thomas Coryat describes his discussion with a Jewish rabbi on the occasion of his visit to the Jewish ghetto in Venice. What began as a relatively cordial exchange of views became "many vehement speeches," and Coryat feared violence at the hands of "some forty or fifty" who had gathered and "began very insolently to swagger with me, because I durst reprehend their religion" (92). In the course of his description of this event, Coryat takes an opportunity to denounce their "insupportable pride" and to call them "unchristian miscreants," for the simple reason that they, like the rabbi with whom he began his discussion, "had confidently resolved to live and die in his Jewish faith" (91).

Over the years, many such collections of letters, diaries, and excerpts from the writings of Shakespeare and his contemporaries have been published, including R. E. Prichard's *Shakespeare's England*, Joel Hurstfield and Alan Smith's *Elizabethan People*, Arthur Kinney's *Elizabethan Backgrounds*, and Leonard Ashley's *Elizabethan Popular Culture*. Any one of these books will provide an actor with countless riches, provided they are read with imagination, sensitivity, and in full voice.

The Language of the Day

The King James Version of the Bible is readily available to any aspiring Shakespearean actor as a handy tool for training the voice and the mind to familiarity with language and thought patterns in tune with Shakespeare's. Less readily available, but conveniently collected and edited by scholars, are examples of other Elizabethan writings that have survived the four hundred years from his time to ours. We are going to be most interested in those writings that were intended to be read aloud, that being in keeping with Shakespeare's writings for the theatre. Letters, broadsides, ballads, announcements, tales, and any other popular-culture artifacts are going to be more valuable than scholarly tomes that made no effort to fit the written grammar to spoken rhetoric.

You will find all sorts of amusing entries that help to bring alive the world of Shakespeare and, if they are read aloud, will condition the mind and tongue in preparation for Shakespeare's prose. For example, here are the first few lines of an entry entitled "Bowling" from John Dover Wilson's collection *Life in Shakespeare's England*:

A bowl-alley is the place where there are three things thrown away besides bowls, to wit, time, money and curses, and the last ten for one. The best sport in it is the gamester's, and he enjoys it that looks on and bets not. It is the school of wrangling, and worse than the schools, for men will cavil here for an hair's breadth, and make a stir where a star would end the controversy. No antic screws men's bodies into such strange flexures, and you would think them here senseless, to speak sense to their bowl, and put their trust in entreaties for a good cast. (19)

Many of the collected writings are satires or social commentary and so may not represent an objective, evenhanded presentation of all aspects of any given subject. Provided that we allow for exaggeration and one-sided reporting, we can use such collections for insights into the lives of ordinary people in Shakespeare's time.

Reproductions of Early Modern Texts

Dedicated historians travel to museums and libraries that hold the surviving manuscripts and first editions of the works that they later cite in their various studies. A significant number of the books that we now assume Shakespeare himself read have been reprinted by modern publishers and so are available to a wider readership.

Barnes and Noble has brought out excellent reproductions of many important publications by Shakespeare's contemporaries in its Elizabethan and Jacobean Quartos series. Garland's series is called The Renaissance Imagination and a growing number of Elizabethan and Jacobean texts are now readily available in facsimile as well as reprinted versions. It is hard to imagine, when one surveys the number of reprinted Elizabethan and Jacobean texts, that there is anything of significance that has not been made available to the modern reader. You can consult the diaries of English ambassadors to Russia when you are playing one of the four lovers in *Love's Labour's Lost* who disguise themselves as Russians; simply make use of Lloyd E. Berry and Robert O. Crummey's index to their *Rude and Barbarous Kingdom* to go directly to the pages on Elizabethan views of Russia.

Publishers vary in their approach to the reprinting of these important historical documents. Some re-create the spelling, punctuation, and even layout of the original texts, while others give their modern readers a bit of a break by replacing the old letter *f* with the letter that represents that sound today, so that "wi*f*e" reads as "wise" and is not therefore mistaken for "wife." Other irritations are created by the usage of *u* and *v*, which is based upon patterns in Roman inscriptions rather than upon the contrast between the vowel and the consonant, and the use of the letter *i* where today we would use either *j* or *y*. Such editors will also regularize the use of these letters in keeping with modern instead of Elizabethan typesetting, but otherwise will not change the original spelling.

There are also modern publishers who update the spelling and even the punctuation so that the modern reader encounters no barriers to easy understanding. Sadly, the reader also receives none of the interesting clues about pronunciation and intonation that the older texts contain. With that in mind, some editors use modern lettering but retain period-specific spelling and punctuation.

While it is not easy to read reproductions of original manuscripts, with a little patience and practice you can become accustomed to the spellings, and the more you can acclimatize yourself to the language, the more Shakespeare's achievement will be set in context. This is the ultimate goal in examining these reprints. There is no real need for an actor to encounter firsthand the sources over which the best scholars have pored and from which have been gleaned all of the interesting bits. There is a need, however, for the modern actor to seek every available opportunity to read aloud from any surviving document, by which action the language of the time is placed into the mouth, to be savored and absorbed as the movement of muscle and the flow of breath. Although we all like the fully modern editions best for the speed with which we can access the material, the original texts do become easier to read quickly with practice and afford the actor a very special opportunity otherwise unavailable in modern editions.

In 1971 the Burt Franklin Research and Source Works series reprinted the 1912 collection *Ballads and Broadsides* edited by Herbert Collmann who had chosen to present his selections in their original spelling and typesetting. The short poem about Henry V looks like this:

> The fyfte Henry of Knyghthod lode ſtarre
> Wyſe and ryght manly, playnely to termyne
> Ryght fortunate, proued, in peace and warre
> Greatly experte, in marcyall dyſſplyne
> Able to ſtande amonge the worthyes nyne
> Reygned ix. yere v. monthes, & xxiiii. daies who lyft regarde
> Lyeth at weſtmynſter, not farre fro S. Edwarde.
> > Crowned the ix. daye of Auguſt,
> > > The yere of our lorde a M. iiii. C. xiii.
> > And dyed the xxxi. daye of Auguſt
> > > The yere of our lorde a M. iiii. C. xxii. (56)

I should mention that the difference between "f" and "ſ" is not as apparent in the book, and only by careful comparison of words could I determine that the second-last word in the sixth line has the former and not the latter.

In consideration of the modern reader, a modern editor might well give you this same text in modern forms, without changing the content.

> The fifth Henry of knighthood lodestar
> Wise and right manly, plainly to 'termine
> Right fortunate, proud, in peace and war
> Greatly expert, in martial discipline
> Able to stand among the worthies nine
> Reigned 9 year 5 months, and 23 days who [left] regard
> Lieth at Westminster, not far from St. Edward.
> > Crowned the 9th day of August,
> > > The year of our Lord 1413
> > And died the 31st day of August
> > > The year of our Lord 1422.

This leaves the modern reader with a number of puzzles, such as inversions, "The worthies nine," ellipsis, " 'termine" for "determine," and the phrase "lyft regard," which doesn't make much sense at all. We can be thankful not to have to puzzle out the strange letters as well.

However, we are denied an interesting opportunity to sound out the language as we attempt to read aloud the unexpected spelling, taking as our basic assumption that the original compositor worked phonetically. Therefore, my preferred style of reprint is one in which the modern editor has removed the needlessly confusing use of *f* for the letter *s* and has regularized to a modern standard the use of *u* and *v* but has not otherwise tampered with the spelling and capitalization. This allows me to read the passage aloud and set into my mouth the broad vowels, the extra syllables, and the clipped consonants as noted in the original spellings. The verse on Henry V might look something like this:

> The fyfte Henry of Knyghthod lode starre
> Wyse and ryght manly, playnely to termyne
> Ryght fortunate, proued, in peace and warre
> Greatly experte, in marcyall dyssyplyne
> Able to stande amonge the worthyes nyne
> Reygned 9 yere 5 monthes, & 23 daies who lyft regarde
> Lyeth at westmynster, not farre fro S. Edwarde.
> > Crowned the 9 daye of August,
> > > The yere of our lorde a 1413 [or one thousand, four hundred, thirteen].
> > And dyed the 31 daye of August
> > > The yere of our lorde a 1422 [or one thousand, four hundred, twenty-two].

With this spelling, and reading aloud, my mouth elongates the first syllable of "Knyghthod" but clips the second. The final sound of "starre" is burred or rolled and very definitely is not transformed into a modern British "ah" sound.

Folger Reprints

As with many other aspects of Shakespeare studies, we have reason to be thankful to the Folger Shakespeare Library for finding ways of sharing its extensive holdings with the general public. It publishes a collection called Folger Documents of Tudor and Stuart Civilization, in which it has reprinted everything from the 1559 Book of Common Prayer to "Advice to a son" precepts written by Lord Burghley, Sir Walter Raleigh, and Francis Osborne, edited by Louis B. Wright. The Book of Common Prayer that was in use in the only recognized church service during Shakespeare's life will give an actor a firsthand encounter with the religious language and spiritual rituals with which the audience, actors, and hence the characters were most familiar. If one has encountered Polonius's precepts to his son Laertes in the third scene of *Hamlet*, it is fascinating to read those written by Lord Burghley, upon whom the character of Polonius might have been based.

Another in this same series is William Harrison's 1587 *The Description of England*, in a lovely modern edition complete with an excellent index for browsing. Here you might acquire firsthand the manner in which Elizabethans described themselves, for Harrison's goal was to preface a historical study of England with a detailed description of the country as it was in his day. Some of Harrison's descriptions are of landscapes, but a significant portion of his writing records the activities of daily life. He has a section on the food and diet of the English and another on their apparel and attire. He also dedicates one section to the punishments to which wrongdoers were sentenced, in which you will find many examples of Harrison's blend of documentation and boosterism. He claims for England an absence of torture as a legal activity, as something that "with us is greatly abhorred, sith we are found always to be such as despise death and yet abhor to be tormented, choosing rather frankly to open our minds than to yield our bodies unto such servile halings and tearings as are used in other countries. And this is one cause wherefore our condemned persons do go so cheerfully to their deaths, for our nation is free, stout, haughty, prodigal of life and blood" (187).

Alert to Harrison's agenda, we can survey his observations of all aspects of society, seeking a portrait of how the Elizabethans wanted to see themselves. Here is his description of ladies of the court, which follows a lengthy paragraph demonstrating the unsurpassable beauty of the great palaces and their occupants:

Beside these things I could in like sort set down the ways and means whereby our ancient ladies of the court do shun and avoid idleness, some of them exercising their fingers with the needle, other in caulwork [ornamental netting], divers in spinning of silk, some in continual reading either of the Holy Scriptures or histories of our own or foreign nations about us, and divers in writing volumes of their own or translating of other men's into our English and Latin tongue, whiles the youngest sort in the meantime apply their lutes, citterns, prick song, and all kind of music, which they use only for recreation sake when they have leisure and are free from attendance upon the Queen's majesty or such as they belong unto. (228)

The editor kindly clarifies that a cittern is a guitarlike instrument and "prick song" is music with a descant or any music in parts.

William Harrison is often quoted by social historians, sometimes as a valuable source, sometimes in order to demonstrate his inaccuracies in light of modern historiography. For our purposes, he is often more useful than a professional historian, because he shares the same interests as we do: painting a vivid picture of his world in keeping with his values.

In 1979 the Folger Shakespeare Library enlisted the services of the eminent Shakespearean biographer S. Schoenbaum in putting together the published book for an exhibition of its holdings. The result, *Shakespeare, the Globe, and the World*, is a marvellous collection of first-rate reproductions of the artifacts held in this important collection. The text takes you through Shakespeare's early years in the small country town of Stratford, with information on schooling, flora and fauna, leisure activities, and the known facts of his family. Then the London years are described, with many fascinating illustrations and information about daily life and social customs. The final section of the book documents some of the many productions of the plays as well as works of art inspired by Shakespeare held in the Folger collection.

John Stow's *A Survey of London*

Quite a different source can be found in the Clarendon Press reprint of John Stow's 1603 *A Survey of London*. Thanks to the well-indexed edition of this 1603 publication, modern actors can supplement information about Shakespeare's London found in scholarly reference texts with a description of the city made by a contemporary of Shakespeare's. Open Stow's survey to any page, and you will walk up and down the streets of London as Shakespeare knew it, and through his eyes see houses, churches, markets, and collections of inhabitants. The index of persons, places, and subjects allows the modern reader to browse for specific allusions and anecdotes, such as the drowning deaths, by accident or as punishment, recorded in connection with various riverside locations. Stow fancied himself a historian, and recorded in his survey is a fascination with the history of the capital city of Britain, one that it is easy to imagine Shakespeare and his fellow actors sharing, in particular as they portrayed the lively events at Eastcheap in the days of Henry IV.

It is fascinating to trace Stow's private opinions and personal experiences despite his apparent dedication to objective description and recording of factual information. For example, he writes of the enclosure of common grounds "that neither the young men of the City might shoot, nor the ancient persons walk for their pleasure in those fields, but that either their bows and arrows were taken away or broken, or the honest persons arrested or indited" (II, 77). Stow records the story from Edward Hall's history of the riots of the early years of the reign of Henry VIII, which effectively ended the hedging of these open lands, but continues, "But now we see the thing in worse case than ever, by means of inclosure for Gardens, wherein are builded many fair summer houses, and as in other places of the Suburbs, some of them like Midsummer Pageants, with Towers, Turrets, and Chimney tops, not so much for use or profit, as for show and pleasure, bewraying the vanity of mens minds" (II, 78). These garden houses, which Stow elsewhere labels "fair houses of pleasure" (I, 129), had a reputation for being just the sort of place where a powerful government official, like Angelo in *Measure for Measure*, might meet a young woman for an activity that would not bear the cold, clear scrutiny of the general public:

> He hath a Garden circummured with Brick,
> Whose western side is with a Vineyard backed;
> And to that Vineyard is a planched gate,
> That makes his opening with this bigger Key:
> This other doth command a little door,
> Which from the Vineyard to the Garden leads,
> There have I made my promise, upon the
> Heavy middle of the night, to call upon him. [4.1.28]

Elsewhere in his *Survey of London*, Stow records a more personal encounter with the ambitions of the land-grabbing gentry, in this case in the person of Thomas Cromwell, who rose to the station of lord high chamberlain under Henry VIII:

This house being finished, and having some reasonable plot of ground left for a Garden, he caused the pales of the Gardens adjoining to the north part thereof on a sudden to be taken down, 22 foot to be measured forth right into the north of every mans ground, a line there to be drawn, a trench to be cast, a foundation laid, and a high brick Wall to be builded. My Father had a Garden there, and an house standing close to his south pale, this house they loosed from the ground, and bare upon Rollers into my Father's Garden 22 foot, ere my Father heard thereof, no warning was given him, nor other answer, when he spake to the surveyors of that work, but that their Master sir Thomas commanded them so to do, no man durst go to argue the matter, but each man lost his land, and my Father paid his whole rent, which was vi.s vii.d. the year, for the half which was left. Thus much of mine own knowledge have I thought good to note, that the sudden rising of some men, causeth them to forget themselves. (I: 179)

This is the sort of private and personal history that sparks the imagination of an actor.

Reprints in Context

Some editors are more successful than others in setting the reprinted material within its larger sociohistorical context. The amount of introductory or accompanying material varies greatly from editor to editor and is as much a matter of editorial taste as the choice of using modern spelling.

As is often the case, we are indebted once again to the Folger Shakespeare Library for John Stubbs's, *Gaping Gulf* a remarkable document that provides an actor not only with examples of the language of the period, but also with a gripping story that would have been well known to Shakespeare's first actors. Because the editors of this series, the Folger Documents of Tudor and Stuart Civilization, have modernized spelling, punctuation, and capitalization, these reprints are a great way to get a feel for Elizabethan syntax. Open the book to any of the letters and read one aloud. This is a marvellous way to feel the shape of the language, and if you do it with some regularity, you will naturally make the necessary adaptations to speaking that will serve you well in acting the plays.

Editor Lloyd Berry's introduction gives the reader a thumbnail sketch of an issue that gripped the nation all the years Shakespeare was growing up: who would Elizabeth marry? The man who came closest, and who was thought to be England's next king, Francis of Valois, duke of Alençon, was first proposed as a suitor when Shakespeare was eight years old. He won the heart of many for his support of the Huguenots, French Protestants then enduring terrible persecutions. His dashing adventures included arrest and imprisonment, escape, rallying of opposition to the Catholic persecutors, and the leading of rebel forces that finally succeeded in forcing the French king, his elder brother, to come to terms with his Protestant subjects. Elizabeth had sent support for his war efforts, and when his envoy visited her court to discuss a political alliance, the talks turned to marriage.

Alençon was neither as tall nor as handsome as his elder brother, bearing the ravages of smallpox on his face, but he clearly had the capacity to instill warm regard in a wide variety of admirers. After serving as the champion of French Protestants, he next went to the Low Countries, what is today Holland and Belgium, that area of Europe that was, during the years when Shakespeare was a teenager, attempting to throw off Spanish (Catholic) rule and establish an independent (Protestant) state. This long-running war provided an opportunity for some of England's shining lights to win glory and honor on the battlefield and, in the case of Sir Philip Sidney, to die. Many young Englishmen, filled with the glory of the Protestant battle against Rome, were happy to serve under Alençon, much as Bertram does in *Much Ado about Nothing*, where the conflict is thinly disguised by setting it in Tuscany and evoking Alençon in the character entitled the duke of Florence.

Elizabeth's council, which was desperate for her to marry, fearing above all the chaos of a throne without an heir, increased its pressure on Elizabeth, and she, still using her marriageability as a political playing card, bought time by announcing that she could never marry someone she had not met in person. This seemed to bring negotiations to a halt, because no one could imagine Alençon dropping everything and travelling to England to pay court to his coy mistress, but this is in fact exactly what he did, and when Shakespeare was fifteen, the country was enjoying the vicarious pleasure of observing its aging virgin queen being wooed like a young girl by this appealing (or appalling, depending upon your point of view) man twenty years her junior. She nicknamed him her frog, but everyone noted that she seemed truly fond of him, and the betting in town shifted. This was the same year that John Stubbs published a tract attacking the match and had his right hand struck off as punishment for his treason. Sir Philip Sidney, who also wrote a letter opposing the marriage, was not punished with anything more than the queen's displeasure.

The plans for the marriage seemed to be moving forward, though slowly, as suited the complex political alliances being negotiated. The year before Shakespeare himself married, Alençon again visited, and he and Elizabeth publicly exchanged rings, kissed, and declared their intention to wed. But it all seems to have been tied up with financial and political support for Alençon's flagging efforts in the Low Countries, to which he returned and from which he fled, disgraced, to die in France in 1584. It was said that Elizabeth wept for this end of her last hope for marriage and children. She was fifty years old, and for the next twenty years, during which Shakespeare emerged as a leading playwright, everyone knew that the Tudor dynasty would end with her death.

Who was John Stubbs, and how might the sacrifice of his right hand have affected Shakespeare and his first actors when, for example, they prepared a production of *Titus Andronicus*, in which the sacrifice of a hand is eagerly undertaken by the title character?

Stubbs was the highly educated and financially coddled son of a prosperous member of the gentry, a lawyer by training, with many connections by marriage and friendship among the nobility. He and many of Elizabeth's loyal subjects opposed the marriage to Alençon in large part because they objected to any alliance with France, and the fact remained that despite his championing of the Huguenots, Alençon was a baptized and practicing Catholic.

In Berry's introduction we find the record of Stubbs's scaffold address, taken down by a witness to the event, which took place in front of a large crowd in the market square at Westminster. Here is how it begins:

What a grief it is to the body to lose one of his members you all know. I am come hither to receive my punishment, according to the law. I am sorry for the loss of my hand, and more sorry to lose it by judgment; but most of all with Her Majesty's indignation and evil opinion, whom I have so highly displeased. (xxxv)

Later in the same address he says,

I pray you all to pray with me that God will strengthen me with patience to endure and abide the pain that I am to suffer and grant me this grace, that the loss of my hand do not withdraw any part of my duty and affection toward Her Majesty, and because, when so many veins of blood are opened, it is uncertain how they may be stayed and what will be the event thereof. (xxxv)

The sheriff of Middlesex, who had been ordered to carry out the punishment, had also received instructions that competent surgeons be present to prevent Stubbs from bleeding to death. It took three blows to sever the hand, and Stubbs fainted, but recovered in time to remove his hat with his left hand and call out, "God Save the Queen," as he left the scaffold. He survived this and his imprisonment, which lasted until Alençon's death, whereupon ironically he came into favor with the leading members of Elizabeth's council, who sought him out to use his considerable skills as a writer of polemics in service of the Crown.

We cannot assume that Shakespeare knew John Stubbs, who died in 1590, but he quite likely knew of Stubbs, as well as other writers whose publications had been ruthlessly suppressed. His dear friend Ben Jonson, along with other playwrights like Thomas Nashe and George Chapman, served prison sentences for their crime of sedition, which seems to have been loosely defined as publicly proclaiming anything nasty about anyone with any power at court. The heavy hand of government control of public discourse was very much part of Shakespeare's daily experience and is something to be remembered in considering the relative political conservatism of his plays. Actors and the writers who scripted their lines risked fines, imprisonment, and even dismemberment for giving voice to an unpopular opinion about current events.

SHAKESPEARE'S LIBRARY

My Library
Was Dukedom large enough.

Prospero [*Tempest* 1.2.109]

A productive subsection of Shakespearean scholarship has traced in his writings the evidence of the books that were readily available and that can be shown to have influenced him in some obvious or indirect manner. Many of the direct sources are reprinted by the editors of individual plays, and actors can count on the scholars to have gleaned these materials for all possible implications. There is nothing to stop an interested actor, however, from encountering the popular books of Shakespeare's England firsthand, simply to absorb the attitudes they convey and the language they use.

Schoolbooks

The premise of A. L. Rowse's *What Shakespeare Read—and Thought* is that we can trace in Shakespeare's plays the patterns of thought that were available to any literate autodidact of his time. Furthermore, by locating the source of the pattern of thought, for example, in a textbook used in schools or a readily available translation, we can observe how Shakespeare manipulated his sources, how he borrowed from many places to create his stories and characters, how he rewrote entire speeches just enough to make them suit the situation but not so much that the original cannot be traced, and how he manipulated the plots he lifted from history and fiction to shape the action of his plays. For scholars, this comparison between the source and Shakespeare's end product is a fascinating area for speculation on the thematic impact Shakespeare intended his plays to have. The actor, concerned with playing the character rather than discussing the ideas, will have an interest in the second part of Rowse's title, provided that we add a third premise to this field of study: that the patterns of thought that influenced Shakespeare would have been shared with his actors and his audience and, to a large extent, with the characters of the plays themselves, if we can imagine them having rich and complex intellects informing what they say and do.

For a general introduction to this aspect of Shakespeare's world, we turn once again to the publications of the Folger Shakespeare Library. In thirty-six pages, Craig R. Thompson's *Schools in Tudor England* gives you the overview and all of the important details that you need to set your imagination working. Unless you have been cast as Holofernes in *Love's Labour's Lost* or the schoolmaster in *The Merry Wives of Windsor*, it will probably not be necessary for you to cover the ground in as much detail as T. W. Baldwin includes in his lengthy studies *William Shakespeare's Small Latine and Lesse Greeke* and *William Shakespere's [sic] Petty School*. Baldwin dominates this subgenre of Shakespeare scholarship, and his books are guaranteed to provide a detailed examination of the public education available to boys of Shakespeare's generation and class in England. Baldwin's theories about just what Shakespeare studied and what impact his education had on his plays might be widely debated, but the collection of historical documents and factual evidence has served as a foundation upon which others have built their contradictory theories.

The Art of Rhetoric by Thomas Wilson was a popular school textbook in Shakespeare's schooldays and has been published in a modern and easily accessible edition. This allows you to discover the power of language as Shakespeare did: through the patterns of words and the manipulation of communication designed to persuade, all of which turns up in Shakespeare's plays, used by his characters to reveal thoughts and feelings and to arouse emotions in the listeners in the audience.

Shakespeare's Sources

Another specialized area of Shakespearean scholarship is the close comparison of the play published under Shakespeare's name with the sources from which he borrowed everything from the plot to words in characters' mouths. Scholars are fascinated by what this reshaping suggests about the thematic interest the source material had for Will; actors are less likely to find this of much help. It is perhaps comparable to being cast in the film adaptation of a novel. It might not be useful at all to know what is in the longer, undramatic source because your job as an actor is to solve the challenge of this particular set of scenes and lines. When the novel is over four hundred years old and has been read by no one but esoteric scholars, it becomes less and less likely to provide any payoff for the work involved. Most scholarly editions of the plays include excerpts from the most important sources and summarize the most significant changes Will made in his dramatization.

Far more interesting for the actor than a discussion of the modifications Shakespeare made to the original, or even the original itself, are the many indirect and subtle sources that are likely to have had an impact on how the first actors and audience responded to Shakespeare's situations, characters, and lines of dialogue. Whether or not Shakespeare had all of these books in his library, the fact that they were published suggests a general interest in and awareness of the subject matter. Modern reprints allow actors to browse and absorb impressions and develop some associations above and beyond the de-tailed comparison of play with sources.

Geoffrey Bullough's eight-volume collection *Narrative and Dramatic Sources of Shakespeare* is the standard reference work for scholars comparing the plays with their sources. Here you will find more of Shakespeare's favorite books: Plutarch, for his Roman plots, Raphael Holinshed and Edward Hall, for his histories, and prose fiction in translation for his comedies. Other books Shake-speare might very well have enjoyed include William Baldwin's *A Mirror for Magistrates* and Castiglione's *The Courtier*, available in English translation during his lifetime. Sources for the plays also include other plays, many known to us only by a record of a performance, and oral traditions that require a greater degree of speculation on the part of the scholar.

We must be careful to include in our consideration of Shakespeare's sources not only the works of history and literature, but also the productions of pop-ular culture, from which he could draw to create events and characters for his plays. An actor is looking to understand this aspect of Shakespeare's world in order to understand how his characters might have understood their world, or, alternatively, to discover the shared assumptions that are at work in the communication between Shakespeare the play shaper and his first actors, em-bedded in the language of the plays but not easily read if the plays are en-countered merely as literary texts or entirely through modern sensibilities. Fortunately for the actor, many of the most significant elements buried in Bullough's and Baldwin's exhaustive studies have been teased out in much more accessible form by scholars who either share an actor's interest or who present the results of their labor in a form that rewards browsing.

The Classical World

In the first part of *Henry VI*, Suffolk meets Margaret on the field of battle, and thus begins the plot that will see this woman Henry's queen and Suffolk's mistress in the second part of *Henry VI*. Suffolk experiences just a momentary hesitation in the face of the betrayal he envisions:

> Oh wert thou for my self: but Suffolk stay,
> Thou mayest not wander in that Labyrinth,
> There Minotaurs and ugly Treasons lurk. [5.3.187]

Here Shakespeare endows the young Suffolk with an awareness of classical mythology that would probably be anachronistic in the medieval setting of the play but was a familiar marker of the educated in the London of Shakespeare's day. Because the Latin curriculum of even the most modest country schools made use of these very stories, Shakespeare was not assuming a university education as a prerequisite for comprehension. Fortunately for the modern actor, many of the stories that caught his imagination continue in the shared cultural experience of today, whether in a Disney animated film or a *Sesame Street* parody. Our understanding of classical mythology is fairly selective, however, and a good general survey of the ancient gods and goddesses will be an important resource book for the Shakespearean actor.

Classical Mythology Reference Books

Every library is sure to have dictionaries or encyclopedias of the classical gods and goddesses who pop up in Shakespeare's plays. I am fond of Penguin's reprinting of Thomas Bulfinch's *Myths of Greece and Rome*. The telling of the essential elements of the myths is straightforward, and the index and table of contents will be all you will need to clarify that a Minotaur did indeed lurk in the labyrinth, that Theseus (he of *A Midsummer Night's Dream*) defeated the monster with the help of Ariadne (mentioned in *Dream* as a former lover of Theseus), and that the love story of Theseus and Ariadne did not have a happy ending (he left her behind on the island of Naxos, deserting her while she slept).

Bulfinch, who first compiled his collections in the mid-nineteenth century, has been reprinted in several modern editions based on the original three books: *The Age of Fable; or, Beauties of Mythology*, *The Age of Chivalry; or, Legends of King Arthur*, and *Legends of Charlemagne; or, Romance of the Middle Ages*. Shakespeare does not allude to King Arthur or Charlemagne with any regularity, but I have still had occasion to consult Bulfinch when I was tracking down associations with the name Rowland de Boys and his second son Orlando for the actors in *As You Like It*. Both the fool in *King Lear* and Glendower in the first part of *Henry IV* speak of Merlin as a prophet and dreamer, and Mistress Quickly confuses Arthur with Abraham when she announces the death of

Falstaff, saying, "Nay, sure, he's not in hell: he's in Arthur's bosom, if ever man went to Arthur's bosom" [*HV* 2.3.9].

Bryan Holme, the compiler of the Penguin edition of Bulfinch, has brought together a lovely collection of pictorial material demonstrating how the stories have inspired visual artists through the ages. It does not matter to an actor if the painting is neither English nor of the correct time period. A vivid image arouses the raw material from which an actor can draw to transform an allusion into a character's thought or need. That, in a nutshell, is what the Shakespearean actor must do for each and every classical allusion. An intellectual understanding is less than useful if it remains only intellectual.

The problem with Bulfinch is that Shakespeare's classical allusions range far and wide and encompass minor characters and lesser-known events. Therefore, a more comprehensive guide, with a detailed index, is necessary. Look for something that has good genealogical tables, because important mythological characters are sometimes introduced obliquely: Phaeton, the well-known driver of the chariot of the sun, is called Merops' son in *The Two Gentlemen of Verona* [3.1.153]. I like Mark P. O. Morford and Robert J. Lenardon's *Classical Mythology* for its genealogies, but for actors who wish to delve into the rich pageantry of the classical myths, there is no better reference book than Robert Graves's *Greek Myths*. Be prepared to encounter every detail and every variation on the predominant myth in this compendium that sets the standard for scholarship in the field. Make use of the table of contents to track down the principal gods and legends, but also check the index. Every bit of information included in the book is given a number or letter, and the references in the index are to these rather than to page numbers of the book itself. You will soon catch on to Graves's system and appreciate the skill with which he has told the stories and collected and arranged all the information. By looking up every single reference in the index you can be sure to locate every single detail about the interconnected cast of characters who turn up in each other's stories with the regularity of a long-running soap opera.

Perhaps the name "Hermione" will catch the eye, and the listing in Graves's index leads us to the sad story of the daughter of Helen and Menelaus, who makes a brief appearance in the legends of the major characters with whom she is associated, her parents and her two husbands, Orestes son of Agamemnon and Neoptolemus son of Achilles. What might it mean to the Hermione of *The Winter's Tale* to bear such a name? Is there an echo of the rivalry between Orestes and Neoptolemus in her husband Leontes' sudden and murderous jealousy of his childhood friend Polixenes?

What I enjoy about books like Arthur Cotterell's *The Encyclopedia of Mythology*, which have been designed for a general rather than a scholarly readership, is their extensive use of full-color reproductions of paintings and sculptures. Paging through Cotterell's book will introduce you to the inspiration artists other than Shakespeare have received from these legends. For example, the 1880

John William Waterhouse painting *Echo and Narcissus* reminds me of Juliet on her balcony:

> Hist Romeo hist: O for a Falc'ners voice,
> To lure this Tassel gentle back again,
> Bondage is hoarse, and may not speak aloud,
> Else would I tear the Cave where Echo lies,
> And make her airy tongue more hoarse, than mine
> With repetition of my Romeo. [*R&J* 2.2.158]

Cottrell's dictionary entry informs me that Echo pined away for love of the disinterested Narcissus until only her voice remained (63).

I do not think that there is any reason to have a scholar mediate between the actor and the great classical myths or even Ovid and Virgil, for that matter. There are many scholarly works that analyze the patterns to be observed in Shakespeare's use of classical allusions, and of these I would recommend *Shakespeare and the Uses of Antiquity* by Charles and Michelle Martindale as the best general introduction. The fifth chapter, "Shakespeare's Stoicism," deals with the concept of constancy and is therefore of particular interest to anyone working on Horatio and his like.

Classical Allusions

Let us pause for a moment to clarify the relationship between the myths of the Greeks and those of the Romans. Serious scholars find a great deal to say on this topic, but their agenda includes tracing the evolution of mythology over time and geographical distance; an actor is looking for explanations of Shakespeare's allusions that enrich the experience of the language, assist in the development of character, and inform the value system at work in the world of the play. Because the Roman culture borrowed wholesale from the Greek pantheon of gods, you will need to learn the double naming system in order to make use of what scholars have to say. Shakespeare used the Latinate form of the Greek names, for example, Jove for Zeus, Juno for Hera, Venus for Aphrodite, and Hercules for Heracles. This reflects Shakespeare's encounter with the legends in Latin schoolbooks like Ovid's *Metamorphoses*.

Ever since Greek and Latin disappeared from the curriculums of schools, young actors have been at a distinct disadvantage compared to earlier generations. If we held national surveys, I wonder what recognition value the old heroes and gods would have with the general public. Probably Jove/Jupiter and Venus/Aphrodite would fare well, along with Hercules and Achilles, but what about Niobe, or Thetis, or Tantalus, or Demeter? Yet these characters and the vivid stories in which they appear form the background for the events of the plays.

As an actor, you can acquire a familiarity with names through footnotes and dictionaries. These allow you to understand the words you are required to say or hear on stage. When Orsino opens *Twelfth Night* with his ode to love, he explains his torment with reference to Actaeon:

> O when mine eyes did see Olivia first,
> Me thought she purged the air of pestilence;
> That instant was I turned into a Hart,
> And my desires like fell and cruel hounds,
> Ere since pursue me. [1.1.18]

Almost every edition will assist the reader with the information that this is a reference to the story of the Greek king who, while out hunting one day, stumbled across the forest glen where Diana, the virgin goddess, was bathing. Because he had seen her naked, he was turned into a stag and was hunted down and killed by his own dogs.

With this information, everyone on stage can "understand" the lines, but can anyone "play" them? Everyone can probably identify with the torments of unrequited love and even see some similarity between those feelings and being chased by a pack of hunting dogs. But why that image and not another? At this point, the association is unspecific, generalized, icing rather than the cake itself. The result is "poetical" acting, beautiful words and images for their own sake.

A few hours paging through books on classical legends will help immensely. There are wonderful pictures to be gazed at that capture one artist's impression of some aspect of the story of Actaeon. There are more details to be learned about the story that the editors have excluded, because how much does a reader need to know? An actor, however, seeks something different than just knowing. Who can say what detail it is that will unlock the allusion for the actor and transform these words from an intellectual to an emotional connection between real human feeling and well-known legend?

Ovid's Metamorphoses

Elizabethan schoolboys used Ovid's *Metamorphoses* as a Latin textbook, and from the number of times that Shakespeare alludes to one of the stories, it is clear that he remembered it well for the rest of his life. Scholars consult the English translation by Arthur Golding published in 1567, but a modern actor will want to acquire a copy of a modern translation of this Latin poem, of which there are many available. My favorite, both for the price and the quality of the translation, is Oxford's The World's Classics edition, translated by A.D. Melville.

Here is Melville's translation of Ovid's description of Diana's reaction to being seen by Actaeon, in the moments before she turns him into a hart, to be pursued by his own hounds:

And as the clouds are coloured when the sun
Glows late and low or like the crimson dawn,
So deeply blushed Diana, caught unclothed.
Her troop pressed close about her, but she turned
Aside and looking backwards (would she had
Her arrows ready!) all she had, the water,
She seized and flung it in the young man's face,
And as the avenging downpour drenched his hair
She added words that warned of doom: 'Now tell
You saw me here naked without my clothes,
If you can tell at all!' (56)

It is the small details in this retelling of the legend that capture my imagination:
Diana/Olivia looking back over her shoulder, flinging water into Actaeon/Or-
sino's face, and the injunction never to tell of seeing her blushing, embarrassed,
emotionally if not physically naked. I find this an invitation to invent a compelling shared history. If we also imagine that this memorable encounter was,
in fact, the last time they saw each other, then it might also be available to
contribute to the subtext during their encounter in the last scene of the play,
when the following exchange takes place:

Olivia: What would my Lord, but that he may not have,
        Wherein Olivia may seem serviceable?
        Cesario, you do not keep promise with me.

Viola: Madam:

Orsino: Gracious Olivia.

Olivia: What do you say Cesario? Good my Lord.

Viola: My Lord would speak, my duty hushes me.

Olivia: If it be ought to the old tune my Lord
        It is as fat and fulsome to mine ear
        As howling after Music.

Orsino: Still so cruel?

Olivia: Still so constant Lord.

Orsino: What to perverseness? you uncivil Lady
        To whose ingrate, and inauspicious Altars
        My soul the faithful'st off'rings have breathed out [2270]
        That ere devotion tendered. What shall I do?

Olivia: Even what it please my Lord, that shall become him. [5.1.101]

There is something about this exchange which gives me the feeling that these
two have some old business between them, other than the obvious: his long
and unwelcome suit to her, and their current rivalry for the loyalty of the page
Cesario. I like to think that Ovid holds the clue.

Virgil's Aeneid

The *Aeneid* of Virgil holds a special place in a proto-Shakespearean bookshelf and rewards the actor who reads passages at random. You can also track down an allusion pointed out by scholarly editors and have a look at the larger passage in which the specific reference can be found. Scholars might be satisfied by the briefest of quotations, but an actor will want to explore the widest possible range of impressions and associations. Some will choose to read the entire poem from cover to cover in one of the excellent modern translations available in paperback or in a university library. I like to use Dryden's beautiful 1694 translation, for its gloriously neoclassical vocabulary and rhythms.

The story of Aeneas's sojourn with Dido clearly caught Shakespeare's imagination, with good reason. It is a compelling story of doomed love in an exotic setting, well suited for use by lovers like Lorenzo in *The Merchant of Venice*:

> In such a night
> Stood Dido with a Willow in her hand
> Upon the wild sea banks, and waft her Love
> To come again to Carthage. [5.1.9]

and also by cynics like Mercutio teasing the lovesick Romeo:

> Now is he for the numbers that Petrarch flowed in: Laura to his Lady, was a kitchen wench, marry she had a better Love to be-rhyme her: Dido a dowdy, Cleopatra a Gipsy, Helen and Hero, hildings and Harlots: Thisbie a grey eye or so, but not to the purpose. Signior Romeo, Bon jour. [2.4.38]

But the *Aeneid* also contained a thrilling story of the fall of Troy. When Hamlet describes a much-enjoyed piece the visiting actors had performed, he remembers, "One chief Speech in it, I chiefly loved, 'twas Aeneas Tale to Dido, and thereabout of it especially, where he speaks of Priams slaughter" [2.2.445]. Here is a bit of Shakespeare's creation of that imaginary play, followed by a bit of Virgil in the 1696 Dryden translation.

> Anon he finds him,
> Striking too short at Greeks. His antique Sword,
> Rebellious to his arm, lies where it falls
> Repugnant to command: unequal match,
> Pyrrhus at Priam drives, in Rage strikes wide:
> But with the whiff and wind of his fell Sword,
> Th'unnerved Father falls. . . .
> But who, O who, had seen the mobled Queen, . . .
> Run bare-foot up and down,
> Threatening the flame
> With Bisson Rheum: A clout upon that head,
> Where late the Diadem stood, and for a Robe

About her lank and all o'er-teemed Loins,
A blanket in th' Alarm of fear caught up.
Who this had seen, with tongue in Venom steeped,
'Gainst Fortunes State, would Treason have pronounced?
But if the Gods themselves did see her then,
When she saw Pyrrhus make malicious sport
In mincing with his Sword her Husbands limbs,
The instant Burst of Clamour that she made
(Unless things mortal move them not at all)
Would have made milch the Burning eyes of Heaven,
And passion in the Gods. [2.2.468]

This said, his feeble hand a javelin threw,
Which, flutt'ring, seem'd to loiter as it flew:
Just, and but barely, to the mark it held,
And faintly tinkled on the brazen shield.
Then Pyrrhus thus: "Go thou from me to fate,
And to my father my foul deeds relate.
Now die!" With that he dragg'd the trembling sire,
Slidd'ring thro' clotter'd blood and holy mire,
(The mingled paste his murder'd son had made,)
Haul'd from beneath the violated shade,
And on the sacred pile the royal victim laid.
His right hand held his bloody falchion bare,
His left he twisted in his hoary hair;
Then, with a speeding thrust, his heart he found:
The lukewarm blood came rushing thro' the wound,
And sanguine streams distain'd the sacred ground.
Thus Priam fell, and shar'd one common fate
With Troy in ashes, and his ruin'd state:
He, who the scepter of all Asia sway'd,
Whom monarchs like domestic slaves obey'd. [Book 2: 742]

With a minimum of effort an actor can gain maximum benefit from the Greek and Latin books that might well have been in Shakespeare's library.

Montaigne

When Hamlet enters about to launch into the famous "To be, or not to be," he might well be reading, as he was the last time he wandered on and Gertrude, seeing him approaching, announced, "But look where sadly the poor wretch comes reading" [2.2.168]. If he is reading a book, that book might well be Montaigne's *Essays*. Scholars have analyzed the threads that can be traced back to Montaigne that run through the plays in general and this speech in particular. An actor might want to have a look at the *Essays* firsthand either in the translation that Shakespeare might have seen, published in 1603 by John Florio, or in a modern translation such as that created by M.A. Screech for

Penguin Books. For the most part they are short contemplations, often referring to classical Greek and Roman models; you can imagine someone with
"small Latine and lesse Greeke" absorbing his classical models secondhand in
just such pleasant packages.

In connection with "To be, or not to be," there are several quite wonderful
essays that Hamlet might have been reading to prompt just such a monologue.
In "On Judging Someone Else's Death" we find a discussion of classical models
of suicide, and among Montaigne's comments, this: "It is to go far beyond
having no fear of death actually to want to taste it, to savour it" (689). There
is also a paraphrase of Seneca: "Not only bad and intolerable mishaps but
merely being sated with living gives us a desire for death" (690).

The essay "On Conscience" contains this passage here as translated by
Screech: "So wondrous is the power of conscience! It makes us betray, accuse
and fight against ourselves. In default of an outside testimony it leads us to
witness against ourselves: *Occultum quatiens animo tortore flagellum* [Lashing us with
invisible whips, our soul torments us"] (412). This seems to offer much rich
background and intellectual context for Hamlet's musings, as does the essay
entitled "On the Inconstancy of Our Actions," the first lines of which could
describe Hamlet himself: "Those who strive to account for a man's deeds are
never more bewildered than when they try to knit them into one whole and
to show them under one light, since they commonly contradict each other in
so odd a fashion that it seems impossible that they should all come out of the
same shop" (373). The richest parallels between Montaigne and Hamlet arise
out of the melancholy that the two shared. Both were educated, thoughtful
men, deeply intellectual and given to a pervasive sadness, which Montaigne
writes of in many of his essays, but most particularly in "To Philosophize Is
to Learn How to Die."

Jestbooks

At the masked ball in *Much Ado About Nothing*, Beatrice is told something
about herself that she is not too happy to hear: "That I was disdainful, and
that I had my good wit out of the hundred merry tales: well, this was Signior
Benedick that said so" [2.1.129]. Happily for the actor who would like to read
first-hand what was reputed to be Queen Elizabeth's favorite collection of jests,
a single copy of *A C. Mery Talys* survived from the original 1525 publication
to be reprinted several times over the next fifty years. There have been several
modern reprintings of this and other jestbooks of the period. Some editions
such as *Shakespeare Jest-books*, edited by W. Carew Hazlitt, or *Shakespeare's Jest
Book*, edited by Hermann Oesterley, re-create the spelling of the original, spar-
ing the modern reader only the old-style *f* for the letter *s*, so that a story might
read as in the Oesterley edition:

A fole there was, that dwelled with a gentylman in the countrey, whiche was called a
great tyraunte and an extorcyoner. But this fole loued his mayster merauylously, be-

cause he cherysshed hym so well. It happened [3 lines missing] to heuen: for I had leuer go to hell. Then the other asked hym why he had leuer go to hell. By my trouthe, quod the fole: for I wyll go with my master; and I am sure my master sall go to hell. For euery man seyth he shall go to the deuyll in hell; and therfore I wyll go thyder with hym. [XLIV]

Even though we can only be disappointed that three lines are missing, we can be thankful to have this little story as an example of the fool as simpleton, quite a different personality trait than the fools we meet in Shakespeare's plays. Did the first actors and audience of *The Merchant of Venice* remember this tale when Launcelot Gobbo debated with himself about leaving his master, Shylock?

Certainly, my conscience will serve me to run from this Jew my Master: the fiend is at mine elbow, and tempts me, Gobbo, Launcelot Gobbo, good Launcelot, or good Gobbo, or good Launcelot Gobbo, use your legs, take the start, run away. [2.2.1]

I would recommend a firsthand encounter with any of the jestbooks from this era, not in search of clues with regard to Shakespeare's plays, for surely we can assume that if there were any such connections, some hardworking scholar would have found them, but as a general introduction to the language of the times, as exercises by individuals less witty and theatrical than Shakespeare's Beatrice or Launcelot. What always strikes me when I sample from these books is just how amusing the little stories are not. They do not correspond to the way in which a modern comedian or comic writer would structure an amusing anecdote in the telling or recording, and so they do not succeed in striking my funny bone in any way. On the other hand, if I read any one of the tales aloud, I am reminded immediately of the flow of prose that sounds just like someone talking, and so I can use these as a way of acclimatizing myself to the language that Shakespeare might have heard on the doorsteps of houses up and down the streets of Stratford.

I am also struck by how vulgar many of these tales can be. Here is a particularly rude one, rewritten with modern spelling from Paul M. Zall's *A Hundred Merry Tales*:

A young gentleman of the age of twenty year, somewhat disposed to mirth and gay, on a time talked with a gentlewoman which was right wise and also merry. This gentlewoman, as she talked with him, happened to look upon his beard which was but young and somewhat grown upon the over lip, and but a little grown beneath as all other young mens beards commonly use to grow, and said to him thus: sir, ye have a beard above and none beneath; and he, hearing her say so said in sport: mistress, ye have a beard beneath and none above. Marry, quod she, then set the t'one against the t'other. Which answer made the gentleman so abashed, that he had not one word to answer. [XXXII]

Such crude stories set Shakespeare's participation in the language of sexuality very much in context. Having found this particular merry tale, let us make a quick trip to *As You Like It*, where Rosalind teases Orlando about his status as a lover, lacking as he does all of the required signs:

A lean cheek, which you have not: a blue eye and sunken, which you have not: an unquestionable spirit, which you have not: a beard neglected, which you have not: (but I pardon you for that, for simply your having in beard, is a younger brother's revenue). [3.2.372]

In this context, what can we make of the exchange between Touchstone and the two princesses earlier in the play?

Touchstone: Stand you both forth now: stroke your chins, and swear by your beards that I am a knave.

Celia: By our beards (if we had them) thou art.

Touchstone: By my knavery (if I had it) then I were: but if you swear by that that is not, you are not forsworn. [1.2.71]

On one level, the joke of this scene is that the two young women do not have even a younger son's minimal facial hair upon which to swear. On another level, there is a lurking potential for a naughty allusion to pubic hair, while on a third level, remembering that the roles were originally played by young men, there is the possibility that they, like the young gentleman in the merry tale, and like Orlando later in the play, could be mocked for their inability to grow a beard just yet.

The collection of merry tales reflects the prejudices and assumptions that permeated Shakespeare's England. You will find xenophobia, sexism, racism, and much mockery of the ignorant and uneducated. I always think of a character like William in *As You Like It* when I read the following story. I reproduce it with the older spelling and invite you to read it aloud, imagining that these are the phonetic re-creations of the country accent of the oral tradition from which the story comes:

There was a certayn plowmans son of the contry of the age of xvi yeres, that neuer coming moche amonge company but alway went to plough and husbandry. On a tyme this yonge lad went to a weddyng with his fader, where he se one lute [play] vpon a lute; and whan he comae home at nyght his moder asked hum, what sporte he had at weddynge. This lad answeryd and syd: by my trouth, moder, quod he, there was one that brought a gose in his armes and tykled her so vpon the neck, that she crekyd the sweetlyest that I hard gose creke in my lyfe. [XLV]

Fools on Fooling

Anyone cast as or with one of Shakespeare's fools might be happy to find a copy of Robert Armin's *Foole upon Foole*. Armin is the actor who joined Shakespeare's company in 1600, and scholars generally attribute to his special skills the creation of Touchstone, Feste, and Lear's fool. It is not clear if Armin wrote some or all of the pamphlets or simply lent his name to help sales. That debate does not interest actors, who might as well assume a connection or leave the document on the shelf. The full title of the book is *Foole upon Foole, or Six Sortes of Sottes: A Flat Foole and a Fatt Foole, a Leane Foole and a Cleane Foole, a Merry Fool and a Verry foole: Shewing Their Lives, Humours and Behaviours, with Their Want of Wit in Their Shew of Wisdome: Not So Strange as True.* Doesn't that sound like Touchstone?

There is no feeling among scholars that Shakespeare used *Foole upon Foole* as a source for characters like Touchstone, but rather that both he and Armin drew upon a well-established tradition of "allowed fools" who had a place in a great household or court and a reputation among the common people who participated in the circulation of the stories of strange personal habits (one prefers to sleep with the spaniels) or ridiculous behavior (one greedy fool steals a quince pie made for guests and puts it in the moat to cool it) as well as the jests, or witty and elaborate jokes that best pleased the master and demonstrated the special abilities of the natural or artificial fool.

One of my favorite stories is about the fat fool Jemy Camber, which reminds me of Falstaff's adventures with the Merry Wives of Windsor.

There was a Laundres of the Towne, whose daughter used often to the Court, to bring home shirts and bandes, which Jemy had long time loved and solicited, but to no ende, shee would not yielde him an inch of her maydenhead: now Jemy vowed he would have it all. Well, she consented at last, and to be short, soone at night, at nine a clocke being in the winter, when she knew her mother to bee gon to watch with a sicke body, hee should come and all that night lye with her: Jemy though witlesse, wanted no knavish meaning in this, thought long till it was night. But in the afternoon, the mayde goes up to the Castle, and gathers a great basked of Nettles, and comming home strawes them under the bed.

Night comes, nine a clocke strikes, Jemy on his horse comes riding forward, sets him up and knockes at the doore, she lets him in, and bids him welcome bonny man: to bed hee goes, and Jemy never was used but to lye naked, for it is the use of a number, amongst which number she knew Jemy was one, who no sooner was in bed, but she her selfe knockt at the doore, and her selfe asked who was there, which Jemy hearing was afraide of her mother: alas Sir sayes she, creepe under the bed, my mother comes. Jemy bustled not a little, under he creepes stark naked, where hee was stung with nettles: judge you that have feeling of such matters, there he lay turning this way and that way, heere he stung his leg, heere his shoulder, there his buttockes: but the Mayde having lockt the doore to him, went to bed, and there lay hee in durance (as they say) till morning: when the day broke, up gets the Mayde, to Court she goes, and tels the Kinges Chamberlaine of the matter, and he tolde the King, who laughed thereat right hartily.

The Chamberlaine was sent to see him there, who when hee came, found him fast a sleepe under the bed stark naked, bathing in nettles, whose skinne when he wakned him, was all blistered greevously. (87)

Here is Falstaff describing his own misadventures in attempted adultery:

Have I lived to be carried in a Basket like a barrow of butchers Offal? and to be thrown in the Thames? Well, if I be served such another trick, I'll have my brains ta'en out and buttered, and give them to a dog for a New-years gift. The rogues slighted me into the river with as little remorse, as they would have drowned a blind bitches Puppies, fifteen i' the litter: and you may know by my size, that I have a kind of alacrity in sinking: if the bottom were as deep as hell, I should down. I had been drowned, but that the shore was shelvy and shallow: a death that I abhor: for the water swells a man; and what a thing should I have been, when I had been swelled? I should have been a Mountain of Mummy. [3.5.4]

Ballads

When Autolycus attends the shepherds' sheep-shearing festival in *The Winter's Tale*, disguised as a travelling pedlar, he carries in his pack not only gloves, bracelets, necklaces, and perfume for the lads to purchase for their loves, but also another popular item:

Clown: What hast here? Ballads?

Mopsa: Pray now buy some: I love a ballad in print, a life, for then we are sure they are true.

Autolycus: Here's one, to a very doleful tune, how a Usurer's wife was brought to bed of twenty money bags at a burthen, and how she longed to eat Adders heads, and Toads carbonadoed.

Mopsa: Is it true, think you?

Autolycus: Very true, and but a month old.

Dorcas: Bless me from marrying a Usurer.

Autolycus: Here's the Midwifes name to't: one Mistress Tale-Porter, and five or six honest Wives, that were present. Why should I carry lies abroad?

Mopsa: Pray you now buy it.

Clown: Come-on, lay it by: and let's first see moe Ballads: We'll buy the other things anon.

Autolycus: Here's another ballad of a Fish, that appeared upon the coast, on Wednesday the fourscore of April, forty thousand fathom above water, and sung this ballad against the hard hearts of maids: it was thought she was a Woman, and was turned into a cold fish, for she would not exchange flesh with one that loved her: The Ballad is very pitiful, and as true.

Dorcas: Is it true too, think you?

Autolycus: Five Justices hands at it, and witnesses more than my pack will hold. [4.4.259]

The Clown resolves to purchase that ballad as well. It is clear that the sophisticated London crowd was being invited to laugh at the gullible country youth, but scholars are quick to point out that ballads were an element of popular culture that flourished equally in rural and urban settings. Some ballads were scandalous, some were ribald, and all were circulated quickly by word of mouth as well as in the cheap broadsides favored by Mopsa.

Many of the popular ballads of Shakespeare's London are known to us today only by title or subject matter; other documents refer to these ballads because of the impact they had on the general public, for good or ill. Those that have survived make for great browsing: they provide a snapshot comparable to any cultural artifact that was created by the people for the people. We might not appreciate all of the jokes or even understand the appeal, but the ballads are part of the cultural context within which Shakespeare's actors prepared and performed these plays.

In 1873–74 Charles Hindley edited and published in two volumes *The Roxburghe Ballads*, the majority of which had been collected by Robert Harley, the first earl of Oxford, in the early 1700s and which had been in circulation between 1560 and 1700. This marvellous collection of historical documents came into the possession of John Ker, the third duke of Roxburghe, and now are in the British Museum. A nine-volume edition of this archival material, edited by William Chappell, was reprinted in 1966 by AMS Press. In 1971 Harvard University Press issued *A Pepysian Garland*, edited by Hyder E. Rollins, a reprint of the ballads collected by Samuel Pepys, whose diary has been invaluable in providing us with a snapshot of theatregoing in the Restoration period.

Dip into Hindley's edition, knowing that this is the sort of song that filled the public airways of Shakespeare's world, and you will find much that resonates with the language of Shakespeare's plays. For example, the second volume contains a ballad entitled "Household Talke; or, Good Councell for a Married Man," in which Simon and Roger sing alternate verses. Simon has come to his neighbor in deep distress because, as his refrain states, "My Cosen makes a Cuckold of me." Roger responds in the manner of many of Shakespeare's characters:

Why, therefore
Shouldst thou deplore,
Or weare stockings that are yellow?
Tush! Be blith, (man!) Grieve no more,
A Cuckold is a good man's fellow. (61)

Later, Roger makes the following astute observation:

> Jealousie's a mad disease,
> and upon the brain it worketh;
> Like tormenting Lice, or Fleas,
> it in secret corners lurketh. (62)

Roger is able to effect a cure on Simon, who resolves to put aside his jealousy, though he has repeatedly, in his verses, expressed the fear that his neighbors, including Roger, scoff at him.

In the same volume we find "The Merry Cuckold," which contains a few verses that make use of the same images to be found in Shakespeare's plays. Compare

> If a man had
>   all Argus his eyes,
> A wife that is bad,
>   will something twise,
> To gull him to's face,
>   then what bootes mistust,
> The Hornes to disgrace,
>   though weare it I must. (466)

with Berowne's fear that his beloved Rosaline will prove wanton:

> Ay, and by heaven, one that will do the deed
> Though Argus were her Eunuch and her guard. [*LLL* 3.1.298]

Portia uses the same image when she teases Bassanio by pretending to want an adulterous relationship with the young doctor of law to whom Bassanio gave Portia's ring. We know what Bassanio does not: that Portia and the young doctor are one and the same.

> Let not that Doctor e'er come near my house,
> Since he hath got the jewel that I loved,
> And that which you did swear to keep for me,
> I will become as liberal as you,
> I'll not deny him any thing I have,
> No, not my body, nor my husbands bed:
> Know him I shall, I am well sure of it.
> Lie not a night from home. Watch me like Argus,
> If you do not, if I be left alone,
> Now by mine honour which is yet mine own,
> I'll have that Doctor for my bedfellow. [*Merchant* 5.1.223]

Or compare

Should I be jealous,
   as other men are,
My breath like to bellowes,
   The fire of care,
Would blow and augment,
   therefore I thinke it best,
To be well content,
   though I were Vulcan's crest. (465)

with Demetrius's subtle reference to cuckolding Lavinia's husband:

Though Bassianus be the Emperors brother,
Better than he have worn Vulcans badge. [*Titus* 2.1.88]

Clearly, the classical allusions to the god Vulcan, whose wife Venus had an affair with the god Mars, and the thousand eyes of Argus, who was set to watch over the wanton Io, were "in the air" whenever the topic of cuckoldry was raised.

From this and other examples we can see how the ballads gave voice to commonly held fears, assumptions, prejudices, or wishful thinking. They also document popularized views of history; in the first volume of Hindley's *Roxburghe Ballads*, for example, there is one entitled "The Woful Lamentation of Mrs. Jane Shore, a Gold-smith's Wife of London, Sometime King Edward the Fourth's Concubine, Who for Her Wanton Life Came to a Miserable End. Set Forth for the Example of All Wicked Livers" (108). There is also "The Second Part of Jane Shore Wherein Her Sorrowful Husband Bewaileth His Own Estate and Wife's Wantoness, the Wrong of Marriage, the Fall of Pride; Being a Warning for Women" (115).

Some of the historical ballads are probably more fantasy than history. In one a northern farmer travels to Whitehall to present to the king himself the farmer's legal problems; in another Edward IV meets a tanner while out hunting. In both ballads, as one might expect, the king learns from the commoner, and all ends with unforeseen good fortune. Another class of ballad reminds a modern reader of contemporary journalism, witness "The Lamentation of Master Pages Wife of Plimmouth, Who Being Enforced by Her Parents to Wed Him against Her Will, Did Most Wickedly Consent to His Murther, for the Love of George Strangwidge; for Which Fact She Suffered Death at Barnstaple in Devonshire. Written with Her Own Hand, a Little before Her Death" (191).

VERBAL AND VISUAL PORTRAITS OF DAILY LIFE

I am sent with broom before,
To sweep the dust behind the door.

Puck [*Dream* 5.1.389]

The modern actor who enjoys finding out what ordinary life was like will benefit from Lena Cowen Orlin's *Elizabethan Households*. This anthology is another in the long list of invaluable resource materials from the Folger Shakespeare Library and was created in connection with the 1995 exhibition of the same name. Each section in Orlin's book is introduced by just the sort of general survey that is most useful to an actor. In "Members of the Household," for example, we learn that on average, men married at twenty-five or twenty-six and women at twenty-three, because a couple needed to be financially self-sufficient before they married and set up housekeeping as an independent family unit in a community. Most households were therefore viable economic units and included servants who were in many cases younger individuals from the same social class as the man and his wife, living in that household in part to learn the skills necessary for success as adults. In other words, social historians have proven that Shakespeare did not always reflect ordinary English customs in his plays. The Verona of *Romeo and Juliet*, where women married and were mothers by fourteen, would have been as foreign to the first actors as to us today.

In the documents with which Orlin fills her book, we find many examples of how published writers of the day discussed domestic issues. To assist in your judicious browsing, Orlin includes a brief introduction to each excerpt, but it is not on her agenda to link these reprints with the plays themselves. The actor can browse for general interest and come upon all sorts of connections. For example, here is Robert Dudley, earl of Leicester, writing to his agent in France about a young kitchen lad whom he has selected for special training under a master chef in Paris:

And look what allowance he will ask for his teaching, and his board shall be quarterly sent over for him to such as you shall nominate. And do pray you to give every earnest charge for his well teaching, as also to have him kept under for royeting [rioting, or carousing] abroad. And as hitherto he hath been of good honest disposition, so being young and lacking some to keep him in awe, he may stray now abroad. But let him know that you have given order that there shall be watch over his behavior and that I have written to you earnestly to advertise me how he shall behave himself. And give charge to his master to keep him under and from liberty; but to set him to work enough. (49)

His instructions might perhaps remind you of Polonius and Reynaldo in *Hamlet*.

Private Letters

One of the great puzzles as we read Shakespeare's plays from the remove of four hundred years is assessing just how Shakespeare might have reflected the language patterns that he heard around him. The few letters that have survived the ravages of time are an invaluable means of comparison. Here is an excerpt from a letter sent from the Jesuit priest Robert Southwell to his father, as edited by Nancy Pollard Brown in *Two Letters and Short Rules of a Good Life*:

Death in itself is very fearful, but much more terrible in regard of the judgment that it summoneth us unto. If you were laid on your departing bed, burthened with the heavy load of your former trespasses and gored with the sting and prick of a festered conscience, if you felt the cramp of death wresting your heartstrings and ready to make the rueful divorce between body and soul, if you lay panting for breath and swimming in a cold and fatal sweat, wearied with struggling against your deadly pangs—O how much would you give for an hour of repentance, at what rate would you value a day's contrition? Then worlds would be worthless in respect of a little respite. A short truce would seem more precious than the treasures of empires; nothing would be so much esteemed as a trice of time, which now by months and years is lavishly misspent. (10)

What an evocative supplementation of Hamlet's famous "Thus Conscience doth make Cowards of us all" [3.1.82].

Here is the same writer expressing his desire for a speedy end to his imprisonment, even if it means the end of his life, in a letter addressed to Sir Robert Cecil:

I have lived thus eight months as one enclosed up in an anchorite's cell, having had no more part of the whole world but the scope of a few paces, no more use of life but to expect and behold my death, no more comfort of mankind but the recourse of a keeper and sometimes of Her Majesty's Lieutenant, whose resort, though it be but seldom, bringeth such content and leaveth so mild a relish as doth not a little qualify the gallish taste of my other aggrievances. . . . But although . . . I have otherwise been left in oblivion to bear my sorrows company and to entertain my thoughts with their own dislikes, yet I know my silence stilleth not the tongue of my heaviest friend, neither doth my absence absent me from his memory, who (I fear me) is more mindful to publish my disgraces than to procure for himself any good opinion. (77)

We can compare this with the musings of Richard II in a similar imprisonment: "I have been studying, how to compare / This Prison where I live, unto the World" [5.5.1]. Southwell was brought to trial for treason on the grounds of his admitted crime of being a Catholic priest sent to England to minister to the spiritual needs of English Catholics and, or so the government feared, to prepare those still faithful to the rule of Rome for open rebellion against their excommunicated queen.

Commonplace Books

When the ghost of Hamlet's father asks to be remembered, Hamlet resolves to remember nothing else. The image he uses would have been a familiar one to his audience:

Yea, from the Table of my Memory,
I'll wipe away all trivial fond Records,
All saws of Books, all forms, all pressures past,
That youth and observation copied there;
And they Commandment all alone shall live
Within the Book and Volume of my Brain,
Unmixed with baser matter. [1.5.98]

Hamlet is here describing the commonplace book, popularly carried by educated young men and women, into which they jotted excerpts from books they were reading, quotations from witty conversationalists they admired, and what today might appear in a diary or private journal. It is tempting to speculate just what might have been in Hamlet's commonplace book, and scholars point, for example, to his cribbing of Montaigne in the famous "To be, or not to be" as a likely entry. It is strange to think of any such private, personal, and youthful documents surviving when so many more seriously created manuscripts have disappeared into the gaping maw of destructive time. However, along with assorted private letters from quite ordinary people, we do have, albeit locked away in special collections, examples of the sort of "trivial fond records" that Hamlet describes. Thanks to the efforts of the Renaissance English Text Society, which has published many important manuscripts, we can look at one such commonplace book, that kept by Lady Anne Southwell-Sibthorpe. The editor, Jean Klene, has included an excellent introduction that, along with a browse through the volume itself, will provide a modern actor with an excellent model for an ordinary young woman who would have been in her early twenties when Shakespeare's plays were first performed.

I particularly enjoyed looking at Lady Anne's collection of "Apothegmes," what we would call proverbs and Hamlet labelled "saws." My favorite is "I had rather be a toad than a flatterer, but had rather be nothing than either of them" (107). I also enjoyed the short bestiary, with an entry on the dromedary or camel that includes the warning "When they come to bucking time they are full of malicious fury, and will remember them that have done them injury and kill them if they can surprise them" (104). This book also includes photographs of some of the pages of the original folios, housed in the Folger Shakespeare Library, so that you can get an impression of the style of handwriting of both professional scribes employed by Lady Anne to copy the selected excerpts and her own commentary and original writings.

OLD BOOKS ANEW

That Book in manys eyes doth share the glory,
That in Gold clasps, Locks in the Golden story.

Lady Capulet [R&J 1.3.91]

One of the most pleasant developments in recent years, from the perspective of those eager to immerse themselves in Shakespeare's world, is the publication of attractive and appropriately modernized versions of the books that existed when Shakespeare was a boy and a young man. These are not scholarly works, though they are often held in academic libraries, and they have been modified too extensively to qualify as reprints. Rather, they represent new strategy on the part of publishers to bring ancient texts to a modern readership. We cannot all travel to the Folger Library in Washington, D.C., or the Bodleian Library at Oxford University in England, but, thanks to the creativity of a variety of authors and illustrators, we can enjoy the experience of encountering the images and the language of these fascinating historical documents. The best of these offer beautiful illustrations and a format that gives the impression of older printing styles but presents no barriers to a modern reader's enjoyment of the words on the page.

Richard Barber has done a double service, for he has not only produced an attractive edition of a medieval bestiary, but has also translated it from the Latin into English and included an excellent introduction. Prior to this beautiful edition, most of us made use of T. H. White's charming *Bestiary*, equally useful but functional rather than an aesthetic inspiration.

Most of us are familiar with the animal fables of Aesop and so are accustomed to the concept that certain animals become associated with a set of human attributes: the fox is sly, the lion is heroic, the owl is wise. A bestiary is a compendium of character descriptions for a variety of animals, far more detailed than a modern reader might expect, with some surprises. We learn, for example, that weasels are cunning and also skilled in healing; they are the thieves of the animal world but have the capacity to bring their dead infants back to life. The source of the personality traits ascribed to each animal is in part that animal's observable behavior, upon which is placed a human interpretation, and in part the references to that animal in classical literature and the Bible.

The cunning weasel, best known for sucking eggs, pops up in Shakespeare's plays five times. Jaques in *As You Like It* and the Bishop of Ely in *Henry V* both make use of the egg-sucking association, Jacques to mock himself, "I can suck melancholy out of a song, / As a Weasel sucks eggs" [2.5.12], and the Bishop of Ely to slander the Scots:

> But there's a saying very old and true,
> If that you will France win, then with Scotland first begin.
> For once the Eagle (England) being in prey,
> To her unguarded Nest, the Weasel (Scot)
> Comes sneaking, and so sucks her Princely Eggs,
> Playing the Mouse in absence of the Cat,
> To tame and havoc more than she can eat. [1.2.166]

In the first part of *Henry IV*, Lady Percy compares her husband Hotspur to a weasel when he refuses to explain his preparations for war, which she is sure are the result of his hot temper: "Out you madheaded Ape, a Weasel hath not such a deal of Spleen, as you are tossed with" [2.3.77]. Pisanio picks up on this same attribute when he is coaching Imogen, the heroine of *Cymbeline*, on how best to play the part of a man:

> You must forget to be a Woman: change
> Command, into obedience. Fear, and Niceness
> (The Handmaids of all Women, or more truly
> Woman its pretty self) into a waggish courage,
> Ready in gibes, quick-answered, saucy, and
> As quarrelous as the Weasel. [3.4.154]

Hamlet teases Polonius by describing a cloud shaped like a camel or a weasel or a whale. We learn from the bestiary that a camel prefers muddy water to clear: if it is offered clear water to drink, it will muddy it before drinking. Although a camel is accustomed to burdens, it is also known for taking on more than it can accomplish. Whales are associated with people who destroy those who take them to be harmless because of the legend, reported in the bestiary, that sailors sometimes mistake whales for islands, land upon their backs, and then are drowned when the whale dives. If we imagine that Hamlet, Polonius, and Rosencrantz and Guildenstern, who are silent observers of this exchange, know their bestiaries, as do the actors and the audience, then the hidden message contains accusations and/or warnings of camel-like, weasel-like, or whalelike behavior. Rosencrantz and Guildenstern are muddying up the waters and are quite terribly overburdened in the task to which Claudius has set them; Polonius is sneaking around trying to suck from Hamlet the secret of his strange behavior; and Hamlet himself appears harmless but is plotting revenge. The Bodleian bestiary translated by Richard Barber dates from the thirteenth century and so represents the folk legends that would have permeated the culture in which Shakespeare and his actors lived; these are just the sort of images that stick in the brain when one is searching for a striking metaphor.

One of my most beloved modern renderings is Marie Collins's edition of William Caxton's *The Description of Britain*. Caxton was a printer and publisher who, in 1480, decided to publish a book about the history of his country. He put together a compilation of miscellaneous information, mostly cribbed from a recent English translation of the Latin *Polychronicon* of Ranulph Higden, which was in itself a group of stories, a few facts and a great deal of fiction, myth, legend, and invented explanations. Caxton, who was, after all, a businessman, had a hunch that his target audience would be interested in owning an edition of what everyone felt to be the true history of their beloved England.

All of this took place a full hundred years before Shakespeare himself might have started to think about English history, but Caxton's publication still had an effect on the imaginations of those Englishmen interested in documenting their history. For example, in *Richard II* the queen stands waiting for her deposed husband and addresses the Tower, where he will be imprisoned, "Ah, thou, the model where old Troy did stand" [5.1.11]. Caxton records the legend that Brutus, the first king of the Britons, founded the city of London to commemorate the ravaged city of Troy.

What is wonderful about Collins's edition of Caxton is the collection of reprints and photographs that have been selected to illustrate Caxton's short text. Here you will find medieval maps and illuminations alongside contemporary shots of some of the landmarks mentioned by Caxton that can be admired today. This is a particularly inspiring resource for anyone working on the history plays.

Thames and Hudson has published a lovely edition of *The Diary of Baron Waldstein: A Traveller in Elizabethan England*, translated and annotated by G.W. Groos. This collection of pictures, drawings, and historical details accompanies a modern English version of the 1600 diary written originally in Latin by the young German visitor. This is a wonderful way to be introduced to the sights of Shakespeare's England, as remembered by a European tourist. My favorite passage is the one in which he and his entourage finally meet Queen Elizabeth. In his entry for July 9 the baron records their journey to Greenwich Palace by boat and their eagerness to see the Queen. They were brought to the Presence Chamber by a guide "sent to us for this very reason at the Queen's command by Mr Secretary Cecil" and joined the crowd "of famous people and noblemen" waiting there.

Then, dressed in white and silver, the Maids of Honour (their beauty and shapeliness had no difficulty in diverting the eyes and minds of some of the spectators) made ready for the entrance of the Queen and of those who were to escort her to the chapel. A procession came first, led by the Chancellor carrying a gold-embroidered purse bearing the royal insignia, and a Knight of the Garter holding a sword before him, and Secretary Cecil following; then she herself, glittering with the glory of majesty and adorned with the jewelry and precious gems, entered into the view of the whole assembly and stretched her arms out wide as if to embrace everybody present. At her entry everyone knelt.

She had already been told of my arrival and asked at once where I was and what language I spoke. Quite soon she identified me, and speaking in English said graciously: "I welcome you." She heard me patiently to the end of what was certainly rather a long speech, and then, very gracious, deigned to give me a most kind reply. And when, among other things, I said that in reality she far surpassed the reports about her, then she interrupted me, putting the wrong meaning on my words, and said: *"This shall be your lordship's punishment—you have perhaps heard more than you are going to see: pay somewhat less attention to rumour."*

Actually, before I could address the Queen, to declare how great her goodness was, she first stretched out her hand for me to kiss, and immediately afterwards she raised me to my feet. (73)

The baron then records in his diary the flowery speeches he had prepared. This exchange was conducted in Latin, the language of the diary and one in which all of the educated were fluent. The exchange between the nineteen-year-old student and the sixty-seven-year-old woman seems to have been charged with sexual, social, and cultural tensions that would not have been identical to those experienced by Rosencrantz and Guildenstern when they first appear in *Hamlet*, but this snapshot of the English court contains much that actors find most inspiring.

THE SHAKESPEARE INDUSTRY

The enduring popularity of all things Shakespearean has created a market for the reproduction of archival material dating from Elizabethan and Jacobean England. Actors can look forward to many more reproductions and reprints with which to enrich their exploration of Shakespeare's plays.

RECOMMENDED READING

General Introductions

Burgess, Anthony. *Shakespeare*. Harmondsworth: Penguin Books, 1970.

Davis, Michael Justin. *The Landscape of William Shakespeare*. Exeter, Devon: Webb & Bower, 1987.

Fido, Martin. *Shakespeare*. Maplewood, NJ: Hammond, 1978.

Frye, Roland Mushat. *Shakespeare's Life and Times: A Pictorial Record*. London: Faber, 1968.

Horizon Magazine, with Louis B. Wright, eds. *Shakespeare's England: A Horizon Carvel Book*. New York: American Heritage Pub. Co., 1964.

Hussey, Maurice. *The World of Shakespeare and His Contemporaries: A Visual Approach*. London: Heinemann, 1971.

Laroque, François. *The Age of Shakespeare*. Translated by Alexandra Campbell. New York: Harry N. Abrams, 1993.

Pinciss, Gerald M., and Roger Lockyer, eds. *Shakespeare's World*. New York: Continuum, 1989.

Schoenbaum, S. *William Shakespeare: Records and Images*. Menston, England: Scolar Press, 1981.

Picture Books

Burke, John. *Life in the Castle in Medieval England*. Totowa, NJ: Rowman and Littlefield, 1978.

Girouard, Mark. *Life in the English Country House: A Social and Architectural History.* New Haven, CT: Yale University Press, 1979.

Johnson, Paul. *The National Trust Book of British Castles.* New York: Putnam, 1978.

McNeill, Tom. *English Heritage Book of Castles.* London: B.T. Batsford, English Heritage, 1992.

Millar, Oliver. *The Tudor, Stuart, and Early Georgian Pictures in the Collection of Her Majesty the Queen.* London: Phaidon Press, 1963.

Platt, Colin. *The National Trust Guide to Late Medieval and Renaissance Britain from the Black Death to the Civil War.* London: George Philip, 1986.

Strong, Roy. *The English Icon: Elizabethan and Jacobean Portraiture.* London: Routledge & Kegan Paul, 1969.

Warner, Philip. *The Medieval Castle: Life in a Fortress in Peace and War.* New York: Taplinger, 1971.

Emblems

Chew, Samuel. *The Pilgrimage of Life.* Port Washington, NY: Kennikat Press, 1973.

Diehl, Huston. *An Index on Icons in English Emblem Books, 1500–1700.* Norman: University of Oklahoma Press, 1986.

Eichenberg, Fritz. *Dance of Death: A Graphic Commentary on the Danse Macabre through the Centuries.* New York: Abbeville Press, 1983.

Green, Henry. *Shakespeare and the Emblem Writers: An Exposition of Their Similarities of Thought and Expression.* London: Trübner & Co., 1870.

Holbein, Hans. *The Dance of Death.* New York: Dover, 1971.

Maser, Edward A., ed. *Baroque and Rococo Pictorial Imagery: The 1758–60 Hertel Edition of Ripa's "Iconologia."* New York: Dover, 1971.

Ripa, Cesare. *Iconology.* New York: Garland, 1979.

Whitney, Geoffrey. *A Choice of Emblemes* (1586). Menston, England: Scolar Press, 1973.

Wither, George. *A Collection of Emblemes, Ancient and Moderne* (1635). Columbia: University of South Carolina Press, 1975.

Wittkower, Rudolf. *Allegory and the Migration of Symbols.* London: Thames and London, 1987.

Anthologies of Elizabethan Documents

Ashley, Leonard R.N. *Elizabethan Popular Culture.* Bowling Green, KY: Bowling Green State University Popular Press, 1988.

Collmann, Herbert Leonard. *Ballads & Broadsides: Chiefly of the Elizabethan Period.* New York: B. Franklin, 1971.

Harrison, George B. *England in Shakespeare's Day* (1928). Freeport: Books for Libraries Press, 1970.

Hurstfield, Joel, and Alan G.R. Smith. *Elizabethan People: State and Society.* New York: St. Martin's Press, 1972.

Kinney, Arthur F. *Elizabethan Backgrounds: Historical Documents of the Age of Elizabeth I.* Hamden, CT: Archon Books, 1975.

Orlin, Lena Cowen. *Elizabethan Households: An Anthology.* Washington, DC: Folger Shakespeare Library, 1995.

Prichard, R.E., ed. *Shakespeare's England: Life in Elizabethan and Jacobean Times.* Stroud, Gloucestershire: Sutton, 1999.

Schoenbaum, Samuel. *Shakespeare, the Globe, and the World.* New York: Oxford University Press, 1979.

Wilson, John Dover, ed. *Life in Shakespeare's England: A Book of Elizabethan Prose.* New York: Barnes & Noble, 1969.

Reprints of Books Published in Shakespeare's England

Berry, Lloyd E., and Robert O. Crummey, eds. *Rude and Barbarous Kingdom: Russia in the Accounts of Sixteenth-Century English Voyagers.* Madison: University of Wisconsin Press, 1968.

Collins, Marie. *Caxton, the Description of Britain: A Modern Rendering.* New York: Weidenfeld and Nicolson, 1988.

Groos, G.W. *The Diary of Baron Waldstein: A Traveller in Elizabethan England.* London: Thames and Hudson, c1981.

Harrison, William. *The Description of England* (1587). Edited by Georges Edelen. Ithaca, NY: Cornell University Press, 1968.

Southwell, Lady Anne. *The Southwell-Sibthorpe Commonplace Book: Folger MS. V.b. 198.* Edited by Jean Klene. Tempe, AZ: Medieval & Renaissance Texts & Studies, 1997.

Southwell, Robert. *Two Letters and Short Rules of a Good Life* (c. 1600). Edited by Nancy Pollard Brown. Charlottesville: University Press of Virginia, 1973.

Stow, John. *A Survey of London* (1603). Edited by Charles Lethbridge Kingsford. Oxford: Clarendon Press, 1971.

Stubbs, John. *Gaping Gulf, with Letters and Other Relevant Documents* (1579). Edited by Lloyd E. Berry. Charlottesville: University Press of Virginia, 1968.

Wilson, Thomas. *The Art of Rhetoric* (1560). Edited by Peter E. Medine. University Park: Pennsylvania State University Press, 1994.

Wright, Louis B., ed. *Advice to a Son: Precepts of Lord Burghley, Sir Walter Raleigh, and Francis Osborne.* Ithaca, NY: Cornell University Press, 1962.

Shakespeare's Library

Baldwin, T.W. *William Shakespeare's Petty School.* Urbana: University of Illinois Press, 1943.

———. *William Shakspere's Small Latine & Lesse Greeke.* Urbana: University of Illinois Press, 1956.

Baldwin, William. *The Mirror for Magistrates* (1559). Edited by Lily B. Campbell. New York: Barnes & Noble, 1960.

Bulfinch, Thomas. *Myths of Greece and Rome.* Compiled by Bryan Holme. Harmondsworth: Penguin Books, 1981.

Bullough, Geoffrey, ed. *Narrative and Dramatic Sources of Shakespeare.* 8 vols. London: Routledge and Kegan Paul, 1957–75.

Castiglione, Baldassare. *The Book of the Courtier* (1562). Translated by George Bull. Harmondsworth: Penguin Books, 1976.

Cotterell, Arthur. *The Encyclopedia of Mythology: Classical, Celtic, Norse.* Ottawa: Prospero Books, 1999.

Florio, John. *The Essays of Montaigne* (1603). 3 vols. New York: AMS Press, 1967.

Golding, Arthur. *Metamorphoses: The Arthur Golding Translation* (1567). New York: Macmillan, 1965.

Graves, Robert. *The Greek Myths.* 2 vols. Harmondsworth: Penguin Books, 1960.

Hoby, Thomas. *The Book of the Courtier* (1561). New York: AMS Press, 1967.

Martin, Richard, ed. *Bulfinch's Mythology.* New York: HarperCollins, 1991.

Martindale, Charles, and Michelle Martindale. *Shakespeare and the Uses of Antiquity.* London: Routledge, 1990.

Montaigne, Michel de. *The Complete Essays.* Translated by M.A. Screech. Harmondsworth: Penguin Books, 1991.

Morford, Mark P.O., and Robert J. Lenardon. *Classical Mythology.* New York: Longman, 1991.

North, Thomas. *Plutarch's Lives of the Noble Grecians and Romans* (1579). 6 vols. New York: AMS Press, 1967.

Ovid. *Metamorphoses.* Translated by A.D. Melville. Oxford: Oxford University Press, 1987.

Thompson, Craig R. *Schools in Tudor England.* Ithaca, NY: Cornell University Press, 1958.

Virgil. *Aeneid and Fourth ("Messianic") Eclogue in the Dryden Translation.* Edited by Howard Clarke. University Park: Pennsylvania State University Press, 1989.

Ballads, Jestbooks, and Bestiaries

Armin, Robert. *Foole upon Foole* (1600). Edited by H.F. Lippincott Salzburg: Institut für Englische Sprache und Literatur, Universität Salzburg, 1973.

Barber, Richard, trans. *Bestiary: Being an English Version of the Bodleian Library, Oxford M.S. Bodley 764: With All the Original Miniatures Reproduced in Facsimile.* Woodbridge, England: Boydell Press, 1993.

Chappell, William, ed. *The Roxburghe Ballads.* 9 vols. New York: AMS Press, 1966.

Collmann, Herbert Leonard. *Ballads and Broadsides: Chiefly of the Elizabethan Period.* New York: B. Franklin, 1971.

Hazlitt, W. Carew, ed. *Shakespeare Jest-books: Reprints of the Early and Very Rare Jest-Books Supposed to Have Been Used by Shakespeare.* London: H. Sotheran & Co., 1881.

Hindley, Charles, ed. *The Roxburghe Ballads.* 2 vols. London: Reeves and Turner, 1873–74.

Oesterley, Hermann, ed. *Shakespeare's Jest Book: An Edition of A Hundred Mery Talys* (1526). Gainesville, FL: Scholars' Facsimiles & Reprints, 1970.

Rollins, Hyder E., ed. *A Pepysian Garland: Black-Letter Broadside Ballads of the Years 1595–1639, Chiefly from the Collection of Samuel Pepys.* Cambridge, MA: Harvard University Press, 1971.

White, T.H., ed. *The Bestiary: A Book of Beasts: Being a Translation from a Latin Bestiary of the Twelfth Century.* New York: GP Putnam's Sons, 1960.

Zall, Paul M., ed. *A Hundred Merry Tales, and Other English Jestbooks of the Fifteenth and Sixteenth Centuries.* Lincoln: University of Nebraska Press, 1963.

ᘓ 5 ᘖ
Famous Players of the World Stage

O For a Muse of Fire, that would ascend
The brightest Heaven of Invention:
A Kingdom for a Stage, Princes to Act,
And Monarchs to behold the swelling Scene.

Chorus [*HV* Prologue, 1]

It was inevitable that the best-known national figures would find themselves reflected, directly or indirectly, in the fictional characters of the popular culture of the age. The finding of reflections went very much out of fashion as scholars became uncomfortable with implications of direct correspondence or intended satire, despite what had previously been considered the obvious similarities between, for example, a character like Polonius and Elizabeth's favorite counsellor, Cecil. The entire practice of finding these parallels came into further disrepute when it was linked to the efforts of some amateur historians to prove that no glover's son could possibly have been responsible for these great works of poetry. The supporters of the earl of Oxford as the alternative author had to reposition the authorship to an earlier decade, suggesting that the earl wrote the plays, and only much later were they premiered on the London public stage. That done, they are eager to find parallels between events at court and in the earl's life and the characters and events of the plays, no matter how farfetched, in order to demonstrate the irrefutable truth of their unprovable assumptions.

Without attempting to participate in any aspect of these esoteric controversies, an actor can find much of interest in the parallels between the events and characters in the plays and the famous players of Shakespeare's social and political scene. Every actor seeks to bring flesh and blood and breath to the plays that have come down to us as Shakespeare's. It really doesn't matter to an actor if Shakespeare intended Polonius to be a satire of Cecil or a satire of a generic type of political advisor given to long-winded speeches and spying on his betters. What matters to an actor is that the possibility that Cecil was the model for Polonius opens up a line of inquiry that might bear rich fruit in the playing of the role.

We would think nothing of this if the play and the reflection were modern. For example, imagine that you have been offered a supporting role in a contemporary drama. Someone mentions, in passing, that your character bears a remarkable similarity to one of Richard Nixon's advisors. There is no way of knowing if the playwright intended this or if the reflection is a generic or specific one: your character could be any ruthless, pragmatic, amoral advisor to any president. There are many to choose from, and it is, after all, something of a stereotypical character.

However, a quick look at some of the information available about Nixon's advisors reveals some very interesting details that bring the character alive for you. Suddenly the role no longer feels like an exercise in playing a stereotype, but has become an opportunity to bring to life and try to make sense of a very real person. In addition, some of the information you have uncovered helps to explain the actions of the character in the play. It is not so much that you were puzzled before, but that now, having read about Nixon's advisors, you have answers to questions you had never even thought to ask. No one will know what you have used to ground your work on the role in the complexities of real life, but you and others will know that the grounding has taken place.

Actors who do not find historical information of any assistance in the development of character quite rightly observe that sufficient riches for character development can be found in the text of the play. Indeed, there is a case to be made about the extraneous quality of some of this factual information. The bottom line is this: if knowing about Cecil would help you to play Polonius, then you need to get your hands on some information about him as quickly and efficiently as possible. For some actors, simply knowing that a real person might have been in Shakespeare's mind when the play was written is all that is needed to keep them honest and specific in their approach to characterization.

REFLECTIONS IN A MIRROR

Scholars have long suggested that the Elizabethan mind was trained to identify correspondences. In church, they heard sermons pointing out how every aspect of the natural world reflects a specific order of importance as mandated by God. In the works of poets and dramatists, they heard metaphors that built upon these correspondences. The stability of the entire kingdom was said to depend upon the familiar system inherited from medieval times. E.M.W. Till-yard's excellent introduction in *The Elizabethan World Picture* to what is called "the great chain of being" suggests just how complex and coherent this system of correspondences had been, though it was all being challenged during Shakespeare's lifetime. In *Troilus and Cressida* Shakespeare has Ulysses, that most wily and thoughtful of counsellors, give voice to the importance of hierarchy in warding off chaos:

> The heavens themselves, the Planets, and this Centre,
> Observe degree, priority, and place,
> Insisture, course, proportion, season, form,
> Office, and custom, in all line of order:
> And therefore is the glorious Planet Sol
> In noble eminence enthroned and sphered
> Amidst the other, whose medicinable eye
> Corrects the ill Aspects of Planets evil,
> And posts like the Commandment of a King,
> Sans check, to good and bad. But when the Planets
> In evil mixture to disorder wander,
> What Plagues, and what portents, what mutiny?
> What raging of the Sea? shaking of Earth?
> Commotion in the Winds? Frights, changes, horrors,
> Divert, and crack, rend and deracinate
> The unity, and married calm of States
> Quite from their fixture? [1.3.85]

In addition to answering questions about the hierarchies at work in Shakespeare's England, the work of Tillyard and others in this field clarifies an important element at work in the creation of characters in the plays. Quite simply, every character can be assumed to serve as some sort of reflection, because everything created and imagined exists as a reflection of whatever link in the chain it corresponds to.

With this sort of habit of mind widely shared among his actors and audience, Shakespeare could construct striking and three-dimensional characters with a few significant details that invited the consideration of correspondences. He did not have to create a detailed satire in order to suggest a well-known and possibly powerful and thus dangerous figure. He could draw upon the profound complexity of a public figure in the service of his play without having to expend stage time showing more than one striking correspondence.

Sadly, this creates a real challenge for the modern actor, who might not spot the parallel between a character and a possible corresponding figure and so might miss out on the wealth of information upon which the first actors and audience could draw. Now that scholarly editors regularly avoid mentioning all but the most obvious contemporary allusions, an actor needs to know something about all of the major players on the great stage of Shakespeare's world.

THE GLASS OF FASHION

He was the Mark, and Glass, Copy and Book,
That fashioned others.

Lady Percy [*2HIV* 2.3.31]

Who were the shining lights of Shakespeare's age, the models for excellence and achievement? How did their public activities and reputations epitomize the values of the day? Were they models for any of Shakespeare's characters?

Historians have generated answers to the first two questions, and Shakespearean scholars have enjoyed debating answers to the third. Actors who are interested in historical biography as grist for the mill of creative character development will find assorted riches in the portraits of those individuals who were, in their day, the glass of fashion, the observed of all observers. We have long been fascinated with the big names of early modern England: Elizabeth herself; Robert Dudley, her longtime favorite later raised to the highest level of the nobility as the earl of Leicester; Robert Devereux, the doomed earl of Essex who became her favorite in the last years of her life; and his and Shakespeare's own patron, Henry Wriothesley, earl of Southampton, a follower of the doomed Essex who was pardoned and became a favorite of the bisexual James.

Shakespeare's Patron

There is plenty of evidence to suggest that Shakespeare had firsthand encounters with the nobility of England, though probably not to the extent that fictional treatments of his life would like to suggest. Whatever his relationship might have been with Southampton, Shakespeare's encounter with the young earl and his family and friends would have provided him with models for the many young gallants who feature in his plays. G.P.V. Akrigg in *Shakespeare and the Earl of Southampton* finds echoes of the Shakespeare/Southampton connection in several of the plays. For example, he argues that the two characters named Antonio, each of whom is presented in a passionate friendship with a young man (Sebastian in *Twelfth Night* and Bassanio in *The Merchant of Venice*), correspond to Shakespeare, noting in particular the difference in class and the loaning of money. Evidently, at the time *The Merchant of Venice* was written, Southampton was so deeply in debt that he was forced to turn the management of his estate over to his attorneys. Akrigg goes so far as to speculate that Southampton's advisors would have recommended his pursuit of a lovely heiress, just as Bassanio pursues Portia.

The first part of Akrigg's book is a straightforward biography of Southampton, which is worth reading for any actor playing one of Shakespeare's young gallants, even if the direct correspondences of the playwright and the patron to the various male characters in the plays remains an unprovable game of "spot the reflection." A.L. Rowse in *Shakespeare's Southampton, Patron of Virginia* comes to the same sort of conclusion as Akrigg: that Southampton's shadow can be spotted in the majority of the plays.

Glorious and Infamous

In 1904 Sir Sidney Lee published a book entitled *Great Englishmen of the Sixteenth Century*, in which grouping he included Sir Thomas More, Sir Philip Sidney, Sir Walter Raleigh, Edmund Spenser, Francis Bacon, and William Shakespeare. An actor will want to roam further afield to include individuals who do not happen to be English and male, as well as broadening the definition of "great" to include those who achieved prominence in less admirable fields of endeavor. We might call this collection of individuals the mirrors of the age.

Sir Thomas More and *The Winter's Tale*

Many of the great molders of form for Shakespeare and his fellow actors were, like Sir Thomas More, already the stuff of history and of popular plays. More's life was problematical for an Elizabethan audience: admired for his erudition and political writings, but distrusted for his unwavering adherence to the supremacy of Rome in matters of faith, he was held up by more than one faction as the model of all that is heinous or honorable. Since the outcome of the political/religious question over which he lost his head, the right of the king of England to name himself head of the Church in and of England, was inextricably tied up with the question of the legitimacy of Elizabeth and so her right to the throne, it is surprising to discover a play in which he is the title character, about his rise from humble beginnings as sheriff of London to the lord high chancellor of England and his subsequent fall from favor, his trial, and his execution. *A Man for All Seasons* this old play is not, being the result of multiple writers, one of whom was Shakespeare himself, and harshly censored by the authorities.

Can we find Sir Thomas More–like characters in Shakespeare's plays? I have always wondered about Camillo, the advisor of the jealous and paranoid Leontes in *The Winter's Tale*. We know very little about this supporting character, though he has a significant function in the plot. If, however, More were a possible source of the reflection, then the biography of one conveniently fills in the gap of the other.

A few of the correspondences line up strikingly: Camillo is the trusted confidant of a king who puts his queen on public trial for adultery. Camillo must choose between his loyalty to his monarch and his personal honor. More made just such a choice, in favor of private belief over loyal service, and King Henry executed not one but two wives for adultery. Although the situation in *The*

Winter's Tale does not match More's actual experience, this similarity is fascinating.

The option of "trying on for size" the reflection of Sir Thomas More while exploring Camillo in rehearsal allows the actor the means of entering the fictional events of the play with one particular supposition: how would someone like More have felt about all this? Given how far he has risen in the king's service, consider how much his voluntary exile hurts. Given his international reputation as the epitome of a saintly and brilliant counsellor, consider how automatic is the trust of others and how painful is the need to choose between two wrongs. Given that this is the author of *Utopia*, how would he view the idyllic pastoral scene in the second half of the play?

I would not recommend too tightly constructed a connection between Camillo and More, for his is just one of the reflections available. Another candidate, whose biography leads the actor in quite a different direction and one equally exciting for the play, is Francis Walsingham, Elizabeth's infamous spy master, brilliant diplomat, and trusted counsellor, who rose from humble beginnings as the son of a lawyer to Elizabeth's secretary of state. His daughter Frances made him the father-in-law of two glorious young men each in his way a mirror of the age, Sir Philip Sidney and Robert Devereux. Walsingham is cast in quite a different mold than More, and his reflection brings to Camillo all of the capacities of the assassin and undercover agent. It makes sense of Leontes' asking him to murder the visiting king of Bohemia and explains Camillo's ability to call upon extensive resources whenever escape plans are required. These darker character traits are just as exciting to explore as the weighty honor and intellect of the first correspondence.

It does not matter to us whether Shakespeare intended this or any other direct reflection of any specific royal counsellor. There is nothing to be gained by trying to prove any of these correspondences, and thank goodness, as actors, we are not required to provide footnotes. In fact, we are not required to pursue any of these connections unless the calibre of the rehearsal process is enhanced by such explorations. If, however, you are drawn to this sort of "trying on" of possible reflections in pursuit of a firm grounding in particular for the supporting characters, then do so wholeheartedly, knowing that your impulses echo those of Shakespeare and his contemporaries.

Sir Philip Sidney

Sir Philip Sidney died in 1586, and the telling of his final days makes a powerful story. He left behind letters as well as his great works of poetry, and a great deal is known about his life. For Shakespeare's contemporaries, he came to be the epitome of great potential cut short in its prime, as well as the living embodiment of what might be called "the Renaissance man," excelling equally in his artistic and his athletic pursuits, truly "the Courtiers, Soldiers, Scholars: Eye, tongue, sword" [*Hamlet* 3.1.151].

For an actor working on one of Shakespeare's brilliant and doomed young men, it is tempting to seek the resonation between fictional character and the real young man who made such an impression on his age. Such an actor might enjoy reading a scholarly biography that captures the drama of Sidney's life, as does Katherine Duncan-Jones in *Sir Philip Sidney, Courtier Poet.* He would probably skip over the analysis of Sidney's great poetic masterpieces, which is Duncan-Jones's primary focus, and go directly for the biographical details that contribute to our understanding of this individual.

Seeking Historical Solutions to Puzzling Characters

Is there any benefit to an actor in pursuing these connections between the fictional and the famous, other than an enrichment of one's individual creative explorations? For the most part, I would have to confess that the reflections are intriguing but not central to our capacity to create exciting theatre, with one important exception, and that is in connection with the character of Bertram in *All's Well That Ends Well.* Rather than proving the rule, I would argue that this exception demonstrates the validity of seeking connections as part of our work on Shakespeare. While it is tempting to proclaim the universality of these plays and thereby escape responsibility for any research, these plays were written in a very specific time and were constructed to be effective within a very specific set of conventions and cultural associations. Some aspects of the plays simply do not work unless we can rediscover and transmit for today's audiences that which allowed Shakespeare's audiences to enjoy the plays.

The trouble with Bertram is that he is, on the page, an entirely unappealing character. It is almost impossible for a modern audience, or even an acting company, to warm to this young man. Look what he does to Helena, the sweet young doctor's daughter who loves him so truly. When, as a reward for curing the king of France, she is invited to choose any young noble of the court as her husband, and she chooses Bertram, he rejects her outright and has to be forced to marry her. He in turn refuses to honor his duties as a husband, clearly setting up the conditions for an annulment as soon as such legal action would be politically expedient. Then he takes off for the foreign wars, where he tries to talk his way into the bed of a sweet young thing named Diana. When he hears that Helena has died, he races back to court in order to offer his hand for the daughter of the king's counsellor, this being the sort of expedient marriage that would best advance his political and economic standing.

The real problem with Bertram is what his nastiness does to our feelings about Helena. Here is this feisty, articulate, endearing young woman who insists on pursuing this unpleasant young man, sacrificing her honor and our respect in the process. It is very difficult to be pleased at the "happy" ending; cynical productions display, in the final reunion of the miraculously restored and pregnant Helena with her suddenly loving Bertram, the prediction that this will be a desperately unhappy marriage.

If Bertram is judged by our standards, then the reflections we place upon him do neither protagonist much credit. If, however, we place an Elizabethan mirror to the young man, we might stand a chance of understanding Helena's obsession. Forgiveness, or even admiration, might well follow such empathy.

There are several models for young Bertram. In his participation in the foreign wars he resembles Sir Philip Sidney. This sheds an entirely new light upon Bertram. Suddenly, his careful consideration of a politically motivated marriage becomes the only unpleasant aspect of the poet-courtier-warrior ideal. No wonder Helena is willing to journey so far and undertake so much for love of him. She exhibits that familiar enthrallment given voice by Emilia as she and Desdemona gossip about Lodovico, who is evidently a very handsome fellow: "I know a Lady in Venice would have walked barefoot to Palestine for a touch of his nether lip" [*Othello* 4.3.38].

Another possible reflection, and one that pleases those who believe that "Shakespeare" was a pseudonym for Edward de Vere, the earl of Oxford, can be spotted in that man's life story. Immediately after his forced marriage, Bertram announces his plans by saying,

> I'll send her to my house,
> Acquaint my mother with my hate to her,
> And wherefore I am fled: Write to the King
> That which I durst not speak. His present gift
> Shall furnish me to those Italian fields
> Where noble fellows strike: War is no strife
> To the dark house, and the detested wife. [2.3.286]

The first audience for this play had a contemporary scandal with which to compare this abrupt development in the plot. The earl of Oxford was the ward of Cecil, Lord Burghley, who forced a match between de Vere and his daughter Anne, and the earl deserted his young wife soon after. He also is thought to have been the father of the illegitimate son of Anne Vavasour, a lady of the queen's bedchamber. All this took place in 1575–80; scholars date *All's Well That Ends Well* to 1602, though some feel that it was written as early as 1594. The fact that Southampton, Shakespeare's patron, was also being urged into marriage with Cecil's granddaughter (and Oxford's daughter) Elizabeth during the 1590s simply brought back into everyone's mind the earlier arranged marriage and the unhappy events that followed. Southampton, however, was more successful in resisting and eventually married the pregnant Elizabeth Vernon, another of the queen's favorites.

We will never know if aristocratic members of the audience had a bit of a chuckle when they figured out the similarities between fiction and fact; it might even be that the actor playing the role dressed, spoke, and moved in a manner to echo Southampton. Modern audiences won't get the joke, even if costume and hair design for Bertram were created from one of the portraits of the young earl. Political satire does not travel well, so even if we knew for sure that was Shakespeare's intention, we have no interest in playing Bertram in order to comment on Southampton or Oxford, or even to summon the ghost of the glorious Sidney.

There is, however, one very significant insight that these reflections afford, and that is a careful consideration of the marriage of Bertram from the perspective of a member of the English aristocracy. In the final scene of *All's Well That Ends Well*, we have an enactment of the delicate negotiations between an heir to a great estate and a senior counsellor of the court, supervised by the king himself, as Bertram is matched to Lafew's daughter following the supposed death of his first and unloved wife Helena. To our modern eye this scene seems the utmost of tackiness. The king, Lafew, and Bertram speak at some length about their love for the dead Helena, but the point of the interview is the formal restoration of Bertram to the king's favor and the settling of the marriage arrangements with Lafew's daughter. When Helena appears and her tricks and stratagems are revealed, she wins Bertram and the alternative match is forgotten.

This is a romantic comedy, and love overcomes the greatest odds. However, the resistance to the happy ending comes not from the disinterest of Bertram, but the great class divide between the two lovers. This is made clear earlier in the play, when Bertram rejects Helena. It does not matter that Helena has saved the king's life, that he has given her great dowries, and that to deny her as a wife is to defy the king's direct command. Bertram is appalled at her class, the fact that she is a poor physician's daughter. Her blood would corrupt his, which is that of one of the great noble houses of the land. But the king responds that he can make her his equal in nobility and wealth.

Poor Helena is an almost mute witness to the debate between the king and Bertram, which mirrors the tension in the aristocracy of Shakespeare's day. Alongside the traditional noble families were those whose wealth and coats of arms were the gift of one or another of the monarchs of the age. Favorites could find themselves empowered over the heads of men and women who could trace their lineage to a far older line of kings. Southampton, Shakespeare's patron, would have been a simple knight's son if his grandfather had not assisted Henry VIII in his quest for various new wives. And who was Cecil before he did such service for Elizabeth?

The blending of old and new bloodlines in the aristocracy was not a symptom of the emergence of democratic sensibilities. The divide between even the lower levels of the aristocracy and the general public was still so extreme that only the very rare and almost magical prowess of extraordinary individuals like Cecil or Helena could transcend it. But once one was ennobled, there was a difference only in degree, not in kind, between old and new aristocrat. Bertram is foolish to reject Helena because a few weeks ago she was a poor physician's daughter; the second she is made his equal in wealth and title, she is an appropriate wife for him to take.

This does not make it any less humiliating for Helena, but it does open the door to a more satisfying ending. Bertram is rejecting the king's interference in inherited status and the marriage market wherein the nobility matches up in self-selected old or new blendings of noble bloodlines. His refusal of Helena as a bedmate is a rebellion against this interference; once he has grown up a little in the foreign wars and has realized that he wants and needs to be reconciled back into the hierarchy of the king's circle, the only impediment to forming a strong alliance with the king's new favorite is removed. As a more mature young noble, he knows that he needs to ally himself through marriage to the center of power, either through Helena to the king or through Lafew's daughter to Lafew to the king. The miraculous return of Helena occurs at the perfect time when Bertram, like the earl of Southampton, realizes that personal and political need not be at odds, and that a successful married relationship can be achieved within the existing pattern of privilege and favoritism.

Reflections of a Woman's Face

Unlike scholars of an early time, who tended to view history as the possession of the notable men of any given age, modern actors are free to partake of the exciting developments in recovering the stories of women. Of necessity, these are often women of the noble classes, the only ones to leave even a partial record of their existence. For insight into the lives of less-well-connected women, we must turn to the broad social histories described in the previous chapter.

But for anyone working on, for example, the countess of Rossillion in *All's Well That Ends Well* or Viola in *Twelfth Night*, seeking an Elizabethan model of a woman of intelligence, sensitivity, and temporal power, biographies of such feminine luminaries as Mary Sidney will provide much inspiration. Margaret Hannay's biography *Philip's Phoenix* untangles the web of interfamily connections, which is of use in understanding the peerage of Elizabeth's court, and provides all you need to know about the complex political maneuverings among the most powerful in the land.

For an introduction to some of the potential models for everyone from Goneril to Lady Macbeth, you might want to look at Pearl Hogrefe's collection *Women of Action in Tudor England*. Here you will find, in addition to Queen Elizabeth herself, historical figures such as Catherine Parr, Catherine of Aragon, and Margaret Beaufort, as well as some wives of powerful and influential men like Lord Burghley and Francis Bacon. Any one of Hogrefe's sketches tells a great story, but my favorite is the chapter on Bess of Hardwick, who married four times, each of them a step up the ladder until the last liaison made her a countess and allowed her to arrange the marriage of her daughter Mary to Charles Stuart which placed her sufficiently high up to maneuver over the years in a failed attempt to place her granddaughter Arabella Stuart on the throne. Hogrefe paints the picture of a complex woman, capable of great love and loyalty, even as she charts Bess's climb from genteel poverty to affluence and influence.

Some of the same material is contained in *Tudor Women*, an earlier book by the same author, but one that casts a wider net in order to include women outside the nobility. The result is a broader and more general study, in which you will find what was "normal" for women and then the many examples of women who did something differently. It may come as a surprise after reading Shakespeare's plays, where the women's experiences tend to be as limited as the number and acting abilities of the boys who played the roles, to learn that there were women in business, women in office, women patrons and writers, and women who ran large estates for their absent husbands or on behalf of their young sons. In the Countess Olivia of *Twelfth Night* we have just such a capable woman. Her brother and father dead, she is surrounded by her retainers and a foolish drunken kinsman, Sir Toby, who is more in need of her care and guidance than capable of assisting her in running her estate. Although she does some unexpected things, being in love, we must conclude, with Sebastian, that she is not insane, for

> if 'twere so,
> She could not sway her house, command her followers,
> Take, and give back affairs, and their dispatch,
> With such a smooth, discreet, and stable bearing
> As I perceive she does. [4.3.16]

Although we can see reflections of several powerful noblewomen in Olivia, the specifics of her situation echo the woman who gave her name to the age. This mysterious, complex, fascinating individual has been the subject of so many biographies, to say nothing of the movies and television shows, that hers is the face most likely to be spotted in the mirror.

Elizabeth

Queen Elizabeth was in the last years of her reign when Shakespeare exploded onto the theatrical scene in London, and her successor James came to the throne in time to ensure that all of Shakespeare's mature works could be claimed for Jacobean studies. But wherever Shakespeare is placed by historians, it is clear that the powerful iconography developed by the last Tudor monarch influenced Shakespeare and his contemporaries long after the remarkable woman was gone from the scene.

Thus it can often vitalize an actor's work on a role to consider just which legend about the infamous Elizabeth his or her character might reflect. For example, we happen to know that Elizabeth in a rage broke the finger of one of her waiting gentlewomen. What are we to make of the fact that Cleopatra does the same thing? We happen to know that *A Hundred Merry Tales* was reputed to be a publication that won Elizabeth's favor; how does that affect our appreciation of Beatrice, who is also associated with that book and, like Elizabeth, resists society's agenda of marriage as the natural state for women?

We can find striking similarities between Portia and Elizabeth, two women who inherited immense estates and a complex barrier to romance in the dead hand of a father. If we consider Elizabeth's immense learning and her easy mastery of the language of diplomacy and the council chamber, we might find more credible Portia's excellence in the courtroom. Although Elizabeth was not in fact as successful as Portia in steering a middle ground between justice and the good of the state, she presented a Portia-like attitude as the ideal toward which she aspired.

There are many excellent biographies available for anyone interested in Elizabeth's life. My personal favorites have been written by Alison Plowden, whose knowledge is scholarly in breadth but entirely accessible in presentation. In addition to *Young Elizabeth* and *Elizabeth Regina*, I enjoyed *The House of Tudor* for the overview it provides. Christopher Hebbert's *The Virgin Queen* is also a book I have found useful.

Fortunately for scholars, and actors, a great number of official and personal documents have survived. Elizabeth's letters are readily available, for example in the selection edited by G. B. Harris, as are transcripts of many of her speeches. Maria Perry has put together an excellent collection in *The Word of a Prince: A Life of Elizabeth I from Contemporary Documents*. It is a wonderful experience to read something that Elizabeth wrote when she was just eleven years old. Marc Shell's edition of *Elizabeth's Glass* reproduces photographs of the little girl's handwriting, as well as a modern-spelling edition of Elizabeth's translation of "The Glass of the Sinful Soul," plus a very important commentary that sets this artifact into the larger context of social and political forces at work in Shakespeare's England.

Arabella Stuart and As You Like It

During a rehearsal of the early scenes of *As You Like It*, the actresses playing Celia and Rosalind might want to consider the story of Arabella Stuart, another shadow who can provide a third dimension to the conundrum facing Rosalind and her cousin.

Arabella Stuart's mother was another granddaughter of Henry VII, along with Elizabeth and Mary, Queen of Scots, Arabella's aunt. For anyone who considered Elizabeth illegitimate, a not unreasonable assumption given that her father's first wife was still alive when she was born, and her parents were only able to marry because her father made himself head of the Church of England and gave himself a divorce, these cousins had a better claim to the throne once Henry's only legitimate children, Edward and Mary, had ruled and died.

Elizabeth was forty-two when Arabella was born. Six years later Arabella was an orphan and the most marriageable young noblewoman of Europe. She was educated to rule, and by the time she was a young woman, she was determined to rule herself, in particular in matters of love. Elizabeth, and later

James, were just as determined that she be barred from any marriage that increased her likelihood of proving a threat.

The romantic events that followed occurred after *As You Like It*, but they included the use of men's clothing to make an escape from near imprisonment, and incarceration and insanity, followed by death, when her plans to marry her beloved were thwarted. As an added bonus, we can read many of the letters she wrote during the long years of her difficult life as a close cousin to the reigning monarch. As with all reproductions, these are a wonderful source of language for reading aloud just to get the sounds and rhythms into the inner ear. Sara Jayne Steen's edition of *The Letters of Lady Arbella Stuart* is beautifully laid out with modern lettering and period spelling, and the introduction that accompanies the letters is a detailed and fascinating retelling of the story of this remarkable woman's life. David Durant's *Arbella Stuart* is a more detailed biography; he, like Steen, uses her official name in his title but the more affectionate and familiar name in telling her story, a fitting reflection of the contradictions in the life of this unfortunate woman.

Arabella's father was the younger brother of that Henry Stuart, Lord Darnley, who married Mary Queen of Scots and fathered James, who became king of England. James and Arabella as first cousins therefore shared the same claim to the throne of England through their paternal grandmother, who was the daughter of Henry VIII's older sister Margaret by her second husband. Arabella married, against James's wishes, another direct heir to the throne, this time through Henry's younger sister Mary, whose second marriage produced two daughters, the elder of whom allowed her daughter Jane to be placed upon the throne as a Protestant alternative to Mary, daughter of Henry VIII, from which high place she was removed a few days later, followed by imprisonment and execution. Her younger sister, Catherine, formed an illegal relationship that produced two sons, the elder of whom in turn produced three sons who survived to adulthood, the eldest of whom formed the unlucky relationship with Arabella. At the time of their marriage, they were no longer well positioned to steal the throne from James, who had three healthy adult children to follow him onto the throne of England. That did not stop James, like the duke in *As You Like It*, from fearing Arabella's potential as a lodestone for rebellion.

Sir Walter Raleigh and *Measure for Measure*

Returning to the list of great names provided by Sir Sidney Lee, we encounter that most romantic of figures, whose placing of a cloak over a mud puddle has come down to us as one of the more enduring images of Elizabeth and her courtiers. How might the glorious Sir Walter Raleigh illuminate characters and events in Shakespeare's fictional worlds?

Modern actors struggle with the strange manipulations of the disguised duke in *Measure for Measure*, who seems to toy with Isabella's sanity by allowing her to believe that her brother has been executed. Compare that manipulation with James I's of Sir Walter Raleigh: having been found guilty of an attempted assassination of James, Raleigh and his confederates were sentenced to the grisly death promised all traitors. On the day of the execution, Raleigh was made to stand at a window overlooking the scaffold to watch the execution of Sir Griffin Markham, Lord Grey, and Lord Cobham, the chief conspirators who had planned to place Arabella Stuart on the throne. James arranged for each to be brought to the scaffold alone, given an opportunity to make a farewell speech, say the appropriate prayers, and prepare to be beheaded, an adjustment made to the more extreme sentence suffered by the nonaristocratic conspirators. Markham, who went first, was told at the very moment of execution to return for further meditation. Lord Grey, after his fiery speech, was informed that the order of execution had been changed and that he would have to wait an hour. The same trick was played on Lord Cobham, and then these three were brought together on the scaffold each stunned to see the others still alive. Only then did the sheriff announce that the king wished to demonstrate his mercy. The impact of this drama was undercut by the holding up of the head of Cobham's younger brother, who had been executed the day before. Raleigh had to wait until the next day to learn that he too had received the same demonstration of mercy. He spent the next thirteen years in the Tower of London, his death sentence not commuted, but merely suspended, and when he again came into disfavor in 1618, it was revived and he was executed.

Actors considering the role of Claudio, who is condemned to death in *Measure for Measure* for the pregnancy of his fiancée Juliet, might want to contemplate another interesting element of Raleigh's life story: his relationship with Bess Throckmorton. When her pregnancy could no longer be hidden, both she and Raleigh, the father of her child, were thrown into the Tower under sentence of treason, for which the penalty was death. No one expected Raleigh to get out of that situation alive. Such was his charm, however, that he survived not only this but a subsequent thirteen-year imprisonment under James. He was finally executed for treason on a trumped-up charge in 1618. For a scholarly biography of this fascinating Renaissance man, I recommend Stephen J. Greenblatt's *Sir Walter Raleigh*. A. L. Rowse's *Raleigh and the Throckmortons* is an older and lighter work, and great fun to read.

Robin Hood

A less dangerous subject for popular drama was *The Death of Robert, Earl of Huntington*, also by Anthony Munday, who is considered the primary author of the Thomas More play. Thanks to the enduring appeal of the outlaw of Sherwood Forest, for ballad writers and filmmakers alike, a modern actor can count on his audience having a vivid set of images upon which to draw, cued by the Third Outlaw in *The Two Gentlemen of Verona* when he delivers his lines:

By the bare scalp of Robin Hoods fat Friar,
This fellow were a King, for our wild faction. [4.1.36]

When the exiled Valentine encounters these forest-dwelling outlaws, they give
him a choice: death or

Say ay, and be the captain of us all:
We'll do thee homage, and be ruled by thee,
Love thee, as our Commander, and our King. [4.1.63]

Valentine wisely takes the second choice and plays Robin Hood to this collection of thieves and murderers, placing upon them a noble restriction:

I take your offer, and will live with you,
Provided that you do no outrages
On silly women, or poor passengers. [4.1.68]

The outlaws readily agree, because, as one says, "We detest such vile base
practises."

Another group of foresters compared directly to Robin Hood lives in the
forest of Arden; this is the exiled Duke Senior and his followers of *As You Like
It*, described by Charles in the first scene of the play:

They say he is already in the Forest of Arden, and a many merry men with him; and
there they live like the old Robin Hood of England: they say many young Gentlemen
flock to him every day, and fleet the time carelessly as they did in the golden world.
[1.1.114]

The familiarity of these allusions is potentially misleading if the actor is not
careful to place the legend of Robin Hood into the historical context; the
embroidery added to the original story by each generation can shift the tone
of the allusion quite radically. Today the heroic self-sacrificing earl is nearly
overshadowed by the tongue-in-cheek vision of men in tights frolicking in
improbable greenery; it appears from these examples that Shakespeare also
had a mixture of admirable and irreverent images upon which to draw.

Fortunately for the modern actor, Robin Hood has proven a subject of
interest to just the sort of scholar most appreciated in our search for the Shakespearean context of the words we might have to say or hear on stage in one
of these plays. For example, J. C. Holt's *Robin Hood* provides us not only the
historical substance of the legend, but also an excellent seventh chapter entitled
"The Later Tradition," in which he brings us forward from medieval England
through Shakespeare's time up to the great romantic traditions of the beginning
of the nineteenth century. Thanks are owed to Holt for a well-researched book
that is also a good read.

A more traditional scholarly approach is taken by Maurice Keen in *The*

Outlaws of Medieval Legend. This book is most useful for its first chapter, which explains the significance of the term "greenwood" in outlaw legends, of some interest to those who sing "Under the Greenwood Tree" in the forest of Arden. Keen also discusses the "real" Robin Hood and the history of outlaws, which will provide the outlaws of *The Two Gentlemen of Verona* with some real-life models.

USING THE PAST TO REFLECT THE PRESENT

> And now I will unclasp a Secret book,
> And to your quick-conceiving Discontents
> I'll read you Matter deep and dangerous.
>
> Worcester [*1HIV* 1.3.188]

On the eve of the ill-fated rebellion led by the earl of Essex, one of the conspirators hired Shakespeare's company to perform *Richard II*, evidently hoping that the portrayal of the deposition of that other flawed and poorly advised monarch would arouse the people in support of the forceful removal of the aged Elizabeth's counsellors in favor of Essex. When the rebellion had collapsed, the actors who had been contacted by the conspirators were hauled in for questioning. Fortunately, they were able to convince the authorities that they had been innocent of any direct involvement. After it was all over, Elizabeth is said to have observed to one of her courtiers, "I am Richard II, know ye not that?"

The connections that the conspirators and Elizabeth were prepared to make between the present and the past suggest that these correspondences were understood to be ever present. Richard and Elizabeth are so little alike that we do not spot the resemblance, as we are happy to do when we consider Cleopatra or Portia. What is at work here is a continuum that links all kings. A vivid portrait of the flaws of any king was therefore, by extension, an opportunity for a piercing and immediately relevant political commentary on the current ruling monarch.

Tudor History

There is another important reason why any examination of English history was politically dangerous: the Tudor claim to the throne was so weak as to make a mockery of either primogeniture (direct inheritance from oldest son to oldest son) or the blood of kings. Elizabeth's grandfather was, before he defeated Richard III at Bosworth Field, simply the earl of Richmond. He had absolutely no claim to the throne. Through his mother he could trace his family back to John of Gaunt, the third son of the powerful Edward III, but only through the illegitimate children Gaunt had with his mistress Katharine

Swynford. As a favor to his uncle, Richard II had retroactively conferred legitimacy upon these children, but only on the condition that they and their descendants would never be in line for the throne. His father Edmund Tudor was the son of Owen, a handsome Welshman who had served in the personal court of Henry V. When that king died, his widow, Katherine of Valois, fell in love with her husband's squire. There were rumors that this relationship, too, was never legalized.

Two factors played into Richmond's hands. He stepped forward at a time when there were no other male contenders to the throne left standing, following the various murders and battle deaths among the legitimate grandsons of Edward III. He also followed a relatively unpopular king and so was able to present himself, like Henry IV, as the restorer of peace and good government. He quickly solidified his position by marrying Elizabeth of York and presenting this as the union of the red and white roses; he took this as the Tudor crest.

For all the turmoil of the Tudor dynasty, England did emerge from a medieval world into the Renaissance during their rule. One component of the transformation of England was the acquisition of a vital literature in the native language, composed of translations of the classical works and also histories of the people of the land. As these were commissioned by the monarchy, it is only natural that they would shape the story of England to suit the propaganda that justified Richmond's stealing the throne. Under this perspective, the English people sinned in deposing Richard II and were subsequently punished by the civil wars until such time as God's instrument brought peace by destroying the most heinous of kings, Richard III.

There are many books by scholars who specialize in the history plays, in any one of which you are sure to find a thoughtful discussion of how Shakespeare absorbed and challenged the prevailing views of recent history, as well as some hints as to why he wrote so many histories early in his career and then turned his attention to what we call his mature tragedies and comedies. Two of my favorites are John Wilders's *The Lost Garden,* which places the plays within an Elizabethan sense of human history as divine history, and Alexander Leggatt's *Shakespeare's Political Drama,* which demonstrates how the way history is told reflects the political and social issues of the people telling and listening to the stories. Graham Holderness's *Shakespeare's History* is the best exploration of how history is created and reflected in the plays.

An actor in the history plays is not obliged to understand the Tudor view of English history, because the character he plays is highly unlikely to view the events of the play he is in from that perspective, unless, like the visionary prelate the bishop of Carlisle in *Richard II* he foresees the future and warns:

And if you Crown him, let me prophesy,
The blood of English shall manure the ground,
And future Ages groan for this foul Act.
Peace shall go sleep with Turks and Infidels,

And in this Seat of Peace, tumultuous Wars
Shall Kin with Kin, and Kind with Kind confound.
Disorder, Horror, Fear, and Mutiny
Shall here inhabit, and this Land be called
The field of Golgotha, and dead mens Skulls.
Oh, if you rear this House, against this House
It will the woefullest Division prove,
That ever fell upon this cursed Earth.
Prevent it, resist it, let it not be so,
Lest Child, Childs Children cry against you, Woe. [4.1.136]

Most editors lay out the important aspects of how the events of any of the histories were understood to have unfolded. For example, in *Richard III* we find the culmination of God's retribution in the reign of terror under Richard, brought to an end only by the godly victory of the earl of Richmond. The genealogical facts are buried under the dramatic showdown between good and evil. The horror days of the civil war form the subject of the three plays of *Henry VI*; the deposition of Richard is the central action of *Richard II*. The uneasy quiet immediately following the deposition is dramatized in the two plays of *Henry IV*, but only in order to set up the emergence of the hero king in *Henry V*. Clearly, the retribution skips a generation: only Henrys IV and VI endure the horrors described so vividly by Carlisle.

A good sense of genealogy is a basic requirement to follow the crown as it skips from one to another of the grandsons and great-grandsons of Edward III. It is also necessary, in a play like *Richard II*, to have a firm grasp of events that predate the start of the play and were dramatized by one of Shakespeare's contemporaries in an anonymous play called *Thomas of Woodstock*. A copy of this play, published as *The First Part of the Reign of King Richard the Second*, survives, though all that remains of many of the other plays of the London stage is the title; the Malone Society issued a reprint in 1929. Again, most editors provide you with all you need to follow the plot.

What is more difficult to grasp is the manner in which the histories act out a concept of divine retribution. As with other issues of belief, the actor, stepping into the shoes of the character he is playing and seeing the world through those eyes and not his own, needs to prime himself to see the hand of God in the events of the play. Here is Bolingbroke, now on his deathbed, having ruled as the title character in the two plays of *Henry IV*, giving voice to the burden of guilt that he has carried since the death of his cousin Richard:

God knows, my Son,
By what by-paths, and indirect crooked ways
I met this Crown: and I my self know well
How troublesome it sat upon my head. [*2HIV* 4.5.183]

Earlier in their relationship, the poison of guilt and the awareness of the hand of God in patterns of retribution was expressed by the father to his wayward son:

> I know not whether God will have it so,
> For some displeasing service I have done;
> That in his secret Doom, out of my Blood,
> He'll breed Revengement, and a Scourge for me:
> But thou dost in thy passages of Life,
> Make me believe, that thou art only marked
> For the hot vengeance, and the Rod of heaven
> To punish my Mistreadings. [*1HIV* 3.2.4]

The actors entrusted with the roles of this father and son can draw upon universal experiences of tension and bitter love, but they also need to explore the more profound implications expressed in such statements as these. Such explorations can be assisted by the excellent overview offered by Robert Rentoul Reed, Jr., in *Crime and God's Judgment in Shakespeare*, in particular in his second chapter, "The Justice of God: Medieval and Renaissance."

Kingship

Shakespeare performed and wrote in a world ruled by kings and queens. Republican Rome was available as a mythical model for an alternative social order, but in the majority of his plays Shakespeare includes at least one king or queen, or equivalent, as a central or significant player.

In addition to finding out about the two monarchs under whom Shakespeare lived, Elizabeth and James, and the English kings about whom he wrote plays, Henrys IV through VI and VIII, Richards II and III, and John, as well as Lear and Macbeth, it is helpful to have a broader impression of how the concept of kingship was played out in other plays. What are we to make, for example, of the king of France in *All's Well That Ends Well* and Don Pedro in *Much Ado about Nothing?* Where does Theseus from *A Midsummer Night's Dream* fit into the mix? Then there are the usurping brothers of deposed rulers: Antonio and Prospero in *The Tempest* and the two dukes in *As You Like It*.

Sandra Billington's *Mock Kings in Medieval Society and Renaissance Drama* provides a two-part overview of just this topic. In the first section Billington traces the conventions of mock-heroic or satirically villainous kings who appear in folk plays; she concludes this section with an excellent chapter on how the serious concepts surrounding the monarchy were advanced or challenged, upheld or undercut during Shakespeare's lifetime. I would recommend this, the fourth chapter, as an excellent overview of the concepts of kingship reflected in the plays. The second part of the book discusses specific plays; use the index to browse for specific references.

One of the dangers inherent in doing a history play is the misreading of Shakespeare's presentation of the complex social and political function of kingship. Actors quite naturally share the audience's tendency to lump all monarchs into one type of authority and power, while Shakespeare and his contemporaries were well aware of the variations to be found in history and even within the long reign of Elizabeth, who experienced quite a different hold upon her council and courtiers at different times in her forty-five years on the throne. We tend to have only a vague understanding of the limits placed upon royal power, assuming that a king can shout, "Off with his head!" like Richard III or the Queen of Hearts, not realizing the gamble being taken by Richard or Henry V in ordering the summary execution of proven traitors. In the case of Henry V, his words clarify his function as the embodiment of English law, not personal revenge:

> Touching our person, seek we no revenge,
> But we our Kingdoms safety must so tender,
> Whose ruin you have sought, that to her Laws
> We do deliver you. Get you therefore hence,
> (Poor miserable wretches) to your death. [2.2.174]

As for Richard III, a close examination of his elimination of Hastings reveals that he is careful first to have approval from the council, voiced ironically by Hastings himself, to put to death anyone guilty of conspiring to bring about Richard's death by witchcraft. When Hastings questions Richard's evidence and accusation, a reasonable reaction given that the only evidence is a withered arm that Richard has presumably had for years, he leaves himself open to being included in the charge, because one of the two women named is his own mistress. Therefore, when Richard leaves the scene with the tag line "The rest that love me, rise, and follow me" [3.4.79], he sets up a silent moment when, by their actions, the rest of the council vote against Hastings and thus make legitimate his execution.

Another common and very modern misperception has to do with the relative merit of the manipulations of the powerful. We are all too ready to lump all successful politicians in with Richard III and assume that any use of authority is, almost by definition, an abuse of power. There is much in the plays to suggest that Shakespeare, along with many of his contemporaries, was fully prepared to admire even a crafty manipulator like Richard and, when political savvy was combined with personal moral courage, admire a consummate politician like Henry V, who stage-manages the denouncing of his trio of traitors even more brilliantly than Richard gets Hastings.

Playing History

There is a reason why the history plays are not performed as often as the comedies and tragedies, even in England, where one might expect the audience and actors to have a special interest in and comprehension of medieval politics. There is also a reason why, despite the absolute disinterest that most audience members have in the subtleties of regal maneuvers, documented so vividly in these plays, they are still performed, even in North America. The juxtaposition of great swaths of history with complex family relationships that creates this paradoxical antipathy and appeal causes certain difficulties for modern actors cast in major or supporting roles in these plays.

It is all very well for the audience to doze quietly while characters on stage negotiate a complex political accord, waiting for the next moving or hilarious scene wherein appealing characters interact in recognizable relationships. The actors on stage must (*a*) know what they are saying, (*b*) know why their character cares, and (*c*) understand the stakes, all of which requires at a minimum a solid understanding of such nuances as rival claims to the throne, the relative prestige of any members of the peerage on stage, and the political and family alliances that not only predate the events of the play but also continue into Shakespeare's England.

The familiarity of Shakespeare's first audiences and actors with the current holders of the ancient titles and the contemporary undercurrents of political brokering in Elizabeth's palace led Shakespeare to alter historical fact in order to make carefully nuanced commentary on his time and place. There is no surprise in this: that is also what a modern director will attempt if she undertakes a production of one of the histories for today's audience. These plays are mirrors we hold up to examine our own faces, not to teach a lesson in history.

It is tempting, given the limitations of the audience's knowledge or interest and the seductive clarity of the relationships in a history play, for the actors to ignore the history entirely. In this they might be aided by the scalpel of the director, cutting away any lengthy discussions of policy, rivalry, and historical detail and collapsing the various members of the peerage into a clump of lords in attendance at certain scenes to signify that the actions of the central characters also affect the well-being of the kingdom. This, after all, is all that the audience will take away, and, to be honest, they won't appreciate the efforts you might want to make to dwell upon the elements of the plot that are merely political or historical.

Henry V provides us with a good example. A war needs to be fought for the dramatic action of the play to work. We need to know who is the enemy (the French). We don't need to understand any more about the "why" of the war than that Henry feels justified in attacking France, and that there is something personal at work. Hence the majority of productions cut to the bone the opening speeches that set up the complex argument of Henry's right to the throne of France and instead kick off the play with just enough of the court ritual to set up the arrival of the tennis balls and the dauphin's insult of the former playboy and newly reformed Henry.

The actor playing the king might well be better served by such a beginning, finding sufficient fuel for the subsequent rousing calls to battle required of the character in the *mano a mano* rivalry with the Dauphin. The attendant lords either dress the stage to provide sufficient courtly outrage for the opening gambit, or they have a close look at the subtle details Shakespeare injects into the scene. The second is more time-consuming, but makes the playing of the various lords more individual and rewarding. The simple fact of the matter is that Henry's claim to the throne of France is not at all straightforward, and the various members of his court have quite different and selfish reasons for supporting or tempering Henry's reaction to the tennis balls.

Challenges for the Actors

The preparation of one of Shakespeare's history plays sets a special challenge to an actor wishing to take advantage of scholarship. In part, this is the result of the flexibility of which Shakespeare took advantage to reflect his time as well as another time, or at least his time's view of that other time. We then layer on top of that a third and even fourth time period, depending on the interpretation of the individual production. Therefore, for example, we might have need to negotiate Elizabethan and medieval as well as contemporary and, perhaps, Edwardian images in working on a production of *Richard II* costumed as if it were set in the imperial Russian court.

Sometimes the negotiations can be quite tricky. Although the relocation of Shakespeare's court plays to an alternative time and place might benefit a modern audience's understanding of the intersection of personal and public in the life of a monarch, this type of directorial choice can set great problems for actors interested in grounding their characterization in a fact-based sense of time and place. Let us take the example of the court of Nicholas and Alexandra, perhaps the last tragic and glorious imperial court in the modern world. No wonder this is a popular choice for directors and designers looking for a visual and emotional home for Hamlet, or Leontes, or King Lear. But what does such a transportation mean for Ophelia, or Hermione, or Cordelia? Attitudes to the education and social role of women had undergone as significant a change from Shakespeare's time to Victoria's or Alexandra's as from theirs to ours.

Even if we frame our exploration of a history play firmly in the time and place being portrayed, we encounter the complexities of Shakespeare's approach to capturing the reality of another time and place. His Rome or Scotland or medieval and ancient Britain is a curious amalgam of what scholars call anachronisms but what we can recognize as the simple strategies of a popular playwright. If we watch films made in the 1930s and 1940s that are set in far-off times and places and contrast them with contemporary portraits of a similar time and place, we can see immediately how the fashions of history have changed in that short time. We can only see another time through our own eyes, and Shakespeare was no different.

Therefore, how are we to make sense of the duke of Kent, who has a social status and a political function that could not possibly have been in place in ancient Britain, more than 1,100 years before the court of King Arthur? How would Shakespeare's audience have "read" his intervention in the banishment of Cordelia, and later his decision to disguise himself as a blunt-spoken man-for-hire whose status as the king's man makes his nightlong imprisonment in the stocks a grave insult to Lear?

Some sensitivity to the status of the man who was duke of Kent in Shakespeare's time will clarify just what sacrifice the character makes when he becomes the masterless man who returns to serve Lear even after his banishment. But it is clear from many other aspects of the play that the court of King Lear is not meant to be England in the early 1600s. Too many things are said and done that simply could not occur in Shakespeare's world. We are clearly in some other, earlier, less complex time, when England could be divided among three daughters, when five hundred knights was a reasonable personal entourage for a retired king, and when a personal fool accompanied the king into private life.

Shakespeare and his contemporaries wrote a significant number of plays set in England's less distant past, which were immensely popular with his audience but are seldom performed today, in large part because they contain frequent allusions to names and events that would have meant something to the first audience but that make sense only if one has access to the footnotes provided by scholars. *Richard III* is probably the most often performed of the history plays because it is such a rip-roaring melodrama, which can be enjoyed whether one understands the historical stakes or not. The two plays set in the reign of Henry IV are more frequently performed because they contain that supremely theatrical character, Falstaff. The dollops of history seem to get in the way of the story of a man, his father, and his fat friend. *King John*, *Henry VIII*, and the three plays about the life and times of Henry VI contain many striking speeches with which an actor might make a good showing at an audition, even with only the vaguest understanding of the story being dramatized, but are rarely staged.

Richard II will be our prototype for making use of historical research because it is a wonderful play that rewards an understanding of history on the part of the actors with a dynamic theatrical event. This could of course be said of any of the history plays, each of which is potentially a theatrical tour de force, but immensely challenging to the performers and the audience who lack a general knowledge of history.

Fortunately, scholars have prepared the way with a wide variety of studies of the social and political structures, the roles of the monarchy, the nobility, and women, and the clothing, patterns of courtship and courtesy, and education of any given historical period in England and around the world. Many of these studies are intensely academic, filled with the minutiae of evidence that make the case for a modern historian. These are of minimal use to an actor, other than to take advantage of the general introduction or the sweeping conclusions that are most likely to be found in the first and last chapters. Of far more use are the general introductions that do not pretend to argue a specific conclusion of the theory of history, but rather capture the spirit of the times. The inclusion of a significant amount of pictorial evidence is often the best sign that the book will be of real use to inspire a sense of the time and a framework within which the words of the play might be placed.

An Actor's Guide to British History

If you are reading a history play looking for good audition speeches, you will appreciate Isaac Asimov's presentation of the plot and the important historical information, all presented with great sensitivity to the sort of questions that the average reader is likely to ask. Who are the people mentioned? What previous event is being referred to? What is at stake politically at this moment? How does Shakespeare's "take" accord with or contradict the historical facts? Another general overview can be found in Peter Saccio's *Shakespeare's English Kings*, in which each of the history plays receives a chapter detailing what we know from history, what we find in the play, and why the discrepancies have occurred. Also note the most admirable of goals expressed by John Julius Norwich who, in his introduction to *Shakespeare's Kings*, after recommending the scholarly editions of the plays to those wanting to know more about texts, dates, and sources, writes, "My own object has been far more modest: simply to provide lovers of Shakespeare, enthusiastic but cheerfully non-expert, with the sort of single volume that I myself should like to have had, when my eyes were first opened to the splendour of these Histories, more than half a century ago" (10).

What does the actor do with these discrepancies? In *Richard III* we find the horrific scene in which Richard woos Lady Anne literally in the presence of the dead body of a man he has killed. Almost everyone assumes that the coffin contains the body of her dead husband, Edward, Prince of Wales, because he is mentioned so often in the scene and was killed by Richard, he claims, as a result of her beauty. But in fact the body is that of Henry VI, also murdered by Richard but more recently so that Richard's older brother Edward of York can sit on the throne. That murder was dramatized by Shakespeare at the end of the third play about Henry VI as the final in a sequence of butcheries that occurred in the Wars of the Roses.

There is every reason to believe, based upon the historical record, that Richard and Anne formed a love match, and that it was her marriage to the Prince of Wales that was a political maneuver on the part of her father, Warwick the King Maker, who switched sides more than once during the civil war between the rival claimants for England's throne. But none of that has any place in Shakespeare's play or in the wooing scene. It is only with some sense of the larger historical picture that the actors can make sense of this shared litany of dead menfolk:

Queen Margaret: I had an Edward, till a Richard killed him:
I had a Harry, till a Richard killed him:
Thou hadst an Edward, till a Richard killed him:
Thou hadst a Richard, till a Richard killed him.

Duchess of York: I had a Richard too, and thou didst kill him;
I had a Rutland too, thou holp'st to kill him.

Queen Margaret: Thou hadst a Clarence too,
And Richard killed him. [*RIII* 4.4.39]

How unfortunate it is for the modern actor that everyone seems to be named either Edward, Richard, or Henry. Margaret refers to her husband, Henry VI, and her son Edward. She also refers to the two young princes, his nephews, whom Richard murdered in the Tower, named Edward and Richard. The Duchess's Richard is her husband, after whom the monstrous murdering Richard was named.

Richard II places an even more difficult historical puzzle before a modern audience. The first scenes of the play raise the question: Who killed the duke of Gloucester? Bolingbroke accuses Mowbray, his widow the duchess of Gloucester points the finger at Richard the king, and then the issue is dropped as the play moves from the banishment of Bolingbroke to Richard's excursion to Ireland, Bolingbroke's return, and the passing of the crown from Richard to Bolingbroke. Then, to the dismay of all, the issue is raised again, but this time the duke of Aumerle is accused of the murder. When the bishop of Carlisle announces that Mowbray has died, it is clear that we will never know for sure who committed the evil deed.

What is not clear to us, but would be clear to Shakespeare's audience, is that everyone on stage knows very well who killed Gloucester and why. Either the scandal was still remembered, or Shakespeare was counting on his audience's familiarity with the recent hit play about Thomas of Woodstock, because he felt no need to explain. The modern equivalent would be a play containing a debate about "who shot John F. Kennedy" in which much is implied but the matter is ultimately dropped because Oswald is dead, and we will never know.

The historical evidence is fairly straightforward. Thomas of Gloucester was arrested, as were the other leaders of the anti-Richard party. All but Gloucester were tried and executed for treason. Gloucester was arraigned for treason but was sent to Calais, then an English protectorate on the French coast, where he died while under close arrest. It is very unlikely that either Mowbray or Aumerle killed him in person, but very likely that anyone loyal to Richard and close to him, as both these men were, would have (*a*) known what happened to Gloucester, (*b*) concurred as to the necessity of his death by means other than a public treason trial, and (*c*) been privy, directly or indirectly, to the murder plan. It is only by knowing something of the events of the eighteen years referred to by Bolingbroke in his accusation of Mowbray that everyone on stage can hope to participate in the hidden tensions that the scene is clearly intended to dramatize.

Fortunately for the actors, if not for the audience, there are several excellent sources for the sort of historical framework *Richard II* requires from the average actor. In addition to the resource books by Asimov and Saccio, a good general introduction can be found in the series of books on the life and times of each of the English kings published by Weidenfeld and Nicolson. These give the reader not only the narrative of the major events of the reign but an introduction to the social, religious, and political issues of the period. There are also a good collection of pictures in each of the books, which can be connected directly to the events of the play, such as one in Michael Senior's *The Life and Times of Richard II* of the execution of Richard's supporters by Bolingbroke's men (179).

You will be able to find a good discussion of the historical events of Shakespeare's kings, though you may not find it worth your while to plow through the small-print, multifootnote academic studies. A quick look at the index will give you an idea if you can make use of the scholarly book to help you to understand the events of the play. Michael Hicks's *Who's Who in Late Medieval England* is particularly user-friendly. But beware. The search will be complicated by the way names are used in the plays and by the historians. There is the family name, the noble title, Shakespeare's version of the name, the spelling of the name in historical documents used by the scholar, yet these can all be the same person. In *Richard II* there is a supporting character named Sir Stephen Scroop whom scholars like Anthony Tuck call Lescrope. Under the same family name in the index of Tuck's *Richard II and the English Nobility* he is listed alongside Sir William Lescrope, who is also the Earl of Wiltshire. Perhaps Shakespeare did not know this, because when Scroop announces the execution of the Earl of Wiltshire, there is no indication that he is describing the death of his uncle.

In the final scene of the play, The Duke of Northumberland announces that he has sent the heads of four conspirators to London. The first named is Salisbury, who has appeared earlier in the play. Next are named Spencer, Blunt, and Kent. This last-named individual proves to have an interesting and potentially significant relationship to the important characters in the play. Tuck lists him under "H" for Holland, Thomas, Earl of Kent, Duke of Surrey. This instantly clarifies something that might otherwise pass us by: that Kent is the same person as Surrey, who steps forward as a witness to Fitzwater's accusations in the first scene of the fourth act.

Gervase Mathew describes in *The Court of Richard II* the unsuccessful conspirators and what became of them in much more detail than Shakespeare. From this book the actor can learn that Thomas Holland, earl of Kent, had been made duke of Surrey by Richard in 1397, but when Richard lost his throne, Holland lost his dukedom and so reverted to being the earl of Kent.

The same thing happened to Aumerle, whose father the duke of York explains to the duchess:

> Aumerle that was,
> But that is lost, for being Richards Friend.
> And Madam, you must call him Rutland now. [5.2.41]

We also learn that this Thomas Holland, executed by Northumberland, is the nephew of another conspirator, John Holland, duke of Exeter and earl of Huntingdon, who was Richard's half brother, the son of his mother Joan by her second husband, Sir Thomas Holland. It is little wonder, then, that the Holland family remained loyal to Richard and staged a rebellion in his favor after he had given up the throne to Bolingbroke.

For all the frustration of using the scholarly sources, there is much of interest to an actor in the historical documents. In the entry on Mowbray in *Who's Who in Late Medieval England* we learn that he was brought up with King Richard. A quick look at the arrival of Rosencrantz and Guildenstern at Elsinore offers some suggestions about the relationships a prince might have with the young noblemen brought to court to share his tutors, his games, and his growing up. In *The Court of Richard II* we can find out the brutal way that Salisbury and Kent were captured by the townspeople of Cicester and butchered in the streets, and how Spencer was thrown off the ship on which he sought to escape and was executed by the people of Bristol. In *Richard II and the English Nobility* we learn exactly what Bolingbroke means when he speaks of his letters of patent in 2.3.130, something that is not explained in the play but is very important to understand the events leading up to his return to England after the death of his father. Richard had given Bolingbroke permission to receive his inheritance if his father died while he was still in exile. This permission was legalized by letters patent, which Richard then revoked, having Bolingbroke declared a traitor and banished for life.

Medieval England

In addition to the general studies of Richard's time, there are many scholarly works on specific aspects of life in late medieval England. As Richard is saying goodbye to his Queen, he instructs her to seek sanctuary in a religious house in France, and for himself.

> I am sworn Brother (Sweet)
> To grim Necessity; and he and I
> Will keep a League til Death. [5.1.20]

This may be a religious brotherhood, but it might also be a reference to the bond between chivalric knights, one of whom here is death himself. Maurice

Keen's *Nobles, Knights, and Men-at-Arms in the Middle Ages* contains a chapter entitled "Brothers-in-Arms" that discusses the chivalric brotherhood, quoting from actual letters that bound knights to lifelong loyalty.

There is little in the way of battle in *Richard II*, unlike the rest of Shakespeare's history plays, but there is sufficient reference to the threat of armed battle and the siege of castles to require a familiarity with medieval warfare. There is also reference to the great military achievements of the older generation, John of Gaunt, the duke of York, and Richard's father the Black Prince, as well as to the Crusades, in which Mowbray dies during his exile. A book like Timothy Newark's *Medieval Warfare* can provide a general introduction, with reproductions and modern artistic renderings of images that bring specific references in the plays to life.

Time-Life Books can be counted on to put together an interesting collection of reproductions and photographs. *Age of Faith* by Anne Fremantle is a good example of the wonderful inspiration available in the historical record. *The Atlas of Medieval Man* by Colin Platt contains maps and reproductions from around the world, including Richard's devotional painting, the Wilton Diptych. This marvellous artifact shows on one side the coronation of Richard and on the other side the Virgin Mary carrying the baby Jesus, surrounded by a corps of angels, each wearing Richard's distinctive badge, the white hart. When Richard says,

> For every man that Bolingbroke hath pressed,
> To lift shrewd Steel against our Golden Crown,
> God for his Richard hath in heavenly pay
> A glorious Angel: then, if Angels fight,
> Weak men must fall, for Heaven still guards the right. [3.2.58]

we suddenly have a picture of the image these words convey.

The first action in *Richard II* is the complex legal, political, and religious event of a chivalric trial by combat. In order to frame the action of the first and third scenes, *The Duel* by Robert Baldick can clarify a great deal of what is going on. Equally important is some understanding of the entire concept of chivalric knights, for which books like *The Knight in Medieval England* by Peter Coss are invaluable.

All of the medieval history plays are set in a time that exhibited specific attitudes to kingship, justice, the procedures of warfare, and the social and political institutions that dominated Britain. W. M. Ormrod's *Political Life in Medieval England* offers a good general introduction to the important events and also those all-pervasive attitudes that seem so foreign to modern actors but were very much a part of the world being re-created on stage.

The Women of the History Plays

Actresses in particular can benefit from the recent developments in social history, as feminist historians have turned their eyes to "herstory," the aspects of a time that are experienced by women in private life. Jennifer C. Ward's *English Noblewomen in the Later Middle Ages* will answer a variety of questions about what life might have been like for women such as the duchess of Gloucester or the duchess of York, who do not have a major role to play in the political action of *Richard II* but who must even so be brought to life by an actress assigned the role. How can it be, for example, that the duchess of Gloucester, whose husband had been declared a traitor, his estate forfeit to the Crown, now lives in near poverty, as she explains to her brother-in-law Gaunt at Plashy with its "empty lodgings and unfurnished walls, / Unpeopled offices, untrodden stones?" [1.2.69]. Yet, a few scenes later, the duke of York can send a servant to borrow a thousand pounds from her [2.2.90]. Could she, as a widow, have private income that could not be touched by the vengeance of King Richard? Ward's book contains information on the rights of widows to hold lands and revenues inherited from their fathers in jointure, even after the death of their husbands. We know that Gloucester married one of the deBohun heiresses (Bolingbroke married the other) and that these women shared the vast holdings of their father, Humphrey. Her mother was Princess Elizabeth, the youngest daughter of Edward I. We have the final will of Eleanor, duchess of Gloucester, which provides some interesting details that might prove useful to the designers and the actress playing the role:

Item, a chronicle of France in French with two silver clasps, enamelled with the arms of the duke of Burgundy. Item, one book of Giles [of Rome], On the Rule of Princes. Item, a book of vices and virtues, and another, in rhyme, of the history of the knight of the swan, all in French. Item, a psalter well and richly illuminated with gold enamelled clasps, with white swans and the arms of my lord and father enamelled on the clasps, and with gold mullets on the binding; this psalter was left to me with remainder to my heirs, and was to pass from heir to heir. Item, a coat of mail with a latten cross on the spot over the heart which belonged to my lord his father. Item, a gold cross hanging by a chain with an image of the crucifix and four pearls round it, with my blessing, as the possession of mine which I loved most. (51)

Ward's collection of documents *Women of the English Nobility and Gentry, 1066–1500*, which she has translated as well as edited, is ideal for browsing because it has a first-rate index, though we might regret that the wives of the great nobles are all listed under their husbands' titles, as well as excellent general introductions before each of the categories into which she has placed the selections: marriage, family, land, wealth and lordship, household, and religion.

In addition to Ward's books, I would recommend two studies of life in the great noble households, each of which includes very important insights into the lives of the duchesses who appear in the histories. Kate Mertes describes vividly the complexities of running a large estate *The English Noble Household* while Margaret LaBarge has created *A Baronial Household of the Thirteenth Century*, a less scholarly book that shares the stories of several fascinating women.

Scholars have covered the late medieval period of English social history with the same thoroughness as Shakespeare's own era. You will find books on the mundane aspects of daily life, such as Richard Britnell's collection of fascinating articles, in *Daily Life in the Late Middle Ages*. A.F. Scott's collection of first-hand accounts *Every One a Witness* includes modern versions of everything from ballads and letters to excerpts from some of the earliest published records. Here is a description of Richard II recorded in Latin by Richard De Maidstone:

Where he sits on his white horse, they draw back so that the good King himself may be seen by his people. How fresh-coloured his face, crowned with yellow hair, his combed locks shining under the garland; gleaming with gold in the red robe that covers too much his fair body. (12)

To supplement these contemporary accounts of the historical figures, we have the full-length scholarly biographies and specific histories of this period. My favorite among these are the biographies by Philippe Erlanger of Margaret of Anjou, who dominates the Henry VI plays and also makes a memorable, if historically impossible, appearance in *Richard III*, and by M.A. Hicks of both Richard and his brother Clarence, who dies so horribly in a wine barrel, Richard's first victim in the same play. Charles Ross and J.R. Lander have each produced a reliable general history of the Wars of the Roses.

Basil Clarke's historical study of mental illness, *Mental Disorder in Earlier Britain: Exploratory Studies*, contains a fascinating study of King Henry VI that might be of interest to actors working on Shakespeare's plays about that king's reign. Because Clarke's approach is cultural as well as medical, he has as much to say about possession by demons as about epilepsy. The later chapters, in which he deals with famous cases from Shakespeare's era, also make for interesting reading. In contrast with these scholarly books, A.J. Pollard's *Richard III and the Princes in the Tower* is filled with fascinating illustrations, including photographs of the bones of the skeletons discovered in the Tower cupboard, as well as details of the portraits of Richard showing the overpainting added to suggest a deformity of one shoulder.

For an introduction to the cultural history of medieval England, I would recommend the second volume of *The Cambridge Cultural History of Britain*, edited by Boris Ford. This nine-volume series, the third volume of which focuses on the sixteenth century, offers a collection of excellent general introductory articles on a wide variety of cultural and social topics. Other volumes can be consulted for the history plays, while the later volumes are useful when your director has reset the production into a later century.

London Weekend Television prepared a series called *The Making of Britain*, for which Lesley Smith edited the companion books. These are beautifully illustrated and as scholarly and entertaining as can be expected, given their genesis. Together, they offer a wonderful introduction to the world of the histories.

When in Rome

The Roman plays pose a special challenge to the modern production company. When these plays are set in togas, we struggle with the tension between the historical Rome as we understand it today, the Rome that the Elizabethans thought existed, and Shakespeare's Rome, which is neither of these. Often, however, these plays are relocated into another historical period so that the political complexities can be used to delve into issues of greater interest to a modern audience than ancient Rome. Because Shakespeare was using ancient Rome to comment on his world, we are following in his footsteps, but the layers of association can become confusing.

Here is a simple example. In *Titus Andronicus* the court goes out on an early-morning hunt, during which many terrible things happen. The setting is clearly the woods outside the city, in which there is talk of panthers as well as deer. It is not easy to find a historically accurate model for such a hunt in the late Roman Empire, at which time the wild forests were far removed from the sprawling urban center that was Rome. It is far easier to find an Elizabethan model, and the language of the opening moments of the scene supports a very English hunt: "The hunt is up, the morn is bright and grey, / The fields are fragrant, and the Woods are green" [2.2.1].

Now let us look at the opening moments of this play. The former Caesar has died, and no heir has been named. From the point of view of Roman history, this is highly unlikely. From the point of view of using Rome to make a comment on contemporary English politics, this is a burning issue: Elizabeth is by this time an old woman without legal heir who refuses to name her choice of a successor. The exchange between the rivals for the imperial crown is a snapshot of the chaos that could be unleashed upon England if Elizabeth were to die suddenly.

In all questions about Roman life and attitudes, the actor will find many opportunities to consider both Roman and Elizabethan realities for inspiration. Rather than dwell upon the tensions between the two realities, marvel at how often they combine to provide multiple points of contact upon which an actor can build a foundation in truth.

Ancient Rome is second only to Elizabethan England as a time and place that attracts the interest of the general public, and the result is a wide variety of books that bring together useful details and inspiring images, based upon strong scholarship but freed from the excessive detail of interest only to specialists.

In contrast, there are some books that deal with an examination of Shakespeare's Rome that focus specifically on the Roman plays: *Julius Caesar, Antony and Cleopatra, Coriolanus,* and, to a lesser degree, *Titus Andronicus* and *Cymbeline*. The most interesting elements of these literary studies are the clarification of the assumptions Shakespeare's actors and audiences would have made about the Romans. However, the primary focus of these books is to discuss the themes of the plays and are of less interest to those who perform Shakespeare than to those who study him. Because the interest is primarily thematic, even the best discussions of the Roman world as understood by the Elizabethans, such as Charles Wells's *The Wide Arch*, focus on the values the Romans were assumed to have. This information is, of course, of interest to actors, but tends to be more self-evident, reflected as it is in the action of the play and the statements of the characters. Concrete details of daily life are not as relevant to this sort of scholarly writing.

The danger of deciding that because Shakespeare was not accurate about Rome, there is no necessity for the actor to know anything about Rome is that the play sits in a never-never world, neither fully Elizabethan nor fully Roman. This is fully satisfactory for the presentation of ideas, but entirely unsatisfactory for the creation of the details of lives truly lived by characters who evoke real people.

Whenever we examine the family relationships of a play, whether it is set in Vienna, Verona, or ancient Rome, we find a portrait of domesticity that would have been familiar to Shakespeare's first audience and actors. However, it is also of interest to some actors to have a look at what the *real* Rome was like, always seeking for artistic inspiration, and only incidentally for historical accuracy. If you want details that assist in the grounding of theatrical action into historical reality, you should have a look at one of the many general introductions to daily life in republican Rome, such as Jo-Ann Shelton's *As the Romans Did* or Jérôme Carcopino's *Daily Life in Ancient Rome*. Horizon Books and Facts on File, both of which published favorite volumes on Shakespeare's era, have also produced *The Horizon Book of Daily Life in Ancient Rome* and Lesley and Roy Adkins's *Handbook to Life in Ancient Rome*, respectively. I have also made great use of an older contribution, O.A.W. Dilke's *The Ancient Romans: How They Lived and Worked*. The first volume of *A History of Private Life, From Pagan Rome to Byzantium*, edited by Paul Veyne is also a resource for this sort of research.

One of the tricks of looking at Rome is ensuring that you are in the right century. There was a continuity to certain aspects of Roman life from the early days of the republic (*Coriolanus*) through to the decadence of the late empire (*Titus Andronicus*). However, there are many aspects of daily life that changed, particularly in the customs of the elites, who dominate the cast lists of the plays. Carcopino's book, for example, examines Rome at the height of the empire, and so his discussion of the business corporations and manual occupations is not as helpful for actors creating the citizens of *Coriolanus* or *Julius Caesar*.

Shakespeare borrowed all of his place names from his sources, although he may have spoken to travellers who could tell of the ancient ruins still visible in sixteenth-century Rome. We are more fortunate than he in that we can take advantage of modern archeology's mapping of the ancient city. O.F. Robinson's *Ancient Rome* offers such a mapping for the imperial era, too late for *Coriolanus* but useful for *Julius Caesar, Antony and Cleopatra,* and *Titus Andronicus.*

DISTORTED IMAGES OF THE PAST

One of the dangers of seeking the grounding of one's character in the reflections of the notables in Shakespeare's world is that our pool is limited by those individuals whose stories have captured the imagination of others before us. We are likely to have some strong images of Queen Elizabeth, from Hollywood or historical fiction, but how many of us know much about James, who ascended the throne midway through Shakespeare's writing career and whose presence was felt upon the political scene even earlier? He was, after all, the most likely heir even though Elizabeth refused to name him formally.

Another problem with Hollywood's and historical fiction writers' versions of Shakespeare's England is that they quite naturally put a very modern spin on the role of women in that culture. It is very difficult for us to imagine, much less enjoy, a world in which women played such a restricted role and, furthermore, in which those restrictions seemed normal to almost everyone. Our modern eye is much more attracted to the anomalies like Elizabeth or Moll Cutpurse, a woman who dressed as a man and was a notorious member of the underworld in Shakespeare's London. There is a lively modern tradition of having young Elizabethan women dress up as boys and run away to the theatre, which makes for great fiction but is not particularly credible from a historical perspective. Geoffrey Trease's 1940 novel *Cue for Treason,* in which the runaway girl ends up as Juliet as well as the main player in the secret service of Sir Francis Walsingham, has been a favorite book of mine since I was a young girl. You can find the same plot device in film and television, from John Mortimer's *Will Shakespeare* to Tom Stoppard's *Shakespeare in Love.*

These fictional treatments of history are immensely appealing and dangerous: the portrait of Shakespeare's world is made so credible that it is difficult to tell what is outright fabrication, for the sake of the story, and what is a tidbit of historical fact well used to ground the story in reality. I am reminded of James Cameron's film *Titanic,* which manufactured much marketing momentum by documenting the historical research that went into props, costumes, scenic details, and the events depicted and then shattered any credibility the film might have had by showing the hero and a friend and later the hero and heroine on the prow of the ship, an area strictly out of bounds to all passengers for reasons of safety. But it made for a wonderful picture, didn't it?

Fortunately, actors are freed from the constraints placed upon scholars or even upon writers and filmmakers whose assumptions can and will be scrutinized closely by experts. An actor's assumptions and imaginings are private. If the image of standing on the prow of a fast-moving ocean liner helps you to bring alive a line of Shakespeare, who has the right to deny you access to that image? Does it matter that it never would have happened in 1912? If *Shakespeare in Love* helps you to believe in the compelling power of Shakespeare's love stories, do we care if the premise of the movie does not bear the cold light of scholarly analysis?

RECOMMENDED READING

Famous Players of the World Stage

Akrigg, G.P.V. *Shakespeare and the Earl of Southampton.* London: H. Hamilton, 1968.
Duncan-Jones, Katherine. *Sir Philip Sidney, Courtier Poet.* New Haven, CT: Yale University Press, 1991.
Durant, David N. *Arbella Stuart: A Rival to the Queen.* London: Weidenfeld and Nicolson, 1978.
Elizabeth I, Queen of England. "The Glass of the Sinful Soul" (1544). In *Elizabeth's Glass*, edited by Marc Shell, 114–144. Lincoln: University of Nebraska Press, 1993.
Greenblatt, Stephen J. *Sir Walter Raleigh: The Renaissance Man and His Roles.* New Haven, CT: Yale University Press, 1973.
Hannay, Margaret P. *Philip's Phoenix: Mary Sidney, Countess of Pembroke.* Oxford: Oxford University Press, 1990.
Harris, G.B., ed. *The Letters of Queen Elizabeth I.* London: Cassell, 1968.
Hibbert, Christopher. *The Virgin Queen: Elizabeth I, Genius of the Golden Age.* Reading, MA: Addison-Wesley, 1991.
Hogrefe, Pearl. *Tudor Women: Commoners and Queens.* Ames: Iowa State University Press, 1975.
———. *Women of Action in Tudor England: Nine Biographical Sketches.* Ames: Iowa State University Press, 1977.
Holt, J.C. *Robin Hood.* London: Thames and Hudson, 1983.
Keen, Maurice. *The Outlaws of Medieval Legend.* Toronto: University of Toronto Press, 1961.
Perry, Maria. *The Word of a Prince: A Life of Elizabeth I from Contemporary Documents.* Woodbridge, England: Boydell Press, 1990.
Plowden, Alison. *Elizabeth Regina: The Age of Triumph 1588–1603.* Stroud, Gloucestershire: Sutton, 2000.
———. *The House of Tudor.* Stroud, Gloucestershire: Sutton, 1999.
———. *Young Elizabeth: The First Twenty-Five Years.* Stroud, Gloucestershire: Sutton, 1999.
Rowse, A.L. *Raleigh and the Throckmortons.* London: Macmillan, 1962.
———. *Shakespeare's Southampton, Patron of Virginia.* New York: Harper & Row, 1965.
Steen, Sara Jayne, ed. *The Letters of Lady Arbella Stuart.* New York: Oxford University Press, 1994.
Tillyard, E.M.W. *The Elizabethan World Picture.* New York: Vintage, 1959.

Shakespeare and History

Asimov, Isaac. *Asimov's Guide to Shakespeare.* Garden City, NY: Doubleday, 1970.
Baldick, Robert. *The Duel: A History of Duelling.* New York: Chapman and Hall, 1965.

Billington, Sandra. *Mock Kings in Medieval Society and Renaissance Drama.* Oxford: Clarendon Press, 1991.

Britnell, Richard, ed. *Daily Life in the Late Middle Ages.* Stroud, Gloucestershire: Sutton, 1998.

Clarke, Basil. *Mental Disorder in Earlier Britain: Exploratory Studies.* Cardiff: University of Wales Press, 1975.

Coss, Peter. *The Knight in Medieval England, 1000–1400.* Stroud, Gloucestershire: Alan Sutton, 1993.

Erlanger, Philippe. *Margaret of Anjou: Queen of England.* Coral Gables, FL: University of Miami Press, 1971.

Ford, Boris, ed. *The Cambridge Cultural History of Britain,* Vol. 2: *Medieval Britain.* Cambridge: Cambridge University Press, 1992.

Fremantle, Anne. *Age of Faith.* New York: Time, 1972.

Hicks, M.A. *False, Fleeting, Perjur'd Clarence: George, Duke of Clarence, 1449–78.* Stroud, Gloucestershire: Alan Sutton, 1980.

————. *Richard III: The Man Behind the Myth.* London: Collins & Brown, 1991.

————. *Who's Who in Late Medieval England, 1272–1485.* Chicago: St. James Press, 1991.

Holderness, Graham. *Shakespeare's History.* New York: St. Martin's Press, 1985.

Keen, Maurice. *Nobles, Knights, and Men-at-Arms in the Middle Ages.* London: Hambledon Press, 1996.

Labarge, Margaret Wade. *A Baronial Household of the Thirteenth Century.* New York: Barnes & Noble Books, 1980.

Lander, J.R. *The Wars of the Roses.* New York: St. Martin's Press, 1990.

Leggatt, Alexander. *Shakespeare's Political Drama: The History Plays and the Roman Plays.* London: Routledge, 1988.

Mathew, Gervase. *The Court of Richard II.* London: Murray, 1968.

Mertes, Kate. *The English Noble Household, 1250–1600: Good Governance and Politic Rule.* Oxford: Basil Blackwell, 1988.

Newark, Timothy. *Medieval Warfare, an Illustrated Introduction.* London: Jupiter Books, 1979.

Norwich, John Julius. *Shakespeare's Kings.* London: Viking, 1999.

Ormrod, W.M. *Political Life in Medieval England, 1300–1450.* New York: St. Martin's Press, 1995.

Platt, Colin. *The Atlas of Medieval Man.* London: Macmillan, 1979.

Pollard, A.J. *Richard III and the Princes in the Tower.* Stroud, Gloucestershire: Alan Sutton, 1991.

Reed, Robert Rentoul, Jr. *Crime and God's Judgment in Shakespeare.* Lexington: University Press of Kentucky, 1984.

Ross, Charles. *The Wars of the Roses: A Concise History.* London: Thames and Hudson, 1976.

Saccio, Peter. *Shakespeare's English Kings: History, Chronicle, and Drama.* Oxford: Oxford University Press, 1977.

Scott, A.F. *Every One a Witness: The Plantagenet Age: Commentaries of an Era.* London: Scott & Finlay, 1975.

Senior, Michael. *The Life and Times of Richard II.* London: Weidenfeld and Nicolson, 1981.

Smith, Lesley M., ed. *The Making of Britain: The Age of Expansion.* London: Macmillan, 1986.

————. *The Making of Britain: The Dark Ages.* London: Macmillan, 1984.

————. *The Making of Britain: The Middle Ages.* London: Macmillan, 1985.

Tuck, Anthony. *Richard II and the English Nobility.* London: Edward Arnold, 1973.

Ward, Jennifer C. *English Noblewomen in the Later Middle Ages.* London: Longman, 1992.

————, ed. *Women of the English Nobility and Gentry, 1066–1500.* Manchester: Manchester University Press, 1995.

Wilders, John. *The Lost Garden: A View of Shakespeare's English and Roman History Plays.* Totowa, NJ: Rowman and Littlefield, 1978.

When in Rome

Adkins, Lesley, and Roy A. Adkins. *Handbook to Life in Ancient Rome.* New York: Facts on File, 1994.

Cantor, Paul A. *Shakespeare's Rome, Republic and Empire.* Ithaca, NY: Cornell University Press, 1976.

Carcopino, Jérôme. *Daily Life in Ancient Rome: The People and the City at the Height of the Empire.* Translated by E.O. Lorimer. New Haven, CT: Yale University Press, 1992.

Casson, Lionel. *The Horizon Book of Daily Life in Ancient Rome.* New York: American Heritage Pub. Co., 1975.

Dilke, O.A.W. *The Ancient Romans: How They Lived and Worked.* Newton Abbot: David and Charles, 1975.

Miola, Robert S. *Shakespeare's Rome.* Cambridge: Cambridge University Press, 1983.

Robinson, O.F. *Ancient Rome: City Planning and Administration.* London: Routledge, 1992.

Shelton, Jo-Ann. *As the Romans Did: A Source Book in Roman Social History.* New York: Oxford University Press, 1988.

Thomas, Vivian. *Shakespeare's Roman Worlds.* London: Routledge, 1989.

Veyne, Paul, ed. *From Pagan Rome to Byzantium: A History of Private Life*, Vol. 1. Series edited by Philippe Ariès and Georges Duby. Cambridge, MA: Belknap Press of Harvard University Press, 1987.

Wells, Charles. *The Wide Arch: Roman Values in Shakespeare.* New York: St. Martin's Press, 1993.

ᘉ 6 ᘉ
The Peopled World

And these same Thoughts, people this Little World
In humours, like the people of this world.

Richard [RII 5.5.9]

Actors and scholars agree that one of the undeniable achievements of Shake-speare is his creation of a vast array of complex, fascinating characters. Some are central to a play's effect and, with large amounts of stage time, reveal multiple facets of personality. Others are functional or even marginal, perhaps only appearing in a single scene, but somehow, with a telling detail or a striking metaphor, Shakespeare is able to suggest not only an individual but an entire section of society. He truly "peoples his little world" with all of the variety and contrast of the real world from which he drew his models.

A modern actor therefore has some responsibility to consider the wide range of characters, not only in their individuality, but also in their contexts. How do the various characters reflect the people whom Shakespeare might have known or observed? In particular, where do these various individuals fit in the organized structure of this particular society?

CLASS

North American actors live with the inferiority complex that comes from the widely held assumption that British actors have a leg up when it comes to performing Shakespeare. Leaving aside the issue of accent and the simple fact that British students seem to recover from their aversion to the plays sooner than their North American counterparts, familiarity in this instance breeding national pride, I would argue that the primary advantage a British actor has over a North American is the profound comprehension of class and the corresponding complexities of interpersonal relationships.

North American actors need to be told, and then reminded repeatedly, that one of the greatest problems facing Helena and Bertram is a difference in their social status that cannot be erased by the favor of the king of France and his offer of a dowry. Bertram will always be the heir to a great and noble family, and Helena will always be the daughter of an itinerant herbalist/surgeon. The idea of their bloodlines mixing to bring forth the next Count of Rossillion, is ludicrous. Or at least this is how it first appears to Bertram, as a representative of the older aristocracy.

Then, just when the concept of class difference is firmly ingrained, we encounter Polonius, whose character echoes in many ways Elizabeth's great advisor William Cecil, whom she raised from the educated servant class to the gentry and then to the nobility, to the horror of those young men of ancient noble families like Bertram in fiction and Robert Devereux, the earl of Essex in real life. In the great confrontation between the two powerful men, Cecil and his sons survived to serve the next monarch; Essex went to the block, and his title was attainted. The movement of individuals up and down the great chain of being was very much a part of Shakespeare's world, on stage and off.

The British actors understand intuitively the paradox of class: that it is so clearly and unequivocally marked that there is never any doubt who stands above or below whom, and at the same time it is porous, so that the charwoman can pull status on the queen, and the most mocked are those pretending to be something they are not. The slumming Lady Margery is just as foolish as Dame Margery trying hard to replace her country accent with the vowels of the hoity-toity of London town.

Even British actors struggle with finding a correct reading on the tensions embodied within the class system of Shakespeare's England. There is comfort in knowing that everyone has a place, but terror in that the world is changing and clear-cut relationships of masters and servants seem to have been replaced with something that shifts toward and away from the old order depending upon the price of corn and the success of the master's latest mercantile venture. There is a constant fear of riot, shared by the nobility and the urban householders alike; in the country there is famine and displacement to challenge the deeply ingrained habits of mutual dependability and respect between the lord of the manor and his tenants and yeomen. In the cities there is disease alongside an economic and cultural explosion that fuels English pride and xenophobia. The threat of invasion is ever present, and England has never enjoyed so long a peace. The nobility are decadent and profligate and finally taking their place among the elite of Europe in the arts of peace and war.

Individuals look to those above them in status and admire, fear, mock, and challenge in equal measure. They look below them and respect, distrust, discount, and cherish. Above all, they rely upon each other, assume a shared set of values one with the other, and can never ignore the sentiments or activities of those above and below, even as they place members of other classes in distinct and separate categories, almost as if they were separate species.

The difference in class affects every single relationship in Shakespeare's plays. Even apparent equals would never have been exactly equal, for every Englishman knew his rights of precedence before or after every other individual with whom he came in contact. It is difficult for us, at this remove, to read the signals as to which of Proteus or Valentine would enter before the other. In Shakespeare's theatre this would have been demonstrated in the first moments of their appearance on stage by all of the various markers of status available to the actors and easily read by the audience.

For a good introduction to the basic social divisions and how they manifest themselves in the plays, Ralph Berry's *Shakespeare and Social Class* is the place to start. But a far more detailed and thoughtful description of this aspect of Shakespeare's England can be found in Peter Laslett's *The World We Have Lost*, a publication initially sparked by a BBC program and geared toward a non-scholarly readership, though it is the result of the painstaking research of a team of historians who have pored over all available records in order to assemble an accurate picture of the demographics of England before the industrial revolution. Laslett's goal is to undo some of the damaging misperceptions that arise, in part, from Shakespeare's plays. For example, after reading *Romeo and Juliet* we might assume that Elizabethans married far earlier than we do today. In fact, the records demonstrate that the average age was closer to twenty-six for men and twenty-three for women.

Laslett has an excellent chapter on social class, though he strongly objects to using the concept of social class, a theory that emerged after the industrial revolution, to analyze the England that Shakespeare knew. What he describes, however, is a culture in which social status or "place" was firmly set and wherein one's place governed all one's interactions with others.

HONORABLE SERVICE

At the very end of his career as a playwright, Shakespeare collaborated on a play about Elizabeth's father, the most recent of the historical conflicts that he dared to bring to the London stage. Elizabeth was safely dead, as were all of the key players in the events dramatized: the dissolution of Henry's marriage to Katherine and the ties of England to the Catholic Church in Rome. The play is seldom performed in the modern theatre, in large part because it is primarily about the maneuverings of the courtiers rather than the relationships that bound King Henry to his former and future queens, all of which has been thrilling dramatized by modern writers. However, buried in this work you will find, alongside some wonderful showcase monologues for Queen Katherine, fascinating evocations of life at court, including this compelling statement of the loyalty and service that the greatest individuals in the land were felt to owe their monarch:

> I do profess,
> That for your Highness good, I ever laboured
> More than mine own: that am, have, and will be
> (Though all the world should crack their duty to you,
> And throw it from their Soul, though perils did
> Abound, as thick as thought could make 'em, and
> Appear in forms more horrid) yet my Duty,
> As doth a Rock against the chiding Flood,
> Should the approach of this wild River break,
> And stand unshaken yours. [3.2.190]

The fact that the speaker, Cardinal Wolsey, is soon to fall out of the king's favor does not diminish the power of this avowal of honorable service.

Ideals of duty and loyalty permeate all master-servant relationships in Shakespeare's plays. Today we might remain suspicious of this sort of unsubtle indoctrination in support of a system which privileged the few at the expense of the many, and it is impossible to know for sure how aware Shakespeare was of the very real oppression all around him. What is far more important, when acting in these plays, is to participate fully in the relationships that are shaped by the hierarchies described, and proscribed, by the words the characters speak.

Here, for example, is Queen Katherine in her last scene. She has now been set aside by Henry, and knows that she is dying. As an indication of her greatness of heart, she has been given this to say:

> My next poor Petition,
> Is, that his Noble Grace would have some pity
> Upon my wretched women, that so long
> Have followed both my Fortunes, faithfully,
> Of which there is not one, I dare avow
> (And now I should not lie) but will deserve
> For Virtue, and true Beauty of the Soul,
> For honesty, and decent Carriage
> A right good Husband (let him be a Noble)
> And sure those men are happy that shall have 'em.
> The last is for my men, they are the poorest,
> (But poverty could never draw 'em from me)
> That they may have their wages, duly paid 'em,
> And something over to remember me by.
> If Heaven had pleased to have given me longer life
> And able means, we had not parted thus. [4.2.138]

Here we have a portrait not only of the economic ties that bound servants to masters, those of personal advancement and gainful employment, but also those emotional ties that placed a burden of care upon those born to great estate for the well being of all who were bound to service there. Servants could hope to be remembered in a master's will; young ladies could find a good husband and, if endowed with beauty of person and soul, perhaps even be raised by marriage to the ranks of the nobility. But the greatest sign of true loyalty is the willingness of the server to remain in service even when the wages are not paid, for no hope of personal gain, but rather out of love.

Clearly, we cannot take such a sentimental portrait at face value. Mark Thornton Burnett's *Masters and Servants in English Renaissance Drama and Culture* is a much more reliable study of the relationship between those who serve and those who are served, as reflected in the historical documents that suggest what it was actually like. His description of this aspect of Shakespeare's world is particularly useful to the modern actor because who among us has ever been a servant or had a servant, unless we count the ministrations of the lowly assistant stage managers in that category? How useful it is, then, to be able to consult Burnett's book when one is working on Malvolio, Speed, or Launcelot Gobbo or Maria, Margaret, or Juliet's Nurse. Burnett has divided his book into sections on apprentices, members of the guilds, male personal servants and female personal servants and finally a chapter on the noble households. Each section begins with a general discussion of the social history. What follows is a discussion of how this is played out on the stage in plays by Shakespeare and his contemporaries. Burnett's index is a useful place to see how the play in which you are performing might figure in his study.

Let us consider *Twelfth Night* as an example of how Burnett's book might assist the actors in the company, whether they be servants or masters. What about Maria? Burnett's fourth chapter, "Women, Patriarchy, and Service," sets out some of the different tasks she might perform in the household and several possible scenarios for how she might have come into service in Olivia's household. A quick look in the index under "maidservants" reveals an entry on the topic of marriages, and suddenly we can place the coy comments about the potential match between Sir Toby (Olivia's uncle) and Maria, at best a poor and distant relation, into the context within which the first actors would have viewed it. Maria is far less grasping and desperate than other marriage-seeking maidservants in plays of the period, but how happy she must be when Toby says, "I could marry this wench for this device" [2.5.182], referring to the duping of Malvolio. That she adores him, Toby has already claimed. What are we to think when Fabian announces, in the process of revealing the entire plot in the final scene, "Maria writ / The letter, at Sir Toby's great importance, / In recompense whereof, he hath married her" [5.1.362]? Let us temper our modern romanticism with a healthy respect for the class difference that such an alliance would represent.

Another entry in Burnett's index is for stewards, who are discussed at length in the first section of the fifth chapter, "The Noble Household." We know that Olivia is a wealthy countess and thus a member of the highest reaches of the nobility of Illyria. Her steward would therefore be a gentleman in his own right, well educated and entrusted with significant responsibilities in the running of a large estate. It is all the more hilarious, then, when this pompous and possibly elegant man dresses up in yellow stockings in the mistaken impression that Olivia enjoys this latest court fashion. Burnett clarifies that it was the steward's responsibility to discipline unruly members of the household, so his reaction to Toby's late-night revelry is a natural extension of his authority. Once again, we must temper our modern love of rebels with a healthy respect for the prudence and right thinking of Olivia's efficient and loyal steward Malvolio.

This brings us to the all-important question, the social mobility of stewards. Just how outrageous is Malvolio's dream of a marriage with his mistress? The leaping across class divisions, from educated gentleman servant to "Count" Malvolio, is clearly a fantasy, though a few well-known spectacular rises from humble farmhouses to great offices, wealth, and even a title gave fuel to Malvolio's "Cinderfella" daydream. As Burnett reminds us in his discussion of the interclass misalliances of *Twelfth Night*, in 1557 Frances, the duchess of Suffolk, married her master of horse following the death of her husband, prompting the then Princess Elizabeth reportedly to remark, "Has the woman so far forgotten herself as to marry a common groom?" (169). Did Elizabeth remember this when she was responding to the marriage ambitions of her own favorite and master of horse Robert Dudley? Such postfuneral marriages seem to have been in the air; three years before the Suffolk scandal, and following a longer period of widowhood, the dowager duchess of Suffolk, stepmother to Frances, married her gentleman usher, who had served as her companion and advisor for many years.

Burnett's index entry for *Twelfth Night* allows us to hop and skip from item to item. We discover, for example, that in reprimanding Sir Toby and then the fool, Maria is taking upon herself activities that are very much the responsibility of the mistress of the house. Perhaps Olivia is too young or too much in mourning (and later too much in love) to notice how Maria oversteps her bounds. The reference to Maria as Penthesilea, queen of the Amazons [2.3.177], takes on new significance when we consider how rare such domineering waiting women were in plays of the period.

Such knowledge can be immensely helpful for those actors who like to endow their characters with a personal history that makes sense of the function they serve in the world of the play. Let us take as an example *Hamlet*'s Reynaldo, whom Polonius sends to Paris with letters for Laertes. Who might Reynaldo be? How did he come to be selected for this particular service? Clearly he is a trusted member of Polonius's household, but not so important that he cannot be spared for the long journey to France. There are as many possibilities as there are actors cast in the role, but I will share my scenario. I like to think of Reynaldo as being somewhat close to Laertes' age, thus making a good potential observer of the social life of such a young man about town. I imagine him as being very much beholden to Polonius and therefore the stuff of which a good servant-spy is made. So I imagine a young Reynaldo growing up on the family estate, much removed from Elsinore, of humble beginnings but demonstrating a lively intelligence that catches the attention of Polonius. Reynaldo is brought into the great manor and educated, thereby allowing the young man to leap from his parents' class to the emerging professional class of personal secretary to a great statesman. Once he has mastered several languages and demonstrated competence in administration, he is brought to the court to serve in Polonius's personal office, assisting rather than running things himself. Reynaldo never for a moment questions Polonius's right to order his activities and even his attitudes, for he owes to his patron his current status and financial security. I suspect that he has his eye on a well-bred young lady's maid and hopes to make a fine match, with the permission and support of his patron, of course. When Polonius is murdered, I have always imagined poor Reynaldo down in Paris, getting the news along with Laertes, and immediately transferring his unquestioning and undying allegiance to the son of the family. For that reason, I am never upset to see the same actor who played Reynaldo reappearing as one of the rebels when Laertes bursts in on the king and queen and demands justice for his father's murder.

If you would like to have a look at another book that gives support to my invented backstory for Reynaldo, check out David Cressy's *Literacy and the Social Order*. Here you will find much to ponder when you are considering poor Peter's dilemma in *Romeo and Juliet*, sent as messenger to a list of invited guests and unable to read the list. The nonscholar might not be interested in Cressy's chapter on "The Measurement of Literacy," but an actor will find much of interest in Cressy's introductory chapter and also "The Acquisition of Literacy" and "Literacy and Loyalty."

OCCUPATIONS

> Sir, I am a true Labourer, I earn that I eat: get that I wear; owe no man hate, envy no mans happiness; glad of other mens good, content with my harm.
>
> Corin [*AYLI* 3.2.73]

One of the important research questions that will send an actor to the dusty bookshelves is that of the few occupations mentioned in the plays. The majority of the characters are members of the leisure classes and their personal servants. There are, however, a scattering of merchants, professional soldiers or sailors, doctors, and schoolteachers and a courtesan, a goldsmith, a dressmaker and a hatmaker, an apothecary, a curate, a vicar, a constable or two, assorted country folk, and the mechanicals of *A Midsummer Night's Dream*: a carpenter, a weaver, a bellows-mender, a tinker, a joiner, and a tailor by trade. In *The Merry Wives of Windsor*, the most middle-class of the plays, we have a country justice, a parson, and a physician among the supporting cast, but the husbands of the merry wives of the title are simply "gentlemen" and have no more occupation than to manage their estates. In *Measure for Measure* we meet an executioner and a bawd, and in *The Winter's Tale* we meet a pedlar. In the histories, in addition to the nobility, we meet a few ordinary folk, including a jailer, an armorer, a gardener, and, in the taverns that Prince Hal loves to frequent, a hostess, drawers, carriers, ostlers, and a beadle. Members of Shakespeare's own profession make an appearance in *Hamlet*, as do a pair of grave diggers, and among the citizens of ancient Rome we find some very English tradesmen, including a cobbler and a carpenter. Musicians put in an appearance in many of the plays, and in *Timon of Athens* we find a poet and a painter, as well as a jeweler, seeking patronage and a quick sale of their handiwork.

The Professions

Because of the stature of Shakespeare in Western intellectual life, experts in a wide variety of fields have turned their eyes to the plays and documented items of interest to their discipline. These fall quite far outside the standard purview of Shakespeare studies because they are neither literary nor theatrical, but they contain many gems of information that are just about exactly what an actor might like to know.

Medicine

In 1980 Dr. E. Wood Hall of the College of Pharmacy at the University of Texas at Austin completed a study that he called *Shakespeare's Pharmacy*, in which he documented Shakespeare's knowledge of drugs, flowers, and folk medicine. Alphabetical lists of names of plants, drugs, and diseases, followed by the Shakespearean references and Hall's analysis of the scientific validity of the allusion, make for fascinating reading.

Similarly, we have Aubrey C. Kail's *The Medical Mind of Shakespeare*, in which this medical doctor takes us through the plays and notes the many references to medical matters, commenting not only on the accuracy of the allusions but also on the broader social history to aid our understanding. Because Kail has no scholarly agenda, and also because the book has been beautifully produced, with excellent illustrations both historical and from theatrical productions, this book provides an excellent introduction to matters medicinal in the plays.

There are a few doctors in Shakespeare's plays, including the Doctor of Physic who observes the sleepwalking of Lady Macbeth and Helena's father, whom we never meet but who significantly influences the action of *All's Well That Ends Well*. What real-life models would have been available to the first actors and audience of these plays?

English Medicine in the Seventeenth Century, by Dr. A.W. Sloan, includes not only brief descriptions of common ailments and their treatments, but also snapshots of various apothecaries, surgeons, midwives, and quacks, all candidates for models for the doctors who appear in the plays. For example, we learn of a Richard Napier, an ordained clergyman with medical qualifications who became well known for his treatment of the mentally ill. This remarkable man was said to communicate with the archangel Raphael for a prognosis for his patients, and we know from his medical records that he consulted the horoscopes for each patient; he also often prayed with the patient when he was seeking a cure. Sloan's book is nicely laid out, and each entry contains just enough information clearly presented to provide information to the newcomer to the topic. Sadly, many entries in this book describe individuals who practiced long after Shakespeare left London, but the general practice of medicine and the diseases that flourished were not greatly changed through the course of the century.

Lucinda McCray Beier covers the same material as Sloan, but in much more detail. *Sufferers and Healers* is the published version of her Ph.D. dissertation, revised for a wider readership than fellow scholars. In this book you will find fascinating case histories as well as reproductions from contemporary medical manuals and data taken from medical records. Thankfully, the prose is relatively free from either scholarly or medical jargon, and the stories she tells are wonderfully dramatic, great fuel for the sparking of an actor's imagination.

Nancy G. Siraisi's *Medieval and Early Renaissance Medicine* reminds us how medieval Shakespeare's contemporaries were in thinking and practice. Siraisi, like the others, includes reproductions of drawings and woodcuts, and her index lists all of the major diseases for efficient browsing. Her examples are taken from all of Europe, but this should not deter us; English doctors of note had often travelled to the great teaching centers in Basel, Padua, Paris, or Montpellier for their training and shared with all of Renaissance Europe a healthy respect for the ancient writings of Galen and Hippocrates.

Images of Disease

There are some aspects of life in Shakespeare's England that so permeate his plays as to make a study of the topics well worth the while of the astute actor or general reader. These topics seldom constitute the primary focus of a plot, but rather permeate the language of the plays. For example, the plague that devastated London on a regular basis becomes a curse for Falstaff, "A plague upon it, when Thieves cannot be true one to another. Whew: a plague light upon you all" [*1HIV* 2.2.27], and a vivid metaphor of malevolence for Queen Margaret, "Thou wast born to be a plague to men" [*3HVI* 5.5.28]. A quick look at the opening pages of Paul Slack's exhaustive study in particular his section on "Plague and Its History," which contains a vivid description of the symptoms and course of the disease, and "Social Repercussions," which describes what happened when an epidemic struck, will reveal the emotional power and sensory associations that this language would have evoked in Shakespeare's London.

It is important to place all of Shakespeare's metaphors of disease and illness within the context of medical thought of the times. What is the fistula the king of France is cured of in *All's Well That Ends Well*? When Kate says, "Then vail your stomachs" [*Shrew*, 5.2.176], what is being implied? A separate and important subcategory of medical metaphor is the role that the humors play in what we today would term the psychology of personality and emotion.

The scholarly editions of the plays can be counted on to provide an actor with some basic information about the medical profession in Shakespeare's England, and for more detailed information there are several excellent sources. I have often used F. David Hoeniger's *Medicine and Shakespeare in the English Renaissance*, both for the general discussions of medical thought and for specific references to various diseases in the plays, making use of his excellent general subject and play-by-play indexes in the back of the book. For example, actors in *Hamlet* find in the index under that play a reference to the "juice of cursed hebenon" [1.5.62] that Claudius poured into Hamlet, Sr.'s ear. In consulting the cited pages, they will learn that doctors have affirmed that certain poisons, including this very one, can in fact be absorbed through the ear directly into the bloodstream and thereupon cause exactly the symptoms described by the ghost, including "acute exfoliative dermatitis" (255), which the ghost describes in laymen's terms as a "vile and loathsome crust" [1.5.72]. Actors who say or hear lines like "But yet so false that he grieves my very heart-strings" [*Two Gents* 4.2.61] will be interested to learn from Hoeniger's vivid description of medical assumptions and research of the time that what is for us today a metaphor of a breaking heart was, for that time, an observable reality recorded by anatomists and understood by the general public, and was captured vividly as a literal diagnosis in this description of intense suffering: "His grief grew puissant and the strings of life, / Began to crack" [*Lear* 5.3.217].

Let us consider the sort of research you might be interested in doing about the symptoms of and treatments for syphilis. There are so many references to the symptoms that, like the plague, it might well be added to the list of general conditions of life about which every actor should familiarize himself, whatever role he is playing. But let us focus on just one character: Jacques in *As You Like It*. After meeting the fool Touchstone in the forest, Jacques asks Duke Senior if he too can wear a fool's motley and spend his days curing the world of its diseases. The duke responds:

> Most mischievous foul sin, in chiding sin:
> For thou thyself hast been a Libertine,
> As sensual as the brutish sting itself,
> And all the embossed sores and headed evils,
> That thou with licence of free foot hast caught,
> Wouldst thou disgorge into the general world. [2.7.64]

Are we to take from this that Jacques himself is exhibiting the symptoms of syphilis? Whether or not this is a metaphorical or a physical comment, the information provided by medical and social historians might be of interest. Claude Quétel's *History of Syphilis* takes us from the beginning to the present day, and so only the first three chapters are applicable; each of these makes for very interesting reading. Johannes Fabricius includes everything from woodcuts to modern medical records in *Syphilis in Shakespeare's England*, and his entire work makes for fascinating, if nauseating, browsing.

Madness

In addition to the many references to illness in the plays, there are those characters who lose their sanity or pretend to do so in order to advance the plot. Whether you are playing Ophelia, Edgar, Hamlet, or Titus Andronicus or playing opposite these characters in major or supporting roles, you will want to know something about how the Elizabethans viewed madness.

There are Shakespearean scholars who have latched onto this clearly defined subject for their academic territory; the result is such books as *Madness and Drama in the Age of Shakespeare* by Duncan Salkeld. These are as likely to describe the scenes of the plays as they are to discuss the historical facts of madness in sixteenth-century England. For that reason, books in other areas of the library are also worth a look.

Alongside general studies of mental illness you will find historical studies, which will give you the perspective of the mental health professionals concerning the origins of their discipline in early modern England. The most useful is Michael MacDonald's *Mystical Bedlam*. Here you will find immensely significant information about popular stereotypes of insanity, including the connection between suicide and madness (for your Ophelia) and the proofs of lunacy (for your Hamlet, Lear, and Titus). On the former topic, MacDonald reminds us, "Legal thought and popular belief insisted that suicide was self-murder, a conscious and premeditated act committed by a fully rational criminal" (133). On the latter topic, MacDonald notes the substantiating proofs of insanity as "frantic energy, fits of wildly inappropriate laughter or rage, restless wandering or aimless running, and titanic physical strength" (139).

MacDonald's study is also of benefit to more than just the performers of the characters who either go or pretend to go insane, thanks to a section entitled "Stress, Anxiety, and Family Life." Here you will find a wealth of information about what people feared, what caused them discomfort or pain in their daily lives, and the social structures that oppressed and supported the individual in just about equal measure. *Mystical Bedlam* is the result, in large part, of MacDonald's exhaustive reading of the almost sixty volumes of medical notes of Richard Napier, an astrological physician who treated a huge number of people from 1597 until 1634. Because Napier recorded all of his patients' symptoms, including their personal conditions, MacDonald is able to contribute to our understanding of what today would be labelled stress, anxiety, or depression. I was particularly interested in all the stories of unhappiness in love, such as that of the cobbler's fiancée:

At first she did not want to marry him: "Her friends rather and mother, liking of a stranger, would persuade her to marry him, but she fancied him not. Yet her friends were very willing thereunto, and it was concluded in a week." When the parents discovered the shoemaker was a debtor, they broke the engagement with equal indifference to the wishes of their daughter, who by this time had fallen in love with him. (93)

Forced marriages, we learn, were not limited to the nobility or Italian patriarchs like Lord Capulet and his Juliet.

In addition to specialized studies such as MacDonald's, general histories often include excellent introductions to the period that interests us. One such book is Walter Bromberg's *From Shaman to Psychotherapist*, which in two chapters treats classical, medieval, and Renaissance attitudes and activities. "Rationalism and Religion" deals with the traditions that England would have inherited from medieval times and also from the recent rediscovery of classical medical textbooks. "The Devil's Dominion" contains many important comments about the connection between madness and the supernatural in the minds of Shakespeare's first actors and audience. Because Bromberg is in a hurry to get to the beginning of a more scientific approach to mental illness, his survey is not detailed; because, however, he is interested in a clear-sighted evaluation of the roots of his profession, these early chapters are an excellent introduction to the Elizabethan mind-set, whether ignorant or educated, toward the insane.

Vieda Skultans includes one chapter on Shakespeare's England in *English Madness*, and it is an excellent introduction to the theory of the humors and how that affected the diagnosis and treatment of madness. This chapter is also worth reading for a better understanding of a character like "the melancholy Jacques" in *As You Like It*.

Lawyers and the Law

Actors can be thankful for the contribution made by medical historians, perhaps especially for those who like to see in Shakespeare's plays evidence of a detailed and sophisticated understanding of their profession. Not surprisingly, the lawyers also want their say, to demonstrate Shakespeare's knowledge of the law and their knowledge of Elizabethan judicial systems. The legal context of the plays does require some help from experts. Exactly how accurate is the trial scene in *The Merchant of Venice*? How would the coroner have ruled on Ophelia's death by drowning? What legal action could have been taken against Angelo for his attempted seduction of Isabella to fulfill the promise of the title, *Measure for Measure*?

Fortunately, several lawyers with a great love of Shakespeare and a vast knowledge of English legal history have gone through the plays and the historical records and have then written books that will answer all your questions.

I have a great fondness for George W. Keeton's *Shakespeare's Legal and Political Background*, in large part because of his wonderful sense of humor. Here is his introduction to an immensely important historical figure:

One of the few eminent Elizabethans to whom the authorship of Shakespeare's plays has not been attributed is Sir Edward Coke, Queen Elizabeth's Attorney-General, and her successor's formidable Lord Chief Justice. This unusual omission may be due, as Lord Campbell suggests, and as the rough language of his legal writings confirms, to the fact that in the whole course of his life, Coke "never saw a play acted, or read a play. Or was in company with a player," nor, it may be added, did he ever give the slightest hint of possessing any glimmering of a sense of humour. (43)

The most exciting thing about Shakespeare-loving lawyers, or law-loving scholars, is the honest enthusiasm they bring to the subject matter. Because they seek a readership of both lawyers and literary scholars, they avoid the jargon of either discipline, and the result is that non-scholars and non-lawyers alike can delve into these books and pull out just what they are interested in knowing. It was in William Hawley's *Shakespearean Tragedy and the Common Law* that I discovered a fascinating piece of jurisprudence: that Hamlet was within his legal rights in stabbing Polonius to death, because the old man had been hiding behind the arrass. Hawley concludes, "The state trials indicate with certainty that one such as Polonius who secrets himself in the Queen's chamber is strictly liable for the act" (48). Daniel J. Kornstein is another Shakespeare-loving lawyer turned author, and has taken as the title of his book a line from Dick, one of Cade's rebels in the first second part of *Henry VI*, who suggests that the first thing they should do, upon seizing power, is "Kill all the lawyers" [4.2.76].

When people ascribe to Shakespeare an attitude toward lawyers, Jack Cade's rebels are often quoted, lines that are sure to demonstrate that Shakespeare is still our contemporary. Weighing in on the other side of the argument, Ian Ward contends in *Shakespeare and the Legal Imagination* that Shakespeare had a fine sense of legal nuance and a healthy respect for the justiciary. Since it doesn't really matter what Shakespeare himself thought and felt about lawyers, we can concern ourselves entirely with the enactment of legal situations, for which the actor will require some concrete information and a general understanding of the function of things legal that will provide the larger context for the world of the play. Ward's *Shakespeare and the Legal Imagination* is a welcome addition to esoteric studies of legal matters in the plays. Because Ward is neither a Shakespearean scholar nor a historian specializing in the British legal system, he simply presents the information he has in language appropriate to the most general readership, talks about each of the plays from the perspective of the legal elements to be found therein, and supplies an index for cross-checking.

In contrast, the traditional historical or literary approach has produced equally interesting, if less accessible, studies. In addition to the books about things legal that focus on Shakespeare, we can turn to legal historians for information that is broader and less skewed by the need to fit the historical evidence to the events of the play in order to comment on the themes or other issues that interest Shakespearean scholars. Books like John Bellamy's *Criminal Law and Society in Late Medieval and Tudor England* and *The Tudor Law of Treason* contain an index that will take the browsing actor directly to the pages that deal with topics of interest, such as seditious tales, when one is preparing for the trial scene in *The Winter's Tale* or civil disorders if one is playing one of Cade's rioters in the second part of *Henry VI*.

One specific aspect of the marriages of the nobility was the wardship of the orphaned children of the great houses of Elizabethan England. This directly affected Shakespeare's patron, and Southampton's rejection of Anne Cecil might have been in part the model for Bertram's reaction to his forced marriage to Helena in *All's Well That Ends Well*. Legal historians can provide some assistance in puzzling out the complexities of the situation. Joel Hurstfield in *The Queen's Wards* includes Southampton in his discussion of this phenomenon.

The Arts of War

Shakespeare invited his audience to imagine everything from Troy to Bosworth Field, from Actium to Agincourt. In his comedies he readily sends his heroes off to war or brings them onstage from some recent conflict, all the better to sharpen their interest in love, to say nothing of their lovers' interest in them. All of these battles challenge the modern actor to acquire an understanding not only of aspects of military conduct and the sequence of events of any battle mentioned in the plays, but also the general patterns of warfare, the machines and marching orders, the relationship between officers and line soldiers, customary at that time. In addition, it is important to know if the specific military leader being portrayed is a brilliant innovator or a rash fool (depending entirely upon whether his armies win the day) or, alternatively, a traditional strategist and commander, following the customary order of battle and winning or losing the day for that reason. In *Henry V* he provides a Chorus to put into words what is so often implied in his theatre, the responsibility of the audience to provide a vivid imaginary picture of warfare: "Work, work your Thoughts, and therein see a Siege: / Behold the Ordinance on their Carriages, / With fatal mouths gaping on girded Harflew" [3.Prologue.25]. A modern actor must be prepared to do no less. Fortunately, the popularity of historical re-creations of specific military conflicts has resulted in the publication of beautifully illustrated overviews and studies of specific battles, guaranteed to answer more questions than you would ever think to ask, whether your role is that of a common foot soldier like Michael Williams in *Henry V* or a famous military leader like the title character of that play.

As with other aspects of Shakespeare's historical dramatizations, we can observe a mixture of historical accuracy and contemporary coloring, much of which has the ring of authenticity. In *Shakespeare's Military World* Paul Jorgensen provides the larger context within which these military scenes were first performed. He blends together a close look at the events and personnel, cross-referenced to published texts on the art of war, and is careful not to forget the popular stereotypes at work in the theatre. *Miles gloriosus*, or the counterfeit soldier, makes an appearance in his index, as do the better-known generals such as Essex and Leicester, the better-known battles such as Agincourt and Philippi, and everything from the pillaging of common soldiers to jealousy in promotion. Many interesting bits of information are presented in this useful resource book. For example, one would wonder what Shakespeare's first actors and audience felt about the hanging of Bardolph, Prince Hal's old drinking companion, for looting a church [*HV* 3.6], knowing as they did that the difference between illegal pillage and honorable ransom was the scale of the theft and the rank of the thief. Elizabeth counted upon the income from her navy, called pirates in other countries, and nothing made her more angry than "embezzling" of her royal plunder by ordinary soldiers (150).

The Art of War and Renaissance England, John Hale's contribution to the Folger Guides to the Age of Shakespeare series, is a volume on all things military, in which he introduces the reader to a broad general discussion of the art of war in England and then reproduces a series of frontispieces, woodcuts, and other illustrations. Hale's discussion of each reproduction on the facing page provides an excellent source of information about attitudes to military conflict and weaponry as well as historical details about the wars fought in Shakespeare's lifetime.

For a more detailed introduction to matters military, C.G. Cruickshank's *Elizabeth's Army* is likely to have the answers to your questions. Cruickshank's index is not particularly helpful, but his book is laid out into chapters for ease of browsing, whether your interest is "Uniforms" in connection with Rosalind's chosen male attire, "A gallant curtle-axe upon my thigh" [*AYLI* 1.3.115], or "Discipline" in connection to the hanging of Bardolph.

These books allow us to see Shakespeare's battles through Elizabethan eyes. Questions will arise in rehearsal, however, about the actual battles, the historical reality of medieval or classical warfare, and the social context of all things military in the era in which the play is set. These questions will lead you to quite a different section of the library, under the letter U, that is dedicated to the history of great battles, famous generals, and the development of the machines of war. Here you will find books like *War Through the Ages* by Lynn Montross and *The Art of War in the Western World* by Archer Jones that can be consulted for their preliminary chapters, as these books deal with war before, during, and after Shakespeare's lifetime. George Gush's *Renaissance Armies* contains a wealth of useful details, supplemented by illustrations of flags, uniforms, and weaponry associated with specific armies of this era. For a general reference book there is *The Hutchinson Dictionary of Ancient and Medieval Warfare*, edited by Matthew Bennett. The same can be said of *The Cambridge Illustrated History of Warfare*, edited by Geoffrey Parker, and *The Encyclopedia of War Machines*, edited by Daniel Bowen.

Henry V *and Military History*

No other play sets quite the challenge of *Henry V*, with its evocation of the famous battle at Agincourt and the siege of Harfleur. Here you will find such specific allusions as Henry's use of the term "a gentleman of the company" to identify himself to the guard while in disguise [4.1.39] and Fluellen's reference to the concavities of the mines created by Macmorris's pioneers [3.2.59]. Who are all these military personnel, what are all these specific activities, and just what did happen at Harfleur and Agincourt?

Although Christopher Duffy does not discuss Henry's French campaigns in *Siege Warfare*, he does include a detailed examination of the continental conflicts in which English soldiers fought during Shakespeare's lifetime. His illustrations are particularly useful for drawing a link between the words of Shakespeare's play and the associations held by the first actors and audience members. Parma's assault of Tournai, in the 1682 drawing by P. Melchor de Novar (75), and the same artist's rendering of Giambelli's destruction of the Spanish bridge at Antwerp (79) are vivid pictures of what Macmorris is unable to achieve, "I would have blowed up the Town, so Christ save me law, in an hour" [3.2.91] and what Fluellen and his comrades have prevented: "Marry, th'athversary was have possession of the Bridge, but he is enforced to retire, and the Duke of Exeter is Master of the Bridge" [3.6.93]. Although Martin Brice does not include a picture of Harfleur in *Forts and Fortresses*, his description of medieval forts and their fortifications helps me to envision just why Henry was held at Harfleur for two months, and only won the city when the governor reluctantly capitulated [3.3.44].

Contamine's *War in the Middle Ages* contains a section titled "Contracts, Salaries and Volunteers," where I can read about the indenture for military service under which Edmund Paston would receive 18 pence a day in exchange for mounting watch and doing guard duty, and otherwise carry out the orders of his commanding officer. However, this is not the only source of income that Paston clearly anticipated, as Contamine explains:

The duke was to receive the thirds of his war gains and the thirds of the thirds (that is about 11 per cent) of his retinue's winnings. Within six days of a capture the duke was to be informed of the name, rank, state, condition, number and value of prisoners. Edmund could keep them unless they happened to be the king of France, the king's sons, dukes, counts, lieutenants or captains in chief, whom he was to deliver either to the king of England or to the duke, in return for suitable recompense. (152)

Is this the sort of gentleman of the company that Henry is claiming to be when he wanders around his camp at night? If such agreements were in place, it casts a slightly different light upon Henry's decision to execute the French prisoners [4.7.63], some of whom would have been worth a considerable sum of money in ransom. Stephen Turnbull's *The Book of the Medieval Knight* suggests an added complexity to this situation in his discussion of the ransoming of a king, something that Henry announces he will not accept [3.6.154] but his soldiers foresee as the natural outcome of defeat [4.1.122].

It is in John Keegan's *The Face of Battle* that I find the most detailed analysis of the events at Agincourt, including a discussion of the complex interweaving of chivalric and Christian codes of conduct and the horrific reality of hand-to-hand combat, described by Michael Williams:

The King him-self hath a heavy Reckoning to make, when all those Legs, and Arms, and Heads, chopped off in a Battle, shall join together at the latter day, and cry all, We died at such a place, some swearing, some crying for a Surgeon; some upon their Wives, left poor behind them; some upon the Debts they owe, some upon their Children rawly left: I am afeared, there are few die well, that die in a Battle. [4.1.134]

The morality of Henry's cause is debated by John Sutherland and Cedric Watts in *Henry V, War Criminal?* Whatever we might think of their conclusions, it remains to each actor playing the role and participating in the production to come to terms with the seductive glory of medieval warfare.

Sailors

Several of Shakespeare's plays feature seafaring language, characters, or even scenes. If you are playing the wrack of the king's ship in the first scene of *The Tempest*, you will want to know something about sailing ships of the time, in addition to the actual meaning of each of the commands shouted by the boatswain. A useful book is Alexander Frederick Falconer's *Shakespeare and the Sea.* Falconer bore the rank of lieutenant commander of the Royal Naval Reserve at the time of publication, and his writing reflects his firsthand knowledge of the long traditions of the British navy. Occasionally it is irritating to encounter his assumption that the reader will understand basic shipboard terminology, but a decent dictionary in hand solves that problem fairly readily. The book includes an index by play as well as by term, which is invaluable in checking for nautical terms buried in land-bound plays.

A wonderful little dictionary that is sadly only to be found in university reference libraries is Falconer's 1965 *A Glossary of Shakespeare's Sea and Naval Terms Including Gunnery.* Here you will find a Royal Navy man's precise definitions as well as the plays in which they occur. There is no index that lists each play and the naval references to be found there, and most editors will have made use of this information in their notes, but the book still makes for fun browsing, especially for those playing members of the frantic crew in the first scene of *The Tempest.*

Artisans

One piece of the puzzle that will help to make sense not only of Shakespeare's acting company, but also the nonnoble characters who appear in the plays, is the economic and social organizations known as guilds. These medieval urban societies were on the cusp of change in early modern England, but the triumph of the merchant class was still in the future in Shakespeare's London, where the great guild organizations continued to oversee the training, marketing, and protection of their members. Although each writer has more to say about the eighteenth and nineteenth centuries than earlier times, both Jasper Ridley in *A History of the Carpenters' Company* and Jennifer Lang in *Pride without Prejudice* capture the glorious history of the great guilds. You can balance Ridley's and Lang's boosterism with R. A. Leeson's more scholarly *Travelling Brothers*. Leeson's first three chapters are an excellent summary of the social and economic status of the skilled craftsman, like Bottom the weaver, Quince the carpenter, Starveling the tailor, Snug the joiner, Flute the bellows-mender, and Snout the tinker. In contrast, Laura Stevenson's discussion of the portrait of this class of individual in the literature of the time is much less helpful. Her first chapter, in which she sets the economic context, is a good general introduction, but her focus is on the conventions the writers used and the themes they explored, rather than upon the real-life models for the characters.

Yeomen

A good introduction to country life has once again been provided by the Folger Shakespeare Library, and in Albert Schmidt's *The Yeoman in Tudor and Stuart England* you will find reproductions of woodcuts and quotations from contemporary sources that illustrate everything from pruning trees and the gathering of fruit to the husbandry of horses and the slaughtering of livestock. Most important, Schmidt disabuses the reader of any notion that there is an automatic equation between yeomen and poverty. This class of individual contained some successful small farmers who were busy acquiring all of the trappings of the emerging middle class, including larger houses, more furniture, and the wherewithal to send their sons to the local grammar school.

Shakespeare's characterization of the assorted country folk in his plays is shaped as much by the comic conventions that require the uncivilized bumpkin to contrast with the overcultivated courtier as with the firsthand knowledge that Shakespeare and his first actors might bring to the roles. Costard, in *Love's Labour's Lost*, seems to have nothing else to do with his time than to carry letters for his betters and misuse fancy words in what might be an indication of his ignorant pomposity, à la Dogsberry, but he just as likely represents a sly critique of the nobility who surround him. In contrast, in *As You Like It* Corin, who lives at the edge of the forest of Arden and tends sheep for a miserly absentee landlord, has much more to say about his working life, though he too still seems to have time to banter amusingly with Touchstone about the difference between country ways and court ways.

So, although a detailed understanding of the husbandry of the sheepcote might be of interest to the actor playing Corin, the real benefit of learning about country life in Shakespeare's England will be for the actor seeking to unlock the richness of Shakespeare's imaginative language. His metaphors and similes are filled with comparisons between a complex human experience and a mundane aspect of simple daily life: the unknowable compared with the familiar, as when Macbeth compares the refreshment of sleep to the knitting up of a raveled sleeve, that most ordinary of housewifely activities [2.2.34].

THE ARISTOCRACY

To sort our Nobles, from our common men.

Montjoy [*HV* 4.7.74]

At the other end of the social scale, we have the members of the nobility and the challenge facing the modern actor in attempting to keep straight the family names, the titles, the personal names, and the many different ways in which a character can be identified or addressed. Who were these people, and what was their life like? One scholar whom you will find cited in general introductions about the nobility of Shakespeare's England is Lawrence Stone, who might be called the grandfather of the social history of early modern Britain. You will find many very useful chapters in his monumental study *The Crisis of the Aristocracy*; I have made great use of the chapters on credit to make sense of Bassanio's situation in *The Merchant of Venice* and have appreciated such interesting information as the fact that between 1560 and 1610 one marquis, eight earls, one viscount, and six barons were known to have fathered children by women other than their wives. This puts the situation of *King Lear*'s Edmund into perspective. In his chapter "The Attractions of the Court" Stone links the economic crisis facing many noble families with the political and social imperatives of living close to the reigning monarch, an aspect of the life of the nobility that has a significant impact upon the experiences of the average Shakespearean actor.

Alongside the scholarly tomes, we have a limited number of wonderful first-hand accounts of Elizabeth's and James's courtiers. These are best when the author is an unashamed gossip, as is Sir Robert Naunton. Here, from his *Fragmenta Regalia*, is his demolition of one of Elizabeth's favorites, if not Naunton's:

Sir Christopher Hatton came to the court (as his opposite Sir John Perrot was wont to say) by the galliard, for he came thither as a private gentleman of the Inns of Court in a masque, and for his activity and person (which was tall and proportionable) taken into the Queen's favour. He was first made vice-chamberlain and shortly after advanced to the place of Lord Chancellor.

A gentleman that beside the graces of his person and dancing had also the additament of a strong and subtle capacity, one that could soon learn the discipline and garb of the times and court. And the truth is he had a large proportion both of gifts and endowment but too much of the season of envy, and he was a mere vegetable of the court that sprung at night and sunk again at his noon. (67–68)

Scholars are reluctant to give any credence to the evidence offered by such biased observers as Sir Robert, but actors can only be thankful that his observations have been preserved.

The Courtier's Life

How many times do the junior members of the company play waiting gentlemen and women? They stand around, as Hamlet says, the mute observers of the fearful scene, whether it be the endgame of *Hamlet* or the early court scenes of *As You Like It.* Who might these characters be? How would they listen to the words of the "observed of all observers," the principal actors of their court world?

Scholars have much to offer actors seeking to invest their silent courtiers with life stories, attitudes, and individual reactions to the words spoken in their presence. Whether the setting is Denmark or France, the frame of reference for Shakespeare's audience would have been the contemporary court world, and a quick look at the personalities and daily life in an English royal palace will provide much raw material for an actor's invention.

All the Queen's Men by Neville Williams is a good place to start. This book will give you just enough history to understand the rise and fall of favorites, the various factions and how they influenced public and private events, and the great noble families who dominated their time. In addition, you will find portraits and brief biographies of individuals upon whom you might model your personal courtier.

For the ladies who silently attend the various queens of England or Denmark or the princess of France, an excellent introduction is Anne Somerset's *Ladies-in-Waiting,* an eminently readable book that will provide you with countless models for your character, either from Shakespeare's time or from later generations if your production has been reset into another century. Details about life at court, if such information will help you invest your lord or lady with a life offstage, can be found in books about palace life. I have found Christopher Hibbert's *The Court at Windsor* helpful, in particular because it provides snapshots of daily life at Windsor Castle from the time of Henry II right through to Elizabeth II. This is most useful if your production has been reset into another century. The illustrations alone make for productive browsing, but Hibbert rewards anyone willing to read at length with compelling anecdotes and vivid descriptions of royal doings. David Starkey's *The English Court* contains an excellent introductory chapter, followed by a chapter on the history plays, then one for Elizabeth's court and one for James's. The book only goes up to the civil war, so actors in plays that have been relocated by directors to a later period will want to explore supplementary information found in Hibbert.

For an alternative approach to the history of one castle, you might want to consider the many royal residences that were scattered around the countryside and in London. Simon Thurley's *The Royal Palaces of Tudor England* contains not only many excellent photographs and reproductions of paintings and architectural drawings, but also many interesting details about palace life such as the workings of the palace kitchens and garderobes (for those actors who never lose sight of the fact that even courtiers have a digestive system). Another book for courtiers, especially if the time period is shifted to another court, is H.D. Molesworth's *The Golden Age of Princes*. This book contains great pictures and lots of details about rituals and the duties of the courtier.

A book that provides another context for the development of supporting characters in court scenes is *The Aspiring Mind of the Elizabethan Younger Generation* by Anthony Esler. In this the junior courtiers might find real-life models for the younger generation of ambitious courtiers whose opportunities were limited until the older generation stepped aside. Robert Devereux, the earl of Essex, is perhaps the individual best known to modern readers, and he appears in Esler's book along with another well-known celebrity, Sir Walter Raleigh; Robert Sidney and Robert Cecil are less well known but in many ways more useful for the playing of supporting courtiers.

Not everyone will want to work his way through Frank Whigham's *Ambition and Privilege*, but those who do will be well rewarded. Whigham blends references to the popular books on a courtier's life that might have been read by an aspiring young man of Elizabeth's court with information about the successful strategies used by some of these courtiers, of which the general public, including Shakespeare and his actors, might well have been aware. This book makes it clear how the choices a courtier made in what he wore, the gifts he gave and received, and even the language he trained himself to use were significant in the never-ending dance of competitive self-glorification. Sadly, the index in this book is not at all useful to the theatrical browser; the table of contents is little better. Flipping through the book will reveal interesting tidbits on almost every page, but answers to specific questions are more difficult to find.

In some ways the courtier's world changed completely with the arrival of James of Scotland; in other ways there was little difference in substance, though styles continued to change with the fashion. The transition from Tudor to

Stuart monarchies remains blurred within the plays because we know only when the plays must have been completed, not when Shakespeare began working on them, and all of them reflect contemporary society and individuals only obliquely.

Most of us have a fairly interesting set of images of life in the Tudor court, gleaned in large part from Hollywood epics and BBC miniseries. However, the intrigues of the courtiers surrounding James and Charles are, if anything, even more melodramatic, lacking only a charismatic central character to attract a full cinematic treatment. For a snapshot of the central characters, I recommend David Lindley's *The Trials of Frances Howard* and Beatrice White's *Cast of Ravens* along with David Bergeron's two books, *Royal Family, Royal Lovers*, and *Shakespeare's Romances and the Royal Family*; this second book draws some fascinating parallels between Shakespeare's late plays and events and personalities at court.

In her collection of articles entitled *The Mental World of the Jacobean Court*, Linda Levy Peck has published a first-rate introduction to the way that the court of James viewed itself; here you will find many themes that also occur in Shakespeare's later plays. Peck's other contribution to the volume, an article entitled "The Mentality of a Jacobean Grandee," is equally useful as an examination of a real-life model for such fictional characters as Gonzalo in *The Tempest*.

G.P.V. Akrigg's *Jacobean Pageant* contains three chapters that are particularly useful in providing details for our courtier-actors. "The New Court Is Formed" yields the long list of courtiers who would have been in residence in any castle; "A Day's Business at Winchester" and "The Courtier's Life" are ideal reading for those looking for a "snapshot" of castle life.

"Courtesie"

One area of scholarly research that has immediate and lasting impact on the work of actors is the study of concepts of courtesy that were prevalent in Shakespeare's England. Scholars working in this area make extensive use of the various handbooks published in English, most of which were translations and/or imitations of *Il Cortegiano* (The courtier) by Baldesar Castiglione. There is, naturally, an English tradition of courtly manners, inherited from medieval codes of chivalric conduct, and astute historians also consider the ambivalence with which stout-hearted true-blue sons of England might accept, or not, imported Italian manners and affectations.

Historians also examine the clash of codes of conduct that reflect the intersection of class identification in early modern England, where the habits of dress, address, and any of a variety of public and private interactions might be governed by contrasting styles. In this sort of study they are aided by the evidence in the dramatic literature of the period, in particular the satiric comedies that mocked the affectations of the socially mobile.

Although Joan Wildeblood and Peter Brinson's *The Polite World* was published in 1965, I would still recommend it as the best introduction to the theory and practice of courtesy in this and any period covered by their study. They begin with a section on the ideals, which includes a chapter on how young people were educated in the cultural mores of their time. This short introduction to their lengthy examination of the details of behavior serves to remind the reader that there is always a gap between what a society claims to admire and what people actually do in a given time and place. Wildeblood and Brinson also remind the reader that manners do not occur in a vacuum by inserting a second preliminary section that sketches the basic considerations of the environment: the domestic furnishings and the activities of the servant classes, which supported the leisure-time pursuit of perfect manners by the members of the elite classes. It is in Wildeblood and Brinson's lengthy third section that an actor will find specific instruction on what they term the "technique" of good manners: how to sit, how to walk, and how to handle fans, hats, gloves, and rapiers. Members of the acting company embarking on the creation of a society can only say, "Thank you, thank you, thank you" for this study.

Unlike his contemporary, Ben Jonson, Shakespeare sets out to satirize the affectations of the excessively mannered only rarely, but inevitably his plays touch upon the way that people interact, and so upon the good, or bad, manners of his time. When Corin, the country bumpkin of *As You Like It*, is comparing court life to country life with his new friend Touchstone, he says, "You told me, that you salute not at the Court, but you kiss your hands; that courtesy would be uncleanly if Courtiers were shepherds" [3.2.48]. How fortunate it is that Wildeblood and Brinson's explanation is available to make sense of what otherwise seems like the strangest possible activity, which has its roots in the veneration demonstrated by a priest during religious ceremonies. It appears to have enjoyed some currency as the height of fashionable courtly behavior in European courts, but seems never to have caught on in England, except among the set of hypercourtiers often mocked by the satirists. The association that the English audience might have made with this as a uniquely French custom could have been sparked by the French locale of *As You Like It*.

Anna Bryson's much more recent work *From Courtesy to Civility* is chock-full of interesting tidbits, but is not nearly as useful for the browsing actor. Almost every page, if it is skimmed, turns up a nugget that amuses or informs, but neither the table of contents nor the index help the actor in search of specific information about some detail of courtesy or good manners. However, Bryson's ability to take in the scholarly developments of the thirty-three years intervening, combined with her witty and accessible writing style, makes this book well worth a close examination by actors seeking to immerse themselves in the manners of the times.

As is often the case in scholarly collections, a promising title turns out to be of little practical use to the browsing actor. Jorge Arditi's *A Genealogy of Manners* has the evocative subtitle *Transformations of Social Relations in France and England from the Fourteenth to the Eighteenth Century*. Although the book is praised as "remarkable for its scope and erudition" on the back cover, the scope and erudition have taken Arditi in the direction of theory (Norbert Elias, Michel Foucault, and Pierre Bourdieu are mentioned) and analysis of the big picture: systems of social relationships and the exertion of power in the interactions between the nobility and the monarch. I suspect that Arditi would be scornful of Joan Wildeblood and Peter Brinson's lack of theorizing and their simple presentation of some of the customs and attitudes. Actors, while acknowledging Arditi's undoubted erudition, can leave his book on the dusty shelf.

FOOLS

> Let me play the fool,
> With mirth and laughter let old wrinkles come.
>
> Gratiano [*Merchant* 1.1.79]

I have always felt great sympathy for the actors cast as one of Shakespeare's fools. Like the clown characters, they are left with the responsibility for saying whichever of the jokes have survived the knife in the cut text the company is using and so have to plow through the scholarly explanations of why what they say was funny four hundred years ago. Is there anything sadder than the serious explanation of why a joke is funny? Clowns have it easier, in my opinion, because their social status (country oaf, village constable, cheeky servant) is enduring, and modern audiences find their existence in the world of the play credible. But what is a fool?

I have vivid memories from my childhood of the Danny Kaye vehicle *The Court Jester*, and the long traditions of motley, bells on cap and toes, bauble and slapstick, and ridiculous behavior to match do fit some of the references and jokes ascribed to the fools. But the real-life court fools, and in fact the entire tradition of the fool, are richer and offer modern actors many more models from which to select a workable persona for the production in which they have been cast.

Enid Welsford's study *The Fool* traces the European medieval heritage as well as specific English practices and examples. She then explores how the phenomenon of the courtly fool is reflected in literary documents, with a chapter on Elizabethan drama so that you can see just how much Shakespeare was working within a stage convention.

John Doran also has a chapter on English court fools in *The History of Court Fools* and records some interesting stories that Touchstone and company might find inspiring. The story is told of John Low, a fool in the court of James V of Scotland, that he was rebuked for not having shown proper bowing and scraping before some great lord. Low claimed not to have recognized such

greatness and was instructed to judge a man's greatness by his dress, specifically, his velvet robes and gold chains. A short time later, Low was seen
bowing deeply to the mules in the courtyard, claiming loudly that these were
clearly great lords, as witness their velvetlike skin and the ornately decorated
halters round their necks. His punch line was "Sure, I shall never learn the
difference between a lord and a beast!" (192).

Sandra Billington's *A Social History of the Fool* is a less scholarly and so less
dense treatment of the topic, but she discusses the broadest general sociological
implications rather than describing any useful details. This is still a good introduction to the concept of an "allowed fool," as Olivia describes Feste [*12th
Night* 1.5.94].

You might also want to have a look at Vicki Janik's sourcebook *Fools and
Jesters in Literature, Art, and History*. Her introduction traces the characteristics
of fools working in a tradition that stretches from the earliest recorded human
activity to the latest film and television, all around the world. She has also
collected articles by a variety of authors on fools that Shakespeare might have
known or known of as well as William Kemp and Robert Armin, the actors
who would have played these roles for Shakespeare. Each article is a clear,
straightforward general introduction with a good bibliography. Some of the
historical information about Archie Armstrong, James's fool, or Will Somers,
the fool of Henry VIII, can help us to comprehend Shakespeare's fools. Have
a look also at the portrait of Sir Thomas More's family, in which his fool
appears, not in a pointed hat with bells, but looking like a wise and elderly
uncle or family friend.

VILLAINS, ROGUES, AND NOTORIOUS FAILURES

> Oh what a Rogue and Peasant slave am I?
>
>   Hamlet [*Hamlet* 2.2.550]

Not all of Shakespeare's characters are kings and princesses or members of
the nobility. Some are quite ordinary citizens or even extraordinary ones, rep-
resentatives of England's underworld, about which we have some wonderful
information thanks to the work of scholars. Gāmini Salgādo's *The Elizabethan
Underworld* is one of many books that can be found in sections of the library
quite removed from the Shakespeare shelves. That is because it contains historical information in a sociological context rather than literary analysis informed by the findings of social historians. Salgādo quotes Shakespeare
occasionally, but more often he makes reference to the plays of Shakespeare's
contemporaries who wrote in the new genre of city comedy and domestic
drama, a genre that apparently held little appeal for Shakespeare.

For a taste of the scholarship that must be completed before a sociological
phenomenon from a different era can be described and discussed in relation

to Shakespeare's plays, have a look at John Pound's excellent study, *Poverty and Vagrancy in Tudor England*. Don't be put off by the many citations and the statistical charts. Pound tells a compelling story of the dispossessed who were very much in evidence on the streets of London as well as in the countryside around Stratford. Here is his description of one aspect of the vagrancy laws:

Any man or woman who lacked means of support and remained unemployed for three days or more was deemed a vagrant as a matter of course. On conviction before two justices of the peace, the beggar was to be branded with a "V" and then given over to the informant as his slave for a period of two years. In return for meals of bread and water, and the occasional luxury of "refuse of meat", he was expected to perform any task his master gave him, however vile it might be. If he refused, he was liable to be whipped, chained and, if necessary, imprisoned with iron rings round his neck and legs. The informant could capitalize on his property whenever he chose to do so either by selling the slave outright or by leasing him for a specified period of time. Should the master become ill, and look like expiring before the two-year period had elapsed, he was authorized to bequeath the slave to his heirs. Life was hardly likely to be congenial for the enslaved vagrants and it was assumed that some, at least, would attempt to escape. In consequence, it was stipulated that a runaway could be enslaved for life for a first offence and executed for a second. (39)

This aspect of normal, everyday life in Shakespeare's England places quite a different cast on the Earl of Kent's decision in *King Lear* to disguise himself as just such a masterless man and seek employment with the man who exiled him.

When Lear is being led into a hovel in the middle of the storm sequence, he appears to come to a realization about the nature of poverty:

Poor naked wretches, where so e'er you are
That bide the pelting of this pitiless storm,
How shall your House-less heads, and unfed sides,
Your looped, and windowed raggedness, defend you
From seasons such as these? O I have ta'en
Too little care of this: Take Physic, Pomp,
Expose thy self to feel what wretches feel,
That thou mayst shake the superflux to them,
And show the Heavens more just. [3.4.28]

For a richer understanding of the dispossessed and alienated in Shakespeare's England, an actor can turn to studies by Shakespearean scholars and by social historians. William C. Carroll's *Fat King, Lean Beggar* is the best general introduction on this topic. Here you will find first a presentation of the seminal works on poverty which shaped the attitudes toward and discussions of poverty at this time, and then a discussion of the poor rebels, the sly scoundrels, and the experiences of disempowerment undertaken by characters like Kent and Edgar in *King Lear*.

Autolycus, who appears in *The Winter's Tale*, leaps off the page without any reference to the social history. But without a quick look at the available resources, it is impossible to know just how outrageous, ingenious, original, or familiar his activities might be. There were in fact a high proportion of excourtiers working as con artists in London in Shakespeare's day, so when Autolycus announces, "I have served Prince Florizel, and in my time wore three-pile, but now I am out of service" [4.3.13], Shakespeare's first audience would not assume that he was lying. The fictional scoundrel's theatrical setup for stealing purses may seem outrageous to us: he pretends to have been beaten by the notorious thief Autolycus, which means that he describes himself in the most negative terms while demonstrating his skill in doing the very deed he is describing. This makes for great fun in the theatre, but when we have a look at the stories recorded in the many pamphlets about the underworld published during Shakespeare's lifetime, we find many examples of equally elaborate cons perpetrated by thieves with a definite gift for the theatrical. These are readily available in collections such as *The Elizabethan Underworld*, edited by A.V. Judges, and *Elizabethan Rogues and Vagabonds*, edited by Frank Aydelotte.

Stories from the Underworld

Robert Greene is an Elizabethan writer best known for his vitriolic attack on Shakespeare, which appeared in *Greene's Groats-Worth of Wit, Bought With a Million Repentance: Describing the Folly of Youth, the Falsehood of Makeshift Flatterers, the Misery of the Negligent, and Mischiefs of Deceiving Courtesans. Written Before His Death and Published At His Dying Request*, a document reputed to be Greene's deathbed musings. This is a reprint well worth reading aloud, to savor the wit and the venom of this remarkable contemporary of Shakespeare. Here is the section in which the insult appears, just three lines after the opening address to Christopher Marlowe, Thomas Nashe, and George Peele, three other playwrights:

Base minded men all three of you, if by my miserie you be not warnd: for unto none of you (like mee) sought those burres to cleave: those Puppets (I meane) that spake from our mouths, those Anticks garnisht in our colours. Is it not strange, that I, to whom they all have beene beholding: is it not like that you, to whome they all have beene beholding, shall (were yee in that case as I am now) bee both at once of them forsaken? Yes trust them not: for there is an upstart Crow, beautified with our feathers, that with his *Tygers hart wrapt in a Players hyde*, supposes he is as well able to bombast out a blanke verse as the best of you: and beeing an absolute *Johannes fac totum*, is in his owne conceit the onely Shake-scene in a countrey. O that I might intreat your rare wits to be imployed in more profitable courses: & let those Apes imitate your past excellence, and never more acquaint them with your admired inventions. I knowe the best husband of you all will never prove a Usurer, and the kindest of them all will never prove a kind nurse: yet whilest you may, seeke you better Maisters; for it is pittie men of such rare wits, should be subject to the pleasure of such rude groomes.

Greene seems to have had a string of popular sellers with his series about con-artists, known as conny catchers, a conny being a rather stupid visitor to London, easily tricked into parting with his money or her virtue. Greene published *Notable Discovery of Coosnage* (1591), *Cuthbert Conny-catcher: The Defence of Conny-catching* (1592), *The Second Part of Conny-catching* (1592), and *The Thirde & Last Part of Conny-catching, with the New Devised Knauish Art of Foole-taking: The Like Cosenages and Villenies Neuer Before Discouered: A Disputation Betweene a Hee Conny-catcher and a Shee Conny-catcher* (1592) before he succumbed to his poverty, venereal disease, and/or the plague. John Marston later cashed in on the fad with *The Scourge of Villanie* (1599) and Thomas Dekker turned out *English Villainies Discovered by Lantern and Candlelight* (1608) and *The Gull's Horn-Book* (1609). Any and all of these make for amusing browsing, and excerpts from these sources are included in collections of prose for modern readers.

Here is a sample from E. D. Pendry's easy-to-read modernized version of *English Villainies Discovered by Lantern and Candlelight* (with glossary for unfamiliar terms in the back):

A *clapperdudgeon* is in English a "beggar born (some call him a *palliard*), of which sorts there are two: first, natural; secondly, artificial. This fellow above all other that are in the regiment of rogues goeth best armed against the cruelty of winter. He should be wise, for he loves to keep himself warm, wearing a patched *caster* a "cloak" for his upper robe, under that a *togemans* a "gown" with high *stampers* "shoes", the soles an inch thick pegged, or else patches at his girdle ready to be clamped on, a great *skew* a "brown dish" hanging at his girdle and a tassel of thrums to wipe it, a brace of greasy night-caps on his head and over them, lest he should catch a knavish cold, a hat or *nab cheat*; a good *filch* or "staff" in his hand, having a little iron peg in the end of it, a *buhar* a "little dog" following him, with a smug *doxy* attired fit for such a roguish companion. (295)

An indication of the popularity of books about the underworld is the number of publications that were printed in such numbers as to ensure survival of at least one copy to form the basis of a modern reprint. What does Hamlet mean when he accuses himself of being a rogue? The reprinted pamphlets, sociological studies, and historical biographies will give you specific and amusing stories to put into your memory, with which to build a strong association, so that Hamlet's self-deprecating comment is never again a bland, generic condemnation, but a vivid and demeaning comparison between a royal prince and the second-rate cheat and con-man so common in London's underworld.

Infamous and Glorious

Shakespeare's England was populated by some very striking individuals very much in the eye of the general public, in addition to the monarchy and the nobility struggling for supremacy in court circles. There are many fascinating individuals whose infamous activities would have been very much "in the air" and so available for Shakespeare's first actors and audience. Arthur Freeman has put together a very entertaining collection entitled *Elizabethan Eccentrics*, well worth a read from cover to cover, though several of his eccentrics lived after Shakespeare's time. You will want to read about the "Roaring Girl," a real-life cross-dresser who lived out Rosalind's fictional goal:

> Were it not better,
> Because that I am more than common tall,
> That I did suit me all points like a man,
> A gallant curtle-axe upon my thigh,
> A boar-spear in my hand, and in my heart
> Lie there what hidden woman's fear there will,
> We'll have a swashing and a martial outside,
> As many other mannish cowards have,
> That do outface it with their semblances. [*AYLI* 1.3.114]

Moll Cutpurse, as she was called, roared around Bankside, up and down the streets outside the Globe, making a spectacle of herself through her defiance of traditional women's roles and clothing. She was the star of her very own play, *The Roaring Girl*, as well as ballads and stories, and thanks to Randall Nakayama's edition of *The Life and Death of Mrs. Mary Frith*, the modern actor can catch a glimpse of the original.

Some of the seedier contemporaries of Shakespeare in the great city of London have brought upon themselves such notoriety that they have become the subject of full-length historical biographies. Why is it that the villains are so much more interesting than the hardworking actor-playwrights who used them for inspiration? While biographies of Shakespeare can prove somewhat tedious, the stories about the notorious are usually entertaining and informative.

Francis Langley is of interest to theatre historians as the owner of the Swan Theatre on Bankside, but he is of even greater interest to William Ingram in *A London Life in the Brazen Age* as an example of a grasping, conniving, struggling, and unfortunate capitalist, an excellent illustration of the shady deals, legal shenanigans, financial manipulations, and triumphs and defeats that were the common experience of an Elizabethan businessman. Ingram tells a fascinating story and, along the way, explains much about life on the edge in Shakespeare's London. This is a valuable book not only for the merchants who populate Venice along with Shylock, but also for the gallant young men who enjoy the freedom of the city of Vienna. One of the latter, Isabella's condemned brother Claudio, explains to his good friend Lucio why he is being taken away in chains to prison:

> From too much liberty, (my Lucio) Liberty:
> As surfeit is the father of much fast,
> So every Scope by the immoderate use
> Turns to restraint: Our Natures do pursue,
> Like Rats that ravin down their proper Bane,
> A thirsty evil, and when we drink, we die. [*Measure* 1.2.125]

Lucio responds to this image of self-indulgence as rats that ravin, or gobble down, their deserved poison or bane with his own attitude and imagery: "If I could speak so wisely under an arrest, I would send for certain of my Creditors: and yet, to say the truth, I had as lief have the foppery of freedom, as the morality of imprisonment" [1.2.131]. Francis Langley was a creditor to many of the young gallants of London, and although his type can be found readily in the London comedies of Shakespeare's contemporaries, we can find echoes of the London scene even when Shakespeare sets his plays in Italy or France.

These notorious, nefarious Londoners have only recently come out from behind the blinding light cast by the big names of the era, the queen and her earls having dominated our attention at the expense of individuals with whom Shakespeare would have had much more in common. It is much more difficult to find out anything about the unnamed many; for the most part we have to be satisfied with general social history studies wherein patterns of behavior are described rather than individuals brought to life.

Leslie Hotson's introduction to *Shakespeare versus Shallow* tells a wonderful story of meticulous scholarship on the part of someone as passionately dedicated to delving as any actor is to theatre. Buried in the Public Record Office were thousands of rolls and bundles of documents dating from the years of Shakespeare's adulthood, more than any one individual could comb in a lifetime of delving. Hotson, following in the footsteps of some great Victorian diggers, set his sights on the rolls of the Queen's Bench and, in particular, the petitions for sureties of the peace, what today we would call peace bonds or restraining orders. The documents offer snapshots of some juicy gossip as one party informs on the other or is informed upon by a third party in order to document the feared threat of physical violence that has motivated the petition.

Hotson's long search resulted in the fortuitous discovery he determinedly sought. In the official records of 1596 we find more than one concrete fact about Shakespeare. On August 11 his son Hamnet was buried in Stratford. On October 20 a coat of arms was granted to his father John. Finally, we have his tax bill marking his residency as the parish of St. Helen's, Bishopgate, London. It is in this year's records that Hotson found evidence of a surety of the peace being taken out against our William.

Immediately, Hotson began pursuing answers to all the questions this tiny entry raises. Who is William Wayte, the person whose name appears as the fearful defendant? Others are named along with William. Who are they? One happens to be an individual about whom Hotson already knew something. This was Francis Langley, notorious moneylender and owner of the Swan Theatre. Since Hotson knew that the swearing of peace bonds was frequently undertaken tit for tat, he now combed the records backwards and forwards from this date. Sure enough, earlier in the same month he found an entry for Langley's petition against Wayte. Hotson includes reprints of the entries, which give the modern reader some idea of the immense eyestrain he must have endured searching for these obscure clues among the handwritten, abbreviated, Latin entries recorded in the disintegrating manuscripts.

A second person was named in Langley's petition, a William Gardiner, and the combination of Hotson's further digging in a variety of other records with his memory of the name appearing in other documents of historical interest resulted in the uncovering of all sorts of information about Gardiner. He was a justice of the peace for Middlesex and Surrey, in which district sat the Swan. It turned out that Gardiner had been involved in the flurry of repressive government responses to Thomas Nashe's *Isle of Dogs*, which had been performed at the Swan and which resulted in the Privy Council requesting that Gardiner and his fellow justices command Francis Langley to tear down his theatre. But all of that took place the following year. It took still further digging in the records of a variety of courts to uncover the events leading up to the pair of peace bonds. Hotson eventually discovered evidence of Gardiner suing Langley for libel, the quoted offense being "He is a false knave, and a false perjured knave; and I will prove him so" (26). Langley's defense was that Gardiner had given false testimony under oath, and therefore to call him a false, perjured knave was truth, not slander. Gardiner abandoned his claims for £2,200 in damages.

Hotson was now hot on the trail of this William Gardiner, and the result is a completely enjoyable biography cobbled together from the few odd scraps of information and much speculation based upon Hotson's extensive readings in the social, political, and economic history of Shakespeare's England. As might be gathered from the title of the book, Hotson sees in Gardiner a model for Justice Shallow, though Gardiner turns out to have been quite a nasty fellow.

Armed with all of Hotson's discoveries, found after such effort and good fortune, all described vividly in his opening chapter, we can follow him into the heart of his theory. There is no denying that he paints a compelling picture, in particular when he suggests that the extra details included in several of Shallow's scenes were placed there in order to create a satire of Gardiner and his buddy Wayte that would be recognized by everyone "in the know." If Hotson is right, then Wayte, a.k.a. Slender, had a slender whey-face and a little yellow beard. The rest of Hotson's book consists of modern-spelling,

English-language versions of the various legal documents that Hotson found in his search for Gardiner in the court records. These are well worth a dip and browse for the vivid stories and wonderful evocation of ordinary language in the testimony of real Elizabethans.

SHAKESPEARE THE MASTER OF ALL ARTS

Steeped in the Colours of their Trade.

Macbeth [*Macbeth* 2.3.115]

Military historians are tempted to give Shakespeare a few years' military service during the years for which we have no other record of his activities, just as lawyers give him legal training and doctors have suggested an apprenticeship to a surgeon. All of these suggestions cancel each other out, because if he can create such sensitive and accurate portraits of so many professions, and since he could not have undertaken them all, we must assume that he acquired the details he used to make the portraits accurate some other way. Therefore, although it is tempting to imagine him participating in one of the skirmishes in which English troops were involved during his lifetime, or apprenticing himself to a law clerk, a gardener, a falconer, or whatever other profession he seems to have mastered, it is more credible to attribute to him a good ear for jargon and an eye for the raw material out of which to fashion exciting scenes. The most obvious conclusion is that he picked the brains of everyone he met and also that he, the greatest autodidact of the millennium, took advantage of the books that had become available in his lifetime thanks to the explosion of relatively inexpensive printing processes and translations into English of the writings of European and ancient writers.

RECOMMENDED READING

Social Class

Berry, Ralph. *Shakespeare and Social Class*. Atlantic Highlands, NJ: Humanities Press International, 1988.

Burnett, Mark Thornton. *Masters and Servants in English Renaissance Drama and Culture: Authority and Obedience*. New York: St. Martin's Press, 1997.

Cressy, David. *Literacy and the Social Order: Reading and Writing in Tudor and Stuart England*. Cambridge: Cambridge University Press, 1980.

Laslett, Peter. *The World We Have Lost: Further Explored*. London: Methuen, 1983.

The Medical and Legal Professions

Beier, Lucinda McCray. *Sufferers and Healers: The Experience of Illness in Seventeenth-Century England*. London: Routledge & Kegan Paul, 1987.

Bellamy, John. *Criminal Law and Society in Late Medieval and Tudor England.* New York: St. Martin's Press, 1984.

———. *The Tudor Law of Treason: An Introduction.* Toronto: University of Toronto Press, 1979.

Bromberg, Walter. *From Shaman to Psychotherapist: A History of the Treatment of Mental Illness.* Chicago: H. Regnery, 1975.

Fabricius, Johannes. *Syphilis in Shakespeare's England.* London: Jessica Kingsley, 1994.

Hall, E. Wood. *Shakespeare's Pharmacy.* Austin: University of Texas at Austin, College of Pharmacy, 1980.

Hawley, William M. *Shakespearean Tragedy and the Common Law: The Art of Punishment.* New York: Peter Lang, 1998.

Hoeniger, F. David. *Medicine and Shakespeare in the English Renaissance.* Newark: University of Delaware Press, 1992.

Hurstfield, Joel. *The Queen's Wards: Wardship and Marriage under Elizabeth I.* London: Frank Cass, 1973.

Kail, Aubrey C. *The Medical Mind of Shakespeare.* Balgowlah, NSW: Williams & Wilkins, 1986.

Keeton, George W. *Shakespeare's Legal and Political Background.* London: Pitman, 1967.

Kornstein, Daniel J. *Kill All the Lawyers? Shakespeare's Legal Appeal.* Princeton, NJ: Princeton University Press, 1994.

MacDonald, Michael. *Mystical Bedlam: Madness, Anxiety, and Healing in Seventeenth-Century England.* Cambridge: Cambridge University Press, 1981.

Quétel, Claude. *History of Syphilis.* Translated by Judith Braddock and Brian Pike. Cambridge: Polity Press, 1990.

Salkeld, Duncan. *Madness and Drama in the Age of Shakespeare.* Manchester: Manchester University Press, 1994.

Siraisi, Nancy G. *Medieval and Early Renaissance Medicine: An Introduction to Knowledge and Practice.* Chicago: University of Chicago Press, 1990.

Skultans, Vieda. *English Madness: Ideas on Insanity, 1580–1890.* London: Routledge & Kegan Paul, 1979.

Slack, Paul. *The Impact of Plague in Tudor and Stuart England.* London: Routledge & Kegan Paul, 1985.

Sloan, A.W. *English Medicine in the Seventeenth Century.* Durham: Durham Academic Press, 1996.

Ward, Ian. *Shakespeare and the Legal Imagination.* London: Butterworths, 1999.

The Arts of War

Bennett, Matthew, ed. *The Hutchinson Dictionary of Ancient and Medieval Warfare.* Chicago: Fitzroy Dearborn, 1998.

Bowen, David, ed. *The Encyclopedia of War Machines: An Historical Survey of the World's Great Weapons.* London: Octopus Books, 1978.

Brice, Martin. *Forts and Fortresses: From the Hillforts of Prehistory to Modern Times: The Definitive Visual Account of the Science of Fortification.* New York: Facts on File, 1990.

Contamine, Philippe. *War in the Middle Ages.* Translated by Michael Jones. London: Basil Blackwell, 1984.

Cruickshank, C.G. *Elizabeth's Army.* Oxford: Oxford University Press, 1968.

Duffy, Christopher. *Siege Warfare: The Fortress in the Early Modern World, 1494–1660.* London: Routledge & Kegan Paul, 1979.

Falconer, Alexander Frederick. *A Glossary of Shakespeare's Sea and Naval Terms Including Gunnery.* London: Constable, 1965.

———. *Shakespeare and the Sea.* New York: Frederick Ungar, 1964.

Gush, George. *Renaissance Armies, 1480–1650.* Cambridge: Patrick Stephens, 1975.

Hale, John R. *The Art of War and Renaissance England.* Washington, DC: Folger Shakespeare Library, 1961.

Jones, Archer. *The Art of War in the Western World.* Urbana: University of Illinois Press, 1987.

Jorgensen, Paul A. *Shakespeare's Military World.* Berkeley: University of California Press, 1973.

Keegan, John. *The Face of Battle.* London: Pimlico, 1991.

Montross, Lynn. *War Through the Ages.* New York: Harper, 1960.

Parker, Geoffrey, ed. *The Cambridge Illustrated History of Warfare: The Triumph of the West.* Cambridge: Cambridge University Press, 1995.

Sutherland, John, and Cedric Watts. *Henry V, War Criminal?: And Other Shakespeare Puzzles.* Oxford: Oxford University Press, 2000.

Turnbull, Stephen. *The Book of the Medieval Knight.* London: Arms and Armour, 1985.

Vale, Malcolm. *War and Chivalry: Warfare and Aristocratic Culture in England, France and Burgundy at the End of the Middle Ages.* Athens: The University of Georgia Press, 1981.

Artisans and Yeomen

Lang, Jennifer. *Pride without Prejudice: The Story of London's Guilds and Livery Companies.* London: Perpetua Press, 1975.

Leeson, R.A. *Travelling Brothers: The Six Centuries' Road from Craft Fellowship to Trade Unionism.* London: George Allen & Unwin, 1979.

Ridley, Jasper. *A History of the Carpenters' Company.* London: Carpenters' Hall; in association with Unicorn Press, 1995.

Schmidt, Albert J. *The Yeoman in Tudor and Stuart England.* Washington, DC: Folger Shakespeare Library, 1961.

The Aristocracy

Akrigg, G.P.V. *Jacobean Pageant; or, The Court of King James I.* New York: Atheneum, 1974.

Bergeron, David M. *Royal Family, Royal Lovers: King James of England And Scotland.* Columbus: University of Missouri Press, 1991.

———. *Shakespeare's Romances and the Royal Family.* Lawrence: University Press of Kansas, 1985.

Bryson, Anna. *From Courtesy to Civility: Changing Codes of Conduct in Early Modern England.* Oxford: Clarendon Press, 1998.

Esler, Anthony. *The Aspiring Mind of the Elizabethan Younger Generation.* Durham, NC: Duke University Press, 1966.

Hibbert, Christopher. *The Court at Windsor: A Domestic History.* London: Allen Lane, 1977.

Lindley, David. *The Trials of Frances Howard: Fact and Fiction at the Court of King James.* London: Routledge, 1993.

Molesworth, H.D. *The Golden Age of Princes.* New York: Putnam, 1969.

Naunton, Sir Robert. *Fragmenta Regalia; or, Observations on Queen Elizabeth, Her Times & Favourites* (1653). Edited by John S. Cerovski. Washington, DC: Folger Shakespeare Library, 1985.

Peck, Linda Levy, ed. *The Mental World of the Jacobean Court.* Cambridge: Cambridge University Press, 1991.

Somerset, Anne. *Ladies-in-Waiting: From the Tudors to the Present Day.* New York: Knopf, 1984.

Starkey, David. *The English Court: From the Wars of the Roses to the Civil War.* London: Longman, 1987.

Stone, Lawrence. *The Crisis of the Aristocracy, 1558-1641.* Oxford: Clarendon Press, 1965.

Thurley, Simon. *The Royal Palaces of Tudor England: Architecture and Court Life, 1460-1547.* New Haven, CT: Yale University Press, 1993.

Whigham, Frank. *Ambition and Privilege: The Social Tropes of Elizabethan Courtesy Theory.* Berkeley: University of California Press, 1984.

White, Beatrice. *Cast of Ravens: The Strange Case of Sir Thomas Overbury.* New York: G. Braziller, 1965.

Wildeblood, Joan, and Peter Brinson. *The Polite World: A Guide to English Manners and Deportment from the Thirteenth to the Nineteenth Century.* London: Oxford University Press, 1965.

Williams, Neville. *All the Queen's Men: Elizabeth I and her Courtiers.* London: Weidenfeld and Nicolson, 1972.

Fools, Rogues, and Misfits

Aydelotte, Frank. *Elizabethan Rogues and Vagabonds.* New York: Barnes & Noble, 1967.

Billington, Sandra. *A Social History of the Fool.* Brighton, Sussex: Harvester Press, 1984.

Carroll, William C. *Fat King, Lean Beggar: Representations of Poverty in the Age of Shakespeare.* Ithaca, NY: Cornell University Press, 1996.

Cutpurse, Moll. *The Life and Death of Mrs. Mary Frith: Commonly Called Moll Cutpurse,* (1662). Edited by Randall S. Nakayama. New York: Garland, 1993.

Dekker, Thomas. *English Villainies Discovered by Lantern and Candlelight* (1608). Edited by E.D. Pendry. London: E. Arnold, 1967.

———. *The Gull's Horn-Book* (1609). Edited by E.D. Pendry. London: E. Arnold, 1967.

Doran, John. *The History of Court Fools.* New York: Haskell House, 1966.

Freeman, Arthur. *Elizabethan Eccentrics: Brief Lives of English Misfits, Exploiters, Rogues, and Failures, 1580-1660.* New York:Dorset Press, 1978.

Greene, Robert. *Cuthbert Conny-Catcher: The Defence of Conny-Catching* (1592). Edited by G.B. Harrison. New York: Barnes & Noble, 1966.

———. *Greene's Groats-Worth of Wit* (1592). Menston, England: Scolar Press, 1969.

———. *A Notable Discovery of Coosnage* (1591). *The Second Part of Conny-Catching* (1592). Edited by G.B. Harrison. New York: Barnes & Noble, 1966.

———. *The Thirde & Last Part of Conny-Catching, With the New Devised Knauish Art of Fooletaking: The Like Cosenages and Villenies Neuer Before Discouered: A Disputation Betweene a Hee Conny-catcher and a Shee Conny-catcher* (1592). Edited by G.B. Harrison. New York: Barnes & Noble, 1966.

Hotson, Leslie. *Shakespeare versus Shallow.* Freeport, NY: Books for Libraries Press, 1970.

Ingram, William. *A London Life in the Brazen Age: Francis Langley, 1548–1602.* Cambridge, MA: Harvard University Press, 1978.

Janik, Vicki K., ed. *Fools and Jesters in Literature, Art, and History: A Bio-bibliographical Sourcebook.* Westport, CT: Greenwood Press, 1998.

Judges, A.V., ed. *The Elizabethan Underworld: A Collection of Tudor and Early Stuart Tracts and Ballads Telling of the Lives and Mis-doings of Vagabonds, Thieves, Rogues, and Cozeners and Giving Some Account of the Operation of the Criminal Law.* New York: Octagon Books, 1965.

Marston, John. *The Scourge of Villainie* (1599). Edited by G.B. Harrison. New York: Barnes & Noble, 1966.

Pound, John. *Poverty and Vagrancy in Tudor England.* London: Longman, 1986.

Salgādo, Gāmini. *The Elizabethan Underworld.* London: J.M. Dent & Sons, 1977.

Welsford, Enid. *The Fool: His Social and Literary History.* London: Faber and Faber, 1935.

ॐ 7 ॐ

Shakespeare's England

Day, night, hour, tide, time, work, play.

Capulet [*R&J* 3.5.176]

We have always known a great deal about the major players of Shakespeare's world, the monarchs, the powerful courtiers, the great adventurers or thinkers, and the famous authors. That is because they were written about by their contemporaries or left extensive documents that could be pored over by historians interested in the important political events, scientific discoveries, journeys, and works of art that serve as either the reflection of an era or the mark of significant change.

Now we have access to a different kind of knowledge, of matters such as the construction of undergarments, the arrangements made in country, village, and city for the disposal of human waste, and cooking methods and dietary habits of the poor and the wealthy. This is in large part because of a shift in the agenda of historians, who, having mined the extraordinary activities of the great, have turned their attention to the ordinary activities of the unimportant but numerous populace.

THE ACTOR'S CONTRIBUTION TO SOCIAL HISTORY

For many years Shakespearean scholars have been visiting the area of the library that contains Elizabethan social history, seeking a richer understanding of some aspect of the plays. Actors can join them in the search, though not unexpectedly they will have a slightly different agenda. The primary purpose of an actor's learning about what life was like in Shakespeare's England is to further our understanding of the language of the plays. When Macbeth says, "They have tied me to a stake, I cannot fly, / But Bear-like I must fight the course" [5.7.1], or Olivia says, "Have you not set mine Honour at the stake, / And baited it with all th'unmuzzled thoughts / That tyrannous heart can think?" [*12th Night* 3.1.117], a modern actor would be denied a great deal of insight if no information were available about the popular Elizabethan sport of bear baiting. If, however, the actor finds a way to partake of the results of the hard work of the diggers and delvers, all sorts of exciting and unexpected riches will come to light.

The scholars find the information, and some of them then use it to comment on literary aspects of the plays. Actors use the information to spark their imaginations. Some like to flesh out the daily life of their characters or develop a backstory. This can be an important activity when one is playing a supporting character. Not only is it a great way to spend rehearsal time while the director is coaching the leading players, it also pushes your courtier or citizen to become an engaged observer of the main action. Are you in debt? Have you heard any good ballads lately? Is your underwear comfortable? Do you prefer hawking or hunting to hounds? Do you follow the French or Italian school of fencing? What did you have for dinner?

These may seem frivolous questions, but they are all elements of the ordinary world that become important to an actor because Shakespeare used them when he created metaphors. We might assume, given his reputation as a poet, that his imagery would be sophisticated and philosophically complex. When we have a close look, however, we find that almost always he chooses to build upon the sensations of the familiar.

Uta Hagen has said that one of the most valuable tools available to the actor is a vivid imagination. Hagen writes in *Respect for Acting* about her strategies for imagining herself actually living in a time other than her own:

If you can't go abroad, or even visit . . . historic spots to find a variety of historical experiences, you can still read biographies and histories. Read them until you *know* you've lived in those rooms with those people, eaten that particular food, slept in that strange bed behind those curtains; danced, jousted and tilted with the best of them. . . . Customs, architecture, fashion, social needs, politics—all change, all come and go, but throughout history people have breathed, slept, eaten, loved, hated and had similar feelings, emotions, needs. Anything which allows for a realization of this by the actor is vital. It must be grasped fully so that if, on stage, you live now or at any other time in history, you will be able to put yourself there rather than be reduced to an illustration of doing what "they" did then. (30)

Fifty years ago Hagen and others did not have access to the wealth of information available to the actor attempting a Shakespearean role today. Social historians of the early modern period of British history have been busy filling in the gaps in our knowledge through painstaking examinations of every single available scrap of evidence about the ordinary activities of daily life. Actors have much to be thankful for, because not only does Shakespeare prompt acting that is physically grounded in the realm of the senses, but scholars have worked for years to assemble hundreds of books filled with exciting details about the sights, smells, sounds, tastes, and textures of Shakespeare's England.

Historical Authenticity

If your production is set in Elizabethan times, this information can assist you in bringing the entire world of the play to life in your imagination. It is, of course, a wonderful source for scenic artists, costume and set designers, and property people striving for historical authenticity. But that is only one benefit to be gained from the work of social historians, and as few productions are set with any historical accuracy in Elizabethan England, an actor could quite rightly conclude that the work needed to seek out these details would not be justified were it not for the fact that Shakespeare fills his plays with direct and subtle references to the ordinary, to simple daily habits, to household objects and activities, to familiar (to him and his audience) sights, sounds, smells, tastes, and sensations.

Some of these we recognize immediately. Our hair still stands on end, though we no longer have guards standing sentinel, and so we understand when Gertrude describes Hamlet's reaction to seeing his father's ghost for the second time:

> Forth at your eyes, your spirits wildly peep,
> And as the sleeping Soldiers in the'Alarm,
> Your bedded hair . . .
> Start up, and stand an end. [3.4.119]

But some of these wonderful details will be lost to us forever if we do not ground ourselves in the reality of Shakespeare's England. The premise that is at work here is that the cultural experiences that surrounded Shakespeare, his actors, and his audiences can be taken as the cultural framework within which every one of his characters lived.

How can we be sure of this? We can't, of course, but we can make an informed guess that Shakespeare's actors would be little different in this regard from actors today. No matter how much you read history and follow the advice of Uta Hagen, you still look at the past through the eyes of the present. None of us can escape the lens provided by the culture in which we live. We can see this quite clearly if we look at movies about, say, the Civil War made in the 1930s and 1940s, in the 1950s and 1960s, or in the last five years. There is quite a different way of looking at these events that is very much influenced by the values and the concerns of the time in which the film was made. Clark

Gable brings all of the sensibilities of his own time to Rhett Butler; if today's heartthrob were to play the role, he would do the same.

We can find plenty of evidence that Shakespeare's theatre viewed all times and places as essentially the same as England of his day. Henry Peacham's sketch of *Titus Andronicus* shows actors wearing contemporary dress, with just the barest costume accessories on a few key characters to suggest the exotic period and locale. And then there are the many anachronisms, suggesting no real interest in historical accuracy, and most important, the characters speak and think and feel strongly about contemporary social issues, whether or not people who actually lived in that time and place would feel the same.

A Character's Past

How well it resembles it the prime of Youth.

Richard [*3HVI* 2.1.23]

The connection between metaphor and social history does not stop with imagining sensations. Metaphors can be used as clues for backstories. Here is Juliet describing her impatience as she waits for her wedding night with Romeo:

So tedious is this day,
As is the night before some Festival,
To an impatient child that hath new robes
And may not wear them. [3.2.28]

Is this not an invitation for the actors playing the nurse and Juliet, and perhaps even Juliet's parents, who enjoy imagining life before the events of the play, to develop an incident involving Juliet's new dress and the excited preparations for Easter morning or Twelfth Night?

For any given play, editors are likely to have tapped the research of social historians to explain images and specific references. It is up to the actor to tie these to the imagined reality of daily life. Here is Kent insulting Regan's trusted steward Oswald in a speech that also served as a snip of social satire for Shakespeare's first actors and audience, who would have recognized contemporary tensions and pretensions in the description:

A Knave, a Rascal, an eater of broken meats, a base, proud, shallow, beggarly, three-suited-hundred pound, filthy, worsted-stocking knave, a Lily-livered, action-taking, whoreson glass-gazing super-serviceable finical Rogue, one Trunk-inheriting slave, one that wouldst be a Bawd in way of good service, and art nothing but the composition of a Knave, Beggar, Coward, Pandar, and the Son and Heir of a Mongrel Bitch, one whom I will beat into clamorous whining, if thou deniest the least syllable of thy addition. [*King Lear* 2.2.15]

The notes explain the social significance of these insults: Kent, an earl of the realm (perched on the topmost rung of the nobility), now disguised as a man-for-hire (as low as you can go without being a criminal), insults Oswald the steward (at the pinnacle of the servant class) by associating him with the lowest type of servant, one who feeds on kitchen scraps, receives a modest annual salary (which includes three changes of livery), and wears woollen stockings instead of gentlemanly silk, whose entire estate can be stored in a trunk, but who looks good in a mirror, has a way with the ladies, prefers taking legal action to the manly art of self-defense, and is altogether a self-serving super-servant of the most despicable sort.

What might it mean to Oswald to be called these things? Is there just enough truth in all of this to wound him deeply? Or is it entirely true, and Kent has discovered all of this by living in the servants' world and observing Oswald from below? What might it be like to have eaten the leftovers from the lords' tables, to work your way up from beggary to a position of responsibility in a noble household, and now to be the confidant (and possibly the lover) of a princess? The editors' notes leave the actors wanting more information through which to explore what these words might mean to the men who speak and hear them.

Unlocking the Mysteries of Character Motivation

> You would pluck out the heart of my Mystery.
>
> Hamlet [*Hamlet* 3.2.366]

Actors tend to feel confident about their ability to discover the heart of the characters they play. They enjoy testifying to the universality of Shakespeare's characters, who, beneath the surface of historical difference, are, after all, very familiar. They speak with confidence about their character's motivations, assuming that people then wanted pretty much what people want today. However, when a society's values have shifted in several important areas, all of these assumptions might be bogus. With more thoughtful consideration, we might discover that certain general drives, such as the desire to be respected and admired, are transformed radically by the available means by which such a goal can be achieved. The longing for love and all of the actions that are connected to the winning of the high regard of the beloved are affected by the prevalent attitudes to gender roles: the beloved fulfills the ideal of woman or man, and love is achieved by fulfilling those ideals in the eye of the one who is the object of your desire.

Look, for example, at poor Julia comparing herself to Silvia's portrait in *The Two Gentlemen of Verona*. She loves Proteus, who used to love her but now loves Silvia, a love triangle that will be sure to resonate in the personal experience of everyone in the cast. But the grounds of comparison are simultaneously age-specific and universal:

> Here is her Picture: let me see, I think
> If I had such a Tire, this face of mine
> Were full as lovely, as is this of hers;
> And yet the Painter flattered her a little,
> Unless I flatter with my self too much.
> Her hair is Auburn, mine is perfect Yellow;
> If that be all the difference in his love,
> I'll get me such a coloured Periwig:
> Her eyes are grey as glass, and so are mine:
> Ay, but her fore-head's low, and mine's as high. [4.4.184]

Which of Julia or Silvia better fulfills Proteus's ideal of womanhood, given the standards that he has absorbed from his culture? The fashionable "tire" or headdress of the age has a role to play, as does the skill of the painter. It is easy to find a parallel in a teenager's encounter with a glossy photograph of a movie star or fashion model. But the more subtle implications are suggested by Julia's supposition "If that be all the difference in his love, I'll get me such a coloured periwig." Everyone on stage and in the audience will know that a wig will not help, because the encoding of feminine values takes place over a wide variety of attributes.

Here is Benedick musing on his resistance to love:

One woman is fair, yet I am well: another is wise, yet I am well: another virtuous, yet I am well: but till all graces be in one woman, one woman shall not come in my grace: rich she shall be, that's certain: wise, or I'll none: virtuous, or I'll never cheapen her: fair, or I'll never look on her: mild, or come not near me: Noble, or not I for an angel: of good discourse: an excellent Musician, and her hair shall be of what colour it please God. [*Much Ado* 2.3.26]

Here we find the need for a more complex range of concepts, for what would be the ideal graces in a woman in Benedick's time and place? Virtue, wisdom, and temperament appear alongside personal attractiveness and wealth. Her bloodlines are as important as her education, but the color of her hair is not an issue. The benefit, therefore, for the actor seeking to ground his work in the discovery of the motivation of the character, of a rich understanding of the perceptions, attitudes, assumptions, and prejudices of the Elizabethans, is the most precise connection between the words the character speaks and those universal drives that provide a bridge between his time and ours.

APOCRYPHA

Because actors are not bound by the same rules as historians, we can glee-fully consume apocrypha and gossip, not caring if the story is factual, provided that it captures the imagination in some profitable way. Of course, it is preferable to know the difference between those unprovable yet compelling yarns and undeniable fact, lest in conversation with a scholarly type we be shamed with the lie direct, as in "Oh, but that's just a myth; we have no evidence of Shakespeare having played the ghost of Hamlet's father, old Adam in *As You Like It*, or any other role, for that matter."

It is also useful to distinguish between stories that were in circulation when Shakespeare's plays were first being rehearsed, and therefore were available to the company and the audience as a source of emotional resonance within the characters and events of the play, and stories that have been invented in the generations following Shakespeare's lifetime. For example, the stories about Richard III, in circulation in part to discredit the last Yorkist monarch in order to elevate Elizabeth's grandfather, who stole the throne out from under the nose of far more direct heirs, are of far greater interest than the facts of the short reign of that historical figure. I am not sure that it does the actors much good to know that recent biographers have suggested that the marriage between Richard and Lady Anne was in fact a love match.

GENERAL INTRODUCTIONS

Everyone can always use a good general introduction to Shakespeare's world. Such a resource rewards repeated browsing, as each new production allows for fresh connections between the historical information and the challenges of the text. The Shakespeare companions, guides, and general introductions described previously contain much useful information, and some of the best overviews are contained in the introductory pages to the collected works so often assigned to university Shakespeare courses. *The Riverside Shakespeare* contains seventy-six pages of introduction, including eight pages of full-color reproductions.

Another good place to start might be the inexpensive paperback *Shakespeare Alive!* put out by Bantam Books under the name of no less than the modern Shakespearean director Joseph Papp, who for thirty-seven years brought free Shakespeare to Central Park in vivid and vigorous productions. This book, coauthored with Elizabeth Kirkland, contains pictures, facts, and cultural considerations that a beginning actor will need to start to put the plays into the time and place in which they were written. Scholars would find much to criticize in *Shakespeare Alive!* because the authors have preferred to paint a clear and vivid picture rather than delve into the complexities and contradictions that scholarship has revealed.

On many occasions I have been grateful to Jo McMurtry for her concise presentation of all sorts of general information that is sure to answer questions of anyone trying to imagine living in Shakespeare's world. Sadly, her book *Understanding Shakespeare's England* is out of print and suffers from the inevitable limitations of time and place. It is amusing today to read her attempt to portray the modern equivalency of Elizabethan money: a pound of butter for $2.29 in 1988; a loaf of American bread for 89 cents (71). How I wish that this volume could be reissued and updated! Students and actors would be ever so thankful. If you can find her book, be sure to read her first chapter on degree and rank, the best explanation I have ever read for a North American requiring an introduction to the entire concept of a nobility.

Another good general introduction to Shakespeare's world is found in the first part of Peter Hyland's *An Introduction to Shakespeare*. In fifty-four pages Hyland gives all the most important historical events and cultural conditions, clarifying every step of the way how little we know for sure of Shakespeare's life and how difficult it is to come to any simplistic conclusions about what he might have thought and felt.

Alison Sim has put together a lovely general introduction to the social and cultural values of Shakespeare's England, *Pleasures and Pastimes in Tudor England*. You might miss this one, given her title and the fact that it is catalogued in neither of our two favorite sections of the library: Shakespeare as literature or Shakespeare's England as history. Instead, it sits alongside books on games and sports; it really belongs in the category of general social history, as it includes an excellent introduction to everything from clothing and fashion to dancing, music, reading, and the theatre.

The Horizon Book of the Elizabethan World by Lacey Baldwin Smith remains one of the best general introductions, filled as it is with detailed overviews of the beliefs, political systems, cultural activities, famous personalities, and noteworthy events of the times, as well as a wealth of illustrations and anthologies of quotations from the writers of the time. I am particularly fond of this treatment because it sets England firmly into a European context, without which it is very difficult to understand much of what the average Elizabethan feared and admired. Although most of Blair Worden's *Stuart England* covers a time after Shakespeare's death, it is another contribution of scholars, with a great collection of pictures and short articles on society and politics.

Even if you are not working on *Hamlet*, Roland Mushat Frye's book *The Renaissance Hamlet*, which sets the play into the context of Shakespeare's England, is an invaluable resource for Shakespearean actors. For example, in his discussion of the famous "To be or not to be" soliloquy, after an examination of Protestant and Catholic theological thought concerning "conscience," Frye explains the traditional views of the nature of human thought. Conscience is one of the rational powers, available only to those creatures with a sense of reason, and the God-given power of conscience is the root source of knowledge and judgment. But in the ongoing processes of conscience are stirred up five different passions or motions of the heart: shame, sadness, fear, perturbation, and desperation (182).

This information will prove invaluable in making sense of the exchange in *Measure for Measure* between the duke, disguised as a friar, and the imprisoned and pregnant Juliet, whose lover Claudio is sentenced to die for their illegal premarital sexual relationship:

Duke: Repent you (fair one) of the sin you carry?

Juliet: I do; and bear the shame most patiently.

Duke: I'll teach you how you shall arraign your conscience
And try your penitence, if it be sound,
Or hollowly put on.

Juliet: I'll gladly learn.

Duke: Love you the man that wronged you?

Juliet: Yes, as I love the woman that wronged him.

Duke: So then it seems your most offence-full act
Was mutually committed.

Juliet: Mutually.

Duke: Then was your sin of heavier kind than his.

Juliet: I do confess it, and repent it (Father).

Duke: 'Tis meet so (daughter) but lest you do repent
As that the sin hath brought you to this shame,
Which sorrow is always towards our selves, not heaven,
Showing we would not spare heaven, as we love it,
But as we stand in fear.

Juliet: I do repent me, as it is an evil,
And take the shame with joy. [2.3.19]

Frye's commentary has pointed the way to understanding how shame can be connected with joy: shame is the symptom of the vigorous workings of conscience and a confirmation of the resilience of the soul that would bring spiritual comfort and rejoicing to anyone living in a culture that experienced all aspects of life within a moral framework.

Historical Scholarship for the Nonacademic Reader

As we might expect, historians can be as dry and dusty as Shakespearean literary scholars, and as caught up in their own private agendas of debating among themselves or presenting every scrap of evidence in order to "prove" their theories. Fortunately, some historians offer general introductions and popularized publications that are wonderfully useful for all of the reasons that their more traditional colleagues will despise them: the absence of any new information or theory, along with a scarcity of footnotes and a relatively short bibliography—in other words, easy and profitable reading for actors.

There are several overlapping designations of the time period that concerns us: Elizabeth was the last of the Tudor monarchs, and some historians have found "the Tudor Age" to be a useful concept. Shakespeare would have found much that was Tudor to be distinctly old-fashioned, coming as he did at the end of the era, but he and his contemporaries were very much a product of their recent history, and so a general introduction like A.H. Dodd's *Elizabethan England* is well worth a look.

One of the dangers of acquiring some historical background for Shakespeare's England is that the era will be inaccurately defined. One temptation is to conflate Shakespeare's England with Elizabethan England; in actual fact Shakespeare came to London during the last years of the old queen's reign, when eyes were already turned north to her most likely heir. Another temptation, and perhaps just as dangerous, is to assume that Shakespeare was unaffected by the lingering traditions of earlier times and by the active memories of his parents and grandparents of significant events from their lifetimes. The evil hunchback Richard III was defeated by Elizabeth's grandfather, and although no one alive in Shakespeare's London could have lived in the time of the War of the Roses, everyone would have family stories passed through the very few intervening generations. In the case of the nobility, the current holder of a noble title might be the direct descendant of the nobleman named in one of Shakespeare's history plays, and families could easily take offense if the characterization of a grandfather or great-grandfather was not in keeping with the version the family wished to promote.

Fortunately, Elizabeth and her father, Henry VIII, have an enduring place in the imagination of the general public, and therefore publishers continue to release accessible introductory books on what is known generally as the Tudor period of English history, usually enhanced by beautiful photographs and reproductions. For example, in *The Tudor Age* Jasper Ridley has blended lovely reproductions with a detailed and general introduction not only to the story of the royal family (all those wives) but also to various aspects of the culture at that time. The table of contents clarifies Ridley's organizational strategy, and the index allows you to locate something about people, places, or things. For example, spotting "mirrors," I turn to his chapter on "Furniture and Food" and learn that wineglasses were used only by the rich and fashionable, that the ordinary people only used glass in their windows, and that their mirrors were made of steel, not glass.

The Stuart kings, the first of whom was Shakespeare's King James, have a hold on our imagination because of their role in the drama of the English civil war. It is important to remember that Shakespeare and his first actors and audience could have no idea that their Parliament would, in a few short years, cut off the head of their anointed king. Historians love to point to the seeds of that decision in Shakespeare's time, but if we are looking for clues as to how it might have felt to live alongside William the actor from Stratford, we have to keep reminding ourselves that seeds are only visible when they have grown into plants. Even so, it is important to remember that this was a time of widespread uncertainty, and *Authority and Disorder in Tudor Times* by Paul Thomas is a good introduction to the conflicts and concerns.

A good general history of the Jacobean era (named after James), which might be included in a book on the Stuarts, will help to remind us that Shakespeare was an active playwright under James as well as Elizabeth. As a very broad overview, I would recommend *The Oxford Illustrated History of Tudor and Stuart Britain*, edited by John Morrill. This book is entirely reputable as scholarship, but is presented in a form that is useful and appealing to a broader readership. The illustrations, as promised by the title, are excellent, and the different chapters have been contributed by specialists in the various fields. As with other general histories, the table of contents will guide you toward discussions of historical events or more general social issues such as education, the family, and the theatre, this last an excellent overview written by the eminent Shakespearean theatre historian Andrew Gurr.

In the 1970s Weidenfeld and Nicolson published its series of books on the English monarchs which remain the best place to start of an illustrated general biography for any one of the English monarchs. To supplement the more sweeping overviews, look for Robert Lacey's *The Life and Times of Henry VIII*, Neville Williams's *The Life and Times of Elizabeth I*, and Antonia Fraser's *King James VI of Scotland, I of England.*

Historical Sociology and Cultural History

In a section of the library removed from history books, you will find the writings of a small group of sociologists and experts in cultural studies who have chosen to write about a time other than the present. It is not clear to an outside observer what difference there might be between a cultural historian and a historical sociologist, except that their books have quite different call numbers. For any actor who becomes fascinated with the minutiae of ordinary life in Shakespeare's England, I can recommend two of the standard cultural history/social history textbooks: J.A. Sharpe's *Early Modern England*, and *Sixteenth-Century England* by Joyce Youings. A.L. Rowse's *The Elizabethan Renaissance: The Cultural Achievement* and *The Elizabethan Renaissance: The Life of the Society* are always enjoyable to read, if now out of date in light of recent scholarship. The same could be said of Ivor Brown's *How Shakespeare Spent the Day*, which is great fun though unrepresentative of any sort of rigorous academic research.

Sometimes experts from other fields make a contribution to some obscure aspect of one of the plays. George V. Zito weighs in with *The Sociology of Shakespeare*, in which he blends sociology's tables, charts, and figures, with an overview of the cultural context within which Shakespeare's plays were written and first performed. Philip K. Bock has considered a more general readership in preparing *Shakespeare and Elizabethan Culture: An Anthropological View*. Experts would find his brief introduction to the era and his discussion of the plays superficial, and perhaps discount his theories, but I would recommend this not only as a general introduction, but also for his thought-provoking chapters on silence, color, body concepts, and Shakespeare's views of the self.

Fortunately for the avid explorer of Shakespeare's England, certain scholars have taken upon themselves the task of digesting the vast amount of material available and producing studies on specific topics that are, in their opinion, of greatest interest to those seeking an understanding of the times in which Shakespeare wrote. The most scholarly of these treatises are heavy going, filled with documentation of the facts that form the basis of the writer's thesis, formulated at least in part, as is often the case in academic circles, in response to the theses of other scholars in this particular subdiscipline. But many writers seek a more general readership, and the results are accessible works that provide a straightforward and thoughtful introduction for an actor seeking the hypertext connections to be found in the plays.

B.L. Joseph's *Shakespeare's Eden* is just such an offering, prepared by an individual with some sensitivity to the requirements of actors playing roles in the plays and a fine way of explaining complex events that does not minimize the contradictions and gaps to be found in the primary source material. *Shakespeare's Eden* is, at first glance, not the most appealing general introduction, lacking as it does any reproductions of paintings and drawings, but the second, third, and fourth chapters of this book contain the most accessible detailed portrait of the functioning of political power at this time and hence serve as an invaluable overview to all of the actors who play royalty and their noble advisors. I would also recommend the sixth chapter, "Man, the Cosmos, and Providence Divine," as an excellent introduction. What Joseph accomplishes, far better than the "snapshot" descriptions, is to clarify that Shakespeare's England was a place of change. Joseph outlines the most significant changes in his first chapter and in his fifth, entitled "Events and Explanations," answers the question: How could a people who seemed so completely to believe in the divine right of kings bring themselves to try a king for treason and then cut off his head? This event was far in the future for Shakespeare, and yet, as Joseph demonstrates, the seeds for that rebellion were sown before the plays were written, and the impetus can be traced in all of the plays.

Modern historians have important concerns about evidence and documentation, whether they are attempting to clarify what actually happened during a significant event or describing the patterns of behavior of a specific time and place and group of people. Actors have much less interest in what is factual, provable, or discernible and so can enjoy approaches to history that are out of fashion or discredited because they have strayed across the boundary between art and research. We can only be thankful that G. B. Harrison was not so concerned about his scholarly reputation that he hesitated to publish *The Elizabethan Journals*. In these wonderful creations Harrison blends a retelling of the information contained in a wide variety of historical sources with an imaginative re-creation of what might have caught the attention of the average individual on a day-to-day basis from 1591 to 1603. You can browse through several months of a specific year and get a feel for the variety of issues, gossip, and events that might reasonably be supposed to have caught the attention of Shakespeare and his fellow actors in London. Harrison had to make educated guesses about the exact dates of various interesting events, and other scholars have shown his guesses to be as often incorrect as correct, but such quibbles about precision cannot detract from the pure pleasure afforded by this manner of bringing Shakespeare's world alive in our imagination.

The modest index might steer you toward something about which you are curious, but this is probably not the best place to go looking for answers to such questions. It is interesting, for example, to trace references to the issue of the succession, which occur occasionally in the early journals and then increase in number and significance as Elizabeth reaches the end of her long life. But Harrison's presentation of historical events in this form reminds us that someone living through those years might well have been deeply impressed by what we would consider insignificant events, and that gossip and the fluctuation of prices in the market would be just as important as the ill-fated rebellion of the earl of Essex.

Practical Application: The Actor Makes Use of *Shakespeare's England*

A massive reference work from the beginning of the twentieth century is the two-volume *Shakespeare's England*, a collection of articles about everything from archery, duelling, and falconry in the section on "Sports and Pastimes" to alchemy, astronomy, and astrology in the section on "The Sciences." Onions completed the editorial work begun by W.A. Raleigh and S. Lee, which had been interrupted by the beginning of the First World War. In the publisher's preface, antiquarian lore is acknowledged as a strength of English Shakespearean criticism. Modern historians have an entirely different approach to the many topics contained in this collection of entries, but an actor is free to enjoy the late Victorian fascination with "the little things that change, and in their change serve as an index to the character of a man or of an age" (vi).

Heavy, dusty books such as these reward browsing, both random and assisted by the indexes of names and terms found at the back of the second volume, and also the reading of any entry that treats a subject about which some information is required. When you are flipping the pages, you will find photographs of samples of handwriting, drawings of the enlarged faces of coins of the era, and reproductions of contemporary woodcuts of jugglers' tricks or a sword-fighting exhibition. The first volume might open to the entry on medicine, where you will find a variety of diseases: gout, palsy, consumption, jaundice, and, of course, the plague. In the index of names you might come upon the lengthy listing of subheadings under "London," in which you will find the Globe Theatre as well as the Dagger Tavern and Shepherd's Bush.

You might also be interested in the index of passages cited. Say you have been cast in *Hamlet* and are curious about possible connections between Denmark and the daily experiences of the first actors. The first reference in the index under that play will take you to the entry on "Actors and Acting," and specifically to a discussion of the information contained in Philip Henslowe's diary. We learn that the author of this entry, Percy Simpson, has concluded that ghosts were costumed in the clothing that they could be assumed to have worn naturally, and, as in the case of the ghost of Hamlet's father, they changed costume according to the location in which the ghost materialized: full armor for the battlements and a nightgown in Gertrude's private rooms. Percy interprets this latter garment to be the sort of dressing gown that a well-bred gentleman would wear in 1916 (II, 268).

The next citation takes us to the entry on "The Navy," submitted to the collection by L.G. Carr Laughton. Here we find a more detailed explanation for the line in the first scene of the play: "Why such impress of ship-wrights, whose sore Task / Does not divide the Sunday from the week" [1.1.75]. The reference to *Hamlet* appears in a footnote listing several references to the customary practice of raising men for military service by their being hired or "prested" in a contract similar to many other forms of employment, which became, subsequent to the degeneration of such service, forced service, and "prest-money" became "press-money" (I, 166).

It was when I was reading the entry on "Falconry" by the Hon. Gerald Lascelles that I discovered a paragraph that illuminated a favorite passage quite unexpectedly. Falconry is, after all, an area of knowledge that is exotic and esoteric today but was clearly common for Shakespeare's first audience and actors, given the number of times he makes use of falconry to build an image or evoke an experience, everything from Petruchio calling Kate his haggard [*Shrew* 4.1.193] to a lengthy discussion of the pleasures of the sport [*2HVI* 1.2.56]. The plays are filled with references that are illuminated by Lascelles's entry. Here, for example, is some information about haggards:

It stands to reason that the longer a bird has been at large preying for herself, and possibly for a young brood also, the more care, skill, and trouble will be required to train her; she may even be untrainable, or more trouble to reclaim than she is worth. Many such have been known. (II, 355)

Here Lascelles quotes Othello's negative use of the term with regard to the beloved wife he fears has betrayed him [3.3.260] and Hero's critique of Beatrice's proud disdain [*Much Ado* 3.1.36] before continuing:

On the other hand, if a fine-tempered, naturally docile haggard be found, there is no great difficulty to a skilled hand in training her, except that it takes a long time to overcome that nervousness and dread of man which is ingrained in her. When the haggard is once trained the falconer finds himself with no amateur like the eyas [taken from the nest by the falconer], which needs first to be tamed and then taught how to fly, but with a professional expert that cannot be defeated by the shifts and artifices, or left behind by the speed, of any feathered fowl. Hence Latham, a great [1615] authority, but in this instance peculiar, extols the haggard, and places her before every other variety of hawk. (II, 355)

In this, Latham would agree with Petruchio, who demonstrates the brilliance of his haggard with a wager: "Twenty crowns? I'll venture so much of my hawk or hound, but twenty times so much upon my wife" [*Shrew* 5.2.71].

Lascelles quotes Petruchio when he describes the process of taming and training a hawk and other nuances of the sport that otherwise would elude the modern reader of such lines as Juliet's call to Romeo, "Hist, Romeo, hist! O, for a falconer's voice / To lure this tassel-gentle back again" [2.2.158], or the chilling portent of evil from *Macbeth*, "On Tuesday last, / A falcon, towering in her pride of place, / Was by a mousing owl hawked at and killed" [2.4.11]. It enriches the emotional resonance of such speeches immeasurably when we learn that tassels were short leather straps attached to the legs of the hawk, on the ends of which were attached little silver rings engraved with the name of the owner, and that a falcon is able to achieve a pitch or height that makes her the greatest of all hunters, unlike the barnyard owl, good only for lowly mousing.

It was the last page of this fascinating article that sent me to another passage in *Macbeth*, that most powerful and puzzling soliloquy that begins:

> If it were done, when 'tis done, then 'twere well,
> It were done quickly: if th' Assassination
> Could trammel up the Consequence, and catch
> With his surcease, Success: that but this blow
> Might be the be all, and the end-all. Here,
> But here, upon this Bank and Shoal of time,
> We'ld jump the life to come. [1.7.1]

It was not until I read Lascelles's closing comments on the less impressive aspects of the sport that Macbeth's words came alive for me. Lascelles reports:

The method of taking larks with the hobby [a small falcon] was known as "daring". The hawk was trained to wait on, above the falconer, just as the falcon gentle was used for flying at the brook or at game. The presence of their swift enemy overhead so terrified or "dared" the larks that they crouched upon the ground and remained almost immovable. Two men then took a trammel net, or oblong net of considerable size, the lower edge of which was weighted with plummets. The net was borne a little above the ground, and as the weighted cord touched and flushed the cowering larks they rose directly into it, and a whole flock could be taken at a haul. (II, 366)

I had always known that the verb "to trammel" referred to catching up in a net, but I had never had a strong image of such an activity. Intellectually, I can use this information to consider what Macbeth chooses to do in the moments immediately after the discovery of the murdered king: he hovers over the gathered thanes like the hobby daring the larks into frozen submission. As he predicted, however, in this earlier musing, it is simply not possible to catch them all, and Macduff, for one, escapes the trammel of Macbeth's imposing presence and natural leadership. Emotionally, I find that this image gives me something even more useful and compelling: a set of sensations that can be imagined, a specific type of anticipation and excitement. The situation as given in the narrative has always suggested a certain type of emotional state for this moment in Macbeth's experience, but suddenly the imagery of his first words sharpens my understanding of and empathy for that experience.

New Historicism

An important contribution to our understanding of the complexities of the relationships that existed between people of similar and different status has been the work of literary scholars who have used the findings of social historians to produce what is generally termed "new historicist" readings of Shakespeare and his contemporary dramatists. Like every other "new" school of criticism, these Shakespearean scholars come in for praise and scorn from their colleagues, depending upon factors well beyond the understanding or interest of actors and other nonacademics. When you are reading a new historicist study, you will be pleased at the inclusion of many useful details about the activities and concerns of ordinary people, among whom you can count the characters you will portray. You will at the same time experience some irritation at the determination of these scholars to fit the story they are telling into a specific mold in order to prove their particular theory of history, often Marxist in orientation. As a general rule, feel free to grab hold of the facts presented, as they are almost always based upon years of painstaking examination of historical documents, and feel equally free to discard the general conclusions unless they fit with what you are already sensing holds true for the world of the play.

To introduce yourself to new historicist scholarship and along the way pick up some very interesting information about Shakespeare's England and the issues that were "in the air" when the plays were first rehearsed, check out Richard Wilson's *Will Power*. Here you will find essays that make a direct connection between at least one of the plays and at least one significant social issue. In the chapter on *As You Like It*, for example, you will learn about the enclosure riots that rocked England in 1596, and generally about the tension between urban or court economies and rural economies. Wilson captures the danger and the thrill of outlaws and rebels who would have been the same age as Shakespeare's actors and would have shared with many of the company, as with Shakespeare himself, a set of countryside memories. In his fifth chapter, "The Quality of Mercy: Discipline and Punishment in Shakespearean Comedy," Wilson paints an evocative picture of the various forms of public punishment that were customarily enacted against offenders, a form of entertainment that Shakespeare's scaffold at the Globe duplicated in certain disturbing ways. Wilson's comments are of great interest to actors seeking to place their finger on the pulse of the age.

The articles of new historicists have been collected into some interesting volumes that are very much worth a look, in contrast to the collections of thematic or literary articles. The table of contents is the place to begin: is there an article on the play you are doing? Is there an article on another play from a perspective that might assist you in rehearsals for your own? For example, in Michael Neill's *Putting History to the Question* you can find "Shakespeare and the Bonds of Service," which includes a wide-ranging discussion equally interesting to characters who are servants (Maria and Malvolio) and to characters who offer service as a token of love and respect, such as Kent in *King Lear* and Ferdinand in *The Tempest*. You can also find "This Gentle Gentleman," of interest to anyone seeking a broad understanding of class issues in Shakespeare's world.

Stephen Greenblatt is one of the best-known new historicists and author of such books as *Renaissance Self-fashioning, Shakespearean Negotiations,* and *Learning to Curse.* You can count on almost anything he has written to begin with an interesting anecdote that might well have been familiar to Shakespeare's first actors and audience, and that vividly evokes the attitudes and experiences that form the cultural background to the plays. Even if Greenblatt does not follow with a detailed application of the story to one of Shakespeare's plays, the issues he raises and the implications he suggests have far-reaching potential when they are added to the creative mix during rehearsals.

Eric Mallin is another new historicist who, in *Inscribing the Time*, places Shakespeare and three of his plays firmly in the context of the times in which they were first performed, in this case the years spent waiting for Elizabeth to die. He links *Troilus and Cressida* to the Essex rebellion, *Hamlet* to the question of succession, and *Twelfth Night* to nostalgia for Elizabeth once she had died and James's flaws as a king had begun to show. Leah S. Marcus provides a similar set of connections with a broader focus in *Puzzling Shakespeare*, ranging far and wide through the plays and exploring England under both Elizabeth and James. She also includes a section on the city of London in which she suggests how the locations given the different plays, such as the Vienna of *Measure for Measure*, could reflect the London in which the first actors lived as well as the exotic European city about which they had heard some interesting stories.

Greenblatt and other new historicists have edited collections of articles that follow Greenblatt's style of using an evocative anecdote to introduce a discussion of a work of literature within the larger context of Shakespeare's England; Greenblatt himself edited *Representing the English Renaissance* and Richard Wilson and Richard Dutton prepared *New Historicism and Renaissance Drama*. These books are well worth a quick browse to glean the stories and a taste of the discussion of the implications. If you find a writer whose jargon and theorizing do not alienate, and whose inclusion of fascinating historical anecdotes to which there is no other easy access inspires you, you can seek other articles and books by this actor-friendly scholar and be sure that your effort will be rewarded by the maximum possible benefit to your creativity.

Enclosure Acts, edited by Richard Burt and John Michael Archer, is an example of a collection of historicist articles on such subjects as enclosures, vagrancy, rebellion, class conflict, and witches. An example of fascinating connections can be found in Richard Wilson's "Observations on English Bodies: Licensing Maternity in Shakespeare's Late Plays," in which he examines the diaries of Shakespeare's son-in-law, John Hall, and relates some of what he finds there to the offstage scenes of birth in plays like *The Winter's Tale*.

David Scott Kastan has brought out a collection of his writings, *Shakespeare After Theory*, that he presents as alternatives to new historicist criticism, but to the uninitiated there is little to differentiate them, containing as they do the same ideal combination of interesting social history applied directly to the situations evoked in the plays. In particular, I recommend his chapter "Is There a Class in This (Shakespearean) Text?" which addresses the issues of class that can be confusing for North American actors.

The difference between a new historicist critic and an actor interested in finding out more about the everyday world within which the plays were first rehearsed is that the critic seeks topical connections that will better illuminate the themes or structure of the play. The actor seeks anything that will spark an intuitive, personal connection with the world of the play and its characters, those to be played and those to be encountered in rehearsal and performance. There is no need for the spark or trigger to be demonstrably connected with the writing of the play, and apocrypha (unprovable and probably fictional anecdotes) can prove as useful to the actor as documented historical events. It is almost impossible to predict exactly what tidbit of background information will send a pulse of creative energy through an actor, though others can suggest the general category of research that will prove worth the effort. Because there is no need to prove the validity of the connection other than with the dictum "If it works, use it," and because there is no need to analyze why the connection works for that particular actor on that day while rehearsing that play, actors' use of the products of historical scholarship bears no resemblance to the academic products within which the useful information is held. This is why an actor will browse quickly through an article or book, skipping paragraphs that discuss, theorize, or quote extensively from the play in question, in search of a bit of history: a story vividly retold, a quotation from someone who lived when Shakespeare did, a reprint of artwork that the first actors might have seen, or ballads they might have heard sung on the street.

ENCYCLOPEDIAS OF ORDINARY LIFE

Sir Toby: Does not our lives consist of the four Elements?
Sir Andrew: Faith so they say, but I think it rather consists of eating and
              drinking.

[*12th Night* 2.3.9]

Thanks to those who have spent countless hours gleaning dusty old diaries, handbooks, woodcuts, and all manner of publications from Shakespeare's England, we now have a great deal of specific and useful information on all sorts of things, compiled in handy reference books. Much of this has been in turn digested and regurgitated with an eye toward a specifically Shakespearean readership, but an actor might well want to have a look at more general studies rather than encounter only what another individual has come to consider important for Shakespeare's plays. After all, Shakespeare might only have mentioned directly a limited number of culinary creations, but many a director will stage a banquet scene, and inevitably someone will want to know what the chef is serving.

The GT area of the library is where you will find reference books that rest at the intersection of history and sociology plus cultural studies, what might be called cultural history. The product of such scholarship makes for fascinating reading for the actor seeking the life truly lived. Georges Vigarello's *Concepts of Cleanliness* is a good example of the riches awaiting you in this section of the library. Have a look at his chapters on "Vermin" or "The Stench of Towns and People" and then consider that when Marcellus suggests that there is something rotten in the state of Denmark, he is speaking, in part, of the smell of death in the air [*Hamlet* 1.4.89].

C. Anne Wilson's *Food and Drink in Britain* is divided into food types, so you can look up her chapter on "Bread, Cakes, and Pastry" or check out "Drinking in Britain." Because hers is a historical study, she then divides each chapter into eras, from Roman times through medieval to early modern. Alternatively, you can zoom in on the index and find out about Falstaff's favorite beverage, sack, a dry amber wine from the south of Spain, sweetened with sugar; the best sack came from the Canary Islands, which may have implications for the host's plan to visit Falstaff: "I will to my honest knight Falstaff, and drink canary with him" [*Wives* 3.2.87].

In 1999 the Folger Shakespeare Library presented a lavish exhibit on food in Shakespeare's England. The accompanying guide, *Fooles and Fricassees*, edited by Mary Anne Caton, is filled with reproductions and reprints, a veritable feast for the eye and imagination. Here you will find everything from recipes to woodprints of kitchen scenes, as well as photographs of glassware and cooking implements that were on display during the exhibition. The book is most useful for the precise explanations that accompany each item.

Elizabethan clothing will be familiar to most actors, but it is always a good idea to balance the creative innovations of your costume designers with some verifiable historical facts, such as those contained in Virginia LaMar's *English Dress in the Age of Shakespeare*. It is also, I think, important to know exactly which articles of clothing you are referring to if you have been cast, for example, as Autolycus in *The Winter's Tale* and find yourself referring to the women and men you have duped by portions of their clothing: "You might have pinched a Placket, it was senseless; 'twas nothing to geld a Cod-piece of a Purse" [4.4.609].

Because horses were so much a part of daily life, and because Shakespeare's imagery is filled with allusions to riding, every actor should try to find a copy of Anthony Dent's *Horses in Shakespeare's England*. How else will you be able to comprehend Rosalind's pick-up line, "I'll tell you who Time ambles withall, who Time trots withall, who Time gallops withall, and who he stands still withall" [*AYLI* 3.2.309]? Once you learn the specifics of each of these riding styles, you will join Orlando in admiration of the perfection of this comic tour-de-force.

A WOMAN'S WORK

Lo, as a careful housewife runs to catch,
One of her feathered creatures broke away,
Sets down her babe and makes an swift dispatch
In pursuit of the thing she would have stay:
Whilst her neglected child holds her in chase,
Cries to catch her whose busy care is bent,
To follow that which flies before her face.

Sonnet 143

The activities and life experiences of women, which are central to the social history of any culture, have, until quite recently, been of little interest to traditional scholars. Actors benefit greatly from the academic revolution that resulted in women's studies departments and publications, for the result has been a flood of information and stories that we might call "her-story."

For an excellent introduction to the lives of women in Shakespeare's England, told with a novelist's skill and a biographer's eye for detail, look for *The Tudor Housewife* by Alison Sim. Here you will find chapters on marriage, childbirth, the education of girls, housework, food and drink, the housewife as doctor, women and business life, and religion. This book rewards a reading from cover to cover in order to uncover such fascinating bits as the estimation that 19% of landed couples died without living heirs either because no children were born to them or all of their children had died (16). Other details about giving birth will be of interest to the cast of *The Winter's Tale*, for Hermione is forced to give birth to her daughter in a prison and then to stand trial, "The Child-bed privilege denied, which 'longs / To Women of all fashion" [3.2.103]. Sim describes the room prepared for Anne Boleyn's lying-in and the elaborate public celebrations that greeted the birth of an English royal child. Sim includes information about the activities of the women who attended the birth and the special care afforded the mother following the birth, which included three days in a darkened room because labor was believed to weaken the eyesight, at the end of which time the woman would sit up for the first time. What a violation of accepted medical practice it would be to rush the new mother to a public trial for her very life!

For a more academic study of the same subject, you will want to look at Anne Laurence's *Women in England*, which contains a wealth of information on marriage, sexuality, motherhood, women's relationships with other women, their experiences of illness, work inside and outside the home, their crafts, their writing, their participation in organized religion, and the customs and beliefs that seem to have been unique to women. Her final section deals with how women experienced the predominantly male jurisdictions of law, politics, and crime. Just as you would expect from first-rate social history seeking "herstory," she depicts the average lives of ordinary women whose activities drew no notice but whose presence was a constant and whose participation was required in those human events of such great interest to dramatists like Shakespeare.

LOVE, MARRIAGE, AND PROCREATION

> You kiss by the book.
>
> Juliet [*R&J* 1.5.110]

If you ever have to play a young lover or the parent of such a creature, you will want to know about courtship in Shakespeare's England. How common was forced marriage? Were young women really considered old enough to marry at fourteen? Ann Jennalie Cook touches upon almost everything of interest to an actor in Shakespeare's plays in her book *Making a Match: Courtship in Shakespeare and His Society*. The only complaint that might be made is that all of the examples of normal behavior in Shakespeare's time come from the plays themselves, almost as if Cook used the plays as her primary source material for what ordinary people thought and felt and did. This dangerous assumption, that the mirror Shakespeare held up to nature was like the one in your bathroom, creating a near-perfect reflection, rather than a medieval or Renaissance mirror that at best shows a distorted and tinted view, is of greater concern to scholars than to actors. Ultimately, in performing a play, it doesn't matter if the events enacted are a realistic representation of Shakespeare's England. For the characters, the events of the play make up the self-contained world of the play. Even so, it can help an actor to commit to the events of the play if they are set against historical events that reveal the true-life situations, people, and attitudes that Shakespeare chose to reflect, albeit altered to suit his stage.

One of the more complex social events that puzzle modern actors is the act of betrothal, which clearly has a great deal more significance legally in Shakespeare's England than getting engaged does today. We know from Buckingham's sly insinuations in *Richard III* that a previous betrothal was sufficient to raise questions of bastardy in the children born of a subsequent marriage to a different woman. Mariana seems to be in a similar situation in *Measure for Measure*: her betrothal to Angelo, once it is consummated through the bed trick, makes her a married woman responsive to her husband's command, though a church ceremony is still an important final step. How on earth do all these disparate events fit together?

The process seems terribly complicated and disorganized to us today, and so we stand to benefit from the careful study of such scholars as David Cressy. Unlike Cook, Cressy has little interest in Shakespeare: his book *Birth, Marriage, and Death* will be found in the history section of the library. The excellent index lists all of the topics covered, and the discussion of each is detailed, specific, and a fascinating read. The book is packed full of information that explains the larger context of a passing comment, allowing an actor to make an informed choice of how to make use of the line within the emotional dynamics of the scene as played.

For example, in *Coriolanus* the house-bound wife of the hero is enticed to visit a neighbor lady who has recently given birth. Cressy's section on childbirth contains a three-page section on "Childbed Gossips," which contains several fascinating tidbits that open up all sorts of possibilities for the actresses in the scene, allowing them to clarify the type of temptation that Valeria is offering and Virgilia is refusing.

Lawrence Stone, whose study of the aristocracy discussed in the previous chapter is useful when one is considering that class of individuals, has also produced an invaluable general study of family structures in all classes of society during this era, *The Family, Sex, and Marriage in England*. Shakespearean scholars, in turn, have built upon just this sort of study. A book that I have found consistently useful for the exploration of family relationships is Marjorie Garber's *Coming of Age in Shakespeare*. She organizes her book into chapters on everything from women's rights to death and dying, and an excellent index will guide you to specific issues or plays. Garber leaps from play to play to weave her portrait of the family relations in the plays; in contrast, *Our House Is Hell* by Max H. James jumps from plays to social history and back again, covering much of the same ground from a different perspective. Together, these two books will answer a great many questions about what would have seemed credible and what extraordinary in the family relationships enacted in the plays.

For example, when modern actors are rehearsing *Romeo and Juliet*, they might find of great interest what James has to say about the conflicting attitudes to corporal punishment for children and parental consent for marriage that were very much "in the air" in Shakespeare's time. James quotes from the memoirs of Anne Halkett, who, though she was born in 1623, records firsthand a Juliet-like battle of wills between parents and children with regard to the choice of a marriage partner. Garber, meanwhile, points out the profound meaning of Romeo's offer to discard his family name, a moment that otherwise might pass by in rehearsal as a quick and almost comic eagerness of the young lover to fulfill any request made by his Juliet, even one as romantically absurd as "Romeo, doff thy name, / And for that name which is no part of thee, / Take all myself" [2.2.47].

Another useful source for information on the social history of the family is Philippe Aries's *Centuries of Childhood*. Here you will find all sorts of useful and specific information about schooling, games, clothing, and family life. I wish there were a book comparable to Shulamith Shahar's *Childhood in the Middle Ages* or Barbara Hanawalt's *Growing Up in Medieval London* about early modern England, though I would strongly recommend *Childhood in the Middle Ages* as a source of information about the practices that were well established and essentially unchallenged when Shakespeare's father was a boy. Hanawalt's book is also excellent, not only for imagining the world of the *Henry VI* plays, but also for a glimpse of the era immediately before Shakespeare's.

PRIVATE MATTERS

It used to be that the most intimate aspects of the private activities of ordinary people were ignored. Now, with a deeper understanding of and comfort with discussing human sexuality, scholars have been able to make an important contribution to the process an actor faces in bringing alive the highly charged as well as the ordinary relationships between these characters from the past. If we are prepared to talk about sex, we can finally answer some of the really important questions, such as those offered by Angus McLaren in *A History of Contraception* and Valerie Fildes in *Wet Nursing*. Contraception and wet nurses might not be important unless you are cast as Romeo, Juliet, or her nurse, but isn't it nice to know that if you have a question about such matters, you now have a place to go to find an answer?

Sexual Pleasure

Of all of the human elements in Shakespeare's plays, it is most tempting to assume that sexuality is part of an unchanging continuum across the four hundred years between his time and ours. After all, human physiology is unchanged, is it not? Actors soon discover that this assumption is one of the most dangerous. Our late-twentieth-century attitudes to masculinity and femininity, to courtship and procreation, and to heterosexual/homosexual definitions consistently create a stumbling block to our understanding of what is going on when Shakespeare ventures into erotic territory.

Scholars have ventured fearlessly into this territory in the last few decades, after suffering from an unspoken moratorium on sexual issues in connection with the Bard of Avon. We still struggle to throw off the restrictions of our late Victorian great-grandparents, and some insights and conclusions are decidedly unwelcome to the homophobic sensibilities of many.

Shakespeare made sexual jokes. Shakespeare created sexy characters. Shakespeare shows men declaring passionate love to other men, and women discussing shared physical intimacy. Some characters reveal that they know how to achieve sexual fulfillment without risking pregnancy. Other characters speak knowingly of the addictive mix of pleasure and pain. This was no Victorian. Nor was this a sophomoric, locker-room "nudge-nudge, wink-wink" crudity. Sexuality was as natural as the hunger for food, and the sins of the flesh were condemned just as gluttony was, being two of the seven deadly sins to which human flesh is heir. The closest modern equivalent we have to the free exchange of sexual energy that flows so purely between young lovers like Romeo and Juliet or Rosalind and Orlando is social dancing. The carefully shaped exchanges and the erotic subtext match the learned steps and the intense connection that is allowed and invited by everything from the tango to the twist.

Many scholars have charted the complex social forces that gave shape to the erotic subtexts of Shakespeare's England. It is very important for a modern actor to discover the ways in which the great sexual dance was learned and viewed, or we risk doing the twist when the tango has been scripted or, worst yet, not even realizing that the characters on stage are dancing.

Perhaps it is tempting to assume that sex underlies all human interactions, in a sort of bastardized post-Freudianism. It is also tempting to bring contemporary morality to all of this sexuality. When is a sexual reference rude and irreverent, and when is it a simple statement of fact? Only by developing some sense of the context within which the great sexual dances take place can a modern actor fine-tune the engine driving the overtly and subtly sexual scenes in the plays.

Michel Foucault is the name that pops up often in studies of the history of sexuality. It was this literary scholar who insisted that attitudes toward human sexuality change radically over time and between cultures, and we should not superimpose our assumptions and blind spots onto the artifacts of another time and place, Shakespeare's plays included. It does an actor little good to know that there are sexual references in the lines if these references are not placed into some sort of larger context. Individuals live as members of societies, and societies have complex attitudes to the significance of sexual activity. Gazing backwards toward Shakespeare's England, several scholars have attempted to provide an overview of the sometimes-contradictory regulations and practices of wooing, wedding, procreating, and just plain fooling around.

A.L. Rowse, a biographer of Shakespeare, has published the diaries of Simon Forman, which are fun reading for any Shakespearean actor. Have a look at Rowse's explanation so that you can follow Forman's cryptic code for sexual dalliances, of which he seemed to have a fair number. Also note how passionately he cared for his books and how he earned his way as an astrologer. This is a fascinating glimpse into the life of an ordinary fellow, just trying to get by and attending the theatre as one of the simple pleasures of life.

It is not simply salacious curiosity that is satisfied by the publication of Alan Haynes's *Sex in Elizabethan England* in Sutton's Illustrated History Paperbacks series. Here you will find excellent, well-researched chapters on homosexuality, premarital sex, and the relationship between sexual pleasure and procreation. Haynes's index lists only people and plays, including Shakespeare's, so you will have to read the relevant chapter to find the specifics that interest you. The reason that so many people are listed in the index is because the book is in large part a document of the sex scandals that were very much in the public eye during Shakespeare's youth. Given his capacity to include sexual attraction and suggest sexual activity, it behooves an actor to consider how such matters would have been discussed by Shakespeare and his contemporaries. I was fascinated to read, for example, about Elizabeth Southwell, a lovely maid of honor, first to the elderly Queen Elizabeth, her godmother, and then to Queen Anne. In 1605 this nineteen-year-old woman disguised herself as a male page and ran away with her lover, Sir Robert Dudley, who happened to have a wife and children already. This Dudley was the illegitimate son of Robert Dudley, earl of Leicester, from whom he inherited not only a considerable estate but also the charm and emotional fire that had won the heart of Queen Elizabeth herself.

Haynes's chapters set out a way of looking at the evidence we have about how Elizabethans functioned sexually. Paul Hair's volume *Before the Bawdy Court* sets out some of the evidence, allowing the browsing actor to discover unexpected echoes and confirmations as well as challenges and revelations. In Hair's collection we find such enticing bits of gossip as this, from Thame, Oxfordshire, in 1608: "Item we present unto you that John Thomlinson and the wiffe of George Ellis were Lockt into a Rome togither very susspiciously by her husbands report" (36), or this, from West Ham, Essex, dated 1589:

Hopkinson appeared and said that he with others were in the companie of a stranger, in the house of John Ward of Westham, a vittelinge house, in the night time; and talking of Mr Eborne, some said that he was jealiouse over his wyf; the said stranger said yf he knewe where he dwelt, he would naile a paire of hornes at his doore; and in further talke this examinant said, that Robert Dickins wold geve him a paire of hornes, and so did, & he nailed them at the said Mr Eborns dore. (137)

Items such as this shed new light on Benedick's response to Don Pedro's prediction that some day he too will wear the yoke of a married man: "The savage bull may, but if ever the sensible Benedick bear it, pluck off the bulls horns, and set them in my forehead, and let me be vildly painted, and in such great Letters as they write, here is good horse to hire: let them signify under my sign, here you may see Benedick the married man" [1.1 262].

Bastardy

Many of the entries in Hair's collection concern the birth of illegitimate children, an aspect of Elizabethan society that directly concerns a few of the characters of the plays. On the surface of things, the situation for illegitimate children of powerful men seems self-evident to the actors playing the roles of the Bastard in *King John* and Edmund in *King Lear*, and to all who play opposite them. Shakespeare makes great use of these and other illegitimate characters to provide the voice of the perennial outside and, in the case of Edmund and Don John in *Much Ado about Nothing*, provides bastardy as sufficient excuse for all manner of villainous envy. Here is Edmund's commentary on his status:

> Why brand they us
> With base? With baseness Bastardy? Base, Base?
> Who in the lusty stealth of Nature, take
> More composition, and fierce quality,
> Than doth within a dull stale tired bed
> Go to th'creating a whole tribe of Fops,
> Got 'tween asleep, and wake? [*Lear* 1.2.9]

Because these men are acknowledged by their powerful families, and because each of them enjoys a fair amount of stage time, it is tempting to place a modern interpretation upon the namelessness of this trio of noble bastards. But that is to ignore the implications of bastardy as a social construct in Shakespeare's England. Blue-blooded bastards were in evidence in the court of Elizabeth and of James, but they were not called bastards. One of them was called the duke of Richmond. That Henry Fitzroy could have been king had Henry VIII divorced his queen to marry Henry's mother, Katherine Blount, instead of Anne Boleyn, might well have aroused the venom expressed by Edmund, but as Henry Fitzroy died of tuberculosis at the age of nineteen, we will never know.

The term "bastard" was reserved for those born outside of wedlock and unprotected by a powerful patron. It carried with it an emotional punch that linked the stage characters as much with the village scandal as with the court's misalliances. Historians have studied the latter in detail; sociologists are more interested in the former. We do not have names, just statistics, for the incidence of illegitimacy in places like Stratford, and at first glance such scholarly works might seem untheatrically reliant upon tables and charts. But there is much of very real interest in a book like *Bastardy and Its Comparative History*, edited by Peter Laslett, in particular a chapter like "The Social Context of Illegitimacy in Early Modern England," by David Levine and Keith Wrightson.

Homosexuality

If you are interested in learning more about the topic of homosexuality in the time of Shakespeare, I recommend Bruce Smith's *Homosexual Desire in Shakespeare's England*. You would not browse this book to find out more about the plays, although his index lists them by title, as well as the sonnets, mentioned in the book. Rather, you would read it for the story the documents tell of the sexual desire felt by some men for other men. Another book that comes at this topic from a different perspective is Jonathan Goldberg's *Sodometries*. I recommend his second chapter, "The Making of Courtly Makers," as being of some interest to an actor playing a character like Le Beau in *As You Like It*.

GAMES AND PASTIMES

> What sport shall we devise here in this Garden,
> To drive away the heavy thought of Care?
>
> Queen [*RII* 3.4.1]

There are three general types of theatrical situations in which an actor will want to know the details of a specific game or pastime. The first is when the main action of the play includes the enacting of such an activity. In this category we would include, for example, the wrestling match in *As You Like It*. The second situation is when the activity is mentioned in the play, either directly, as when the dauphin of France sends the new King Henry tennis balls, or indirectly, as in a metaphorical reference to the game of bowls. The third situation is when the director of the production suggests that supporting or principal characters might be passing the time on stage doing something, and the search begins for an appropriate game for this time and place, for these characters, to say nothing of some concrete information on how to play it. Not surprisingly, scholars have mined the history of games and pastimes as thoroughly as any actor might wish. We have at our fingertips not only the rules of the various games but also the subtle nuances of the social significance of the activity.

Passing the Time on Stage

Perhaps your director wishes you to play a game of cards while you are on stage in Elizabethan costume, or perhaps you would like to understand what

Table 7.1
The First Round of Hazard

Main Roll	5	6	7	8	9
Chance Roll Wins	5	6 or 12	7 or 11	8 or 12	9
Chance Roll Loses	2, 3, 11, or 12	2, 3, or 11	2, 3, or 12	2, 3, or 11	2, 3, 11, or 12
Throw Again	4, 6, 7, 8, 9, or 10	4, 5, 7, 8, 9, or 10	4, 5, 6, 8, 9, or 10	4, 5, 6, 7, 9, or 10	4, 5, 6, 7, 8, or 10

Falstaff means when he says, "I never prospered, since I forswore myself at Primero" [*Wives* 4.5.101]. *The Oxford Guide to Card Games* by David Parlett will direct you to an appropriately historical variation of poker, bridge, or rummy.

Cards were generally played by the wealthier members of society; soldiers were more commonly associated with dice. Hazard was a popular game, perfect for passing the time playing while you were besieging castles or waiting for your intended murder victim to happen by. The rules are easy enough for speedy mastery and just complex enough for suspense. The word came to be associated with chance or fate, and so when Cassius says, "Why now blow wind, swell Billow, / And swim Bark: / The Storm is up, and all is on the hazard" [*JC* 5.1.67], he is drawing upon the metaphor that provoked the expanded uses of the word.

The dice are thrown to establish the Main, which cannot be less than five or greater than nine, or the dice are passed to the next player. Bets are placed, and then the one who threw the Main rolls again, in what is called the Chance. Table 7.1 shows which rolls of the Chance win against which Main, and suggests the element of complexity. The soldier with the dice stands to collect the bets of all the others if the second roll of the dice falls his way, but he must cover all the bets if he loses. If, however, he has thrown a number which neither wins nor loses, then the dice are rolled again until either the Main or the Chance appears a second time. Throwing the Main at this point in the game means bad news for the thrower; the Chance is good news. Anything else means the play goes on, but more bets can be placed before each roll.

With these terms in mind, have a look at Enobarbus's advice to Antony on the eve of the great sea battle at Actium:

> Most worthy Sir, you therein throw away
> The absolute Soldiership you have by Land,
> Distract your Army, which doth most consist
> Of War-marked-footmen, leave unexecuted
> Your own renowned knowledge, quite forego
> The way which promises assurance, and
> Give up your self merely to chance and hazard,
> From firm security. [*A&C* 3.7.41]

Antony's response, "I'll fight at sea," has all of the reckless energy of the gambler placing his month's pay on the single throw of the dice, evoked by Enobarbus's use of two terms from the well-known game, an image that we will get whether we know the rules or not. Knowing the rules allows the concept to become a concrete metaphor, and the words to be associated with a specific activity and perhaps even a shared memory between the two men of long hours spent winning and losing with the flick of a wrist and the tumble of the dice.

We are so used to thinking of Shakespeare as an Elizabethan writer that we forget that his history plays are set firmly in England's medieval world, and that the folk traditions that spanned the century had their roots firmly in an earlier time. Comedies like *All's Well That Ends Well*, with its religious pilgrimage, and *Measure for Measure*, with its chaste nun, or tragedies like *King Lear* lend themselves to medieval staging. For that reason, Teresa McLean's enjoyable overview *The English at Play in the Middle Ages* is well worth a look. The index and table of contents will help you to browse efficiently.

Dancing

The re-creation of the specific dance steps and patterns, including the festive dances of the hobby horse or morris, the court dancing at which Elizabeth excelled, and the country dances of the manor and town, has been made possible by the 1651 publication of John Playford's *The English Dancing Master*, which was reissued as *The Dancing Master* at regular intervals for the next sixty-seven years. Dances that can be traced to Shakespeare's England are recorded here, some only in the later issues. Taken all together, and placed beside the other evidence we have, these sources allow us not only to relearn the dances but also to understand how people felt about dancing and the role dancing played in their ordinary and politically charged interactions.

In John Fitzhugh Millar's *Elizabethan Country Dances* you will find an excellent general introduction that includes a clear definition of such terms as "casting" and "gypsy," even if you couldn't perform them, and a list of references to specific dances in literature. *Romeo and Juliet* makes it onto this list with the reference to "heartsease." The largest number of references is in Thomas Heywood's *A Woman Killed with Kindness*. There is also an index, and the dances are presented with the melody and the steps, if they are known, or a brief general description if that is the only information available. "Heartsease" is listed as an easy dance set to twenty-four bars of music, designed for a two-couple square set. A verse is provided, and at the bottom of the page Millar lists the books in which the dance is described.

For another example of esoteric scholarly interests, have a look at Skiles Howard's *The Politics of Courtly Dancing in Early Modern England*. Here you will find a description of dance forms, the teaching of European dance steps in England, how male and female bodies were held, and how their feet moved in stately or riotous measures. All of this will be interesting when you are preparing for the masked ball in *Much Ado about Nothing*, which is introduced with a set of dance references as Beatrice advises Hero on how to respond to her father's matchmaking:

For, hear me Hero, wooing, wedding, and repenting, is as a Scotch jig, a measure, and a cinque pace: the first suit is hot and hasty like a Scotch jig (and full as fantastical) the wedding mannerly modest, (as a measure) full of state and ancientry, and then comes repentance, and with his bad legs, falls into the cinque-pace faster and faster, till he sink into his grave. [2.1.72]

Another place to go for the identification of these different dances, if not details on the steps, is the sister discipline of music, and in particular historians of music, those scholars who have prepared such invaluable reference books as the many volumes of *The New Grove Dictionary of Music and Musicians*, edited by Stanley Sadie.

Music

Shakespeare's plays contain not only songs and musical airs, but also musical terminology blended into Shakespeare's imagery. Editors of the plays will give you a preliminary definition, but questions you might have that arise out of need to own the language of your character. As an alternative to the twenty volumes of the *New Grove Dictionary*, you will be happy to discover that historians of music have prepared reference books that apply directly to Shakespeare's era. I have made great use of Graham Strahle's *An Early Music Dictionary* as well as Jeffrey Pulver's *A Dictionary of Old English Music and Musical Instruments*. You will find all of these resources helpful if you have to be on stage during the music-lesson scene in *The Taming of the Shrew*. Hortensio, disguised as the music master Litio, woos Bianca with a revision to the "gamut" or diatonic scale with which modern audiences are familiar thanks to "Do, a Deer" from *The Sound of Music*. But here is Hortensio/Litio's version:

> *Gamouth* I am, the ground of all accord:
> *A re*, to plead Hortensio's passion:
> *Be me*, Bianca take him for thy Lord,
> *C fa ut*, that loves, with all affection:
> *D sol re*, one Clef, two notes have I,
> *E la mi*, show pity or I die.

Bianca's response to this lover's suit?

> Call you this gamouth? tut I like it not,
> Old fashions please me best, I am not so nice
> To change true rules for old inventions. [3.1.73]

It will take more than a few footnotes to make sense of this sequence; in *New Grove* you will find that "gamut" is a term for any system for learning the notes of a scale. The entry contains a cross-reference to "solmization," the use of syllables associated with pitches to learn musical intervals. Under this second term you will find a great many more details, probably too many, but there are also illustrations, including a reproduction of the drawing of a hand showing how the notes can be traced on the finger tips. Is Hortensio playing with Bianca's hand as she reads his love letter?

This is the same information contained in *The New Harvard Dictionary of Music*, edited by Don Michael Randel, under "gamut" and the cross-referenced "Guidonian hand," and though the illustration is not as striking, the basic information is all that is included, and there is no danger of being drowned in highly expert musical knowledge. In Pulver's dictionary the entry for "gamut" quotes from *The Taming of the Shrew*, but there is no cross-listing, and so unless you know to look up "Guidonian hand," you will not be directed to still another cross-listing, "Aretinian syllables," and will miss the reprint of the original Latin verse that Hortensio has expropriated:

Ut queant laxis Resonare fibris,
Mira gestorum Famuli tuorum,
Solve polluti Labii reatum
Sante Johannes. (10)

Could the love letter have been set to music? You will need to consult *The Oxford Companion to Music* by Percy Scholes to discover the melody written out under the cross-listed entry "hexachord." Perhaps Bianca sings Hortensio's letter, having learned the melody when she first learned her notes.

SPORTS

When we have matched our Rackets to these Balls,
We will in France (by Gods grace) play a set,
Shall strike his fathers Crown into the hazard.
                                        Henry [*HV* 1.2.261]

It is not surprising that Shakespeare blends into his plays many allusions to athletic activities in which characters might participate or that provide an evocative metaphor. You will want to understand the game of bowls in order to say a line like Petruchio's "Thus the bowl should run, / And no unluckily against the Bias" [*Shrew* 4.5.24], even if your modern audience won't catch the reference to the weighted ball used in the Elizabethan version of lawn bowling. It might require a further leap of imagination to appreciate two of the more popular forms of recreation, fencing and hunting, as each of these activities inevitably blends in with a less pleasant pastime: fighting for one's life or poaching in order to live.

Fencing

Brawl Ridiculous: Swordfighting in Shakespeare's Plays by Charles Edelman is a scholarly book that can be consulted just like the more practical handbooks such as J.D. Martinez's *The Swords of Shakespeare* for information on weaponry, the stylization of stage fighting in Shakespeare's theatre, and the Elizabethan fascination with medieval trial by combat, as well as tidbits buried in descriptions of the various fights to be found in the plays. For example, we learn that if Romeo woos by the book, according to Juliet, then Tybalt challenges by another book, *Vincentio Saviolo His Practice*. Mercutio has a bit of good fun mocking Tybalt as a follower of this ultra-fashionable import that irritated the more blunt, manly English swordsmen of Shakespeare's day:

Oh he's the Courageous Captain of Compliments: he fights as you sing pricksong, keeps time, distance, and proportion, he rests me his minim, one, two, and the third in your bosom: the very butcher of a silk button, a Duellist, a Duellist: a Gentleman of the very first house of the first and second cause: ah the immortal Passado the Punto reverso, the Hay. [*R&J* 2.4.19]

Benvolio's interjection "The what?" always gets a laugh at this point, in part because the audience shares his confusion at the barrage of terms coming at them. With something of a demonstration, they can understand that Tybalt fights as if he were playing music, though they might not understand that the house referred to is a fencing school, nor that the causes are occasions upon which a gentleman was obliged to take offense and challenge the offender to a duel. The "passado" and the "punto reverso" are easily illustrated as specific forehand and backhand thrusts. Mercutio now continues with his diatribe:

The Pox of such antic lisping affecting fantasies, these new tuners of accent: Jesu a very good blade, a very tall man, a very good whore. Why is not this a lamentable thing Grandsire, that we should be thus afflicted with these strange flies: these fashion Mongers, these pardonme's, who stand so much on the new form, that they cannot sit at ease on the old bench. O their bones, their bones. [2.4.28]

Here the actor can play all the different voices or "accents," including the lisping admirers and the disapproving grandfathers, all with their fake French "pardonnez-moi" and "bonne! bonne!" All this is fairly clear even without the notes, though the fact that "duellist" is also a newly coined word might not leap off the page at a modern actor.

Three scenes later, Tybalt demonstrates his command of a duellist's causes. To call someone a villain or traitor is not, in fact, to be the challenger in a fight, for the challenger must respond to such an insult with a challenge. Therefore Tybalt, like his servants in the first scene, is careful to stay on the right side of the law.

Tybalt: Romeo, the love I bear thee, can afford
No better term than this: Thou art a Villain.

Romeo: Tybalt, the reason that I have to love thee,
Doth much excuse the appertaining rage
To such a greeting: Villain am I none;
Therefore farewell, I see thou know'st me not.

Tybalt: Boy, this shall not excuse the injuries
That thou hast done me, therefore turn and draw.

Romeo: I do protest I never injured thee,
But loved thee better than thou canst devise:
Till thou shalt know the reason of my love,
And so good Capulet, which name I tender
As dearly as my own, be satisfied.

Mercutio: O calm, dishonourable, vile submission:
Alla stucatho carries it away.
Tybalt, you Rat-catcher, will you walk?

Tybalt: What wouldst thou have with me?

Mercutio: Good King of Cats, nothing but one of your
nine lives, that I mean to make bold withal, and as
you shall use me hereafter dry beat the rest of the
eight. Will you pluck your Sword out of his Pilcher
by the ears? Make haste, lest mine be about your ears
ere it be out.

Tybalt: I am for you. *Drawing* [3.1.60]

When Romeo has been called "villain," a name that should prompt him to respond with a challenge, his conciliatory reply is entirely out of keeping with the code of the first house. It falls to Mercutio to accept the insult on Romeo's behalf and to place the challenge with the words "Will you walk?" Tybalt's response, "I am for you," marks the beginning of the duel proper. "Alla stoccata," which appears in the folio as "alla Stucatho," is a fencing term meaning "at the thrust," Mercutio using the imported fencing terms as a direct mockery that Tybalt, as a gentleman, will not be able to bear.

Hunting

In *As You Like It*, as in many of Shakespeare's plays, we see scenes of what was a common pastime for the Elizabethan nobility, the pursuit of game with the bow, with hounds, or with a hawk. Two interconnected social realities are suggested by the references by the exiled duke's courtiers to the hunt: that of the noble recreation of the chase and that of poaching, an activity for which Shakespeare is said to have had to leave Stratford rather quickly.

In addition to the sort of introductory description that is to be found in Raleigh, Lee, and Onions's *Shakespeare's England*, we can venture into quite a different section of the library to find the products of still another branch of scholarship, the SK call numbers that contain books on hunting and fishing. If you are in a university library, these will often be historical studies and therefore will be sources of specific information about just what Shakespeare is describing when he sends the princess of France out to shoot deer with Navarre's forester, or when Curio invites Orsino to break free from his music-induced melancholy by going out to hunt the hart.

Roger Manning's *Hunters and Poachers* is just such a book, and in it you will find a chapter on the Purlieu Men and the controversy surrounding their rights to hunt in the royal forests. That there is a real connection between these men and the foresters of *As You Like It* is suggested not only by the way that the exiled duke and his men hunt in the forest of Arden, but also by the use of the term "purlieus" by Oliver when he first ventures into this part of the countryside [4.3.76].

For specific applications to Shakespeare, we can look at a book first published in 1897, D.H. Madden's *The Diary of Master William Silence*. This lovely volume manages to blend the storytelling of fiction with a scholar's attention to factual detail, for Madden has written a diary of William Silence, who, in Madden's imagination, turns out to be a dedicated sportsman, equally interested in hunting the hart and the hare and in hawking or in angling, and enjoying all the pleasures of country courtesy. Here you will find a vivid description of how to man the haggard, mentioned by Petruchio in *The Taming of the Shrew*, and a discussion of different kinds of horses such as nags at one end of the scale or a roan Barbary at the other, so when Hotspur says of mincing poetry, " 'Tis like the forced gait of a shuffling Nag" [*1HIV* 3.1.133], or when Richard II and his groom discuss Bolingbroke's Barbary roan [5.5.78], you will have at the very least William Silence's opinion of their relative worth.

Another lovely volume that contains all sorts of interesting information about hunting, hawking, and fishing is T.R. Henn's *The Living Image*. Here you will find details such as the fact that birds of prey eat the feathers and fur of their victims and disgorge this matter in the form of small, hard pellets. The falconer offers his bird trays of small, smooth stones, which the bird also "casts," to avoid indigestion and keeps a close eye on the captive bird's castings and "mutes" or droppings to monitor its health (36). Henn links this with a quotation to describe Angelo, the hypocritical puritan of *Measure for Measure*: "His filth within being cast, he would appear / A pond, as deep as hell" [3.1.92]. Among his sources Henn lists T.H. White's *The Goshawk*, which anyone fascinated by hawking must read from cover to cover. White brings all of a novelist's skill to this moving memoir of his experiences as an amateur falconer just before the Second World War.

Michael Billett's *A History of English Country Sports* takes the reader well into the nineteenth century, but he includes much information that would be accurate for Shakespeare's day. This is another of those books that benefit from the work of scholars but present the information for a more general readership.

There are lovely illustrations plus all of the important facts, without the excessive detail and footnotes that are required to support the scholar's primary agenda. Billett's chapters on "Falconry" and "Bear Baiting" are particularly useful.

John Cummins's *The Hound and the Hawk* rewards a close reader with much important information about hunting in the era before Shakespeare. As with other medieval studies of cultural history, there is much to be said for becoming familiar with the activities and associations that would have been familiar to Shakespeare's father, and that had not really changed much in the years during which Shakespeare grew to manhood. Of particular interest is the chapter on the symbolism of falconry, where we find the interesting bit of information that although sparrowhawks were associated with the carrying of love messages, the desire of a man for a sensual and strong-willed woman found expression in medieval poetry about the haggard. Is that what Petruchio has in mind when he calls Kate his haggard [*Shrew* 4.1.193]? Here is one stanza of the poem quoted by Cummins:

> By Lure then, in finest sort,
>   He seekes to bring her in:
> But if that she ful gorged be,
>   He cannot so her win:
> Although her becks and bending eies,
>   She manie proffers makes:
> 'Wo ho ho!' he cries, awaie she flies,
>   And so her leave she takes. (228)

With such powerful images at his disposal, it is little wonder that this aspect of the natural world supplies so much of Shakespeare's vivid language.

HOLIDAYS

> If all the year were playing holidays,
> To sport, would be as tedious as to work.
>
> Hal [*1HIV* 1.2.204]

Although Shakespeare and his contemporaries lived in a country in which religious observance was strictly regulated, the rich and varied associations between days of the year and special celebrations were woven in and around the sanctioned holy days. Different districts preserved different folk legends and celebrations, which would have been known to Shakespeare's audiences and upon which he draws when he has a character refer to a specific day of the year. Four hundred years later it is sometimes difficult to trace the associations. For example, in *Richard II* the king sets St. Lambert's Day for the duel between Bolingbroke and Mowbray. This is September 17, which of itself is of little interest unless it is connected with the associations that might have been in place for the first actors and audiences.

Robert Chambers's two-volume Victorian compendium *The Book of Days* is a good place to start when you are looking up a specific calendar reference. In this work each month of the year is introduced with an article that marks the general associations with that season, including, under the heading "Historical," astrological notes and, for September, a reminder that when the year was said to begin in March, September was the seventh month, and so its name made sense.

Under the date in question, more than one saint is listed, in addition to St. Lambert, who was murdered on this day in 708 or 709. Then follow stories associated with this day, some from the centuries after Shakespeare's, others more appropriate. None of the stories for September 17 happen to be of use, though one of them, telling of an infamous case in 1663, makes for interesting reading. Other dates include more interesting legends and anecdotes. On September 4 we find the story of St. Cuthbert's tomb at Durham and the Northumbrian legend of St. Cuthbert's beads. Fortunately Chambers supplies a detailed index, so stories and legends can be located even if you don't know the day of the year with which they might be associated.

Ronald Hutton's *The Rise and Fall of Merry England: The Ritual Year, 1400– 1700* also provides an overview on the ritual year and then discusses how the shifts in official religious teaching and regulation created tensions and change experienced by Shakespeare and his contemporaries. The opening chapter is a good all-purpose introduction to the seasonal entertainments; the rest of the book is pretty heavy going if you are looking for inspiration. Thankfully, Hutton has published a nonscholarly treatment of this subject, *The Stations of the Sun*, which contains all the strengths of his breadth of scholarship and an excellent index and is written in a dry but otherwise accessible manner.

Hutton's index is the best tool for the interested actor. When you encounter a reference to a specific festival, delve into his book at the pages noted in the index, and you will discover all sorts of interesting glimpses into the familiar associations upon which Shakespeare was drawing when he first presented the manuscript to his fellow actors. For example, we can consult Hutton to learn about the Midsummer Day custom of setting bonfires of mixed wood and bones as a focus for the merrymaking and also to drive away the evil spirits that can bring disaster to a rural community. These bonfires were thought to guard against the heavy rains and resulting blight that could destroy a harvest, as well as warding off late summer diseases, including the plague.

Folk Festivals

Shakespeare shared with some of his actors and many of his audience the experience of being a country mouse in the big city of London. Even the most complacent urban dweller lived within smelling distance of the farms that surrounded the city and could retain an awareness of the changing seasons, if not share the firsthand experiences of festivals and fairs that marked the calendar year for country folk. But the folk customs of the small towns and villages are featured in the plays, and many scholars mark the residue of ritual celebrations in the professional plays of the London stage. If you are playing Julia in *The Two Gentlemen of Verona*, you can look up Pentecost (or Whitsun, as it was commonly known) and find out about the Maid Marian plays that were the more familiar entertainment. A play about Theseus and Ariadne is either an invention on Julia's part or the mark of a very upscale entertainment. Selections from songs and copies of woodcuts enrich Hutton's detailed historical study, and it is the factual details that delight the actor. The analysis of the plays themselves is better left to scholars who don't get to interact with the plays in the rehearsal hall.

A slightly different approach is taken by François Laroque in *Shakespeare's Festive World*. The first part of this book contains an excellent overview of the many festival occasions and activities that were part of Shakespeare's world. Laroque also includes a good index, so have a look under the title of your play or the specific holiday to which your character refers.

For example, I looked in Laroque's index to see what he might have to say about *Hamlet* and discovered a fascinating section on the cannibal banquet, which Laroque presents as a contemporary folk image drawn from the allegory of Death as the great leveller. Laroque traces the image of the cannibal banquet from *Titus Andronicus*, where it is enacted literally at the end of the play when Titus serves up Tamora's evil sons in a pastry, through the horror of Shylock's intended revenge in *The Merchant of Venice*, where a pound of flesh is not just a metaphor, but something to be cut from the body of the hapless Antonio, to *Hamlet*, where "The funeral baked meats / Did coldly furnish forth the marriage tables" [1.2.180], so quickly did Gertrude marry after the death of her husband the king. Laroque illumines the imagery of cannibalism in the riddle of Polonius:

Claudius: Now Hamlet, where's Polonius?

Hamlet: At Supper.

Claudius: At Supper? Where?

Hamlet: Not where he eats, but where he is eaten. [4.3.16]

Laroque's point is that tragedies partake of the shared folk images of perverted celebrations even as the comedies cash in on the holiday spirit of England's festivals. For the actor, information such as that Laroque provides supplements the dry references by editors in connection to the obvious and direct allusions to seasonal folk customs.

Scholars have brought together information from a variety of sources to examine the celebratory associations that surround specific plays. David Wiles's *Shakespeare's Almanac* touches on *The Merry Wives of Windsor* and *Love's Labour's Lost* as well as *The Tempest*, but is primarily a study of *A Midsummer Night's Dream*, and his chapters on the symbolism of midsummer, Valentine's Day, and May Day, as well as popular astrology are filled with interesting associations that enrich an actor's appreciation of the very special atmosphere evoked by this popular play.

Saints' Days

In addition to holidays, the names of saints figure in Shakespeare's writing as reference points by which characters mark some form of significance. St. George, St. Francis, St. Valentine, St. Patrick, or St. Peter might already be familiar to the average actor, but what about St. Gregory or St. Anne, St. Martin or St. Stephen? This is the time to get your hands on a reference book like *The Oxford Dictionary of Saints* by David Hugh Farmer. You are being offered information of some significance when a character makes use of a specific saint in moments of heightened emotion.

About St. Lambert, whose name is taken by September 17, the reference books on saints' lives inform us that he was born of a noble family and was educated by St. Theodard, then bishop of Maestricht, who nominated Lambert to succeed him. Theodard was murdered in 668. While Lambert was bishop, he apparently backed the wrong party and lost his position, whereupon he was exiled and spent seven years in a monastery. He was reinstated by Pepin of Herstal when the murder of Lambert's nemesis placed Pepin in a position of power, but Lambert did not hesitate to denounce Pepin for his adulterous affair with the sister of his wife. While Lambert was praying at the tomb of Theodard in Lieges, the brother of these two women, who was also Pepin's attendant, murdered Lambert with a javelin.

Dictionaries like Farmer's and John Delaney's *Dictionary of Saints* can be consulted for a variety of associations between seasons and saints. I was interested to discover, for example, in the *Oxford Dictionary of Saints* that St. Valentine had no connection with lovers. He was an early Christian of Rome who seems to have come within a hair's breadth of converting Claudius to Christianity before being martyred by that emperor. His best-known miracle was healing the blind daughter of the prefect guarding him as he awaited his execution. Somehow, his feast day on February 14 became associated with the Roman festival of Lupercalia, enacted in the first scenes of *Julius Caesar*, and folk legend has it that birds pair up on that day, which is what prompts Theseus to say, when he discovers the four young lovers asleep together in the woods, "Saint Valentine is past, / Begin these wood-birds but to couple now?" [*Dream* 4.1.139].

It is clear from this reference that part of knowing about the saints is becoming familiar with the calendar of saints' days and other festivals that still marked the passing of the seasons even if England no longer officially recognized all of the traditional Roman Catholic customs and beliefs. For that reason, you might want to consult general reference books on folk customs. For example, books like Christina Hole's *British Folk Customs* will inform you about the noise of the May horns, blown to scare away fairies and witches, to prevent the fairies from enticing children away. The Indian child over whom Titania and Oberon fight so fiercely is just such a changeling, and knowing this particular folk custom places quite an interesting implication on Theseus's dawn command, "Go bid the hunts-men wake them with their horns" [*Dream* 4.1.137].

I am always curious about associations with the few specific dates that appear in Shakespeare's plays, such as the first of May or Midsummer Day, both of which are mentioned, along with St. Valentine, in *A Midsummer Night's Dream*. For a specifically English take on such festivals, be sure to look at Charles Kightly's *The Customs and Ceremonies of Britain*, where you will learn of the strong association between the two celebrations and some specific suggestions as to the activities associated with them: the lighting of large bonfires, the maypole and other dances, and the gathering of special woodland bouquets. On the first of May, young girls would go out before dawn to wash their faces in the May dew, and if they wished hard enough during the ceremony, they would be married within the year. Is this perhaps the activity referred to by Theseus, trying to explain the appearance of the lovers in the forest at dawn: "No doubt they rose up early, to observe / The rite of May" [*Dream* 4.1.132]. The dew was thought to be most powerful if it was collected from beneath an oak tree, perhaps even the great oak where Peter Quince and his players agree to meet.

THE NATURAL WORLD

> And this our life exempt from public haunt,
> Finds tongues in trees, books in the running brooks,
> Sermons in stones and good in every thing.
> I would not change it.
>
> Duke Senior [*AYLI* 2.1.15]

Shakespeare's plays are filled with references to plants and animals, and it is always interesting to find out more not only about what these might look like, if you don't already know, but also what associations these aspects of the natural world might have had for an Elizabethan actor and audience member. Fortunately, many scholars and enthusiasts have compiled just this sort of information. The best of these works contain good indexes and straightforward descriptions of each flower, bird, or beast and include information that can be used to discover what is being communicated through the image or reference. Even the less successfully organized studies contain compelling word pictures of the wide variety of plants and animals mentioned in the plays.

Three books for and by bird lovers are excellent examples of the information that is available. James Edmund Harting's book *The Birds of Shakespeare* contains an index by play and by bird, a useful service to browsers, but Peter Goodfellow's *Shakespeare's Birds* contains lovely drawings and a first-rate introduction. I have enjoyed looking at H. Kirke Swann's *A Dictionary of English and Folk-Names of British Birds* because of his fascination with folklore.

Gardens

Many a scene takes place in a garden, noted quickly and effectively by a comment from one of the characters. In the garden scene in *Richard II*, Shakespeare has the gardener spin an elaborate and extended allegory comparing the good government of England to the nurturing of a garden. The placing of scenes in a garden seems to locate them in a particularly English setting, one familiar to many of the first actors and audiences because of the popularity of formal gardens in the houses of the great noblemen and those more recently arrived among the gentry. In London proper the general public could admire the gardens of the great houses from the river, though the size of the house itself seemed to be more significant, if John Stow's description is any indication. Here he mocks the pretensions of one landowner:

This house being so large and sumptuously builded by a man of no great calling, possessions or wealth, (for he was indebted to many) was mockingly called *Fishers folly*, and a Rhyme was made of it, and other the like, in this manner.

> *Kirkebyes Castell, and Fishers Follie,*
> *Spinilas pleasure, and Megses glorie.*

And so of other like buildings about the Cittie, by Citizens, men have not letted to speak their pleasure. (I, 165)

Here is Stow making once again a thinly-veiled criticism of the enclosure of public areas for private use:

Then East from the Curriers row, is a long and high wall of stone, inclosing the north side of a large Garden adjoining to as large an house, builded in the reign of king Henry the eight, and of Edward the sixth, by sir William Powlet, Lord Treasurer of England: through this Garden, which of old time consisted of diverse parts, now united, was sometimes a fair foot way, leading by the west end of the Augustine Friars church straight North, and opened somewhat West from All Hallows Church against London wall towards Moregate, which footway had gates at either end locked up every night, but now the same way being taken into those Gardens, the gates are closed up with stone, whereby the people are forced to go about the saint Peters church, and the East end of the said Friars Church, and all the said great place and Garden of sir William Powlet to London wall, and so to Moregate. (I, 176)

Orchards, herb gardens, and the ubiquitous kitchen garden were a feature of daily life for all of society, even within the city of London. It is difficult for a modern actor to remember just how easy it was for people to get to the open countryside, either to the north or across the river to the south. Every householder would have at the very least a small plot of tended land as part of his leasehold, on which he could raise the necessaries for his table alongside a few examples of God's wonder in a flower garden, now a popular art, the practice of which was no longer limited to professional gardeners and followers of the cloistered life. From Ellen Eyler's study *Early English Gardens and Garden Books*, another of the Folger Shakespeare Library booklets on Tudor and Stuart civilization, we also learn such interesting things as the recommended freshness of horse dung for a melon patch, "not above eight or ten days old and not exceeding fourteen" (48), as recorded in one of the many gardening books from the period, from which she quotes at length.

Flowers

One significant subcategory of folklore and folk knowledge is the language of flowers. Modern performers find this a greater challenge than did our Victorian forbears, who still understood the secret messages that could be conveyed by the well-chosen bouquet sent to an old flame. But once you buy into the pleasure to be gained from indirect communication, the great flower scenes can be fun to play, provided everyone understands the complexity and emotional power of the imagery of flowers. The two great flower scenes are Ophelia's and Perdita's, but flowers are scattered throughout the plays and provide almost everyone with an opportunity to give or receive a full-senses jolt along with the intellectual meaning of the moment.

Fortunately for modern performers, aficionados have mined the imagery of flowers, and a variety of sources allow us to access the content of the message. Jessica Kerr's study of Shakespeare's flower references, *Shakespeare's Flowers*, contains lovely drawings and a first-rate introduction. The same scholar and publisher who produced *Shakespeare's Erotic Word Usage* turned to still another aspect of the natural world to create *Shakespeare's Imagery of Plants*. From J. Barry Webb we learn the connection between lettuce and one's "salad days" [1.5.73], mentioned by Cleopatra to describe her youth. This phrase has come to mean "the good old days," with a connotation of sexual liveliness, but in fact Cleopatra is referring to a time when her blood was cold, when she was not capable of the hot passion she now feels for her Antony. Under the heading of "Lettuce" we learn that the Elizabethans believed that lettuce was under the government of the goddess of chastity and therefore mitigated desire, as well as being generally good for health and often eaten before or after a meal, a "cold" herb to combat the "heat" of meat (120).

But plant and flower references fall flat on stage when they are delivered with a simple intellectual understanding of medicinal import. These images are predominantly sensory, almost always involving not only a vivid visual memory but also touch, smell, and even taste. Webb tells us that lettuce was usually eaten with vinegar, oil, and a little salt, a very definite taste. Let's have our Cleopatra imagine picking away at a salad back in the old days but now, with Antony, enjoying sumptuous banquets of rich foods. Back then, an ice princess, cold and untouchable; now, a glutton for all the pleasures of the flesh.

Clearly, simply reading the notes for each of the citations in Webb's book will do little to assist an actor unless an entire sensory experience is built around the metaphor. Webb's book can help build little bouquets of memory to surround each image, transforming it from an archaic form of communication into a living, felt connection. If both actors share this enriched understanding of the sensuality of flowers, the beauty of the image will be more than skin deep.

Another example of a great Victorian collector of folklore whose work proves surprisingly useful when one is performing Shakespeare is Henry N. Ellacome, vicar of Bitton and author of *In a Gloucestershire Garden* who in 1896 published the third edition of *The Plant-Lore and Garden-Craft of Shakespeare*. Each entry, arranged alphabetically, begins with the various quotations from Shakespeare in which the plant is cited, and then Ellacome proceeds to record whatever bits of information he has collected, including a goodly portion of his personal experience gardening in the English countryside. There is nothing academic and everything scholarly about this book. It is clearly a labor of love, and the collection of quotations and information is a major achievement. Great care is taken to direct the reader to the source of information, but no attempt is made to place the observations within a larger thesis or theoretical framework. I always enjoy reading the entries, although I feel under no obligation to subscribe to every one of his assertions, as his was not a time of factual documentation and theorizing.

TRAVEL

> I'll make a journey twice as far, t'enjoy
> A second night of such sweet shortness, which
> Was mine in Britain, for the Ring is won.
>
> Jachimo [*Cymbeline* 2.4.43]

The episodic freedom of the Elizabethan stage allowed Shakespeare's characters to disappear out of one location and reappear in another, with no attention paid to how they got there and the time that must have passed for the journey. Occasionally they announce their arrival with a brief reference to the toil of the journey, as when Rosalind, Celia, and Touchstone arrive in the forest of Arden complaining of hunger and weariness, and in a few plays Shakespeare actually shows us travellers in midjourney, as in *The Winter's Tale* when we see the two messengers discussing where they have been and how soon they will arrive at their destination.

It is comforting to the actors to know that in the rush of the events of the play, the audience is not overly concerned with details of the journeys that have been made by the characters, but actors cannot be this complacent. Inevitably, when one is playing a character who has travelled between scenes, the mind drifts toward questions about how long, how far, and how difficult the trip was. Maps are pulled out, means of transportation are considered, and clocks are adjusted accordingly, to reveal on many an occasion that the timing of events within the plays does not bear close scrutiny.

There were dramatic conventions associated with travel that are clearly of more importance to the plays than the mundane logistics. For example, sea voyages are associated with psychological change. Both Hamlet and Richard II return from their adventures at sea so transformed that they seem like different people. Land journeys, in contrast, seem more functional: a character needs to get from A to B for the plot to proceed, and so Romeo, for example, is seen leaving Juliet's bedroom in Verona, then hearing of her supposed death in Mantua, then sneaking into her family's crypt back in Verona.

Even without benefit of maps and mileage charts, Shakespeare's first actors would have had a vivid and specific image of the human effort required to bring this frantic young man hurtling, one would assume on horseback, the twenty miles that separate the two cities. To assist a modern actor in assessing exactly what Romeo has just experienced when he reappears in the final scene of the play, we can turn once again to a publication of the Folger Shakespeare Library, Virginia A. La Mar's *Travel and Roads in England*, and learn that the fastest pace on horseback, set by the professional riders employed by the government, was seven miles per hour, five in winter, but that this standard was seldom met. We can learn about the discomfort of saddles and the dangers of the road, including but not limited to the absence of any markings and the frequency with which someone who did not know the roads quite simply got lost. As usual with the Folger publications, La Mar's booklet contains reprints and quotations that provide wonderful details that are very useful for imagining just what it would have been like to journey long or short distances alongside the characters of the plays.

COMMERCE

Even economics has a historical arm of scholarship, and it is to that section of the library that we can go in search of specific information about money. An excellent publication in the New Appreciations in History series is C.E. Challis's pamphlet *Currency and the Economy in Tudor and Early Stuart England*; if you can get hold of that, you will not want to plow through a book as detailed as his study *The Tudor Coinage*. If the latter is the only title you can find, look at his fourth chapter, "The Circulating Medium," for the answers to questions like "What sort of money would I carry and how would I get paid?" R.D.

Connor's *The Weights and Measures of England* can be consulted for its pictures of coins. You will also find useful Sandra Fischer's dictionary of economic terms *Econolingua*, which includes the relative values of the various types of money mentioned in the plays as well as useful definitions of a variety of verbs and nouns associated with commercial transactions. For the most specific of details, you might consult Ronald Edward Zupko's handbook *British Weights and Measures* in which you will learn that twenty troy grains make a scruple, three scruples make a dram, eight drams make an ounce, and twelve ounces make a pound (155).

ANACHRONISMS

Even though Shakespeare set his plays almost always in another time and/or place, such as the England of the history plays or various Italian cities, or ancient Rome and Egypt, or exotic places like Bohemia, Illyria, Ephesus, or Denmark, scholars have spotted the references to contemporary England and, specifically, the London of Shakespeare's day in almost everything he wrote. This is no surprise. If you look at the script for any fantastical or historical drama, you will find the imprint of the time and place of the writer's own life: we use the familiar to make sense of the unfamiliar or imagined, even if we are not consciously aware of doing so. For that reason, we can find great help in understanding the social and economic function of some of Shakespeare's characters in books about Shakespeare's London.

LONDON

I hope to see London, once ere I die.

Davy [*2HIV* 5.3.60]

Many of Shakespeare's contemporaries scored theatrical hits with hilarious satires of contemporary London life, a genre of plays that modern scholars label "city comedies." The closest Shakespeare came was a gentle mockery of middle-class concerns in *The Merry Wives of Windsor*; he preferred to set the majority of his comedies in more fairy-tale settings such as Illyria or Bohemia. Perhaps he wished to be freed from the constant danger of arrest for straying too close to the bone; his colleague Ben Jonson on more than one occasion felt the heavy hand of the law for offending some powerful people.

Even though none of Shakespeare's plays are officially set in the London of his time, his customary disregard for historical or geographical authenticity allowed for the inclusion of anachronistic touches in classical Rome or medieval England, and for that reason some of the resource books created to enhance the study of Ben Jonson's plays, such as D. Heyward Brock's *A Ben*

Jonson Companion or Fran C. Chalfant's *Ben Jonson's London*, can be useful for a Shakespearean actor. In addition, Shakespeare festivals do on occasion include a city comedy such as *The Alchemist* or *Bartholomew Fair* by Jonson or *The Knight of the Burning Pestle* by Francis Beaumont, for which such information is invaluable.

Plays like Jonson's *Bartholomew Fair* or Beaumont's *The Knight of the Burning Pestle* contain marvellous tidbits of information about life in Shakespeare's London and are also great theatrical pieces. These London plays are well worth looking at because they help us to understand the world in which Shakespeare lived, provided we take into account that these are plays, not docudramas. If they are comedies, we can expect satirical exaggeration; if they are dramas, heightened events. Even so, there is something wonderfully theatrical and evocative of life in the city.

London in History

The first 120 pages of Felix Barker and Peter Jackson's *London*, a collection of pictures accompanied by concise and informative commentary, describe London up to and including Shakespeare's era. This makes their contribution an excellent resource for Shakespearean actors. The authors have attempted to portray not just the geography and architecture, but also the political and cultural events of note. In the chapter on Elizabethan London, there are sections on "Threats against the Queen's Person," "Elizabeth's Navy," and "Birth of the Theatres."

The London Encyclopaedia, edited by Ben Weinreb and Christopher Hibbert, is an example of a parallel reference resource, emerging from the interests of historians rather than literary scholars. As with any general historical work, the actor will need to check carefully that the information he is discovering is in fact from Shakespeare's era. The entry on Tyburn contains such fascinating information as the following:

- The first permanent triangular gallows were erected in 1571 (the accompanying picture dates from 1747).

- Condemned prisoners were driven to Tyburn by cart.

- In 1447 five condemned prisoners had already been hanged, cut down while still alive, stripped, and marked out for quartering when their pardon arrived, but the hangman, whose fee included the clothes of the condemned, refused to give up his perk and sent them home naked. The executioner also sold the rope for six pence an inch.

- The hangman was known commonly as the Lord of the Manor of Tyburn. (897)

Even though *Measure for Measure* is set in Vienna, I cannot help but think of the executioner Abhorson when I read those facts.

The London Encyclopaedia can be used for looking up a location mentioned in one of the plays, and the editors have made use of the "funeral gothic" font for those sites that can only be imaged on the basis of historical documents. One such listing is Paris Garden, Southwark, which was infamous as a location of gambling, bear baiting, and theatrical establishments. It is also interesting to look up such general categories as cemeteries or gardens, under which listings the editors have supplied a compendium of such locales.

Two general studies of London which provide a useful backdrop against which to imagine Shakespeare writing and performing in his plays are *London 1500–1700*, edited by A.L. Beier and Roger Finlay, and *Worlds Within Worlds*, by Steve Rappaport. Here you will find well-written scholarly studies which have emerged from the academic discipline of cultural history.

Historical Maps

My one regret when I consult *The London Encyclopaedia* is the absence of a good map of the city. But what city? The London of Shakespeare's day was quite a different place than the London of Dickens, even if we leave aside the expansion of boundaries that resulted from the population growing from 120,000 in 1583 to 7,252,000 in 1911. I get these numbers from Hugh Clout's *The Times London History Atlas*, a wonderful publication that includes excellent maps, reconstructions, historical illustrations, and commentary.

We are fortunate to have access to historical maps that can add a very specific sense of reality to a rehearsal hall. Every university library can be counted on to have a good collection of historical and modern maps in a permanent collection, usually housed in or near the Reference section. Of course not everyone is equally handy at reading a modern map, and a historical one can be uninspiring. In addition, our modern way of making and reading maps would not have been something that Shakespeare and his contemporaries encountered. Compare, for example, a reproduction of the Höfnagel map of London, such as the one which appears in Felix Barker and Peter Jackson's *The History of London in Maps* (13) with the product of modern scholarly cartography to be found in a series such as *The British Atlas of Historic Towns*, the third volume of which was edited by Mary D. Lobel and W.H. Johns and shows us London from prehistoric times until 1520. These in turn can be compared with modern maps of London. Even if you are not interested in his discussion of the history of cartography, you might enjoy the many lovely full-color reproductions of the maps themselves in P.D.A. Harvey's *Maps in Tudor England.*

I happen to love maps, modern or historical, and am always thankful for those publishers who have collected first-rate reproductions for my perusal. I like to bring a detailed map of England to rehearsals of Shakespeare's history plays so that everyone can see just where they are. The Automobile Association published an *Illustrated Guide to Country Towns and Villages of Britain*, filled with full-color modern photographs of historical buildings, and therefore a wonderful source for images to correspond to the pictures painted by Shakespeare's language. Many of these of course are from the centuries after Shakespeare's death, but a significant number of them would have been just the sort of humble dwelling or great manor that would have been familiar to Shakespeare's actors and audience.

The academic discipline of historical geography has opened to our understanding many of the realities of daily life in the distant past, for which there are no records other than a few surviving documents and the land itself. Many of the publications by such scholars are filled with detailed analysis of very specific data in language created for the discipline. But the effort of these scholars lays the foundation upon which we all build.

Two contrasting books will give the actor a glimpse of the immense wealth of information unearthed by historical geographers, upon which literary scholars draw when linking Shakespeare's plays to the world in which he lived. Robert Bearman has edited *The History of an English Borough: Stratford-upon-Avon*, which is filled with great chunks of historical data rather than lovely pictures and general, introductory articles written for the non-academic reader. There are two chapters that deal with the town during Shakespeare's lifetime, and both are of real interest for anyone seeking the richest possible portrait of the age from which to draw inspiration when one is reading the plays. As always, going to the scholarly resource lessens an actor's reliance upon an editor of the plays to provide relevant information. Ann Hughes's chapter on religious tensions in the town is of particular interest, as this is a topic that Shakespeare could not deal with directly in his plays, given the censorship under which he worked, but that would have been very much in the minds of his actors and audience. The zealous Puritans described by Hughes might have influenced Shakespeare's portrait of Malvolio in *Twelfth Night*; the mixture of strict with lax observers is captured in the clown's description of Perdita's preparations for the sheep-shearing feast in *The Winter's Tale*:

She hath made me four and twenty Nose-gays for the shearers (three-man song-men, all, and very good ones) but they are most of them Means and Bases; but one Puritan amongst them, and he sings Psalms to horn-pipes. [4.3.41]

Placing these portraits alongside the studies in Bearman's book suggests that some fascinating characters could be in attendance at Perdita's sheep shearing.

Perhaps you are preparing a production of *As You Like It* and are attempting to understand just what the original actors would have imagined when Rosalind says, in answer to Orlando's question where she dwells, "Here in the skirts of the forest, like fringe upon a petticoat" [3.2.336]. If you are looking for information about patterns in population, farming, and forests, or if you think that historical geography might interest you, I would recommend a general textbook or introductory survey, such as H.C. Darby's *A New Historical Geography of England before 1600*. The chapter on England around 1600, by F.V.

Emery, is a straightforward description based upon the painstaking gathering of evidence undertaken by Emery and others, with no effort to present the evidence firsthand, except in a few easy-to-read maps. Similarly, the chapters on England in the time covered by Shakespeare's history plays, written by R.E. Glassock and Alan R.H. Baker, are useful for anyone interested in a detailed portrait of those days and, perhaps more important, just how things changed between 1334 and 1600.

THEATRICAL TIME MACHINES

There is no escaping the modern framework within which a historical period will be viewed. There is no way to recapture a "real" Elizabethan theatrical event, as we are no longer Elizabethans. We can be instructed to mimic some of their theatregoing habits, and we can attend a performance in a space that re-creates the actor-audience relationship that they enjoyed, but we cannot erase our world view, much less replace it with theirs, even if we could know for sure what it was and re-create it in all its complexity.

Therefore, at the very least, every production has a minimum of two historical and theatrical contexts at work: that of our day and that of Shakespeare's. We then begin to add more layers. Shakespeare himself layered his plays with a double set of references. The histories and many of the tragedies are set in the past; the comedies and romances often have the feel of either a fairy-tale time and place, such as Illyria or the forest of Arden or outside Athens, or a strange and exotic locale such as Venice, Cyprus, or an island only accessible by a combination of fate and a good tempest.

We know that Shakespeare's actors performed in the clothing that was familiar to his audience. In fact, they often modelled sumptuous and fashionable garments in keeping with the glamour of their public presentation and the social status of their characters. The few touches of historical costuming were worn and viewed alongside what was, for them, modern dress.

Modern-dress productions of Shakespeare in our day, however, run into a few basic problems. What do you do with all those references to swords, which were standard accoutrements for the Elizabethan gentry but can only be found in theatres and fencing academies today? What do you do about that language, which was flamboyant, heightened, but comprehensible for Shakespeare's first audience but is virtually a foreign language for us today?

Many directors have turned their back on the elaborate clothing of Shakespeare's England, and not only on account of the expense of such costumes. They fear that audiences will find it almost impossible to "read" such signals of status and position. When someone enters and speaks, everyone needs to know if this is a high-status earl or a slightly-less-high-status knight. In addition, the characters all look so fabulous and historical, in keeping with their strange and beautiful manner of speaking, that it is difficult to imagine any link between their concerns and ours today, and directors fear that such productions will be beautiful but ultimately meaningless theatrical events. As a result of these fears, legitimate or groundless, half a century of Shakespearean production has experimented with setting the plays in still another time and place, so that setting and costuming suggest not only a larger social context within which these events make sense, but also the rich and compelling meanings to be found in these increasingly aged texts.

This leaves the actor who is interested in that social context with a considerable puzzle. The production will make reference, say, to India under the British raj, as did John Barton's 1976 production of *Much Ado about Nothing*. If you are going to wear the uniform of a British regiment, and the play has you returning from a war, you might want to know something about British military action in the Indian subcontinent during that time. I can think of one question that I, for one, would want answered: how likely was it that I would die in such a battle? The mood of the civilians in inquiring about and greeting the returning soldiers has always suggested to me that not many of their "set" have actually died, and that the point of going to war seems to be how well you do in gaining glory:

Leonato: I learn in this letter, that Don Peter of Arragon, comes this night to Messina.

Messenger: He is very near by this: he was not three Leagues off when I left him.

Leonato: How many Gentlemen have you lost in this action?

Messenger: But few of any sort, and none of name.

Leonato: A victory is twice itself, when the achiever brings home full numbers: I find here that, Don Peter hath bestowed much honour on a young Florentine, called Claudio.

Messenger: Much deserved on his part, and equally remembered by Don Pedro, he hath borne himself beyond the promise of his age, doing in the figure of a Lamb, the feats of a Lion: he hath indeed better bettered expectation, than you must expect of me to tell you how.

Leonato: He hath an uncle here in Messina, will be very much glad of it. [1.1.1]

This exchange sets a serious problem to the entire company if, for example, the play has been repositioned to a Civil War or 1920s setting, following wars that involved a horrific loss of life. However, the British army in India was more likely than not to have returned from just such a skirmish, in which unnumbered natives might have died but "few of any sort, and none of name," that is, no white men. The Indian raj setting allowed the company to evoke a credible atmosphere of postwar relaxation as well as setting up a characterization of the night watch as native policemen, complete with accent, to mangle the English language in such lines as "Is our whole dissembly appeared?" [4.2.1].

Of course, for every problem that is solved by a shift in setting, another is created. What is to be done with Don Pedro in the British raj? First there is his name, which, along with the other Italian references, does not allow us to forget that the play has been arbitrarily transported to India. Then there is his very specific social status, which is important for understanding the function he serves in acting as matchmaker and for the significance of the following exchange, which takes place immediately after the match between Hero and Claudio has been successfully made:

Beatrice: Good Lord, for alliance: thus goes every one to the world but I, and I am sun-burned, I may sit in a corner and cry, heigh ho for a husband.

Don Pedro: Lady Beatrice, I will get you one.

Beatrice: I would rather have one of your fathers getting: hath your Grace ne'er a brother like you? your father got excellent husbands, if a maid could come by them.

Don Pedro: Will you have me? Lady.

Beatrice: No, my lord, unless I might have another for working-days, your grace is too costly to wear every day: but I beseech your Grace pardon me, I was born to speak all mirth, and no matter.

Don Pedro: Your silence most offends me. [2.1.318]

Neither the British raj nor our modern world contains a model for Don Pedro's exact combination of temporal power and social status. The actors in this scene might want to gain some familiarity with the models that would have been available to the first company of actors, which would have included both English and European princes. My personal favorite is Henry of Navarre and Burgundy, who became Henry IV of France. This individual actually makes an entirely unhistorical appearance in Love's Labour's Lost, where he entirely lacks the sophistication and maturity exhibited by Don Pedro. In life he was a much more complex and striking figure, and one very much in the mind's eye of the average Elizabethan, as he came to the French throne in 1589. He was admired not only for his courage and gallantry in battle and his religious tolerance as a ruler, but also for his many love affairs, and is well described in any general introduction to the history of France.

   Actors are saved from insanity by the simple fact that the entire world of the play is, after all, fictional, even if actual historical events are being represented. The Messina of Much Ado about Nothing serves the requirements of the play to tell a story about certain characters and certain events and has been constructed out of an amalgam of the familiar, pure fantasy, and a reflection of something that might be called history and/or travelogue. In this, Shakespeare's first company performed a similar juggling act to the one asked of actors today, as do modern actors in contemporary plays. If a member of the Much Ado cast has to put a few more objects up into the air, the juggling might grow more challenging, but it is still juggling the real with the imagined, the known with the historical or exotic.

A modern actor might have an even more complex intellectual mosaic to create in a production of one of Shakespeare's Roman plays for a modern audience. In addition to our world view and Shakespeare's, we have the values of ancient Rome as Shakespeare saw them, and the values of ancient Rome as contemporary historians suggest them to us today. In some productions, when the director might have reset the play in, say, Prohibition Chicago, there are the values of that time and place as well.

Take, for example, the relationship between a husband and wife as portrayed in *Julius Caesar*, to be enacted in a Chicago gangster version of the play. Let's imagine that the director wants to portray Portia and Brutus as having a good marriage, but Calpurnia is to appear a very much younger second wife, a "trophy wife." These are the modern, contemporary allusions upon which the actors must base their work. Layered on top of that are the images provided by costumes and props selected to suggest Prohibition Chicago. These include, for Calpurnia, a stereotypical "gangster's moll" look, and for Portia, a contrasting housewife ensemble. But the actress playing Portia makes reference to her father Cato, so some research reveals information about educated wives and daughters of republican Rome, as well as Shakespeare's sources for his culture's attitude toward Romans, confirmed by the women who appear in his other Roman plays. None of these sources match up in any way with a gangster's moll, a trophy wife, or even a modern marriage. What on earth are we to make of Portia's swallowing fire to kill herself? And what attitude should we take to Calpurnia's barren state that Caesar announces to the assembled crowds? Significantly, both wives kneel to their respective husbands, which clearly arouses a strong response in both Brutus and Caesar.

Clearly, the historical research undertaken by a Shakespearean actor cannot be used to limit a performance to those actions that would be authentic for only one time in history. Often we will discover that an action or an attitude that is completely inauthentic for one time or place is one that best serves the production. If blended well, the result can be a layering effect whereby the various times and places evoked by the text each can be glimpsed or sensed beneath the surface. We will become accustomed to putting aside modern attitudes that get in the way of Shakespeare's story. Therefore, if the actor playing Brutus says that if his wife were to kneel to him, he would burst out laughing, we know that he simply must put aside that perspective to make Brutus come alive. But sometimes an attitude that was prevalent in Shakespeare's time is similarly set aside. Therefore, the modern director of the Prohibition *Julius Caesar* might want the assembled crowd to smirk at Caesar when he announces Calpurnia's barren state, because in Chicago in the 1930s people have caught on to the fact that the absence of children might be attributed to an inability of the husband to father a child. This reaction would have no place in Shakespeare's theatre. It is also a historical fact that Julius Caesar acknowledged more than one young man as his natural child (i.e., one born out of wedlock to a mistress), although none of his legal wives ever bore him a child.

Historians place a great deal of value on things like accuracy; fortunately, actors are freed from the need to justify their eclectic sources of inspiration on historical grounds. If information about the social life of the period into which the director has transported the play solves one moment, and information about the customs of Shakespeare's England helps to make sense of another, while modern assumptions and understandings inform the development of the internal landscape of the character, the result will have as much or as little theatrical validity as can be achieved through the rehearsal and production process. It is by these standards that the performance will be judged.

RECOMMENDED READING

General Introductions to Shakespeare's England

Bock, Philip K. *Shakespeare and Elizabethan Culture: An Anthropological View.* New York: Schocken Books, 1984.

Brown, Ivor. *How Shakespeare Spent the Day.* London: Bodley Head, 1963.

Dodd, A.H. *Elizabethan England.* New York: G.P. Putnam, 1973.

Fraser, Antonia. *King James VI of Scotland, I of England.* London: Weidenfeld and Nicolson, 1974.

Frye, Roland Mushat. *The Renaissance Hamlet: Issues and Responses in 1600.* Princeton, NJ: Princeton University Press, 1984.

Harrison, G.B. *The Elizabethan Journals: Being A Record of Those Things Most Talked of During the Years 1591–1603: Comprising: An Elizabethan Journal 1591–4, A Second Elizabethan Journal 1595–8, A Last Elizabethan Journal 1599–1603.* London: Routledge & Kegan Paul, 1938.

Hyland, Peter. *An Introduction to Shakespeare: The Dramatist in His Context.* New York: St. Martin's Press, 1996.

Joseph, B.L. *Shakespeare's Eden: The Commonwealth of England, 1558–1629.* New York: Barnes & Noble, 1971.

Lacey, Robert. *The Life and Times of Henry VIII.* London: Weidenfeld and Nicolson, 1972.

McMurtry, Jo. *Understanding Shakespeare's England: A Companion for the American Reader.* Hamden, CT: Archon Books, 1989.

Morrill, John, ed. *The Oxford Illustrated History of Tudor and Stuart Britain.* Oxford: Oxford University Press, 1996.

Papp, Joseph, and Elizabeth Kirkland. *Shakespeare Alive!* New York: Bantam, 1988.

Raleigh, W.A., S. Lee, and C.T. Onions, eds. *Shakespeare's England: An Account of the Life and Manners of His Age.* 2 vols. Oxford: Clarendon Press, 1916.

Ridley, Jasper. *The Tudor Age.* London: Constable, 1988.

Rowse, A.L. *The Elizabethan Renaissance: The Cultural Achievement.* New York: Charles Scribner's Sons, 1972.

———. *The Elizabethan Renaissance: The Life of the Society.* London: Macmillan, 1971.

Sharpe, J.A. *Early Modern England: A Social History, 1550–1760.* London: Edward Arnold, 1987.

Sim, Alison. *Pleasures and Pastimes in Tudor England.* Stroud, Gloucestershire: Sutton, 1999.

Smith, Lacey Baldwin. *The Horizon Book of the Elizabethan World.* New York: American Heritage Pub. Co., 1967.

Thomas, Paul. *Authority and Disorder in Tudor Times, 1485–1603.* Cambridge: Cambridge University Press, 1999.

Williams, Neville. *The Life and Times of Elizabeth I.* London: Weidenfeld and Nicolson, 1972.

Worden, Blair, ed. *Stuart England.* Oxford: Phaidon, 1986.

Youings, Joyce. *Sixteenth-Century England.* London: Allen Lane, 1984.

Zito, George V. *The Sociology of Shakespeare: Explorations in a Sociology of Literature.* New York: Peter Lang, 1991.

New Historical Scholarship

Burt, Richard, and John Michael Archer, eds. *Enclosure Acts: Sexuality, Property, and Culture in Early Modern England.* Ithaca, NY: Cornell University Press, 1994.

Greenblatt, Stephen J. *Learning to Curse: Essays in Early Modern Culture.* London: Routledge, 1990.

———. *Renaissance Self-fashioning: From More to Shakespeare.* Chicago: University of Chicago Press, 1980.

———, ed. *Representing the English Renaissance.* Berkeley: University of California Press, 1988.

———. *Shakespearean Negotiations: The Circulation of Social Energy in Renaissance England.* Berkeley: University of California Press, 1988.

Kastan, David Scott. *Shakespeare After Theory.* London: Routledge, 1999.

Mallin, Eric S. *Inscribing the Time: Shakespeare and the End of Elizabethan England.* Berkeley: University of California Press, 1995.

Marcus, Leah S. *Puzzling Shakespeare: Local Reading and Its Discontents.* Berkeley: University of California Press, 1988.

Neill, Michael. *Putting History to the Question.* New York: Columbia University Press, 2000.

Wilson, Richard. *Will Power: Essays on Shakespearean Authority.* Detroit: Wayne State University Press, 1993.

———, and Richard Dutton, eds. *New Historicism and Renaissance Drama.* London: Longman, 1992.

Daily Life

Caton, Mary Anne, ed. *Fooles and Fricassees: Food in Shakespeare's England.* Seattle: University of Washington Press, 1999.

Dent, Anthony. *Horses in Shakespeare's England.* London: J.A. Allen, 1987.

Lamar, Virginia A. *English Dress in the Age of Shakespeare.* Ithaca, NY: Cornell University Press, 1964.

Vigarello, Georges. *Concepts of Cleanliness: Changing Attitudes in France since the Middle Ages.* Translated by Jean Birrell. Cambridge: Cambridge University Press, 1988.

Wilson, C. Anne. *Food and Drink in Britain: From the Stone Age to the 19th Century.* Chicago: Academy Chicago, 1991.

Family Matters

Aries, Philippe. *Centuries of Childhood: A Social History of Family Life.* New York: Knopf, 1962.

Cook, Ann Jennalie. *Making a Match: Courtship in Shakespeare and His Society.* Princeton, NJ: Princeton University Press, 1991.

Cressy, David. *Birth, Marriage, and Death: Ritual, Religion, and the Life-Cycle in Tudor and Stuart England.* Oxford: Oxford University Press, 1997.

Garber, Marjorie. *Coming of Age in Shakespeare.* London: Methuen, 1981.

Hanawalt, Barbara A. *Growing Up in Medieval London: The Experience of Childhood in History.* New York: Oxford University Press, 1993.

James, Max H. *Our House Is Hell: Shakespeare's Troubled Families.* Westport, CT: Greenwood Press, 1989.

Laurence, Anne. *Women in England, 1500–1760: A Social History.* New York: St. Martin's Press, 1994.

Shahar, Shulamith. *Childhood in the Middle Ages.* London: Routledge, 1990.

Sim, Alison. *The Tudor Housewife.* Montreal: McGill-Queen's University Press, 1996.

Stone, Lawrence. *The Family, Sex, and Marriage in England, 1500–1800.* New York: Harper & Row, 1977.

Private Matters

Fildes, Valerie. *Wet Nursing: A History from Antiquity to the Present.* Oxford: Basil Blackwell, 1988.

Goldberg, Jonathan. *Sodometries: Renaissance Texts, Modern Sexualities.* Stanford, CA: Stanford University Press, 1992.

Hair, Paul, ed. *Before the Bawdy Court: Selections from Church Court and Other Records, Relating to the Correction of Moral Offences in England, Scotland, and New England, 1300–1800.* London: Elek, 1972.

Haynes, Alan. *Sex in Elizabethan England.* Stroud, Gloucestershire: Sutton, 1997.

Laslett, Peter, ed. *Bastardy and Its Comparative History.* Cambridge, MA: Harvard University Press, 1980.

McLaren, Angus. *A History of Contraception: From Antiquity to the Present Day.* Oxford: Blackwell, 1990.

Rowse, A.L. *Simon Forman: Sex and Society in Shakespeare's Age.* London: Weidenfeld and Nicolson, 1974.

Smith, Bruce R. *Homosexual Desire in Shakespeare's England: A Cultural Poetics.* Chicago: University of Chicago Press, 1991.

Pastimes and Pursuits

Billett, Michael. *A History of English Country Sports.* London: Robert Hale, 1994.

Cummins, John. *The Hound and the Hawk: The Art of Medieval Hunting.* New York: St. Martin's Press, 1988.

Edelman, Charles. *Brawl Ridiculous: Swordfighting in Shakespeare's Plays*. Manchester: Manchester University Press, 1992.

Henn, T.R. *The Living Image: Shakespearean Essays*. London: Methuen, 1972.

Howard, Skiles. *The Politics of Courtly Dancing in Early Modern England*. Amherst: University of Massachusetts Press, 1998.

Madden, D.H. *The Diary of Master William Silence: A Study of Shakespeare and of Elizabethan Sport*. New York: Haskell House, 1969.

Manning, Roger B. *Hunters and Poachers: A Social and Cultural History of Unlawful Hunting in England, 1485–1640*. Oxford: Oxford University Press, 1993.

Martinez, J.D. *The Swords of Shakespeare: A Heavily Illustrated Guide to Stage Combat Choreography in the Plays of Shakespeare*. Jefferson, NC: McFarland & Co., 1996.

Millar, John Fitzhugh. *Elizabethan Country Dances*. Williamsburg, VA: Thirteen Colonies Press, 1985.

Playford, John. *The English Dancing Master, 1651*. Edited by Margaret Dean-Smith. London: Schott, 1957.

Pulver, Jeffrey. *A Dictionary of Old English Music and Musical Instruments*. London: Kegan Paul, Trench, Trubner, 1923.

Randel, Don Michael, ed. *The New Harvard Dictionary of Music*. Cambridge, MA: Belknap Press of Harvard University Press, 1986.

Sadie, Stanley, ed. *The New Grove Dictionary of Music and Musicians*. 20 vols. London: Macmillan, 1980.

Scholes, Percy A. *The Oxford Companion to Music*. Oxford: Oxford University Press, 1970.

Strahle, Graham. *An Early Music Dictionary: Musical Terms from British Sources, 1500–1740*. Cambridge: Cambridge University Press, 1995.

White, T.H. *The Goshawk*. Harmondsworth: Penguin Books, 1963.

The Ritual Year

Chambers, Robert, ed. *The Book of Days: A Miscellany of Popular Antiquities in Connection with the Calendar, Including Anecdote, Biography, and History, Curiosities of Literature, and Oddities of Human Life and Character*. 2 vols. Detroit: Gale Research Co., 1967.

Delaney, John J. *Dictionary of Saints*. Garden City, NY: Doubleday, 1980.

Farmer, David Hugh. *The Oxford Dictionary of Saints*. Oxford: Oxford University Press, 1987.

Hole, Christina. *British Folk Customs*. London: Hutchinson, 1976.

Hutton, Ronald. *The Stations of the Sun*. Oxford: Oxford University Press, 1996.

Kightly, Charles. *The Customs and Ceremonies of Britain: An Encyclopaedia of Living Traditions*. London: Thames and Hudson, 1986.

Laroque, François. *Shakespeare's Festive World: Elizabethan Seasonal Entertainment and the Professional Stage*. Trans. Janet Lloyd. Cambridge: Cambridge University Press, 1991.

McLean, Teresa. *The English at Play in the Middle Ages*. London: Kensal Press, 1983.

Parlett, David. *The Oxford Guide to Card Games*. Oxford: Oxford University Press, 1990.

Wiles, David. *Shakespeare's Almanac: A Midsummer Night's Dream, Marriage, and the Elizabethan Calendar*. Woodbridge, Suffolk: D.S. Brewer, 1993.

The Natural World

Ellacombe, Henry, N. *The Plant-Lore and Garden-Craft of Shakespeare.* London: Edward Arnold, 1896.

Eyler, Ellen C. *Early English Gardens and Garden Books.* Ithaca, NY: Cornell University Press, 1963.

Goodfellow, Peter. *Shakespeare's Birds.* Woodstock, NY: Overlook Press, 1983.

Harting, James Edmund. *The Birds of Shakespeare.* Chicago: Argonaut, 1965.

Kerr, Jessica. *Shakespeare's Flowers.* New York: Thomas Y. Crowell, 1969.

Swann, H. Kirke. *A Dictionary of English and Folk-Names of British Birds: With Their History, Meaning, and First Usage, and the Folk-lore, Weather-lore, Legends, etc., Relating to the More Familiar Species.* Wakefield, England: EP Publishing, 1977.

Webb, J. Barry. *Shakespeare's Imagery of Plants.* Hastings, East Sussex: Cornwallis, 1991.

Economic Life

Challis, C.E. *Currency and the Economy in Tudor and Early Stuart England.* London: Historical Association, 1989.

———. *The Tudor Coinage.* Manchester: Manchester University Press, 1978.

Connor, R.D. *The Weights and Measures of England.* London: Her Majesty's Stationary Office, 1987.

Fischer, Sandra K. *Econolingua: A Glossary of Coins and Economic Language in Renaissance Drama.* Newark: University of Delaware Press, 1985.

La Mar, Virginia A. *Travel and Roads in England.* Washington, DC: Folger Shakespeare Library, 1960.

Zupko, Ronald Edward. *British Weights and Measures: A History from Antiquity to the Seventeenth Century.* Madison: University of Wisconsin Press, 1977.

London and Stratford

Automobile Association of Great Britain. *Illustrated Guide to Country Towns and Villages of Britain.* Basingstoke, Hampshire: Drive Publications, 1985.

Barker, Felix, and Peter Jackson. *The History of London in Maps.* London: Barrie & Jenkins, 1990.

———. *London: 2000 Years of a City and Its People.* London: Cassell, 1974.

Bearman, Robert, ed. *The History of an English Borough: Stratford-upon-Avon, 1196–1996.* Stroud, Gloucestershire: Sutton, 1997.

Beier, A.L., and Roger Finlay, eds. *London 1500–1700: The Making of the Metropolis.* London: Longman, 1986.

Brock, D. Heyward. *A Ben Jonson Companion.* Bloomington: Indiana University Press, 1983.

Chalfant, Fran C. *Ben Jonson's London: A Jacobean Placename Dictionary.* Athens: University of Georgia Press, 1978.

Clout, Hugh, ed. *The Times London History Atlas.* New York: HarperCollins, 1991.

Darby, H.C., ed. *A New Historical Geography of England before 1600.* Cambridge: Cambridge University Press, 1976.

Harvey, P.D.A. *Maps in Tudor England.* Chicago: University of Chicago Press, 1993.

Lobel, Mary D., and W.H. Johns, eds. *The City of London: From Prehistoric Times to c. 1520.* The British Atlas of Historic Towns, vol. 3. Oxford: Oxford University Press in conjunction with the Historic Towns Trust, 1989.

Rappaport, Steve. *Worlds Within Worlds: Structures of Life in Sixteenth-Century London.* Cambridge: Cambridge University Press, 1989.

Weinreb, Ben, and Christopher Hibbert, eds. *The London Encyclopaedia.* London: Macmillan, 1983.

⋙ 8 ⋘

Beliefs

What I did, I did in Honour,
Led by th'Imperial conduct of my Soul.

Lord Chief Justice [*2HIV* 5.2.35]

One of the most difficult questions to answer for an actor is, "What would my character have believed about . . . ?" Then might follow a reference to angels, devils, heaven, hell, oracles, fate, conscience, sin, or damnation. The easy answers are the most dangerous. It is probably an error to assume that your character would have believed what you yourself believe. But it is equally an error to assume that everyone in Shakespeare's England believed absolutely and without question one of the set doctrines available from established religious organizations. Certain concepts and attitudes, however, can provide a broad framework when you are seeking to create a credible inner world for your character.

First of all, issues that today we would designate "religious" were, in Shakespeare's time, far more encompassing, serious, and emotionally charged. There was available for all a compelling and vivid vocabulary for the discussion of matters of faith. The public theatres were careful to avoid engaging in any of the religious debates of the era, but Shakespeare made use of the vocabulary regularly; hence the questions of actors when their characters make statements such as King John's self-condemnation:

O, when the last account 'twixt heaven and earth
Is to be made, then shall this hand and Seal
Witness against us to damnation! [4.2.216]

Just what is King John imagining when he makes this reference to the Last Judgment?

Just as it behooves us to venture into the history stacks to find out about historical personages, and into the medical stacks to find out about attitudes to disease, we can find important works on the popular systems of belief in Shakespeare's England. Philosophical concepts, issues of faith, and superstitions will all figure in any overview of what people believed. An actor's job is to place herself into that world, unequivocally, without standing apart and passing judgment on those beliefs, while at the same time recognizing that there could never exist a single world view that would be held by every member living in that time and place.

Some of the beliefs held by Elizabethans were not very different from ideas we accept or know to be accepted by people today. But some were so completely at odds with our modern world view that additional care is required to ensure that we allow the characters of the play to adhere to what the playwright has scripted them to believe; scholars can assist in this process by clarifying the range and complexity of the belief system suggested by the language.

Let us consider superstitions as an example of the most easily bridged gap between the modern and the Elizabethan. Although we pride ourselves in being rational (as did the Elizabethans), we all know of very real beliefs in the supernatural that are held by ourselves or people we know. Even if we retain some scepticism, as does Horatio in the first scene of *Hamlet*, we still love the thrill of ghost stories and perhaps even have had a spooky experience or keep an open mind that such experiences as reported by others might be true. Rather than simply taking it for granted that Shakespeare's contemporaries believed in fairies, ghosts, and witches, why not introduce yourself to some details of the range of belief that existed in Shakespeare's England and the details of the superstitions upon which Shakespeare built his plays?

INTELLECTUAL HISTORY

Scholars can be immensely helpful in providing actors with a richer awareness and understanding about the religious vocabulary that permeates the plays. This is an aspect of what is called intellectual history, and there are several useful books that set out the central facets of the belief system of Shakespeare's England.

Most general introductions to Shakespeare's plays contain something about the beliefs of his age. Even more helpful are the general introductions to Shakespeare's England, most of which include a wealth of material on superstitions, prejudices, religious practices and controversies, and value systems. I have made great use of John Erskine Hankins's *Backgrounds of Shakespeare's Thought*, which includes an index by play, allowing me to check out whatever connections he has made, and also a detailed table of contents so that I can pursue any questions I might have about specific topics. I have found his explanations of complex ideas to be neither embarrassingly simplistic nor needlessly convoluted.

C.A. Patrides's contribution *Premises and Motifs in Renaissance Thought and Literature* is narrower in focus and is particularly useful for ideas like heaven and hell, angels, Satan, and numerology, to name just a few of his chapter headings. Shakespeare is not central to this book, being mentioned just six times in the index, which is something of a relief. I have found, however, that I am able to make connections even if Patrides is not interested in regularly applying his observations directly to the plays.

SHAKESPEARE'S PERSONALITY

A fascinating subcategory in Shakespearean studies can be found in books entitled something like *Shakespeare's Personality*. This genre of literary/historical criticism is out of fashion these days, but the older works such as Edward Wagenknecht's *The Personality of Shakespeare* and Harold Grier McCurdy's *The Personality of Shakespeare* attempt to place under examination the complex web of social and cultural influences, beliefs, attitudes, life experiences, and individual genius that might have been at work within the individual who produced the primary linguistic energy that resulted in the plays we perform today. It doesn't matter to an actor that the author has been declared dead, and that this type of scholarship is a humanist illusion in the eyes of poststructuralist deconstructionists (whatever they might be). The actor can find much of interest in the blending of modern psychological theories of personality with historical examinations of Elizabethan attitudes to selfhood when he is seeking to understand that thing we call the character with which an actor is entrusted in performance. Here is an example of the connections between performance and scholarship afforded by this sort of study. When you are playing Viola or Sebastian in *Twelfth Night*, consider that Shakespeare was himself the father of a boy/girl pair of twins, and that the boy, Hamnet, died in 1596; scholars date *Twelfth Night* to 1601 or 1602. Unlike those scholars who discredit the significance of such data about the playwright, actors regularly work closely with playwrights and know that the person who wrote the words they speak is paradoxically both deeply connected with and quite extraneous to the printed version of the play.

THE HISTORY OF POPULAR BELIEFS AND IDEALS

The popular culture of a time and place serves an important function in the creation of characters. We must assume that not only the actors and audience partake of the images and values encoded in the popular culture, but so too, to a greater or lesser degree, do the characters in the plays. One of the challenges facing a modern actor is the replacing of Clint Eastwood with Achilles, or whatever the appropriate equivalent might be.

This is an area in which scholars can be most helpful. Because some of them have undertaken a detailed study of not only Shakespeare's plays but the popular culture of his time, they can draw our attention to just how these powerful indicators might illuminate events and characters in the plays. More importantly for the actor, they can provide insight into possible sources of encoding behavior, allowing the actor to make his own leaps of association.

One such study comes from Reuben A. Brower. His *Hero and Saint* provides one answer to the question: Whom would a young Elizabethan man have admired? Achilles and Aeneas set the standard that someone like Hamlet finds so hard to meet. Max James, in *Scarce Truth Enough Alive*, works from the opposite perspective. He takes a close look at Troilus and Timon, two characters who, on the surface of things, would seem to have little in common with people today, and finds striking similarities between contemporary American values and those of Shakespeare's England.

Justice, Mercy, and Revenge

Shakespeare's characters have a great deal to say about justice and mercy, and some of them have things to do if, like Hamlet, they find themselves caught up in a revenge plot. Every character in the history plays is knowingly or unknowingly working within a system of divine retribution that was visible in hindsight and, not surprisingly, justified the Tudor monarchy. Literary scholars have therefore had much to say on these topics, and the scholarly editions of the plays in which these themes play an important part always include a good general introduction to the belief systems that provide a context for the events of the play.

Honor

There is one closely connected concept, however, about which the characters care a great deal and have a great deal to say, and that is that thing known as "honour." In *The Harvard Concordance to Shakespeare*, compiled by Marvin Spevack before Internet Shakespeare sites with good search engines made such scholarly endeavors obsolete, the listing for "honour" and associated words makes up nine columns of very small print in which Spevack lists 681 uses of the word "honour," 128 of "honourable," 7 of "honourably," 44 of "honour'd" and 10 of "honoured," 32 of "honour's," and 81 of "honours." If we add other associated words, most particularly "dishonour," the number of citations climbs. Clearly, this was a word upon which Shakespeare and his contemporaries drew for a significant proportion of the theatrical impetus of the plays.

A modern actor has some work to do to reposition himself into a nonmodern view of this concept. It is refreshing to encounter Falstaff's mocking riff:

Can Honour set to a leg? No: or an arm? No: Or take away the grief of a wound? No. Honour hath no skill in Surgery, then? No. What is Honour? A word. What is in that word Honour? Air: A trim reckoning. Who hath it? He that died a Wednesday. Doth he feel it? No. Doth he hear it? No. Is it insensible then? yea, to the dead. But will it not live with the living? No. Why? Detraction will not suffer it, therefore I'll none of it. Honour is a mere Scutcheon, and so ends my Catechism. [*1HIV* 5.1.131]

But Falstaff is, in this as in so many other profound beliefs, very much outside the norm of respected behavior, and modern actors must, with Hotspur, be prepared to say without irony,

> Send danger from the East unto the West,
> So Honour cross it from the North to South,
> And let them grapple: O the blood more stirs
> To rouse a Lion, than to start a Hare!
> . . .
> By heaven, me thinks it were an easy leap,
> To pluck bright Honour from the pale-faced Moon,
> Or dive into the bottom of the deep,
> Where Fathom-line could never touch the ground,
> And pluck up drowned Honour by the Locks:
> So he that doth redeem her thence, might wear
> Without Co-rival, all her Dignities. [*1HIV* 1.3.201]

At the end of the first part of *Henry IV*, in which both these characters proclaim these words on "honour," only the fat and irreverent Falstaff will be left standing. The heroic Hotspur will lie dead on the field of battle, proof positive of Falstaff's supposition that honor cannot cure a man of a mortal wound. However, the crown prince Hal, the sun/son around whom both Falstaff and Hotspur circle, has this to say of Hotspur:

> When that this body did contain a spirit,
> A Kingdom for it was too small a bound:
> But now two paces of the vilest Earth
> Is room enough. This Earth that bears thee dead
> Bears not alive so stout a Gentleman. [5.4.89]

and this of Falstaff:

> Death hath not struck so fat a Deer to-day,
> Though many dearer in this bloody Fray. [5.4.107]

By the end of the second part of *Henry IV*, Hal, now King Henry V, will forever reject both his companion Falstaff and his world view in favor of the heroic and honorable.

To a great extent, an actor's understanding of the concept of honor in Shakespeare's England can be gleaned from the references to honor made by the various characters in the plays themselves. However, scholars can supplement this understanding by setting the word and the concept into a larger context, that of the thoughts of other writers and the actions of well-known individuals that were "in the air" and so provided a framework within which the plays were first rehearsed and performed.

A fine introduction to this topic is provided in the opening chapter of Norman Council's *When Honour's at the Stake*. This book examines the ideas about honor not only in the first part of *Henry IV*, quoting as I did both Hotspur and Falstaff, but also in *Julius Caesar*, *Troilus and Cressida*, *Hamlet*, *Othello*, and *King Lear*, and his chapters on these plays are well worth reading if you have been cast in one of them. But the introduction is all-purpose: useful for any play because all the plays treat matters honorable and dishonorable.

It is almost impossible to enter into a discussion of Elizabethan and Jacobean concepts of honor without discussing the career of Robert Devereux, earl of Essex. He, along with other famous and infamous contemporaries of Shakespeare, is discussed in Anthony Esler's *The Aspiring Mind of the Elizabethan Younger Generation*, which describes the political careers of the most prominent men of Shakespeare's age, in the final years of the reign of Elizabeth, from the perspective of intergenerational conflict. *Society, Politics, and Culture* by Mervyn James is a scholarly work that examines the tensions surrounding the concept of honor and just how honor mattered to people. James takes us far back in time to lay the groundwork for his careful study of just how things changed so that Essex could declare his rebellion "honourable" without feeling that he had stated an absurdity. I would recommend starting with James's chapter on the Northern Rising of 1569, which surely must have been a vivid collective memory for Shakespeare's audience. There is a great deal here that will prove invaluable, in particular for an actor assigned one of the major roles in a history play, where concepts of honor and England are so central as to be virtual characters alongside Henrys and Richards.

Machiavelli

Lest we fall into the trap of ascribing to Shakespeare's era a nobility that nostalgia would have us believe marks "the good old days," we should familiarize ourselves with that most cynical of philosophers, Niccolò Machiavelli. Modern English translations of his seminal works abound, such as Peter Bondanella and Mark Musa's *The Portable Machiavelli*, but what is far more important than a firsthand encounter with his treatise *The Prince* is a clear understanding of how Elizabethans read these ideas, in other words, how these ideas shaped the lens through which they might view events, fictional or actual. A literary study that lays out the contrast between the heroic and the Machiavellian role models is Wyndham Lewis's *The Lion and the Fox*. For a discussion of the impact Machiavelli had upon English political theory and practice, you could consult Felix Raab's study *The English Face of Machiavelli*.

The best general introduction to Machiavelli's life and ideas has been created by Patrick Curry and Oscar Zarate, *Machiavelli for Beginners*. I am not ashamed to confess that I have used a number of these Beginners series books to acquire a clear, firm overview of a difficult and complex philosopher or theorist. The combination of vivid and evocative illustrations with a text provided by an expert who can set aside all scholarly considerations is, for me, irresistible.

D.C. Biswas in *Shakespeare in His Own Time* presents a straightforward and wonderfully accessible introduction to Machiavelli through a discussion of Hal as presented in *Henry IV, Part I*. He also looks at the influence of the writings of Montaigne through an examination of *Troilus and Cressida*. His useful book also considers the administration of justice, beliefs about witches, and the debt Shakespeare owed to the English author John Lyly and is well worth looking at if you are rehearsing *Measure for Measure, Macbeth*, and *Love's Labour's Lost*, respectively.

THE ENGLISH CHURCH

> If men could be contented to be what they are, there were no fear in marriage, for young Charbon the Puritan, and old Poysam the Papist, how some'er their hearts are severed in Religion, their heads are both one, they may jowl horns together, like any Deer i' the Herd.
>
> Clown [*All's Well* 1.3.50]

Although his personal beliefs are subject to much debate, Shakespeare does, occasionally, make use of some general terms describing religious affiliation. We can take from this example, and others like it, that Puritans and Papists were as far apart, for religious reasons, as anyone could be in Shakespeare's England, for all that they might be alike with regard to the horns of cuckoldry.

The best-known Puritan in Shakespeare's plays is Malvolio of *Twelfth Night*, whose religious beliefs are associated with his unwillingness to party into the wee small hours of the night. The fun-loving Sir Toby's rebuttal to Malvolio's intervention includes the rhetorical question, "Dost thou think, because thou art virtuous, there shall be no more cakes and ale?" [2.3.114]. The editorial explanations of this line in the Oxford, the Cambridge, and the Arden editions all make reference to the Puritans' rejection of church festivals. This seems on the surface to be sufficient to make sense of the tension between Malvolio and the other servants, but surely there must be larger issues at stake in a world that forbids the exploration of the issues in the theatre and still executes heretics on a regular basis.

This is where the Folger Shakespeare Library booklet on the topic proves valuable. In a clear summary of the most significant events in English history,

Craig Thompson in *The English Church in the Sixteenth Century* sets out the complexities of the religious tensions in Shakespeare's England. There is the Church of England, the policies of which are reinforced by the powers of the state, threatened simultaneously by "old Poysam the Papist" and "young Charbon the Puritan." There is no such thing as religious freedom or toleration of different theological points of view. Elizabeth executed Puritans and Catholics alike whenever they publicly challenged the teachings of the Church of England. Because we associate England with the Protestant resistance to the Catholic powers of Europe, we forget that the Puritans and other extreme Protestant groups, dissatisfied with the inability of the Church of England to reform itself, broke away and became as much a threat as Catholic spies from Spain.

The main complaint that the Puritans had against the Church of England was just that it had been declared the only church of England. Rome might no longer be in the picture, but the Anglican Church remained a hierarchical and highly politicized social institution. The Puritans sought to undercut the power of bishops and archbishops, and hence of the church as an arm of the policies of the state, by placing at the center of the spiritual experience the interaction of the individual with the Bible and of the congregation with itself as a community of believers. In 1593 such congregations were declared illegal, and the execution of unrepentant Puritans began in earnest.

Scholars have been able to generate a fair number of academic publications considering the question of Shakespeare's personal religious beliefs. Was he secretly still an adherent to the old faith, someone who perhaps attended church to avoid the fines levied against recusants? There is evidence that members of his immediate family were secret Catholics with ties to members of the nobility playing the dangerous games with the Catholic claimant to the English throne, Mary Queen of Scots. There is also evidence of an abhorrence for certain of the Roman Catholic tenets, expressed, for example, in an aversion to celibacy or the unflattering portrait of the papal delegate in *King John*. Was there any significance in the fact that Hamlet studied at Wittenberg, Luther's hometown? What about the many friars that make an appearance in the Italian plays? Are they simply local color, or do they reflect Shakespeare's reactionary Catholicism?

Ultimately, it does not matter what Shakespeare himself believed, but rather what attitudes toward religious belief were "in the air," so to speak, and thus available to be used by the first actors to individualize the characters in the play. A modern actor might be more comfortable concluding that religious beliefs in general, and adherence to one specific subset of the Christian religion in particular, have no significance in these plays. But that is to ignore an important aspect of Shakespeare's world and to place modern suppositions onto these plays, perhaps thereby missing some important nuances of personal behavior.

Let us return to *Twelfth Night*, where we can agree that the tension between Toby and Malvolio has as much to do with their differing attitudes to having a good time as to any religious controversy. But what about the religious beliefs of others in the play? Let's have a look at an exchange between Feste the fool and Viola regarding her mourning for her dead brother:

Feste: Good Madonna, give me leave to prove you a fool.

Olivia: Can you do it?

Feste: Dexterously, good Madonna.

Olivia: Make your proof.

Feste: I must catechise you for it Madonna: good my Mouse of virtue answer me.

Olivia: Well sir, for want of other idleness, I'll bide your proof.

Feste: Good Madonna, why mournest thou?

Olivia: Good fool, for my brothers death.

Feste: I think his soul is in hell, Madonna.

Olivia: I know his soul is in heaven, fool.

Feste: The more fool (Madonna) to mourn for your brothers soul, being in heaven. Take away the Fool, Gentlemen. [1.5.57]

Olivia, as a woman of the nobility, without father or brother to guide her, nonetheless orders the affairs of her household, which would have included the form of worship to which all would have subscribed or have been denied her protection. Toby's inability to get up in the morning might well have included a reluctance to put in an appearance at divine service, but skipping church was never a politically neutral act in Shakespeare's world.

Olivia becomes Elizabeth-like in this as in other matters. Like Elizabeth, she mourns the dead brother, rules without the assistance of a male protector, and feels the oppression of unwelcomed suitors. Within her household she gives space to both "young Charbon the Puritan, and old Poysam the Papist" in the person of Malvolio and Sir Toby, respectively, though each in his own way causes her great discomfort and embarrassment. She is not immune to religious error, but is capable of receiving instruction and, when the most important event in her young life finally takes place, evokes the sanctity of a priest to ensure the endurance of her bond of love with Sebastian.

It might be tempting to a modern actor to see these brief allusions to matters of faith as plot devices or character images (Malvolio is like a Puritan; therefore play him uptight and pompous) rather than placing the religious tensions alongside the character interactions in seeking a more comprehensive view of how someone like Olivia might see the world. *Twelfth Night* is a comedy, and as such, in it the weighty issues of religious martyrdom seem out of place. Malvolio the heretic Puritan is punished with imprisonment but is freed to vow revenge on the rest of the cast. The images of dismemberment, horror, shame, and confusion that permeate the tragedies, on the other hand, can be traced in part to the displays of religious martyrdom captured in such documents as John Foxe's *Acts and Monuments*. It is here that we can see a woodcut of Archbishop Cranmer thrusting his right hand into the fire to burn first, because with it he had signed a recantation of his Protestant opinions. The story that accompanies the woodcut is powerfully theatrical: in a public gathering at which he was expected to repeat his recantation, he surprised all by denouncing his weakness in bowing to the will of the Roman Catholic Mary and her husband Philip of Spain. He was taken immediately to his public execution at the stake.

Shakespeare's Bible

The Elizabethans were surrounded by the rich cultural heritage of the Christian world. Bible stories were a shared currency upon which to build a cohesive web of allusion and direct reference. A modern actor can benefit from a familiarity with this web and use it to infuse a character and the spoken word with not only a spiritual energy but also resonating emotional associations.

Shakespeare's Bible is not readily available to modern readers. The two Bibles most in use in Shakespeare's lifetime were the Bishops' Bible, published in 1568, which was the book required to be read in English churches, and the Geneva Bible, first published in 1560 and reprinted often with short marginal notes that greatly influenced how people thought about what they read daily from privately owned copies of these editions. These two were the accepted Protestant Bibles; those who still practiced the Roman Catholic faith privately in their homes might use the Rheims translation of the New Testament, published in 1582, or, after 1609, the complete Bible published in Douay.

Although the King James Bible was published in 1611 after Shakespeare stopped writing for the theatre, it uses language contemporary to Shakespeare's and provides therefore a good acclimatization for the actor's tongue. As with Shakespeare, read aloud, savor the rhythms and the way thoughts are put together, and you can gain much of service to your speaking of Shakespeare's plays. You will also find a rhetorical use of punctuation similar to that found in the First Folio.

In addition to a general familiarity with the language of the Bible, including imagery and syntax, it is important to have a firsthand encounter with the great stories of the Bible that resonate in the Elizabethan psyche and therefore, inevitably, in the psyche of the character of the play that an actor must bring alive. When Hamlet addresses Polonius with "O Jephthah Judge of Israel, what a Treasure hadst thou?" [2.2.404], he is alluding not only to a popular ballad, but also to the story told in Judges 11. On the eve of a great battle, Jephthah vowed that if he were victorious, he would make a burnt offering of thanks, selecting as his sacrifice whatever came to the door to greet him. His enemies were defeated, but when he returned home, his daughter, his only child, came out to meet him. This much of the story is given by most editors. It is only by reading the whole chapter that we can access all of the additional connections that might exist between Polonius and Jephthah, such as the fact that Jephthah was the son of Gilead by a harlot, and that the legitimate sons drove Jephthah out of Israel until they were threatened by the Ammonites, whereupon they came begging to Jephthah to lead their armies. Might this provide a clue to Hamlet's attitude to Polonius, or even something about the man's rise to power in Elsinore?

At a time when readings from the Bible formed a significant portion of the weekly church service, which everyone attended as a matter of habit, law, and/ or religious principle, and additional Bible readings occurred in most family homes as a daily ritual, the language of the day was permeated with direct and indirect allusions, consciously made as a type of shorthand communication or unconsciously woven into the flow of images, the construction of sentences, and the selection of words. The availability of the Bible in English, along with the widespread literacy that resulted from Tudor attitudes to public education, was relatively new, and it is little wonder that the Bible provided a linguistic backdrop against which Shakespeare's characters struggled to give voice to thoughts and feelings of great significance in their fictional world.

The allusions to the stories in the Bible are easily documented and almost always present an actor with an additional element of emotional complexity that well rewards the slight extra effort required to read not only the exact verse quoted but the complete story that has been encoded in the shorthand reference. Remember that Shakespeare was counting on his actors and his audiences sharing his society's familiarity with not only the narrative elements of the stories but also the imagery used in the telling. Assistance in locating the most subtle biblical allusions can be found in the scholarship of Naseeb Shaheen, whose exhaustive study *Biblical References in Shakespeare's Plays* will provide you with the biblical allusions in each play. Consider this an invitation to delve into the Bible for some good stories as well as the oft-quoted proclamations of Christian ethics and faith.

Along with the scholarly works that chart for us the biblical references in Shakespeare's plays, and a general reading of the Bible, it is worthwhile to have a look at the other standard religious texts that would have provided a constant source of imagery and association for Shakespeare's actors and audience. For example, *The Book of Common Prayer* can be consulted for such important rituals as Holy Communion, baptism, confirmation, matrimony, and burial. The Folger Shakespeare Library has published a lovely reprint of the edition used in Shakespeare's lifetime, edited by John E. Booty, which allows you to read the text in clean, clear print with modern spellings.

Stories and Legends from Christian History

As we have seen, an understanding of Shakespeare's Bible can open for an actor some powerful emotional contexts for many allusions and images as well as relationships and situations in the plays. But we should not limit our research to the religious books. The plays are sprinkled with references to saints and holy places, and a familiarity with the medieval legends that grew up around church history can be inspiring. The Master of the Revels would not license any play that addressed religious controversies directly, but that did not stop Shakespeare or his contemporaries from portraying characters who were members of religious orders currently outlawed in England, or from alluding to places like St. Gregory's well in *The Two Gentlemen of Verona* [4.2.84]. At times these allusions form part of the local color of the Italian or pre-Protestant historical setting, but they also crop up as anachronisms in the plays set in the classical world as when Duke Theseus, ruler of ancient Athens, greets the young lovers of *A Midsummer Night's Dream* with "Good morrow, friends. Saint Valentine is past: / Begin these wood-birds but to couple now?" [4.1.139]. George Every's *Christian Mythology* contains lovely pictures of woodcuts and carvings to illustrate his discussion of the most important legends and artifacts that fueled the imagination of people like Shakespeare.

One of Richard's favorite phrases in *Richard III* is "By St. Paul." At first glance, this might seem a simple toss-off, a nod of the head in the direction of piety from a notably impious villain. But a quick survey of reference material and medieval liturgical drama reveals a popular stage character customarily portrayed as either a short, bald, and bandy-legged figure of ridicule or a fiery-tempered knight, hot to persecute those enemies of the state, the early Christians, only to be thrown off his horse on the road to Damascus. In some plays there are more scenes of Paul before his conversion than after, excuses for entertaining enactments of all manner of wickedness. Suddenly "By St. Paul" becomes a subtle way of appearing pious while sneering at the weakness of those who do not share the world view of preconversion Paul, as well as a recurring reminder of the well-known ending on Bosworth Field: "A Horse, a Horse, my Kingdom for a Horse" [5.4.7]. Is it possible that Richard also mimics Paul's bandy legs?

Personal Faith

In addition to a relatively straightforward tracking of biblical allusions, it is important for an actor to delve into the spiritual world of the characters. Shakespeare's England was still deeply divided by religious allegiances, and so Shakespeare was careful to avoid any direct reference to an article of faith that would call down the wrath of the censors. Even so, his characters frequently give voice to lengthy statements of spiritual belief, and even those who are reticent in matters of faith make use of specific words or phrases that have spiritual significance.

We are on much shakier ground when it comes to analyzing the belief systems at work in the plays. Individual characters might quote directly a moral sentiment, as does Richard II in his final scene, when he muses about his own thoughts:

> The better sort,
> As thoughts of things Divine, are intermixed
> With scruples, and do set the Faith it self
> Against the Faith: as thus: Come little ones: and then again,
> It is as hard to come, as for a Camel
> To thread the postern of a Needles eye. [5.5.11]

Does Richard have his Bible open to Matthew 19, where he can read "But Jesus said, Suffer little children, and forbid them not, to come unto me: for of such is the kingdom of heaven" [14], and "Again I say unto you, It is easier for a camel to go through the eye of a needle, than for a rich man to enter into the kingdom of God" [19]? Even this does not prove that the character is free from an ambivalence towards the morality expressed. Often that ambivalence is the source of the dramatic power of the moment or the entire character, as when Richard continues his musings:

> Thoughts tending to Ambition, they do plot
> Unlikely wonders; how these vain weak nails
> May tear a passage through the Flinty ribs
> Of this hard world, my ragged prison walls:
> And for they cannot, dye in their own pride.

Despite the promise of welcome, and the warning of the need to divest worldly concerns, Richard is not able easily to put aside his ambition and pride.

There might have been very good reason for Shakespeare to flood his plays with an element of ambiguity with regard to religious issues. England during his life was still a place of martyrdom and political treachery on matters of faith. Catholic admirers of the Bard might intuit that Shakespeare, like Hamlet, had "something in his soul / O'er which his Melancholy sits on brood" [3.1.164], and that the immense power of the plays rests in part on the subliminal messages that somehow the great master has been able to communicate to those receptive few who can read him aright. I suspect that it is much more likely that we all hold these famously great plays up to ourselves, like the hand-tapped brass mirrors in museums, and see reflected back something that we take to be the heart of the mystery, but that is really some aspect of our personal nature that the mirror of the fictional world catches and tosses back to us. There is no denying, however, that Shakespeare lived and wrote in a time when certain profound religious beliefs permeated the very air, to be absorbed and expelled in countless ways that can be noted in the plays. Because we do not breathe the same air today, though some of us may share the same beliefs, we need to prepare ourselves to feel the depth of the significance that can only come from such a belief.

That is not to say that everyone in Shakespeare's England thought the same about concepts of grace, conscience, or damnation, to name just three "hot" words in the vocabulary of the age. In fact, I would argue that it is better for an actor to avoid at all costs limiting the meaning of such loaded terms to a simple belief or rational definition. It is better to let the word resonate deeply in the uncharted realms of unknowable significance. But you must acknowledge that these are powerful concepts, deeply embedded in the characters' view of the world and all that really matters.

We will often find characters questioning or even mocking the teachings of the Bible, as does Emilia when Desdemona announces that she would never betray her husband, no, not for the whole world, echoing Matthew 16:26: "what shall it profit a man, though he should win the whole world, if he lose his own soul?" Emilia responds, "The world's a huge thing: / It is a great price, / for a small vice" [*Othello* 4.3.68]. This scene has a very modern feel, secular, comfortable in its divorce from the heavy hand of simplistic moralizing associated with organized religion. But that is not the world of the play, and assuming such an attitude to the final moments in the play will rob them of their tragic power. When Othello speaks of the jewel that he threw away, he is talking not only of his wife, but also of his soul, and the horror of this realization will only work for the others on stage if they allow their characters to believe in the significance of damnation.

A good introduction to the wide variety of beliefs and philosophical thought that formed the intellectual and religious environment within which Shakespeare's audiences would have viewed his plays, and his first actors would have perceived his characters, is Peter Milward's *Shakespeare's Religious Background*. Of course, Milward's assumptions about Shakespeare's theology may not appeal to everyone, but his grasp of the issues of the time is strong and is presented well for the novice reader.

Doomsday

One of the most compelling images from Christian mythology is that of the Final Judgment. Several different sections of the Bible contain vivid descriptions of what was predicted to occur at the end of the world as we know it. Every actor of Shakespeare should engage in a firsthand encounter with the entire Book of Revelation, reading aloud from the King James translation from start to finish, simply to feel the shape of the language when it is spoken aloud and to absorb the rush of images, of which the following is just one small taste:

And before the throne there was a sea of glass like unto crystal: and in the midst of the throne, and round about the throne, were four beasts full of eyes before and behind. And the first beast was like a lion, and the second beast like a calf, and the third beast had a face as a man, and the fourth beast was like a flying eagle. [Revelation 4:6]

This is the beginning of John's vision, which continues for another seventeen chapters. His vision is the major source of the imagery of the apocalypse, but a wide range of biblical passages provided additional details. Here is Peter's image of the apocalypse: "The heavens shall pass away with a great noise, and the elements shall melt with fervent heat, the earth also and the works that are therein shall be burned up" [2 Peter 3:10]. Paul prophesied, "For the Lord himself shall descend from heaven with a shout, with the voice of the archangel, and with the trump of God" [1 Thessalonians 4:16].

Apocalyptic imagery is threaded into Shakespeare's plays, and a modern actor would do well not only to have a close acquaintance with this language, but also to make a strong connection between the images and the emotions they were intended to arouse. This is no time to indulge in ironic scepticism. It is far better to allow every character you play to be deeply affected by any reference, no matter how subtle, to the Judgment Day, even if you yourself consider such reactions the most primitive of superstitions.

It might be that you are playing one of the supporting players in *Antony and Cleopatra*, and in the fourth act you play one of the guards who rushes in upon the terrible scene of Antony's botched suicide. Shakespeare has given you and your colleague, playing the other guard, two simple lines that would have sent chills of horror and an awed sigh of recognition, far greater and more specific for his first audience than ours today. You say, "The Star is fallen," and your partner answers, "And time is at his Period" [4.14.106]. The death of this great warrior is like the end of the world itself, the universal apocalypse that will mark the end of human time, to be followed by the Judgment Day and the beginning of our experience of eternity.

Perhaps you are one of the silent assembled onlookers when Duncan's body is discovered in Macbeth's castle, and you must seek an appropriate response to Macduff's alarum:

> Awake, awake!
> Ring the Alarum Bell: Murder, and Treason,
> Banquo, and Donalbain!: Malcolm awake,
> Shake off this Downy sleep, Deaths counterfeit,
> And look on Death it self: up, up, and see
> The great Dooms Image: Malcolm, Banquo,
> As from your Graves rise up, and walk like Sprites,
> To countenance this horror. Ring the Bell. [2.3.73]

In addition to the surprise and shock, Shakespeare is asking for a far greater and more spiritual emotion, that of horror, and the specific horror felt when one is contemplating the very face of doom itself.

King Lear is threaded through with subtle hints of the sensation that the onlookers experience when they are witnessing the terrible sequence of events, and though Edmund the bitter and sceptical bastard rejects his father's super-

stitions, Gloucester's words resonate four acts later at Edmund's dying reformation and attempted redemption. Gloucester has observed:

These late Eclipses in the Sun and Moon portend no good to us: though the wisdom
of Nature can reason it thus, and thus, yet Nature finds it self scourged by the sequent
effects. Love cools, friendship falls off, Brothers divide. In Cities, mutinies; in Countries,
discord; in Palaces, Treason; and the Bond cracked, 'twixt Son and Father. This villain
of mine comes under the prediction; there's Son against Father, the King falls from bias
of Nature, there's Father against Child. We have seen the best of our time. Machina-
tions, hollowness, treachery, and all ruinous disorders follow us disquietly to our
Graves. [1.2.103]

In Luke's record of Jesus' description of "the days of vengeance," when "all
things which are written may be fulfilled" [Luke 21:22], we find images that
Gloucester uses: "Nation shall rise against nation, and kingdom against kingdom: And great earthquakes shall be in divers places, and famines, and pes-
tilences; and fearful sights and great signs shall there be from heaven," and
also "And there shall be signs in the sun, and in the moon, and in the stars;
and upon the earth distress of nations, with perplexity; the sea and the waves
roaring; Men's hearts failing them for fear, and for looking after those things
which are coming on the earth: for the powers of heaven shall be shaken."
Mark's version is even closer: "Now the brother shall betray the brother to
death, and the father the son; and children shall rise up against their parents,
and shall cause them to be put to death." In Mark's version Jesus speaks of
"the abomination of desolation" and then says, "But in those days, after that
tribulation, the sun shall be darkened, and the moon shall not give her light,
And the stars of heaven shall fall, and the powers that are in heaven shall be
shaken" [Mark 13:12, 14, 24–25].

I have made repeated use of Harry Morris's *Last Things in Shakespeare*, having
found his blend of cultural history and literary analysis fascinating and informative. His book is filled with reproductions of woodcuts that capture the
profound connection between religious teachings about death and the Last
Judgment and the images found in the plays. He has chapters on *Hamlet, Othello,
King Lear, Macbeth*, and *Romeo and Juliet* that are well worth reading if you are
working on these plays. What is surprising is to find chapters on comedies (*A
Midsummer Night's Dream* and *As You Like It*) and three of the histories: the two
parts of *Henry IV* and *Henry V*. Morris's book rewards the browser seeking a
general introduction to images of doomsday. Look in particular for the woodcuts illustrating the fifteen signs preceding doomsday, and then read Lennox's
description of the terrible storm the night that Duncan is murdered by Macbeth:

And (as they say) lamentings heard i' th' Air;
Strange screams of Death,

And Prophesying, with Accents terrible,
Of dire Combustion, and confused Events,
New hatched to th' woeful time.
The obscure Bird clamoured the live-long Night.
Some say, the Earth Was feverous,
And did shake. [2.3.56]

Shakespeare had a vast array of images upon which to draw, ones that were readily available in the public eye as a result of the work of a variety of visual artists.

The Terror of Chaos and the Terror of Civil War

So powerful an image was civil war that the 1574 *Homily against Disobedience and Wilful Rebellion*, created to indoctrinate Elizabeth's subjects against the very idea of opposition to her rule, summons up images of civil war breaking the bonds of blood, an event of unsurpassed horror dramatized by Shakespeare in the third part of *Henry VI*. In the fifth scene of the second act, the king has withdrawn from active fighting but serves as witness to a matched pair of battlefield discoveries. First, a young man drags on the body of an enemy soldier, only to discover that it is his own father he has killed in battle. Then an older soldier, bringing on a second body, discovers that he has killed his only son. The soldiers are given matching speeches of discovery and grief; the father's includes this condemnation of civil war:

O pity God, this miserable Age!
What Stratagems? how fell? how Butcherly?
Erroneous, mutinous, and unnatural,
This deadly quarrel daily doth beget [*3HVI* 2.5.88]

Elizabethans had good reason to fear the death of Elizabeth, for the absence of a strong and unquestioned heir opened the door to the horrors of civil war, made even more terrifying in the imagination because of the blending of the prophecy of doomsday and the moralizing legends of recent history.

When Othello, declaring his love for Desdemona, vows, "When I love thee not, / Chaos is come again" [3.3.91], he is participating in an analogy between the overturning of everything valued in his life and the biblical meaning of the word chaos: "The 'formless void' of primordial matter, the 'great deep' or 'abyss' out of which the cosmos or order of the universe was evolved," as the *OED* defines it. What most terrified Shakespeare's contemporaries in any prophecy of chaos was the loss of order, the overturning of the entire system of nature, the removal of every code of conduct, for animals as well as humankind. They used an image of deformity or misshapen ugliness, in contrast with the glorious framework dictated by God and enacted in every aspect of nature. Therefore, when the hunchback Richard contemplates what terrible curse he experienced in his mother's womb, he imagines an event:

> To shrink mine Arm up like a withered Shrub,
> To make an envious Mountain on my Back,
> Where sits Deformity to mock my Body;
> To shape my Legs of an unequal size,
> To dis-proportion me in every part:
> Like to a Chaos, or an un-licked Bear-whelp,
> That carries no impression like the Dam. [*3HVI* 3.2.156]

The images of chaos were well established: the stars and the moon itself would break free and go where they willed, the seasons would blend into a confused mixture, the winds would die and the clouds would cease to release rain over the parched earth, and all vegetation would become dust. Animals would violate their natural patterns; even fish would come out of the water to feed.

We can find these images in the writings of Shakespeare's age, and also in its visual arts, in particular in the murals that decorated English churches. A surprising number of churches had such paintings, and they usually occupied the most impressive location, over the chancel arch, so that week after week the congregation would sit in contemplation of these powerful images of St. Michael weighing souls, the damned tormented at the gates of hell by all manner of fiends, and the dead emerging from their graves. There was just such a painting in Trinity Chapel in Stratford, and though there is evidence that it was covered over with whitewash in 1562, there is also evidence that the vivid murals underneath still showed through to irritate the Puritans for another century. For an actor seeking to imagine what it would be like to soak in such visual riches for a few hours every Sunday, there could be nothing better than to visit just such a church, but for those of us who do not have easy access to such buildings, there is the detailed scholarship available in books like M.D. Anderson's *History and Imagery in British Churches*, in which you will also find a map listing suitable churches if an opportunity for a visit ever arises.

After browsing through the pictures in Anderson's book and rereading our Bible (aloud, of course), let's see just how these images are borrowed by Shakespeare and imagine the fear and awe associated with them. Prospero, describing his career as a magus, concludes his list with "graves at my command / Have waked their sleepers, oped, and let 'em forth / By my so potent art" [5.1.48]. Because the dead in their shrouds and the damned souls were portrayed partially or entirely naked, Edgar's disguise as Poor Tom the Bedlam beggar continues the series of doomsday images woven into the storm scene of *King Lear*. When Lear meets Tom, he considers the implications of nakedness:

Why thou wert better in thy Grave, than to answer with thy uncovered body, this extremity of the Skies. Is man no more than this? Consider him well. Thou owest the Worm no Silk, the Beast, no Hide; the Sheep, no Wool; the Cat, no perfume. Ha? Here's three on 's are sophisticated. Thou art the thing it self; unaccommodated man, is no more but such a poor, bare, forked Animal as thou art. [3.4.101]

With this, Lear begins to tear off his own clothes. The souls in the doomsday pictures are portrayed as naked men and women, stripped of all worldly signs of power and authority. To this combination of thunder and lightning and near-naked men stripped of name, status, and even sanity, Shakespeare adds still another ingredient, the tormenting devils. Edgar has chosen as his disguise a madman "whom the foul fiend hath led through fire and through flame, and through ford and whirlpool e'er bog and quagmire" [3.4.51]. This is like a doomsday mural come to life.

That Lear has undergone something like a journey into hell itself is clarified by more images from the doomsday murals when he recovers. He mistakes Cordelia for another spirit who has died and says,

> You do me wrong to take me out o' th' grave,
> Thou art a Soul in bliss, but I am bound
> Upon a wheel of fire, that mine own tears
> Do scald, like moulten Lead. [4.7.44]

Modern actors can participate in the emotional wrenching of the reunion of Cordelia and her father on many levels. Images such as this assist even the most secular minds to grasp something of the grandeur and the terror evoked by these words in Shakespeare's first actors and audiences.

Damnation

The simple word "damnation" that is heard so often in modern settings that it scarcely retains its status as an expletive was, for the Elizabethans, a word to summon a massive association of images and sensations. In addition to the priestly intoning of passages from the Bible, Shakespeare's actors and audience would have had many opportunities to encounter the sort of horrific details that fueled the imaginations of such painters as Hieronymus Bosch and such writers as Dante. A modern actor might not have the time or linguistic skill to encounter Dante's *Inferno* it its original compelling form, but every library will afford firsthand a glimpse of *The Garden of Earthly Delights*.

English schoolboys were also at this time encountering the images of the pagan afterlife described vividly by Virgil in the *Aeneid* when Aeneas seeks advice from his dead father through the agency of the Cumaean Sibyl. He is magically protected from the horrors, but is free to report back to his companions, giving the lie to Hamlet's "from whose Bourne No Traveler returns" [3.1.78]. An excellent book that brings together visual imagery with an introduction to the attributes of the afterlife, both pagan and Christian, is Alice K. Turner's *The History of Hell*.

Lurking in the shared memory of the older actors and audience members, in which number we might well include Shakespeare himself, would be the unforgettable performances of *The Harrowing of Hell* as part of the great cycle plays of the guild festivals. We can only imagine, from the texts of the plays and the medieval drawings of the mouth of hell, how the guild actors would have portrayed the torments of the damned.

The Medieval Institute at Western Michigan University regularly publishes monographs on early drama, art, and music, two of which, *The Iconography of Heaven*, edited by Clifford Davidson, and *The Iconography of Hell*, edited by Davidson and Thomas H. Seiler, are collections of articles that remind us of the immense power of associated images that had collected around the words "heaven" and "hell," in large part because of the traditions of medieval drama. I recommend these collections for anyone seeking a truly theatrical set of images for such moments as this from *The Tempest*:

> All but Mariners
> Plunged in the foaming brine, and quit the vessel;
> Then all a fire with me the Kings son Ferdinand
> With hair up-staring (then like reeds, not hair)
> Was the first man that leaped; cried hell is empty,
> And all the Devils are here. [1.2.210]

Who might all these devils be? In *The Iconography of Hell*, Barbara D. Palmer's article "The Inhabitants of Hell" will give you the answer that would have occurred to actors remembering the great plays of their youth. *Macbeth* in particular is filled with opportunities for theatrical echoes, for example, from the comic porter, who invites the audience to remember the medieval traditions when he announces, "But this place is too cold for hell. I'll devil-porter it no further" [2.3.16]. The murky hell, filled with the dunnest smoke, is Lady Macbeth's invitation to remember the excuse for theatrical pyrotechnics that hell will always present, described vividly by Philip Butterworth in his contribution, "Hellfire."

DEATH

> Thou art deaths fool,
> For him thou labour'st by thy flight to shun,
> And yet runn'st toward him still.
>
>   Duke [*Measure* 3.1.11]

The reality of life expectancy is just one aspect of attitudes toward death that might prove of interest to both a scholar and an actor. Before we assume that the universality of human experience precludes anything other than tapping ourselves in order to bring alive lines like Romeo's "Thus with a kiss I die" and Juliet's "O happy Dagger, / This is thy sheath" [5.3.120, 168] or even Flute/Thisbe's "Come blade, my breast imbrue" [*Dream* 5.1.344], we might want to see what the scholars have to say about how the early modern world differed from ours in this regard, as in so many others.

Shakespeare himself is as insightful a source as any for the fears someone might have when facing death, or the preparation one might undergo to achieve the readiness of the truly courageous. Scholars can supplement these insights with discussions of the belief systems that sustained a hope in a life after death, all the while flooding the mind with images of the horror of perpetual damnation; scholars can also document the customs surrounding the death of a loved one.

Onstage funerals, such as Ophelia's or Juliet's, require of the production company some consideration of the ceremonies attendant upon such events that would have been normal in the world of the play, sometimes to fulfill them and sometimes to deny them. When Juliet is discovered apparently dead on the morning of her wedding to Paris, her father describes what is to follow:

> All things that we ordained Festival,
> Turn from their office to black Funeral:
> Our instruments to melancholy Bells,
> Our wedding cheer, to a sad burial Feast:
> Our solemn Hymns, to sullen Dirges change:
> Our Bridal flowers serve for a buried Corse:
> And all things change them to the contrary.[4.5.84]

Everyone on stage will want to know if this is an unusual or customary event. For Ophelia, we are told by the officiating priest,

> Her Obsequies have been as far enlarged,
> As we have warrantise, her death was doubtful,
> And but that great Command, o'ersways the order,
> She should in ground unsanctified have lodged,
> Till the last Trumpet. For charitable prayers,
> Shards, Flints, and Pebbles, should be thrown on her:
> Yet here she is allowed her Virgin Rites,
> Her Maiden strewments, and the bringing home
> Of Bell and Burial. [5.1.226]

What we are not told is exactly what ceremonies have taken place in this funeral, which Hamlet has described for us when he said:

> Who is this they follow,
> And with such maimed rites? This doth betoken,
> The Corse they follow, did with desperate hand,
> For do its own life, 'twas of some Estate. [5.1.218]

An excellent resource book that will answer all of these questions and others that may crop up in staging the ceremonies of death that might conclude a tragedy, mark a transition in a history, or set the stage for a comic reversal is Clare Gittings's *Death, Burial, and the Individual in Early Modern England*. This slender book has emerged from exhaustive research but is unburdened with scholarly debate; the information is communicated with minimal extraneous comment, and the documentary evidence is presented in vivid stories rather than citations of historical proof. Here is a quotation from a notebook kept by Thomas Hardy:

Girl who committed suicide—was buried on the hill where two roads meet: but few followed her to her unblest grave: no coffin: one girl threw flowers on her: stake driven through her body. Earth heaped round the stake like an ancient tumulus. (This is like Mother's description to me of a similar burial on Hendford Hill, when she was a child.) (72)

Gittings's book is filled with such vivid and dramatic anecdotal information; the statistics necessary for historical scholarship are gathered in an appendix at the end.

As we have seen, a very important contribution to the general social history resources available to actors is David Cressy's *Birth, Marriage, and Death*. Cressy's scholarship is guaranteed to answer any questions you might have about anything from wet nurses to burial fees. There is probably more information on any given topic than you would think you would ever need, but the richness of historical details provides the rock-solid support for the creation of a reality that can be reflected in the language of the plays.

THE SUPERNATURAL

> Fairies black, gray, green, and white,
> You Moon-shine revellers, and shades of night.
> You Orphan heirs of fixèd destiny,
> Attend your office, and your quality.
> Crier Hob-goblin, make the Fairy Oyes.
>
> Mistress Quickly [*Wives* 5.5.47]

When the merry wives of Windsor torment the foolish Falstaff by arranging for their family and friends to pretend to be fairy creatures of the forest, a modern audience might be forgiven for mocking the fat old lover's terror. And yet we laugh just as hard when Bottom seems as oblivious to the fairy nature of his new-found love as to the transformation of his selfhood into assdom. Our complacent assurance of superiority is based, in both cases, in our assumptions about the absolute fiction of both portraits. Would Shakespeare's audience have been so sure?

It is impossible in this, as with any of the other beliefs we have discussed, to speak of the various members of this audience as if they shared a common and absolute world view. What we can demonstrate, with some assurance, is that magic, witchcraft, and demonology were topics for serious discussion, and that folklore was replete with tales of real fairies as well as with reports of excellent practical jokes based upon the victim's superstition.

Magic

People remain fascinated with magic, superstitions, and arcane information about plants, animals, and systems that order the universe, like astrology and numerology. This is fortunate for actors of Shakespeare, because Shakespeare's plays are filled with references to the extraordinary. Whether it is the witches in *Macbeth*, Prospero's incantations in *The Tempest*, or the description of ghosts and ghouls in *Romeo and Juliet* and *A Midsummer Night's Dream*, popular books on magic provide invaluable assistance to anyone required to play, describe, or hear of anything from the world of the supernatural.

Many of these resources, such as the *Encyclopedia of Magic and Superstition* and the *Encyclopedia of Witchcraft and Demonology*, both published by Octopus Books, cover a variety of cultures and times; careful reading is required to avoid superimposing onto Shakespeare's England the beliefs of another time and place. However, there is much evidence to suggest that the mythical constructs that shape Elizabethan imagination are part of a vast and species-specific pattern of archetypal patterns of mythology.

A fine, detailed, but dense compendium can be found in Keith Thomas's *Religion and the Decline of Magic*. You might want to skip the first half of the book and go directly to his chapters on astrology, witchcraft, and ghosts and fairies. As an alternative to Thomas's dense prose, have a look at Grillot de Givry's *Witchcraft, Magic, and Alchemy*, a great source for reprints of striking images and imagination-provoking details, and the result of as meticulous a scholar as any in the world. In the literary section, a book like Anthony Harris's *Night's Black Agents* is a great place to begin, as he provides an enjoyable overview in his first chapter, "The Social Setting," as well as chapters on *Macbeth* and *The Tempest*. Though both Barbara Traister in *Heavenly Necromancers* and John Mebane in *Renaissance Magic and the Return of the Golden Age* include a chapter on *The Tempest*, their books are really most useful for broader background, in particular Mebane's fifth chapter, "Magic, Science, and Witchcraft in Renaissance England," and Traister's introduction on popular stereotypes of magicians. Traister describes several notorious contemporary magicians who would have been available for use as "life studies" by actors in Shakespeare's company, and I find the woodcuts and reprints scattered through the book inspiring and evocative.

Witches

Publications about the doings of famous witches and even more famous witch catchers also make for interesting reading, especially for those actors cast in *Macbeth*. *Witchcraft and Hysteria in Elizabethan London*, edited by Michael MacDonald, is worth a look simply for the introduction to this volume, which contains three publications concerning the infamous case of Mary Glovers. Everyone in London in 1602, and for some years after, would have heard a great deal about this incident, what with the terrifying symptoms of blindness, inability to speak or even swallow, and wild fits, and the chilling events leading up to the curses of the old witch upon the fourteen-year-old victim, to say nothing of the tortures the accused, Elizabeth Jackson, endured in an effort on the part of the city government to prove her capacity for supernatural evil. MacDonald tells the story well and also sets the event into the larger context of Elizabethan superstitions and medical and judicial practice in the face of apparent diabolical activity.

For specific studies of the phenomenon of witchcraft trials in England, the best product of the scholarly work can be found in Barbara Rosen's collection *Witchcraft in England, 1558–1618*. For a detailed overview of the subject, James Sharpe's *Instruments of Darkness* is a good place to start, and his bibliography will steer you to the best scholarship in the field if you are so inclined. This is where you will encounter more and more esoteric studies, such as Alan Grant Macfarlane's *Witchcraft in Tudor and Stuart England*, an exhaustive study in cultural geography and historical sociology. Macfarlane's book, like others you will find in this section of the library, is filled with wonderful details as well as complex charts, maps, and theoretical arguments.

Of the other reprints of contemporary publications on the occult, I would recommend Nicolas Remy's *Demonolatry* and Francesco Maria Guazzo's *Compendium maleficarum*. These were the most important "handbooks" for prosecutors of witches published during the years that Shakespeare was writing plays in London. Of course England had its own publications on this topic, and an actor can have a look at modern reprints of King James's *Daemonologie*, published in 1597, and Reginald Scot's *The Discoverie of Witchcraft*, first published in 1584.

You will find resources about witches and all things magical scattered around a university library, some books lurking in cultural history alongside studies of folk legends and fairy tales, others in theology, in the subsection dedicated to demonology. There are historical studies, and of course literary studies. At the other end of the scale, there is the Time-Life series which is so popular and accessible as to scarcely count as scholarship, although it is based upon the work of scholars and can both inspire and inform.

Although witches were very much in the public eye during Shakespeare's years in London, they do not make much of an appearance in his plays. The three weird sisters of Macbeth might be labelled first, second, and third witch in your acting text, but they are only addressed as witches once, as reported by the first sister:

> A Sailors Wife had Chestnuts in her Lap,
> And munched, and munched, and munched:
> Give me, quoth I.
> Aroint thee, Witch, the rump-fed Ronyon cries.
> Her Husband's to Aleppo gone, Master o'th'Tiger:
> But in a Sieve I'll thither sail,
> And like a Rat without a tail,
> I'll do, I'll do, and I'll do. [1.3.4]

Edgar uses the same phrase in his disguise as Poor Tom, the Bedlam beggar:

This is the foul fiend Flibbertigibbet; he begins at Curfew, and walks till the first Cock: He gives the Web and the Pin, squints the eye, and makes the Hare-lip; Mildews the white Wheat, and hurts the poor Creature of earth.

> *Sings.* Withold footed thrice the old,
>   He met the Night-Mare, and her nine-fold;
>   Bid her alight, and her troth-plight,
>   And aroint thee Witch, aroint thee. [3.4.115]

What is much more common in Shakespeare's plays is the label of "witch" applied to women who have offended the speaker in some way, which is why the first weird sister in *Macbeth* sends the storm to kill the chestnut woman's husband. In *The Winter's Tale* Leontes calls Paulina a witch when she dares to confront him with the stupidity of his jealousy and with his infant daughter. Antony calls Cleopatra a witch when he believes that she has betrayed him during the sea battle at Actium. Both men are wrong: Paulina and Cleopatra intend no harm, and if they have power, it is that of any strong-willed and intelligent woman. When the identical twins of *The Comedy of Errors* encounter the friends and family of their opposites, they quite naturally come to the conclusion that they are being pursued by witches. We, who know the truth, can laugh at this misperception.

The potency of witchcraft is an effective metaphor for other destructive powers, such as might prompt Don Pedro to betray his young friend Claudio by wooing the lovely Hero for himself, prompting Claudio to fear:

> Friendship is constant in all other things,
> Save in the Office and affairs of love:
> Therefore all hearts in love use their own tongues.
> Let every eye negotiate for it self,
> And trust no Agent: for beauty is a witch,
> Against whose charms, faith melteth into blood. [*Much Ado* 2.1.175]

This leaves us with two portraits of witches, one comic and one serious. In *The Merry Wives of Windsor* Mistress Ford persuades Falstaff to escape the jealous wrath of her husband by disguising himself as Mother Prat, thereby ensuring that he endures a sound beating as Ford rages:

A witch, a Quean, an old cozening quean: Have I not forbid her my house. She comes .
of errands does she? We are simple men, we do not know what's brought to pass under
the profession of Fortune-telling. She works by Charms, by Spells, by the Figure, and
such daubery as this is, beyond our Element: we know nothing. Come down you
Witch, you Hag you, come down I say. [4.2.172]

Mistress Ford has told us a little more about this unseen character: that she is her maid's aunt, that she is a woman large enough that her dress fits Falstaff, and that she is known as the Old Woman of Brentford. The label of witch is her husband's. Mistress Page, her accomplice in the tricking of Falstaff, adopts the same label for Falstaff in disguise.

Lest we assume that Shakespeare shared our attitude to accusations of witch-craft, that harmless old women like Mother Prat and Elizabeth Jackson were wrongly accused of supernatural powers by jealous husbands and hysterical girls, let us have a look at the characterization of Joan of Arc, called Joan La Poucelle in the first part of *Henry VI*. Here we see an English portrait of the French heroine, and she is everything that one might expect from a witch: seductive, destructive, and ultimately betrayed by her devilish supporters. In fact, Shakespeare shows Joan calling up her supernatural powers with lines like "Then take my soul; my body, soul, and all, / Before that England give the French the foil" [5.3.22]. Only witchcraft could explain the defeat of the English at the hands of a simple shepherd girl. As the great English warrior Talbot discovered near the beginning of the play:

> A Witch by fear, not force, like Hannibal,
> Drives back our troops and conquers as she lists:
> So Bees with smoke, and Doves with noisome stench,
> Are from their Hives and Houses driven away.
> They call'd us, for our fierceness, English Dogs,
> Now like to Whelps, we crying run away. [1.5.21]

We might want to dismiss Talbot's lines as England's rewriting of history, but in the world of the play Joan is a witch, Talbot's encounter with her is charged with supernatural implications, and the actors playing the roles might want to know just what demonology was thought to be. The cast of *The Merry Wives of Windsor*, on the other hand, would find greater interest in the stories of false persecution.

Along with *Macbeth*, the other great magical play is *The Tempest*. When Prospero introduces Caliban to the castaways, he explains Caliban's deformity:

> This mishapen knave;
> His Mother was a Witch, and one so strong
> That could control the Moon; make flows, and ebbs,
> And deal in her command, without her power. [5.1.268]

Earlier in the play Prospero and Ariel have discussed Caliban's mother at length, providing us with a few additional details, such as her name and appearance. She is "the foul Witch Sycorax, who with Age and Envy / Was grown into a hoop" [1.2.258].

We learn that she was born in Algiers, from whence she was banished "for mischiefs manifold, and sorceries terrible / To enter human hearing." But they could not kill her because she was pregnant with Caliban, "(a freckled whelp, hag-born) not honoured with / A human shape," suggesting that his father might well have been a supernatural creature, confirmed by Prospero when he introduces Caliban as "this demi-devil; / (For he's a bastard one)." As a sample of her nastiness, Prospero describes her punishment of Ariel:

> She did confine thee
> By help of her more potent Ministers,
> And in her most unmitigable rage,
> Into a cloven Pine, within which rift
> Imprisoned, thou didst painfully remain
> A dozen years. . . . It was a torment
> To lay upon the damned, which Sycorax
> Could not again undo: it was mine Art,
> When I arrived, and heard thee, that made gape
> The Pine and let thee out. [1.2.274]

White Magicians

Sycorax is the most powerful and exotic witch imaginable, but she still cannot rise to the power of the Magus or white magician, Prospero. When it is time to set aside the immense power he has acquired, Prospero provides us with a compendium of his magical repertoire:

> I have bedimmed
> The noontide sun, called forth the mutinous winds,
> And 'twixt the green sea and the azured vault

Set roaring war: to the dread rattling thunder
Have I given fire and rifted Jove's stout oak
With his own bolt; the strong-based promontory
Have I made shake and by the spurs plucked up
The pine and cedar: graves at my command
Have waked their sleepers, oped, and let 'em forth
By my so potent art. [5.1.41]

Several scholars have charted just the sort of information an actor needs to connect these words with a belief system that would have been available to Shakespeare's company. *Prospero's Island*, Noel Cobb's study of the play, is filled with illustrations and connections between Shakespeare's imaginative creation and the events and beliefs of Shakespeare's day. In particular, he draws our attention to the similarities between Prospero and Dr. John Dee. We are fortunate to have access to a document reported to have been written by that most infamous of white magicians. *John Dee's Conversations with Angels*, by Deborah Harkness, sets in context the surviving fragments of Dee's record of his conversations with angels. This is an invaluable introduction to Dee's religious beliefs, his intellectual training, and the events of his life. I have made use of Harkness's index to browse through this book, and because she tells such a good story, every page is great fun to read. I was interested to learn about anything Dee or his angels might have said about the conversion of the Jews. Dee was not untypical of his time and place. He expressed all of the anti-Semitism one might expect, distrusting the Jews as a stubborn and spiteful race, fearing them and yet envying their secret teachings, and longing for and fervently believing in the ultimate reunification of Christians, Jews, and Muslims at the completion of human time. As a philosopher and mystic, he was hopeful of learning from his angels if he could acquire, from any Jew he might be so fortunate to meet, some word of the whereabouts of the lost books of the Bible. Dee, for one, would have been thrilled at Antonio's spontaneous demonstration of Christian forbearance at the end of the trial scene in *Measure for Measure*. The conversion of Shylock by the force of law and the state was exactly the plan that Dee tried to interest Elizabeth in undertaking; she did not respond positively, in part because she ruled over a country that had expelled its Jews in 1290. There is no evidence that his angel conversationalists shared his prejudices.

I recommend Peter French's *John Dee: The World of an Elizabethan Magus* to any actor fascinated by the shadow that would have been cast across the role of Prospero by such a well-known contemporary figure. Nicholas Clulee offers a good introductory chapter in *John Dee's Natural Philosophy* that presents the facts of Dee's life in an unsensational manner, and then a careful and detailed examination of his scientific writings, set within the context of religious, mathematical, occult, and scientific experimentation and theory. Otherwise, his book is pretty heavy going, but very important for our understanding of the white magician as a type of scientist. Prospero's intense study of books, that are not necessarily occult texts but perhaps ancient scientific treatises, suggests to Clulee that his extraordinary skills are a manifestation of Prospero's command of the natural elements through a mastery of scientific fact. Astrology as a means of predicting the auspicious opportunity, as when Prospero observes,

> By my prescience
> I find my Zenith doth depend upon
> A most auspicious star, whose influence
> If now I court not, but omit, my fortunes
> Will ever after droop, [1.2.180]

merges with astronomy as a means of navigation. The charting of the night sky, shared in primitive form with Caliban who was taught how "to name the bigger light, and how the less, / That burn by day and night" [1.2.335], provides the juncture for science and magic.

Spells and Ceremonies

I find the documents about conjuring even more interesting than the historical studies of white magicians. I have used both Arthur Edward Waite's *The Book of Ceremonial Magic* and Claire Fanger's *Conjuring Spirits* for ideas for staging Prospero's spells and invocations. Neighboring shelves hold books on alchemy, astrology, and numerology, all of which resonate in the world that Shakespeare considered normal. Don Cameron Allen's *The Star-crossed Renaissance* explores some of the controversies about such subjects, reminding us that a single belief system did not exist, so that at one and the same time Edmund's scepticism and his father's forebodings could coexist as credible world views on the Elizabethan stage. Old Gloucester fears, "These late Eclipses in the Sun and Moon portend no good to us" [*King Lear* 1.2.103], but as soon as he has left the stage, Edmund scoffs:

This is the excellent foppery of the world, that when we are sick in fortune, often the surfeits of our own behavior, we make guilty of our disasters, the Sun, the Moon, and the Stars, as if we were villains on necessity, Fools by heavenly compulsion, Knaves, Thieves, and Treachers by Spherical predominance. Drunkards, Liars, and Adulterers by an enforced obedience of Planetary influence; and all that we are evil in, by a divine thrusting on. An admirable evasion of Whore-master-man, to lay his Goatish disposition to the charge of a Star. My father compounded with my mother under the Dragons tail, and my nativity was under Ursa Major, so that it follows, I am rough and Lecherous. I should have been that I am, had the maidenliest Star in the Firmament twinkled on my bastardizing. [1.2.118]

We must be careful not to fall into the trap of assuming that because Edmund's attitude matches our own, his was the true expression of Shakespeare's beliefs.

Fairies

Social historians have successfully demonstrated a pervasive trust in the workings of astrology in Shakespeare's England, and the witch trials confirm that the fears and persecutions stemmed from the workings of a deeply held faith. But what about fairies? Here we must venture into the territory of the anthropological study of folk legends for exciting resources. There is simply no way of proving what people generally scoffed at or believed. It is, however, possible to have a look at the stories and legends in circulation during Shakespeare's lifetime.

Katharine Mary Briggs's updating of F. J. Norton's survey of oral traditions, *A Dictionary of British Folk-tales in the English Language*, is a two-part, four-volume work that contains retellings of literally thousands of legends, tales, and anecdotes. Each part has its own index of tale types and migratory legends, which is useful if you are a folklorist; tales are then listed alphabetically by title. The best way to find interesting legends is to browse the appropriate section. The first part is fictional stories, such as fables (animal stories), nursery tales, and funny stories. The second part is dedicated to folk legends, in other words, stories that were believed to be true at the time they were told. Here you will find collections of tales about ghosts, witches, giants, saints, dragons, fairies, and local and historical legends. In connection with *A Midsummer Night's Dream*, I enjoyed reading some of the tales about changelings and about fairy glens and fairy dances, but found the story of the fairy funeral the most significant. It is all too easy for us to forget that Oberon and Titania are mortals and will some day die. In the legend that Briggs records, the queen of the fairies, a tiny and beautiful creature, is being buried in a small crevice near the altar of the local church. The hapless witness barely escapes with his life, so fairies clearly are not entirely benign, but how wonderful it is that they have chosen a church for her resting place. Briggs has also prepared two excellent introductions that link the contents of her massive survey specifically to Shakespeare's plays. *The Anatomy of Puck* and *Pale Hecate's Team* provide a compendium of examples from ballads, broadsheets, plays, and poems.

Most scholarly editions of *A Midsummer Night's Dream* have a good selection from these sources, but for the sake of space these are edited to reveal the most important and striking debt that Shakespeare owes the source. There are always additional insights to be gained by having a look at the entire source, particularly when it represents what might best be termed Elizabethan popular culture. There are always a great many more peripheral sources than can be directly attributed. A case in point is the set of Robin Goodfellow stories, songs, and poems collected in 1845 by J.O. Halliwell-Phillipps for the Shakespeare Society of London and reissued in 1966 as *Fairy Mythology of a Midsummer Night's Dream*. Here you will find a great collection of material that sheds light on how Shakespeare's Puck fits into a long and lively tradition. The older studies such as Lewis Spence's *The Fairy Tradition in Britain* and Minor White Latham's *The Elizabethan Fairies* are often more useful than more recent studies, as the collection of folk legends through contemporary references was for Latham sufficient; there is no attempt to analyze the legends within the context of anthropology, ethnography, or cultural history. John Brand's three-volume *Observations on the Popular Antiquities of Great Britain* reflects the fascination that fairies held for the Victorians. There is an index in the third volume, but the table of contents for each volume is a good indicator of the riches to be found by the browsing actor. I was fascinated by his entry on the child's caul or silly how, wherein he notes advertisements for the sale of same that he saw in papers in the 1790s. The advertisement was specifically addressed to gentlemen of the navy and others going on long voyages, or generally "to prevent trouble." W. Carew Hazlitt's two-volume dictionary version, *Faiths and Folklores of the British Isles*, contains far less detail but is often found in the reference section of a university library.

For an example of a literary and historical exploration of this material, I recommend Linda Woodbridge's *The Scythe of Saturn*. Woodbridge roams far and wide in her discussion of the many superstitions and irrational beliefs that permeated Shakespeare's England and hence can be traced in his plays. Browse the index to discover the topics touched upon, everything from hunchbacks and human sacrifice to topsy-turviness and saturnalia.

PREJUDICES

> How much methinks, I could despise this man.
>
> Wolsey [*HVIII* 3.2.297]

> I hope I shall see an end of him; for my soul
> (yet I know not why) hates nothing more than he.
>
> Oliver [*AYLI* 1.1.165]

Some of the beliefs of the average member of Shakespeare's audience might best be classified as prejudices, particularly with regard to national characteristics. A.J. Hoenselaars's *Images of Englishmen and Foreigners in the Drama of Shakespeare and His Contemporaries* will provide you with a general overview of things like climate theory, whereby the national temperament is viewed to have been set by the climate of one's birthplace, as well as individual comments on national types and on specific plays. The book is divided into time periods, as the prejudices of the xenophobic Londoners changed with contemporary events, and also into sections on "Foreigners in England" and "Englishmen Abroad." Hoenselaars will help you to put Shakespeare's portrait of Shylock within the larger context of the presentation of Jews on the London stage at that time, so that you can see just how much of Shakespeare's creation challenges and how much fulfills audience expectations.

For a broader study of attitudes to a foreign country, I recommend *The Elizabethan Image of Italy* by John Lievsay, another of the wonderful booklets published under the auspices of the Folger Shakespeare Library. Italy figures in so many of Shakespeare's plays that it seems imperative for the modern actor to have some idea of how much of what appears in the plays is in the category of "local color," in other words, fulfilling audience expectations of what life in Italy should be like, and how much is specific to the world of this particular play, in other words, Shakespeare ringing a variation on the expected Italian content. Of course, we can expect to find in all of these plays much that is quite simply a reflection of the world that Shakespeare and his actors knew and considered normal, much as a Hollywood portrait of other times and places features American values and character notes. It quite defies our modern expectations to realize that Italy was not in fact a country, but a shared set of attributes divided into distinct locales: Milan, Venice, Florence, Naples, and Rome itself. Therefore, we should use "Italian" the way we might use "European" today, to mark something that is different from American, but not by any means a homogeneous culture.

The next thing to realize is that the English had a profoundly ambivalent attitude toward Italy. Despite their intense patriotism and xenophobia, they felt all of the inferiority of a relatively new culture toward one that had flourished for centuries. Italy was the home of all of the great writers, painters, architects, and influential thinkers that English children studied in school. When Sir Walter Raleigh, imprisoned in the Tower, was allowed the trappings of a gentleman, he brought into his prison cell his library of Italian books.

The choice of Italy as a destination for English travellers did not decrease when England broke with Rome. The great universities attracted the intellectuals as well as those interested in the latest advancements in scientific thought and medicine; the shining stars of each generation of the nobility, such as Philip Sidney, had the allure enhanced by their Italian adventures.

In Italy, too, one would find oneself daily in direct contact with the great civilizations of the classical world, a natural reinforcement of the love affair that even the modestly educated English gentleman enjoyed with Latin. Shakespeare might have mocked such sentiments, as when he has the country schoolmaster Holofernes respond to Jaquenetta's simple request that he read a letter for her by saying:

Facile precor gellida, quando pecus omnia sub umbra ruminat, and so forth. Ah good old Mantuan, I may speak of thee as the traveller doth of Venice, *venchie vencha, que non te vede, que non te perreche.* Old Mantuan, old Mantuan. Who understandeth thee not, *ut, re, sol, la, mi, fa:* Under pardon sir, What are the contents? or rather as Horace says in his, What, my soul verses? [*LLL* 4.2.93]

Here I have reproduced the folio spelling, incorrect as it may be, as it suggests just how badly Holofernes mangles pronunciation. Alongside such mockery, there is a clear admiration for all things Italian and Latin woven through the plays. In particular, Shakespeare seems to have had a fascination with the various cities about which he might have heard a variety of tales. Venice, still a great commercial power, was rivalled by Naples for grandeur and wealth, but both these cities were notable for their open indulgence in the pleasures of the flesh; Florence, though smaller than London, boasted 8,000 courtesans out of a population of 100,000. This reinforced for the English the popular tales of jealousy and murder that presented the hot-blooded Italians as unmatched for carnality and diabolical revenge. The *duello* captured the popular imagination, and the many treatises available on the art of fencing were Italian in origin. It is little wonder, then, that Italy became a favorite location for plays about jealousy, revenge, and any excuse for a spectacular stage fight.

MISOGYNY

The various scholars who write about women in Shakespeare's world and in his plays often make reference to some of the many pamphlets and treatises written for or about women. As with all such reprints, these are interesting to read (aloud) simply for the sound of the words and the rhythms of the sentences. You might also want to have a look yourself at the texts that are often quoted by scholars. A representative collection can be found in *Half Humankind* by Katherine Usher Henderson and Barbara F. McManus. Here you will find a section on the social contexts that identifies the common stereotypes of women, all of which we can find at work in Shakespeare's plays.

At first glance, a tract like Joseph Swetman's "The Arraignment of Lewd, Idle, Froward, and Unconstant Women or the Vanity of them, Choose you Whether, with a Commendation of Wise, Virtuous, and Honest Women, Pleasant for Married Men, Profitable for Young Men, and Hurtful to None," first published in 1615 and reprinted in *Half Humankind* with modern spellings, is pure misogyny. Here is a sample of Swetman's diatribe:

For women have a thousand ways to entice thee and ten thousand ways to deceive thee and all such fools as are suitors unto them: some they keep in hand with promises, and some they feed with flattery, and some they delay with dalliances, and some they please with kisses. They lay out the folds of their hair to entangle men into their love; betwixt their breasts is the vale of destruction; and in their beds there is hell, sorrow, and repentance. Eagles eat not men till they are dead, but women devour them alive. For a woman will pick thy pocket and empty thy purse, laugh in thy face and cut thy throat. They are ungrateful, perjured, full of fraud, flouting and deceit, unconstant, waspish, toyish, light, sullen, proud, discourteous, and cruel. (201)

When Rosalind, disguised as a saucy young lad, describes how she could pretend to be a woman, she says something very similar:

He was to imagine me his Love, his Mistress: and I set him every day to woo me. At which time would I, being but a moonish youth, grieve, be effeminate, changeable, longing, and liking, proud, fantastical, apish, shallow, inconstant, full of tears, full of smiles; for every passion something, and for no passion truly any thing, as boys and women are for the most part, cattle of this colour: would now like him, now loathe him: then entertain him, then forswear him: now weep for him, then spit at him; that I drave my Suitor from his mad humour of love, to a living humour of madness, which was to forswear the full stream of the world, and to live in a nook merely Monastic. [*AYLI* 3.2.407]

Now the audience, hearing this, knows that Rosalind loves Orlando, and she has just pointed out the simple truth, that

Love is merely a madness, and I tell you, deserves as well a dark house, and a whip, as madmen do: and the reason why they are not so punished and cured, is that the Lunacy is so ordinary, that the whippers are in love too. [3.2.400]

A darker expression of revulsion at women's nature is expressed by the various husbands who believe, each of them incorrectly, that their wives have been unfaithful. Here is Posthumus, from *Cymbeline*:

> Could I find out
> The Womans part in me, for there's no motion
> That tends to vice in man, but I affirm
> It is the Womans part: be it Lying, note it,
> The womans: Flattering, hers; Deceiving, hers:
> Lust, and rank thoughts, hers, hers: Revenges hers:
> Ambitions, Covetings, change of Prides, Disdain,
> Nice-longing, Slanders, Mutability;
> All Faults that name, nay, that Hell knows,
> Why hers, in part, or all: but rather all
> For even to Vice
> They are not constant, but are changing still;
> One Vice, but of a minute old, for one
> Not half so old as that. I'll write against them,
> Detest them, curse them: yet 'tis greater Skill
> In a true Hate, to pray they have their will:
> The very Devils cannot plague them better. [2.5.19]

Shakespeare arranges it so that some of his comic misogynists end up falling in love, and each with a woman most likely to give them a taste of all they hate and fear. Here are two of the wittiest of that breed: Berowne, from *Love's Labour's Lost*, and Benedick from *Much Ado about Nothing*:

> What? I love, I sue, I seek a wife,
> A woman that is like a German Clock,
> Still a-repairing: ever out of frame,
> And never going a-right, being a Watch:
> But being watched, that it may still go right.

Nay, to be perjured, which is worst of all:
And among three, to love the worst of all,
A wightly wanton, with a velvet brow.
With two pitch balls stuck in her face for eyes.
Ay, and by heaven, one that will do the deed,
Though Argus were her Eunuch and her guard.
And I to sigh for her, to watch for her,
To pray for her, go to: it is a plague
That Cupid will impose for my neglect,
Of his almighty dreadful little might.
Well, I will love, write, sigh, pray, sue, groan,
Some men must love my Lady, and some Joan. [*LLL* 3.1.174]

That a woman conceived me, I thank her: that she brought me up, I likewise give her most humble thanks: but that I will have a recheat winded in my forehead, or hang my bugle in an invisible baldrick, all women shall pardon me: because I will not do them the wrong to mistrust any, I will do my self the right to trust none: and the fine is, (for the which I may go the finer) I will live a Bachelor. [*Much Ado* 1.1.238]

Benedick's respect for women lives alongside his distrust of their sex and his lack of eagerness to accept the yoke of marriage.

Returning to Swetman, it might surprise us to find that his treatise also contains expressions of the profound connection between men and women and the admiration a man must feel when he contemplates certain other aspects of women's nature:

Amongst all the creatures that God hath created, there is none more subject to misery than a woman, especially those that are fruitful to bear children, but they have scarce a month's rest in a whole year, but are continually overcome with pain, sorrow, and fear. As indeed the danger of childbearing must needs be a great terror to a woman, which are counted but weak vessels in respect of men, and yet it is supposed that there is no disease that a man endureth that is one half so grievous or painful as childbearing is to a woman. (213)

This is the context within which we must see the strength of Shakespeare's women, whether it be Kate's shrewishness, Viola's patience, or Hermione's pain, sorrow, and fear. The stereotypes of the day were not so narrow as to preclude as many admirable women as despicable ones.

LAYERS OF MEANING

In her autobiography, *Pentimento*, Lillian Hellman describes the painters' term she has taken as her title:

Old paint on canvas, as it ages, sometimes becomes transparent. When that happens it is possible, in some pictures, to see the original lines: a tree will show through a woman's dress, a child makes way for a dog, a large boat is no longer on an open sea. That is called pentimento because the painter "repented," changed his mind. Perhaps it would be as well to say that the old conception, replaced by a later choice, is a way of seeing and then seeing again. (3)

I have often had occasion to make use of Hellman's image as I attempt to find a workable metaphor for the effect that an awareness of social history has upon the playing of Shakespeare on the modern stage. I believe that audiences are capable of sensing, even if they do not catch sight of the old conceptions, the presence of an earlier way of seeing that has shaped the plays we bring to life today.

RECOMMENDED READING

Patterns of Belief in Shakespeare's England

Brower, Reuben A. *Hero and Saint: Shakespeare and the Graeco-Roman Heroic Tradition.* New York: Oxford University Press, 1971.

Hankins, John Erskine. *Backgrounds of Shakespeare's Thought.* Hamden, CT: Archon Books, 1978.

James, Max H. *Scarce Truth Enough Alive: Shakespeare's Contemporary Search for Truth and Trust.* Pittsburgh, PA: Dorrance Publishing Co., 1995.

McCurdy, Harold Grier. *The Personality of Shakespeare: A Venture in Psychological Method.* New Haven, CT: Yale University Press, 1953.

Patrides, C.A. *Premises and Motifs in Renaissance Thought and Literature.* Princeton, NJ: Princeton University Press, 1982.

Wagenknecht, Edward. *The Personality of Shakespeare.* Norman: University of Oklahoma Press, 1972.

Honour

Biswas, D.C. *Shakespeare in His Own Time.* Delhi: Macmillan, 1979.

Bondanella, Peter, and Mark Musa, eds. *The Portable Machiavelli.* Harmondsworth: Penguin Books, 1979.

Council, Norman. *When Honour's at the Stake: Ideas of Honour in Shakespeare's Plays.* New York: Barnes & Noble Books, 1973.

Curry, Patrick, and Oscar Zarate. *Machiavelli for Beginners.* Cambridge: Icon Books, 1995.

Esler, Anthony. *The Aspiring Mind of the Elizabethan Younger Generation.* Durham, NC: Duke University Press, 1966.

James, Mervyn. *Society, Politics, and Culture: Studies in Early Modern England.* Cambridge: Cambridge University Press, 1986.

Lewis, Wyndham. *The Lion and the Fox: The Role of the Hero in the Plays of Shakespeare.* London: Methuen, 1955.

Raab, Felix. *The English Face of Machiavelli, a Changing Interpretation, 1500–1700.* London: Routledge & Kegan Paul, 1964.

Matters of Faith

Anderson, M.D. *History and Imagery in British Churches*. London: J. Murray, 1971.

Booty, John E., ed. *The Book of Common Prayer, 1559: The Elizabethan Prayer Book*. Charlottesville: University Press of Virginia, 1976.

Cressy, David. *Birth, Marriage, and Death: Ritual, Religion, and the Life-Cycle in Tudor and Stuart England*. Oxford: Oxford University Press, 1997.

Davidson, Clifford, ed. *The Iconography of Heaven*. Kalamazoo: Medieval Institute Publications, Western Michigan University, 1994.

———, and Thomas H. Seiler, ed. *The Iconography of Hell*. Kalamazoo: Medieval Institute Publications, Western Michigan University, 1992.

Every, George. *Christian Mythology*. Twickenham: Hamlyn, 1970.

Foxe, John. *Acts and Monuments, 1563*. 8 vols. Edited by George Townsend. New York: AMS Press, 1965.

Gittings, Clare. *Death, Burial, and the Individual in Early Modern England*. London: C. Helm, 1984.

James I, King of England. *The English Bible, Translated out of the Original Tongues by the Commandment of King James the First, Anno 1611*. New York: AMS Press, 1967.

Komroff, Manuel, ed. *The Apocrypha; or, Non-canonical Books of the Bible: The King James Version*. New York: Tudor Publishing Company, 1936.

Milward, Peter. *Shakespeare's Religious Background*. Bloomington: Indiana University Press; 1973.

Morris, Harry. *Last Things in Shakespeare*. Tallahassee: Florida State University Press, 1985.

Rickey, Mary Ellen, and Thomas B. Stroup, eds. *Certaine Sermons or Homilies, Appointed to Be Read in Churches, in the Time of Queen Elizabeth I, 1547–1571* (1623). Gainesville, FL: Scholars' Facsimiles & Reprints, 1968.

Shaheen, Naseeb. *Biblical References in Shakespeare's Plays*. Newark: University of Delaware Press, 1999.

Thompson, Craig R. *The English Church in the Sixteenth Century*. Washington, DC: Folger Shakespeare Library, 1979.

Turner, Alice K. *The History of Hell*. New York: Harcourt Brace, 1993.

The Supernatural

Allen, Don Cameron. *The Star-crossed Renaissance: The Quarrel about Astrology and Its Influence in England*. New York: Octagon Books, 1973.

Brand, John. *Observations on the Popular Antiquities of Great Britain: Chiefly Illustrating the Origin of Our Vulgar and Provincial Customs, Ceremonies, and Superstitions* (1849). 3 vols. Detroit: Singing Tree Press, 1969.

Briggs, K.M. *The Anatomy of Puck: An Examination of Fairy Beliefs among Shakespeare's Contemporaries and Successors*. London: Routledge & Kegan Paul, 1959.

———. *A Dictionary of British Folk-tales in the English Language, Incorporating the F. J. Norton Collection*. 4 vols. Bloomington: Indiana University Press, 1970.

———. *Pale Hecate's Team: An Examination of the Beliefs on Witchcraft and Magic among Shakespeare's Contemporaries and His Immediate Successors*. London: Routledge & Kegan Paul, 1962.

Clulee, Nicholas H. *John Dee's Natural Philosophy: Between Science and Religion*. London: Routledge, 1988.

Cobb, Noel. *Prospero's Island: The Secret Alchemy at the Heart of The Tempest*. London: Coventure, 1984.

de Givry, Grillot. *Witchcraft, Magic, and Alchemy*. Translated by J. Courtenay Locke. New York: Dover, 1971.

Encyclopedia of Magic and Superstition: Alchemy, Charms, Dreams, Omens, Rituals, Talismans, Wishes. London: Octopus Books, 1974.

Fanger, Claire, ed. *Conjuring Spirits: Texts and Traditions of Medieval Ritual Magic*. University Park: Pennsylvania State University Press, 1998.

French, Peter J. *John Dee: The World of an Elizabethan Magus*. London: Routledge & Kegan Paul, 1972.

Guazzo, Francesco Maria. *Compendium Maleficarum* (1608). Edited by Montague Summers. Secaucus, NJ: University Books, 1974.

Halliwell-Phillipps, J.O., ed. *Fairy Mythology of a Midsummer Night's Dream: Early Documents Illustrative of Shakespearian Fairy Mythology*. Nendeln, Liechtenstein: Kraus Reprint, 1966.

Harkness, Deborah E. *John Dee's Conversations with Angels: Cabala, Alchemy, and the End of Nature*. Cambridge: Cambridge University Press, 1999.

Harris, Anthony. *Night's Black Agents: Witchcraft and Magic in Seventeenth-Century English Drama*. Manchester: Manchester University Press, 1980.

Hazlitt, W. Carew. *Faith and Folklore of the British Isles: A Descriptive and Historical Dictionary of the Superstitions, Beliefs, and Popular Customs of England, Scotland, Wales, and Ireland, from Norman Times to the End of the Nineteenth Century, with Classical and Foreign Analogues*. New York: Benjamin Blom, 1965.

Holzer, Hans, ed. *Encyclopedia of Witchcraft and Demonology: An Illustrated Encyclopedia of Witches, Demons, Sorcerers, and Their Present Day Counterparts*. London: Octopus Books, 1974.

James I, King of England. *Daemonologie, 1597*. New York: Barnes & Noble, 1966.

Latham, Minor White. *The Elizabethan Fairies: The Fairies of Folklore and the Fairies of Shakespeare*. New York: Octagon Books, 1972.

MacDonald, Michael, ed. *Witchcraft and Hysteria in Elizabethan London: Edward Jorden and the Mary Glover Case*. London: Routledge, 1991.

Macfarlane, Alan Grant. *Witchcraft in Tudor and Stuart England: A Regional and Comparative Study*. London: Routledge & Kegan Paul, 1970.

Mebane, John S. *Renaissance Magic and the Return of the Golden Age: The Occult Tradition and Marlowe, Jonson, and Shakespeare*. Lincoln: University of Nebraska Press, 1989.

Remy, Nicolas. *Demonolatry* (1595). Edited by Montague Summers. Secaucus, NJ: University Books, 1974.

Rosen, Barbara, ed. *Witchcraft in England, 1558–1618*. Amherst: University of Massachusetts Press, 1991.

Scot, Reginald. *The Discoverie of Witchcraft* (1584). East Ardsley, Wakefield: EP Pub., 1973.

Sharpe, James. *Instruments of Darkness: Witchcraft in England, 1550–1750*. Harmondsworth: Penguin Books, 1996.

Spence, Lewis. *The Fairy Tradition in Britain*. London: Rider and Company, 1948.

Thomas, Keith. *Religion and the Decline of Magic: Studies in Popular Beliefs in Sixteenth and Seventeenth Century England*. London: Weidenfeld and Nicolson, 1971.

Traister, Barbara. *Heavenly Necromancers: The Magician in English Renaissance Drama*. Columbia: University of Missouri Press, 1984.

Waite, Arthur Edward. *The Book of Ceremonial Magic: The Secret Tradition in Goetia, Including the Rites and Mysteries of Goetic Theurgy, Sorcery, and Infernal Necromancy*. New Hyde Park, NY: University Books, 1961,.

Woodbridge, Linda. *The Scythe of Saturn: Shakespeare and Magical Thinking*. Urbana: University of Illinois Press, 1994.

Prejudices

Henderson, Katherine Usher, and Barbara F. McManus. *Half Humankind: Contexts and Texts of the Controversy about Women in England, 1540–1640*. Urbana: University of Illinois Press, 1985.

Hoenselaars, A.J. *Images of Englishmen and Foreigners in the Drama of Shakespeare and His Contemporaries*. Rutherford, NJ: Fairleigh Dickinson University Press, 1992.

Lievsay, John L. *The Elizabethan Image of Italy*. Ithaca, NY: Cornell University Press, 1964.

❧ 9 ❧

Shakespeare in the Theatre

As in a Theatre, whence they gape and point
At your industrious Scenes and acts of death.

Bastard [*John* 2.1.375]

THEATRICAL CONVENTIONS

The more we know about the conventions of Shakespeare's theatre, as well as the makeup of the audience, the experience of attending the theatre, the composition of his company of players, the physical attributes of the theatrical spaces for which the plays were written, and the production practices, including casting, rehearsing, and acting, the better we can understand the language of the plays specifically and, more generally, how these plays might work in today's theatre. Please do not think that I am recommending that we return to a "Shakespearean" staging of these plays. I do not value the authentic at the expense of creativity and have no particular commitment to museum theatre. Rather, I would not want to see actors wasting time on passages that appear difficult only because the actor is attempting to superimpose our modern theatrical conventions onto a play written for a specific theatre and actors and audience. In addition, it is only by understanding the older conventions that modern actors can find exciting ways to bridge the gap between what Shakespeare's audiences would have expected, accepted, and appreciated and the expectations, assumptions, and taste of the patrons who pay the bills.

Let us agree that no interpretation that works in the living crucible of a theatrical performance can possibly be "wrong," no matter how puzzled Shakespeare would be if he could be magically transported into a modern theatre.

But why ignore the insights and inspirations that emerge from the work of historians and archeologists who work in this area of Shakespeare studies? Academic libraries contain many sources of information that can change the way a modern actor thinks about the plays. An important category of research involves scholars of theatre history who attempt to piece together the evidence we have with what we can surmise from the plays themselves to come up with a model of the theatres for which Shakespeare wrote his plays.

Another important category, most exciting when it is undertaken by scholars who combine an in-depth knowledge of the plays and a firsthand experience of play production, is the analysis of Shakespeare's stagecraft or dramaturgy. These terms are used to describe the way Shakespeare put his plays together so that they worked theatrically. J. L. Styan's *Shakespeare's Stagecraft* over and over reminds us that Shakespeare was an actor, that rehearsal time was limited, and that the plays are filled with guidelines, hints, controls, and suggestions for the actors in the company.

I very much enjoyed John C. Meagher's *Shakespeare's Shakespeare*, which takes us back to the First Folio and quartos for clues about how the plays were intended to be performed, clues that are difficult to read since we are cut off from the conventions of that theatre. Meagher makes these conventions come alive by demonstrating the theatrical "payoff" of, for example, the fact that actors would have to play more than one role. His book answers many questions you might have had about why things happen the way they do in the plays. Why is the nurse not present in the final scene in *Romeo and Juliet?* Why didn't Benvolio take the message to Romeo, seeing that he is such a close friend? Shakespeare's audience would not have had these questions if the actors playing these roles were visible on stage playing other characters. Of course, that is all very well, but what do we do today? Do we bring them on, with no lines? The nurse, silent? Imagine that. Or do we send her home, along with the actor playing Mercutio, midway through the evening? What a waste of great acting talent. No easy solution seems available for modern production companies. Peter J. Smith has taken an unusual and exciting approach to performance criticism in *Social Shakespeare*. He begins with an analysis of trends in modern interpretations, and then makes some fascinating comparisons between the challenges we find in the plays today and the social and cultural issues that would have aroused the interest of Shakespeare's audience. For example, in his chapter on racism in *The Merchant of Venice*, "The Eternal Mushroom of Humanity," he describes the concerns raised by modern critics about the antisemitism in even the most sympathetic of portraits of Shylock, and then discusses some of the popular Elizabethan myths and assumptions that make their way into the text of the play.

Pauline Kiernan has documented some of the experimentations in "authentic" staging being undertaken at the New Globe in *Staging Shakespeare at the New Globe*. She includes interviews with actors, the director, and the voice and movement coach for the production of *Henry V* that she observed, and there is much here that suggests how different acting might have been for Shakespeare and his colleagues in the first Globe.

The whole idea of theatrical conventions is well explained in M.C. Bradbrook's *Themes and Conventions of Elizabethan Tragedy*. I found that reading about the conventions in Shakespeare's time helped me to realize that the modern theatre contains as many strange ways of doing things that are so familiar that we don't realize how contrived and how bizarre they are. This keeps us from laughing up our sleeves too much at those conventions we find strange in Shakespeare's plays. Four hundred years from now people will find our conventions just as ridiculous.

Recent archeological activity at the site of the first Elizabethan theatres has produced a wealth of evidence about what Shakespeare's theatre was really like, so Bradbrook's book is not nearly as useful as it once was. Still, it contains an important message for today's actors: Shakespeare wrote within a set of theatrical conventions, only some of which we share. If you understand how conventions work and how his conventions were different from ours, you will be less likely to mistake great bits of theatre for silliness. An example is the death of Desdemona. What is a modern actress to do with the way that poor girl just refuses to die? Just when you think that she has finally expired, she pops up one last time to lie in order to save her husband/murderer's reputation. Such a sequence of events would not be out of place in a Monty Python skit; in the penultimate scene of a great tragedy it causes real problems for the actors who have to commit to the reality of the moment. Absorbing Bradbrook's ideas can help.

PRODUCTION HISTORY

Another type of scholarship that appeals to some actors a great deal and to others not at all is the documentation of productions of a specific play, performances of a specific role, or trends in Shakespearean production. Theatre historians have collected a great deal of information about how Shakespeare's plays have been performed over time, but for the purposes of this discussion I will divide the scholarship into four distinct categories.

First, we have the studies of how Shakespeare's plays were performed in his lifetime, which we will stretch to include the years following his death up to the restoration of the public theatres in 1660, following the closing of the theatres by the Puritan government. Some people argue that this forced closure means that there is a clear and undeniable break between the acting of Shakespeare's company and the acting that starts off the next period, as a generation of apprentices, otherwise trained under actors who had been trained under actors who had acted in the premier productions, were now being trained by actors who had been trained in the French classical theatre and were brought in by the restored King Charles II. Thus 1660 marks the arrival of actresses, perspective scenery, and an entirely new style of English play writing and play making on the London stage.

However, when the public theatres were closed by the Puritans, the actors sought employment in private theatricals or in touring troupes that performed in Europe. Also, the two actor-managers who were awarded the royal patents for public theatre performances in 1660 offered, as evidence of their suitability for this very special responsibility, the fact that they had acted on the English professional stage and so could restore the traditions of that great theatrical tradition.

Ultimately this doesn't matter all that much to a modern actor, because it was a long time ago and the way Shakespeare was performed between 1660 and the early part of this century was so very different from how we approach the plays today that only historians find the records fascinating. It is comforting to think of an unbroken acting tradition, and sometimes the insights from actors who tackled the great tragic roles can spark an exciting train of thought for someone facing the same daunting task today. Carol Carlisle has collected some insights in *Shakespeare from the Greenroom.*

The third period begins with the emergence of modern Shakespearean productions and dates from whichever production a particular historian sees as being of central importance to the emergence of whichever style that scholar has deemed truly modern. For today's actor, it doesn't really matter which production is the landmark; there is an overwhelming sensation, however, that our work is part of a tradition of great productions, under the shadow of which we all labor. The third-period productions establish the "straight-up" version of any given play, and the great actors and great productions form a standard of excellence as well as a "proper" interpretation that seems most obviously in keeping with the obvious themes, mood, and style of any given play. All other productions either fall into the traditional modern interpretation or are offered as contrasts, as "fresh and new," and form the fourth period of Shakespearean production.

It is in the fourth period that we find *Much Ado about Nothing* set at the end of the American Civil War or in imperial India. We find *Measure for Measure* as a dark, disturbing play with a bitterly ironic ending. We find all sorts of productions in which an undeniable but secondary theme is teased out into the dominant thrust of the play, and in which alternative interpretations of character challenge our expectations of protagonist and antagonist. This period has been in place almost as long as the third period, because as soon as a powerful traditional production established itself as the "correct" approach, there immediately followed a slate of challenges to that interpretation. We have now a sense that there can't really be anything new to do with any given play, and there is nothing striking or outlandish to tease out of any given plot or set of relationships. The depressing thought that any bright idea you might come up with in rehearsal has already been done can cut the heart out of an actor's exploration of a role.

Some actors assiduously avoid any discussion of how Olivier, Gielgud, Branagh, or Val Kilmer approached his role, or how Vanessa Redgrave's Rosalind might be compared with Katharine Hepburn's. They try not to study the pictures included by the editors of the Oxford, New Cambridge, or Arden editions of the play and would never rent the video or borrow the library's copy of the BBC version of the play. In this manner, they attempt to avoid the insidious "ur-character" of the "correct" interpretation, and also to avoid the depressing sensation of merely duplicating the great ideas of others. After all, does it matter if your insight is shared by another actor? It is a brand-new insight for you and can be cherished and nurtured if it is allowed to grow naturally in the rehearsal process.

Other actors devour all of the studies they can find, look at pictures and films, and read biographies of the great and glorious and reviews of the latest productions from all around the world. They eagerly appropriate any great idea that catches their eye, like magpies collecting brightly colored objects with which to make a nest. They are encouraged by the multiplicity of approaches: there are so many ways to make the role and the play work that there can never be one "correct" way, and the infamous "ur-character" loses its potency to restrict intuitive exploration. They know that there is nothing wrong with being a magpie. Individuality and creativity come from the testing and absorbing and modifying of a unique collection of bits and pieces, molded into a composite characterization that could only be created by that actor at that time and place in that particular production.

Only regular Shakespearean theatregoers are positioned to judge the relative originality of an interpretation. Sitting out there in your audience might be a gaggle of scholars, including theatre historians and specialists in contemporary Shakespearean staging. There might also be a few actors who have played the same role you are attempting. There will be people who can impress others by comparing your performance with Olivier or Gielgud in the same role, and others who will rank your approach within the list of seventeen other productions of the same play that they have seen. They are intimidating, but they are also a tiny minority.

The majority of the audience will be seeing the play for the first time. Some of them will never have read the play and might not even know how the play ends. They won't know whether you are doing the role "correctly" or "in a new and innovative manner, challenging the traditional readings of the character." They will not know whether you are playing the hero or the villain until they see and hear you and judge you and your performance as it unfolds before them.

It often happens in the theatre that an actor is stumped by a moment in a play and is trying to work out an approach to carry it off. If it is a new play, and the playwright is available and helpful, the actor need feel no shame in accepting help that begins, "Well, when I wrote that bit I was thinking that it would go something like this." When the playwright is Shakespeare, and the production of necessity is being rehearsed within the most detailed, complex, and lengthy of theatrical traditions, older actors frequently suggest to younger actors that the solution to their struggle to solve a specific moment might lie in a well-known strategy that is known to have worked over time. This is quite a different impetus from the slavish devotion to doing Shakespeare "correctly," which can deaden an actor's ingenuity and personal contribution to the role. This is taking advantage of the community of actors, the inherited strategies for good stagecraft, and the efficiency of borrowing successful techniques if they will work for you.

I would urge those of you who wish to avoid the dead hand of tradition to clarify in your own mind what is the "ur-character" that already lingers in the back of your mind so that you can resist its insidious restricting of your intuitive, fresh, interactions with the play. For those of you who value traditions of performances and are inspired by the magpie approach, it is important to encounter as many different interpretations as possible so that you no longer believe that any one interpretation is the "correct" one. You will also be looking for books that record specific acting choices rather than more thematic and general studies of trends in Shakespearean productions.

PERFORMANCE CRITICISM

Those scholars who defy the dominant thrust of traditional literary studies of Shakespeare, which have a tendency to forget entirely that these were originally plays to be performed, have established a subcategory of Shakespeare studies known as performance criticism. Publications in this field tend to be relatively less interesting to actors, as the scholars too often expend great effort analyzing the sorts of theatrical discoveries that actors make every day in rehearsal. At the same time, because they bring a great deal of love and sometimes a bit of understanding about rehearsing and performing, their interests and enthusiasms can be shared by theatrical readers. Ann Slater set the standard for intelligent performance criticism in *Shakespeare, the Director*. It is fascinating to read an academic book detailing the theatrical tricks that seem to be understood intuitively or passed down as part of theatrical tradition in professional Shakespeare companies.

Philip McGuire is another example of this new breed of critic. He brings a very theatrical sensibility to *Speechless Dialect*, his thematic study of the significance of silent onlookers and, in particular, the silence of major characters at key moments of the plot. For example, he delves into just what might be suggested by the fact that Isabella is given no responding speech when the duke proposes marriage at the conclusion of *Measure for Measure*. Scholars like Slater and McGuire demonstrate that the division between those who do and those who discuss can result in perceptive observation from the sidelines, should the scholar choose to take that position.

The majority of performance criticism is written from the perspective of the audience. All Shakespearean scholars attend performances, but only the more eccentric among them might have played a role in a production at their university or attended rehearsals of a professional production as an observer. Although an actor might be interested in how audiences perceive the plays, there is not much here in the way of practical advice. At best, such books contain vivid and detailed descriptions of what the scholar remembers about favorite productions. At worst, these are dry and dusty studies that bring together the history of the theatre and the texts of the plays in a manner that makes it difficult to imagine a production that you would ever want to rehearse and perform. Fortunately, you can usually catch wind of the dustiness of the contents even if the title is intriguing. *Stages of Play: Shakespeare's Theatrical Energies in Elizabethan Performance* by Michael W. Shurgot is probably an excellent piece of scholarship, but a quick glance revealed a writing style and a focus that are not going to be particularly inspiring for a modern actor.

In contrast, Albert Bermel's approach in *Shakespeare at the Moment* is lively and eclectic. As he explains in his introduction, he comes to the plays as a playwright-critic rather than a scholar-critic; he is also aware that he is not an actor-critic or a director-critic. His perceptions, influenced by his wide-ranging encounter with scholar-critics as well as with actors and directors in the working theatre, are performance criticism at its most engagingly theatrical.

E.A.J. Honigmann in *Shakespeare: Seven Tragedies* discusses what actors experience firsthand, but in a manner that is refreshingly accurate in evoking what actually goes on in a performance. His focus is the analysis of the theatrical tricks used by the playwright to manipulate the audience's response to characters, and though he generally imagines the role being played "straight," in other words, without any overt challenge to the conventions being employed, he has much to say that makes quite good sense in theatrical terms.

In a similar vein, David Richman traces the reactions of audiences to the comedies, dividing his book *Laughter, Pain, and Wonder* into chapters on laughter, pain, wonder, moods, and endings. An actor might find Richman's prescriptions irritating, as he, like Honigmann, seems incapable of imagining the multiplicity of nuanced emotion that can be aroused by different approaches to the same moment in a play.

SHAKESPEARE IN PERFORMANCE

Fortunately, the subcategory of performance criticism has yielded rich fruit in the form of detailed and thought-provoking studies of how the plays actually work in performance. The Shakespeare in Performance series can be counted on to provide a solid overview of trends in producing the play under discussion, though the breadth of coverage precludes any richness of detail. Each volume contains an introductory survey of the history of performance from whatever records exist from Shakespeare's time to the modern theatre, followed by an intelligent discussion of one or two landmark productions, usually from the British professional theatre. The various scholars contributing to the series have some useful things to say about the theatrical appeal and challenges of the plays, and the editors of the series have been remarkably successful in selecting scholars who have not only a great love of these plays on the stage, but also an honest appreciation of the work of actors and directors. At the other end of the scale is Marvin Rosenberg's series of *Masks* books, a moment-by-moment record of choices available to an actor, with detailed reference to a limited number of interestingly contrasted productions, supported by exhaustive research demonstrated by the lengthy bibliography of sources used, so that a vast number of productions have "entered the mix" that results in Rosenberg's presentation of the play.

The Masks of Shakespeare

Every actor knows his or her own creative processes best, and concerning stage histories there is the same variety of reactions as to any other scholarly resource: some actors enjoy reading all about other productions, while others find the oppressive weight of famous interpretations something to be alleviated by avoidance. My experience is not unusual: I have, when I was directing a play, seen a single photograph or read a single description and afterwards found myself unable to get that image out of my mind, even though I knew full well that it had nothing to do with this cast, these actors, and this particular production process. When I read Charles Marowitz's description of the "ur-character" in *Prospero's Staff* it was with a recognition and retroactive reflection on the acting choices I had made, or rather had not made but had had thrust upon me by the weight of tradition: I was either rebelling against the "correct" interpretation of a character just to rebel, or I was slipping, with the barest consciousness of doing so, into the easiest, that is, correct, approach, and in neither case was my acting based upon any honest interaction with the words of the play or the other performers on stage.

That is the negative impact of stage history. The positive result is the result of being forced, in graduate school, to write an essay on the stage history of one of Shakespeare's plays. In rebellion I chose the most obscure play I could think of, only to discover a most fascinating series of productions of *Pericles*. With this came the discovery that the huge number of productions of even the least well-known plays tended, at the end of the day, to cancel each other out. How could there be a single "correct" interpretation when so many striking and memorable theatrical moments were created by contrasting, diametrically opposed interpretations? In some ways, we are blessed with the knowledge that everything one might think of when one is seeking a "new" way of doing Shakespeare has probably already been done, and therefore, as an alternative to originality, one is free to seek something that simply works for the company assembled to explore this particular play in this time and place.

I am quite fond of Marvin Rosenberg's *Masks* books, for his exhaustive record of how a variety of productions "solved" moment after moment of *Hamlet* clarifies immediately that there are as many solutions as there are creative teams at work on these immense theatrical challenges. These dense books reward the cover-to-cover reader, but an actor in the throes of a production might not want to risk drowning in the almost one thousand pages of small print and might elect rather to dip a toe in specific scenes, using Rosenberg's organizational structure. He begins with the first moments and concludes with the closing, with brief digressions for discussions of characters: in the case of *Hamlet*, Horatio, the Ghost, Claudius, Gertrude, Ophelia, Laertes, and Polonius. These chapters include Rosenberg's own analysis of the craft of characterization, for example, how Shakespeare has shaped the audience's encounter with character, and how that in turn has influenced how critics and scholars have written about Ophelia or Polonius. But he quickly moves on to comment as an observer on various production choices and to report the perceptions of various actors who have undertaken the role. If nothing else, these chapters set before the actors the landscape of the challenges facing them during the rehearsal process and suggest the central choices they will be making as they find their personal and therefore unique way into a role.

Naturally, Rosenberg's own interpretation of the play influences every paragraph of his writing, and his selection of productions upon which to draw for extensive examples is limited not only by the availability of detailed production records but also his taste in "valid" as opposed to "illegitimate" interpretations. Of necessity, he and other production historians build more and more of their scholarship upon the film or television productions for which there exists a record that can be examined again and again by scholars around the world. Actors, however, know that the process and production of live theatre events is so different as to make the film and television productions merely theoretically of interest for interpretive choices, more the director's sphere than the actors' search for a way to play the role repeatedly, without any possibility for repeated takes, and all in one go.

But these are minor quibbles that should not diminish the achievement of Rosenberg's books, and I would recommend them wholeheartedly to actors who enjoy such discoveries as mine when I wondered about just how Hamlet's comments to Ophelia during the Mousetrap might have been played in the different productions Rosenberg draws upon for *The Masks of Hamlet*. The scene that interests me is discussed in forty-two densely printed pages, and in them I find all sorts of interesting bits of stage history and theatrical analysis. What I appreciate most about Rosenberg's strategy is that he includes what he calls "naive spectators" in his research. These are individuals who are encountering a production of the play for the first time, and who are questioned about what they think is going to happen next, what they think of events, characters, and relationships, and what they find clear and what puzzling as the play unfolds. This is the person who does not know that Ophelia will go mad and drown but watches the Mousetrap hoping for a happy ending to the love story. In playing the role, there are possibilities for finding the roots of the vulnerability to madness without forgetting that Ophelia too is more likely to still be hoping for a happy ending to the small story in which she is the heroine.

Here is Rosenberg on some of the options open to Ophelia upon entering:

Ophelia has come in divided: not wanting to be exposed to Hamlet's cruelty again yet hoping to help in any way she can. She has had to be pulled in by Polonius; she has run in late, as if only at the last minute she could bring herself to participate. She has locked eyes with Hamlet; she has refused to look at him. (568)

Rosenberg asks the question we all must ask on Ophelia's behalf: "Why does Hamlet treat Ophelia so? Why does Shakespeare?" (569). There does not seem to be any answer to this question. But there are many possible answers to the question, How might Ophelia respond to Hamlet's sexual innuendo?

Modest, she has been shy, hurt, in tears, has tried to smile, has looked down, turned away; power Ophelias, like Warner's and Sarkola's, have been angry, combative, and made of the beat of this dialogue a build that could lead to blows. (570)

Rosenberg's compendium of options is richest, of course, for the actor playing Hamlet. I am very fond of the multiple strategies listed for portraying the antic disposition that Hamlet promises to put on at the end of act 1; when we finally see him again midway through the second scene of act 2, after everyone has discussed his insanity, we can't help but eagerly anticipate how this Hamlet will "play" madness. What fun! My favorite is the actor who entered chewing the pages of the book as Gertrude says, "But look where sadly the poor wretch / Comes reading" [2.2.168]. Costumes have ranged from a jester's bells to a woman's dress, pajamas, or not much at all.

Sadly, Rosenberg has completed his studies of only four of the great tragedies: *Othello, Hamlet, King Lear,* and *Macbeth.* However, he has published a collection of short pieces on a variety of subjects, all of which are theatrical and insightful. Rosenberg has also published a collection of various articles and lectures on such topics as "Lady Macbeth's Indispensable Child" and "Subtext in Shakespeare." This volume entitled *The Adventures of a Shakespeare Scholar* is well worth browsing, for although not every article is equally theatrical, and every article has as much scholarly residue as theatrical verve, Rosenberg can always be counted on to approach a topic very much from a theatrical point of view.

Gary Williams's study of *A Midsummer Night's Dream,* entitled *Our Moonlight Revels,* contains an excellent first chapter in which he examines the play within the context of Elizabethan staging conventions and a wonderful final chapter in which he draws upon examples of a wide variety of productions in order to demonstrate how many different ways the play can be performed for a modern audience. In between, he takes the reader through the history of this play's productions.

Ronald Watkins and Jeremy Lemmon published four books in their In Shakespeare's Playhouse series, three of which are a vivid description of just how they imagine the first production of *Hamlet, Macbeth,* and *A Midsummer Night's Dream* might have gone. Their fourth title, *The Poet's Method,* is a more general study. They have drawn upon the work of theatre historians and also upon their own experience in producing Shakespeare, and the books are a great pleasure to read. Scholars have found much to criticize in such speculative writing, in large part because the authors do not differentiate between ideas based upon factual evidence and ideas based upon theatrical intuition. Those of us without an academic agenda can enjoy these for what they set out to be: books that attempt to capture the excitement and thrill of the first performance. It is important, however, not to fall into the trap of thinking that Watkins and Lemmon's description is how the play in question should be performed. Here is a sample from their book on *Hamlet,* describing their imagined scene when the players first arrive in Elsinore:

The entry of the Players makes a welcome invasion of colour and movement upon the Stage. Perhaps they push a hand-wagon full of their properties and costumes; we have no difficulty in recognising at least the Humorous Man (a sort of Armado-Jacques-Malvolio), the Clown and my young Lady (who is of course a boy). (67)

Watkins and Lemmon are of course guessing that the players are a welcome invasion, just as they are imagining color and movement and lots of props. Their knowledge of the conventions of acting companies leads them to speculate about "the Humorous Man," and they assume that the clown would reveal himself by some clownish activity or attire. They are on quite firm ground in identifying "my young Lady" as a boy. Here is what they have to say about the first player's performance:

The First Player is not a figure of fun nor is his performance absurd: indeed he is very accomplished, in the stylistic convention which is his fashion: this may be that of the neighbouring and rival company, the Admiral's Men, but we may assume that Shakespeare and Burbage were not insensitive to the skill and power of Edward Alleyn's acting. (67)

Again, Watkins and Lemmon blend theatre history, in Alleyn and the Admiral's Men, with pure speculation about contrasting acting styles and mutual respect. Every book in the series is just such a vivid, entertaining, and imaginative speculation and a welcome break from dusty, if reliable, scholarship.

One of the best of the scholarly-theatrical hybrids is James Lusardi and June Schlueter's *Reading Shakespeare in Performance: King Lear*. Here we have a fascinating blend of agendas: to consider a variety of interpretations offered by scholars as a result of close reading of the plays in the study, while also considering some of the many choices made by various productions. The result is a combination of quotations from scholars who have quite contradictory ideas about what is going on at any given moment in the play with descriptions of interesting acting choices and staging strategies. Sadly, in the discussion of productions they are limited by their use of film and video versions that can be studied exhaustively in a manner comparable to reading the play over and over. Even so, this is a bridging of two worlds that does much to remove any illusion that there exists a single, correct interpretation for any aspect of this or any other great play.

Directors of Shakespeare

Books by and about directors of Shakespeare sometimes contain interesting insights into approaches that actors might take when they are rehearsing the play. More often they are about that thing we call the director's concept; in other words, they are concerned with a single interpretation of a play rather than how to interpret and play in a play. They also contain much about dealing with the politics of a theatrical organization and the director's personal development. The approach that John Barton and Peter Hall take to the speaking of Shakespeare's verse, for example, is described in detail in Barton's *Playing Shakespeare*; Peter Hall's autobiography *Making an Exhibition of Myself* and Michael L. Greenwald's biography of Barton, *Directions by Indirections*, are comparatively disappointing on that topic. Tina Parker's work with Shakespeare and Company in Lennox, Massachusetts, is greatly influenced by Kristin Linklater's, who has documented her approach to Shakespeare in *Freeing the Shakespearean Actor's Voice*. Helen Epstein's book on Parker, *The Companies She Keeps*, offers few insights about verse-speaking. You will learn more about Joseph Papp's approach to Shakespeare from his *Shakespeare Alive!* than from Helen Epstein's biography. Even so, the biographies of Barton, Papp, and Parker and the autobiography of Sir Peter Hall make for interesting reading and do contain nuggets of useful information about "how" as well as "why" these directors do Shakespeare.

The story of some of the great modern Shakespeare festivals might prove of interest to some actors, particularly those performing in or hoping someday to perform in such a setting. John Houseman and Jack Landau's *The American Shakespeare Festival*, Tom Patterson and Allan Gould's *First Stage: The Making of the Stratford Festival*, and Sally Beauman's *The Royal Shakespeare Company*, are just three such offerings. At the opposite end of the scale, for a fascinating record of producing Shakespeare in Moscow, have a look at Guy Sprung's *Hot Ice*.

For a collection of interviews with directors, with mixed results, Ralph Berry's *On Directing Shakespeare* is the best by far. Barry has also contributed other collections of articles on different productions and approaches to Shakespeare in the modern theatre in *Changing Styles in Shakespeare* and *Shakespeare in Performance*. His books reveal detailed study of historical documents, more than an average familiarity with how actors do their work, and a Britain-centered view of modern Shakespearean production.

Michael Scott takes a very similar approach to Ralph Berry's in *Renaissance Drama and a Modern Audience*. He includes chapters on *The Comedy of Errors* and *Measure for Measure*, as well as *Volpone*, *The Changeling*, and other plays by Shakespeare's contemporaries.

Because most of the women directors in her book had not yet been invited to direct for the Royal Shakespeare Company, Elizabeth Schafer's *MsDirecting Shakespeare: Women Direct Shakespeare* offers a refreshing snapshot of alternative Shakespearean production in Britain and Australia. Sadly, she did not visit North America, where women are making important and interesting contributions from the margins, at the top, and just slogging away in the trenches alongside their male colleagues.

The Royal Shakespeare Company has made many contributions to library shelves. In addition to the various histories of the theatre and essays written from the audience's point of view, it supported what had been hoped to be a series entitled Directors' Shakespeare, but only *Approaches to Twelfth Night*, edited by Michael Billington, has appeared. This is one of the most interesting books from the perspective of directing, as Billington has interviewed four directors of RSC productions of *Twelfth Night*, in which they do not always agree with each other, and during which they tackle some very specific and theatrical questions, such as the social structure of the play, naturalism and its limits, and discovering Shakespeare's world.

Secondhand accounts can also provide interesting insights, though when the reporter has no experience as an actor, the record can be disappointingly bare of insights about acting Shakespeare. Tirzah Lowen's *Peter Hall directs Antony and Cleopatra*, which documents Hall's obsession with language, never describes his methods for approaching text in rehearsal, and so is little help to an actor seeking inspiration from this great director. But it is always fun to be a fly on the wall, along with those writers who were allowed to sit in on the rehearsal process and have recorded in some detail the atmosphere, the interpersonal dynamics, the struggles and of course the challenges. David Selbourne's *The Making of A Midsummer Night's Dream* lets us in on some of the nastier things that occurred during the creation of this landmark production; Kristina Bedford, in *Coriolanus at the National* and Roger Warren, in *Staging Shakespeare's Late Plays*, are more discreet, though it is possible to read between the lines and imagine the tensions suggested in their documentation of the complex process of bringing Shakespeare's great plays to life in the modern theatre.

Actor's Insights

I have always enjoyed reading biographies about actors, justifying my salacious interest in the details of personal lives by claiming that I was looking
for insights into acting. Such insights can be buried, fleeting, illusionary, or
subsumed by the writer's agenda of celebrating the mystery of the great talent.
"Let's celebrate how great she was in this role, but we're not going to tell you
anything useful, like how she did it, because only she could do it, and who
are you, you lowly creature reading this book, to think you could ever even
attempt what she did so effortlessly?" I found Brian Cox's *The Lear Diaries* and
Maurice Good's *Every Inch a Lear* equally fascinating, and I was deeply moved
by *Woza Shakespeare!*, in which Antony Sher and Gregory Doran contribute
alternating chapters to their diary of rehearsing *Titus Andronicus* in post-
apartheid South Africa.

Those actors who do share the nuts and bolts of their approach to Shakespeare usually demonstrate that there are tricks to help just about anyone get
to the heart of the mystery. But what you do when you get there is another
matter, and that is where the great actors of yesterday and tomorrow emerge
from among the crowd of visitors to the Shakespeare stage.

I have some favorite firsthand accounts. I remember laughing aloud during
Antony Sher's *Year of the King*, and I regularly tell my students stories from
Jonathan Miller's autobiography, *Subsequent Performances*. Any theatrical autobiography can contain a few nuggets of concrete advice buried in the mountains of anecdote and name-dropping, but these have to be viewed as a pleasant
and generally unexpected bonus in addition to the real reason for reading the
book from cover to cover: unashamed eagerness to devour the anecdotes and
read the famous names. Despite its promising title, John Gielgud's *Acting Shakespeare* was not filled with nuggets, in part because attitudes toward Shakespeare
and tastes in acting style have changed so radically, but more because Gielgud's
memories were seldom of the specifics of any aspect of production, and he
was never inclined toward verbalizing his way of approaching a role.

In contrast, the Royal Shakespeare Company's *Players of Shakespeare*, with
four volumes in the series, edited, respectively, by Philip Brockbank, Russell
Jackson and Robert Smallwood (volumes 2 and 3), and R.L. Smallwood, can
be counted on to provide interesting comments by leading performers talking
about their experiences with major roles. Carol Rutter has a more specific
agenda in *Clamorous Voices*: to reveal the unique experiences of actresses in what
is still a male-dominated cultural industry. For a "thumb-your-nose" style of
diary, have a look at Steven Berkoff's record of playing Hamlet, *I Am Hamlet*.
I particularly enjoyed his exploration of the mind-numbing "To be or not to
be" and all of the wild and crazy ways he considered delivering this too, too
familiar soliloquy.

Judith Cook's books are an appealing blend of a taste of theatre history with
a few interesting quotations from an actor who has tackled a particular role.

Her focus is very much on what the actor experiences in playing the major roles in the modern theatre. In *Shakespeare's Players*, as well as obvious "big-name" roles—Hamlet, Shylock, Falstaff, Lear, Macbeth—she also includes groupings of roles, such as the lovers (Proteus, Mercutio, Berowne, Benedick) and the jealous husbands (Leontes, Othello, and Iago), as well as clowns and kings. The best chapters in *Women in Shakespeare* are on Lady Macbeth and Cleopatra, but Cook creates interesting groupings of the young lovers, the historical women, the victims of male injustice, and the practical women.

For a document that is as unique as the performance experiences it captures, have a look at *Shakespeare Comes to Broadmoor*, edited by Murray Cox, in which actors and psychiatrists discuss a performance of *Hamlet* for patients at the infamous English hospital for the criminally insane, the permanent home of some of England's most notorious murderers. What happens to an actor's approach to playing the murderer Claudius when he knows that he will be watched by murderers who can spot the real thing?

The published diaries of actors provide an interesting contrast with observers' records of the rehearsal process. There are some insights that only an actor can provide, but the simple truth is that most actors are either unskilled at the description and analysis of the process or reluctant to submit their intuitive creativity to the potentially debilitating scrutiny of reasoned explanation. This makes their published diaries frustrating for scholars, but actors who know firsthand the rehearsal process being described will be well equipped to fill in the blanks with comparable personal experiences and can sit back and enjoy a good gossip with a colleague.

Whose Shakespeare?

Despite countless demonstrations of the inappropriateness of the assumption, from everyone from John Barton to Joseph Papp, the crippling conclusion that the Brits do Shakespeare best has come to haunt still another generation of young actors. Despite the excitement generated by Hollywood's ventures into Shakespeare's canon, there remains that lurking suspicion that the "serious" student of Shakespeare needs to have a look at the BBC series to understand what the plays are really about. Mel Gibson makes a sexy Hamlet who speaks the language very well because he received traditional (i.e., British) classical training before his role as Mad Max catapulted him to cinematic stardom, and he is Australian, which is almost British, right? When Julie Taymor took on *Titus Andronicus*, she brought together an international cast dominated by British (Anthony Hopkins, Alan Cumming, Jonathan Rhys-Meyers) and almost British (Colm Feore from Canada, among others) actors.

Shakespearean scholars contribute as much to a Brit-centered view of Shakespeare in production when they base entire books of performance criticism upon productions seen only at the Royal Shakespeare Company or the National Theatre. This is not to deny the excellence of some of the actors and some of the productions. But not every actor who has mastered that particular accent and has been cast in a significant role on one of those stages can be said to be, ipso facto, a brilliant Shakespearean actor. Far too many scholars write as if the only interesting discoveries to be made through the examination of productions of the plays can be made through British productions. This snobbery is as misplaced as that which drives the "Oxford wrote the plays" machine.

There are productions of Shakespeare all around the English-speaking world, and although few companies have access to the funding or the clout of the RSC, many have found a way to make Shakespeare come alive for their audiences. Scholars, and even critics, might sneer at the pedestrian, the predictable, the un-British approach, but they forget that when they see a production, their attention is taken up primarily with comparisons; for the majority of the audience this is the first production they have seen, and some of them do not even know what is going to happen next.

Actors are fortunate in being able to have a direct connection with the naïve spectators who dominate their audiences. Weeks of laughter and tears can ease the wounds of a snotty, comparative review. However, when they venture into performance scholarship, the dangerous effects of the elitist bias return. If you read a sufficient number of books and articles on productions of your play, you may begin to think that it is time to develop a British accent and watch every episode of *Playing Shakespeare* six or seven times in order to model yourself after one of those great RSC actors. Despite my enjoyment of Albert Bermel's *Shakespeare at the Moment*, I wondered why he seemed oblivious to exciting North American productions despite his many years in the United States. In his introduction I found the clue: "As a Briton by birth, I grew up on Shakespeare," he announces, and it seems as if his tastes in Shakespearean production and his assumptions about how best to act the plays were formed by this early imprinting and have remained unchallenged since.

Another source of a horrifying lack of confidence in a natural, even naïve, venture into Shakespeare is the diaspora of RSC actors into classrooms and studio workshops around the world. These veterans of some of the best Shakespearean productions have much to teach students about playing the roles, speaking the language, and acting the classics. However, there is simply not a comparable interest on the part of administrators of such programs in bringing in non-British or even non-RSC actors to give comparable workshops that would illuminate how Shakespeare can come alive in a variety of cultural contexts.

The lingering fear that only the Brits can do justice to Shakespeare can also be eradicated by a first-rate stage history of any of the best-known or less often performed plays in the canon. True, the production factory that is the Royal Shakespeare Company will figure largely in any scholarly work and entirely dominate the writings of almost all British and many North American scholars. But all around the world actors and directors are cracking open the complexity of these cultural artifacts and reclaiming them anew. This, combined with the scholar's reminder that the cultured English accent is not, in fact, suitable to the language of Shakespeare (he wrote for a spoken English that would sound to a modern North American like someone from Appalachia or Newfoundland), should free us at last from an inappropriate inferiority complex with regard to the great British actors, directors, and scholars. Let us honor their achievements, but let us not feel that theirs is the only way.

Shakespeare Archives

Another perverse bias is emerging in performance criticism as a result of the availability of productions for exhaustive study. This has resulted in another subgenre of scholarship: Shakespeare on film, which in itself is an interesting subject for debate along the lines of "When should Shakespeare be taken off the writing credits?" But in the specific area of performing Shakespeare, those scholars who wish to write in general terms about how the plays are constructed for performance turn to those productions that have been recorded and thus preserved for repeated viewing. The very limited number of "legitimate" productions (here defined as using only and almost all of Shakespeare's text) is dominated by the BBC series, which contains some very interesting and some excruciatingly bad performances. I am not sure who in the business of doing theatre would want the discussion of the performance of Shakespeare to be framed by this particular selection of documents. Even as astute and theatrical a writer as Albert Bermel fills *Shakespeare at the Moment* with examples from the BBC videos and films by Kenneth Branagh.

ACTING SHAKESPEARE

When my cue comes, call me, and I will answer.

Bottom [*Dream* 4.1.200]

The many books about Shakespeare written by working actors, directors, and teachers have no pretensions to be considered scholarly works and so do not fall easily into the academic disciplines that dominate Shakespeare studies. For actors, however, these are usually the best place to start in your search for concrete, useful strategies for performing Shakespeare in the modern theatre.

Pearls of Wisdom

We are fortunate to have available a growing number of books by master directors and teachers, following in the footsteps of the first of this number to publish the insights based upon years of rehearsing Shakespeare's plays. *Playing*

Shakespeare by John Barton contains countless gems. If you can see the video version, watching the actors work is like watching a professional sports team practice. The excellence, the training, the enthusiasm, the risk taking, and the growing and learning are all captured for us firsthand. For that, I am willing to accept the fact that the book rambles, some things are never fully explained, and the great mystery at the heart of it all—how an actor makes it work— remains a mystery, a function of the unique abilities of these actors and, for those of us who are not British, of the specific accent they use when they are speaking the texts. I have found that students, after watching the tapes, feel a renewed sense of awe for Shakespeare's language, but also an overwhelming sensation that you would have to be one of that magic breed to pull it off.

Even so, Barton remains for me an example of the payoff when scholarship and theatre experience merge in a single individual. I know that he is not everyone's cup of tea. No one director or scholar can ever be that, and in the hothouse of Shakespeare studies, where passions run high as individuals develop strongly held beliefs about "correct" and "incorrect" approaches, anyone with any credibility is going to have vehement detractors. All I can say is that when I first read the book, I was thrilled at the insights it afforded and the scholarship without tears.

Although Barton remains my personal favorite, he is working in a well-established tradition. For example, Bertram Joseph brought what he had learned from doing research into Elizabethan acting styles to theatre companies around the world; you can read all about his discoveries in his book *Acting Shakespeare*. Because his was the first, he grabbed the most obvious title, and everyone else has had to find an alternative way of saying the same thing. You will notice, if you have a look at the book, that 1960 was a long time ago in terms of acting, and students have dismissed this book by saying that it would have been easy for Joseph to help actors to act Shakespeare, "because way back then they all acted in a fake, melodramatic style, right?"

To balance Barton's and Joseph's books, I send students to master teachers whose work is firmly grounded in a contemporary American approach to realist acting. Four recent books are still readily available: Robert Cohen's *Acting Shakespeare*, Malcolm Morrison's *Classical Acting*, Kurt Daw's *Acting Shakespeare and His Contemporaries*, and Wesley Van Tassel's *Clues to Acting Shakespeare*. These authors are first and foremost teachers of acting and secondly actors and/or directors of Shakespeare working in academic or professional settings. As none is a scholar, each has produced a book that essentially documents the process and content of his courses. These books contain many interesting observations and exercises, and although there is some overlap, each master teacher has developed his own approach to the teaching of classical acting. Adrian Brine's *A Shakespearean Actor Prepares*, written with Michael York, is a recent addition to this list. Janet Suzman's *Acting with Shakespeare* is perhaps not as systematic as those by experienced teachers, but the firsthand experience of this successful Shakespearean actor tells on every page.

Actors' Guides to Shakespeare's Language

Although these experienced teachers and directors have much to say about many aspects of acting Shakespeare, a significant proportion of each of their books is dedicated to the challenges that Shakespeare's language presents the modern actor, as are my own two books, *Shakespearean Language* and *Shakespearean Characterization*, prepared as companion texts to *Shakespearean Scholarship*. An actor needs to understand what her character is saying. This requires a firm grasp of the emotional content and the relationships within which the speech act is occurring, all of which is conveyed by or allowed within the intellectual content of the speech. When actors are acting in a modern play, interpretation and exploration of the possibilities suggested by the word on the page are the primary activities of the rehearsal period. Only occasionally does a director or actor have to puzzle through how the sentence conveys what the sentence conveys.

In acting Shakespeare, the emphasis is, at first glance, reversed. Actors feel that they have a firm grasp of the general content, both intellectual and emotional, based in large part upon the traditional portrait of the assigned character and that moment in the play. Therefore, Juliet is clearly expressing love for Romeo in the balcony scene. The challenge to the actor is to figure out why those words in that order convey that particular thought.

It has been my experience that provided an actor actually does expend the intellectual effort to figure out how the language works in the scene, she will discover that there is just as much interpretive richness, complexity, and room for exploration as in a modern text. The greatest danger to less experienced actors is that they will speak the text as a sort of flowing musical accompaniment to a generalized wash of preordained emotion, in full confidence that because they have always thought that the balcony scene was a romantic love scene, that is the full sum of what they should be conveying with these words in this order.

What does it take for a modern actor to discover why those words in that order mean what they do? In order to act Shakespeare, do we have to master such dense scholarly tomes as are found in the history-of-English section of the library, or in that section of the Shakespeare shelves dedicated to lengthy analyses of Shakespeare's language, which are almost impossible to read unless you have a background in linguistics? The answer, fortunately, is "No."

Practical Guidance

The most basic introduction to Shakespeare's language can be found in John Doyle and Ray Lischner's *Shakespeare for Dummies*, which contains a chapter entitled "Why Does Everyone Talk So Funny?" as well as one on jokes and another advice-filled chapter, "How to Read Shakespeare's English." Because the book was created by a director and an actor, the information and the advice are appropriate, specific, and a good place for "dummies" to start.

The most practical introductions for actors to the language of Shakespeare are found, not surprisingly, in books written by professional voice teachers. At the top of this list I would place Cicely Berry's *The Actor and His Text*, followed by Kristin Linklater's *Freeing Shakespeare's Voice*. A third important contributor to this category of book is Patsy Rodenburg, who has not collected her ideas on performing Shakespeare into a single book, but whose observations and exercises in *The Need for Words, The Actor Speaks*, and *The Right to Speak* regularly draw upon Shakespeare and apply directly to classical acting.

What these books have in common is a firm grounding in the physiology of speaking. That is no surprise, because these are voice teachers and coaches, not scholars, not actors, not directors. From that unique vantage point they have been able to acquire a sensitivity toward Shakespeare's language that is deeply informed by the work an actor must do to speak these words convincingly in the modern theatre, and a knowledge of how to glean the text as well as to prepare the vocal instrument to deliver the text. Their ideas have been crystallized through their work with some of the best Shakespearean actors performing in our time. Cicely Berry has long been associated with the Royal Shakespeare Company and Patsy Rodenburg with the National Theatre of Britain. Kristin Linklater's professional credits are American, though she received her training in Britain. Edward S. Brubaker's *Shakespeare Aloud* is now out of fashion, but it remains a useful guide to the very specific challenges of Shakespeare's verse. Even older and less valued, but still insightful and a good general introduction, is *Speaking Shakespeare* by David Hedges and Mita Scott Hedges.

None of these books is the product of scholarship, for which we may be thankful. However, if we are looking for ways of accessing the products of years of activity on the part of specialists in language, then we will want to return to the drier and dustier sections of the library.

General Introductions

A book that stands on the dividing line between dense scholarly studies and pragmatic advice from teachers and coaches is Gert Ronberg's *A Way with Words*. Scholars are quick to sneer at a book like this because it summarizes and generalizes rather than analyzing in depth and entering into the subtleties and complexities that provide grist for the academic mill of debate, rebuttal, confutation, and other excuses for publication. However, if you are looking for an introduction to topics such as rhetoric, sentence structure, or vocabulary, *A Way with Words* contains a richness of detail about Shakespeare's language and is an important resource for any actor seeking an understanding of the mechanics underlying the great theatrical effects described vividly in the books of practitioners.

A relatively recent and wonderfully accessible overview can be found in W.F. Bolton's *Shakespeare's English*. For examples, Bolton uses the history plays, which are some of the least familiar to modern actors. I think that this is a good thing, because the discussion of language can be kept separate from the overlay of preconceived notions about the tragic or comic oratory or wordplay. Also, the histories are relatively early in Shakespeare's writing career, and in them we can see him using the tricks of the trade available to him from the conventions of oratory and dramatic poetry already blended into the muscular and flexible instrument for presenting character and emotion by playwrights like Christopher Marlowe.

Specialized Language Books

There are several books that reward the reader with perseverance, but resist browsing and require the acquisition of a minimal vocabulary for parts of speech and syntactical units. These are the language books that best explain what the scholars have to say about Shakespeare's language, rather than present new theories or the results of the painstaking studies that produce the theories, none of which I would recommend to an actor.

Brian Vickers has published two books that will assist an actor determined to taste firsthand the enriched analysis of language made possible by the work of scholars. *Classical Rhetoric in English Poetry* is like a standard textbook of classical rhetorical forms; by the end you feel like you have received the same sort of schooling that Shakespeare probably did, and if he can do it, why can't you? *The Artistry of Shakespeare's Prose* explains and demonstrates the complex patterns found in prose passages in an effective and striking manner.

Sister Miriam Joseph's books, from an early period of scholarship, are an excellent supplement to Vickers's texts, as she provides the reader of *Shakespeare's Use of the Arts of Language* with a compendium of rhetorical devices and examples of their use taken from the plays. In *Rhetoric in Shakespeare's Time*, Joseph has created a guide to the classical rhetorical devices, their names, and traditional applications, with examples from Shakespeare that illustrate his skill in using well-established word patterns for dramatic effect.

For a thorough survey of Shakespeare's language, I recommend that the brave reader start with N.F. Blake's *Shakespeare's Language: An Introduction.* This is an exhaustive discussion of Shakespeare's use of language, full of the sort of jargon you associate with boring grammar lessons. However, if you can see it through, you will walk away with a firm grasp of the essential building blocks of language and how Shakespeare manipulated them to greatest effect.

Without a doubt, the best book on Shakespeare's verse patterns is George Wright's *Shakespeare's Metrical Art.* A careful and complete reading of this book will remove all of the mystery of scansion and clarify the beauty and complexity of Shakespeare's dramatic poetry. This book is tough going for non-scholars, but if you stick with it, you will find that all of your questions about scansion are answered.

The majority of books on Shakespeare's poetic devices are literary in approach and of no great help to an actor, who very much needs to create personal and active connections between images and emotions. One scholarly book, however, can serve as a sort of dictionary. Caroline Spurgeon's *Shakespeare's Imagery and What It Tells Us* is the first complete catalogue of every image Shakespeare ever used, collected in general categories and analyzed for recurring patterns. A decent index and table of contents make this a useful resource for actors, but the writing style and perspective are poetical rather than theatrical. An actor armed with Kristin Linklater's advice about muscular metaphors can survive the onslaught of Spurgeon's exhaustive lists with heart and energized intuition intact.

Expert and Esoteric Language Studies

For the most part, in preparing this book, I have not included works of scholarship that I felt were excessively specialized or unbearably alienating. In the area of language studies, however, I have included more such titles because of the very specific challenges that face an actor attempting to master the complexities of Shakespeare's language. Even so, I have eliminated a significant number of publications that are even more heavy going than the following products of intense scholarship.

Hilda Hulme's scholarly *Explorations in Shakespeare's Language* is filled with fascinating information about the word usage in specific plays and also with general patterns in language usage. The index and table of contents can help you bypass information you don't need. *A Reader in the Language of Shakespearian Drama*, edited by Vivian Salmon and Edwina Burness, was published in the series Amsterdam Studies in the Theory and History of Linguistic Science, but this collection includes articles that are specific and useful as well as articles filled with the jargon that scholars have developed for the analysis of language. In *Renaissance Perspectives in Literature and the Visual Arts*, Murray Roston sets Shakespeare's use of language in the context of the heritage of visual as well as literary arts; the shared imagery proves captivating and suggests the use of surviving pictorial art to spark acting explorations.

In *Shakespeare's Dramatic Speech*, Anthony J. Gilbert presents an application of modern theories of conversation to the plays of Shakespeare. All of the things that actors are most intuitive about, and most right about, are here accessed in an entirely scholarly manner, a stating of the obvious in fancy language. Bruce R. Smith has produced an interesting study of the sounds that would have been heard inside and out of the theatre, *The Acoustic World of Early Modern England: Attending to the O-factor*, and he writes in an evocative, freewheeling style, but his is not a book for browsing, and although the back cover presents a quotation from a professional voice coach claiming that the book "provides extremely valuable background information for actors," it is so dense and esoteric that only the dedicated specialist is likely to appreciate Smith's achievement.

Grammar

A book that you will often find cited in scholarly notes, and often in notes that are otherwise unintelligible and seemingly unimportant for an actor, is

E.A. Abbott's *A Shakespearian Grammar*. The publication date on this little book is 1886, and at first glance it would seem to be just the dry and dusty sort of tome an actor should most avoid. Thank goodness you can, as all scholarly editors have consulted Abbott extensively and use him regularly to explain the different ways in which word usage in Shakespeare's time followed different grammatical rules than are viewed as correct today. Even so, a quick glance will reveal the pesky problems of those simple words that we assume mean the same today as they did for Shakespeare, when in fact some are used in quite different ways. For example, Abbott informs us that "so" can be used to suggest "on condition that" or "provided that" when it is combined with the future tense, in a form of conditional, or it can be used to mean "in this way, exactly in this manner." "So" is also used as a relative intensifier, as in "I was so angry that . . . ," much as it is today. Abbott is most useful for tricky little words like "that" and "which" and "so" and "were." He records how Shakespeare shifts the tense of verbs, and how he uses prepositions and conjunctions. Of course, to read Abbott, you have to have at your fingertips all of the terminology of grammar, which few of us do these days.

Sometimes Abbott's insights open up the potency of an image that is muted by a modern actor's incorrect assumptions about grammatical usage. For example, Abbott points out that the past participle of a verb used as an adjective can have a greater meaning than we would allow it today. He cites Claudio's speech about death from *Measure for Measure*:

> This sensible warm motion, to become
> A kneaded clod; And the delighted spirit
> To bathe in fiery floods. [3.1.121]

"Kneaded" and "delighted" are past participles of the verbs describing the action of preparing bread dough and taking delight, so we automatically imagine clumps of earth that were once pounded like bread dough and the human spirit that once delighted in the pleasures of the flesh. But Abbott points out another significance of the passive participle: that which was might still be now and is capable of being in the future. In other words, -ed is equivalent to -able. The spirit is now and will always be capable of experiencing delight, but will be doomed to an eternity of fiery floods; the body will experience a future where it is joined forever with the earth, tilled every spring from now to the Judgment Day (275). Abbott's comments offer a subtle difference in meaning, one that is not a requirement for understanding the image Claudio uses, and an actor would be excused for thinking that his first, intuitive reading of the line will do just fine for the purposes of playing the scene. Why undertake the study of grammar unless it is absolutely necessary?

In the style of Abbott, but not as detailed and so less oppressive, is G.L. Brook's *The Language of Shakespeare*. This is not as useful as a dictionary resource, but rewards a skimming look at his lists of words that were used in a

different manner then as compared to now. This is the sort of study that frees
the actor from the tyranny of the footnotes. By absorbing the information set
out by Brook, you can begin to find the four-hundred-year-old language patterns customary rather than off-putting.

The Language of Shakespeare's England

Scholars who edit Shakespeare's plays and help a modern actor to untangle
the unfamiliar language are serving as intermediaries between a wide variety
of specialists and those with entirely theatrical considerations. Although the
most detailed and scholarly introductions to early modern English are not
likely to attract even a casual glance, they sometimes contain buried nuggets
of gold that fascinate and illuminate. For example, in Charles Barber's *Early
Modern English* there is a fascinating section entitled "Written and Spoken Language" in which are reproduced excerpts from the published transcripts of the
trial of Charles I in 1649, which seem to record something very close to what
was actually said, in other words, with less than the usual tidying up and
formalizing after the fact. He also surveys the plays of the period, looking for
scenes that might be credible evocations of everyday talking. He then analyzes
these snippets, noting how colloquialisms, common proverbs and oaths, and
broken sentences give the illusion of "lively speech." Barber also suggests those
markers of ordinary talk that appear in modern naturalistic scripts but that are
notably missing from his examples. These include all of the pause fillers (um,
ah, er) and the mindless repetitions that come out of the mouth mechanically
as the mind races, searching for words to express thoughts. Is this because
Elizabethans had different habitual activities to cover the disjunction of mind
and mouth, or because the conventions of stage representation valued speed
and forward movement over the evocation of the halting, tedious language
use of the street and kitchen? Barber feels under no obligation to suggest an
answer, but the question is an important one for actors to keep in mind.

Barber's next section, "Language Written for Oral Delivery," draws upon
the evidence of published sermons, which sometimes were circulated days after
the public delivery by the well-known priest. Here is the opening of Hugh
Latimer's "Sermon of the Plough," with the spelling and punctuation from the
first printing:

Moyses was a meruelous man, a good man. Moyses was a wonderful felowe, and dyd
his dutie being a married man. We lacke suche as Moyses was. Well, I woulde al men
woulde loke to their dutie, as God hath called them, and then we choulde haue a
florishyng christian commune weale. And nowe I would aske a straung question. Who
is the most diligent bishoppe and prelate in al England, that passeth al the reste in
doinge his office? I can tel, for I knowe him, who it is: I knowe hym well. But nowe
I thynke I se you lysting and hearkening, that I shoulde name him. There is one that
passeth al the other, and is the most diligent prelate and precher in al England. And
wl ye knowe who it is? I wyl tel you. It is the Deuyl. (58)

To assist a modern reader in standing up and saying these words in full voice, here is the same text with modern spellings:

Moses was a marvellous man, a good man. Moses was a wonderful fellow, and did his duty being a married man. We lack such as Moses was. Well, I would all men would look to their duty, as God hath called them, and then we should have a flourishing Christian commonweal. And now I would ask a strange question. Who is the most diligent bishop and prelate in all England, that passeth all the rest in doing his office? I can tell, for I know him, who it is: I know him well. But now I think I see you listing and harkening, that I should name him. There is one that passeth all the other, and is the most diligent prelate and preacher in all England. And will ye know who it is? I will tell you. It is the Devil.

Barber's commentary on the language of this sermon suggests that this is popular oratory at work, in contrast to the learned rhetoric of the sophisticated and carefully constructed formal speechifying. Barber goes so far as to suggest that this might well be a record of "an unscripted performance by a highly skilled and experienced preacher, reconstructed afterwards from the performer's notes and the transcripts of shorthand writers" (59). A modern actor, coming upon such information and analysis, can only be thankful for Professor Barber's lifelong research in this specialized field. For anyone interested in exploring this highly specialized branch of scholarship, I recommend Manfred Görlach's *Introduction to Early Modern English.*

SHAKESPEARE'S FIRST THEATRES

> Pat, pat, and here's a marvellous convenient place for our rehearsal. This green plot shall be our stage, this hawthorn brake our tyring house, and we will do it in action, as we will do it before the Duke.
>
> Peter Quince [*Dream* 3.1.2]

In addition to learning about Shakespeare's language, the modern actor will need to know something about Shakespeare's theatre practice. As this is a particularly productive area of Shakespearean scholarship, you will have little difficulty finding good general introductions as well as works on specific topics.

Although it does not benefit from recent developments in scholarship following archeological excavations in London, the third volume of the series published by Methuen under the title *The Revels History of Drama in English,* edited by J.L. Barroll, contains a useful introduction to the production of Shakespeare's plays from the perspective of the theatre historian. Here you will find lists of plays performed at court and in the various public theatres, a fascinating snapshot of what must have been a vibrant and thrilling theatrical environment for Shakespeare the young actor. You will be immediately struck by how many of the titles are of plays forever lost to us. We will never know, for example, what might have been the plot of *The Witch of Islington*, which received one performance in July of 1597. We also will never know if Shakespeare had a hand in the creation of any of the lost plays, or what he might have borrowed shamelessly from them. Collections of information such as are found in these books remind us of the danger of coming to conclusions about Shakespeare's theatrical career, given the absence of so many important documents.

The bedrock of most theatrical history of Shakespeare's era is the painstaking collection of documented evidence compiled by E.K. Chambers in his four-volume work *The Elizabethan Stage*. Here you will find every scrap of concrete information available to theatrical historians as they attempt to answer some of the essential questions: How were the plays performed, by whom, for whom, under what conditions of rehearsal and production, with what sort of economic success, within what sort of organizational structure? Gerald Bentley undertook a similarly exhaustive study (seven volumes) of *The Jacobean and Caroline Stage*, also of interest because Shakespeare's career spans the monarchies of Elizabeth and James. These many volumes are invaluable when you are looking for answers to specific questions.

One of the dangers of general introductions to Shakespeare's theatre found in the various companions, guides, general introductions, and complete works, is that they do not have the mandate of placing Shakespeare's theatre into a larger historical context, that of the development of drama in England. Much of what would have influenced the actors in the first productions would have come from the inherited traditions of theatrical performance that would have encompassed plays and performance settings that predate the Globe, Blackfriars, and royal entertainments for Elizabeth and James. I recommend J.L. Styan's *The English Stage*. Here you will find a straightforward history greatly influenced by Styan's own scholarly interest in the staging of Shakespeare's plays. I also recommend Tiffany Stern's *Rehearsal from Shakespeare to Sheridan* for a persuasive theory about rehearsal practices in Shakespeare's Globe.

Also housed near Chambers and Bentley you will find reproductions of many of the documents to which theatre historians often refer. I happen to enjoy looking at reproductions of Philip Henslowe's diary, a reprint of which by R.A. Foakes and R.T. Rickert, along with other surviving documents, provides the scholars with the few bits of factual information that they must weave into a coherent theory about exactly how the plays were staged.

Documents of Court Performances

Another source of information about how Shakespeare's plays were performed comes to us from court documents in association with the fairly regular theatrical entertainments supervised by the Office of the Revels. For those who enjoy direct contact with actual historical artifacts, the *Materialien zur Kunde des älteren Englischen Dramas* series has been published, *Documents Relating to the Office of the Revels in the Time of Queen Elizabeth,* edited by Albert Feuillerat. Here you can open up a folded page and read about the various items purchased, including "Rushes . . . mosse, holie, and Ivie" or "A paire of Silvered ffoiles." The accounts also include fascinating details like lists of performances, bringing to mind the courtly entertainments offered Theseus in response to his cry:

> Come now, what masques, what dances shall we have,
> To wear away this long age of three hours,
> Between our after-supper, and bed-time?
> Where is our usual manager of mirth?
> What Revels are in hand? Is there no play,
> To ease the anguish of a torturing hour? [*Dream* 5.1.32]

Here are two items from 1584:

An invention of three plays in one prepared to have been showed before her highness on Shrove Sonday at night and to have been enacted by her majesty's servants at Somerset place. But the Queen came not abroad that night, yet was employed on the same one house and battlement. (365)

An antique play and a comedy showed presented and enacted before her highness on Shrovetuesday at night at Somerset place by her majesty's servants wheron was employed one house. (365)

Does this not sound very much like Theseus's options for entertainment? They include "The battle with the Centaurs to be sung by an Athenian Eunuch, to the harp," "The riot of the tipsy Bacchanals, tearing the Thracian singer, in their rage," "The thrice three Muses, mourning for the death of Learning, late deceased in beggary," and, his choice for the evening's entertainment, "A tedious brief Scene of young Pyramus, and his love Thisbe; very tragical mirth" [*Dream* 5.1.46]. We are reminded too of the range of performances suggested by Polonius when he announces the arrival of the players in Elsinore: "The best Actors in the world, either for Tragedy, Comedy, History, Pastoral: Pastoral-Comical-Historical-Pastoral: Tragical-Historical: Tragical-Comical-Historical-Pastoral: Scene individable, or Poem unlimited. Seneca cannot be too heavy, nor Plautus too light" [*Hamlet* 2.2.396].

Here is another list of items supplied by the propertymaker John Carow in 1574:

Monsters, Mountaynes, fforestes, Beastes, Serpentes, Weapons for warr as gunnes, dagges, bowes, Arowes, Bills, holberdes, borespeares, fawchions daggers, Targettes, pollaxes, clubbes headdes & headpeeces Armor counterfet Moss, holly, Ivye, Bayes, flowers quarters, glew, past, paper, and suche lyke with Nayles hoopes horsetailes dishes for devells eyes heaven, hell & the devell & all the devell I should saie but not all. (241)

One can only imagine the extravaganza being performed.

There are many summaries of the information contained in the court documents, for which you will be thankful if you try to find useful information from Feuillerat's book, which contains no indexes or table of contents. On the other hand, there is something to be said for having a look yourself, rather than letting the scholars suggest what is important in the source according to their values and agendas, which can be quite different from an actor's.

The Old Globe

Academic books on Shakespeare's theatres are some of the best examples of the scholarly agenda at work. The demands of this particular discipline require that the author demonstrate, in exhaustive detail, the source of any facts used to build a theory, and further that the author defend this particular theory against other scholars' speculations. This can make for a tedious experience for the non-specialist. Of the many, many books in this field, I find the writing of Andrew Gurr to be the most theatrical and accessible, and would recommend in particular *Rebuilding Shakespeare's Globe* and the book he wrote with Mariko Ichikawa, *Staging in Shakespeare's Theatres*. I also enjoyed Peter Thomson's *Shakespeare's Theatre*, and John Orell's contribution to the scholarly debates, *The Quest for Shakespeare's Globe*. Recent archeological explorations in London, and the reconstruction of the Globe based upon the most recent victors in the scholarly debates, makes obsolete any book on this topic published before 1980. In no other area of scholarship has the older generation been so completely dethroned.

The New Globe

Any discussion of the Globe Theatre must now take into account Sam Wanamaker's project of rebuilding the Globe. J.R. Mulryne and Margaret Shewring have put together *Shakespeare's Globe Rebuilt*, a collection of articles that document the controversies and compromises, complete with insights from acheologists and carpenters and discussions about implications for performers when the past is considered in light of the present. Although I am sceptical about our capacity to replicate a Shakespearean performance by inviting a group of tourists to pretend to be Elizabethans (the encouragement of vocal responses seems to result in the replication of hissing the villain and cheering the hero from an old melodrama), without doubt this book will arouse nothing but respect and admiration for Wanamaker's vision and strength of will.

The Acting Companies

Of less usefulness for the practical considerations of rehearsing and performing the plays, but of interest nonetheless to actors of Shakespeare, are the many excellent scholarly books on the theatrical companies of Shakespeare's time. Occasionally Shakespeare does make reference to his occupation when he can draw a useful comparison between the character's situation and an actor's, as when Beatrice chides a stunned Claudio with, "Speak Count, 'tis your cue" [*Much Ado* 2.1.305], or Coriolanus says when he, too, is taken by surprise, "Like a dull Actor now, / I have forgot my part, / And I am out, even to a full Disgrace [5.3.40].

But these general references to the experience of acting seem generic, equally as applicable to the amateur thespians like Bottom or Holofernes in the audience as to the newly established companies of professional players. The economic and organizational structure of the Lord Chamberlain's Men does not seem to have provided much metaphoric material for Shakespeare's creative musings.

Andrew Gurr has made a major contribution to the historical scholarship on this topic, and I would recommend *The Shakespearian Playing Companies* for its fifth chapter, entitled "Settled Practices," which provides an actor with an overview of the working conditions of an actor in Shakespeare's time. Michael Hattaway's *Elizabethan Popular Theatre: Plays in Performance* is another book that will provide you with more details than the basic introductions mentioned earlier. In the second part of his book, Hattaway discusses five plays, only one of which, *Titus Andronicus* is by Shakespeare, so it is for the first section that I would recommend his work. The layout of the theatre, the logistics of performing, and the makeup of the acting companies are clearly explained.

Another good introduction to the life of the average actor in Shakespeare's theatre can be found in Gerald Bentley's general introductions to his field of study, *The Profession of Dramatist in Shakespeare's Time* and *The Profession of Player in Shakespeare's Time*, handy alternatives to his seven-volume *The Jacobean and Caroline Stage*. Bentley is obliged to document for his scholarly readers the source of his information, which slows down the story he tells of the working conditions, various financial considerations, and the hierarchy of the theatre companies. His seventh chapter in *The Profession of Player*, "London Companies on Tour," might be of interest to actors in *Hamlet*, for example, to assist in the creation of a credible troupe of players arriving in Elsinore, with the attending uncertainties, interpersonal relationships, and city-bred reputation. In *The Profession of Dramatist* he must address the fact that Shakespeare is an anomaly in that he was both an actor and a playwright, and, more importantly, that he was a shareholder in the company and therefore enjoyed a completely different, more advantageous financial and contractual relationship. If you are interested in this aspect of an Elizabethan playwright's life, you will want to read Bentley's chapters on relationships with acting companies, methods of payment, and contractual obligations.

Bentley has some very straightforward and general things to say about collaborations between playwrights, which are a burning issue for scholars and less than significant for actors, particularly anyone who has participated in a workshop of a new script. The more exciting and vigorous the process, the less likely it is that anyone will be able to remember who contributed what, and yet everyone is quite satisfied to see the name of a single playwright on the program or published text.

It is impossible for scholars to decide how political Shakespeare was, and how much contemporary social commentary his plays contained. Some point to his powerful patrons and his success as a court writer, suggesting that he actively promoted the interests of the powerful at the expense of the very real injustices experienced by ordinary folk. Others, like Annabel Patterson, argue persuasively that Shakespeare, like all of the popular writers of the era, knew just how to signal to the general public the real message hidden so that the censors could not pin the crime on the company performing. In *Shakespeare and the Popular Voice* you can read Patterson's vivid portrait of Shakespeare as guerilla playwright, speaking out on important issues during an oppressive reign of right-wing reactionaries who set up systems of all-encompassing censorship and then could not trap our tricky wordsmith, though everyone else in the audience was in on the joke. Along the way, you will learn about all sorts of contemporary events that were very much "in the air" and would have influenced the first actors' attitudes to the characters and events of the plays, even if Patterson's Shakespeare is a figment of her longing that the great playwright not be a puppet of the establishment.

Shakespeare quite wisely kept his head down and avoided the sort of scandal that saw his good friend Ben Jonson in prison for writing *The Isle of Dogs*, which dared to make some rude and critical comments about powerful people. As a reward, he and his troupe received patronage from the most powerful nobles in the land and performed regularly for Elizabeth; when James ascended to the throne, they became the King's Men.

Considering the potential for antiauthoritarian risk taking on the part of Shakespeare's first actors can serve to challenge our assumptions about the tone of certain scenes. For example, one of the more tedious scenes to play in *Macbeth* involves Macduff and Malcolm in the testing scene. We leave behind the horrors of Scotland for this duet, as Macduff in England tries to find out if Malcolm, son of the murdered King Duncan, will return at the head of an army to defeat the evil Macbeth. Malcolm, for some strange reason, tests Macduff by describing himself as an absolutely hideous individual who will make a terrible king. As he adds sin upon sin, Macduff tries to argue that he would still be better than Macbeth, until the pile grows too large and Macduff is forced to give up hope for his beloved Scotland. Malcolm then reveals that the entire list was a hoax, that he is pure and good and everything you would want in a king, and it is time to go kill that murdering usurper, right?

It takes a bit of intellectual maneuvering for the actor playing Malcolm to figure out why he would do this to loyal, heartsick Macduff. It doesn't help that we know that Macduff's wife and children have just been butchered back in Scotland, and his cousin is about to arrive to tell him the news. It is bad enough having to provide filler between these two scenes, but what sort of pointless filler is this?

The task is even more difficult if the director refuses to cut the references to the king of England, in whose court Malcolm has taken refuge and who is providing the exiled Scots with an army. Shakespeare has inserted a discussion of this man's God-given ability to cure a type of skin disease just by touching the sufferer. Scholars gleefully tell you all about James I and this old superstition, and how Bill was clearly setting out to flatter the new king with several references to his ancient royal lineage in the play.

None of that will help a modern actor put much zing into the scene. But listen to this interesting historical aside. Take the list of despicable characteristics that Malcolm attributes to himself. Each and every one of these was attributed to James. So instead of being the saintly royal Scot, he was actually the evil horror that Malcolm is describing. Now, imagine being the poor actor in the role playing Macbeth at the court before James. As Malcolm starts the scene, he knows that everyone in the court, including the king, will catch the insulting references to James's shaky morality. Will the king pretend that he doesn't get it? Or will he rise, like Claudius in *Hamlet*, and cry for lights [3.2.270], as Elizabeth once did to interrupt a court performance that did not please her? Will the players be arrested and thrown in the Tower? As each sin is added to the list, it might be the one that forces James to retaliate. Similarly, each sin might be the one to tip Macduff over the edge. Suddenly, the actor playing Malcolm realizes just what a dangerous game he is playing, toying with volatile and armed men who have a great deal to lose and little patience with psychodrama.

Nothing has changed in the basic interpretation of the scene. Macduff is still being tested, and what is at stake is still the definition of kingship. But the test is now a dangerous one for the actor as well as the character, and Malcolm is gambling more than just an intellectual one-upmanship. We can never know if this interpretation of Macbeth at the court is historically correct, but it doesn't matter. We do know that the play appears to flatter a king who was not a very nice human being in exactly the ways that Malcolm describes. The rest is exciting conjecture that fuels an actor's creative work on a role, and we shall let the ends justify the means, as we are not historians but artists. No one need ever know what we used to give the scene its cut and jab, its danger and emotion. We just thank the history books that we found something that got us out of a dull, "correct" reading of the scene.

Leonard Tennenhouse sets each of Shakespeare's genres into the context of contemporary royal politics in *Power on Display: The Politics of Shakespeare's Genres*. The opening pages of each section are the most valuable for actors because they provide an interesting grouping of historical bits and pieces. Unfortunately, what follows is then a discussion of various plays that moves into that territory of interpretation that muddies the waters, as do all of the thematic "readings" of the plays.

Censorship

Bentley also includes some information about the regulations governing theatrical performance. Censorship, both overt and indirect, is one aspect of stage production that needs to be understood by the modern actor, not as an example of cultural history, but as one of the conditions that affected directly what Shakespeare could include in his plays and what he had to imply in order for his play to be passed for performance, for his troupe to be selected for court appearances, and for him to avoid arrest and punishment for blasphemy, libel, or treason.

The Boy Players

As a specialized category of Shakespearean theatre history, there are a number of books on the presentation of female characters by the young apprentices of the company. I have always found that the consideration of this aspect of Shakespeare's theatre practice creates layers of confusion for modern actors, for even if you happen to be cast in an all-male production, the way a modern audience "reads" drag today does not seem to have any correspondence to the way Shakespeare's first audience made sense of boy actors playing girl characters, a significant number of whom then disguise themselves as boys.

For those interested in this topic, I would recommend Stephen Orgel's *Impersonations*, as he is as much interested in social history and theatre history as he is in literary analysis. Michael Shapiro also includes this sort of information in his more traditional literary analysis of the cross-dressing heroines in Shakespeare's plays, *Gender in Play on the Shakespearean Stage*.

Upon hearing of a troupe of players, Hamlet lists the members of the company before he even knows which company it is. From this we gain a snapshot of the expected line of business for which the leading players would become known, and an audience member's enthusiastic response:

He that plays the King shall be welcome; his Majesty shall have Tribute of me: the adventurous Knight shall use his Foil and Target: the Lover shall not sigh gratis, the humourous man shall end his part in peace: the Clown shall make those laugh whose lungs are tickled o'the sere: and the Lady shall say her mind freely; or the blank Verse shall halt for't. [2.2.319]

All of this is, of course, a direct contrast to real life in Elsinore, where kings are murdered or conspired against, knights hesitate, lovers are separated, humor-infected individuals like Claudius are marked for murder, the court fool Yorick is dead, and the women are almost completely silenced by the oppressive love of the men who rule their world.

What follows next is almost always cut as a digression into the war of the theatres that theatre historians find interesting but that leaves modern audiences entirely in the dark. The actors playing the roles of these visiting players will want to have a look, for the lines contain great clues for the backstory of these characters. First of all, Hamlet himself was clearly a patron of their city theatre, and by consulting some books on performances at the Globe you will be able to come up with many specific images of just where he might have sat (on the stage itself), how he might have demonstrated his enjoyment (with presents for his favorite performers), and how familiar his face would be to the players for both those reasons.

Buried in the digression are some interesting clues about the life of the players. We learn, for example, that it is possible for a troupe to fall out of favor with the general public by growing rusty; this surely will affect the manner in which the players respond to Hamlet's question about their capacity to play *The Murder of Gonzago* with twenty-four hours' notice. They are not rusty, no sir! We also learn that boy players grow up to become common players, another clue for the backstory the actors might develop. The boy travelling with the company, who plays the wife in *The Murder of Gonzago*, comes in for special attention from Hamlet, who greets him with "What, my young Lady and Mistress? By'r lady, your Ladyship is nearer to Heaven than when I saw you last, by the altitude of a Chopine. Pray God, your voice like apiece of uncurrent Gold be not cracked within the ring" [2.2.424]. An intimacy and familiarity with life in the theatre is suggested by this greeting and by his address to the other player he greets personally: "O, my old friend" [2.2.422].

THE SWAN OF AVON

> Thou art a Monument, without a tomb,
> And art alive still, while thy Book doth live,
> And we have wits to read, and praise to give.
>
> Jonson, *The First Folio*

We cannot conclude our survey of Shakespeare's acting companies without considering William himself, who was an actor and shareholder in the company in addition to being the resident playwright. It is fashionable these days for scholars to conclude that he was not a good actor and to assume that he was content with minor roles such as Adam in *As You Like It* or the ghost of Hamlet's father, roles that would allow him plenty of time to sit out front and coach the others or sneak away for some additional writing time. There is much to be said, however, for the alternative view that Shakespeare was a skilled performer, though Richard Burbage was the star of the company, and that his plays are so actor-friendly because he was one himself. We will never know, of course, because the records do not contain that sort of information. What we do know for sure about the man is so limited that biographers have plenty of room for speculation, thus fueling the production of annual additions to this section of the academic library.

Biographies of Shakespeare

Every library will contain a biography of Shakespeare, and a university library will have an entire collection. These fall into two general styles. Some strive to tell the story of this man's life, making use of the known facts and filling the gaps with reasonable speculation based upon the social history of the times. The theory is that Shakespeare, being a man of his times, would have lived his life relatively normally. Other biographers link what is known about Shakespeare with the plays themselves, seeking always to find reflections of a life lived in the fantasies the man created for the theatre. Either style of biography will be a useful source for an actor looking for the information on the general social history of the times. The indexes of the nonliterary biographies can be used to track down information on such topics as "usury," for which Shylock is so roundly condemned in *The Merchant of Venice* but which both Shakespeare and his father undertook as a way of putting their money to work for them in the expanding economy of early modern England.

My personal favorite happens to be Russell Fraser in *Young Shakespeare* and *Shakespeare, the Later Years*, who blends just enough social history with interesting links to the plays themselves to satisfy what I am looking for in a biography. His indexed comments on usury fill me in on current laws, actual practices, and the facts of Shakespeare's and his father's involvement in the lending of money for interest. I find it fascinating that Shakespeare was such a good businessman. It helps me to reread *The Merchant of Venice* in a refreshingly new way, without assuming that Shylock is a monster simply because Antonio smugly announces, "I neither lend nor borrow / By taking, nor by giving of excess" [1.3.61].

Park Honan's contribution to the biography sector of Shakespearean scholarship, *Shakespeare: A Life*, is, as might be expected from a publication of Oxford University Press, a scholarly work of eminent respectability. He has followed in the literary tradition, and his index lists each of the plays and also the poems, with individual listings for twelve of the sonnets. For *Hamlet* there are scattered references and a twelve-page chunk of the book dedicated to the play. The twelve pages begin with a discussion of a significant contemporary event mentioned in the play (the Poets' Wars) and end with reference to the success the play enjoyed. Sandwiched in the middle is a discussion of the elements of the plot and theme set in the context of the biographical facts, a general category that includes attitudes, conventions, biblical references, and the documented events in Shakespeare's personal and working lives. In *Shakespeare, the Evidence* Ian Wilson sets the available evidence into the broadest possible context, one created by a careful consideration of the plays, the events in England at the turn of the century, and social and cultural conditions within which the plays were written and performed. I have found his book to be the most compelling rebuttal to any suggestion that the plays were actually written by someone other than the glover's son from Stratford.

Another favorite biographer is Peter Thomson, who has chosen to include in *Shakespeare's Professional Career* a greater amount of social history and a correspondingly lesser amount of speculation about the gaps in the documented life of Shakespeare. For example, his second chapter includes a fascinating short history of the Stanley family, invaluable for anyone playing a courtier in one of the royal plays.

Another historian who has as much to say about Shakespeare's theatre as about the life of the man himself is Samuel Burton. His book *Shakespeare's Life and Stage* contains a useful overview of the very few known facts of the life and the far greater amount of information we have about how the theatres worked. Burton has written a straightforward and enjoyable story of personalities, economics, excitement, and theatrical competition, with minimal participation in scholarly debates.

As an alternative to a biography that fills in the gaps with general social history, we have books like Leeds Barroll's *Politics, Plague, and Shakespeare's Theater*, which places Shakespeare and his plays into the margins so that those events and concerns that dominated his years in London can be examined in detail. Barroll tells a compelling story of Shakespeare the London theatre man and Shakespeare the court entertainer, weaving together the few bits of documented evidence about Shakespeare with the far greater amount of detail that we know about the city, the court, and the monarchs. His index lists comments on the various plays, but is far more useful if one is looking up the name of a well-known individual. He also has a great deal to say about the plague, as might be expected from his title, and I would recommend this book for that reason alone.

Another entry in the literary biography canon that makes all of the obvious connections between the plays and the man's life is Dennis Kay's *Shakespeare: His Life, Work, and Era*. It also boasts an excellent index in which each play has a listing with separate citations for the different places in the book where a connection has been made. Perhaps because this is not the product of a university press, Kay has been able to tell the story and let the footnotes fall where they may, in this case in a very general discussion of sources for each chapter at the end of the book. Kay's discussion of *The Merchant of Venice* is representative of the benefits actors can enjoy in a literary biography. The first listing in the index is the five-page discussion of the play, which occurs in Kay's seventh chapter, "Right Happy and Copious Industry," in which Kay deals with the flourish of plays from *King John* to *Much Ado about Nothing*. Kay's index then goes into the details of the connections he has made, which include the commercial issues in the play, its relationship to Christopher Marlowe's *The Jew of Malta*, the portrait of learned women, and various topical references, in which category Kay includes the trial and execution of the queen's physician

Dr. Roderigo Lopez, accused of attempted assassination of the queen by poison, the presence in the queen's corps of musicians of members of the Bassiani
family, and an allusion to Essex's capture of the famous treasure ship *San
Andres*, known popularly as the *Andrew*. It is here that Kay points out Shakespeare's familiarity not only with the recovery of debts in a court of law, but
also with the practice of usury. Kay also lists in his index references to purely
literary aspects of the play, as well as its performance at court and an assess-
ment of its popularity with Shakespeare's audiences. None of these issues are
entered into in any detail, so his book can be used for just the sort of general
introduction that best suits an actor seeking relief from scholarly overkill.

I recommend a cover-to-cover reading of a literary biography to any actor
who has received inspiration knowing that, like Viola and Sebastian in *Twelfth
Night*, Shakespeare's own children Judith and Hamnet were male/female twins,
or who has found in Shakespeare's own less-than-happy marriage (perhaps
following an unexpected pregnancy) an explanation of Prospero's stern injunction to Miranda and Ferdinand:

> If thou dost break her Virgin-knot, before
> All sanctimonious ceremonies may
> With full and holy rite, be ministered,
> No sweet aspersion shall the heavens let fall
> To make this contract grow; but barren hate,
> Sour-eyed disdain, and discord shall bestrew
> The union of your bed, with weeds so loathly
> That you shall hate it both: Therefore take heed. [*Tempest* 4.1.15]

Any attempt to understand the plays themselves that relies upon information
about the private life of the writer is very much out of fashion in literary
circles, but that need not stop an actor whose development of character is
assisted by such connections. Those of us who have a working relationship
with a living playwright know firsthand that the relationship between the writer
and the words on the page is never as simplistic as self-indulgent autobiography
might be: there is always a bond between what the writer has experienced and
what the words evoke on the stage. Literary scholars hate such connections
because they can never be clarified or ascertained as true. Actors love such
connections because they inspire richly without setting limits.

The little factual evidence we have about Shakespeare ensures a steady diet
of biographies, each of which fills in the gaps to suit the theories and assumptions of the author. About one part of his life, however, none can do any more
than fantasize, because we have absolutely no record of any sort between 1585,
when his twins Hamnet and Judith were baptized, and 1592, when he is mentioned in Robert Greene's attack on rival writers as "in his own conceit the
only Shake-scene in a country." Certain assumptions about his life in Stratford
are generally held, in large part because we know a fair amount about his

father, John. Almost every biographer has young William attending the local grammar school but not university, forming a relationship with the older Anne Hathaway and marrying her a few months before the birth of their first child, Susanna, and then leaving Stratford and his young family in order to have established a theatrical career by 1592.

Many scholars and amateur historians have spent years combing all available sources for the slightest possible mention of anyone who might have been William Shakespeare. This provides the modern biographer with assorted bits and pieces of memorabilia, gossip, anecdote, and elusive notation in house records, diaries, and wills, either to discount and exclude or to use as the foundation for some version of events as Russell Fraser does in *Young Shakespeare*. E.A.J. Honigmann theorizes that Shakespeare was a schoolteacher, that he began his theatrical writing quite a few years before 1592, and that he was a Catholic. But as his primary purpose in *Shakespeare: The Lost Years* is proving his case, his book is representative of a third category of biography that is not much use to an actor: the detailed presentation of factual evidence for the sole purpose of discounting the theories of others. In this, Honigmann is following in the tradition of an older generation of biographers, best represented by E.K. Chambers and Samuel Schoenbaum, who set the highest possible standard for the meticulous sifting of documents and verification of evidence.

The long history of Shakespearean biography is itself the subject of some scholarly works. I very much enjoyed the way that Jonathan Bate took me through the shifts and changes in attitudes towards Shakespeare's achievement in *The Genius of Shakespeare*.

The most extensive study, updated as recently as 1991, is S. Schoenbaum's *Shakespeare's Lives*, which will take you from those things recorded about the man during his life through the various legends that were passed around in the years following his death to the great biographers of the intervening years, not forgetting the extremes of bardolatry and rival claimants for the position of the true author of these plays. Scholars like Schoenbaum might sneer at the less scholarly biographers, deeming their books "pop bios" because they represent nothing new in research or illuminating theory. However, for an actor they are the ideal means of acquiring an overview of the man and his world, minus the boring presentation of documentation and the furious decrying of the theories of others.

Gossip

Many of the stories about famous people in Shakespeare's England are very likely apocryphal. Either the narrated event did not happen or the anecdote that has come down to us is highly exaggerated. One such story concerns the joke Shakespeare is said to have played on his leading performer Richard Burbage. Burbage was starring as the hunchback Richard III, and one day a very merry wife of London town was in the audience and made it clear that

she would be interested in a liaison with the energetic actor following the
performance. Somehow, Shakespeare got wind of this and hurried away from
the theatre while Burbage was removing his costume and hunchback. When
Burbage arrived at the generous lady's bedroom door, it was locked, so he
knocked and announced himself. From inside the room he heard the voice of
Shakespeare calling out, "William the Conqueror came before Richard the
Third."

There is much that is suspect in this story. Gossip about lusty actors and
immoral wives has a tendency to be exaggerated; we will never know if either
Burbage or Shakespeare took advantage of their theatrical reputation to win
conquests from among their audience, much less use such a conquest to make
a joke about the historical lineage of England's kings. But what is enjoyable
about this story is that it might be true, and the fact that it was thought to be
true by people who lived only a generation or two from that age gives it added
attraction.

A collection of such gossiping anecdotes, most of them shamelessly apoc-
ryphal, has been published by the Penguin English Library in *Aubrey's Brief
Lives*, edited by Oliver Lawson Dick. The "Brief Lives" collected by John
Aubrey, along with his autobiographical "Life and Times," contains countless
character sketches, often rude, frequently entertaining, and never accurate.
William Shakespeare's is one of the lives Aubrey describes, and we learn:

Though, as Ben Jonson sayes of him, that he had little Latine and lesse Greek, he
understood Latine pretty well: for he had been in his younger yeares a schoolmaster
in the countrey. He was wont to say that he never blotted out a line in his life. Sayd
Ben Jonson, I wish he had blotted out a thousand. (335)

From Aubrey's brief entry about Edward de Vere, earl of Oxford (he whom
some claim to be the true author of the plays), we learn:

This Earle of Oxford, making of his low obeisance to Queen elizabeth, happened to
let a Fart, at which he was so abashed and ashamed that he went to Travell, 7 yeares.
On his returen the Queen welcomed him home, and sy, My Lord, I had forgott the
Fart. (357)

We will never know if this event did indeed take place, but I find it more
credible that this occurred than that de Vere wrote the plays we call Shakespeare's.

The Oxford Controversy

The books that have been written "proving" that the plays we admire today
were in fact not written by the glover's son from Stratford can be found sitting
on the library shelf next to the literary or historical biographies of William

Shakespeare. The various biographers no longer even bother to debate each other; each side is so firmly entrenched in the view that the facts are best interpreted by such radically opposing explanations that an onlooker can only marvel that both sides find their own view so credible. The contrary explanations cannot both be true.

I have always thought that any effort to reassign authorship of the plays stems from class prejudice combined with a misperception of the status of playwrights in early modern England. We are so used to thinking of these plays as the flower of English literature that we forget that they were never created for publication, that in-house playsmiths working in the new professional theatres were not members of the intelligentsia, and that the work was immensely time-consuming contract writing, not the leisure artistic activity of a well-educated member of the elite. The thought that a love of language, a sensitivity to a wide variety of human experiences, and a flair for the theatrical could not possibly emerge from an ignoble autodidact, but only from someone with noble blood and a classical education, is mocked by the evidence of great writers from all over the world. I have read many of these books and enjoyed them, but they have left me entirely unconvinced. I am happy to live with not knowing for sure, or rather knowing that many possible stories fit the available facts, but in all of them the plays were written by a glover's son from Stratford.

Although the books in support of Oxford as the author of these plays make for interesting reading, an actor is not particularly concerned with the relative validity of either claim. Kristin Linklater, a voice teacher whose book *Freeing Shakespeare's Voice* contains many important insights, concludes with a chapter stating her conviction that Oxford wrote the plays:

Oxford's life seems to root and anchor the plays, and I include this glimpse of Edward DeVere because of the delight and excitement I experienced when the man behind the plays came to life in my mind. He was a passionate man, romantic and rash and intellectually profound. His story brings flesh and blood and breath to the voice I hear throughout the plays of William Shake-speare. (213)

Nothing she says in this final chapter, however, changes in any way the implications of all the rest of what she has to say about performing the plays.

An entirely new set of historical assumptions comes into play if you wish to recast the author as a member of the nobility, writing as many as fifteen years earlier than we have assumed these plays to have been written, and influenced by a completely different set of life experiences. In this reading, the dark spirit of the late comedies and great tragedies is thought to reflect the author's depression at the remarriage of a mother rather than the death of a son. The standard pattern of topical allusions adopted by the Oxfordians is set out in Eva Lee Turner Clark's *Hidden Allusions in Shakespeare's Plays*, and a brief look at the chapter on *Much Ado about Nothing* will provide a sample of the topicality that can be superimposed upon the plays if one desires.

When Claudio's success in the recent wars is described to Leonato and his family, the Messenger says, "He hath borne himself beyond the promise of his age, doing in the figure of a Lamb, the feats of a Lion: he hath indeed better bettered expectation, than you must expect of me to tell you how," to which Leonato responds, "He hath an uncle here in Messina, will be very much glad of it" [1.1.1]. This uncle never appears and has no function in the plot of the play; in fact, when Claudio needs the assistance of an older man in the pursuit of his love interest, he turns not to his uncle who lives relatively nearby, but to his mentor Don Pedro. Oxfordians jump upon this rather puzzling reference in order to build their case that the play is holding a mirror up to Philip Sidney and his uncle, the queen's favorite, Robert Dudley, earl of Leicester. At the time they set the first performance, 1582, Sidney was twenty-eight and still unmarried. It takes no effort at all to find in Sidney a possible model for the attractive young Claudio. However, the rest of Clark's allusions require some mental contortions. She sees parallels between Elizabeth's problems with Henry Howard, who was confined to the Tower for suspected or real treason off and on over the years, and Don Pedro's troubles with his bastard brother Don John. The brief sketch we are given of Don John suggests quite a different relationship and tension, something comparable to that experienced by Edmund and Edgar in *King Lear*, but it is not too difficult to accept that any and all of the problematical relatives of a ruling monarch might find their reflection in Don John.

In order to make the rest of the allusions a tidy one-on-one correspondence, Clark suggests that Leonato is Lord Burghley and his brother Antonio is Francis Walsingham, although a reversal of the "casting" would be just as likely, given that she assigns to Hero Walsingham's daughter and to Beatrice Burghley's daughter. Her reason? The dialogue between Don Pedro and Leonato sounds like one that might have taken place between the queen and Lord Burghley. Clark's imagination is in full flower with such statements, though she does draw to our attention the echo that might be heard in a prince's arrival at a country estate, an honor that effectively bankrupted more than one of Elizabeth's nobles. Here is the exchange that Clark quotes:

Don Pedro: Good Signior Leonato, you are come to meet your trouble: the fashion of the world is to avoid cost, and you encounter it.

Leonato: Never came trouble to my house in the likeness of your grace: for trouble being gone, comfort should remain: but when you depart from me, sorrow abides, and happiness takes his leave. [1.1.96]

This could be any of Elizabeth's courtiers, but the echo is indirect rather than a topical allusion. There is also not much of a "payoff" in the linking of Beatrice to Anne Cecil, except that it allows Clark to link Benedick to the earl of Oxford. These two had in fact been unhappily married for some years. If the Elizabethan court afforded a model for the merry war of wits, it is not likely to have been provided by these two. Perhaps there were several models, for we have lots of stories of flirtations of long standing that gave the court its sexual zip, including but not limited to Elizabeth's verbal engagement with a whole series of attractive young men.

For a short and cogent debunking of all of the theories, have a look at Jonathan Bate's *The Genius of Shakespeare*, specifically the third chapter, "The Authorship Controversy." Bate is also very insightful in his commentary on the Shakespeare industry, to which he is also an outstanding contributor. Another writer who can take the reader through the sad story of the development of the Shakespeare industry is Kenneth Mcclellan, whose *Whatever Happened to Shakespeare?* points the finger firmly at the madness of theatrical production, reminding us that the stage as well as the library has some skeletons in closets.

THE MEDIEVAL HERITAGE

If a modern actor thinks about the prevailing influence of Laurence Olivier and Humphrey Bogart, Vivien Leigh and Bette Davis, whose acting is as far removed from ours as the late medieval theatre is from Shakespeare, and if you trace the influence of the great nineteenth-century stars on British and American acting traditions, you will know that there inevitably existed a similar link between the new and improved strategies being developed at the Globe and the long traditions of medieval theatre. For example, we can trace the immense energy of a character like Falstaff or Richard III to the Vice characters and the comic devils that entertained the crowds when Shakespeare was a boy. Robert Weimann's *Shakespeare and the Popular Tradition in the Theater* explains all of the links, and Bernard Spivack's *Shakespeare and the Allegory of Evil* demonstrates how this heritage played out in the creation of some of Shakespeare's most memorable characters.

The sounds and smells of heaven and hell, in their theatrical manifestations, remind us that when Marcellus announces, "Something is rotten in the state of Denmark" [1.4.90], he is inviting the audience to participate in the old traditions of theatrical evocations of hell, complete with sensory effects that had been memorably supplied by the tanners' guild in the old cycle plays, back in the days when all the actors were amateurs.

AMATEUR SHAKESPEARE

Just at the point when you feel that you cannot bear to open another earnest or scholarly book on Shakespeare in the theatre, may I suggest that you refresh yourself with Michael Green's *The Art of Coarse Acting*. This book will be most amusing for those who are now or have ever been participants in an amateur theatre venture and still have a sense of humor. Green documents the fiery collision between pretension and incompetence in a wide variety of productions, including but not limited to Shakespeare. Many of his insights are refreshingly iconoclastic; for example, he is convinced that Will Kemp and the other clowns hated the unfunny things Shakespeare wrote for them to say and started putting in gags that got the sort of laugh that "Ye are as addle-pated as a coxcomb" never gets unless it is accompanied by a rude gesture.

RECOMMENDED READING

Shakespeare in the Theatre

Bate, Jonathan. *The Genius of Shakespeare*. Oxford: Oxford University Press, 1998.

Bradbrook, M.C. *Themes and Conventions of Elizabethan Tragedy*. Cambridge: Cambridge University Press, 1935.

Carlisle, Carol Jones. *Shakespeare from the Greenroom: Actors' Criticisms of Four Major Tragedies*. Chapel Hill: University of North Carolina Press, 1969.

Kiernan, Pauline. *Staging Shakespeare at the New Globe*. Basingstoke: Macmillan, 1999.

McClellan, Kenneth. *Whatever Happened to Shakespeare?* London: Vision, 1978.

Meagher, John C. *Shakespeare's Shakespeare: How the Plays Were Made*. New York: Continuum, 1997.

Styan, J.L. *Shakespeare's Stagecraft*. Cambridge: Cambridge University Press, 1967.

Performance Criticism

Bermel, Albert. *Shakespeare at the Moment: Playing the Comedies*. Portsmouth, NH: Heinemann, 2000.

Honigmann, E.A.J. *Shakespeare: Seven Tragedies: The Dramatist's Manipulation of Response*. New York: Barnes & Noble Books, 1976.

Bulman, James C., and J.R. Mulryne, with Margaret Shewring, general eds. *The Shakespeare in Performance Series*. Manchester: Manchester University Press, 1984–present.

Lusardi, James P., and June Schlueter. *Reading Shakespeare in Performance: King Lear*. Rutherford, NJ: Fairleigh Dickinson University Press, 1991.

McGuire, Philip C. *Speechless Dialect: Shakespeare's Open Silences*. Berkeley: University of California Press, 1985.

Richman, David. *Laughter, Pain, and Wonder: Shakespeare's Comedies and the Audience in the Theater*. Newark: University of Delaware Press, 1990.

Rosenberg, Marvin. *The Adventures of a Shakespeare Scholar: To Discover Shakespeare's Art*. Newark: University of Delaware Press, 1997.

———. *The Masks of Hamlet*. Newark: University of Delaware Press, 1992.

———. *The Masks of King Lear*. Berkeley: University of California Press, 1972.

———. *The Masks of Macbeth*. Newark: University of Delaware Press, 1978.

———. *The Masks of Othello*. Berkeley: University of California Press, 1961.

Slater, Ann Pasternak. *Shakespeare, the Director*. Brighton, Sussex: Harvester, 1982.

Smith, Peter J. *Social Shakespeare: Aspects of Renaissance Dramaturgy and Contemporary Society*. New York: St. Martin's Press, 1995.

Watkins, Ronald, and Jeremy Lemmon. *Hamlet*. Newton Abbot, England: David and Charles, 1974.

————. *Macbeth*. Totowa, NJ: Rowman and Littlefield, 1974.

————. *A Midsummer Night's Dream*. Newton Abbot, England: David and Charles, 1974.

————. *The Poet's Method*. Newton Abbot, England: David and Charles, 1974.

Williams, Gary Jay. *Our Moonlight Revels: A Midsummer Night's Dream in the Theatre*. Iowa City: University of Iowa Press, 1997.

Directors of Shakespeare

Beauman, Sally. *The Royal Shakespeare Company: A History of Ten Decades*. Oxford: Oxford University Press, 1982.

Bedford, Kristina. *Coriolanus at the National*. Selinsgrove, PA: Susquehanna University Press, 1992.

Berry, Ralph. *Changing Styles in Shakespeare*. London: George Allen & Unwin, 1981.

————. *On Directing Shakespeare: Interviews with Contemporary Directors*. London: H. Hamilton, 1989.

————. *Shakespeare in Performance: Castings and Metamorphoses*. New York: St. Martin's Press, 1993.

Billington, Michael, ed. *Approaches to Twelfth Night*. London: Nick Hern, 1990.

Epstein, Helen. *The Companies She Keeps: Tina Packer Builds a Theater*. Cambridge, MA: Plunkett Lake Press, 1985.

————. *Joe Papp: An American Life*. Boston: Little, Brown, 1994.

Greenwald, Michael L. *Directions by Indirections: John Barton of the Royal Shakespeare Company*. Newark: University of Delaware Press, 1985.

Hall, Peter. *Making an Exhibition of Myself*. London: Sinclair-Stevenson, 1993.

Houseman, John, and Jack Landau. *The American Shakespeare Festival: The Birth of a Theatre*. New York: Simon and Schuster, 1959.

Lowen, Tirzah. *Peter Hall Directs Antony and Cleopatra*. New York: Limelight Editions, 1990.

Miller, Jonathan. *Subsequent Performances*. New York: E. Sifton Books/Viking, 1986.

Patterson, Tom, and Allan Gould. *First Stage: The Making of the Stratford Festival*. Toronto: McClelland and Stewart, 1987.

Schafer, Elizabeth. *MsDirecting Shakespeare: Women Direct Shakespeare*. London: Women's Press, 1998.

Scott, Michael. *Renaissance Drama and a Modern Audience*. London: Macmillan, 1982.

Selbourne, David. *The Making of a Midsummer Night's Dream: An Eye-witness Account of Peter Brook's Production from First Rehearsal to First Night*. London: Methuen, 1982.

Sprung, Guy, with Rita Much. *Hot Ice: Shakespeare in Moscow: A Director's Diary*. Winnipeg: Blizzard Publishing, 1991.

Warren, Roger. *Staging Shakespeare's Late Plays*. Oxford: Clarendon Press, 1990.

Actors of Shakespeare

Berkoff, Steven. *I Am Hamlet*. New York: Grove Weidenfeld, 1990.

Brockbank, Philip, ed. *Players of Shakespeare: Essays in Shakespearean Performance*. Cambridge: Cambridge University Press, 1985.

Cook, Judith. *Shakespeare's Players: A Look at Some of the Major Roles in Shakespeare and Those Who Have Played Them*. London: Harrap, 1983.

———. *Women in Shakespeare*. London: Harrap, 1980.

Cox, Brian. *The Lear Diaries: The Story of the Royal National Theatre's Productions of Shakespeare's Richard III and King Lear*. London: Methuen, 1992.

Cox, Murray, ed. *Shakespeare Comes to Broadmoor: The Actors Are Come Hither: The Performance of Tragedy in a Secure Psychiatric Hospital*. London: Jessica Kingsley Publishers, 1992.

Good, Maurice. *Every Inch a Lear: A Rehearsal Journal of "King Lear" with Peter Ustinov and the Stratford Festival Company, Directed by Robin Phillips*. Victoria, BC: Sono Nis Press, 1982.

Jackson, Russell, and Robert Smallwood, eds. *Players of Shakespeare 2: Further Essays in Shakespearean Performance*. Cambridge: Cambridge University Press, 1988.

———. *Players of Shakespeare 3: Further Essays in Shakespearian Performance*. Cambridge: Cambridge University Press, 1993.

Rutter, Carol. *Clamorous Voices: Shakespeare's Women Today*. London: Routledge, 1989.

Sher, Antony. *Year of the King: An Actor's Diary and Sketchbook*. London: Chatto & Windus, 1985.

———, and Gregory Doran. *Woza Shakespeare! Titus Andronicus in South Africa*. London: Methuen Drama, 1996.

Smallwood, R.L., ed. *Players of Shakespeare 4: Further Essays in Shakespearian Performance by Players with the Royal Shakespeare Company*. Cambridge: Cambridge University Press, 2000.

Acting Shakespeare

Barton, John. *Playing Shakespeare*. London: Methuen, 1984.

Brine, Adrian, and Michael York. *A Shakespearean Actor Prepares*. Lyme, NH: Smith & Kraus, 2000.

Cohen, Robert. *Acting in Shakespeare*. Mountain View, CA: Mayfield, 1991.

Daw, Kurt. *Acting Shakespeare and His Contemporaries*. Portsmouth, NH: Heinemann, 1998.

Joseph, Bertram. *Acting Shakespeare*. London: Routledge & Kegan Paul, 1960.

Morrison, Malcolm. *Classical Acting*. Portsmouth, NH: Heinemann, 1996.

Suzman, Janet. *Acting with Shakespeare: Three Comedies*. New York: Applause Theatre Book Publishers, 1996.

Van Tassel, Wesley. *Clues to Acting Shakespeare*. New York: Allworth Press, 2000.

Actors Guides to Shakespeare's Language

Abbott, E.A. *A Shakespearian Grammar: An Attempt to Illustrate Some of the Differences Between Elizabethan and Modern English*. London: Macmillan, 1886.

Barber, Charles. *Early Modern English*. London: Andre Deutsch, 1976.

Berry, Cicely. *The Actor and His Text*. London: Harrap, 1987.

Blake, N.F. *Shakespeare's Language: An Introduction*. London: Macmillan, 1983.

Bolton, W.F. *Shakespeare's English: Language in the History Plays*. Oxford: Basil Blackwell, 1992.

Brook, G.L. *The Language of Shakespeare*. London: Andre Deutsch, 1976.

Brubaker, Edward S. *Shakespeare Aloud: A Guide to His Verse on Stage*. Lancaster, PA: E.S. Brubaker, 1976.

Doyle, John, and Ray Lischner. *Shakespeare for Dummies*. Foster City, CA: IDG Books Worldwide, 1999.

Gilbert, Anthony J. *Shakespeare's Dramatic Speech*. Lewiston, NY: Edwin Mellen Press, 1997.

Görlach, Manfred. *Introduction to Early Modern English*. Cambridge: Cambridge University Press, 1978.

Hedges, David, and Mita Scott Hedges. *Speaking Shakespeare: A Handbook for the Student Actor and Oral Interpreter*. New York: American Press, 1967.

Hulme, Hilda M. *Explorations in Shakespeare's Language: Some Problems of Lexical Meaning in the Dramatic Text*. London: Longmans, 1962.

Joseph, Sister Miriam. *Rhetoric in Shakespeare's Time: Literary Theory of Renaissance Europe*. New York: Harcourt, Brace & World, 1962.

———. *Shakespeare's Use of the Arts of Language*. New York: Hafner, 1966.

Linklater, Kristin. *Freeing Shakespeare's Voice: The Actor's Guide to Talking the Text*. New York: Theatre Communications Group, 1992.

Rodenburg, Patsy. *The Actor Speaks: Voice and the Performer*. London: Methuen, 1997.

———. *The Need for Words: Voice and the Text*. New York: Routledge, 1993.

———. *The Right to Speak: Working with the Voice*. New York: Routledge, 1992.

Ronberg, Gert. *A Way with Words: The Language of English Renaissance Literature*. London: E. Arnold, 1992.

Roston, Murray. *Renaissance Perspectives in Literature and the Visual Arts*. Princeton, NJ: Princeton University Press, 1987.

Salmon, Vivian, and Edwina Burness, eds. *A Reader in the Language of Shakespearian Drama*. Amsterdam: J. Benjamins, 1987.

Smith, Bruce R. *The Acoustic World of Early Modern England: Attending to the O-factor*. Chicago: University of Chicago Press, 1999.

Spurgeon, Caroline. *Shakespeare's Imagery and What It Tells Us*. Cambridge: Cambridge University Press, 1935.

Vickers, Brian. *The Artistry of Shakespeare's Prose*. London: Methuen, 1968.

———. *Classical Rhetoric in English Poetry*. London: Macmillan, 1970.

Wright, George T. *Shakespeare's Metrical Art*. Berkeley: University of California Press, 1988.

Shakespeare's Theatre

Barrol, J.L., et al, eds. *The Revels History of Drama in English, Volume 3: 1576–1613*. London: Methuen, 1975.

Bentley, Gerald Eades. *The Jacobean and Caroline Stage*. 7 vols. Oxford: Clarendon Press, 1941–1968.

———. *The Profession of Dramatist in Shakespeare's Time, 1590–1642*. Princeton, NJ: Princeton University Press, 1971.

———. *The Profession of Player in Shakespeare's Time, 1590–1642*. Princeton, NJ: Princeton University Press, 1984.

Chambers, E.K. *The Elizabethan Stage*. 4 vols. Oxford: Clarendon Press, 1923.

Feuillerat, Albert. *Documents Relating to the Office of the Revels: In the Time of Queen Elizabeth*. Nendeln/Liechtenstein: Kraus Reprint, 1968.

Foakes, R.A., and R.T. Rickert, eds. *Henslowe's Diary.* Cambridge: Cambridge University Press, 1961.

Gurr, Andrew. *The Shakespearian Playing Companies.* Oxford: Clarendon Press, 1996.

———, and Mariko Ichikawa. *Staging in Shakespeare's Theatres.* Oxford: Oxford University Press, 2000.

———, with John Orrell. *Rebuilding Shakespeare's Globe.* New York: Routledge, 1989.

Hattaway, Michael. *Elizabethan Popular Theatre: Plays in Performance.* London: Routledge, 1982.

Mulryne, J.R., and Margaret Shewring, eds. *Shakespeare's Globe Rebuilt.* Cambridge: Cambridge University Press, 1997.

Orgel, Stephen. *Impersonations: The Performance of Gender in Shakespeare's England.* Cambridge: Cambridge University Press, 1996.

Orrell, John. *The Quest for Shakespeare's Globe.* Cambridge: Cambridge University Press, 1983.

Patterson, Annabel M. *Shakespeare and the Popular Voice.* Oxford: Basil Blackwell, 1989.

Shapiro, Michael. *Gender in Play on the Shakespearean Stage: Boy Heroines and Female Pages.* Ann Arbor: University of Michigan Press, 1994.

Stern, Tiffany. *Rehearsal from Shakespeare to Sheridan.* Oxford: Clarendon Press, 2000.

Styan, J.L. *The English Stage: A History of Drama and Performance.* Cambridge: Cambridge University Press, 1996.

Tennenhouse, Leonard. *Power on Display: The Politics of Shakespeare's Genres.* New York: Methuen, 1986.

Thomson, Peter. *Shakespeare's Theatre.* London: Routledge, 1992.

Shakespeare's Life

Barroll, Leeds. *Politics, Plague, and Shakespeare's Theater.* Ithaca, NY: Cornell University Press, 1991.

Burton, S.H. *Shakespeare's Life and Stage.* Edinburgh: Chambers, 1989.

Fraser, Russell. *Shakespeare, the Later Years.* New York: Columbia University Press, 1992.

———. *Young Shakespeare.* New York: Columbia University Press, 1988.

Green, Michael. *The Art of Coarse Acting; or, How to Wreck an Amateur Dramatic Society.* London: Arrow Books, 1964.

Honan, Park. *Shakespeare: A Life.* Oxford: Oxford University Press, 1998.

Honigmann, E.A.J. *Shakespeare: The Lost Years.* Manchester: Manchester University Press, 1985.

Kay, Dennis. *Shakespeare: His Life, Work, and Era.* New York: William Morrow, 1992.

Mcclellan, Kenneth. *Whatever Happened to Shakespeare?* London: Vision, 1978.

Schoenbaum, S. *Shakespeare's Lives.* Oxford: Clarendon Press, 1991.

Spivack, Bernard. *Shakespeare and the Allegory of Evil: The History of a Metaphor in Relation to His Major Villains.* New York: Columbia University Press, 1958.

Thomson, Peter. *Shakespeare's Professional Career.* Cambridge: Cambridge University Press, 1992.

Weimann, Robert. *Shakespeare and the Popular Tradition in the Theater: Studies in the Social Dimension of Dramatic Form and Function.* Baltimore: Johns Hopkins University Press, 1978.

Wilson, Ian. *Shakespeare, the Evidence: Unlocking the Mysteries of the Man and His Work.* New York: St. Martin's Press, 1994.

❧ 10 ❧
Final Thoughts . . . for Now

You do look (my son) in a moved sort,
As if you were dismayed: be cheerful Sir,
Our Revels now are ended.

Prospero [Tempest 4.1.146]

It is time for this particular Sisyphus to walk away from the rock. I know that in the months between the time I send this book to the publisher and its appearance in print, it will become outdated. I can only hope that it will serve to guide some actors into the labyrinth that is a university library, there to find the riches that will inspire and challenge. I cannot complete my labors, however, without some consideration of the latest development in Shakespeareana: the Internet.

THE BARD IN CYBERSPACE

My husband became a "mouse potato" long before I began to explore the Internet, and as I dragged him away from another lengthy session surfing the Net, he would attempt to mitigate his addiction by promising that if I would only try it, I too would surely like it and become not only as fascinated, but as adept as he in finding interesting sites, building a collection of useful bookmarks, and keeping up-to-date on the expanding resources at our fingertips.

The first obstacle I had to overcome was my resistance to removing myself from the sensory pleasure of the university library. What could ever replace the joy of browsing along those overstuffed shelves, breathing in the dust, alone in the silent, empty stacks in search of still another esoteric scholarly tome? Well, I still hang out in libraries, but I also happily surf the Net, having discovered that the same detectivelike mentality that sent me delving through ancient editions of scholarly journals now has me clicking my way through a tangled web of links embedded in hypertext.

The next obstacle I had to overcome was my irritation at the result of a global search. My husband had shown me the icon upon which to click, and I had dutifully entered "shakespeare" in the blank provided. Then I began to work my way through the several thousand entries, everything from high-school students trying to get someone to do their homework assignment for them ("Why did Macbeth kill Duncan? Can anyone help me?" in a chat-room string) to a personal page of someone who professed to love reading Shake-speare's plays as an alternative to television viewing (the Web as dating service?).

Buried in that first long list of findings were what became the first entries on my personal list of bookmarks of favorite sites on the Net: the MIT col-lected works, searchable for keywords or scene by scene through each of the plays (http://tech-two.mit.edu/Shakespeare/) and "Mr. William Shakespeare and the Internet (http://daphne.palomar.edu/shakespeare/).

This second site introduced me to the single most important discovery about navigating the Web: find and make use of the listing of links created by other users of the Net who share your interests. I have since added a few other favorite sources of links, several of which have been "published" on the Web as part of a course package for university or even high-school classes.

The problem with the Internet is one of discernment: how is one to tell the well-researched, reliable posting from the ramblings of the ignorant, well-meaning, or self-promoting? The vast majority of what is available on the Web is geared toward easy access and general information, so an actor will not have to wade through scholarly refuse and theoretical ramblings. Instead, you might find yourself wading through bovine excrement as one barely informed self-aggrandizing owner of a high-speed modem after another holds forth on the topic under discussion or the subject about which he or she has chosen to create a Web site.

On my various searches for things like Elizabethan heraldry and anything about the earl of Essex, I kept landing on the Renaissance home page (http://renaissance.dm.net/), a location of all sorts of interesting bits and pieces of information. This is a perfect example of the bliss and blaring error into which the Internet can lead the unwary.

On its home page, the site contains a hypertext link entitled "Life in Eliza-bethan England: A Compendium of Common Knowledge 1558–1603." Click on this, and you will find yourself in an excellent source of detailed information about everything from fashion and education to food, games, and money. Click on the hypertext link labelled "Author and Designer," and you will discover the credentials of the compiler of this information: twenty-plus years of participating in Renaissance fairs and the Society for Creative Anachronisms. I doubt if there is anyone in the world, except perhaps for a fusty old scholar, who would want such sources of information to disappear from sight. This particular Web page is beautifully laid out and thoughtfully edited, so that each entry is, I am sure, of real use to the improvisers who grace the popular re-creations of medieval and Renaissance life. The only danger is that the site will be mistaken for something it is not and was never intended to be. For actors, this is an excellent introduction to the world that was familiar to the first actors of the plays, rich in detail and erring only in transforming certain complexities into broad generalizations, which is also of course its most pleasing aspect, for the creators have a firm sense of when excessive complexity would alienate the nonscholarly reader.

Also on the home page is the hypertext "The Trial of the Earls of Essex and Southampton, 1601," which appears to be the transcript of the actual trial. The editor, Maggie Secara, has created a beautiful electronic document and has clarified precisely the archival source of what appears: it is from a document published eighty years after the event, a document that does not agree with the state papers and that, she concludes, was contrived for dramatic effect.

Not every contributor to the Web is as precise and truthful as Secara. In the absence of such information, the naïve surfer of the Web might conclude that everything posted is more than likely to be authentic and legitimate, just as everything in the newspaper is more than likely to be true. More sensible explorers of both the Internet and the print media are aware that misinformation, ignorance, error, and outright dishonesty have a statistically high occurrence in such poorly mediated exchanges. My conclusion is that, barring discussion groups, the sites that appear on a page of interesting links are more than likely to be generally correct, if superficial, and most useful in the manner in which they collect information and allow for effective browsing through hypertext links.

The most significant service being provided by the Internet is the publication of electronic texts. The list of resources expands exponentially every month. You can find everything from Thomas Bulfinch's *Myths* to Shakespeare's quartos and the First Folio. You can use an Internet site to search the Bible in any of a number of translations or to cut and paste quotations from Sir Thomas More and Machiavelli, in English or Italian.

I now cannot survive without my high-speed Internet access, and my personal bookmarks run into the hundreds. Every time I log on, I find additional Web sites sponsored by universities or private individuals that contain just the sort of information I used to seek in my university library. Now if I could only figure out how to get connected while I am sitting in the rehearsal hall.

SHAKESPEARE IN THE REHEARSAL HALL

What is the responsibility of an actor cast in a role in a modern production of a play by William Shakespeare? First and foremost, it is the same as her responsibility in any production: to find her way into the heart of the play, to position herself so that the actions of her character can be performed vividly, honestly, and coherently in service of the theatrical event in which she is collaborating. But additional responsibilities rest on an actor in a play by William Shakespeare. Suddenly, there is the burden of playing a role that has been played many times before and toward which our culture has developed a profound ambivalence. If it is a minor role, the ambivalence is that directed toward any aspect of the Bard of Avon and his writings. If it is a major role, the ambivalence can be even more specifically directed to the play and the character.

This cultural ambivalence is a mixture of adoration and antipathy. We acknowledge that playing Hamlet or Rosalind might well be the Everest of acting challenges, and yet somehow we are quick to condemn anyone who falls short of some imagined ideal performance. Almost all of us can remember a deadly dull encounter with a Shakespearean play on the page or stage, and yet we continue to describe Shakespeare as the greatest dramatist who ever lived. We are counting on our actors to access these great plays for us, and yet we place any of their offerings against a yardstick that is so exalted, made up as it is of the best bits of every production ever seen or described, that it is impossible to be anything but disappointed, even if we are thrilled by the opportunity to see such a great play alive again in the theatre.

Far too little attention has been paid to the tremendous burden this places upon actors, who must overcome personal ambivalence, attempt to perform the role vividly, honestly, and coherently, and then endure the ambivalence in the audience's response. We ask actors to perform Shakespeare in front of school audiences made up at least in part of students who are being forced to study a four-hundred-year-old "masterpiece" that bores them to tears. We ask actors to perform Shakespeare in front of scholars, who may or may not love Shakespeare, and ardent fans, who may or may not be up-to-date on the latest academic debates on any given play. If the production brings fresh insights to the text, someone is sure to complain that the director has taken far too many liberties with a play so great that it needs no such theatrical tricks, and if the production is conservative in staging, there will be as many or more complaints that this was a boring museum piece.

It is almost impossible to come to a play or a role for the first time. Even a person who is seeing or reading one of the less often studied or performed plays still brings all of the associated expectations simply because the name of the playwright is front and center during this first encounter. Yet we long for an opportunity to have the familiar become unfamiliar, strange, new, captivating our attention and imagination in just the way we have always suspected or assumed that we should or could be by the world's greatest dramatist.

When you come right down to it, the ambivalence we feel toward these plays matches the reality of what an actor encounters in rehearsal: there is much that makes these plays wonderful theatre, but they are well past their shelf life. The actors discover that the responsibility for disconnecting the deadly elements in the mix from those that are still manifestations of living theatre rests on them, and they are the ones who will die a thousand deaths in front of audiences if they guess incorrectly.

To assist in this complex process of bringing alive a four-hundred-year-old play, the actor has three tools, each of which is as likely to do harm as good, being each of them double-edged and dangerous. The first tool is the traditions of theatrical performance that allow actors to benefit from famous and infamous productions around the world. There is no need to reinvent the wheel. Thousands of actors have struggled with the same complex task, and their strategies are shared within the community of theatre professionals and in countless documents, including diaries, promptbooks, and formal discussions of their craft. Much of this shared wisdom is packaged for actors during their training years, so that most can start off with at least a sense of a map for getting from first reading to opening night.

The danger of this collected wisdom is that it is also the dead hand that stifles a personal, perhaps naïve but nevertheless fresh, approach to the role. How can we expect a young actor to breathe new breath into a role when strategies are presented as "you should" instead of "you could"? But the alternative, putting actors to the task of performing Shakespeare without any support from the traditions of the theatre, results in great numbers of productions in which actors travel down roads that others have tried already. The great discoveries, by which I mean performances that bring alive these outdated masterpieces, emerge from actors who are well supported by the shared wisdom of countless efforts, innumerable failures, and modest victories, and who somehow, with the perfect combination of play, company, time, place, and opportunity, come out with something greater than the sum of its component parts.

The second double-edged tool is the modern actor's modern sensibilities. This is particularly true of relatively naïve actors, and by that I mean those whose academic encounters with Shakespeare have been minimal. These actors bring to the complex task just the right sort of iconoclasm that refuses to accept deadly theatrical effects simply because "we've always done it that way," or "it's Shakespeare, you know." They don't know, and they don't want to know, because they offer no concessions to bad theatre simply because it has been written by the world's greatest dramatist, and who said he was that, anyway?

The danger of the naïve rebellious iconoclast is that when he encounters some aspect of the play that appears to be mere deadwood but is in fact an unfamiliar stage convention with great potential even on the modern stage, the tendency is to jettison regardless of what riches will be lost. I would argue, however, that those actors who can retain the energy of the iconoclast even as they acquire the shared wisdom of theatrical traditions are the most likely to be contributors to the sort of great-discovery performance of which we dream.

The third tool is the subject of this book. It is the great wealth of scholarship that has been contributed by scholars and lovers of Shakespeare, who sometimes make the worst audiences for plays and often work without any apparent regard for the concerns of those entrusted with keeping the plays alive in the theatre. Much of what has resulted from their gargantuan labors is of interest only to those who share their untheatrical concerns, but their findings, absorbed into the theatrical world by means of the creativity of the actor, can offer a tool to assist in the process of reviving what can be saved and demonstrating that even four hundred years later, these are still good pieces of theatre.

The dangers of the scholarly tool are similar to those of the shared wisdom of the theatrical traditions, multiplied a hundredfold. Acting under the shadow of past greats is a terrible burden; acting under the weight of many literary analyses of the character and the play will cripple even the strongest of actors. Ironically, even though actors often share with the "experts" a great love of the idea of Shakespeare's plays, the experts' love and the actors' love often lead them into direct conflict. If you love something, you preserve it and admire it, say the experts out there in the audience. Meanwhile, the actors say that if you love it, you do whatever you have to do to get it into some sort of shape where it can demonstrate once again that it is worthy of admiration, the way it can never be if you leave it pure and unchallenged on the page.

In writing this book, I have tried to clarify my own very personal ambivalence about Shakespeare, which comes from observing firsthand some of the best and much of the worst that can be written about and done with Shakespeare. I think, first of all, that it is time to acknowledge that the plays are, as they appear in the collected works, so far past their "best-before" date that they can only be viewed as examples of great theatre if they are revived by the efforts of actors who make extensive and reckless use of the tools of theatrical wisdom and creative anarchy. Any effort to restrict the experiments of the resuscitation crews will ensure the death of the patient. It is only by the most courageous and daring of explorations that we rediscover what makes these plays worth preserving. Therefore, I have tried to create a reference work that offers suggestions rather than guidelines, in the spirit of might, could, perhaps, in some cases, maybe, and possibly rather than should, must, of necessity, always, and of course.

The simple fact of the matter is that it is impossible to encounter Shakespeare without scholarly interference. Every edition of the play has been edited by a scholar. Every note represents a choice of the editor to translate, to explain, to shape the reader's perception and understanding. All of the well-known plays and characters are firmly set into interpretive boxes, which the production will either challenge or reinforce. No reading is ever truly naïve or neutral, or even personal and open-ended.

By empowering the actor with access to the widest range of scholarly input, one of two things will happen. Either I will be contributing to the deadly burden of bardolatry that quickly destroys an actor's creativity, or I will be arming the actor to cut through the tangled undergrowth as she finds her own way through the mess into something that works for her in that time and place and production. I wish to acknowledge the danger of the first even as I embark upon a project in hopes of accomplishing the second.

I am sufficiently allied with the theatre world to believe, with all my heart, "If it works, it is justified." I would never argue ideologically for or against editing or even rewriting huge chunks of the plays if that is what it takes to create a successful piece of theatre. If Shakespeare requires such concessions as bad acting, stupid staging, and boring productions to stay alive, then it is time to turn off the life support. But I suspect that if we refuse to make concessions and expect every production of Shakespeare to be good theatre first and good Shakespeare only by chance, then the patient is much more likely to continue to experience extraordinary longevity. Not every innovation will work, but every innovation should be tried if there is a chance it might work. Nothing should be denied the creative artists simply because "it's Shakespeare, you know."

On the other hand, I am sufficiently allied with the world of academia to realize that a modern actor who attempts a Shakespearean role without recourse to the support available is more likely to be masking ignorance and laziness than carving out a legitimate acting strategy. If we continue our medical metaphor, such an actor is like the neighbor who read about a health cure in *Reader's Digest* and then attempts to prescribe for every illness on the street. The actor who comes to the work with vague memories of high-school English class and a few courses during his training years is like someone who reads all of the popular books on diet and nutrition and is quite able to make commonsense suggestions about healthy eating. The actor who brings years of experience playing the roles and absorbing the insights of actors older and younger is like a great healer, intuitive and deeply in touch with the folk wisdom that is more likely to ensure wellness than the scalpels and drugs of the modern student of medicine. Best of all, however, would be a doctor who combines folk wisdom, a healthy respect for traditional medicine, and the skill of the scalpel supported by the CAT scan and dialysis machines, the research labs, and even the fancy prescription drugs when only they will save the patient.

Of course this metaphor privileges the scholarly technology over the folk wisdom and so appears to denigrate the contribution of theatrical traditions. My only reason for choosing scholarship over theatre is the fact that these plays are so old, the language has changed so completely, and the distance between the theatrical conventions that worked for Shakespeare and those within which a modern actor works are so extreme that I honestly do not feel that a young actor can do it with just the tools of the theatre and the iconoclast.

We place tremendous expectations on actors of Shakespeare. We expect them to carry the entire burden of our ambivalence. We expect them to be innovative and fresh while not violating the idealized vision we have of the play, one that is impossible to achieve and has perhaps not even been articulated. We expect them to act in a way that is entirely within the conventions that mark the credible for us, that we otherwise encounter in film, television, and the performance of modern plays, and we also expect them to act in a way that might be called "Shakespearean," though we have no real idea what that might be except that it isn't modern. But we will be the first to decry anything that isn't entirely credible or is entirely too credible. We want natural tragedy and unnatural familiarity. We know exactly what we want because we never see it, and we know exactly how every offering fails, though we still love Shakespeare and believe without question that he is the greatest dramatist in the world.

Works Cited

Abbott, E.A. *A Shakespearian Grammar: An Attempt to Illustrate Some of the Differences Between Elizabethan and Modern English.* London: Macmillan, 1886.

Arditi, Jorge. *A Genealogy of Manners: Transformations of Social Relations in France and England from the Fourteenth to the Eighteenth Century.* Chicago: University of Chicago Press, 1998.

Armin, Robert. *Foole upon Foole* (1600). Edited by H.F. Lippincott. Salzburg: Institut für Englische Sprache und Literatur, Universität Salzburg, 1973.

Asimov, Isaac. "The Immortal Bard." In *A Shakespeare Merriment: An Anthology of Shakespearean Humor,* edited by Marilyn Schoenbaum, 187–190. New York: Garland, 1988.

Barber, Charles. *Early Modern English.* London: Andre Deutsch, 1976.

Barker, Francis. "Treasures of Culture: *Titus Andronicus* and Death by Hanging." In *The Production of English Renaissance Culture,* edited by David Lee Miller, Sharon O'Dair, and Harold Weber, 226–261. Ithaca, NY: Cornell University Press, 1994.

Bawcutt, N.W., ed. *The Oxford Shakespeare: Measure for Measure.* Oxford: Oxford University Press, 1991.

Bencard, Mogens, ed. *Denmark's Coronation Carpets.* Copenhagen: Royal Collections, Rosenborg Palace, 1987.

Bevington, David, ed. *The New Cambridge Shakespeare: Antony and Cleopatra.* Cambridge: Cambridge University Press, 1990.

Borgeson, Jess, Adam Long, and Daniel Singer. *The Reduced Shakespeare Company's The Compleat Works of Wllm Shkspr (Abridged).* Edited by J.M. Winfield. New York: Applause Book, 1994.

Bradley, David. *From Text to Performance in the Elizabethan Theatre: Preparing the Play for the Stage.* Cambridge: Cambridge University Press, 1992.

Brissenden, Alan, ed. *The Oxford Shakespeare: As You Like It.* Oxford: Oxford University Press, 1993.

Brown, John Russell, ed. *The Arden Shakespeare: The Merchant of Venice*. London: Routledge, 1988.

Burnett, Mark Thornton. *Masters and Servants in English Renaissance Drama and Culture: Authority and Obedience*. New York: St. Martin's Press, 1997.

Buzacott, Martin. *The Death of the Actor: Shakespeare on Page and Stage*. London: Routledge, 1991.

Carroll, William C. *Macbeth: Texts and Contexts*. Boston: Bedford/St. Martin's, 1999.

Charney, Maurice. *Shakespeare on Love and Lust*. New York: Columbia University Press, 2000.

Clark, Eva Lee Turner. *Hidden Allusions in Shakespeare's Plays: A Study of the Early Court Revels and Personalities of the Times*. Port Washington, NY: Kennikat Press, 1974.

Clark, Sandra, ed. *Hutchinson Shakespeare Dictionary: An A–Z Guide to Shakespeare's Plays, Characters, and Contemporaries*. London: Hutchinson, 1986.

Collmann, Herbert Leonard. *Ballads & Broadsides: Chiefly of the Elizabethan Period*. New York: B. Franklin, 1971.

Contamine, Philippe. *War in the Middle Ages*. Translated by Michael Jones. London: Basil Blackwell, 1984.

Cummins, John. *The Hound and the Hawk: The Art of Medieval Hunting*. New York: St. Martin's Press, 1988.

Dekker, Thomas. *English Villainies Discovered by Lantern and Candlelight* (1608). Edited by E.D. Pendry. London: E. Arnold, 1967.

Dent, Anthony. *Horses in Shakespeare's England*. London: J.A. Allen, 1987.

Dent, R.W. *Shakespeare's Proverbial Language: An Index*. Berkeley: University of California Press, 1981.

Dick, Oliver Lawson, ed. *Aubrey's Brief Lives*. Harmondsworth: Penguin Books, 1982.

Diehl, Huston. *An Index on Icons in English Emblem Books, 1500–1700*. Norman: University of Oklahoma Press, 1986.

Dollerup, Cay. *Denmark, Hamlet, and Shakespeare: A Study of Englishmen's Knowledge of Denmark towards the End of the Sixteenth Century with Special Reference to Hamlet*. Salzburg Studies in English literature, Elizabethan and Renaissance Studies, 47. Salzburg: Institut für Englische Sprache und Literatur, Universität Salzburg, 1975.

Dominic, Catherine C., ed. *Shakespeare's Characters for Students*. Detroit: Gale Research, 1997.

Doran, John. *The History of Court Fools*. New York: Haskell House, 1966.

Doyle, John, and Ray Lischner. *Shakespeare for Dummies*. Foster City, CA: IDG Books Worldwide, 1999.

Edwards, Philip, ed. *The New Cambridge Shakespeare: Hamlet*. Cambridge: Cambridge University Press, 1985.

Epstein, Norrie. *The Friendly Shakespeare: A Thoroughly Painless Guide to the Best of the Bard*. New York: Viking, 1993.

Erickson, Peter B. "Sexual Politics and the Social Structure in *As You Like It*." *Massachusetts Review*, 23:1 (Spring 1982): 65–83.

Evans, G. Blakemore, ed. *The Riverside Shakespeare*. Boston: Houghton Mifflin, 1974.

Eyler, Ellen C. *Early English Gardens and Garden Books*. Ithaca, NY: Cornell University Press, 1963.

Feuillerat, Albert. *Documents Relating to the Office of the Revels: In the Time of Queen Elizabeth*. Nendeln/Liechtenstein: Kraus Reprint, 1968.

Frijlinck, Wilhelmina Paulina, ed. *The First Part of the Reign of King Richard the Second; Or,*

Thomas of Woodstock. London: Printed for the Malone Society at Oxford University Press, 1929.

Furness, Howard Horace, ed. *A New Variorum Edition of As You Like It.* Philadelphia: Lippincott, 1890.

———. *A New Variorum Edition of Hamlet.* 2 vols. New York: Dover, 1963.

Gibson, William. *Shakespeare's Game.* New York: Atheneum, 1978.

Gielgud, John, with John Miller. *Acting Shakespeare.* New York: Scribner, 1992.

Graham-White, Anthony. *Punctuation and Its Dramatic Value in Shakespearean Drama.* Newark: University of Delaware Press, 1995.

Greene, Robert. *Greene's Groats-Worth of Wit* (1592). Menston, England: Scolar Press, 1969.

Groos, G.W. *The Diary of Baron Waldstein: A Traveller in Elizabethan England.* London: Thames and Hudson, 1981.

Hagen, Uta. *Respect for Acting.* New York: Macmillan, 1973.

Hair, Paul, ed. *Before the Bawdy Court: Selections from Church Court and Other Records Relating to the Correction of Moral Offences in England, Scotland, and New England, 1300–1800.* London: Elek, 1972.

Halio, Jay L., ed. *The Oxford Shakespeare: The Merchant of Venice.* Oxford: Oxford University Press, 1993.

Hardy, Barbara. *Dramatic Quicklyisms: Malapropic Wordplay Technique in Shakespeare's Henriad.* Salzburg Studies in English Literature, Elizabethan and Renaissance Studies, 85. Salzburg: Institut Für Englische Sprache und Literatur, Universität Salzburg, 1979.

Harrison, William. *The Description of England* (1587). Edited by Georges Edelen. Ithaca, NY: Cornell University Press, 1968.

Hawley, William M. *Shakespearean Tragedy and the Common Law: The Art of Punishment.* New York: Peter Lang, 1998.

Hellman, Lillian. *Pentimento: A Book of Portraits.* New York: New American Library, 1973.

Hibbard, G.R. "Love, Marriage, and Money in Shakespeare's Theatre and Shakespeare's England." In *The Elizabethan Theatre VI*, edited by George Richard Hibbard, 134–155. Hamden, CT: Shoe String (Archon), 1977.

———, ed. *The Oxford Shakespeare: Hamlet.* Oxford: Oxford University Press, 1987.

Hindley, Charles, ed. *The Roxburghe Ballads.* 2 vols. London: Reeves and Turner, 1873–1874.

Hinman, Charlton. *The First Folio of Shakespeare.* New York: W.W. Norton, 1968.

Hoeniger, F. David. *Medicine and Shakespeare in the English Renaissance.* Newark: University of Delaware Press, 1992.

Hotson, Leslie. *Shakespeare versus Shallow.* Freeport, NY: Books for Libraries Press, 1970.

Hubbard, Frank. *The First Quarto Edition of Romeo and Juliet.* Madison: University of Wisconsin, 1924.

Hutton, Ronald. *The Rise and Fall of Merry England: The Ritual Year, 1400–1700.* Oxford: Oxford University Press, 1994.

James, N.D.G. *A History of English Forestry.* Oxford: Blackwell, 1981.

James I, King of England. *The English Bible, Translated out of the Original Tongues by the Commandment of King James the First, anno 1611.* New York: AMS Press, 1967.

Jenkins, Harold, ed. *The Arden Shakespeare: Hamlet.* London: Routledge, 1989.

Jorgensen, Paul A. *Shakespeare's Military World.* Berkeley: University of California Press, 1973.

Keeton, George W. *Shakespeare's Legal and Political Background*. London: Pitman, 1967.

Kettering, Sharon. "The Household Service of Early Modern French Noblewomen." *French Historical Studies* 20 (Winter 1997): 55–85.

Knapp, Robert S. *Shakespeare, the Theater and the Book*. Princeton, NJ: Princeton University Press, 1989.

Laroque, François. *Shakespeare's Festive World: Elizabethan Seasonal Entertainment and the Professional Stage*. Cambridge: Cambridge University Press, 1991.

Lascelles, Gerald. "Falconry." In *Shakespeare's England*, Vol. II, edited by W.A. Raleigh, S. Lee, and C.T. Onions, 351–366. Oxford: Clarendon Press, 1916.

Laughton, L.G. Carr. "The Navy: Ships and Sailors." In *Shakespeare's England*, Vol. I, edited by W.A. Raleigh, S. Lee, and C.T. Onions, 141–169. Oxford: Clarendon Press, 1916.

Lee, Sidney. *Great Englishmen of the Sixteenth Century*. Port Washington, NY: Kennikat Press, 1972.

Lever, J.W., ed. *The Arden Shakespeare: Measure for Measure*. London: Methuen, 1965.

Lukacher, Ned. *Daemonic Figures: Shakespeare and the Question of Conscience*. Ithaca, NY: Cornell University Press, 1994.

MacDonald, Michael. *Mystical Bedlam: Madness, Anxiety, and Healing in Seventeenth-Century England*. Cambridge: Cambridge University Press, 1981.

Mahood, M.M., ed. *The New Cambridge Shakespeare: The Merchant of Venice*. Cambridge: Cambridge University Press, 1987.

Marienstras, Richard. *The Forest, the Wild and the Sacred: New Perspectives on the Shakespearean World*. Translated by Janet Lloyd. Cambridge: Cambridge University Press, 1985.

Marowitz, Charles. *Prospero's Staff: Acting and Directing in the Contemporary Theatre*. Bloomington: Indiana University Press, 1986.

———. *Recycling Shakespeare*. New York: Applause Theatre Book Publishers, 1991.

Maser, Edward A., ed. *Baroque and Rococo Pictorial Imagery: The 1758–60 Hertel Edition of Ripa's "Iconologia."* New York: Dover, 1971.

McMurtry, Jo. *Understanding Shakespeare's England: A Companion for the American Reader*. Hamden, CT: Archon Books, 1989.

Montaigne, Michel de. *The Complete Essays*. Translated by M.A. Screech. Harmondsworth: Penguin Books, 1991.

Montrose, Louis Adrian. "'The Place of a Brother' in *As You Like It*: Social Process and Comic Form." *Shakespeare Quarterly* 32:1 (Spring 1981): 28–54.

———. *The Purpose of Playing: Shakespeare and the Cultural Politics of the Elizabethan Theatre*. Chicago: University of Chicago Press, 1996.

Morrill, John, ed. *The Oxford Illustrated History of Tudor and Stuart Britain*. Oxford: Oxford University Press, 1996.

Mortimer, John. *Will Shakespeare*. London: Hodder and Stoughton, 1977.

Naunton, Sir Robert. *Fragmenta Regalia; or, Observations on Queen Elizabeth, Her Times & Favourites* (1653). Edited by John S. Cerovski. Washington, DC: Folger Shakespeare Library, 1985.

Nicoll, Allardyce, ed. *Shakespeare in His Own Age: Shakespeare Survey, 17*. Cambridge: Cambridge University Press, 1964.

Norman, Marc, and Tom Stoppard. *Shakespeare in Love: A Screenplay*. Westport, CT: Hyperion Press, 1999.

Norwich, John Julius. *Shakespeare's Kings*. London: Viking, 1999.

Olson, Donald W., Marilynn S. Olson, and Russell L. Doescher. "The Stars of *Hamlet.*" *Sky and Telescope* 96:5 (November 1998): 68–73.

Orlin, Lena Cowen. *Elizabethan Households: An Anthology.* Washington, DC: Folger Shakespeare Library, 1995.

Ovid. *Metamorphoses.* Translated by A.D. Melville. Oxford: Oxford University Press, 1987.

———. *The Metamorphoses.* Translated by Sir Samuel Garth, John Dryden, et al. New York: Garland, 1976.

Paolucci, Anne. "Marx, Money, and Shakespeare: The Hegelian Core in Marxist." *Mosaic* 10:3, 139–156.

Popp, Margret. "How Should One Read Shakespeare's Verse?" *Shakespeare Studies* 17, (1985): 189–207.

Pound, John. *Poverty and Vagrancy in Tudor England.* London: Longman, 1986.

Praetorius, Charles. *Romeo and Juliet: The Second Quarto* (1599). London: C. Praetorius, 1886.

Rackham, Oliver. *Trees and Woodland in the British Landscape.* London: Dent, 1990.

Ribner, Irving, and George Lyman Kittredge, eds. *The Complete Works of Shakespeare.* New York: John Wiley & Sons, 1971.

Ridley, Jasper. *The Tudor Age.* London: Constable, 1988.

Ridley, M.R., ed. *The Arden Shakespeare: Antony and Cleopatra.* London: Routledge, 1988.

Roberts-Baytop, Adrianne. *Dido, Queen of Infinite Literary Variety: The English Renaissance Borrowings and Influences.* Salzburg studies in English literature, Elizabethan and Renaissance studies, 25. Salzburg: Institut Für Englische Sprache und Literatur, Universität Salzburg, 1974.

Rosenberg, Marvin. *The Masks of Hamlet.* Newark: University of Delaware Press, 1992.

Rowse, A.L. *What Shakespeare Read—and Thought.* New York: Coward, McCann & Geoghegan, 1981.

Ryden, Mats. *Shakespearean Plant Names: Identifications and Interpretations.* Stockholm Studies in English 43. Stockholm: Almqvist & Wiksell International, 1978.

Saunders, Corinne J. *The Forest of Medieval Romance: Avernus, Broceliande, Arden.* Cambridge: D.S. Brewer, 1993.

Scott, A.F. *Every One a Witness: The Plantagenet Age: Commentaries of an Era.* London: Scott & Finlay, 1975.

Shurgot, Michael W. *Stages of Play: Shakespeare's Theatrical Energies in Elizabethan Performance.* Newark: University of Delaware Press, 1998.

Sim, Alison. *The Tudor Housewife.* Montreal: McGill-Queen's University Press, 1996.

Simpson, J.A., and E.S.C. Weiner, eds. *The Oxford English Dictionary.* 20 vols. Oxford: Clarendon Press, 1989.

Simpson, Percy. "Actors and Acting." In *Shakespeare's England*, Vol. II, edited by W.A. Raleigh, S. Lee, and C.T. Onions, 240–282. Oxford: Clarendon Press, 1916.

Southwell, Robert. *Two Letters and Short Rules of a Good Life* (c. 1600). Edited by Nancy Pollard Brown. Charlottesville: University Press of Virginia, 1973.

Spevack, Marvin. *The Harvard Concordance to Shakespeare.* Cambridge, MA: Belknap Press of Harvard University Press, 1973.

Stevenson, Laura Caroline. *Praise and Paradox: Merchants and Craftsmen in Elizabethan Popular Literature.* Cambridge: Cambridge University Press, 1984.

Stow, John. *A Survey of London* (1603). 2 vols. Edited by Charles Lethbridge Kingsford. Oxford: Clarendon Press, 1971.

Stubbs, John. *Gaping Gulf, with Letters and Other Relevant Documents* (1579). Edited by Lloyd E. Berry. Charlottesville: University Press of Virginia, 1968.

Tilley, Morris Palmer. *A Dictionary of the Proverbs in England in the Sixteenth and Seventeenth Centuries: A Collection of the Proverbs Found in English Literature and the Dictionaries of the Period.* Ann Arbor: University of Michigan Press, 1950.

Todd, Malcolm. *Everyday Life of the Barbarians: Goths, Franks, and Vandals.* New York: Dorset Press, 1988.

Trease, Geoffrey. *Cue for Treason.* Oxford: Blackwell, 1970.

Virgil. *Aeneid and Fourth ("Messianic") Eclogue in the Dryden Translation.* Edited by Howard Clark. University Park: Pennsylvania State University Press, 1989.

Ward, Jennifer C., ed. *Women of the English Nobility and Gentry, 1066–1500.* Manchester: Manchester University Press, 1995.

Watkins, Ronald, and Jeremy Lemmon. *Hamlet.* Newton Abbot, England: David and Charles, 1974.

Webb, J. Barry. *Shakespeare's Imagery of Plants.* Hastings, East Sussex: Cornwallis, 1991.

Weinreb, Ben, and Christopher Hibbert, eds. *The London Encyclopaedia.* London: Macmillan, 1983.

Wells, Stanley. *A Dictionary of Shakespeare.* New York: Oxford University Press, 1998.

Whitney, Geoffrey. *A Choice of Emblemes* (1586). Menston, England: Scolar Press, 1973.

Wilson, John Dover, ed. *Life in Shakespeare's England: A Book of Elizabethan Prose.* New York: Barnes & Noble, 1969.

Wilson, Richard. "Like the old Robin Hood: *As You Like It* and the Enclosure Riots." In *Will Power: Essays on Shakespearean Authority,* 66–87. Detroit: Wayne State University Press, 1993.

Wright, Louis B. "The Britain that Shakespeare Knew." In *National Geographic,* May 1964, 613–665.

Zall, Paul M., ed. *A Hundred Merry Tales, and Other English Jestbooks of the Fifteenth and Sixteenth Centuries.* Lincoln: University of Nebraska Press, 1963.

Zupko, Ronald Edward. *British Weights and Measures: A History from Antiquity to the Seventeenth Century.* Madison: University of Wisconsin Press, 1977.

General Index

Index of Plays and Characters

About the Author

LESLIE O'DELL is Associate Professor of Theatre and English at Wilfrid Laurier University and Text Consultant for the Stratford Festival in Ontario.